DESIGN & DRAFTING PROJECT MANAGEMENT

Taken from:

Essentials: Microsoft Office Project 2003
by Dawn Parrish Wood and Mary E. Pascarella

Planning, Performing, and Controlling Projects: Principles and Applications, Third Edition
by Robert B. Angus, Norman A. Gundersen, and Thomas P. Cullinane

Images; EyeWire/Getty Images; and

... Microsoft Office Project 2003
by Dawn Parrish Wood and Mary E. Pascarella
Copyright © 2004 by Prentice Hall, Inc.
A Pearson Education Company
Upper Saddle River, New Jersey 07458

Planning, Performing, and Controlling Projects: Principles and Applications, Third Edition
by Robert B. Angus, Norman A. Gundersen, and Thomas P. Cullinane
Copyright © 2003, 2000, 1997 by Pearson Education, Inc.
Published by Prentice Hall

This special edition published in cooperation with Pearson Custom Publishing.

All trademarks, service marks, registered trademarks, and registered service marks are the property of their respective owners and are used herein for identification purposes only.

Printed in the United States of America

10 9 8 7

ISBN 0-536-53213-3

2007760002

KL

Please visit our web site at www.pearsoncustom.com

PEARSON CUSTOM PUBLISHING
501 Boylston Street, Suite 900, Boston, MA 02116
A Pearson Education Company

This textbook, *Design & Drafting Project Management*,
combines content from two leading publications into one custom textbook
specifically chosen for this course. The following is a summary of the book chapters.

PART 1

PART 2

PART 1

Taken from
Planning, Performing, and Controlling Projects:
Principles and Aplications, Third Edition,
by Robert B. Angus, Norman A. Gundersen, and Thomas P. Cullinane

Preface

This text is an introduction to the theory and practice involved in the design and management of technically oriented projects. It is a merger of our personal experiences as designers, engineers, and technical managers of projects whose values have ranged from several thousand to a few million dollars. We have assumed that you are

- A student studying science, engineering, or technology
- Interested in the planning, performing, and monitoring of projects
- Expecting to become involved in projects that will grow in size and complexity

Other texts discuss project design and technical management. However, many of these texts are theory oriented and lack practical examples. (Texts that we feel would be useful to you as references are noted in the bibliography.) We have tried to achieve a balance between theory and practice by including a major case study that is introduced in chapter 1 and continues through chapter 5.

Our years of experience have taught us that the best theoretical knowledge is of little value until you apply it to practical problems. These problems include

- Estimating costs and schedules accurately at the beginning of a project
- Determining and fulfilling the expectations of the client
- Imparting theoretical and practical knowledge to new employees
- Guiding diverse groups of people toward a common goal
- Earning a profit so other projects can be pursued
- Enjoying the work as it progresses

What is the value of life experiences if they do not include (1) learning, (2) having fun while learning, and (3) earning the trust and respect of your superiors, fellow employees, subcontractors, and clients? Not much, we say!

The Northeastern University Cooperative Education Department's motto is "Learn while you earn." We add, "Enjoy your work, enjoy your employ," and prepare for your next opportunity. Test your new skills outside the classroom and practice the theoretical principles you have learned.

The philosophical basis of this book is the systematic approach to project design and management. This approach requires continually considering and reevaluating how each portion of a project interacts with the entire project. Its use can lead to an efficient, useful, and cost-effective product, process, or service.

A typical project using the systematic approach consists of four phases:

1. The Conception Phase, in which ideas are devised and brainstormed
2. The Study Phase, in which potential designs are investigated
3. The Design Phase, in which the system is actually designed in detail
4. The Implementation Phase, in which the system is constructed and delivered

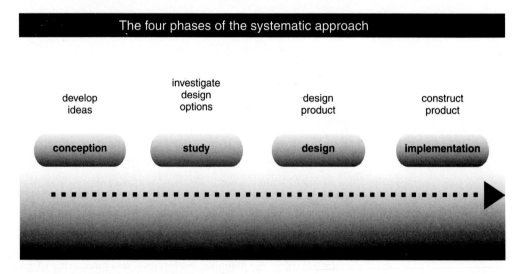

The four phases of the systematic approach

These phases may overlap. However, for discussion purposes, we consider them to be separate in time and cover them in separate chapters.

Chapters 2, 3, 4, and 5 each deal with one of these phases. The four chapters have the same organizational structure, with the following sections:

1. Purpose and goal of the phase
2. Activities occurring during the phase
3. Documentation for the phase
4. Defining the completion of the phase
5. Exercises

The example we use for the major case study is the result of our experiences in working with local business, industry, government agencies, and charitable foundations. In this example, Northeastern University engineering and technology students become involved in a community project in the town of Bedford, Massachusetts. The names of students used in the case study are fictitious.

Chapters 6, 7, 8, and 9 are specialty chapters. They describe our approach to systematic management, documentation, documentation interaction, and modeling. These chapters are an introduction to topics that may be of value to you in later years.

Colleges and universities using this book may need to adapt the sequence in which information is presented so that it dovetails with a variety of courses. The topics covered in the appendixes allow for the flexibility in presentation. The topics are

Appendix A	Value Analysis and Engineering
Appendix B	Objectives, Task Descriptions, and Active Verbs
Appendix C	Specification for the Town of Bedford: "An Activity Center"
Appendix D	Bedford Activity Center Contract
Appendix E	Bedford Activity Center Contract Change Notice (CCN)
Appendix F	Records and Their Interactions
Appendix G	System-Level Specifications
Appendix H	Student Activity Center As-Built Plans

Note that appendixes C, D, E, and H relate specifically to the major case study, the activity center for the town of Bedford.

A free full-product 120-day evaluation version of Microsoft Project 2000 software is provided on a CD-ROM at the back of the text. This CD-ROM allows users to apply the project management and documentation concepts presented in the text using this powerful project management software tool. Sample printouts from Microsoft Project are included in chapter 7.

Acknowledgments

We thank the following who have contributed to the third edition:

> Michelle Churma, who guided us and shepherded all the changes
>
> Robert Mager, who reviewed Appendix A and suggested several constructive changes and, most especially, for his development of behavioral objectives for educational application
>
> Dawn Hawkins, Art Institute of Phoenix; Joseph A. Phillips, DeVry Institute of Technology (OH); and Mr. Kyle B. Smith, Assoc. AIA, ICBO, the reviewers of the third edition

We wish to thank again the following persons who assisted us in the preparation of the second edition:

> Marilyn Prudente, copy editor, who worked closely with us to improve the readability, especially where ESL students are concerned
>
> Thomas E. Hulbert, who rewrote the creativity and brainstorming material and then wrote a new Appendix A
>
> Judith W. Nowinski, who reviewed and edited the entire manuscript
>
> Tom Bledsaw, ITT Technical Institute (Indianapolis, IN); Stephen Howe, Wentworth Tech (retired); David A. McDaniel, ITT Technical Institute (Norfolk, VA); and Duane Nehring, ITT Technical Institute (Earth City, MO), who reviewed the second edition manuscript

We also want to repeat our thanks to those who contributed to the first edition:

> Marilyn H. Steinberg, Science Coordinator for the Northeastern University libraries, for her assistance in locating research material
>
> Judith W. Nowinski, Technical Editor for Bowen's Publishing
>
> Janet Battiste, copy editor
>
> Mark D. Evans, Assistant Professor of Civil Engineering at Northeastern University, and Eric W. Hansberry, Associate Professor of Design Graphics at Northeastern University, who acted as reviewers during manuscript development
>
> Sunand Bhattacharya, ITT Educational Services, Inc.; J. Tim Coppinger, Texas A&M University; Charles H. Gould, University of Maine; David Hanna, Ferris State University; Roger Killingsworth, Auburn University; Peggy A. Knock, Milwaukee School of Engineering; Steven M. Nesbit, Lafayette College; Hirak C. Patangia, University of Arkansas at Little Rock; David Wagner, Owens Community College, who reviewed the final manuscript
>
> Cleveland Gilcreast, Visiting Professor at Merrimack College, who reviewed the management details
>
> Sunand Bhattacharya, ITT Educational Services, Inc., who provided valuable assistance and suggestions for illustrations, design, and pedagogy
>
> Stephen Helba, Editor in Chief at Prentice Hall
>
> Beverly Cleathero and Bill D'Annolfo for their contributions, especially to the specifications appendix
>
> Those family members who have been patient while we worked on this book
>
> Barbara Coleman, who cheerfully assisted us in proofreading every word and diagram at least three times; we especially thank her for her patience and accuracy

The writing of a book is a difficult task that we have enjoyed—with their support.

Bob Angus
Norm Gundersen
Tom Cullinane

English may be a difficult or second language for you.
The words in this book have been carefully chosen to ease the reading.

Contents

The Systematic Approach

The Conception Phase

The Study Phase

The Design Phase

The Implementation Phase

1. Why are planning, performance, and control important in the execution of projects?

2. What is a project, and what is a program?

3. How are projects managed and evaluated?

4. Why is teamwork important on projects?

5. What are the steps in the life cycle of a project?

6. What are the four phases of a project that uses a systematic approach?

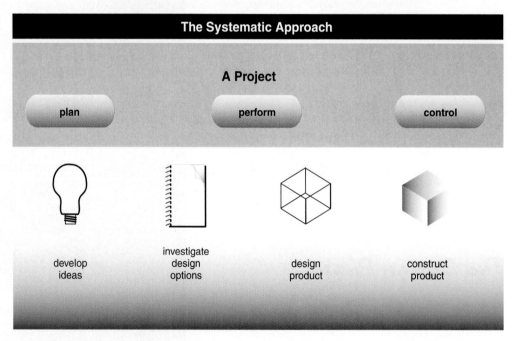

It is best to do things systematically, since we are only human, and disorder is our worst enemy.

Hesiod, 8th century B.C.

This book is intended to provide information on methods to plan, perform, and control a project.

Large and small projects require planning and control so they are completed

1. On time
2. Within budget
3. According to specifications

The achievement of these three goals enhances the reputation of the team, the manager, and the organization. Those who have successfully completed a project are in a better position to obtain new projects from any person or organization that wants quality work. In this book, we will discuss how projects can be initiated, planned, and controlled so that they are completed on time, within budget, and according to specifications. The specifications need to describe a product that is functional and constructable, as well as safe.

SECTION 1.1   THE PURPOSE AND GOALS OF THIS BOOK

*The purpose of this book is to present a systematic approach to the **planning, performance,** and **control** of projects.*

PLANNING AHEAD

You will see this symbol in many places within this text. It indicates some of the important areas where you should pause and plan ahead.

The purpose of this book is to present a systematic approach to the **planning, performance,** and **control** of projects. One goal of this book is to introduce you to techniques that will allow you to start, develop, and complete projects more efficiently and effectively. Another goal is to guide you in working as a member of a team. This is important because the global workplace requires people who are team workers.

Planning is the development of a method for converting ideas into a product or service. Scientists, engineers, and technologists learn to organize a collection of ideas into plans as part of their training. Projects are most successful when plans are carefully developed and prepared well in advance of design initiation (start).

Performance of a project requires a team of people working together to achieve the desired goal. Each team member needs to understand the plans and problems of other team members. As you study the material in the following chapters, you will become more aware of the relationship between your contribution and the successful performance of the entire project.

Control of a project includes seeing that it proceeds according to a well-prepared plan. However, we human beings do not devise perfect plans, since every possible circumstance cannot be known in advance, nor do we execute plans perfectly. Therefore, control includes recognizing when and why a project is not proceeding according to plan. Control also includes knowing if the plan needs to be revised or replaced with one that is more realistic, particularly if the client's expectations have changed.

Our approach in this book has three parts, as shown in figure 1.1:

The case-study project will assist you in understanding the general concepts.

1. Describe the general requirements for planning, performing, and controlling projects.
2. Explain how those requirements are applied through use of an example, a case study that we follow through several chapters.
3. Assign exercises that assist you in learning as you work on your own project.

The example project we have chosen is a combination of our personal experiences and those of others with whom we have worked. This project will assist you in understanding the more general concepts described in chapters 2 through 5 by means of a concrete example.

Figure 1.1 General approach of this book

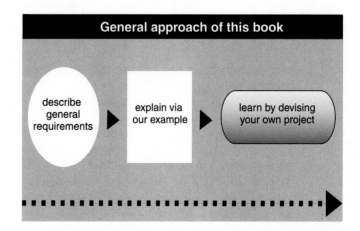

SECTION 1.2   PROJECTS, PROGRAMS, AND PEOPLE

There are three reasons for initiating a project:
- *A bright idea*
- *A perceived need*
- *The need to improve a product*

What Is a Project?   A project is an organized effort to do something useful or attain a useful end result. It is sometimes referred to as a plan, venture, or enterprise. A project is usually guided by a leader known as the project manager.

There are three general reasons for initiating a project:

1. Someone has a bright idea worth being considered.
2. There is a perceived need to be fulfilled.
3. A product needs to be improved.

These reasons lead to the seven steps described in section 1.3.

Results may include such items as designs, plans, procedures, software, equipment, and structures. We later discuss how projects are initiated (conceived and started), planned (studied and designed), and accomplished (implemented and delivered).

How Do You Organize a Project Administratively?   To be successful, a project needs the following: (1) the project must be staffed with people who are able to direct it; (2) there must be sufficient funds to accomplish the project; and (3) there should be potential customers (clients and/or owners) to purchase and use the end product. A staff is required to plan, perform, and monitor the project. Experts are needed to provide advice. Performance of a project requires materials, equipment, and workspace (figure 1.2). These are *internal* influences. Administering a project is discussed at length in Fisk (1992). This and all other references are given in the bibliography.

Someone must be chosen to lead and guide a project. Committees can offer advice; however, they do not provide leadership. We will refer to the project leader as the **manager** of the effort. The manager's role is to organize **people, parts,** and **procedures.** The project manager must firmly establish the project's purpose and goal, as well as organize the group's resources. These resources include staff, ideas, experts, materials, workspace, and equipment. The manager must also focus on the needs of the customer and the funds available for the project.

Figure 1.2   The interrelated parts of a project

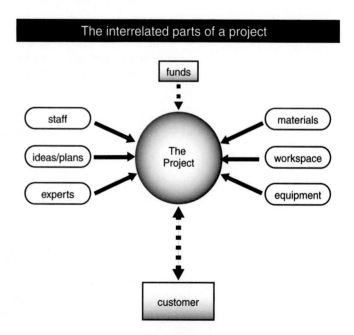

Figure 1.3 External influences that affect a project

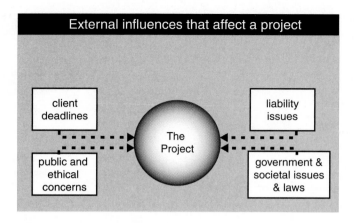

There are *external* influences that affect a project. Among them are the following:

- Client deadlines
- Liability issues
- Public and ethical concerns
- Government and societal issues and laws

It is the responsibility of the project team to continually weigh all these interrelated parts and external influences (figure 1.3) so that the final product is appropriate from both a technical and a social viewpoint.

A project is organized into portions that can be easily understood, accomplished, and controlled.

How Do You Organize a Project Technically?   A project is organized into portions that can be easily understood, accomplished, and controlled. For instance, a building to be constructed is organized as an overall shell having one or more floors. The plan for each floor is then designed separately. The floors require common subsystems, such as electrical power, air conditioning, and stairs, which are designed into an integrated system. A manager watches over the total system design, while technical specialists design the various common subsystems. Skilled drafters and designers lay out each floor and prepare a complete set of construction plans.

A project's success is judged by the project's design usefulness and its cost.

How Do You Evaluate a Project?   The performance evaluation of small projects is usually accomplished via performance reviews conducted by a senior staff member. The performance evaluation of large projects may require a separate staff of specialists who report to higher management. A project's success is judged by its design usefulness and its cost. Other factors involved in project evaluation will be discussed in this book in chapters 2, 3, 5, 6, 7, and 9.

What Is a Program?   A program is a group of related projects. A program usually requires a management team to oversee each of the projects and ensure that all the projects are coordinated. A program title might be "Devise and Implement a Housing Redevelopment Plan." That plan might consist of a group of projects, such as a revitalization of the community center, park improvements, and building painting. Each of these related projects is considered a separate project within the overall housing redevelopment program.

As a project or program becomes more complicated, the time required to accomplish it increases. Successful performance requires not only a plan, but also continual monitoring to verify that it is being followed or to identify when and where the plan must be modified as new information becomes available. For example, the assistance of additional people may be needed to complete a project. The effective coordination of people, parts, and procedures requires experienced management.

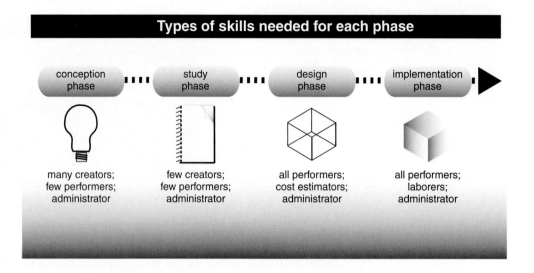

Types of skills needed for each phase

conception phase	study phase	design phase	implementation phase
many creators; few performers; administrator	few creators; few performers; administrator	all performers; cost estimators; administrator	all performers; laborers; administrator

What Types of Skills Do Team Members Need?

The skills of team members should relate to the types of projects being planned and to the status of the project design. Examine figure 1.4, which is discussed in detail in chapter 6.

It is highly desirable for those involved in a project to understand technical subjects besides one's own specialty. Team members can then better evaluate the contributions of fellow team members whose skills may be different from theirs. Priest, Bodensteiner, and Muir (1994, p. 13) wrote that "[a] major study was conducted of over 1000 professionals from 22 high-technology companies to assess the educational and training needs of technical professionals engaged in the transition process from design to production. Eighty-six percent of the respondents believe that a technically based and multidisciplined engineering approach is fundamental to ensure a successful transition."

Another skill that is necessary is the ability of contributors to document and explain their work. Clear, concise, and timely documentation allows individuals' work to be evaluated, revised, and continued by other team members. For larger projects, the documentation is usually extensive. For some larger projects, the cost and quantity of documentation may be greater than the cost and size of the system being designed.

The project manager's skills must include the ability to (1) communicate with team members, clients, and other managers; and (2) evaluate and balance a variety of priorities as presented by others.

A project is devised, designed, managed, and performed by a group of people interacting with one another. These individuals are expected to place the needs of the team above their personal needs.

How Do Teams of People Work Together?

A project is devised, designed, managed, and performed by a group of people interacting with one another. These individuals are expected to place the needs of the team above their personal needs. This does not mean that the personal preferences and directions of each person should be ignored. On the contrary, each team member must learn to recognize that other people approach their work differently. All persons should respect the right of others to perform their assignments in different ways, as long as they contribute to the timely and successful completion of the project and do not interfere with the overall project effort. Each individual must realize that, when people work together, a better product will result, and it will contain the best ideas and efforts of each team member.

> For the many . . . when they meet together may very likely be better than the outstanding few, if regarded not individually but collectively . . . for each individual among the many have their share of virtue and prudence, and when they meet together, they become, in a manner, one [person], who has many feet and hands and senses . . . for some understand one part, and some another, and among them they understand the whole.
>
> Aristotle, 4th century B.C.

SECTION 1.3   PLANNING FOR PERFORMANCE

Steps in a Project

The seven steps of a project start with an idea and extend through sales and distribution:

1. Idea
2. Applied research
3. Design
4. Development
5. Marketing
6. Production (or construction)
7. Sales and distribution

This text is concerned with the first six steps. The steps for successful project performance are iterative rather than linear and are explained below. The sequence of steps may differ from one project to another.

Idea.   An idea is a concept first formulated in the mind of one or more persons. It may be a concept that can be designed or developed immediately, or it may require further study.

Applied Research.   Research, from "search again," is careful, patient, systematic, diligent, and organized inquiry or examination in some field of knowledge. It is undertaken to establish facts or principles. It is a laborious or continued search after truth or information. Applied research is an investigation whose goal is to convert an idea into a practical plan. If the applied research produces negative results, then the project will be terminated without further expenditure of funds and time.

Design.   Design refers to the conversion of an idea into a plan for a product, process, or procedure by arranging the parts of a system via drawings or computer models so that the parts will perform the desired functions when converted to an actual product.

Development.   Development refers to the activity of modifying a design, product, process, or procedure. It may include new features, a different appearance, or only minor cosmetic changes as it progresses from an idea to an actual product, process, or procedure. Development starts with a design and converts it into a product, process, or procedure. There may be several stages of experimental models, breadboard models, experimental prototypes, and production prototypes. The redesigned product, process, or procedure is now ready for production.

Marketing.   Marketing (or market research) involves determining the need for a new product, process, or procedure, and the amount of money that potential customers are willing to invest in that new product, process, or procedure. It is from a marketing study that the number of potential sales is estimated. The focus of the marketing effort is to determine if the new product will sell in sufficient quantities to meet the total project costs, as well as earn a profit. Marketing may occur prior to or during the design and development efforts.

Production.   Production is the act of making numerous, identical copies of an item that has been designed and developed. Production is more efficient and less costly when specialized manufacturing equipment and processes are used to produce the quantities required. However, the quantities to be produced must be great enough to justify the expense of specialized equipment and processes.

The life cycle flow

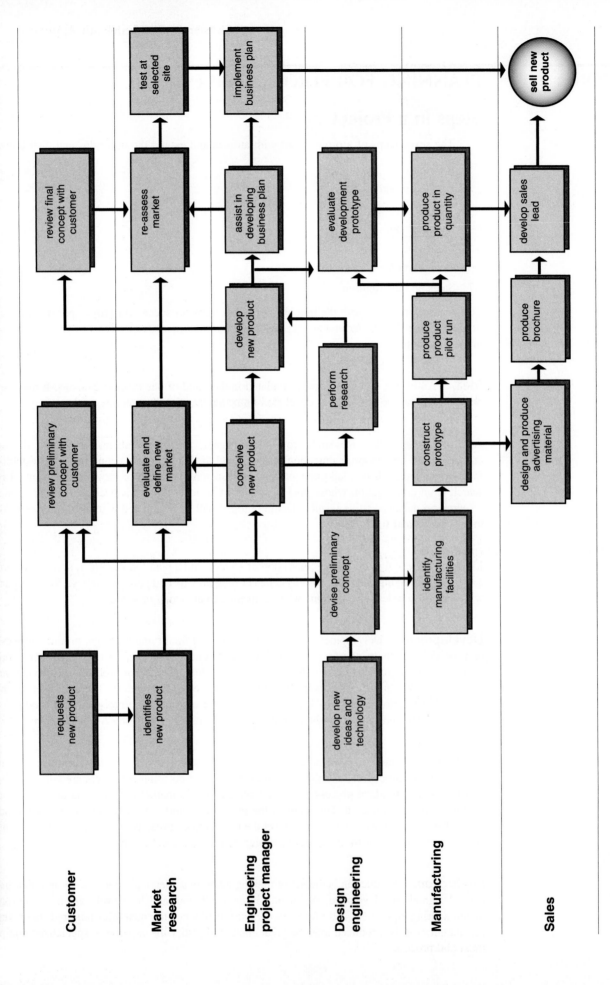

Figure 1.5 The life cycle flow

Sales and Distribution. Selling is required if a project is to be financially profitable. For items manufactured in small quantities, sales consists of contacting those select customers who are willing to pay for the item. For items manufactured in large quantities, many customers are involved. Items often are packaged and sent to distributors, who then supply the products to retail outlets for final sale of the item to customers.

The Life Cycle

The life cycle of the project plan is complete when the initial idea has been converted, via applied research, design, development, marketing, production, and sales and distribution, into a successful and profitable product.

The life cycle of the project plan is now complete. The initial idea has been converted, via applied research, design, development, marketing, production, and sales and distribution, into a successful and profitable product. To accomplish this result, effective planning is necessary. The life cycle flow is shown in figure 1.5.

Concurrent Engineering

Concurrent engineering is a systematic approach that integrates the initial idea for a project with its applied research, design, development, marketing, production, sales, and distribution. Concurrent engineering leads to a more efficient and shorter design cycle while maintaining or improving product quality and reliability. See Banios (1992). Incorporated are:

- customer requests and ideas,
- market research regarding the potential product,
- design and development of models,
- manufacturing prototypes and a pilot run, and
- sales-material preparation and testing.

See figure 1.5 for an example of the overall cycle.

Concurrent engineering compresses the schedule; thus, many activities can be performed either simultaneously or with some overlap. The result is a shortening of the overall cycle time without adversely affecting the project quality, material delivery, and customer sales.

Schedules are devised that indicate when the normally sequential steps and phases of a project can be performed concurrently—that is, overlapped. Planning is based upon interim and final project goals; methods are then devised to achieve these goals. Next, the results are coordinated, and priorities are assigned and tied to customer needs. Engineering, manufacturing, and marketing must work together from the outset to anticipate problems and bottlenecks and to eliminate them promptly. However, no matter how streamlined the schedule, it needs to be remembered that a design actually desired by potential customers succeeds much better in the marketplace than a design that is merely acceptable.

Concurrent engineering recognizes the roles of marketing, manufacturing, and servicing in bringing products to market and in supporting them throughout their life cycle. It emphasizes the need for shared understanding of problems to be solved—as well as meeting the customer expectations as they evolve.

By using electronic communications networks, engineers have greatly reduced the time spent in reviewing designs with remotely located manufacturers. Technology allows design changes to be reviewed and implemented in a quick and systematic manner.

SECTION 1.4 APPLYING THE SYSTEMATIC APPROACH

This section describes in more detail the **systematic approach** to projects and programs first documented by Goode and Machol (1957). When applied wisely to both design and management, this approach most often leads to a less costly and more acceptable, efficient, and effective product or process.

*The life cycle of a typical **system** consists of research, conception, engineering, production, operation, and, finally, retirement or decommissioning.*

Applying the system concept requires maintaining an objective view of how each portion of a project interacts, or fits in, with the entire project. The life cycle of a typical **system** consists of research, conception, engineering, production, operation, and, finally, retirement or decommissioning. These steps are described in more detail in *An Engineering Practices Course* by E. W. Banios (1992). Our presentation focuses upon the conception, engineering, and production portion of the life cycle.

Definitions

As you progress through this book, you will encounter new words and phrases, as well as many words that are familiar to you from other contexts but that are used in the book in a specialized, or technical, way. To aid your understanding, here is a list of technical definitions of basic terms used in this book. These words have special meanings for scientists, engineers, and technologists.

Our Definitions

A **function** is the capability of an individual or equipment to perform in a given manner.

A **system** is any combination of things that actively work together to serve a common purpose. Systems are composed of combinations of parts, people, and procedures.

A **subsystem** is any portion of a system that performs one or more functions that can, alone or in a system, operate separately.

A **device** is that portion of a subsystem that can, alone or in that subsystem, perform an identifiable function.

A **component** or **part** is a portion of a device that normally performs a useful function only when used within that device.

Definitions of all other terms are given in the glossary.

Figure 1.6 shows how aircraft components, devices, and subsystems relate. The aircraft is the primary system for the aircraft designers. Three of its subsystems consist of the airframe, the internal electronics, and the people involved. The **airframe** subsystem consists of the body, wings, tail, and engines. The **electronics** subsystem consists of communications, navigation, and control devices. The **people** subsystem consists of the crew, passengers, and support personnel.

Here is another example from the aviation industry. The Federal Aviation Authority considers its traffic management system to be the primary system. Each participating airline and airport is a subsystem to be managed. Thus, at this level of consideration, each aircraft is a device to be guided, whether the aircraft is on the ground taxiing, taking off, in the air, or landing.

Figure 1.6 Component interrelation

Phases of Project

PPCP 1

A typical project or program that utilizes the systematic approach consists of four phases.

A typical project or program that uses the systematic approach consists of four phases between the consideration of an original idea and its delivery as a product or service. The four phases with their general descriptions are shown in figure 1.7 and are explained below.

Conception Phase: Ideas are developed and evaluated. Such practical considerations as technical feasibility and sources of funding need to be kept in mind.

The definition of an activity is given following the listing of the activities for the four phases. For the Conception Phase, they are:

- Organize a Team
- Formulate a Concept and Select the Project
- Initiate Conception Phase Documents
- Expand Team and Identify Supporting Organizations
- Complete the Planning of the Next Phases of Work
- Convert Document Drafts into Final Documents

Study Phase: Ideas developed in the conception phase are studied. One idea (or solution or direction) is selected and becomes the chosen system. Potential designs are investigated. Where necessary, applied research is performed.

For the Study Phase, the activities are:

- Organize the Study Phase Work
- Establish Ground Rules for Study and Design Phases
- Study Solutions to be Considered for Design
- Gather and Evaluate Information
- Select and Plan One Solution to the Project
- Document the Selected Solution
- Verify and Obtain Funding

Design Phase: The chosen system is designed in detail so that it can be constructed. Parts of the system design may need to be modified. More detailed cost information is available. Marketing can now establish a price and determine if the product will sell at that price.

Figure 1.7 The four phases of the systematic approach

For the Design Phase, the activities are:

- Organize the Design Phase Work
- Select the Solution Details to be Implemented
- Document the Design Solution
- Prepare for the Implementation Phase Work
- Obtain Implementation Phase Funding

Implementation Phase: The chosen system is constructed and delivered.

Implementation Phase Activities are:

- Obtain Implementation Phase Funds
- Review Design Phase Documents
- Allocate Tasks to the Implementation Phase Team
- Prepare to Produce the Designed Article
- Produce and Evaluate Product
- Revise, Review, and Deliver Final Documentation

and, where applicable

- Operate and Maintain Customer-Contracted Articles
- Review the Results of the Implementation Phase
- Pursue New Projects

When a new project consists simply of a slight modification of a previously completed project, the Conception Phase will require less time and attention. Also, the Study Phase can either be shortened or merged with the Design Phase.

The four phases of a project that uses the systematic approach—Conception, Study, Design, Implementation—may overlap.

In chapters 2 through 5, the activities associated with each phase are described in detail. Even if a project is a small one, it will involve all or most of the activities described in these chapters. These phases may overlap. For discussion purposes, we will consider them to be separate in time, as mutually exclusive phases.

In chapters 2 through 5, we will discuss the purpose and goal for each phase. First, let us examine the definitions of the words *purpose* and *goal*.

Purpose: That which one proposes to accomplish or perform; the reason that you want to do something; an aim, intention, design, or plan.

Goal: An object of desire or intent; that which a person sets as an objective to be reached or accomplished; the end or final purpose; an ambition, aim, mark, objective, or target.

Note that there is some overlap between these two definitions. *Purpose* indicates the direction in which you want to proceed; *goal* indicates the end you want to achieve.

Before a project can be completed, it must be selected and started; the project must be **initiated.** We will discuss how projects are initiated in chapter 2 and include a case study as an example. In subsequent chapters, we will cover project planning, performance, and control—through a discussion of project phases and a project example.

Project Activities

We have divided a project into four phases—conception, study, design, and implementation. Each phase is subdivided into activities with one group of activities per phase. An **activity** is an active process, such as searching, learning, doing, or writing, that involves the application of both mental and physical energy. Each activity is further subdivided into smaller, more manageable steps or components until the deliverable products and documents are defined in enough detail to allow better management control.

The Case Study—Project Example

We have devised an example that will be used to illustrate the project phases, described in chapters 2, 3, 4, and 5. In the project example, first-year engineering and technology students apply their skills, capabilities, and interests to a project of their selection. We have selected Northeastern University in Boston as their school. The cities and towns described are suburbs of Boston, Massachusetts. All the student names are fictitious.

CHAPTER OBJECTIVES SUMMARY

Now that you have finished this chapter, you should be able to:

1. Explain the importance of planning, performance, and control in the execution of projects.
2. Define a project and a program; explain their similarities and differences.
3. Explain how projects are managed and evaluated.
4. Explain why teamwork is important on projects.
5. Name the steps in the life cycle of a project.
6. Describe the four phases of a project that uses a systematic approach.

EXERCISES

1.1   Choose a system that you have encountered during your daily activities. For that system, list some of its subsystems, devices, and components. Sketch a figure that presents the relationship among the subsystems, devices, and components. Consider what parts of your system could be considered a subsystem or device in another primary system.

1.2   Acquire a technical dictionary if you do not already have one. Compare the definitions given in section 1.4 with those given in your technical dictionary. Discuss with other students how and why they differ from the ones we have offered in this book.

1.3   List at least five projects and programs that you have either encountered or read about recently. For those projects and programs, write a brief paragraph on why they are labeled *project* or *program*.

   Projects and programs might involve one or more of the following engineering and science specialties:

   architectural, chemical, civil, computer (hardware and/or software), electrical, electronic, environmental, industrial, information systems, marine science, mechanical, systems engineering, and transportation.

1.4   Prepare a list of your personal interests and skills that would apply to working as a member of a team on a class project. Describe your previous experiences in performing and documenting work that you have accomplished. Consider at least the following questions:

   Do you enjoy writing and sketching?

   Are you able to devise and document original material?

   Do you prefer to edit the writing of others?

1.5   With your instructor or faculty advisor, organize one or more teams to search for one or more class projects. Each project should require the application of more than one specialty. In the search for a project, ask, "Who will verify that all of the designs and activities are accomplished satisfactorily?"

The Systematic Approach

The Conception Phase

The Study Phase

The Design Phase

The Implementation Phase

1. Systematic Approach

2. Conception Phase

Conception Phase Purpose and Goal

Conception Phase Activities

Conception Phase Documents

Defining Phase Completion

3. Study Phase

4. Design Phase

5. Implementation Phase

1. What are the purpose and goal of the Conception Phase of a project?

2. What tasks are involved in the Conception Phase of a project, and what activities or steps are performed to complete these tasks?

3. What is the process of selecting a project? How is brainstorming involved in the process? What criteria can be used to evaluate the choice of projects?

4. How are teams for projects organized, utilized, and expanded?

5. What kinds of risks may be involved in projects, and how are alternative solutions found?

6. How are tasks, schedules, and budget constraints identified for a project?

7. What documents are prepared during the Conception Phase?

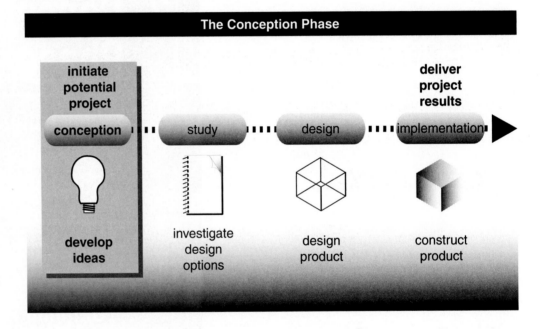

I have learned throughout my life as a composer chiefly through my mistakes and pursuits of false assumptions, not by my exposure to founts of wisdom and knowledge.

Igor Stravinsky, 1966

This chapter discusses how projects are first selected, how teams are assembled, and how tasks, costs, and schedules are estimated so project funding can be pursued.

CONCEPTION

SECTION 2.1   CONCEPTION PHASE PURPOSE AND GOAL

The **purpose** of the Conception Phase is to develop ideas for projects that are of interest and value to you, to potential funding sources, and to your project team. The **goal** of the Conception Phase is the preparation of a list of practical ideas that will lead to a viable project.

At the end of the Conception Phase, you should know how to accomplish the following:

- Define a problem and the risks involved.
- Identify both your customers and potential funding sources.
- Improve your skills and abilities, as well as those of the team, to meet the needs of the project.
- Identify others who have the skills and abilities that you and your team lack.
- Prepare documentation for your proposed solutions.
- Devise a plan that includes the work you must perform.

The plan produced at the initiation of a project will determine the remainder of the Conception Phase, as well as the work to be accomplished during the Study, Design, and Implementation Phases. The associated costs for converting the plan to practical ideas must be included during the Conception Phase. If the project is not selected until the beginning of the Study Phase, then the approximate costs of all plans must be included here.

During this phase, you will continually revise all plans, including cost estimates, when you obtain significant new information or when you develop new ideas. If you are part of a profit-oriented organization, you must plan to earn money in excess of your expenditures so that you and your team will have the financial resources to identify, propose, and accomplish new projects at a later time.

The project team for the Conception Phase consists primarily of diverse creators.

The project team for the Conception Phase consists primarily of diverse creators (Kim, 1990). (See figure 1.4.) A few performers are added later to provide the necessary details. As a project progresses from one phase to another, the number of creators is decreased. They are replaced by planners, performers, and administrators who are experienced in (1) working with the ultimate users and (2) performing various aspects of the project life cycle. (The project life cycle was discussed in sections 1.3 and 1.4.)

Once the creators' work on a project is over, the manager who does not want to lose their expertise must provide different work for them. This way they will be available as creators for future projects. Thus, the organization chart showing the interaction among people is often a fluid one. It must be adapted to the work being performed at the moment.

SECTION 2.2   CONCEPTION PHASE ACTIVITIES

The activities for the Conception Phase consist of the following:

Activity 1: Organize a Team and Formulate a Concept

Activity 2: Select the Project

    2A: Identify customers with a need to be fulfilled.

    2B: Locate sources of funds to fulfill that need.

    2C: Brainstorm to select projects to be considered.

    2D: Identify risks for each potential project.

    2E: Select one project and gather more information.

    2F: Search for and document alternative solutions.

Activity 3: Initiate Conception Phase Documents

    3A: Prepare the Project Selection Rationale.

    3B: Prepare the Preliminary Specification.

    3C: Prepare the Project Description.

    3D: List task, schedule, and budget constraints.

Activity 4: Expand Team and Identify Supporting Organizations

Activity 5: Complete the Planning of the Next Phases of Work

Activity 6: Convert Document Drafts into Final Documents

The sequence of activities given below may change from one project to another. However, all of these activities must be completed during the Conception Phase.

Activity 1: Organize a Team and Formulate a Concept

The tasks of the Conception Phase are these:

- *Develop ideas for projects*
- *Prepare budget and schedule estimates*
- *Write task descriptions*
- *Organize a team*

During the Conception Phase, you develop ideas, prepare accompanying budget estimates, write approximate task descriptions, and devise approximate schedules for each of the projects under consideration. If the project is complicated, you may devise a model. See chapter 9.

You must also select and organize a project team. The team members should be compatible, with complementary skills and abilities. They must all contribute to and investigate the proposed ideas.

Some individuals prefer to work alone on an assignment. However, someone must monitor the work of these individuals so that it remains on schedule, within budget, and is performed to meet the technical requirements of the project. These "loners" should be encouraged to interchange ideas with the other team members.

Realize in advance that the members of your team may have to be changed. Personnel changes are often required to meet the changing needs of your proposed project so that the project remains viable. Changes may also have to occur if significant personality conflicts arise. Remember—a team that can work together *effectively* is being assembled, organized, and assessed.

One team member must be designated as team leader or project manager. This person has the responsibility of organizing and directing the efforts of all the other team members, as described in chapter 6. This manager (or leader) should be a decisive person with both technical and people skills. The manager directs, controls, and verifies project performance and status. The manager also adds new team members as the need for new skills and abilities is identified and terminates or transfers them to other projects when they are no longer needed.

The typical sequence for project conception is shown in figure 2.1. Your proposed projects should focus upon those ideas that

Projects must be practical. They should

- *Meet the needs of the community*
- *Improve skills of team members*
- *Be capable of being funded*

1. Consider the needs of the local community;

2. Use and improve your personal and team skills, abilities, and interests;

3. Concentrate on what you and your team can do well;

4. Identify projects that can be funded by interested people and organizations.

Figure 2.1   Project conception

During this phase you will continue to gather applicable technical data that will assist you in arriving at a realistic concept while you prepare rough plans, and cost and schedule estimates. Later, you will examine how to use the brainstorming concept to expand upon your initial ideas for projects in a positive way. Brainstorming occurs before you select a specific project. Brainstorming is the most commonly applied of the many varied techniques for idea generation. Some of these techniques are described in appendix A.

While you consider and evaluate a variety of projects, you are actually developing ideas that might become the selected project. Expand all ideas and gather enough information for each potential project to allow you and your team to select one project to pursue in detail. Team members should refrain from criticizing evolving ideas during the brainstorming or any other idea-generation process. As you consider potential projects, you should also explore related projects and gather additional information associated with them.

PLANNING AHEAD

As you plan a project, your plans will include answers to questions that start with *who, what, when, where, why,* and *how* (see figure 2.2):

Who will be responsible for the work?

What is to be accomplished and by whom?

When is it to be implemented?

Where is it to be performed?

Why should it be performed?

How will the performance of the project be controlled?

Before you formally initiate a project, you must justify that project. Consider these questions:

Who would be the potential customer and is the proposed project worthwhile to the potential customer?

What will be the approximate cost of the project?

When does the customer require the project to be completed?

Where will the funds for the project originate?

Why should this project be pursued instead of another project?

How will be the project be accomplished?

You and your team must answer these questions, and perhaps other questions, before a significant amount of money and effort is expended.

Convene meetings during which various proposed projects are compared and the questions *who, what, when, where, why,* and *how* are asked. Often, if you combine several proposed projects,

PPCP 2

CONCEPTION

Figure 2.2 The key questions in project planning

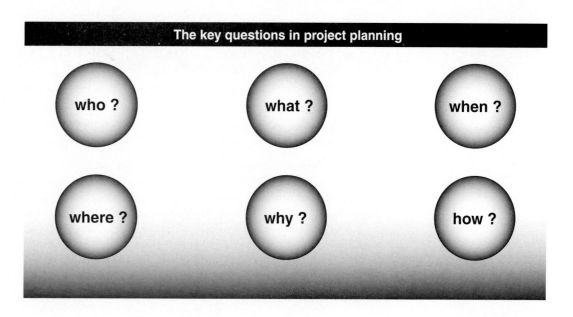

The key questions in project planning

who ?   what ?   when ?

where ?   why ?   how ?

the combined project will lead you to a better one. You should make such decisions only after you have gathered and compared enough information. (How much information you gather and compare requires a qualitative judgment.)

Teams must review all potential projects prior to extensive planning for any one project.

For each proposed project, you must prepare rough plans that provide details concerning the additional work required for you to perform the next three phases. Your plans should include the best available approximations to the required tasks, schedules, and costs. (These three interrelated documents are described in chapter 7.) While you prepare rough plans, and cost and schedule estimates, you will continue to gather applicable technical data to assist you in arriving at a realistic plan. Consider such factors as project cost and complexity, and identify potential customers. Your estimates will change as more data and ideas are gathered, but you must review all potential projects prior to extensive planning. Who will be helpful during such reviews? The manager must choose these people carefully.

The shaded portion of this text, starting below, presents a project example (major case study) that provides specific examples of the general activities described. If you desire to examine only the case study material, then read just the shaded portions of this and succeeding chapters. They flow together and provide a consecutive description of our project approach.

PROJECT EXAMPLE

Professor Thomas E. Hulbert has organized a team of six first-year engineering technology students from Northeastern University in Boston, Massachusetts. Under his guidance, they investigate several local cities and towns in search of a project to perform. Their participation in the project is designed to enhance their skills and abilities in the civil, electrical, mechanical, and industrial fields of engineering and technology.

The team must identify customers, locate sources of money, and select a project in the first six weeks.

Starting October 1, this team is allowed six weeks to perform the Conception Phase activities. They must first identify customers who have a need that could be fulfilled by a project. Then they must locate sources of money that could fund the project. Their selected project must be implemented within a twenty-six-week school term that begins on March 1 and continues through the end of August.

The initial team consists of students from a variety of backgrounds:

Roger Stein had a paper route; worked in a supermarket; is friendly; likes being around people.

Alice D'Annolfo worked with her father and uncle in construction; enjoys working outdoors.

Laura Drake was involved in high school band and field hockey; is creative and is fascinated by science and technology.

Jose Hernandez worked in a pizza parlor; is expressive; likes to work with his hands and with computers.

Kim Wong worked in her parents' restaurant; is friendly; has an interest in chemistry.

Ellery Kistler is a Russian immigrant with drafting experience; is shy and retiring; enjoys designing and constructing model ships.

After three ballots, the students' choice for team leader is Roger Stein.

Roger organizes the six of them into three teams of two persons. Their initial assignment is to discuss potential projects with local business leaders and members of Northeastern's Industry Advisory Committee for Engineering Technology. The teams are to provide interim written reports to Roger; these reports document each of their discussions. Then the group is to determine which potential projects could be performed within the given time. The students will meet formally with Professor Hulbert within three weeks and report the combined results of their activities.

After comparing their personal interests, the team members decide that a small construction or repair project could be accomplished within the time allotted and with the skills available.

Next, they consider the *who, what, when, where, why,* and *how* questions:

Who *will be responsible for searching for a project?* Roger assigns that responsibility to Alice because of her family background and her own personal interests.

What *is to be accomplished and by whom?* Roger will search for funding sources, with the guidance of Professor Hulbert. Ellery is asked to work with Laura in developing sketches of any ideas to be considered.

When *is it to be implemented?* The group agrees that the entire project must be accomplished within the remaining twenty-six weeks of the school year.

Where *is it to be performed?* The project must not require more than twenty miles of travel because there are only two persons with cars.

Why *should it be performed?* The project must use and improve the skills of the six team members. It should also apply the skills, abilities, and interests of other students in their first-year class if they become team members.

How *will the performance of the project be controlled?* Jose and Kim are assigned to develop the necessary tasks, schedules, and budgets. They may later become responsible for monitoring the project tasks, schedules, and budgets once these are defined. Roger will be responsible for ensuring that the quality of the finished product meets whatever specifications are agreed upon by the team members and the potential client.

The team members note that the Conception Phase has been allotted only six weeks. Thus, they decide to explore potential projects for the first two of those six weeks.

They also decide, in advance, to concentrate on small renovation or construction projects, as these will best utilize their skills. Three categories of nearby potential customers are established: business, government, and industry—one for each of the three teams. Each team is to work through the contacts of their professors and establish potential projects.

Formal project initiation will occur after all the information has been gathered, and each potential project justified. The group prepares a list of questions—an informal questionnaire—and obtains appointments with local business, government, and industry officials through the university's Industrial Advisory Board. The questions include these:

Who would be the potential customer, and is the proposed project worthwhile to that customer?

What will be the approximate cost of the project?

When does the customer require the project to be completed?

Where will the funds for the project originate?

Why should this project be pursued instead of another project?

How will the project be accomplished?

Is the project composed of parts that will fit together smoothly?

Is there a definite sequence for optimum performance of the project?

Can the project be completed within a time acceptable to the customer?

Are the team members able to accomplish the necessary work within available funds?

Will the completed project improve team members' skills and abilities?

Is there a technical or financial risk in pursuing the proposed project?

Three categories of nearby potential customers are established for the student teams: business, government, and industry—one for each of the three teams. Each team is to work through the contacts of their professors and establish potential projects.

On a weekly basis, Professor Hulbert meets with each team to assess its progress and guide it toward its final goal. He insists that the students prepare a trip report for each meeting, whether the visits are single or team visits. The team members feel apprehensive about interviewing persons unknown to them and about the amount of effort and writing they anticipate. Professor Hulbert indicates that this work is an important part of the Conception Phase initial research. He also informs them that they may feel more comfortable by first talking with and interviewing people they know personally regarding ideas for potential projects. Following these experiences, they can then visit and interview persons unknown to them and have a greater feeling of confidence.

On Monday afternoon of the third week, Roger convenes a meeting where the potential projects are compared and the answers to the questions *who, what, when, where, why,* and *how* are examined.

Each of the three teams is given one week to develop preliminary plans that provide details regarding the work that will be required for the next three phases of the potential project. The teams are instructed to develop approximations of the required tasks, schedules, and costs. Professor Hulbert invites three of the Industrial Advisory Board members to attend the review of the team efforts.

Activity 2: Select the Project

During this activity, you perform the following tasks:

1. Identify customers who indicate they have a need; establish the technical problems and risks associated with their need.
2. Determine if the potential customers have the funds for fulfilling that need and separate from the stated "need" their actual desires and luxuries.
3. Locate the source of those funds.
4. Brainstorm to determine what projects should be considered.
5. Identify the problems and risks associated with each project.
6. Search for acceptable alternative solutions to each proposed project.

The process of selecting a project is often known as *synthesis* (Pugh, 1993, p. 68). The synthesis process includes two major cyclical components:

- The generation of concepts that are solutions to meet the stated need.
- The evaluation of these concepts to select the one that is most suited to matching the stated need.

Concepts are often best generated by individuals; concept selection and enhancement is often best performed in groups. The outcome of the [Conception] Phase is a complete concept, engineered to an acceptable level to establish its practicality. Details are saved for the Study and Design Phases.

Activity 2A: Identify Customers with a Need to Be Fulfilled

If money is a significant factor in developing a project, then project requirements must be separated into needs, desires, and luxuries.

Your projects must have a useful purpose. Therefore, as you evaluate potential projects, members of your team should determine the requirements of the local community and industry. These requirements are often categorized as needs, desires, or luxuries. If money is no object, then the distinctions between needs, desires, and luxuries are unimportant. If money is a significant factor, then the requirements must be separated into needs, desires, and luxuries.

What are the applicable definitions of needs, desires, and luxuries?

Needs.   A need is something that is considered necessary or essential. During World War II, Dr. Abraham Maslow studied the hierarchy of needs. He claimed that certain needs become dominant when more basic needs are satisfied. Thus, the lower-level needs must be satisfied before the higher-level needs become apparent. The list below indicates his hierarchy:

- Physiological needs: air, food, water
- Safety needs: protection against danger, threat, deprivation, arbitrary management decisions; the need for security in a dependent relationship
- Social needs: belonging, association, acceptance, giving and receiving of love and friendship
- Ego needs: self-respect and confidence, achievement, self-image, group image and reputation, status, recognition, appreciation
- Self-fulfillment needs: realizing self potential, self-development, creativity

Some persons or groups may believe that they have a need. The following questions may help you test if a need is real or imagined:

- Can you determine if the need is real or imagined?
- Are they or you able to express that need in writing?
- Can the need be separated into parts?
- Is each part important enough to continue to be considered as a separate need?
- How serious are you about committing funding to fulfill the need?

The persons or groups may wish to have their "need" fulfilled, yet they may not be able to justify the time and money to do so. In this case, the "need" may be merely a desire.

Desires.   A desire is similar to a wish. It is a longing for something that promises enjoyment or satisfaction. A desire, by definition, is not a need. A strong desire may eventually become a need; a weak desire may be considered a luxury.

Luxuries.   A luxury is the use and enjoyment of the best and most costly things which offer the most physical, intellectual, or emotional comfort, pleasure, and satisfaction. A luxury is considered to be unnecessary to life and health.

The interrelationship of needs, desires, and luxuries is illustrated in figure 2.3. The three definitions given are qualitative, not quantitative. One of your most difficult tasks during the

Figure 2.3 Comparing needs, desires, and luxuries

Comparing needs, desires, and luxuries

most **significant** least

needs	desires	luxuries
housing	purchase car	purchase sports car
food	purchase home	purchase 2nd home
clothing	join health club	visit France

Conception Phase is to assign numerical values to needs, desires, and luxuries, and to weigh them with regard to the total system concept as described by von Oech (1993). However, if the customer (client) is willing to pay for it and the luxury is ethical, then the project can include the luxury.

Systems are normally implemented to provide for needs, rather than for desires and luxuries.

Systems are normally implemented to provide for needs. However, if you, the contractor, can include the desires and luxuries at minimal additional cost, you may be selected as the winning bidder. You must use judgment to determine the proper emphasis among needs, desires, and luxuries because it is unlikely that the potential customers will express their requirements in a clear and concise manner. The proposal evaluator, or team of evaluators of all competing proposals, will also be using judgment regarding the selection of the winning proposal. As Wilde (1978) notes: "As in life, instinct often precedes wisdom."

Market research is best initiated during the Conception Phase. People who specialize in market research have abilities that range from examining patents, trademarks, registered designs, copyrights, scientific journal proceedings, and reference books to less technical skills that include determining the need for a new product, process, or procedure—a new item—and the amount of money that potential customers are willing to invest in that new item. Because market researchers must often estimate the sales potential of a proposed item, they must try to determine if the new item will sell in sufficient quantities to meet the expected total project costs and earn a profit for the company. They must be involved in, or kept informed of, the total design status. However, they are often not trained in a background of total design and are thus unlikely to ask the right questions. See Pugh (1993, pp. 155–157). Some typical questions to ask potential customers or clients are the following:

- What performance do you require, and in what operating environment?
- What are you prepared to pay for this performance?
- How soon do you want the product, process, or procedure?
- What are your expectations regarding quality, reliability, life expectancy, and level of maintenance and documentation?
- What do you like best, or dislike most, about your competitor's designs?
- What safety factors and ergonomic features do you expect to be a part of the new product, process, or procedure, and how are they to interact with your related systems?

All design should start with a need that, when satisfied, will either fit into an existing market or create a market of its own. From the statement of that need, a Preliminary Specification is prepared during the Conception Phase that will evolve into the Design Specification in the Study Phase. Pugh (p. 104) provides a design sequence that starts with a market analysis, includes study, design, development, and production, and ends with selling the product.

PROJECT EXAMPLE

Alice discovers, through her uncle, that the planning board of the town of Bedford, Massachusetts, has devised a town redevelopment plan that is being circulated to contractors for review. Her uncle sends Alice a copy of the plan. There are five projects (figure 2.4) in the plan that the team might have the skills to implement:

- Pave walkways
- Improve playground
- Improve swimming pool
- Construct children's activity center
- Replace old carousel

The team meets and considers these five projects. They visit officials in Bedford to obtain additional information and to see if it is possible to separate needs, desires, and luxuries. They are told that *price* will greatly influence what Bedford can do and will determine the separation among needs, desires, and luxuries.

Town officials note that some town and state money is available, but it is not enough to accomplish any one project. The team must determine the availability of other money and its sources. The team decides to follow the path indicated in bold type in figure 2.4.

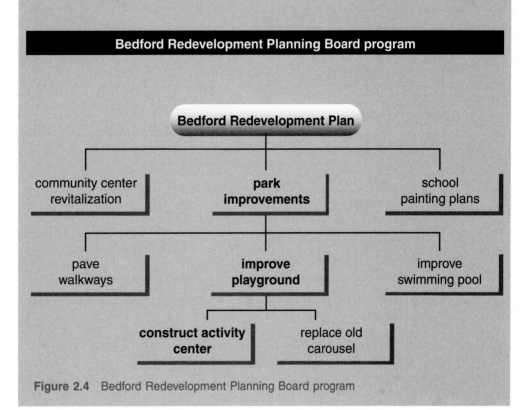

Figure 2.4 Bedford Redevelopment Planning Board program

Activity 2B: Locate Sources of Funds to Fulfill That Need

*There are three types of funding sources to be considered: **government, charitable organizations,** and **lending institutions.***

There are three types of funding sources to be considered: **government, charitable organizations,** and **lending institutions.** Money to fund the project may come from one or more local, state, or federal government agencies. It may be an investment from a bank or other funding or lending agency. It may also be a donation from a corporation or foundation.

When foundations **donate** funds to a worthy project, the foundation executives must believe that the image of their foundation will be enhanced in the minds of the general public when its donation to that project is announced. Organizations that donate money usually want to see the results of their donation within a preestablished length of time. They want their gift to provide something useful to the world as they envision it; they want to know that their donation was not wasted.

Institutions that **invest** their money want it repaid within an agreed time and with interest payments for its use—their **return on investment** (Heyne, 1991). The borrower may also be required to pay for a perceived risk, which would originate from the lender's worry that the borrower might not be able to repay the borrowed funds if the project should fail. In a case of perceived risk, some lenders may require that the borrower provide loan collateral, a security given as a pledge for the repayment of an obligation. This security may be in the form of bonds, stock certificates, or other property of value, and the loan would then be referred to as a "secured loan." Other lenders may rely on the reputation of the borrower, the credit rating of those involved, or the perceived merits of the project itself to guarantee repayment.

PROJECT EXAMPLE

Before the team selects a project, the following information is gathered:

The town of Bedford has only enough funds for the school painting plans and the swimming pool improvement. The selectmen (the town governing body) prefer to use the funding for new construction rather than the funding of repairs.

The Commonwealth of Massachusetts has $15 000 allotted to assist in projects that will provide summer work for young people. All the projects proposed by the selectmen cost more than the allotted $15 000.

An additional $5 000 was discovered to be available from a fund provided to the town via the will of Eleanor Kewer, a retired teacher. The money from this fund must be used for the construction and maintenance of facilities for school-age children.

Roger Stein approaches Professor Hulbert, who then calls both a selectman in Bedford and the attorney responsible for the commitment of the funds of Eleanor Kewer. The attorney encourages the team to work through Northeastern University, which would be responsible for the effort. Professor Hulbert sends to the selectman and the attorney a brochure that summarizes the types of community-oriented projects previously performed by other teams of students at Northeastern University. The selectman and attorney ask that Northeastern prepare a proposal for their consideration. They indicate a priority interest in either constructing a children's activity center or replacing the old carousel.

Normally you must acquire a small amount of funding from an initial funding source for all or most of the Conception Phase. If the labor of team members is your only significant initial requirement, then perhaps all the funding you need would be to pay for office supplies. These supplies might be borrowed. For example, you may be able to utilize computers on a time-available basis from other projects.

Authorization must be obtained from the funding source before money can be transferred from the source to a project.

At the same time that you are seeking funding for the Conception Phase, you are also identifying potential sources of funding for the entire project. Your project can begin when money is available for it. You must obtain authorization from your funding source before money can be transferred from the source to your project.

Activity 2C: Brainstorm to Select Projects to Be Considered

The team must develop project options that are acceptable to all members. One technique for devising new ideas is **brainstorming,** defined as an *unrestrained* offering of ideas or suggestions by all members of a group, typically during a meeting that focuses upon a predetermined problem or a range of items.

Brainstorming is the unrestrained offering of ideas and suggestions by all members of a team during a meeting that focuses on a predetermined range of potential projects.

Brainstorming involves **creativity,** which is an important part of the Conception Phase (Kim, 1990). We use the word "creativity" to indicate a new way of thinking or looking at a problem. When new ideas are being considered, they often lead to an invention or innovation. Albert Szent-Györgyi once said, "Discovery consists of seeing what everybody has seen, and thinking what nobody has thought." The invention or innovation may be a new product, process, or procedure, or it may be the improvement, revision, or redesign of an existing one.

Young children are naturally creative because their minds are relatively unrestrained. In adulthood, our range of thinking narrows because we have been trained to conform, "play it safe," and follow the rules. Roger von Oech, in his book *A Whack on the Side of the Head*

(1993), provides a list of common ways of thinking that block creativity and explains why these ways of thinking should be discarded when we are trying to generate new ideas:

1. Find the "right" answer: There's often more than one "right" answer.

2. That's not logical: Note that logic can eliminate alternatives that seem to be contradictory, but they may turn out to be good ones.

3. Follow the rules: Change or break those rules that are no longer sensible.

4. Be practical: Ideas initially need the wide realm of the possible rather than the narrow realm of the practical. Think: "what if . . . ?" because useful ideas often occur to people while considering many useless ideas.

5. Don't be foolish: Behavior that is silly or humorous often leads to new ideas.

6. Don't make mistakes: Mistakes can be stepping stones in the creative process.

7. That's not my area: This attitude often keeps people from trying new paths. You already know what cannot be done and this can restrict the creative process. New ideas often originate when you venture outside your field of specialization.

8. I'm not creative: Self-esteem is essential to being creative; you must be willing to take risks and accept the consequences, which may be ridiculed by less creative people. If you believe that you are creative, or can be creative, then you will be creative!

Most adults need to be stimulated into new thinking; it seldom occurs spontaneously. We need to perform exercises to remove the mental blocks to new thinking. Here are some techniques you can use to help yourself to become more creative:

1. Stimulate your thinking by reversing the sequence in which you put on your clothes, such as shoes, underwear, shirts, sweaters. Reverse the right and left sequence for inserting hands and feet; it will stimulate your rusty brain cells.

2. Imagine (or observe) how a preschool child thinks about something. Children are less limited in their creativity because their school peers have yet to tease them and discourage their creativity.

3. Record your ideas as soon as you think of them. For instance, have a pad and pencil beside your bed and document your dreams.

4. Eliminate the mental blocks that prevent you from being creative. Focus upon positive thoughts. There is an old song that starts, "Accentuate the positive; eliminate the negative. . . ."

5. Prepare questions that will stimulate a variety of answers. Remember: Answers depend upon the questions asked.

6. Read something outside your area of specialty, preferably something different that you will enjoy, such as fiction or poems.

7. Laugh at yourself. A sense of humor helps because acting silly can lead to new ideas.

For your team project, initiate a nonjudgmental brainstorming session to develop a list of potential projects. The session can be structured or unstructured. A structured session requires that each person in the group be solicited in sequence and provide an idea each time, or "pass" until the next time. An unstructured session allows group members to offer ideas spontaneously. In order for the session to be successful, the team must agree to follow certain rules that have been found to be effective in promoting the uninhibited flow of ideas. In his book *Applied Imagination* (1993), Osborn recommends that brainstorming groups follow these four basic rules:

1. Defer all criticism of ideas: Participants must withhold negative judgments about suggestions. Osborn writes, "When driving for ideas, you go farther if you keep your foot off the brake."

2. Encourage a "free-wheeling" approach: The wilder the idea, the better; it is easier to tame down than to think up.

3. Go for quantity: The greater the number of ideas, the more likely there will be some winners in the bunch.

4. Combine and improve on others' suggestions: In addition to contributing ideas of their own, participants should try to add their own ideas to the suggestions of others.

In addition to Osborn's four rules, the authors and other practitioners experienced in organizing brainstorming sessions recommend the following guidelines published in the ASEE *Prism* magazine (March, 1998). These techniques have proven effective when applied to both large and small projects:

1. Carefully define the problem at the start of the brainstorming session to avoid wasting time on the wrong problem.

2. Allow individuals five minutes to consider the problem before the group tackles it to prevent a "follow-the-leader" thought process.

3. Create a comfortable, casual environment where participants do not feel intimidated so they won't speak up. A circle arrangement is a good setup. If a non-circular table is used, have the "leaders" sit in the middle of a long side to reduce any intimidation that may occur from sitting at the "head" of the table.

4. Record all suggestions. Suggestions may be lost otherwise, and documenting each one lets the participants know that the group accepts and acknowledges every idea.

5. Appoint someone, a group member or another individual, to serve as a facilitator. This person ensures that all members are following the rules.

6. Encourage participants to combine and piggyback if idea generation lags after a session starts. Ideas begin as traditional and tend to become more innovative later in the meeting.

7. Stop the session before the group fades on idea generation. Identifying the best stopping time requires practice and experience on the part of the leader.

8. Keep brainstorming groups small, from six to twelve members. It is also helpful to have participants whose backgrounds range from total familiarity with the problem to total separation from the problem.

9. After the session, classify the solutions using ABC: *A* for feasible solutions, *B* for ideas requiring further development, and *C* for long-term development and technology.

10. Report results to participants and thank them for their time and effort.

Checklists help brainstorming participants develop a budding idea or alter an old one. Run through a checklist of ways to change a current product or process. Osborn has developed the following checklist for change:

Adapt: What else is like this? What other idea does this suggest? Does the past offer a parallel? What could I copy? Whom could I emulate?

Modify: Could I add a new twist? Could I change the meaning, color, motion, sound, odor, form, or shape? What other changes could I make?

Magnify: Could I add something, such as more time or greater frequency? Could I make it stronger, higher, longer, or thicker? Could I add more ingredients? Could I duplicate, multiply, or exaggerate it?

Minify: Could I subtract something? Could I make a condensed or miniature version? Could I make it lower, smaller, shorter, or lighter? What if I omit something or streamline, divide, or understate it?

Put it to other uses: Are there new ways to use this as it is? Does it have other uses if I modify it?

Substitute: What if I used a different ingredient, material, person, process, power source, place, approach, or tone of voice?

Rearrange: Could I interchange components? Could I use a different pattern, layout, or sequence? What if I transpose the cause and effect? What if I change the pace or the schedule?

Reverse: Could I transpose positive and negative? What if I tried the opposite or reversed roles? What if I turn it backwards, upside down, or inside out?

Combine: Could I use a blend, an alloy, an assortment, or a combination? Could I combine units, purposes, appeals, or ideas?

Brainstorming can be performed at two levels. The first level concerns brainstorming ideas that could become projects. All ideas are documented and studied later so the better ones can be pursued in more detail. Once a potential project is selected, brainstorming can be applied to devising clever solutions for the selected project (see chapter 3). This second level concerns developing the details within the selected project (figure 2.5). The brainstorming approach is the same for both levels.

The following examples of projects require different sets of skills. Choosing one of these projects represents the first level of brainstorming.

- Design land usage for a housing project
- Design and construct a community center
- Design and build a model railroad control system
- Design and construct a solar-powered car
- Develop equipment for handling hazardous waste materials
- Develop procedures for handling recyclable materials
- Write new software program for . . .
- Develop a better procedure for . . .

On completion of the brainstorming session for these projects, each idea must be evaluated. Now reality must be added to the creative effort resulting from the brainstorming session.

Developing a list of project selection criteria such as the following represents the second level of brainstorming.

- What are the needs of the local community and industry?
- Are funds available to support the selected project?
- Where are potential sources for funds?
- Which projects are of interest to the team?
- Do these projects apply and improve the team members' skills and abilities?
- For the skills that the team needs, can the team acquire them through outside assistance?

Figure 2.5 The brainstorming concept

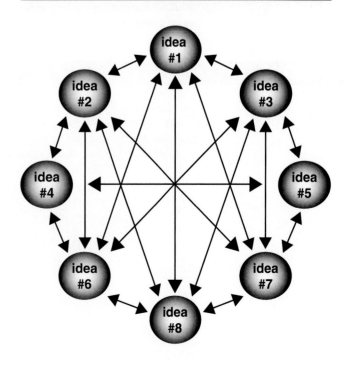

- Approximately how long will it take to study, design, and implement the project?
- Can each project be completed within the time and funds available?

The team should try to invest a minimal amount of time in the effort of deciding on one project and see that project selection is performed as efficiently as possible.

There are, of course, other criteria depending on the projects you are considering. You can assign quantitative values (rating numbers) for these criteria to assist in the project selection process. You should try to invest a minimal amount of time in this effort and see that one specific project is selected as efficiently as possible.

Each project under consideration is evaluated in terms of the criteria. As your group evaluates its combined skills, various team members will recommend projects that can be accomplished with these skills. Your team must also identify those skills they lack. You may have to revise your list of projects and the plans associated with each one depending upon the skills of team members. Sometimes a project concept may grow beyond the funds available to implement it. Again, the plans for the project may have to be revised.

Finally, select a project that you believe is worthy of the investment in planning time, people resources, and client money.

The following are descriptions of additional approaches for solving problems. They are the bionic approach and the Delphi method.

Bionics, also known as nature analysis, uses analogies that involve animals and plants. An example of creativity that has applied the bionic approach is the study of how birds are able to fly. That information was used to design aircraft.

The **Delphi** method may be used when numeric measures are applied to potential problem *solutions*. A qualitative questionnaire is devised by a coordinator to solicit each participant's independent opinion. (The coordinator must remain neutral in questionnaire preparation, analysis, and revision.) Participants are selected whose skills are different, yet their experiences are applicable to the problem. They are asked to "weigh" or "rank" each potential solution. The coordinator then analyzes the results and distributes them again to the participants. The participants vote again on the presented alternatives, and these results are then analyzed and distributed once more. This process continues until at least 75 percent of the participants agree on the design direction to be pursued.

Brainstorming is often used to devise new (creative) solutions to selected projects. It has become a formalized approach that allows only positive contributions to devising solutions to a problem. Another approach to devising solutions is the bionic approach, sometimes known as nature analysis. These and other approaches can be evaluated using the Delphi method. Project solutions are more apt to be practical if one or more of these approaches is applied to the problem under consideration.

PROJECT EXAMPLE

Roger schedules a two-hour brainstorming session for the six team members. He lists the five potential Bedford projects. The team members shout out to Roger ideas about how the projects could be implemented. Laura writes each idea on a chalkboard under its appropriate project heading. Everyone has a good time because there are no restrictions on what can be suggested, nor are there any judgments of suggestions.

The categories and the related ideas developed by the students are listed below:

- Pave walkways

    Buy buckets of asphalt from a wholesale house and apply manually.

    Let a contractor do all the paving and spend the difference on pizza.
- Improve playground

    Smooth all rough spots with a rake and roller.

    Remove the medium- and large-size rocks; build a fence with them.

- Improve swimming pool
    Drain the pool and lengthen it with concrete.
    Construct a smaller children's wading pool near it.
    Design and install a diving board.
- Construct a children's activity center
    Design and build a wood-frame house with toilet facilities.
    Purchase a prefabricated kit and assemble it on town property.
- Replace old carousel
    Use a large version of Erector™-set materials to build a new carousel.
    Design a new carousel using parts from the old one.

Copies of this list are supplied to each team member. The team members are asked to provide their comments in writing by the next Monday.

The team develops a list of project selection criteria. The criteria include the following questions:

- What does the community need?
- Is there money available for such a project, or can the team raise the money needed?
- What are the skills and interests of the team members?
- For those skills they lack, where can the team acquire outside assistance?
- Can they complete the project before they graduate or move on to other courses?

Each of the three student groups is assigned one or two of these five potential projects. The groups are to prepare a Potential Projects document, which includes a narrative and rough estimates of the tasks, schedules, and budgets for their assigned projects. (See chapter 7 for documentation details.) They are to present their results at the beginning of week 5.

Once the team brainstorms ideas, each project must be analyzed according to a set of criteria, which includes the need for the project, the funding available, and the skills of team members.

Activity 2D: Identify Risks for Each Potential Project

Formulate a list of the problems and risks involved for each potential project. To formulate a problem is to convey your ideas via words and diagrams—you prepare a document describing your ideas and opinions. Technical problems require quantitative descriptions that can be assessed by you and others. List the areas, for each potential project, that will require later detailed analysis. Prepare a document that identifies and describes these problems to the extent that they are now known. Indicate how the risks can be evaluated during the Study Phase.

High-risk areas are those portions of a proposed solution that may be difficult to implement and may cause the project to fail. High-risk areas require further investigation. High-risk areas generally fit into one of the following four categories:

High-risk areas are those portions of a proposed solution that may be difficult to implement and may cause the project to fail. For example, new technology may need to be developed.

1. An unusual approach must be considered.
2. Advances in technology are required.
3. Personnel must develop new skills.
4. New equipment, forms, and procedures must be developed and tested.

It is essential that you study and resolve each high-risk area before you proceed with the more expensive Design and Implementation Phases. Therefore, at the beginning of the Study Phase, you must assign a high priority to the investigation of all high-risk areas.

PROJECT EXAMPLE

The various projects described in the town of Bedford redevelopment plan are listed by the groups assigned to each project, along with the risks involved:

Projects	Risks
Pave walkways	Difficult material handling
Improve playground	Team lacks experience; no enthusiasm
Improve swimming pool	Chemical-handling training required
Construct children's activity center	Complicated; time-consuming
Replace old carousel	Special parts must be fabricated

Common risks for all five projects include these:

- Possible competition by local contractors
- Available funds vanishing prior to project initiation
- Lack of enthusiasm for any project by some team members

Professor Hulbert notes that Northeastern has achieved an enviable record on similar projects performed by previous classes of students. The university has been able to obtain projects because it offers work at a low cost since the students work for no wages. Thus, the school's reputation will transfer to the team's effort if the team's plans are well prepared and are convincing.

Compare the problems and associated risks of each potential project. Select one project from the list based upon your evaluation of the technical risks involved and the availability of funding. During this portion of the Conception Phase, the teams continually revise their plans as soon as significant amounts of new information or new ideas are either obtained or proposed.

Activity 2E: Select One Project and Gather More Information

Before large amounts of time and money are invested in the selection process, it is advisable to focus on one project. This is not always possible. However, one project should be selected as soon as possible, but no later than near the begining of the Study Phase.

Once the project is selected, the information-gathering process focuses on obtaining detailed information for that project.

More detailed information that directly concerns the selected project should now be gathered. Questionnaires can be developed so that interviews can be conducted with applicable personnel. Where people will be using a facility, demographic information should be obtained. Where equipment is to be designed, existing and proposed technology must be investigated. A model for simulation of all or a portion of the proposed equipment design may be necessary. (See section 9.3.) This information will be required so that practical design alternatives for implementing the project can be proposed and tested.

PROJECT EXAMPLE

At the Monday meeting for week 5, the team decides to concentrate on the activity center project. It must be affordable, and there must be money available for any contracted work and for any materials that are to be purchased. A cost limit is established:

The activity center project must cost less than $20 000.

Funding must be available in advance for the purchase of materials and services that the first-year students are not able to provide. Any money remaining in excess of the overall expenditures will be donated to a Northeastern fund for student projects so that first-year students, in subsequent years, can pursue similar ventures. Professor Hulbert negotiates with the town of Bedford and the attorney for Miss Kewer's estate for the receipt of funds. The two sources inform Professor Hulbert that they will grant funds, the decision being based on the good reputation earned by the university on previous projects.

Additional data are gathered by all six team members, who now concentrate on the activity center as the team project. The work to be performed, prior to Professor Hulbert's review, includes expanding on all the gathered data (figure 2.6) and determining if other funding sources can assist in the effort, should the $20 000 not be enough.

The team evaluates the new data gathered and decides to continue with the project of constructing an activity center for local community use. The team has previously examined its skills as a group. The members now decide that the team should be able to construct a wood-frame activity center. They proceed in the following way:

Local town leaders are contacted. They offer a parcel of public land on which the activity center could be constructed. The use of private land that could be donated to the town is also explored. Several small-business contractors in the town volunteer their expertise in those areas where the team lacks the capability. Roger first discusses this information with Professor Hulbert and later with the team.

The requirements now established by the team lead it to investigate and analyze activities that can assist children in the community to develop their abilities, skills, and positive self-image. The activity center would be designed to provide activities that promote such development on the part of children who use the center.

The team next investigates ideas for children-oriented activities that could occur within an activity center structure. They interview members of the Bedford community, including school and town administrators, teachers, parents, and children. They discover that two nearby towns have structures where children can play and learn. They also discover that, while some parts of these structures are very successful, other parts of the designs needed to be changed once the structures were in use.

The team members next organize and develop a list of potential child-oriented activities for those who might use the activity center. A demographic study of the ages, gender, and interests of the children for whom the activity center is to be designed is determined by a survey. Parents whose children are in the selected age group are surveyed for their opinions and preferences.

Conception Phase: additional effort for potential project

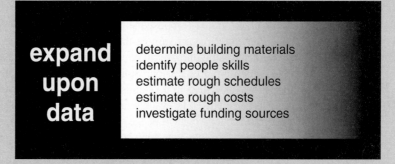

expand upon data

determine building materials
identify people skills
estimate rough schedules
estimate rough costs
investigate funding sources

Figure 2.6   Conception Phase: additional effort for potential project

The purpose of constructing the activity center becomes a combination of exercise, entertainment, and education. The team now realizes that there is more work to accomplish than there is time available. They ask Professor Hulbert for, and receive, an extra amount of time to perform these information-gathering tasks.

The consensus of the team is to offer to design and construct a wood-frame activity center. Thus, the activity center project is now definitely selected. The four phases for the activity center project are shown in figure 2.7.

A rough schedule for the activity center project is devised by Jose and Kim. One week is allotted for completing the remainder of the Conception Phase. This time includes a Conception Phase progress review to be held with Professor Hulbert.

The remainder of the week is allotted to preparing the documentation for the Conception Phase, and for preparing the estimates related to the remaining three phases. The remaining three phases are to be accomplished by the next-to-last week of August. (The last week of August is set aside for delivery of the activity center and of project documentation.) Drafts are exchanged via e-mail.

Figure 2.7   The four phases of the activity center project

Activity 2F: Search for and Document Alternative Solutions

Initiate a second brainstorming session. Prepare a list of alternative solutions for the selected project to be examined during the Study Phase. At the conclusion of this brainstorming session, identify those proposed solutions that will satisfy both your customer and your funding source. See the Project Example that follows for more detail on how this step works.

By determining the overall requirements of a project, you can apply restrictions to the results of your brainstorming session. Split your team into smaller groups so each group can pursue information that will help it establish the project requirements. Prepare an outline of a questionnaire that can be used to evaluate alternative solutions during the Study Phase. You should also establish the general content of the questionnaire at this time.

The strategy that you apply to solve a problem often depends upon your education and experiences.

- Scientists solve problems by analyzing to try to arrive at a solution.

- Designers choose solutions and try to see if one fits the problem.

Design problems cannot be stated precisely. Therefore, solutions cannot be derived directly from them. Designers have to suggest tentative solutions. The solution and problem are then explored in parallel. You need self-confidence to define and redefine a given problem. People who seek structured, well-defined problems will never appreciate the thrill of being a designer!

PROJECT EXAMPLE

A second brainstorming session is scheduled by the team members. The brainstorming results are merged, and the following list of questions related to implementing the project is assembled:

- Will the activity center require a basement?

    If there is a basement, should it be a partial or full basement?

    Should the foundation consist of concrete block or poured concrete?

- Will it be a one-story or two-story activity center?

- How many rooms should there be within the activity center?

    What uses are to be considered for each room?

    Should some activity center rooms be designed for special age or interest groups?

- Will the activity center be constructed to blend in with other local structures and the land, or should it stand out for reasons of its uniqueness?

- Are termites, snow, etc., problems in this area of the country?

Other questions can be added later as team members think of new design directions. Preliminary design requirements are established prior to extensive planning. Rough cost estimates are obtained so that the design direction can be determined during the next phase. Note that these are rough cost estimates. More detailed estimates are determined during the Study Phase (see chapter 3).

Preliminary design require-ments are established prior to extensive planning.

The establishment of requirements and design for a project is an iterative process, as will be discussed later in this book. This means the requirements are constantly being reevaluated and revised.

The general content of a design specification must now be established. Questions such as the following are asked:

- For the activity center, what locations (sites) are available?

- What are the ranges of environmental conditions, such as temperature, humidity, wind, and noise levels, that occur in this area?

- What kinds of building materials are locally available?

- What skilled labor is available locally?

- What companies and their employees might be willing to contribute labor, materials, advice, or guidance?

Some parts of the specification are initiated and written at this time. (See sections 7.1 and 8.1.) Existing local or state building codes are referenced, instead of being included in the Preliminary Specification documentation. Alice examines building codes further to ensure correct interpretation and compliance. She visits the local building, electrical, and plumbing inspectors to determine which parts of each code are stressed by the local inspectors. She also interviews contractors who are known to her father and uncle, who have worked in or near the town of Bedford. She inquires about conforming to building codes and how to determine more precisely which parts of the building codes apply to the activity center project.

Activity 3: Initiate Conception Phase Documents

Develop project plans that again include questions such as *who, what, when, where, why,* and *how:*

Who will be responsible for the work?

What is to be accomplished and by whom?

When is it to be implemented?

Where is it to be performed?

Why should it be performed?

How will the performance of the project be controlled?

The answers to these questions may have changed now that one project has been selected and more information relating to that project has been gathered.

Outlines for the documents for the Conception Phase should now be prepared. If the outlines are begun now, they can be expanded and revised to become the final documents for the Conception Phase. See activity 6 later in this chapter for a more complete discussion of the final documentation.

Activity 3A: Prepare the Project Selection Rationale

The Project Selection Rationale lists the tasks to be performed, the time required to accomplish each task, and the cost of performing each task.

The Project Selection Rationale document explains and justifies the selected project. It also contains an outline for performing that project. In order to plan the remainder of the Conception Phase and the three remaining phases, all team members involved must assume that the work will proceed as described in this evolving document. They have examined, and are examining the following questions:

1. Who investigated alternatives?
2. What led to the accepted conclusion?
3. When should one project be selected?
4. Where did we search for data?
5. Why did we select this particular project?
6. How do we plan to proceed from here?

The answers to these questions justify choosing the selected project.

The completed Project Selection Rationale document lists the tasks that were performed during the Conception Phase, explains the time and costs expended to perform them, and also explains why they were performed. (See sections 7.1 and 7.5.) See activity 6 of this chapter for an example of an outline of a Project Selection Rationale document that could be produced for the activity center project.

PROJECT EXAMPLE

Professor Hulbert advises the team to devise project plans and include revised answers to questions such as *who, what, when, where, why,* and *how.* The answers to these questions may have changed now that one project has been selected and more information relating to that project has been gathered:

Who will be responsible for the work?

What is to be accomplished and by whom?

When is it to be implemented?

Where is it to be performed?

Why should it be performed?

How will the performance of the project be controlled?

The decision to design and construct an activity center will use and develop the skills of the team. It will also provide recreation and learning opportunities for children of the community. Now the team expands the details of the *who, what, when, where, why,* and *how* questions, with the activity center project specifically in mind.

Who will be responsible for various portions of the work? Ellery, with the assistance of Alice and Kim, will be responsible for the design and construction of the activity center foundation and walls. Jose, with the assistance of Laura, will be responsible for the design layout and installation of the activity center wiring. They request assistance from the University Architecture Department on the applicability of their software.

What is to be accomplished? The team next devises a set of tasks that start with the study of potential activity center design directions (chapter 3) and end with the delivery of the completed activity center (chapter 5). The tasks are the following:

Prepare Site

Excavate Site

Erect Foundation

Cap Foundation

Erect Rough Framing (and Sheathing)

Shingle Roof

Install Windows

Install Heating

Finish Exterior Siding

Install Sheetrock™

Plaster Interior

Lay Floors

Install Interior Finish

Paint Interior Finish

Laura is assigned the responsibility for determining the risks for each of these potential tasks.

When is it to be implemented? A date is established for the official ground-breaking ceremony. The completion and delivery dates are planned to occur during week 25. Week 26 is saved for the final project documentation effort.

Where is the activity center to be constructed? Steps made of concrete will be fabricated at a supplier's site; activity center construction and assembly will occur at the Bedford Park site location. (When a circuit, device, building, or system is constructed, it is often divided into several portions, each of which is fabricated at a different location.)

Why should it be constructed? The activity center, when complete, will have provided valuable training for each team member who has participated in the project. The activity center will also add to the quality of life in Bedford by offering a place for young people of the community to exercise, play, and learn.

PPCP 2

CONCEPTION .

How will the performance of the project be controlled? Coordination and control of the entire effort will be the responsibility of Roger. All projects require that people learn to work together. All persons involved must understand their portion of the total assignment and how those portions relate to all other portions of the project. Professor Hulbert notes that Northeastern requires the responsible faculty member to review—on a weekly basis—the status, problems, and plans for resolving the problems for each project.

Activity 3B: Prepare the Preliminary Specification

The Preliminary Specification establishes the bounds of investigation for the Study Phase. Specifications traditionally fall into one of six categories:

- Residential
- Commercial
- Municipal
- Industrial
- Military
- Aerospace

Contents of typical specifications are given in section 8.1. Design specifications are considered to be complete at the end of the Study Phase.

Specifications should not be confused with **requirements.** Specifications, as described in this book, are documents that contain, among other things, a description of the work to be accomplished. Specifications include requirements, but they contain more than just requirements. Requirements are conditions that *must* be fulfilled in order to complete a task or project. Design specifications also include design preferences.

PROJECT EXAMPLE

The Preliminary Specification for the activity center is being prepared by Alice. The following parameters for the project were developed during the Conception Phase:

The activity center will be designed to the specification entitled "Specification for the Town of Bedford, Massachusetts: An Activity Center." (The final version of this document is given in appendix C.)

The activity center will be used by children from ages 4 through 10.

The activity center must cost less than $20 000.

These three sentences are the introduction to the Preliminary Specification.

Alice and Ellery develop the outline of the Preliminary Specification as follows:

General Specifications

General Requirements

Architectural Requirements

Intent of Contract Documents

Subcontractors
Project Meetings
Cleaning (of Site)
Workers' Compensation and Insurance
Project Closeout
General Site Work
Earthwork
Landscaping
Site Utilities
Concrete Formwork
Cast-in-Place Concrete
Dampproofing (Moisture Barriers)
Subsurface Drainage System
Framing and Carpentry
Roof
Window and Door Schedule
Exterior Trim and Siding
Plumbing and Heating
Electrical
Walls, Floors, and Ceilings
Locks
Landscaping, Driveway, Ramp, and Walks

Alice and Ellery are assigned to write and coordinate this document. (The Specification is to be completed during the Study Phase.)

Activity 3C: Prepare the Project Description

The Project Description document describes the Project Plan. It divides the remaining work for the Conception Phase into two parts:

1. Formal task descriptions, which include skills, schedule, cost information, and the risks involved for each task

2. The plans for the Study, Design, and Implementation Phases

See section 2.3 for requirement details in the Project Description.

Descriptions of tasks required to complete the project are now ready to be written. The tasks are arranged in a logical sequence, with time and cost estimates included.

Team members use their combined skills to identify the work to be performed and completed. (This is also known as the Work Breakdown Structure. See chapter 7.) The following procedures are a guide.

• Identify and document the work to be accomplished in the form of tasks. See appendix B.

• Decide where one task ends and another begins, based upon the ease with which it becomes obvious when the task has to be started and when the task is complete.

• Write the descriptions of these tasks so that a logical sequence exists.

• Describe, for each task, the skills required to perform that task.

• Identify and list the materials and equipment required to perform each task.

- Estimate the time required to perform each task (East and Kirby, 1990; Lewis, 1991).
- Estimate the cost to perform each task, using the various cost categories given in section 7.5.

Solicit the skills of consulting specialists, where necessary, to work with team members during the writing of task descriptions. Tasks are first listed in an outline format. The interaction of one task with all others can be expressed via a schedule that connects the start, performance, and completion of each task. Then begin initiating task *descriptions,* which are improved on a continuing basis as more information becomes available.

Miles (1972) notes that the Conception (problem-setting) Phase and the Study (problem-solving) Phase often overlap. Team members must gather much information before the actual problem to be solved can begin to be identified. The task descriptions indicate the understanding of the problem at a given moment in time.

The search for more information and problem (value) analysis continues. (See appendix A.) As the project progresses, there are fewer questions and fewer missing partial solutions. The existing problem may be divided into two or more separate problems, or changed altogether. Disciplined thinking, combined with creativity, leads to solving the remaining portions of a problem until it evolves into the *actual* problem and its solution. Thus, the Project Description is a living, changing document that evolves during the Conception Phase. It becomes the Design Description during the Study Phase. The Design Description is modified during the Study Phase as more information becomes available. The Design Description is the guide to the development of Working and Detail Drawings. The content of these drawings will be discussed during the Design Phase.

For this Conception Phase, include the following for each task description within the Project Description document:

- The identity and objective of the task
- The relation of the task to the overall project
- A description of the work to be accomplished
- The skills required to accomplish each task
- The specifications that define the quality of work and materials
- A schedule for the performance of the tasks
- The costs associated with accomplishing each task

Connect the tasks to skilled individuals and organizations willing to participate in implementing the project.

Carefully review how each task interacts with all others. Identify those tasks whose completion will affect the overall costs and schedule so they can be carefully monitored.

Examine the costs for each task. How do you know what is a reasonable cost estimate? Experience is the best teacher. Therefore, retain good records of previous work and examine these records for applicability to the new project. Gather and consult catalogs containing information regarding materials and their costs. Obtain, where practical, a range of costs and schedule times for each task. Investigate alternative solutions by comparing schedule and costs. Also realize that costs control choices, and choices control costs.

Tabulate the estimated income and expenses for the project during this planning stage. This tabulation is a financial statement that summarizes the assets, liabilities, and net worth of a project, business, or individual at a given date. By preparing these tabulated data using a computer spreadsheet program, you will be able to obtain immediate information on the effect of changes on the project. (See section 6.5.) If a spreadsheet program is not available, then prepare the cost estimates manually. Only ruled paper and a calculator are necessary. However, considerable time is required, and mathematical errors are more likely to occur when the spreadsheet is prepared manually.

PROJECT EXAMPLE

The team members initiate the Project Description document for the activity center. The work for constructing the activity center must now be divided into tasks. (Tasks, their objectives, and their accompanying task descriptions are discussed in appendix B.) Laura, who enjoys writing, is given the assignment of developing a list of activity center tasks by examining the work to be accomplished. Jose and Kim work with Laura to devise an accompanying schedule. Kim, who has an understanding of bookkeeping, volunteers to obtain prices for the various materials that are to be considered. Jose agrees to investigate the scheduling software available on the University computer system. Roger assumes the responsibility for determining the design preferences of the persons who will be funding this effort.

The initial tasks, with their accompanying risks, devised by Laura, are the following:

Tasks	Risks
Prepare Site	Environmental restrictions
Excavate Site	Ledge, soil, water (such as a spring)
Erect Foundation	Temperature, weather conditions
Cap Foundation	Temperature, weather conditions
Erect Rough Framing (and Sheathing)	Quality of lumber, wind
Shingle Roof	Wind, rain, snow
Install Windows	Quality of lumber and window frames
Install Heating	Consistent availability of selected fuel
Finish Exterior Siding	Wind, temperature, humidity, rain
Install Sheetrock™	Humidity, temperature
Plaster Interior	Humidity, temperature
Lay Floors	Condition of rough flooring
Install Interior Finish	Temperature, humidity
Paint Interior Finish	Temperature, humidity

Laura realizes that this list of tasks is likely to be revised during the Study and Design Phases.

Activity 3D: List Tasks, Schedule, and Budget Constraints

All projects are finite in time and costs. Identify those parts of a planned project that are most likely to deviate from your plan or will require further study. Identify especially any areas that will require detailed analysis during the Study Phase. These areas, along with the involved time and costs, are the constraints on this project.

Approximate costs and schedules are developed based on the initial list of tasks needed to implement the project.

Approximate schedules need to be devised based upon the list of tasks developed. See chapter 7 for information on this topic.

The expression **contingency fee** is used in cost estimating to cover unforeseen expenses. It describes the amount of money that is set aside to cover the cost of complications that are suspected or likely to arise, but have not yet been isolated and resolved. For the Conception Phase, these categories are the project uncertainties. The greater the expectation that all design complications have not yet been identified and resolved, the greater the contingency amount.

It is customary to add a percentage to the initial cost estimates to include items whose complexity is not yet understood. The greater the risk involved, the greater the contingency percent. This helps ensure that the final estimates, which are determined during the Implementation Phase, are likely to be within the original estimates determined during the Conception Phase. The actual percentage chosen depends upon the experiences of the estimators and the degree of uncertainty of the data used for estimating.

PROJECT EXAMPLE

The tasks to implement the project, with their associated risks, have been previously listed by Laura. Jose and Kim work with Laura to devise a rough schedule, using her initial list of tasks for the Implementation Phase. The time indicated to accomplish each task is noted to the right of each task in figure 2.8.

Note that the schedule requires approximately six months to accomplish the Implementation Phase. This is a constraint imposed by the school year.

Sample of a rough schedule for the Implementation Phase

initial tasks	Mar	Apr	May	Jun	Jul	Aug
prepare site						
excavate site						
erect foundation						
cap foundation						
erect rough framing						
shingle roof						
install windows						
finish exterior siding						
install Sheetrock™						
plaster interior						
lay floors						
install interior finish						
paint interior finish						

Figure 2.8   Sample of a rough schedule for the Implementation Phase

Kim works with the other members of the team to obtain costs for the various materials to be considered during the Study Phase. Jose and Laura work to convert the materials costs into a total budget, which includes labor and other categories, as discussed in section 6.6. For each entry in the rough cost estimates given in figure 2.9, the students include appropriate contingency amounts as advised by Professor Hulbert. (See chapter 7.)

Note that the total money available is $20 000; the extra $800 (4%) is for contingencies. This is a constraint imposed by the contributing funding sources. It is assumed that there will be no significant costs associated with the Study and Design Phases. The team members and Professor Hulbert are contributing their labor.

↓ ITEM / MONTH →	MAR	APR	MAY	JUN	JUL	AUG	TOTALS
Initial Tasks							
prepare site	600						0
excavate site	1400						0
erect foundation		1700					1700
cap foundation		400					400
erect rough framing			4800				4800
single roof				1000			1000
install windows				1800			1800
finish exterior siding				400	400		800
install Sheetrock™				300	500		800
plaster interior					600		600
lay floors					2200		2200
install interior finish					600	1200	1800
paint interior finish						1300	1300
totals	2000	2100	4800	3500	4300	2500	19200

When using an electronic spreadsheet, it is possible to insert a check cell (I17) to verify that the entries were totalled correctly, because the horizontal row and vertical column are the same. Changes in any of the values will automatically change the two totals.

	A	B	C	D	E	F	G	H	I
1	↓ ITEM / MONTH →	MAR	APR	MAY	JUN	JUL	AUG	TOTALS	
2	Initial Tasks								
3	prepare site	600						0	
4	excavate site	1400						0	
5	erect foundation		1700					1700	
6	cap foundation		400					400	
7	erect rough framing			4800				4800	
8	single roof				1000			1000	
9	install windows				1800			1800	
10	finish exterior siding				400	400		800	
11	install Sheetrock™				300	500		800	
12	plaster interior					600		600	
13	lay floors					2200		2200	
14	install interior finish					600	1200	1800	
15	paint interior finish						1300	1300	
16	**totals**	2000	2100	4800	3500	4300	2500	19200	across:
17								(down)	19200

Sample of a rough cost estimate for the Implementation Phase							
initial tasks	**Mar**	**Apr**	**May**	**Jun**	**Jul**	**Aug**	**totals**
prepare site	600						600
excavate site	1400						1400
erect foundation		1700					1700
cap foundation		400					400
erect rough framing			4800				4800
shingle roof				1000			1000
install windows				1800			1800
finish exterior siding				400	400		800
install Sheetrock™				300	500		800
plaster interior					600		600
lay floors					2200		2200
install interior finish					600	1200	1800
paint interior finish						1300	1300
totals	2000	2100	4800	3500	4300	2500	19 200

Figure 2.9   Sample of a rough cost estimate for the Implementation Phase

Activity 4: Expand Team and Identify Supporting Organizations

Toward the end of the Conception Phase, the skills required to perform the chosen project are reevaluated, as are the skills of existing team members. New team members may be added, and sources of outside help are identified.

Identify additional persons who want to be members of the team for the remainder of the project. Establish a formal organization of all team members. Decide upon a time and place for these new persons to get together and meet the existing team members. This initial meeting is often referred to as a project "kickoff meeting."

Verify your choice of team leader. For some projects, the team leader may be appointed by the organization involved in overseeing the project. The team leader should have both technical and managerial skills and should be a decisive person. For groups of individuals whose focus is on learning to work together, it may be desirable to periodically change the team leaders. This provides good training for those who want to test their management and organizing skills. It also allows the team members to become acquainted with different management styles.

Designate the team leader as **manager** if the team size exceeds nine persons. (This principle derives from management texts and is referred to as the "rule of ten.") At this point, skills and abilities needed to complete the project are reexamined, and additional ones needed are identified. Once again, the manager may need to invite additional persons to become team members. New members are often recommended by existing team members. Projects conceived by college teams may attract retired individuals, who may contribute their skills at a very low cost or at no cost. There also may be other options that could be considered.

Identify other persons or organizations who have the additional skills and abilities required to perform the planned project. These persons or organizations may become involved via a contract, as discussed in section 8.3. Someone may discover that the required additional skills are available from a local company that has access to funds available for the planned project.

PROJECT EXAMPLE

It is time to examine the composition of the project team. The initial six team members examine their skills and abilities.

Roger: Enjoys the leadership role and is accepted by his fellow students; he wants to locate a spreadsheet program that will assist him in comparing the estimated time and costs with (later) actual expenditures.

Alice: Wants to work on the actual design; her father has volunteered the time of a civil engineer who can advise in site layout and heavy-equipment requirements. She is comfortable with converting the Conception Phase ideas into designs during the Study Phase.

Laura: Is creative and enjoys organizing information; she realizes that she has no idea as to how much time will be required to perform the work of each task. She locates a third-year student in accounting to assist with the next phases.

Jose: Likes to work with his hands; he needs assistance to determine sources of information regarding foundation forms and how they are used.

Kim: Is interested in chemistry; she needs information regarding lumber and concrete. There is no first-year student with that information. She contacts a fourth-year student who desires to specialize in these areas during his graduate-school studies.

Ellery: Has drafting experience; he would like to advance his skills by utilizing a computer CAD program for preparing the Study and Design Phase drawings. He seeks advice from Jose.

The team members discover that, to continue, they must add new members to the team for the Study Phase. Where there are no skills or abilities available within the university, they must develop contacts with potential contractors.

Two more first-year students are added to the team in preparation for the Study Phase: Manuel Cardoza, a computer technology major with software experience; and Joseph O'Neil, formerly a carpentry student at a vocational high school.

At the progress review meeting, held with Professor Hulbert, these two new members meet the other team members, are informed of the status of the Conception Phase, and receive their assignments for the Study Phase. Professor Hulbert addresses the issues involved with expanding the six-member team to an eight-member team. He also notes that the coordination required among members for teams containing more than three persons can be significant. The individuals in a larger team have fewer individual responsibilities. However, the increase in team size requires an increased coordination effort.

Activity 5: Complete the Planning of the Next Phases of Work

Plans should be realistic with regard to timely performance and reasonable cost. Meeting these criteria ensures that the actual project will be performed successfully within the scheduled time and financial constraints.

Good planning requires (1) that there is sufficient information available for planning purposes and (2) that the person or persons planning have sufficient experience to use the information wisely. Plans should be realistic with regard to timely performance and reasonable cost. Meeting these criteria ensures that the actual project will be performed successfully within the scheduled time and financial constraints. Information useful to planning, such as actual schedules and costs from similar projects, is often gathered during the Conception Phase. It is then available for use during the Study, Design, and Implementation Phases.

Determine the approximate amount of work necessary to perform the Study, Design, and Implementation Phases. Prepare schedules and estimate costs for performing the remaining activity (final documentation) of the Conception Phase, review all of the activities for the Study, Design, and Implementation Phases, and prepare documentation. The documentation at this point should be restricted to rough estimates until the Study Phase is in progress.

PLANNING AHEAD

The documents for the Design and Implementation Phases are considered to be approximate in content. They are often labeled "Draft," because further information is necessary to expand and complete plans. The time and cost to do more in-depth evaluations, and the effect of these evaluations on the project, will be examined in more detail during the Study Phase.

The managers and reviewers within the organization will want to know that the project will cost no less than, and no more than, specific dollar amounts. Establish the boundaries of low and high project costs before beginning the Study Phase. This process is referred to as **bracketing** the project costs.

- The low-end costs can often be established by examining the data from previously completed projects whose tasks are comparable; unusual development effort is not required.

- The high-end costs can be roughly estimated by interviewing those persons who will be responsible for performing those new tasks whose content requires research and development effort. It then becomes the responsibility of the manager to decide upon a final price for the project. Managers should include contingency funds (see activity 3D) where they suspect the research and development personnel have not provided realistic estimates.

It then becomes the responsibility of the manager to decide upon a final price for the project. Why? Because most funding agencies respond more favorably when only one amount of money is requested. For a funded project, enough money must be earned in excess of expenditures to fund the first stages of future projects that may be identified and proposed later.

Often, funding for only the Study Phase will be authorized. The reason for withholding funds for later phases is that persons responsible for allotting funds want to be assured that the cost of the later phases will not exceed the available money.

Identify any areas that may require detailed analysis during the Study Phase. The time and cost to evaluate these areas, and the impact the results will have upon the project, must be identified now. As an example, human-factor requirements should be included. (See section 9.2.) Revise all plans as soon as significant amounts of new information are obtained or new ideas are conceived and developed.

At some point, the chosen leader must decide when the Conception Phase will end. It is possible that new information may be gathered during the Study Phase that may require briefly reviewing the results of the Conception Phase.

PROJECT EXAMPLE

Planning the activity center project requires the development of a flowchart showing the sequence of the tasks, as shown in figure 2.10.

Figure 2.10   Sequence of events for activity center

The purpose of planning is to ensure that the project, including the drawings and specifications, meets the following criteria:

- The proposed structure is in compliance with the zoning regulations. (Zoning approval is required before a construction permit can be issued.)
- The site work, clearing, and rubble disposal plans are acceptable to authorities.
- The activity center location meets local building codes and other requirements.
- A realistic base is used for determining costs.
- On-schedule completion of the job can be accomplished.
- The project can be completed with the available funds.
- The work is acceptable to the funding sources.

These factors are interrelated. Each day the world becomes more complicated as there are more restrictive regulations and guidelines to consider.

The time between mid-November and the end of December is allotted to the Study Phase. The months of January and February are assigned to the Design Phase. The sequence of events for the project is devised and reviewed. The overall schedule for the project is shown in figure 2.11.

Overall schedule of project phases

initial tasks	Mar	Apr	May	Jun	Jul	Aug
prepare site	▬					
excavate site		▬				
erect foundation		▬				
cap foundation		▬				
erect rough framing			▬			
shingle roof				▬		
install windows				▬		
finish exterior siding					▬	
install Sheetrock™					▬	
plaster interior					▬	
lay floors					▬	
install interior finish						▬
paint interior finish						▬

phase	Oct	Nov	Dec	Jan	Feb	Mar	Apr	May	Jun	Jul	Aug
conception	▬	▬									
study			▬								
design				▬	▬						
implementation						▬	▬	▬	▬	▬	▬

Figure 2.11   Overall schedule of project phases

Activity 6: Convert Document Drafts into Final Documents

Documents for the Conception Phase typically include the following:

- *One that explains why the project was selected*
- *One that contains all the specifications for the project*
- *A general document that describes the project and that contains preliminary proposed costs and schedules*

A phase is not finished until the documentation (paperwork) is complete. Here are the documents to be completed during the Conception Phase:

1. Project Selection Rationale
2. Preliminary Specification
3. Project Description (with an artist's concept)

Simple projects may merge these documents. More complicated projects may require additional documents. The content of each of the above documents is described in section 2.3. These documents can be modified to become portions of the Study Phase documents; see section 3.3.

PROJECT EXAMPLE

As noted above, documentation of activities should be prepared as each of these activities occur. Documentation should *never* wait until all the activities of the Conception Phase are completed.

All involved team members and Professor Hulbert agree that the document for Project Selection Rationale for the activity center project needs to consist of the following:

1. A description of the potential projects explored
   - 1.1   Pave existing walkways
   - 1.2   Improve playground
   - 1.3   Improve swimming pool
   - 1.4   Construct children's activity center
   - 1.5   Replace old carousel
2. Attributes of each potential project
3. Approximate tasks, schedules, and budgets for each project explored
   - 3.1   Pave walkways: $4 500 requiring nine weeks
   - 3.2   Improve playground: $4 200 requiring fourteen weeks
   - 3.3   Improve swimming pool: $7 500 requiring ten weeks
   - 3.4   Construct children's activity center: $20 000 requiring twenty-six weeks
   - 3.5   Replace old carousel: $28 500 requiring forty-two weeks
4. Justification of the project selected
   - 4.1   The need by the town of Bedford for the project
     Why is the activity center needed?
     What activities will occur in the activity center?
     How will these activities meet the needs?
   - 4.2   The schedule and money available
   - 4.3   The complexity of the project
   - 4.4   The skills of the team
   - 4.5   The type of technical and administrative assistance required

Written text, with the appropriate charts and other figures, accompanies each of the above descriptions. Laura is assigned to coordinate the writing of this document. She requests the e-mail addresses from each team member.

For discussion of the Preliminary Specification, see section 2.3.

Figure 2.12   Artist's concept of student activity center

The Project Description document for the activity center contains the following:

- Justification for the project (from the Project Selection Rationale document)
- Semitechnical description of the range of Study Phase options, including an artist's concept of the activity center. (See figure 2.12.)
- Estimated schedule for the Study, Design, and Implementation Phases
- Estimated costs for the Study, Design, and Implementation Phases
- The sources of funding to achieve the $20 000 needed to implement the project
- Directions for the Study Phase

  Ideas to be investigated

  Building-size options

  Types of siding

  Types of roofing

  Landscaping

  Questions to be answered

    What locations in Bedford Park are available?

    What are the ranges of environmental conditions, such as temperature, humidity, wind, rain, snow, and noise levels, of this area?

    What types of building materials are available locally?

    What skilled labor is available locally from companies and employees who might be willing to contribute labor and materials—or perhaps just advice and guidance?

What types of lumber and concrete should be considered?

What foundation construction techniques are applicable?

What are the Bedford water and sewage connection requirements?

Where is electrical power available during construction?

- Staffing skills required for the Study, Design, and Implementation Phases

internal: Manuel and Joseph

external: materials vendors and construction subcontractors

- Resources needed for the next phases:

Facilities

Equipment

Computation support

Ellery is assigned to prepare artist's concepts of the activity center. These are used to explore the design options during the Study Phase. Roger agrees to coordinate the writing of this document and to write the justification paragraph.

It is the first Monday in November. Professor Hulbert informs the team that the Conception Phase must end in eleven days.

SECTION 2.3   CONCEPTION PHASE DOCUMENTS

The Conception Phase begins when an idea is conceived or a need is identified. There may be more than one idea or need and several solutions being considered. Eventually, the project team selects one idea or need and begins to develop a project. The flow from the idea or need to the Conception Phase documents is shown in figure 2.13.

Team members compare their concepts of how the project should progress. Papers are written, circulated, and criticized. Meetings are held to compare the various concepts; meeting reports (see section 8.3) are written. These papers and meeting reports eventually lead to the three Conception Phase documents (figure 2.13).

At the end of the Conception Phase, the completed documents are the following:

1. The Project Selection Rationale: an explanatory document

2. The Preliminary Specification: the beginning of the specification for the project

3. The Project Description with Artist's Concept: the first drawings and plans

The content of each of these documents is described below. (More complicated projects and programs may require additional documents.)

The **Project Selection Rationale** consists of the following:

1. An analysis of the market, where applicable

2. A description of the potential projects explored

3. The attributes of each potential project

4. Approximate tasks, schedules, and budgets for each project explored

5. Justification for the project selected

This document typically consists of less than fifty pages for a modest-size project. For a large program, this document may consist of several volumes of information.

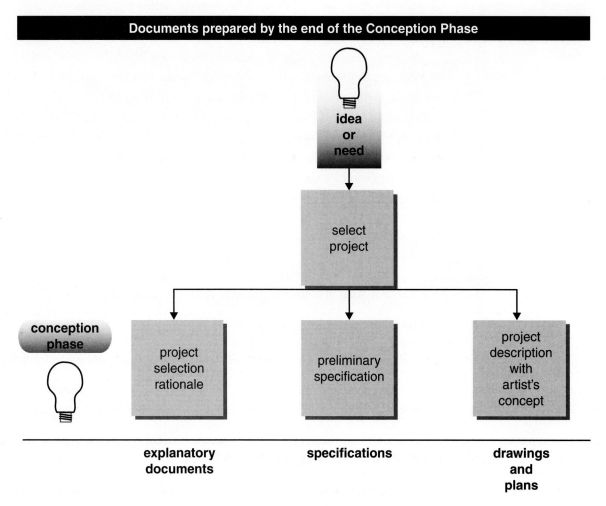

Figure 2.13   Documents prepared by the end of the Conception Phase

The Conception Phase documents contain preliminary information about a project:

- *The **Project Selection Rationale** explains why the project was chosen and contains a preliminary list of tasks, schedules, and budgets.*

- *The **Preliminary Specification** document establishes the bounds of investigation for the Study Phase.*

- *The **Project Description** contains the first drawings or plans.*

The **Preliminary Specification** document establishes the bounds of investigation for the Study Phase. Specifications traditionally fall into one or more of these four categories:

1. Residential or Commercial
2. Municipal or Industrial
3. Military
4. Aerospace

Specifications are documents that contain, among other things, a description of the work to be accomplished. There are standard contents for specifications written for each of these categories. Specifications are described in section 8.1.

Specifications should not be confused with requirements. Specifications contain requirements, as indicated in chapter 8. Requirements are conditions that must be fulfilled in order to complete a task, project, or program. However, specifications may also contain preferences for the way the project is to be implemented.

The **Project Description with Artist's Concept** consists of the following:

1. Justification for the project from the Project Selection Rationale document
2. A semitechnical description of the project that nontechnical financial persons can comprehend

3. An estimated schedule per phase

4. Estimated costs per phase

5. Potential sources of funding

6. Directions for the Study Phase

   ideas to be investigated

   problems to be explored

7. Staffing skills required for the next phases

   internal: persons either available or to be hired

   external: vendors and subcontractors

8. Resources needed for the next phases

   facilities

   equipment

   computer support

The artist's concept of the selected project's physical appearance should be included where applicable. For software projects, a sample of the expected hard-copy output is often supplied. For physically large projects or programs, a scale model of the artist's concept is often constructed, or a computer model may be devised.

When preparing three separate documents, it is important that the contents overlap. For small projects, only one combined document is necessary.

SECTION 2.4

Sometimes the end of the Conception Phase occurs when the documentation for the phase is completed; the manager must decide when the phase is complete, or a schedule may signal its completion.

DEFINING PHASE COMPLETION

The moment when the Conception Phase can be considered complete may not be obvious to those directly involved. Sometimes its end is defined by the completion of the required documents (see previous activity 6). Other times, the team may continue to examine potential projects or continue to evaluate the cost of the chosen project.

The team could now be split into two groups. One group, primarily consisting of creators, would continue to explore alternatives. (These efforts are known as *feasibility studies.*) The second group, primarily consisting of performers, would begin to study one or two selected projects and their potential solutions. This approach, however, can be very dangerous because it can lead to conflicts between the two teams. Also, any new ideas that the first group of creators presents may cause the performers to realize that they have been performing tasks that may no longer be relevant to the project.

The manager must:

• decide when and how the Conception Phase will be terminated,

• insist that all participants proceed on mutually acceptable paths, and

• be certain that all plans are documented in the appropriate reports described in activity 6.

The Conception Phase schedule should indicate specifically when each output document is to be ready in draft form, when the review cycle will occur, and when these documents are ready to be published.

CHAPTER OBJECTIVES SUMMARY

Now that you have finished this chapter, you should be able to:

1. Describe the purpose and goal of the Conception Phase of a project.

2. Explain the tasks involved in the Conception Phase of a project and the six activities or steps through which these tasks are performed.

3. Describe the process of selecting a project, including brainstorming and the criteria for evaluating projects.

4. Describe the process of organizing a team, utilizing skills of team members, and expanding the team when needed.

5. Explain the nature of risks involved in projects and how to search for alternative solutions.

6. Explain the process of listing tasks, schedules, and budget constraints for a project.

7. Describe the documents prepared during the Conception Phase.

EXERCISES

2.1   Revise the Purpose and Goal statement given in section 2.1 to match each of your (multidisciplinary) class project options.

2.2   Examine the activities listed and described in section 2.2 carefully; adapt them to each of your options for a class project.

2.3   Select a team leader by secret ballot. Assist that chosen leader in formulating a team for developing the class project options.

2.4   Devise a matrix for comparing the skills and interests versus the specialty of each potential team member. Apply weights, from 1 to 5, for each entry in the matrix, where 5 is the most important and 1 is the least important. Use these weights to assign team members to portions of the Conception Phase.

2.5   Develop a project concept statement that requires minimal support from outside the team. Expand upon the ideas offered and gather additional information associated with these ideas.

2.6   Identify projects that are related to the initial list of class projects under consideration. Brainstorm to develop plans that answer the questions: *who, what, when, where, why,* and *how.*

2.7   Identify those individuals who will be the most capable of judging the details of the initial list of class projects.

2.8   Visit those individuals or organizations that might participate in the funding of each of the projects on the initial list of class projects. Prepare a written report that describes each visit.

2.9   Initiate the development of a list that can be used to establish the actual needs, desires, and luxuries for each of the customers who indicate they have a need to be fulfilled. For each entry, indicate the risks involved in meeting these needs.

2.10   Match the list of potential funding sources with your initial list of class projects. Prepare a simple presentation that describes each project from your initial list of class projects. Visit the potential funding sources and deliver your presentation.

2.11   Convene a meeting of all team members with your faculty advisor. Discuss all of the project selection criteria listed in activity 2C. Use these criteria to assist in selecting a project for each team.

2.12   Formulate the problems for each project and identify the associated risks. Attempt to answer these questions:

Are we certain that we have identified the problems to be solved?

Are these the actual problems or the perceived problems?

How can we distinguish between the actual and the perceived problems?

2.13   Select one project from that list based on your evaluation of the technical risks and the availability of funding. Search for and propose alternative solutions to the selected project.

2.14   Identify high-risk areas for the selected project. Indicate the effort necessary to analyze those areas during the Study Phase.

2.15   Determine the work to be accomplished that will lead to the proposed solution. Develop approximate tasks, schedules, and budgets for the Conception Phase work. (See appendix B.) Indicate any constraints that must be imposed upon the planned effort.

2.16   Enhance your project team to fulfill the work to be performed during the Study Phase. Identify any supporting organizations needed to perform your project. Contact those organizations and verify their willingness to participate.

2.17   Prepare the approximate tasks, schedules, and budgets for the Study, Design, and Implementation Phases. Establish low and high project cost estimates. Identify those areas that will require detailed analysis during the Study Phase.

2.18   Document the proposed solutions for the selected project and the reasons for their choices. Prepare the three documents described in activity 6.

2.19   Identify the responsibilities for each member of the project team and for any supporting organizations.

2.20   Identify the actual sources that will fund your selected project. Prepare and deliver a presentation to them. Obtain written verification that they will fund your project, including a list of their criteria for project-funding acceptability.

2.21   Review all of the Conception Phase effort. Complete all documents referred to in the exercises above. Terminate the Conception Phase.

2.22   Describe how you would identify the optimum time to terminate the Conception Phase.

PPCP 2

CONCEPTION

chapter 3

1. What are the purpose and goal of the Study Phase of a project?

2. What tasks are involved in the Study Phase of a project, and what activities or steps are performed to complete these tasks?

3. What is the process of reviewing the Conception Phase and planning for the Study Phase?

4. How can team members' skills be utilized to complete the Study Phase, and what can be done to manage team members so they keep to the overall goals of the project?

5. What are the ground rules for a project, and how they are established?

6. How are various solutions for implementing a project investigated and studied, and how are the associated risks and trade-offs evaluated?

7. How can the selection among design alternatives be performed as a group process?

8. What relationships are there with funding sources and potential vendors during the Study Phase?

9. What documents are prepared during the Study Phase, and how do they evolve from the Conception Phase documents?

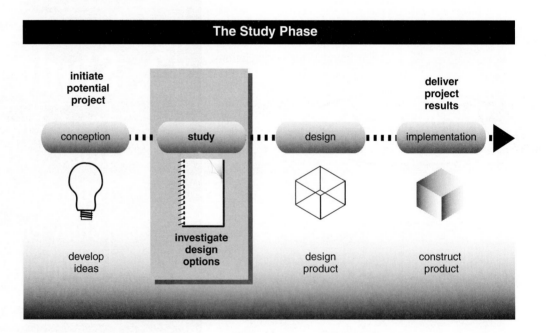

Crafty men [despise] studies; simple men admire them; and wise men use them.

Sir Francis Bacon (1561–1626)

This chapter evaluates the possible directions that the project may pursue. It is less costly to evaluate these directions at this time and select one approach to the following phases.

SECTION 3.1   STUDY PHASE PURPOSE AND GOAL

During the Study Phase, the ways to implement the project chosen in the Conception Phase are studied and developed.

The **purpose** of the Study Phase is to develop and evaluate ways to implement the project selected during the Conception Phase. The **goal** of the Study Phase is to produce a study that effectively directs the final design of a chosen project, which is developed in the Design Phase. The probability of successfully completing a project is lowest, and hence the risk and uncertainty are highest, at the start of a project. The probability of successful project completion should improve as the Study Phase continues.

At the end of the Study Phase, you should know how to accomplish the following:

- Review the Conception Phase results and organize the Study Phase work.
- Establish alternative solution requirements and accompanying constraints.
- Devise criteria for judging the Study Phase outcomes that are compatible with the expectations of the client and funding sources.
- Develop solution alternatives that satisfy the devised criteria.
- Identify and evaluate risks and trade-offs for each proposed alternative.
- Contact and involve vendors and subcontractors that will support the team.
- Prepare documentation describing proposed design alternatives.
- Refine previously devised task descriptions, schedules, and cost estimates for the Design and Implementation Phases.
- Obtain approval, and funding, for the Design Phase.

During the Study Phase, you must continually revise all plans related to your selected project as you develop new solutions.

Note: The Study and Design phases may overlap. See section 3.4.

SECTION 3.2   STUDY PHASE ACTIVITIES

The activities for the Study Phase consist of the following:

Activity 1: Organize the Study Phase Work

    1A: Review the Conception Phase effort.

    1B: Develop the Study Phase details.

    1C: Organize teams into small groups.

    1D: Assign each group a set of tasks to investigate.

Activity 2: Establish Ground Rules for Study and Design Phases

Activity 3: Study Solutions to Be Considered for Design

    3A: Study potential solutions.

    3B: Determine functions to be included in the solutions.

    3C: Determine risks and trade-offs.

Activity 4: Gather and Evaluate Information

    4A: Contact potential vendors for their input.

    4B: Evaluate design alternatives and refine estimates.

Activity 5: Select and Plan One Solution

    5A: Select a solution.

    5B: Plan the Design and Implementation Phases.

PPCP 3

STUDY

Activity 6: Document the Selected Solution

    6A: Refine the task, schedule, and budget documents.

    6B: Document the proposed solution and rationale.

Activity 7: Verify and Obtain Funding

    7A: Verify actual availability of funding.

    7B: Obtain Design Phase funding.

As is true for the Conception Phase, the purpose and goal you define for the Study Phase determine the activities that you are to accomplish. You may change the sequence of the activities described in this chapter from one project to another. However, you must accomplish all of the activities before the Study Phase is complete.

For small, well-defined projects that require a minimum of conception and study, the Conception Phase may be merged with the Study Phase. However, all the activities must be examined and considered. For those projects that require a minimum of study and design, the Study Phase may be merged with the Design Phase. Again, all activities must be considered.

Activity 1: Organize the Study Phase Work

During this activity, you will focus upon reviewing the Conception Phase documentation, developing the details for the Study Phase, organizing the team members into small groups, and assigning each group a set of tasks.

Activity 1A: Review the Conception Phase Effort

Team members need to review documents from the Conception Phase so that everyone understands the overall nature of the project and the proposed solutions.

Read and review the content of the Project Selection Rationale, Preliminary Specification, and Project Description documents. Some statements in them may seem new to you because time has elapsed since they were written. Also, new members may have been added to the team for this phase. At this time, the team needs to evaluate the results of any feasibility studies (alternative approaches) as well. Some team members may be stimulated to suggest new ideas or paths for the Study Phase, many of which can be very useful to the project. Review the tasks, schedules, and budgets prior to the start of the Study Phase work. Prepare and issue a memorandum, if necessary, that indicates your revisions to the original Study Phase plans.

You must now review these questions:

Who will be responsible for each portion of the work?

What is to be accomplished and by whom?

When is it to be implemented?

Where is it to be performed?

Why should it be performed?

How will the performance of the project be controlled?

You must determine if the answers to these questions (figure 3.1) have changed from the Conception Phase.

Request a meeting and review project status on a periodic basis. This is often referred to as a progress or status review meeting. If the team is a large one, the group leaders may be the only ones who attend this review. At such a progress or status meeting, you are all expected to express your opinions regarding the direction being followed. Project redirection should also be considered.

The word consensus implies that all the persons involved in the project agree on a common goal. It is the best approach for project decision making because all persons involved are more willing to work towards that common goal.

Work towards consensus. The word *consensus* implies that all the persons involved in the project agree on a common goal. It is the best approach for project decision making because all persons involved are more willing to work towards that common goal. However, factors over which designers have no control may require the managers to select a nonconsensus option.

Figure 3.1 The continuing key questions for a team

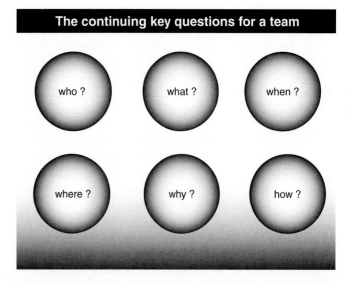

The continuing key questions for a team

who ?   what ?   when ?

where ?   why ?   how ?

PPCP 3

PROJECT EXAMPLE

It is now Friday afternoon in mid-November. Manuel and Joseph have been added to the team since the Conception Phase. The team members meet after classes to assess their school assignments, note their mutual availability, and plan the beginning of the Study Phase.

Roger Stein provides copies of the three Conception Phase documents to each Study Phase team member. Their weekend assignment is to read them and list any changes that they feel should be considered. These lists, and any other comments, are to be delivered to Laura, via e-mail or compatible computer disks and programs, by 8 A.M. Monday morning. Laura has no morning classes and has agreed to incorporate all lists and comments into one memorandum.

Roger has a separate list of Study Phase tasks; he provides a copy to each team member. Each team member is asked to rate these Study Phase tasks from 1 (least interesting) to 5 (most interesting), according to personal preferences. Roger collects these lists.

STUDY

Activity 1B: Develop the Study Phase Details

Review the planning information that was gathered during the Conception Phase. Determine if the Study Phase tasks (appendix B), schedules, and budgets should be revised. Constrain the schedules to a time span, and budgets to an amount, that is equal to or less than was estimated during the Conception Phase.

Prepare the tasks in an outline format. The interaction of each task with all others can be expressed via a schedule. The schedule connects together the start, performance, and completion of each task. (See chapters 6 and 7.) Task descriptions are begun and improved on a continuing basis as more information becomes available.

Continually examine the cost of the overall project, particularly those of the Design and Implementation Phases. As the Study Phase progresses, the complexity of your project usually becomes more apparent. With a growth in project complexity, costs will grow proportionally. If the money required to complete the project increases significantly, then there is a greater chance that the project will be terminated by the funding source.

PLANNING AHEAD▶

Visit the personnel at the funding source on a periodic basis. As the project progresses, sometimes the people at your funding source will have decided to invest the money set aside for your project in a more advantageous project, may have changed their priorities, or perhaps the money they allotted is not available to them as quickly as they had expected. Thus, even if your project team has stayed within their previously allotted funds, those funds may no longer be available.

Devise your plans for the later phases so that there is some versatility to those plans. These are often referred to as **design options** or **planning with performance measures** (Nadler, 1970, p. 768). The tasks are arranged in such a way that one or more of them may be eliminated without a serious effect on the entire project. That is a reason for continuing to plan your design functions so that they are arranged according to the apparent needs, desires, and luxuries as perceived by the people within your funding source. Avoid the temptation to prejudge the changing priorities of your client but continually monitor those changes.

Plans should be devised so that they are versatile and so that one or more tasks may be eliminated without a serious effect on the project. This will allow for completion of a project if some expected funding is lost.

The versatility of your plans for the later phases should not be openly noted in any presentation that precedes later-phase funding. Otherwise, the personnel at the funding source may decide to retain some of the funds desired for your project and let you work with a less versatile design.

Continue to compare your Study Phase project expenditures with your total accomplishments and overall goals of the projects. The project manager is held responsible for the effects of accumulated costs and projected cost estimates. Time also represents money. How much time should be allotted for project design and implementation? The longer the time a project requires—from conception to delivery—the greater are its costs. As noted in chapter 2, the written documentation must be clear and concise. It is the only material usually available to the project evaluators at the funding source.

PROJECT EXAMPLE

The memorandum prepared by Laura is distributed at the Monday afternoon meeting. After three hours of intense discussion, its content is merged into one flowing document to be printed and given to all team members the next day. Also added to the memorandum are the expanded details generated during the Monday afternoon meeting regarding the team's new understanding of the Study Phase work. Jose agrees to merge the newly developed details into the Study Phase task descriptions, schedules, and budgets.

Activity 1C: Organize Teams into Small Groups

One of the important steps in the Study Phase is to organize the work to be done during the phase and to assign team members to the various tasks.

Examine the work to be accomplished during the Study Phase, as modified during the above activities 1A and 1B. Examine further the skills, compatibility, and availability of your team members. Organize your team into small groups in preparation for activity 1D. Choose a leader for each group.

It is the project manager's responsibility to assign people to the activities to be performed during the Study Phase. At this time, the manager may also decide to add more people with a wider variety of skills to the Study Phase team. Recall from chapter 2 that the specific types of skills required for the Study Phase are more performers and fewer creators and that the coordination required among members for teams containing more than three persons can be significant (figure 3.2).

You need to consider two groups when planning the Design and Implementation Phases:

- One group for project needs for these two later phases
- One group for your client who will be using the final product

These two groups of people, working together, will contribute to a more orderly product transfer at the end of the project.

The plans for your project groups may lead to the hiring of new members or reassignment of some of your existing team members. It may lead you to search further for vendors who are more adaptable and less costly than are other members of your team. Consider employing some

Figure 3.2 Types of skills
needed for each phase

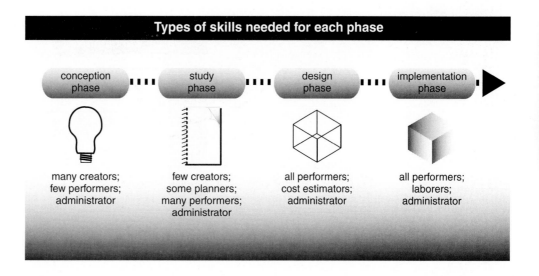

of the people who will eventually use your product as members of your Design Phase team or at least include some of them on your periodic review panel. Thus, they will gradually accept responsibility for ownership of the project.

If there are too many persons involved during the Study Phase who are primarily creators, they may continue to conceive new ideas. That may inhibit the progress of the Study Phase. It is important to maintain the balance between creators and planners for a given project (figure 3.2).

Progress begins by getting a clear view of the obstacles. Lenkurt Electric Co., Demodulator, Vol. 19, No. 4

Organize your project team into small groups. Ask the following questions to assist in this process:

- What are the necessary skills for performing the Study Phase?
- Which of the team members' skills apply to completion of the Study Phase?
- What local applicable skilled labor could assist you?
- Who would supervise the work?

In all probability, the composition of your groups will change as the Study Phase progresses.

STUDY

PROJECT EXAMPLE

During the weekend, Roger and Jose meet with Professor Hulbert. They examine the Study Phase work to be accomplished, and decide on how to group the team members to perform that work. Roger and Jose then prepare a list of potential group assignments with Professor Hulbert. Alternative assignments are noted only on Roger's copy. The proposed groups are these:

Roger and Jose

Alice and Joseph

Laura and Kim

Ellery and Manuel

This list is issued as a matrix. The Study Phase activities are listed vertically and the names of the eight team members are listed across the top of the sheet. (See figure 3.3.)

Figure 3.3   Partial work matrix

Activity 1D: Assign Each Group a Set of Tasks to Investigate

Distribute work assignments to each group of team members. Explain to each group how its work relates to that of all the other groups. Allot each team both time and money to perform its part of the Study Phase.

Synthesize your project so the parts can be individually examined and brought together into a coordinated unit. New ideas often occur as each group studies its assignments while noting the work to be performed by the other groups. Periodic review sessions, often referred to as design reviews, are required to ensure that you and all other team members are aware of the progress of the other groups, and how this progress relates to the overall project plan.

PROJECT EXAMPLE

Roger next distributes a list of potential group assignments for discussion. After a few minor changes to satisfy the personalities involved, the groups and their assignments for the remaining activities (beginning on the next pages) in the Study Phase are as follows:

Study Phase Activities	Group
3A	Laura and Kim, with help from Alice
3B	Ellery and Manuel
3C	Laura and Kim
4A	Alice and Joseph
4B	Ellery and Manuel
5A	All team members
5B	Alice and Joseph
6A	Ellery and Manuel
6B	All team members
7A	Roger and Jose
7B	Roger and Jose

The team members all agree to meet each Monday afternoon to review status. Any documents that are to be reviewed by the entire team will be provided to Laura via a computer disk or e-mail by 8 A.M. each Monday morning for printing and distribution that Monday afternoon.

Activity 2: Establish Ground Rules for the Study and Design Phases

Ground rules govern how the group is to function and interact during the next phases and how the work of various members is to be evaluated.

Prepare the output of the Study Phase in a manner that is acceptable to those who will be reviewing the project's progress and its output. In technical matters, a set of rules—often referred to as **ground rules**—governs the conduct, the procedures, and the final products of the Study Phase, as well as the work for the Design Phase (Hosny, Benjamin, and Omurtag, 1994). Ground rules are an established guide for the conduct of the various remaining activities.

When developing ground rules for a *product,* it is important to agree in advance on that product's attributes. Cross (1944, p. 150) notes that product attributes include:

- Utility—performance aspects such as capacity, power, speed, accuracy, or versatility

- Safety—secure, hazard-free operation

- Ease of use—more user friendly (See human factors, section 9.2.)

- Aesthetics—the appearance: color, form, style, surface finish, feel to the touch

- Reliability—freedom from breakdown or malfunction; performance under a variety of environmental conditions

- Maintenance—simple, infrequent, or no maintenance requirements

- Lifetime—except for disposable products, a long lifetime offers good value for the initial purchase price

- Pollution—little or no unpleasant or unwanted byproducts, including noise and heat

Ground-rule examples are given in the case study. When should ground rules be established?

PLANNING AHEAD▶

Establish the ground rules in advance so that all team members involved will know what the parameters of the projects will be and how their work will be judged. Sometimes you must establish the ground rules during the Conception Phase, modify them during the Study Phase, and further modify them during the early portion of the Design Phase. Thus, team members can examine their work in advance of the formal design reviews to see if they are designing to meet the ground-rule requirements.

As the ground rules are being established, the objectives prepared during the Conception Phase task preparation can be expanded. For smaller projects, most of these objectives are merely stated. For larger projects, where there may be a variety of choices, alternative objectives are prepared, documented, and compared.

One way to assess and compare alternative objectives is known as **weighting** objectives (Cross, 1944, pp. 128–139). He presents a system, with an example, of quantitatively evaluating alternative objectives so you can select the appropriate one. Objectives can include technical and economic factors, user and safety requirements, and so on. **Scores, weights,** or **rankings** may be allocated to each entry, including the qualitative entries.

PROJECT EXAMPLE

At a Monday afternoon meeting, Professor Hulbert asks the team to complete a questionnaire that he has developed. It is a list of how the eventual results of the Design Phase of the activity center could be judged. The team members are asked to add their comments for discussion at a meeting to be held Thursday afternoon. (This list, when modified, will become the ground rules for the activity center project.)

At the Thursday afternoon meeting, Professor Hulbert stands at the chalkboard. Team members propose ground rules, and Professor Hulbert writes them on the board. After one hour of intense discussion, the group agrees on a draft of these ground rules.

The draft of the ground rules for the activity center project is as follows:

- The activity center project must be completed by next August.
- The cost of the activity center project must not exceed $20 000.
- The project must be performed primarily by using the skills of the team members.
- Contractors to be involved must be approved by Professor Hulbert, and their credentials verified by the Northeastern University treasurer's office.
- All documentation must be prepared as work progresses and be corrected at the end of each phase.

These ground rules will be continually reviewed by all and revised by Alice and Joseph during the remainder of the Study Phase.

Activity 3: Study Solutions to Be Considered for Design

During this activity, you will investigate potential solutions or ways to implement the project and determine the functions to be included in each potential solution. Brainstorming or a similar creative technique (chapter 1) can be applied to devise alternative solutions. You must also determine the risks associated with each potential solution.

Activity 3A: Study Potential Solutions

A key part of the Study Phase occurs when various groups investigate ways to implement the project.

Investigate a variety of solutions to implementing the project. Most ideas can be implemented in more than one way. Where the new solutions represent significant changes in project direction, you should require each group to devise accompanying tasks, schedules, and budgets. The new information, along with the new technical direction, is then evaluated as a part of activity 4B.

Devise approaches that remove the need for technological improvements for projects to be accomplished. If complicated portions of a project concept require a significant improvement in technology, materials, or software, they may be high-risk areas. A simulation may be required. See section 9.3.

Investigate whether potential solutions have been previously devised for other projects. Perhaps no one ever considered applying them to the specific problem involved in your project.

As an example, in electronics, a new type of integrated circuit with a new set of specifications may be needed for the project. You may be asked to prove that this new integrated circuit

- Will be satisfactory
- Can be manufactured in the desired quantity and at a reasonable cost
- Will continue to perform satisfactorily as it ages

The testing effort could require much more investigative time than is available. However, standard accelerated aging processes have been devised and accepted via such organizations as the EIA (Electronics Industries Association). End-of-life characteristics can be approximated through an accelerated aging process so that the time required to force the aging of an integrated circuit is but a fraction of its normal expected life.

Avoid investigating approaches that require excessive expenditure of time and money. Where money is in short supply and time frames require prompt solutions, innovative, untested approaches are usually best avoided. However, some very creative solutions that have been authorized by a team manager have resulted in the savings of large amounts of time and money. For such situations, simpler solutions are often pursued simultaneously along with the more creative solutions that at first seem more risky. Thus, the project will not fail or be terminated because of the risk involved in pursuing only one solution.

Illustration: An electronic component and its testing equipment and procedures were developed by a design team. Considerable testing time was required to verify the performance characteristics of the component. The analysis of the data occurred after the component was shipped to the customer; it required several additional weeks of analysis.

A separate design team of software specialists devised a method to monitor the component as it was being assembled and tested; the acquired data were then analyzed as it was gathered. The results were available to ship with the component, thus saving production-and-shipping time and increasing customer satisfaction.

PROJECT EXAMPLE

Laura and Kim have been assigned to investigate ideas and issues associated with designing an activity center. A second brainstorming session is scheduled. The results are evaluated and the team agrees to explore the following options:

- What locations in Bedford Park are available?
    - What are the soil characteristics of the locations?
    - What are the building code restrictions?
- What are possible time schedules for construction?
- Have nearby communities developed similar activity centers?
    - What do the children using these activity centers think of them?
    - What do the teachers, parents, and town and school administrators think of these activity centers?
- How will the goal of meeting children's needs and addressing children's safety issues affect the design?
- How large an activity center can actually be constructed for $20 000?
- What type of activity center should be designed?
- What are the kinds of materials that could be used?
    - What types of plumbing materials are available and applicable?
    - What are the various types of paints suitable to the activity center exterior and interior, as well as the costs of the paints?
    - Will the materials used be available later for repair and maintenance of the center?
- Will landscaping of the grounds be included in the cost?
- What are the possible uses (functions) of the activity center?
- What skills does the team lack that local contractors could supply?

These questions are presented at the next meeting for all team members to analyze. The above list does not change appreciably because it is intentionally vague so it will not become too restrictive during the remainder of the Study Phase. However, during activity 3B below, it is expanded upon as details become available from interviews with individuals experienced in building construction, particularly those contractors and building inspectors who have worked in or near the town of Bedford.

Ellery and Manuel are assigned the task of obtaining copies from the State House Bookstore of the appropriate building, plumbing, and electrical codes that will apply to the activity center structure.

Alice volunteers to investigate alternative foundation designs. She examines textbooks and also interviews Professor Ernest Spencer of the university's Civil Engineering Department regarding the status of concrete foundation designs.

As time passes, the actual outcomes of the original project may either be forgotten or may need to be evaluated again. Team members may become so involved with their particular tasks that they forget to consider how their work will meet the needs of the overall project.

Activity 3B: Determine Functions to Be Included in the Solutions

Continually examine the functions of your project with respect to all ongoing tasks. As time passes, the actual outcomes of your original project may either be forgotten or may need to be evaluated again. Team members may become so involved with their particular tasks that they forget to consider how their work will meet the needs of the overall project. The goals of the overall project must be continually examined with respect to the assigned tasks to ensure that tasks are directly and efficiently contributing to the accomplishment of the overall project.

Illustration: In the 1960's, the president of a supermarket chain requested the designers of a major high-tech corporation to devise a system (1) for placing coded labels on grocery-store products and (2) for scanning and reading those labels. The system was to be connected to the cash register. The objective was to decrease customer check-out time.

After spending $1.5M of company funds, the treasurer of the same chain indicated that the more important need was to keep track of inventory leaving the store. Thus, the sold inventory could be replaced overnight on the shelves. At that time, the storage capacity of computing equipment could not handle the additional inventory-tracking requirement, so the design was terminated.

PROJECT EXAMPLE

Ellery and Manuel carefully examine the questions developed in activity 3A. They now convert these questions into functional statements, known as the **system functions.** These functions will guide the Design Phase team.

- The activity center will be located in the northwest corner of Bedford Park.
- The soil consists of 4" to 6" of rocky topsoil with a clay and rock subsoil.
- The building codes that apply are on file at the Bedford Town Hall.
- Construction must start no later than March 1 and must be finished by the end of August because of school term requirements.
- The work will be supervised by the Superintendent of Public Works of the town of Bedford.
- The activity center must be constructed for $20 000. The known variables are these:

    year-round versus summer use

    the number and size of rooms

    the number of floors, including a full or partial basement

    types of roofing, such as slate, wooden, or asphalt shingles

    exterior walls, such as cedar shingles, clapboards, and vinyl or aluminum siding

    exterior trim, such as pine boards, soffits with vents, vinyl, and aluminum

    interior ceilings, such as plaster, drywall, and hung ceilings

    interior walls, such as plaster, drywall, and panels

    interior floors, such as oak, fir, rubber tile, and carpet

    type of heating (such as oil, electricity, and natural gas) if the facility is to be used year-round as an activity center

    landscaping, such as rough grading with sifted existing or purchased loam

    seeding, such as Kentucky blue, rye, and fescue grasses

- The activity center is to provide, for children ages four through ten, recreation opportunities that also develop simple skills such as these:

    sweeping, cleaning, and dusting

    picking up after themselves

manners, such as greeting and thanking others and proper etiquette for eating

sharing and consideration of others during both individual play and team efforts

personal grooming, such as combing hair, brushing teeth, and washing face, ears, neck, and hands

- The team lacks skills and equipment for excavation and foundation construction.

Thus, all the questions in activity 3A that apply to the activity center have been converted to functions that must be considered by the project team.

Activity 3C: Determine Risks and Trade-offs

PLANNING AHEAD

Develop alternate solutions to the high-risk areas identified during the Conception Phase. Evaluate these solutions by performing a **risk analysis.** During the Conception Phase, the problems and their associated risks were identified. Assess the risks for each proposed alternate solution during this Study Phase. A risk analysis is an analytical technique. It is a quantitative approach used to compare a variety of potential solutions versus their probability of success as a solution. It is a branch of engineering science. For further technical information, see Chase (1974), chapter 9.

Duncan (1996) notes that risk identification consists of determining which risks are likely to affect the project. Each of these risks is then documented and assessed. Risk identification is not a one-time event; it should be performed on a regular basis throughout the project phases. Risk identification is concerned with both opportunities (positive outcomes) and threats (negative outcomes). Checklists are often devised and used for comparison purposes during trade-off studies.

*Determine trade-offs among your problem solutions. A **trade-off** is an exchange; it is the sacrificing of one benefit or advantage to gain another benefit or advantage that you consider to be more desirable.*

Determine trade-offs among your problem solutions. A **trade-off** is an exchange; it is the sacrificing of one benefit or advantage to gain another benefit or advantage that you consider to be more desirable. List and compare the advantages and disadvantages of each potential solution. A trade-off is a qualitative version of a risk analysis.

In performing a trade-off analysis, you are behaving in a manner similar to a circus tightrope walker. Tightrope walkers sometimes have a safety net under them to catch them if they fall. Projects seldom contain safety nets. There are many competitors—the equivalent of lions and tigers on the circus floor—waiting for your project to falter or fail so they may acquire the work. Therefore, those persons involved in active projects must continually walk the four tightropes noted below.

1. *Staffing: the selection of individuals who can plan and perform a project.* The staff is a combination of (1) highly skilled people who can visualize money-saving changes during implementation and (2) unskilled people who are less costly and need more supervision. Tightrope walking, as related to staffing, is the selection of the optimum combination of these people.

2. *Documentation: the drawings and written descriptions of a project.* It is frequently the desire of some designers to be more specific than is necessary. They overdocument a design to please financial and legal people.

Other designers tend to underdocument in order to save time, provide flexibility, and reduce cost. Tightrope walking, as related to documentation, is the balancing of the amount of documentation desired versus its cost and risks.

3. *Pricing: the cost of labor, material, and services to be involved in a project.* An estimator may prefer to overestimate the cost of various portions of a potential project in order to avoid cost overruns. At the same time, the person who is to manage the project may prefer to underprice a project in order to be competitive and win the contract.

Tightrope walking, as related to pricing, is the weighing of the possibility of being awarded a project that loses money versus losing the project that might have earned a profit. This decision is probably the most critical decision to be faced by the team leader and the team.

STUDY

4. *Cost control: the project manager's concern once the project is funded.* It is the responsibility of the project manager to watch every penny that is being spent and how it is planned to be spent. Some managers may not observe that many dollars are being wasted while only a few pennies are being saved. Other managers allow some flexibility in group expenditures so that the ingenuity of the team members may be used to keep total expenditures to a minimum.

Tightrope walking, as related to cost control, is the balancing of authorized expenditures versus the work to be performed. It is a nontechnical activity and depends greatly upon the attitudes of the manager and team members concerning money.

Select the best option for each of the above categories. Examine the result of combining these options. Verify that this combination is the optimum combination. This effort is known as performing a trade-off among the various options. The selection of the optimum combination of these options continues to be more of an art than a science.

PROJECT EXAMPLE

Laura and Kim carefully examine the activity 3B list of system functions. They assess the potential risks associated with each proposed system function.

- What are the problems with locating the activity center in the northwest corner of Bedford Park with respect to water, sewage, electricity, or natural gas access?

- Where is electrical power available during construction?

- Are there available locations within Bedford Park for temporary storage and further processing of the excavated soil?

- Which portions of the Bedford Building Codes apply to this project?

- What are the ranges of environmental conditions, such as temperature, humidity, wind, and noise levels, that occur in this area for either year-round or only summer-use considerations?

- What are the cost comparisons for constructing more than one floor level and the effect upon construction and heating costs?

- Which building materials are locally available—including their prices—for the roof, exterior walls, interior walls, ceilings, and floors?

- Should landscaping be included as a part of the project, or should this work be performed by the Bedford Public Works Department?

- What local companies and employees might be willing to contribute materials, labor, or only advice and guidance?

- What foundation construction techniques are applicable?

A trade-off study is sometimes required. As an example, concrete floors are of a thickness that may require steel mesh within the concrete for structural support. If the concrete floor is 20 percent thicker than is normally used in this type of building design, then the internal steel mesh (or reinforcing rods) will not be required. Both approaches must be evaluated in terms of cost and risk.

A trade-off study is performed by Kim Wong, assisted by a fourth-year technology student. Test materials are prepared, and stress testing and other measurements are performed to determine the resistance of the floor to cracking. That fourth-year student seems more interested in the results of his tests than in the activity center schedule. In order to get him to complete the tests on time, Kim has to continually remind him that the activity center schedule must be followed.

PPCP 3

Activity 4: Gather and Evaluate Information

During this activity, you will contact potential vendors for their technical and financial input, and then evaluate design alternatives. Along with this evaluation, you will be refining your cost estimates.

Activity 4A: Contact Potential Vendors for Their Input

The input of vendors or subcontractors can be invaluable in guiding a project. If they expect to be awarded work as a result of their participation, they may offer advice at no cost.

Identify other persons or organizations who have the additional skills and abilities needed to assist in the performance of your project. They may be **vendors** or **subcontractors.** Their contributions may prove invaluable, particularly if you involve them in the Study Phase effort. They will then feel they are a part of your team. They may frequently offer excellent suggestions based on their experience. If they expect that a subcontract may be offered to them, they may also provide the Study Phase input at no cost to your project.

PROJECT EXAMPLE

Alice and Joseph are given a list of the skills of the team. They then develop a list of the skills necessary to construct the various designs of the activity center. They are now able to identify those skills and the equipment that will be necessary to both design and construct the activity center.

Alice's uncle offers to work with the Northeastern University faculty in reviewing the activity center design as it progresses. Professor Hulbert identifies and urges other faculty members to act as design reviewers. He recommends that the students study the architectural and construction options given in Muller, Fausett, and Grau (1999). For the Study Phase, Joseph contacts several local contractors who can either loan or rent the necessary earth-moving equipment. He also obtains construction cost estimates from them. Alice locates a contractor who will assist in the construction of the concrete foundation, if that is the design path chosen. No commitments are offered at this time because the design path has yet to be selected.

Activity 4B: Evaluate Design Alternatives and Refine Estimates

Cost estimates need to be reviewed to ensure that pricing data are up-to-date and realistic. This activity is primarily a technical activity, with some emphasis on cost and schedule changes.

Examine the outcomes of your previous Study Phase activities. Value analysis may be helpful. (See appendix A.) Compare all of the proposed solutions to your project with one another. Prepare comparison documentation in one standard format in preparation for the work of activity 5A on page 72. The designers will evaluate these alternatives. If cost estimators are involved, they will provide information that will guide the designers. Review cost estimates to ensure that pricing data are up-to-date and realistic. This activity is primarily a technical activity, with some emphasis on cost and schedule changes.

PROJECT EXAMPLE

At their next Monday afternoon meeting, all activity center design alternatives are examined and evaluated. The ground rules are used as the judgment vehicle for both the team members and the work they accomplished. On the board, a matrix is developed that compares each alternative solution with the previously devised ground rules. It is noted that no one has evaluated the effect of the applicable building codes upon each proposed design solution.

Ellery and Manuel obtain a copy of the local and state building codes, including the plumbing and electrical codes. They discover that the various

STUDY

applicable codes originated with the Council of American Building Officials. The applicable codes are the following:

- National Electric Code
- CABO One- and Two-Family Dwelling Code
- BOCA National Building, Plumbing, and Mechanical Codes

They extract the following information that may be of value to the designers:

- Foundation drainage grade: $\geq 6''$ per $10'$
- Stud drilling & notching $\leq 25\%$ of width; on-load bearing $\leq 40\%$ of width; doubled studs $\leq 60\%$ of width
- Window air filtration < 0.5 CFM per linear ft with $\Delta p = 1.56$ psf (CFM = cubic ft per minute; psf = pounds per square ft)
- Handicapped access ramp, slope 1:8 maximum and 1:12 minimum; landing $\geq 3' \times 3'$; guard rails $\geq 36''$ high
- Stairway $\geq 42''$ wide; handrails $\leq 34''$ high; landings $> 3' \times 3'$
- Hallway width $\geq 36''$
- Smoke detectors: all floors—for new construction, permanently wired to 115V

Manuel is assigned to devise a schedule for completing the Study Phase work and to prepare the cost spreadsheet for completing that work.

Activity 5: Select and Plan One Solution

During this activity, you will select one solution for your project, and then plan the Design and Implementation Phases based upon your solution.

Activity 5A: Select a Solution

For selection of solutions or ways to implement a project, the following criteria should be considered:

- *Complexity and cost of the solution*
- *Time to implement solution*
- *Preferences of clients*
- *Availability of materials*

Select the project solution from your previously devised options and design alternatives by comparing the following factors:

- Complexity (technically complicated and intricate)
- Costs (labor and material)
- Urgency (time to investigate versus limited time available)
- Preferences of clients
- Availability of materials

Such decisions are often nontechnical ones.

Your options represent choices that must be weighed both separately and together because they interact, as noted in figure 3.4.

Decision making is a continuous effort of analyzing, assessing, and choosing. Technical information is gathered and compared. Financial information may fluctuate rapidly or may change slowly. The perceptions of your client may be different from your team's preferred technical solution—the client's input must also be considered. The project manager must "smooth the ripples" of change so that team members do not frequently proceed in different directions. During the decision-making process, individuals may become confused and frustrated and no longer perform as a team!

When you are involved in large projects or programs, a formal mathematical or statistical model may be needed for making decisions. See chapter 9. For smaller projects, you can develop a matrix of information in the form of a decision tree for comparison and consideration purposes.

Figure 3.4 Decision basis for project choices

PROJECT EXAMPLE

All team members participate in devising the design direction for a project. This may be a day-long process. By the end of the day, the team members can produce a sketch of the activity center they propose.

All team members participate in devising the design direction, which is to be followed during the next phase of the activity center project. The decisions require so much uninterrupted time that an entire day is set aside for a solution selection. A matrix of information, in the form of a decision tree (figure 3.5), is prepared by Ellery and Manuel as a part of performing activity 4B.

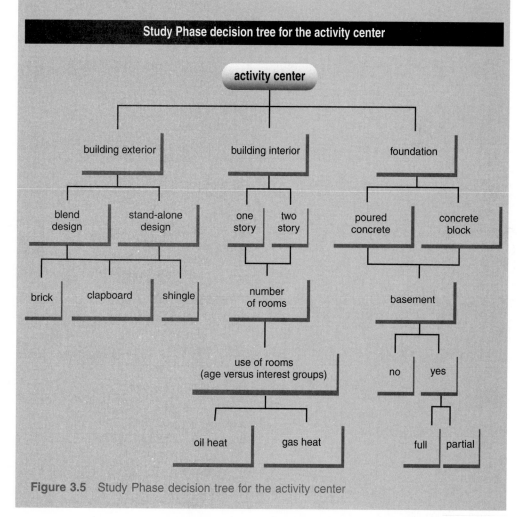

Figure 3.5 Study Phase decision tree for the activity center

Several questions (see chapter 2, activity 2F) are considered during this session:

- Will the activity center be constructed to blend in with other local structures and the land, or should it stand out for reasons of its uniqueness?
- Should the exterior finish be brick, clapboard, or shingle?
- Will it be a one-story or two-story activity center?
- How many rooms should there be within the activity center?
- What uses are to be considered for each room?
- Should the activity center rooms be designed for special age or interest groups?
- Should the central heating system be oil- or gas-fired?
- Will the activity center require a basement?
- Should the foundation consist of concrete block or poured concrete?
- If there is a basement, should it be a partial or full basement?

The work of Kim regarding foundation and concrete floors is examined first because it affects the design choices for the remainder of the activity center. It is decided to use the thicker 6″ concrete floor; it will cost less and will not crack under normal conditions of use.

The decisions agreed on at the meeting that affect the Design Phase (covered in chapter 4) are the following:

- The activity center will be constructed for year-round use.
- It will have a first floor with three rooms, one toilet per room.
- The center will have a basement that can be used for a furnace and for storage of toys that are used outdoors.
- The foundation and first-floor walls will be constructed to allow for later roof raising and the addition of a second floor.
- Roofing will be asphalt shingles.
- Exterior walls will be clapboards.

Figure 3.6 Preliminary sketch of activity center design

- Exterior trim will be pine boards.
- Interior ceilings will be drywall.
- Interior walls will be drywall.
- Interior floors will be rubber tile throughout.
- The type of heat will be natural gas.
- Landscaping will use existing loam $\geq 4''$ deep for finished grading.
- The seed will be supplied by the Town Department of Public Works.

Professor Hulbert reminds the team members to compare these decisions with the ground rules devised in activity 2. A preliminary sketch is shown in figure 3.6.

Activity 5B: Plan the Design and Implementation Phases

Review and revise the Conception Phase plans for the Design and Implementation Phases. Include applicable results from the Value Analysis (see appendix A). Ensure that the revised plans remain realistic with regard to task description content, schedules, and budgets.

The task descriptions, costs, and schedules for the project can now contain more detail, as the project moves nearer to the Design Phase.

For the task descriptions, state the content of each task in enough detail that there are no misunderstandings among the potential workers and managers. Task descriptions define the content that is indicated in the task title. See appendix B.

More detail must be added to the schedules devised during the Conception Phase. Potential vendor and subcontractor plans must also be included in the revised schedules. Schedule headings should coincide with the task headings. Often the titles for the task descriptions are used as headings in schedules so that schedules and tasks coincide. They are often shortened so they fit in the space available.

Budgets must be updated with justification provided in the form of price quotations from both vendors and materials suppliers. These budgets should include headings that coincide with the task and schedule headings.

PROJECT EXAMPLE

Alice and Joseph work closely with Ellery as he writes the task descriptions, and with Manuel, who is revising the schedules and budgets. They need to identify the work to be accomplished during the Design Phase, as well as the human skills and resources needed. They must also estimate the human skills and resources needed for the Implementation Phase. For these two phases, they identify either team members or vendors who can provide time and skills, facilities, equipment, and computation support. The task descriptions, schedules, and budgets are now reviewed by all the team members and revised as necessary. Roger prepares a plot plan (figure 3.7). He has to remind them that, even though vacation week is approaching, there is still work to be done.

PLANNING AHEAD

Professor Hulbert notes that this is the time to learn how to prepare the following documents.

- The Letter of Transmittal, which for the activity center will be a contract letter
- A Design Specification for the activity center, which describes each item to be constructed
- The working and detail drawings, produced with a CAD program

STUDY

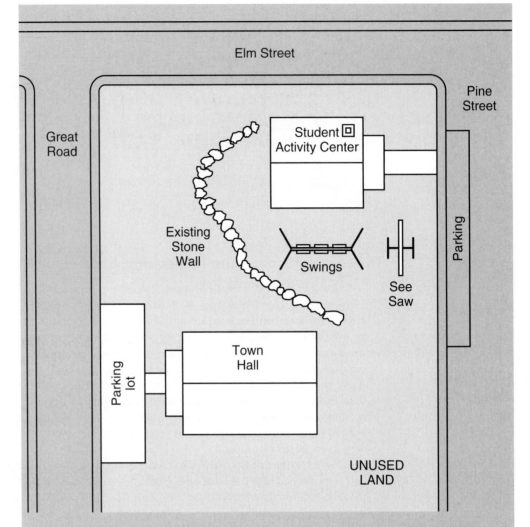

Figure 3.7   Activity Center Plot Plan

He requests that each team member reexamine the requirements of the Design Phase (chapter 4) and indicate where they can either apply their existing skills or can quickly learn new skills.

Roger Stein is overwhelmed by the variety of work to be performed in the Design Phase and wonders where the team will locate the people with the necessary skills.

Alice D'Annolfo believes that she can write most of the Design Specification because of her experience in working with her father. However, she is not comfortable with the legal language involved.

Laura Drake would like to learn how to use a CAD program to devise working drawings, but she worries about how many she can produce during the eight weeks of the Design Phase.

Jose Hernandez prefers to work on revising material costs during the Design Phase, as he is going to have an increased class load next term.

Kim Wong wants to work on foundation and concrete specifications and to continue to refine the cost estimates.

Ellery Kistler agrees to help the other students learn the CAD program.

Manuel Cardoza prefers to concentrate on applying the CAD program.

Joseph O'Neil wants to learn the CAD program and to assist in refining the lumber and related estimates.

Professor Hulbert offers to contact the University Law School for the assistance of one professor or lecturer who has had extensive experience in either writing or reviewing contracts and specifications for both private and commercial buildings.

Activity 6: Document the Selected Solution

As a part of your documentation, you will refine your tasks, schedules, and budgets for the Design and Implementation Phases. You will also prepare a description of your proposed solution and the rationale for its choice.

Activity 6A: Refine the Task, Schedule, and Budget Documents

Documentation becomes more crucial as more people are involved in a project. Descriptions of tasks and subtasks must be easily understood by the Design Phase designers and the Implementation Phase builders.

Individual team members, and groups of team members, have developed the details regarding the selection of the Study Phase project solution and the Design Phase options. Refine your tasks, schedules, and budgets for the Design and Implementation Phases. (See chapter 7.) Note within your documentation that the Implementation Phase documents are best estimates based on available information.

Rearrange your tasks and subtasks so they are more easily understood by the Design Phase designers and the Implementation Phase builders. Information that you gather and examine during this Study Phase may cause new tasks to replace tasks previously documented. Thus, your task descriptions, schedules, and costs for the next phases may change in both content and sequence.

PROJECT EXAMPLE

STUDY

Ellery and Manuel realize that they must work with the other teams to determine design directions and details investigated by these teams and to determine the various associated costs. They decide not to write task descriptions except for those areas that are firm. They discover that it is wiser to invest their time pursuing the costs for firm items and to estimate the accompanying schedule changes rather than to write all the task descriptions at one time.

By the middle of December, with exams over and the vacation week very near, Manuel has devised a modular computer program that can process the inserted changes in cost and schedule (chapters 7 and 8) and display these changes without the need to print another copy. This is of tremendous assistance to the team in rapidly examining the effect of suggestions for modifications in design.

As the Study Phase nears completion, Ellery and Manuel realize that they cannot write all the task descriptions for the Design Phase within the time remaining. Joseph assists Ellery and Manuel in writing these descriptions. The entire team agrees to review the results each evening prior to vacation.

The task descriptions change. Various subtasks are regrouped so they "make more sense" to the ultimate designers and builders. New tasks are added. Sometimes tasks are eliminated. (It should be noted that even these tasks, schedules, and budgets may change again during the Design Phase.) Compare these two lists of tasks:

Tasks from the Conception Phase	Tasks from the Study Phase
Prepare Site	Prepare Site
	Cut and Remove Brush
	Remove Protruding Ledge
Excavate Site	Excavate Site
	Define Foundation Corners
Erect Foundation	Erect Foundation
	Waterproof Exterior Foundation Walls
	Backfill Completed Foundation
	Remove Excess Dirt
Cap Foundation	Cap Foundation
Erect Rough Framing and Sheathing	Erect Rough Framing and Sheathing
	Erect Exterior and Interior Studs
	Erect Roof Rafters
	Board in Walls and Roof
Shingle Roof	Shingle Roof
Install Windows	Install Windows
Install Heating	Install Heating
	Install External Doors
Finish Exterior	Finish Exterior
	Apply Prime Coat of Paint to Exterior
Install Sheetrock™	Install Sheetrock™
Plaster Interior	Plaster Interior
Lay Floors	Lay Floors
	Install Vapor Barrier
	Install Flooring
Install Interior Finish	Install Interior Finish (Doors, Windows, Baseboards)
	Install Stair Treads and Risers
Paint Interior Finish	Paint Interior Finish (Ceilings, Walls, Trim, Floors)

Once the above task details are established, the schedule of tasks is revised. The new schedule shown in figure 3.8 should be compared with that in figure 2.8 in chapter 2 (the upper schedule in figure 3.8). The lower schedule in figure 3.8 has been modified to reflect the knowledge acquired during the Study Phase.

Similarly, the cost-information details are refined as the tasks and schedules are developed in greater detail. Figure 3.9 should be compared with figure 2.9 in chapter 2 (the upper estimate in figure 3.9). Figure 3.9 has been modified to reflect the knowledge acquired during the Study Phase.

Roger asks Professor Hulbert if the tasks should be numbered so it would be easier to follow them as the team progresses into the Design Phase. Professor Hulbert considers the question and then decides they should wait because the changes in task sequence and content during the Design Phase will most likely

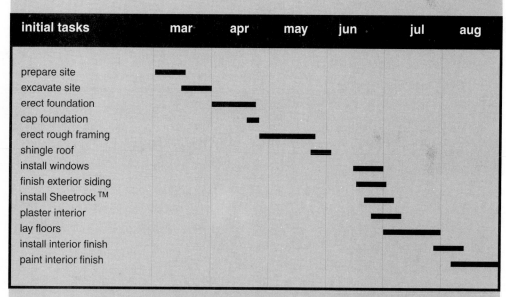

Figure 3.8   Sample of old and revised schedules

be significant. Numbering the initial tasks at this point could cause confusion because the numbers will change when the design is in progress. He suggests that they should use letters at this time so they can more easily compare the Study Phase lettered initial tasks with the Design Phase numbered tasks.

The final task descriptions, schedule, and budget are refined. Professor Hulbert notes that there seem to be no *significant* changes since these budgets, tasks, and schedules were developed during the Conception Phase.

Ellery Kistler asks for the opportunity to write the details of the task descriptions so that he can extend his English writing abilities to technical English. (See appendix B.) Two examples of his writings are given below to help you understand the concept.

Sample of old and revised cost estimates

initial tasks	mar	apr	may	jun	jul	aug	totals
prepare site	600						600
excavate site	1400						1400
erect foundation		1700					1700
cap foundation		400		.			400
erect rough framing			4800				4800
shingle roof				1000			1000
install windows				1800			1800
finish exterior siding				400	400		800
install Sheetrock™				300	500		800
plaster interior					600		600
lay floors					2200		2200
install interior finish					600	1200	1800
paint exterior finish						1300	1300
totals	2000	2100	4800	3500	4300	2500	19 200

initial tasks	mar	apr	may	jun	jul	aug	totals
prepare site	600						600
excavate site	1400						1400
erect foundation		1700					1700
cap foundation		400					400
erect rough framing			4800				4800
shingle roof				1000			1000
install windows				1800			1800
install heating							0
install exterior doors					400		400
finish exterior siding				400	400		800
install Sheetrock™				300	500		800
plaster interior					600		600
lay floors					2200		2200
install interior finish					600	1200	1800
paint interior finish						1300	1300
totals	2000	2100	4800	3500	4700	2500	19 600

Figure 3.9   Sample of old and revised cost estimates

Prepare Site

Survey the site, with Registered Land Surveyors or Civil Engineers, to establish grade levels of the basement floor. Place a stake at each corner of the foundation with "depth of cut" noted on each stake. Install batter boards at each corner and mark them with the location for each foundation wall.

Excavate Site

Excavate the basement and foundation footings, with a minimum of 1' clearance beyond the exterior walls of the foundation. If interfering ledge outcroppings are discovered, then drill with 2" diameter rock drill bits to a depth of 1' below the designed finished-floor level, and blast to remove that ledge.

Note that the first task description (Prepare Site) directly leads to the second task description (Excavate Site). All other task descriptions connect to at least one previous task description and lead to at least one other task description.

The entire set of task descriptions, schedules, and budgets is again reviewed; the review lasts an entire afternoon.

Activity 6B: Document the Proposed Solution and Rationale

The documents for the Study Phase are similar to those from the Conception Phase, except they are much more detailed.

The documents for the Study Phase are the following:

- The Project Description with design options
- The Design Specification
- The Design Description with preliminary sketches

The content of each of these documents is described in section 3.3 on page 83. Preliminary sketches from the solution section process are included. (See activity 5A.) The Design Description should also avoid assumptions that direct the Design Phase team toward considering only one design.

STUDY

PROJECT EXAMPLE

Roger assigns each member a portion of the following documents to be written:

- The Project Description for the activity center, with design options
- The Design Specification
- The Design Description with preliminary sketches

Roger notes that he has been reviewing portions of these documents for two weeks. He states that it is time to write the missing paragraphs and sections and to read each document for its content and the flow of ideas. Here are the assignments for preparation of the documents:

- Roger and Jose turn over the Project Description for the activity center to Alice for review.
- Alice and Ellery turn over the Design Specification to Laura for review.
- Roger agrees to write the Design Description.
- Ellery agrees to prepare the preliminary sketches of the activity center.

They plan for one last meeting before the week-long school vacation.

Activity 7: Verify and Obtain Funding

During this activity, you will first verify the actual availability of the funding identified during the Conception Phase, and then request the Design Phase funding in an official manner.

Activity 7A: Verify Actual Availability of Funding

The continuing availability of funds from sources needs to be constantly monitored, so that the project can obtain funds when they are needed.

Confirm periodically how much funding continues to be available for your selected project. Determine the latest time that it will be available. During the Study Phase, this activity should be performed by the team manager or a small group of individuals from your Conception Phase team. Why? Because funding may be reassigned to other financially needy groups or organizations while your Study Phase team is still working to devise a project solution that will satisfy both your team and the funding source.

PROJECT EXAMPLE

Roger and Jose discover that the Commonwealth of Massachusetts has reduced the $15 000 in funding to $10 000 because of state budget changes. Miss Kewer's $5 000 continues to be available. Thus, the Study Phase team must either revise its options and construct an activity center for $15 000 or else seek an additional $5 000 elsewhere. Roger, Jose, and Professor Hulbert investigate other sources that would be willing to contribute the needed additional $5 000.

The current status of the project can be summarized as follows:

- The activity center lacks $5 000.
- Other funding sources are not yet committed to contributing to the activity center.
- The skills of team members remain applicable to the various designs for the activity center.

Even though an additional $5 000 needs to be raised to construct the $20 000 activity center, a $20 000 activity center seems to be the preferred project level.

Although the team members seem frustrated and discouraged, Professor Hulbert explains that such a funding problem is not unusual. He instructs the team to keep the $15 000 as a lower bound for the Design Phase while he, Roger, and Jose investigate other options for obtaining more funding.

Activity 7B: Obtain Design Phase Funding

Provide a presentation to the previously identified funding source. Verify that your project can be funded promptly. It is customary for funding sources to retain control over their funds until their personnel have reviewed the results of your Study Phase. Now revise those portions of the project as requested by the personnel from the funding source. If it is necessary to have no lost time between the Study and Design phases, then provide a preliminary presentation to the funding source prior to the completion of your Study Phase work.

Funding authorization may occur in one of two ways. Such authorization is usually in the form of a letter. For foundations, a check for the agreed amount is often included with the letter of authorization. This, in effect, pays for the work in advance. For government agencies or within the parent organization of the project team, a purchase order may be issued to authorize the project to proceed.

PROJECT EXAMPLE

In conjunction with Professor Hulbert, Roger obtains the additional no-cost services of vendors for the Design Phase, who later hope to participate in the construction of the activity center. Many of these are contractors who have worked together before in the construction of both private and industrial projects in the Bedford area. They are instructed by Professor Hulbert to be careful *not* to perform work that should be a learning experience for the team.

The team members agree to meet on Tuesday afternoon following their last classes to see if they have discovered any significant errors in the documentation of the Study Phase and the proposed solutions. All the vendors agree to meet at Northeastern University on the Wednesday evening following the year-end school vacation to review the Study Phase documentation.

An important note: The group of Professor Hulbert, Roger Stein, and Jose Hernandez realize that all of the work to date will be wasted if the necessary additional $5 000 is not acquired soon. Otherwise, the Design Phase must limit implementation costs to $15 000. They agree to talk to friends and family during the University vacation for ideas relating to, and sources for, the additional $5 000.

It is late December. Now it is time for Roger to terminate the Study Phase so that they can proceed into the Design Phase when they return and so that all team members can enjoy a well-deserved one-week vacation.

SECTION 3.3   STUDY PHASE DOCUMENTS

During the Study Phase, the ideas developed and documented during the Conception Phase are examined in more detail. Using the Project Description with Artist's Concept and Preliminary Specification as guides, members of the project team proceed with further investigation. In order to more accurately estimate the tasks, schedules, and costs needed to design and construct the selected project, team members propose and pursue a variety of solutions to the selected project.

As the Study Phase progresses, more ideas are circulated via papers and memoranda; more meetings are held to compare and evaluate the various proposed solutions, and more meeting reports (section 8.2) are written. These memoranda and meeting reports eventually lead to three Study Phase documents. The documents completed by the end of the Study Phase are the following:

1. The Project Description (with design options): explanatory documents
2. The Design Specifications: the second phase of specification development
3. The Design Description with preliminary sketches: more detailed drawings and plans

The content of each of these documents is described below. The flow from the Conception Phase documents to the Study Phase documents is shown in figure 3.10.

The **Project Description** consists of the following:

1. A description of the potential project solutions that were explored
2. The attributes of each explored potential project solution
3. The tasks, schedule, and budget for the selected project solution
4. Justification for the selected project solution

This document is often a modified and expanded version of the Project Selection Rationale document from the Conception Phase. This new document typically consists of less than fifty pages for a modest-size project. For a large, complicated program, this document may consist of several volumes of applicable information.

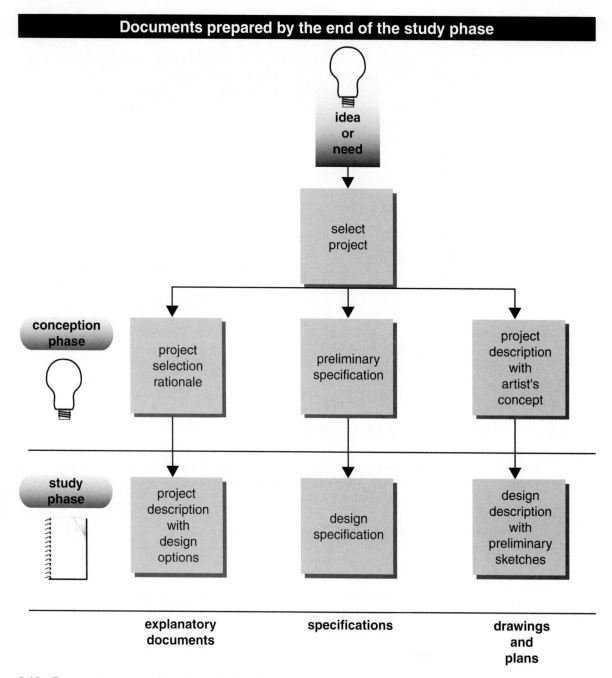

Figure 3.10   Documents prepared by the end of the Study Phase

*The documents from the Study Phase guide the Design Phase. The **Design Specification** document establishes the constraints for the Design Phase.*

The **Design Specification** document establishes the constraints for the Design Phase. It evolves from the Preliminary Specification. The content of the Design Specification is described in chapter 8. The Design Specification must reflect only those functions desired for the selected solution. However, it should avoid directing the Design Phase team toward only one design approach.

The **Design Description** should contain the following:

1. Justification for the project selection developed from the Project Description document
2. A semitechnical description that nontechnical persons can comprehend
3. Estimated schedules per phase
4. Estimated costs per phase

5. Directions for the Design Phase

6. Staffing skills required for the Design Phase

7. Resources needed for the Design Phase

Preliminary sketches for proposed solutions that evolve from the Study Phase should be included. However, the Design Description must avoid guidance that directs the team toward only one solution during the Design Phase.

SECTION 3.4 | DEFINING PHASE COMPLETION

The Study Phase is considered complete when the documentation has been written, reviewed, and revised as recommended during its review. The review team should include individuals from your funding source.

The Study Phase is considered complete when the documentation has been written, reviewed, and revised as recommended during its review. The review team should include individuals from your funding source. Wherever it is possible, include as reviewers some experts in the field who will not be responsible for the funding of the later phases. Why? Because they have not been "close" to the project on a daily basis and may notice problems that have not been considered.

Someone within your organization needs to monitor the total project costs on a continuing basis. This is necessary for all phases of a project because you do not want to overspend, you must stay on schedule, and you want your total effort to be performed according to the specifications previously developed.

The completed documents for the Study Phase consist of an expansion and revision of documents originally devised during the Conception Phase. They are the following:

•   The Project Description with design options, which has evolved from the Project Selection Rationale and includes the refined cost estimates

•   The Design Specification, which has evolved from the Preliminary Specification

•   The Design Description with preliminary sketches, which has evolved from the Project Description (with the artist's concept)

Often, these three documents are initiated during the beginning of the Study Phase. They gradually evolve into their final content by the end of the Study Phase.

The Study and Design Phases may overlap as some members begin to prepare more detailed designs for the project.

The Study and Design Phases may overlap because of the following:

•   Some members of the group are still investigating questions remaining from the Conception Phase

•   Other group members are starting to sketch potential designs and select the materials needed for the Design Phase

•   Other group members are starting to prepare the Design Specification

•   Other group members are writing portions of the Production Specification

Decide when the overall Study Phase will end. Realize that more information may need to be gathered as the design is being developed.

Revise the entire project if very unusual information suddenly becomes available. However, such a revision may discourage the funding source. Thus, a significant project revision should be avoided except during extreme situations. Personnel from the funding source should be kept aware of any significant changes, as well as of the reasons for those changes.

Increase the detail of the tasks and task descriptions devised during the Study Phase as more information is gathered. For some projects, the tasks may also be resequenced. The first three phases of a project may interact as shown in figure 3.11.

Start at the top of figure 3.11 where the concept is determined. For a Yes answer to Concept Determined, you may proceed to the Study Phase. However, if the answer to Concept Determined is No, then you must return to the Conception Phase and revise the appropriate activities. Once the project is selected during the Study Phase, you may proceed to the Design Phase.

Figure 3.11 Interaction of the first three phases of a project

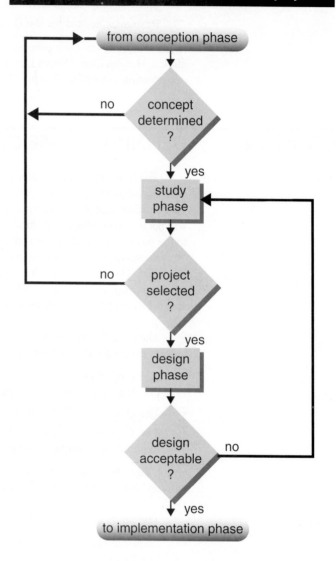

Interaction of the first three phases of a project

There will be times when, during the Design Phase, the design may not be acceptable. If the answer to Design Acceptable is No, then you must return to the Study Phase and revise the appropriate activities.

Continue to walk the tightrope of deciding when a phase is complete. Note any problems that linger from the Study Phase that could adversely affect your Design Phase. Assign problem-solving responsibility to a small but proficient team to rapidly resolve the remaining problems.

CHAPTER OBJECTIVES SUMMARY

Now that you have finished this chapter, you should be able to:

1. Describe the purpose and goal of the Study Phase of a project.

2. Explain the tasks involved in the Study Phase of a project and the activities or steps through which these tasks are performed.

3. Describe the process of reviewing the Conception Phase and planning for the Study Phase.

4. Describe the process of utilizing skills of team members to complete the Study Phase and managing team members to achieve the overall goals of the project.

5. Explain what ground rules for a project are and how they are established.

6. Explain how to investigate and study solutions for ways to implement the project and to evaluate the risks and trade-offs involved with various solutions.

7. Describe how to select among design alternatives as a group process.

8. Discuss relationships with funding sources and potential vendors during the Study Phase.

9. Describe the documents prepared during the Study Phase and how they evolve from the Conception Phase documents.

EXERCISES

3.1   Revise the Purpose and Goal statement given in section 3.1 to match each of your class-project options.

3.2   For your revised Purpose and Goal statement, review your Conception Phase results and organize your Study Phase work. Establish alternative solution requirements and accompanying constraints.

3.3   Carefully examine the activities listed and described in section 3.2; adapt them to each of your options for a class project.

3.4   Write and review the ground rules (criteria) for judging your Study and Design Phase results. Verify that these ground rules are compatible with the expectations of your client and funding sources.

3.5   Review your Conception Phase effort with all team members and other interested parties. Develop the Study Phase content details with all individuals concerned.

3.6   Organize the team into small groups based on their skills, compatibility, and availability. Verify or revise your choice of team leader. Assign each small group a set of tasks to investigate. Develop alternative solutions that satisfy the devised criteria.

3.7   Identify and evaluate risks and trade-offs for each of your proposed alternative solutions.

3.8   Examine the effort required to revise the Conception Phase tasks, schedules, and budgets. Compare this effort with the time and personnel available. Discuss how you might perform this effort without a significant loss of end-product quality.

3.9   Study potential solutions to the selected class project. Develop a list of functions and investigate those forms (solutions) that will satisfy those functions.

3.10   Determine the necessary risks and trade-offs required to implement the project solutions. Devise new tasks, schedules, and budgets where necessary. Contact potential vendors for their technical and financial input.

3.11   Request that the previously identified judges evaluate your proposed solutions. Evaluate accepted design alternatives and refine cost estimates where necessary. Select a project solution.

3.12   Verify the continued existence, actual availability, and method of receiving funding.

3.13   Refine all task, schedule, and budget documents for the Design and Implementation Phases. Document the proposed project solution and the reasons for its choice.

3.14   Prepare documentation describing your proposed design alternatives.

3.15   Obtain Design Phase funding and terminate the Study Phase.

3.16   Describe how you would determine the optimum time to terminate the Study Phase.

The Systematic Approach

The Conception Phase

The Study Phase

The Design Phase

The Implementation Phase

1. Systematic Approach

2. Conception Phase

3. Study Phase

4. Design Phase ▶

Design Phase Purpose and Goal

Design Phase Activities

Design Phase Documents

Defining Phase Completion

5. Implementation Phase

1. What are the purpose and goal of the Design Phase of a project?

2. What tasks are involved in the Design Phase of a project, and what are the activities or steps through which these tasks are performed?

3. What is the role of a manager in the Design Phase?

4. How can a team be organized for the Design Phase and tasks be assigned to individual team members?

5. What is a typical schedule for the Design Phase of a project?

6. What human factors are involved in designing a product?

7. How are function and form linked in developing design plans?

8. What are make-or-buy decisions, and how are they decided?

9. What documents should be prepared for the Design Phase?

10. Who should participate in reviewing and approving the documents from the Design Phase?

11. What are the uses of the documents prepared in the Design Phase?

12. How can it be determined when the Design Phase is completed?

...[D]esign is a polishing job. Much as the potter's wheel is used to mold and shape the first-hewn piece of clay, so the system-design process, through repetition of its steps, molds and shapes the final system.

H. H. Goode and R. E. Machol, 1957

This chapter emphasizes the development of the plans for the project introduced in Chapter 2 and expanded in Chapter 3.

SECTION 4.1

The Design Phase of a project develops the working plans.

DESIGN PHASE PURPOSE AND GOAL

The **purpose** of the Design Phase is to develop the details for the working plans for your proposed project solution. The **goal** of the Design Phase is to prepare a complete set of working plans for the selected design. During this phase, it will be necessary to continually review the working plans for the selected design, including cost estimates, as the design evolves.

At the end of the Design Phase you should know how to accomplish the following:

- Organize your teams into groups for performing design tasks.
- Study potential implementation solutions.
- Develop a design that will satisfy you, your funding source, and the users of your product.
- Refine your previously estimated task, schedule, and budget documents so that they are well developed for the Implementation Phase.
- Document your proposed project design and the reasons for its choice.
- Verify that both your customer and your funding source will accept the Implementation Phase solution.
- Verify availability of funding for the Implementation Phase.

SECTION 4.2

DESIGN PHASE ACTIVITIES

The activities for the Design Phase consist of the following:

Activity 1: Organize the Design Phase Work

   1A: Review the Study Phase effort.

   1B: Develop Design Phase details.

   1C: Organize teams and assign design tasks.

Activity 2: Select the Solution Details to Be Implemented

   2A: Study potential implementation solutions.

   2B: Contact vendors for make-or-buy information.

   2C: Determine make-or-buy decisions.

Activity 3: Document the Design Solution

   3A: Prepare the Production Specification.

   3B: Prepare the Working and Detail Drawings.

   3C: Refine tasks, schedules, and budgets.

   3D: Document the design and reasons for its choice.

Activity 4: Prepare for the Implementation Phase Work

   4A: Review the Design Phase results.

   4B: Verify availability of Implementation Phase funds.

   4C: Plan the Implementation Phase.

Activity 5: Obtain Implementation Phase Funding

As is true for the Conception and Study Phases, the purpose and goal you define for the Design Phase determine the activities that you are to accomplish. The sequence of activities given in this chapter may change from one project to another. However, all the activities must be accomplished before the Design Phase is complete.

As was true during the Study Phase, there will be (design) risks involved with each alternative solution you consider. You will have to assess those risks in relation to their benefits.

DESIGN

Activity 1: Organize the Design Phase Work

Prior to initiating the actual work of the Design Phase, you should review your Study Phase effort and develop Design Phase details with all team members. Then you are in a position to organize the teams and assign them the actual tasks that are to be performed.

It is the role of the manager to see that the work flows well. For a large program, the manager will have a group of people in a systems office handling one or more project and support functions.

It is the role of the manager to see that the work flows well. The manager must be concerned with everyday details, including the following:

*   Providing additional systems-related information where lacking
*   Assisting in resolving system uncertainties
*   Assisting in resolving new-member personnel conflicts
*   Creating an atmosphere of open-mindedness

System-related information and uncertainties occur from the interaction of component parts of projects or programs of all sizes. For a small project, the manager will perform all the above functions. For a large program, the manager will have a group of people in a systems office handling one or more project and support functions.

Activity 1A: Review the Study Phase Effort

The Design Phase requires team members skilled in preparing documentation. Potential contractors are also added. Since the end of your Study Phase, time may have elapsed while the Design Phase funding is being approved. Review the Study Phase effort and its documentation in a project meeting with all involved persons.

Many of the added team members are responsible for preparing the design documents. They are often referred to as technicians, even though their skills may include design and development. These experienced individuals ensure that no technical or semilegal information is missing from documents. However, they are often accustomed to working with considerable guidance from the designers regarding design content.

PROJECT EXAMPLE

It is now the first Monday afternoon in January. Roger Stein, Jose Hernandez, and Professor Hulbert meet informally to discuss the situation of the additional $5 000 that is needed. Their results to date are not promising. They decide how Roger will present this information to the team the next day.

It is now the first Tuesday afternoon in January. Several potential new members have been invited to this first meeting of the Design Phase. Also invited by Professor Hulbert are two faculty members who have been consultants to local industry in the review of technical and semilegal documentation. Roger welcomes all returning team members back from vacation, and he introduces and welcomes the potential new members of the team. Most of the team members have already decided on their class schedules for the school term and share this information.

The team has heard rumors regarding the funding problem. Roger informs the team that a goal of $15 000 had better be set for the construction of the activity center. The additional $5 000 will have to include items that can be canceled without affecting the overall activity center construction and design costs.

Roger distributes the applicable Study Phase documentation to all students in attendance. He reminds them that their Design Phase details will be determined and assigned at their next meeting.

PPCP 4

Activity 1B: Develop Design Phase Details

Develop the Design Phase content, where necessary, by performing the following:

PLANNING AHEAD ▶

• Preparing more detailed Design Phase task descriptions

• Devising a more extensive Design Phase schedule

• Allotting the Design Phase budget to individual groups

The groups are organized in activity 1C on the following page.

For most projects, delivery at or below the previously accepted cost is usually a requirement. However, some projects have deadlines that must be met. For these projects, the client may be willing to accept a cost greater than that originally contracted in order to meet a required schedule. Before spending additional money, obtain written agreement for any verbally discussed cost increase.

During the Design Phase, the design team must explore trade-offs between preplanned approaches and new ones now available. The Implementation Phase should proceed with a minimum (negligible) risk of significant change.

During the Design Phase, the design team must explore trade-offs between preplanned approaches and new ones now available. The Implementation Phase should proceed with a minimum (negligible) risk of significant change. Therefore, design trade-offs are examined to the level of detail required to minimize changes at a later stage. Design trade-offs must also be cost effective—the client wants the most "bang for the buck." Thus, all functions must be satisfactorily fulfilled at the least cost. Remember that sometimes an extra initial cost is acceptable to obtain a higher quality product that will have lower than expected maintenance costs.

Some tasks may require all the time allotted; other tasks can be performed faster. It may be possible to perform a task more quickly but at an additional cost. Thus, it becomes the responsibility of the project manager to decide the trade-offs among tasks, schedules, and budgets for the entire project.

Think about the nervousness that an astronaut must feel sitting in a complicated spacecraft on top of a rocket, knowing that all the craft's components were fabricated and assembled by the lowest bidders. The total system succeeds because the specifications, drawings, and plans have been carefully prepared by systems engineers who are responsible for devising a least-cost, high-quality, cost-effective system. You are learning to devise such designs via much smaller projects.

PROJECT EXAMPLE

Roger leads the team in devising a more detailed schedule for the next two months. The team members decide to assume an eight-week Design Phase because of the loss of days at the beginning of January as a result of the New Year holiday. The Design Phase tasks and budgets are also revised to match the detailed schedule. The new schedule is shown in figure 4.1.

DESIGN

Figure 4.1 Design Phase schedule

Professor Hulbert and William D'Annolfo, Alice's uncle, meet and discuss how to guide the students during the Design Phase. They decide to invite two members of the school's Industrial Advisory Board who have been involved in many construction projects to become advisors and reviewers of the team's designs.

Roger and Jose agree with Professor Hulbert that they must focus on acquiring the additional $5 000. The team votes to keep Roger as team leader. For the Design Phase, he is considered to be the team manager. Therefore, he must also focus on seeing that the Design Phase schedule is met by all team members. Roger feels frustrated by this because he will not have much time to devote to the technical details. Professor Hulbert tells him that this is a common complaint of technical people when they are assigned the responsibilities of manager.

Activity 1C: Organize Teams and Assign Design Tasks

During the Design Phase, all of the Study Phase documentation is converted into the output documents that will guide the Implementation Phase.

Examine the skills, experience, and personalities of those who will be directly involved in the remaining activities of the Design Phase. Include in each group at least one person who has been involved in the Study Phase, to provide continuity from one phase to another.

Assign the various team members to developing each task, or group of tasks, for the Implementation Phase. This effort will convert all of the Study Phase documentation into the documents that will guide the Implementation Phase.

Develop the project plans for the selected project. Define the tasks in more detail so that each team member knows what is to be accomplished. Task descriptions are written and reviewed by the Design Phase group leaders and by those persons who will perform the tasks. Ideally, team members should have no questions about the following points relating to their assigned tasks:

- When a task should start
- What is to be accomplished by that task
- Which other tasks are to be coordinated with that particular task
- When that task is complete

Ensure that each group understands how its assigned design tasks interact with the design tasks of all other groups. The work breakdown structure and content of task descriptions are described in section 7.1 and appendix B.

Human factors (ergonomics) must be considered during the design of both equipment and software. The interactions of human operators or users with equipment and the environment are examined. These factors include the following:

- Location of displays and controls, meters, dials, and knobs on equipment
- Use of color coding
- Shape coding in both display icons and control knobs
- Work space design, including seating, location of work space, and illumination
- Effect of the environment on the users' performance and well-being
- Physical capabilities of human beings who will use the design; consider such factors as chair design, wrist position (to avoid carpal tunnel syndrome), and spinal column and back injuries
- Avoidance of distracting noises and colors where possible
- Expected sociological atmosphere and its effect upon operators

The physical capabilities and limitations of the human beings who will use your design must be recognized. The relationship between the effectiveness of operations of the system and the users' safety, comfort, and well-being must be kept in mind. See section 9.2 for further discussion of the influence of human factors on design.

PROJECT EXAMPLE

It is the second Monday afternoon in January. Roger writes the six design tasks on the chalkboard. He asks the team members to write their names beside each of the tasks they prefer for their assignment. He revises the resulting list, with their agreement, as follows:

Design Phase Task	Assigned Personnel
Develop Design Details	Alice, Laura, Kim, Ellery, and Manuel
Compare Materials Costs	Laura, Jose, Manuel, and Joseph
Compare Labor Costs	Jose, Kim, and Joseph
Document Design	Alice, Laura, Kim, Ellery, Manuel, and Joseph
Review Design with Funding Sources	Roger, Jose, and Alice
Revise and Complete Design Documents	Alice, Ellery, Manuel, and Joseph

The team agrees to meet on Friday afternoons to evaluate status, problems, and plans. Laura agrees to document these meetings so any revised assignments are noted and equally distributed. Most of the team members agree to work on weekends when the CAD work stations at the university are more available. They will e-mail their progress to Laura on or before 8 A.M. on Monday mornings so that she can complete her memoranda for the Monday afternoon meetings. Thus, it is agreed that the team will also meet briefly on Monday afternoons to note any changes in status as a result of the weekend work.

Alice and Manuel interview Professor MacNevers, who teaches CAD. They discover that for construction of an activity center a series of drawings, known as a top-down breakdown, is needed. These drawings provide the required guidance for a contractor. Professor MacNevers notes that experienced contractors do not require a large amount of detail; however, students new to construction will need it (Shepherd, 1991). So it is decided that the students will prepare detailed drawings. The top-down breakdown list, with assignments, is as follows:

Plot Plan

    Landscaping (on a contour map):

        Alice and Laura

    Utilities Locations (water, sewer, gas, and electricity):

        Alice and Ellery

Building Plan

    Foundation Plan (with basement layout, including a natural gas burner location):

        Alice and Kim

    Framing Plan (with main floor and second floor—attic and ridge vent—including corner bracing and studding for doors and windows):

        Jose, Joseph, and Manuel

    Side Elevation:

        Manuel

Laura, Kim, and Ellery examine their class schedules and decide that Manuel will train them, as well as other interested team members, in the use of the CAD program. If they have trouble with learning the details, nonteam student assistants assigned to the CAD facility will help them in their use of the CAD program.

Remember: an important goal of the student project is to help the students gain project experience while providing more recreation for the children in the town of Bedford.

Remember: an important goal of this project is to help the students gain project experience while providing more recreation for the children in the town of Bedford.

Kim's Uncle Don, a retired human factors specialist, attends the second Monday afternoon meeting. He discusses how human factors considerations would apply to the activity center design (Sanders and McCormick, 1992; and Salvendy, 1997). They include the following from the ADA:

- Ramps for the handicapped and the range of slopes
- Space around toilets and sinks
- Colors that alert children to danger
- Location of doorknobs so that they are easily accessible to children
- Latches that are easy to use for doors children need to open
- Latches that are hard to use for doors that small children should not open
- Avoidance of sharp corners and edges that could injure the children
- Knobs that children with sight problems can distinguish by "feel"

Uncle Don also tells them of some of his experiences with human factors applications. The students invite him to attend their design review meeting, scheduled for the conclusion of the Design Phase.

The students decide to construct the foundation and first floor strong enough to support a usable second floor if the town ever decides to raise the roof and add a second floor.

Activity 2: Select the Solution Details to Be Implemented

A variety of implementation solutions should be examined before one solution is chosen. Vendors who will be providing materials must be contacted to determine the best schedule and cost options for their products. Make-or-buy decisions must first be identified and then one solution selected. Only after careful study of the entire design is it advisable to select one solution for the design.

Activity 2A: Study Potential Implementation Solutions

Studying implementation solutions involves analyzing required or desired functions and how they can be most efficiently implemented. The project is beginning to take shape via detailed drawings.

Examine each Study Phase document and then develop a design. Test this design against the Project Description, Design Specification, and Design Description that were prepared during the Study Phase. As each part in the design evolves, start to prepare the Production Specification. Test all recommended design changes against the original task descriptions, schedules, and cost estimates and against the expectations of your clients. Prepare a plan to develop the Working and Detail Drawings. Compare the effect of the recommended design changes and their details with your original task descriptions, schedules, and budgets from previous project phases (Nadler, 1970, p. 768).

Before proceeding to the design of a specific item or system, it is necessary to examine the availability of new materials, circuitry, and software that may not yet be described in even the most recent technical handbooks or literature. Changes occur so rapidly that it may be necessary to investigate "what's new" via the World Wide Web (Pugh, 1993, p. 177).

Begin the preparation of a schedule for assigning personnel and for delivery of materials for the Implementation Phase. The schedule should include the following:

*   Project personnel assignments
*   Contractors' performance
*   Materials deliveries
*   Vendor deliveries

It is this second and more detailed schedule that may cause changes in the preliminary schedules. Why? Because people (including contractors) may not have the staff or facilities to work on more than one project at the same time. Merge all schedules into one master schedule before you complete the Design Phase.

For the Implementation Phase, the following items should be analyzed:

*   Estimates of project staffing and additional personnel needed
*   Estimates of work space needs
*   Required project furnishings, fixtures, and equipment
*   Needed project-support supplies and materials, such as portable toilets

Indicate these items in a separate document rather than as a portion of the actual product implementation documents. They are considered as a part of your project overhead. As such, the costs are not presented to the client.

PROJECT EXAMPLE

Professor Hulbert reminds the team members that they must examine each Study Phase document and recommend any needed changes.

*   Alice reviews the Project Description. She recommends some changes relating to activity center costs and schedules.
*   Laura reviews the Design Specification. She recommends a few changes regarding the concrete foundation design.
*   Roger reviews the Design Description. He recommends minor changes regarding the worker skills required to assist the team.

Three potential design directions are considered. Each design direction is tested against the revised Project Description, Design Specification, and Design Description documents prepared as a part of the Study Phase effort.

Roger initiates early preparation of the Production Specification as each design form evolves from its predetermined function.

Here is an example of how "form follows function" in the activity center project:

Function: Children require "busy" activities to learn; amusement is intertwined with learning.

Form: An activity center provides a physical structure where children can meet, learn, and "have fun" while learning.

Thus the function of the activity center is established, and the form of the solution then follows.

The exact building materials to be used are examined. The following questions are asked:

What functions (uses) can be accomplished by the various designs, and which functions must be revised, deleted, or added?

Is the total cost of the project still between $15 000 and $20 000? (Additional money may not be obtainable from the funding sources.)

What type of foundation will be required? Will it contain steel reinforcing rods and less concrete, or only concrete?

What is the type of soil and/or ledge, and how will it affect design and costs? (Several holes must be dug, and earth extracted and tested. Local contractors may have knowledge of the soil conditions.)

Could a second floor be added later? (This is considered because the town has recently noted a possible future need.)

Will the partitions be fixed or movable?

Roger reminds all the team members that the project may not be funded if the costs become excessive.

Roger assigns Jose, Kim, and Manuel the extra responsibility for monitoring the changes in materials costs and labor costs by applying Manuel's newly devised computer program. Manuel developed it for a software class and designed it to meet the needs of the activity center project.

Each design change under consideration is tested weekly. The test is against these factors:

- The original task descriptions
- Schedules
- Cost estimates
- The expectations of the town of Bedford representatives
- The expectations of Miss Kewer's attorney

The team members are told they must assess the effect of their recommended design changes against the above list. Their recommended changes will be considered during the weekly Monday afternoon meetings. They are told to provide them to Laura via e-mail on or before 8 A.M. Monday. This time allows her to prepare a hard copy for each person attending the afternoon meeting.

Ellery agrees to begin preparation of a Personnel Assignment and Materials Delivery Schedule for the activity center Implementation Phase. This more detailed schedule is to include the following:

- Project personnel assignment dates
- Contractor performance dates
- Material delivery dates
- Vendor delivery dates

Ellery also agrees to provide estimates for the following:

- Project staffing and additional personnel needed
- Work space needs during construction
- Project furnishings, fixtures, and equipment
- Project-support supplies and materials (such as portable toilets)

Alice and Joseph agree to review Ellery's effort each Monday at noon.

One area that must be investigated is how to connect the carrying beams to the exterior wall studs. One suggestion is that metal plates be used. Alice and Joseph have some background knowledge about this construction issue. They agree to perform the following tasks:

- Determine sources for metal plates
- Investigate availability of metal-plate length, width, and thickness
- Determine the bolt size and type needed to fasten the various metal plates
- Estimate the time required to purchase and install metal plates
- Estimate the labor required to install the metal plates with their associated bolts

Manuel agrees to review their effort every other Monday at noon.

Manuel also agrees to investigate the following:

- Types of plumbing materials available
- Types, brands, and cost of paint

Joseph agrees to review his effort every other Monday at noon.

Ellery is assigned to document all changes to the Implementation Phase schedule. Alice and Joseph are assigned to review the vendor data and recommend which vendors will be used for the Implementation Phase.
Roger offers to outline the contents of the Working and Detail Drawings.

Activity 2B: Contact Vendors for Make-or-Buy Information

Explain to your potential vendors, by means of both meetings and documents, those areas where you may purchase an item from them rather than fabricate it yourselves. Obtain vendor input regarding costs and delivery schedules for each item you are considering for a make-or-buy decision.

PROJECT EXAMPLE

At this point in the project development, vendors can be contacted for bids and the extent of work they will perform can be determined.

Alice and Joseph receive copies of the drawings in their draft form from team members who are preparing them. The pair will deliver the drawings to the vendors for use when they prepare their initial bids for the project. Vendors' reputations are examined through the local Better Business Bureau, and the team assesses the vendors for potential use as part of the final selection process within the Design Phase. Potential vendors are informed that they will be selected or rejected on or before March 10. Information about each vendor should include the following points:

- Quality of work
- Dependability regarding schedule
- Excuses offered that increase costs
- Willingness to adapt to schedule and design changes that may occur

The vendors are requested to respond within two weeks and note on their return bids/quotes: "These prices are firm for 60 days."

Figure 4.2 Make versus buy comparison: set of stairs

Make versus buy comparison: set of stairs

make

design stairs
purchase lumber
construct stairs

buy

select standard design
purchase prefabricated stairs
install stairs

Figure 4.3 Make-or-buy sequence

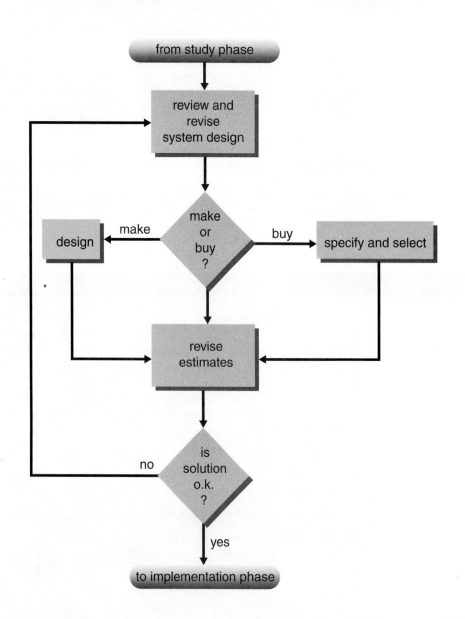

Make-or-buy sequence

from study phase

review and
revise
system design

make
or
buy
?

make → design

buy → specify and select

revise
estimates

is
solution
o.k.
?

no

yes

to implementation phase

Activity 2C: Determine Make-or-Buy Decisions

Examine all the make-or-buy information you have gathered. With this information, you can now do the following:

- Develop design details for the project
- Review and revise the overall design where necessary
- Decide what portions will be fabricated by the designers ("Make")
- Decide what portions will be purchased from vendors ("Buy")

Revise the content of the task descriptions, as well as estimates of costs and schedules, to agree with your make-or-buy decisions.

A "make-or-buy" decision concerning the construction of a set of stairs can serve as an example. (See figure 4.2.)

Make: Students design the stairs, purchase the lumber, and construct the stairs.

Buy: Students (school) purchase prefabricated set of stairs from a lumber supplier.

All the following factors must be considered: total labor and materials costs, convenience, and availability. If the cost differential is close between using the original contractor versus buying an item from another source or performing the work oneself, it may not be worth the effort to "go outside" to a contractor. Also be careful not to invest more time (and, therefore, money) in reaching a decision than will be saved by awarding the work to a contractor.

The make-or-buy decision sequence is given in figure 4.3.

PROJECT EXAMPLE

Laura and Kim devise a matrix of information comparison for the activity center trade-off decisions. For the activity center, the areas for decision making are shown in figure 4.4.

Information comparison matrix

item	initial costs labor material	annual cost of maintenance	life expectancy	exterior appearance
framing lumber:				
pine				
white cedar				
concrete blocks				
poured concrete				
roof shingles				

Figure 4.4   Information comparison matrix

DESIGN

- Which will cost less—lumber, concrete block, or poured concrete—for the foundation? (Labor and material costs, as well as appearance, must be considered.)

- Where is the best trade-off regarding the quality of roof shingles? (Cost versus life expectancy is primarily a quality judgment.)

- What is the preferred exterior finish: clapboards or wood—such as white cedar—shingles? (Consider initial cost, maintenance costs, and desired appearance.)

At this point in the project, design trade-offs are examined to the level of detail required to ensure that implementation can proceed with little risk of significant change.

These and other design trade-offs are examined to the level of detail required to ensure that implementation can proceed with little risk of significant change.

Laura and Kim distribute an "Activity Center Make or Buy" document that they have developed. It is reviewed during a Friday afternoon meeting. The decisions are documented and the results are distributed. Then the appropriate vendors are informed.

Activity 3: Document the Design Solution

It is time to prepare the Production Specification, as well as the Working and Detail Drawings. In effect, the project design and the reason for its choices are being documented.

It is time to prepare the Production Specification, as well as the Working and Detail Drawings. Refine the forthcoming Implementation Phase tasks, schedules, and budgets. (See chapter 7.) In effect, you are documenting your project design and the reason for its choices.

Activity 3A: Prepare the Production Specification

The Production Specification originates from the Design Specification, prepared during the Study Phase. Here are suggested steps for preparing this document:

1. Study the Design Specification.

2. Devise, as necessary, an outline of the Production Specification.

3. Extract, wherever possible, the appropriate portions of the referenced specifications for inclusion. The Design Specification may only refer to environmental and other more general specifications, rather than contain the actual wording.

4. Modify the Design Specification paragraphs to become new paragraphs within the Production Specification.

5. Refer to the Working and Detail Drawings where appropriate.

6. Review and revise the results, where necessary, during activity 3D.

The Production Specification may include the applicable excerpts from the referenced general specifications. Typical specifications contain the following paragraphs or groups of paragraphs:

- Scope of Specifications

- Applicable Documents

- Requirements

- Quality Assurance Provisions

- Preparation for Delivery

- Notes and Appendixes

Government specifications are the most complex; industrial specifications are usually much simpler. See section 8.1, page 205.

PROJECT EXAMPLE

Specifications, including those for construction, follow standard formats. They ensure that contractors perform their portions of the project according to what the client wants.

Alice and Ellery convert the Design Specification into the Production Specification. The content evolves, with paragraph headings added, as noted below. Refer to the specifications for the activity center given in appendix C. Each section consists of paragraphs identified by letter. Subparagraphs are identified by number.

The following sections in specifications are often referred to as nontechnical boilerplate. They are standard in project documents.

General Specifications contain the nontechnical definitions required to avoid misunderstandings later. This section also identifies the organizations and persons who are specifically responsible for the performance and monitoring of the project.

General Requirements contain nontechnical information on who will do what. This section also defines the legal responsibilities, as required by the appropriate local, state, and federal agencies. Workmanship is described, along with how the selection of "equivalent" materials or equipment will be approved.

Intent of Contract Documents is included. Thus if there are errors or duplications that have been overlooked during the other phases of the project, they are to be immediately brought to the attention of all parties involved. At that time, the issues can be promptly resolved.

Subcontractors should not become the problem of the client. This section specifically states that the (prime) contractor is totally responsible for the actions of any and all hired individuals and organizations.

Project Meetings are the responsibility of the contractor. Thus, the contractor assumes full responsibility for coordinating all efforts to ensure that work is performed correctly and on time.

Cleaning requires a separate section because many contractors will leave a mess for others to remove unless they are told otherwise.

Workers' Compensation and Insurance has become important because workers may become injured while working on the project. Legal action in the form of lawsuits can be filed against all parties involved with a project. Contractors must purchase liability insurance for their protection.

Project Closeout must also be defined, and proof given to the client that there are no outstanding debt claims that could be filed against the client. Operating and maintenance manuals and warranties must be delivered to the client so the fixtures and equipment can be properly operated and repaired.

The following sections form the technical content of specifications.

General Site Work is the beginning of the technical portion of the specification. This section is an overview of the remaining technical sections.

Earthwork describes the preparation of the site prior to construction of the foundation and includes specifications for later grading, drainage, and soil-and-rock storage and removal.

Landscaping describes how the earthwork around the buildings shall be finished, graded, and seeded.

The **Site Utilities** section defines the responsibilities of the contractor regarding installation of sewer, water, natural gas, electricity, and telephone service.

Concrete Formwork is an overview of the next three sections. It also notes that forms shall be properly installed and braced, which is a safety feature.

Cast-in-Place Concrete describes the exact sizes, strengths, and consistencies of the footings, walls, and floors, and what to do when ledge is encountered.

Dampproofing is important because many structures are being constructed in areas where water is either present or can accumulate during and after rainstorms or snowstorms.

Subsurface Drainage System requirements exist to remove any water that may accumulate around and under the foundation.

The **Framing and Carpentry** section contains all the wording required to constrain the contractor in the construction of floors, ceilings, roof, and walls. It also, where appropriate, suggests preferred types and sources of material, such as grades of lumber. It also refers to the accompanying drawings.

The **Roof** section describes the types of roof materials to be used and how they are to be installed.

Window and Door Schedule lists the windows and doors to be purchased and how they are to be installed and sealed.

Exterior Trim and Siding defines the type of exterior trim and siding to be installed and the sealing material to be applied.

Plumbing and Heating describes the materials and procedures for water and sewer installation; installation of bathroom and kitchenette fixtures; equipment, materials, and procedures for installation of a furnace and ducts or pipes; the type of central heating, or other form of heating, ventilation, and/or air conditioning (HVAC), as well as related equipment and its installation, to be used to control the environment.

The **Electrical** section lists the equipment and service to be provided via an underground service pipe.

The **Walls, Floors, and Ceilings** section defines the materials to be used on the bathroom and other walls, floors, and ceilings.

Locks are described in detail. (For the activity center, for example, provision is made so access may be controlled by a town employee through a master key to a deadbolt lock.)

Landscaping, Driveway, Parking, Ramp, and Walks are carefully specified in order to provide for vehicle access and parking, walkways, and removal of water.

There are standard specifications and contract forms for construction projects, which may be purchased from the AIA (The American Institute of Architects, 1735 New York Avenue NW, Washington, D.C. 20006) at www.aia.org or the AGCA (Associated General Contractors of America, 333 John Carlyle Street, Suite 200, Alexandria, VA 22314) at www.agc.org.

Activity 3B: Prepare the Working and Detail Drawings

Study your Design Description. Devise, as necessary, a list of drawings to be prepared, typically entitled "Top-Down Breakdown." (The development of this list of drawings is usually iterative.) Expand your preliminary sketches. See figures 4.8 and 4.9 on pages 112 and 113. Provide details for each of the portions of your project, as well as interface information between and among interconnecting and interrelated items. Refer to the Production Specification where appropriate. Review and revise your results, as necessary, during activity 3C on the next page.

The Working and Detail Drawings originate with the Design Description in the Study Phase and its accompanying preliminary sketches. The Design Description should contain general information. The Working and Detail Drawings include specific information as needed.

PROJECT EXAMPLE

The Working and Detail Drawings, as assigned in the Project Example for activity 1C, should use a set of notation standards so all team members use the same layout techniques and notations. Professor Hulbert recommends that decisions regarding format be documented and distributed so all team members will be able to understand the individual drawings. The following drawings are prepared and reviewed:

Plot Plan (a perspective view that defines the boundaries of a parcel of land and the location and orientation of the structure to be built)

> Landscaping

> Location of Utilities (water, sewer, gas, and electricity)

Building Plan

> Foundation Plan (including basement layout with furnace location)

> Framing Plan (with main floor and potential second floor—attic and ridge vent—including corner bracing and studding for doors and windows)

> End and Side View

The above drawings are reviewed by Professor Hulbert, all team members, and Professor Jacobs (who is also an Architectural Engineer). There is now enough documentation to allow the preferred vendors to prepare final bids for construction of portions of the activity center.

Activity 3C: Refine Tasks, Schedules, and Budgets

The final documentation for the Design Phase must include revised and detailed descriptions of tasks, schedules, and budgets.

Review the Implementation Phase task descriptions with respect to any changes that result from your review with the funding source. Revise the task descriptions where necessary. Verify that the individuals and groups who will be responsible for the Implementation Phase agree on the meaning of their assigned task descriptions. (See sections 7.1, 7.2, and appendix B.)

Prepare your final Implementation Phase tasks, schedules, and budgets after questioning those persons who will be responsible for each task. Verify or revise total costs after examining the new budgets. Review how tasks and schedules intertwine. Revise the tasks and schedules as required. Then negotiate any necessary task and schedule changes with those team members or contractors who will be responsible for them.

Review all costs related to the completed design. Verify that the costs are acceptable to the team members or contractors to whom each task will be assigned. Only then is it possible for you to be certain that no one can later say, "I didn't know that" or "It cannot be done for that amount of money."

PROJECT EXAMPLE

The work of the design for the activity center as reviewed is considered complete. During the latter part of the seventh week and the entire eighth week of the Design Phase, the final documentation must be prepared. As the team members review the results of the previous activities, they discover, to their embarrassment, that an extra two weeks of time will be needed to construct the activity center, and the project will extend into September. The team members

DESIGN

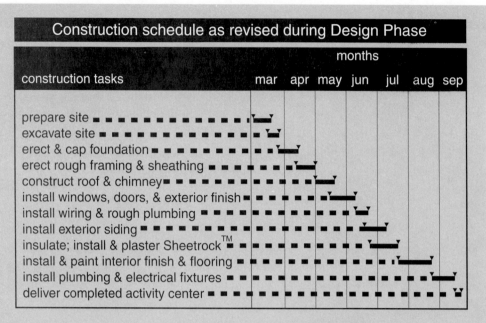

Figure 4.5   Construction schedule as revised during Design Phase

have contacted many vendors of materials and contractors of specialty areas. The new schedule for the Implementation Phase is shown in figure 4.5.

Note that the titles of some of the tasks have been revised slightly. Thus, the titles of the Implementation (Construction) Phase cost estimates also have to be revised so they agree with the new schedule titles. The cost estimates must also be changed so these estimates indicate when the contractors are to be paid, as shown in figure 4.6. Contractors are normally paid at the end of each major task or at the end of a month.

Revised summary estimate for the Implementation (Construction) Phase

construction tasks	mar	apr	may	jun	jul	aug	sep	totals
prepare site	600							600
excavate site	1400							1400
erect & cap foundation		1700						1700
erect rough framing & sheathing		600						600
construct roof & chimney			5100					5100
install windows, doors, & exterior finish				1500				1500
install wiring & rough plumbing				1400				1400
install exterior siding					1600			1600
insulate; install & plaster Sheetrock™					1300			1300
install & paint interior finish & flooring						2000		2000
install plumbing & electrical fixtures							1800	1800
deliver completed activity center							1000	1000
task totals	2000	2300	5100	2900	2900	2000	2800	20 000

Figure 4.6   Revised summary estimate for the Implementation (Construction) Phase

Note: Jim Sullivan (plumber) and Jim Stander (electrician) offer to donate some of their time to keep the total costs within the $20 000 allotted for the project.

Had two contractors not offered to donate their services, the total Implementation Phase costs would have been greater than $20 000. In order to avoid losing the project, two contractors who live in Bedford—one skilled in plumbing (Jim Sullivan) and the other in electrical work (Jim Stander)—offer to donate their services so that the children of the town will have an activity center. (Stander has agreed to perform all wiring and fixture installation, using the labor of various team members.) After discussing the offers with the appropriate town officials, the team accepts the offers of donated labor. A note on the proposals indicates that contribution as a part of the contract.

A decision is made, as advised by Professor Hulbert, to include the actual cost of donated labor as a zero-cost item in those estimates where labor is a separate subtask item (not shown). Thus, for student learning purposes, a more realistic cost estimate of the total project exists.

Activity 3D: Document the Design and Reasons for Its Choice

The completed documents from the Design Phase are sent to the contractors who will use them during the Implementation Phase. These consist of a Letter of Transmittal, the Production Specification, and Working and Detail Drawings.

The completed documents from the Design Phase consist of the following:

- Letter of Transmittal, which for the activity center will be a Contract Letter
- Production Specification
- Working and Detail Drawings

The content of each of these documents is described in section 4.3.

Prepare the Letter of Transmittal (or Contract Letter). The contents of this document are described in section 4.3. Before this document is signed, it should be reviewed by the client, the team manager, and by appropriate legal personnel.

Complete the Production Specification. Contents for this document are described in detail in section 8.1 on page 205.

Devise either a bill of materials or a parts list, and prepare the Working and Detail Drawings. The Working and Detail Drawings consist of the following:

- Presentation Drawing, containing little or no structural information
- Models where appropriate
- Working Drawings, containing all necessary details

Depending on the product or software to be delivered, the drawings may require several sheets. See the next section for more information. When only experienced contractors are allowed to bid on a project, the need for detailed information may be greatly reduced.

As noted in chapters 5 and 7, documents must be prepared at the end of every phase. All *deliverables* must be defined and prepared. What are deliverables? According to Duncan (1996) a "deliverable" is a tangible, verifiable product such as a feasibility study, a detailed design, or a working prototype. The conclusion of a project phase is generally marked by a review of deliverables (such as end-of-phase documents) and project status. Thus, it is possible to (a) determine if the project should continue into its next phase and (b) detect and correct errors in a cost-effective manner. *Deliverables* include both equipment and documents that are *delivered* to the client.

Deliverables that may not be quite so obvious include copies of government-required permits for wiring and plumbing, equipment and its operation and maintenance manuals, recycling data to be implemented at the end of equipment life, and copies of warranties for equipment purchased by the contractor. These items are installed as part of the project implementation; their warranties are passed along to the client to protect the client in the case of a failure.

Costs for the Implementation Phase are now known quite accurately. Also, the money that was spent during the first three phases is known. Now Marketing can establish a price for any product that will be produced in quantity and determine if the product will sell at that price and provide a profit.

PROJECT EXAMPLE

Laura contacts a professor at the Northeastern School of Law to assist in writing the Contract Letter. See appendix D for a copy of the final version of this document. The letter is reviewed by each team member before it is shown to the town of Bedford selectmen. The legal wording is new to most of the team members, so the students discover that reviewing it is a good learning activity.

Alice and Ellery prepare copies of the Production Specification that they have been developing as described in activity 3A. The document's contents are given in appendix C. The copies are distributed to all members of the team, the law professor, and all involved contractors for review. Alice and Ellery revise the specifications as required.

Roger decides to review and coordinate the final Working and Detail Drawings so he can feel he has participated in some of the technical effort for this phase. A computer-generated plan view drawing of the activity center, without dimensions, is given in figure 4.7.

All three sets of documents are gathered together, reviewed by the team, and prepared for distribution to contractors. A letter that explains the contents of the package is included. The letter also reminds all involved parties that the schedule must be followed and the costs kept within budget. It also indicates that Roger, Jose, or Professor Hulbert is to be contacted immediately if any questions arise.

SKETCH OF FIRST FLOOR
(SCALE: 1/8" ≈ 1'0")

Figure 4.7   Plan views of activity center

SKETCH OF BASEMENT FLOOR
(SCALE: 1/8" ≈ 1'0")

PLANNING AHEAD ▶

Activity 4: Prepare for the Implementation Phase Work

It is time to review the Design Phase results. You should also verify the availability of Implementation Phase funding and then complete the planning for the Implementation Phase.

Activity 4A: Review the Design Phase Results

As the design is being developed, it needs to be reviewed by experts and clients for revisions and oversights.

The Design Phase results must be carefully reviewed and compared with the Study Phase documents. Here is one sequence for accomplishing this task:

1. Examine your newly designed product or software from a total system viewpoint.
2. Compare this design with the Study Phase documents: Project Description, Design Specification, and Design Description.
3. Verify that the Design Phase forms match the Study Phase functions.
4. Verify that the ground rules (Study Phase activity 2) were followed.
5. Review any revised ground rules.

PROJECT EXAMPLE

Roger requests a formal review meeting with Professor Hulbert and other faculty members chosen by the professor. These faculty members are given a copy of the design ground rules so they can compare the results to the original requirements. Two administrators from towns adjacent to Bedford are invited to attend the review because of their experiences with similar structures for children.

The meeting occurs at the end of the fourth week of the Design Phase so that any recommended changes can be included prior to presentation to the funding sources. Only five significant changes are recommended during the four-hour review meeting. They are included as design changes during the fifth week.

Activity 4B: Verify Availability of Implementation Phase Funds

The detailed design and plans need to be presented to the funding sources for approval and review.

Inform funding sources regarding the status of the Design Phase. Prepare and give a presentation if necessary. Obtain both general and detailed reactions from the representatives of the funding source. Verify the availability of the needed Implementation Phase funds and their payment schedule.

PROJECT EXAMPLE

Roger reports that the existing $15 000 funding has remained firm. He further notes that an additional $2 000 has been pledged by last year's Northeastern team, which had a surplus of funds from their project. An additional $1 000 is pledged by five faculty members at $200 per faculty member. Roger reminds the team that $2 000 more needs to be raised for the desired $20 000 required to implement the existing plans. He also stresses to team members that they must continue to keep costs under careful control.

At the beginning of the sixth week of the Design Phase, Roger gives presentations to those groups and individuals who will be responsible for the funding of the Implementation Phase. A briefing is scheduled for the participants for Wednesday evening at the university. At that time, Roger describes the drawings for the activity center, shows a scale model of the center, gives a summary of the center specifications, and distributes the Contract Letter for review. He asks the attendees to determine if anything has been overlooked. He also presents the team's assumptions regarding the personnel who will be occupying and working at the activity center. He notes the other items that still need to be prepared include the following:

- An estimate of staffing and additional personnel needed to complete the project
- An estimate of work space needs for the activity center
- A description of preferred furnishings, fixtures, and equipment
- An estimate of needed toilet facilities and storage space, such as bathrooms for adults and children, shelving for worker use, lockable closets and cabinets.

The persons involved in the funding agree, in advance, that the design looks acceptable. (Thus, there is less of a chance that changes will be requested once construction is in process.) The meeting ends with all participants eager to see construction start, and they offer to assist in locating the additional $2 000 needed.

Activity 4C: Plan the Implementation Phase

Before the Implementation Phase begins, the plans should be reviewed to see that they are realistic. All participants should realize that design work stops once the Implementation Phase begins.

Verify that the sequence of work to be accomplished during the Implementation Phase is realistic. Devise and verify the content of a schedule of personnel assignments and material delivery that coincides with the Implementation Phase tasks and schedules. Management subtasks (Implementation Phase activity 3A) should be planned at this time.

Once the Implementation (Construction) Phase starts, any revisions to previous phases will be both expensive and time-consuming. You should make every effort to have all your designs and documentation completed during the Design Phase. The team should not continue designing once the Implementation Phase is initiated.

There is an expression often used by engineers and technologists: "Never deliver drawings and specifications to a manufacturing organization and then go away and forget them." Personnel in manufacturing may need assistance to interpret the words and drawings developed by the design team. Why? Because English is *not* a precise language for communication purposes. Thus, some design-team members and project management personnel need to be a part of the Implementation Phase to ensure project continuity.

PROJECT EXAMPLE

It is the eighth week of the Design Phase. As the final documents are being prepared and reviewed, Roger, Jose, and Professor Hulbert decide to offer their "secret" plan to the team for raising the remaining $2 000. They are going to have a weekend open house in Bedford at the high school gymnasium and request a minimum donation of $5 from individuals and $10 from families to see the plans and model on display. The Bedford Farms Dairy has agreed to donate soda and ice cream for the open house. The local Bedford newspaper provides free advertising for the event.

At the open house, the construction plan is presented once every half hour by Roger and Alice. In addition, Manuel gives a continuing computer demonstration so that the children and parents may see how changes to the activity center design can be quickly documented. His computer is connected via a modem to a Northeastern University work station. (Jose assisted in the development of Manuel's demonstration.) As a result of the event, an additional $3 500 is raised. The team and Professor Hulbert are delighted.

The final assignments for the Implementation Phase can now be scheduled. All funding sources, town selectmen, vendors, Alice's uncle, supporting faculty, and the president of Northeastern are informed of the fund-raising success.

The Personnel Assignment and Materials Delivery Schedule for the Implementation Phase are prepared by Ellery Kistler. They include the following:

- Individual work assignments and schedules for team members
- Contractors' schedules
- Materials delivery schedules
- Vendor delivery schedules

It is this more detailed schedule that may cause changes in the more general Implementation Phase schedule. Vendors, including contractors, may not have the staff to work on two or more projects at the same time. Alice contacts the selected vendors and contractors to ensure that they will be available as needed according to the now final Implementation Phase schedule.

The plans for the Implementation Phase can now take the form of numbered tasks and subtasks to which precise budgets and schedules are assigned. The documentation for the project is now the most complete and accurate.

Ellery and Alice decide that the tasks and subtasks are now specific enough to be numbered. As a result, Manuel can easily connect them to the budget and schedule. Together the three prepare and publish the following information in the form of a schedule:

1. Prepare Site
    1.1   Grade a rough roadway to the activity center site
    1.2   Clear and remove excess soil, trees, and brush as necessary
    1.3   Establish a water supply and portable toilets for workers
    1.4   Provide temporary electrical power for the construction equipment
    1.5   Locate municipal sewage line or sewage-disposal tank
    1.6   Survey and install stakes to identify location of the activity center foundation

2. Excavate Site
    2.1   Excavate for footing, foundation, and chimney base
    2.2   Survey and install batter boards with reference nails and outline twine
    2.3   Establish top level of footings; excavate for spread footings

3. Erect and Cap Foundation; Install Sills
   3.1   Install spread-footing forms
         Pour spread footings
         Remove forms for spread footing
         Install foundation forms and reinforcing bars
         Pour foundation walls
         Remove forms from foundation walls
   3.2   Install wooden foundation sills

Figure 4.8   Ridge vent and its cross section

4. Erect Rough Framing and Sheathing

    4.1   Install floor joists and bridging

    4.2   Install rough flooring on floor joists

    4.3   Erect exterior side walls (including studs with openings for windows and doors)

    4.4   Erect interior walls (with openings for interior doors) and rough stairs

    4.5   Install wall caps

    4.6   Install ceiling joists

    4.7   Install exterior wall material (sheathing on studs)

5. Construct Roof and Chimney (See figures 4.8 and 4.9)

    5.1   Erect roof rafters

    5.2   Erect end wall studs to roof rafters; sheath ends of roof

    5.3   Close in the roof and install vent-pipe flashing

    5.4   Construct chimney with roof flashing

    5.5   Install shingles on the roof

6. Install Windows, Doors, and Exterior Finish

    6.1   Install prehung windows and flashing

    6.2   Install prehung exterior doors and flashing

    6.3   Install finish molding or boards at corners and roof edge

    6.4   Install soffits and fascia

Figure 4.9   Roof details

DESIGN

7. Install Wiring and Rough Plumbing

7.1 Install external kilowatt-hour-meter base

7.2 Install interior circuit-breaker panel

7.3 Install internal wiring, including boxes for outlets, switches, and lighting fixtures

7.4 Install rough plumbing and plumbing vent pipes

8. Install Exterior Siding

8.1 Install exterior finish on walls

8.2 Prime and paint exterior finish, walls, doors, and windows

9. Insulate; Install and Plaster Sheetrock™

9.1 Install interior insulation between studs of exterior walls

9.2 Install insulation and strapping in ceiling

9.3 Install and plaster ceiling Sheetrock™

9.4 Install and plaster wall Sheetrock™

10. Install and Paint Interior Finish and Flooring

10.1 Install finish on exterior door and window frames

10.2 Install baseboards

10.3 Install finish flooring

10.4 Sand, seal, and paint floors

10.5 Hang prehung interior doors

10.6 Paint interior ceilings, walls, and finish

11. Install Plumbing and Electrical Fixtures

11.1 Install plumbing fixtures

11.2 Install electrical fixtures, including switches and outlets

11.3 Install gas heater

Manuel modifies a computer program related to construction to prepare the project documentation. He adds columns that include the names of individuals, vendors, and contractors with their delivery dates.

Activity 5: Obtain Implementation Phase Funding

All the steps necessary to obtain funding and to obtain formal agreement to the plans from funding sources and clients must be completed at this time in the project.

At this time, the tasks, schedules, and budgets for a project will be the most accurate. Any further changes will occur during the Implementation Phase. Now it is imperative to obtain funding for that phase. The typical steps to obtain that funding are the following:

1. Review refinement of tasks, schedules, and budgets; design documentation; and Implementation Phase plans with your client and/or funding source. See Design Phase activities 3C, 3D, and 4C.

2. Agree on the content of your Letter of Transmittal or Contract Letter.

3. Obtain signatures from those individuals who are designated to be legally responsible for the work and its payment.

4. Review your construction and/or delivery and payment schedule as applicable.

5. Prepare to initiate the Implementation Phase.

Terminate the Design Phase effort as soon as the work has been completed and reviewed. A purchase order or other authorization should have arrived for funding the Implementation Phase. If a foundation is a source of funds, then a check for the Implementation Phase will be provided at this time.

PROJECT EXAMPLE

A Letter of Transmittal, including the Letter Contract previously reviewed (see activity 3D), is hand-carried to each authorized person within the state and town and to Eleanor Kewer's trust-fund attorney. Once all signatures are obtained, signed copies of the contract are mailed to each funding participant.

A charge number for expenditures is opened by Professor Hulbert with the university treasurer. A workplace trailer-office and a portable toilet are located. They will be delivered to the Bedford construction site on March 1. A bank account is opened via the university so the university treasurer can verify all invoices and authorize their payment.

It is the end of February. Roger terminates the Design Phase. He sends letters of thanks to all team members, to all those who donated to the project Implementation Phase, to the Bedford Farms Dairy, and to the local newspaper for publicizing the team's open house.

SECTION 4.3   DESIGN PHASE DOCUMENTS

The documentation prepared during the Design Phase will be used to guide the Implementation Phase. Typically the Design Phase documentation is delivered from the engineering team to the manufacturing team. As noted in figure 4.10, manufacturing personnel may be assigned to the Design Phase team to participate in the development of documentation. Since humans read and interpret documents, documents run the risk of being misinterpreted. When the document users are involved in document preparation, this helps to reduce the chances of misinterpretation. Likewise, engineering personnel are assigned to the Implementation Phase manufacturing team to assist in documentation interpretation.

There are at least two approaches to ensuring a quality product. One approach is to invite some of those persons who will be involved in the manufacturing process to become a part of the design team. Another approach is to designate in the early phases of the project those individuals who are involved in the design phase as persons who will become a part of the manufacturing team. Include persons familiar with the various aspects of maintenance necessary for support of the final product. This may include **out-year** requirements (after warranty expiration). Illustration: Many a kitchen in a slab-foundation ranch-style home has been ruined by leaking pipe joints buried in concrete. No one planned for out-of-warranty access to these potential failures.

Figure 4.10 Interaction between the design and manufacturing teams in preparing documentation

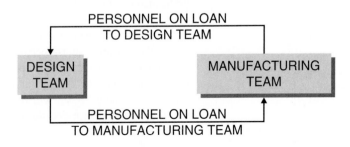

DESIGN

Figure 4.11   Maintenance factors

Consider both the hierarchy (level) and class (type) of maintenance needed (figure 4.11). Audio units, such as CD players, mixers, speakers, and receivers connected together become a specific audio system. Unit vendor warranty is of no use until system maintenance determines a malfunctioning unit. On-scene, or vendor, maintenance personnel must test internal circuitry to isolate unit failures. Circuitry may be located on replacement type subassemblies or hard-wired motherboards. Maintenance time is reduced when unit developers plan for ease of access. Identified faulty subassemblies or individual components are then replaced. Orientation, physical size, and electronic specifications must be duplicated. Good maintenance planning ensures these parts are available for a specific time frame.

Illustration: After a motor burned out in an HVAC system for the third time, customer service representatives began their own research. Nowhere in the prototype-system test documentation was this defect recorded. Neither was it recorded as a problem in any literature. They discovered that the documentation delivered to the client did not contain any user, or operator, requirements to lubricate this motor's unsealed bearing every ninety days (normally found in maintenance manuals). No engineering change for this different type of motor (due to load requirements) had ever been submitted during the system design phase. The end result was incomplete documentation with no contract change being submitted to the client. Once the client followed the user requirements for lubrication, no further burn-out was ever noted.

Be prepared for those clients, purchasing agents, or individual contractors who never think about the important question "Who will fix it?" Discover maintenance requirements as early as a make-rather-than-buy situation. Determine the level of maintenance that will be needed. Obtain answers to the now-familiar questions:

Who will perform the maintenance?

What type of maintenance will be required?

Where will it be performed?

When will it be performed?

Why will it be necessary?

How will it be accomplished?

> (Include the requirements of the manufacturer warranty, and also what maintenance the warranty states that the user **not** do initially.)

Use answers to the above questions to determine the class, or level, of maintenance to be performed (figure 4.11).

Plan for the level of maintenance to be recommended. Will the user perform it? Will the client plan for an in-house person to perform periodic maintenance and testing? Is an outside contractor's customer service representative needed? Will the client need to develop a maintenance team? Will the devices, units, or the total system ever need to be returned to the manufacturer or vendor? If so, will replacement items maintain customer conscientiousness? Note that these maintenance decisions in all end-of-phase reports are included in the documentation delivered to the client.

Ask how an item will be fixed during the Conception and Study Phases. In the Design Phase, the answers to the "who, what, when, where, why, and how" maintenance questions should become an integral part of the design process. Plan maintenance access to key parts of the system (including its software), and determine those points of access prior to manufacturing. This will save repair time and money at some future date. Be ready to present the client with procedures or, with large systems, total maintenance requirements, including specifications and maintenance manuals.

Use maintenance planning to impress a client, to enhance sales, and to capture repeat business. Team leaders must remember to budget for maintenance planning in addition to other normal expenses.

During the Design Phase, the solutions proposed and documented during the Study Phase are examined in more detail. Using the Design Description with Preliminary Sketches and the Design Specification as a guide, the team proceeds with developing and completing the design.

During the Design Phase, the solutions proposed and documented during the Study Phase are examined in more detail. Using the Design Description with Preliminary Sketches and the Design Specification as a guide, the team proceeds with the design. The tasks, schedules, and costs to construct the selected project are estimated and modified as a variety of design details are proposed and pursued. The chosen design details lead to a final design. Estimates are now as accurate as is possible.

Proposed project designs are circulated in the form of reports and drawings. More meetings are held to compare and evaluate the various proposed designs, and more meeting reports (section 8.2) are written. These reports and drawings eventually lead to three Design Phase documents. The documents completed during the Design Phase are the following:

1. The Letter of Transmittal or Contract Letter: the explanatory document
2. The Production Specification: the final specification
3. The Working and Detail Drawings: the drawings and plans

The content of each of these documents is described below. The flow from the Conception Phase documents and the Study Phase documents to the Design Phase documents is shown in figure 4.12.

The Letter of Transmittal or Contract Letter summarizes the obligations of the client and group implementing the project. It includes information on the nature of the project, costs, and payment schedules.

The **Letter of Transmittal** or **Contract Letter** contains both legal and technical terminology. Typically, its content includes the following:

1. The identity of the client
2. The identity of the group implementing the project
3. A list of the applicable documents (such as specifications)
4. The documents that describe the project and a scale model where appropriate
5. The means for ownership transfer
6. Warranties, actual or implied
7. The cost of the project to be implemented and a payment schedule
8. How task, schedule, and cost changes will be processed
9. The signatures of those persons representing the client and the team or its parent organization

Before it is signed, this document should be reviewed by both the client and the project manager, as well as by appropriate legal personnel. An example Contract Letter, one for the activity center project used in chapters 2 through 5, is given in appendix D.

The **Production Specification** content is described in detail in section 8.1 on page 205. A typical Production Specification contains the following paragraphs or groups of paragraphs:

1. Scope of the Specification
2. Applicable Documents
3. Requirements

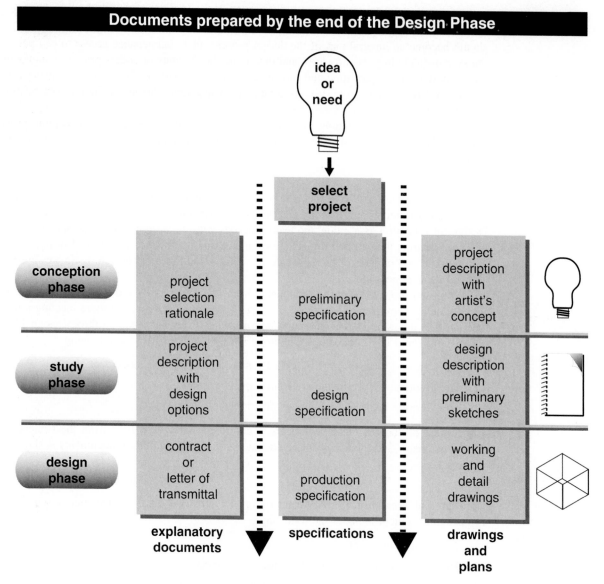

Figure 4.12   Documents prepared by the end of the Design Phase

    4.   Quality Assurance Provisions

    5.   Preparation for Delivery

    6.   Notes and Appendixes

Government specifications are more complex; industrial specifications are usually simpler.

The **Working and Detail Drawings** consist of the following:

    1.   A Presentation Drawing, similar to artist's sketches, that contains little or no structural information

    2.   Models where appropriate

    3.   Working Drawings, containing all necessary details

Depending on the product or software to be delivered, these drawings may require several pages or sheets or may require several volumes. When only experienced contractors are allowed to bid such a project, the detailed information may be significantly reduced.

SECTION 4.4   DEFINING PHASE COMPLETION

The Design Phase is considered "complete" when the documentation has been written, reviewed, and revised as recommended during the review. Again, the review team should include individuals from the funding sources and, wherever possible, experts in the field who are not responsible for the funding of the Implementation Phase. As noted in section 6.7, a designated person should continually monitor the expended costs and the projected remaining costs for the total effort.

The completed documents of the Design Phase consist of an expansion of documents originally devised during the Study Phase. These are the following:

- The Letter of Transmittal or Contract Letter
- The Production Specification
- The Working and Detail Drawings

Often, these three documents are initiated during the beginning of the Design Phase. They gradually evolve into their final content by the end of the Design Phase. See activity 3D on page 107.

Many project managers feel that the Design Phase is not complete until those individuals designated to be legally responsible for the work and its payment have signed the contracts.

Many project managers feel that the Design Phase is not complete until those individuals designated to be legally responsible for the work and its payment have signed the contract. Only then can the Design Phase be considered complete and the Implementation Phase initiated. Sometimes it is more realistic to terminate the Design Phase and reassign personnel until Implementation Phase funding is received. The project manager may save money in the short term. However, after a lapse of several weeks, obtaining the services of those who have previously worked on the project may not be possible. Then the cost of training new personnel represents a significant increase in the cost. So deciding when the Design Phase is ended may be a complicated decision.

Again note that, once the Implementation (Construction) Phase starts, any revisions to previous phases may be both expensive and time-consuming. Therefore, every effort should be made to have all designs and documentation completed during the Design Phase and before the start of the Implementation Phase.

CHAPTER OBJECTIVES SUMMARY

Now that you have finished this chapter, you should be able to:

1. Define the purpose and goal of the Design Phase of a project.
2. Explain the tasks involved in the Design Phase of a project and the activities or steps through which these tasks are performed.
3. Describe the role of a manager in the Design Phase.
4. Explain how a team should be organized for the Design Phase.
5. Outline a typical schedule for the Design Phase of a project.
6. Explain why human factors need to be considered in designing a product.
7. Describe how function and form are linked in developing design plans.
8. Define make-or-buy decisions, and explain how they are determined.
9. Describe the documents that should be prepared for the Design Phase.
10. List those who should participate in reviewing and approving the documents from the Design Phase.
11. Describe the documents prepared in the Design Phase and their uses.
12. Describe when the Design Phase is completed.

EXERCISES

4.1   For each of your options for a class project, revise and include the general Purpose and Goal statements given in section 4.1.

4.2   Examine the activities listed and described in section 4.2. Adapt them to each of your options for a class project.

4.3   Review the Study Phase effort with all team members; develop any required additional Design Phase details with the assistance of all team members. Organize the team into groups for the Design Phase. Assign each group a set of design tasks to perform.

4.4   Develop a design that will satisfy yourselves, your funding source, and the users of your product. Review the design with your previously identified judges. Evaluate their suggestions; decide which suggestions to incorporate into your design.

4.5   Study potential implementation solutions for the project design. Prepare the Contract Letter or Letter of Transmittal, Production Specification, and Working and Detail Drawings.

4.6   Contact potential vendors regarding make-or-buy information; determine make-or-buy decisions.

4.7   Review the Design Phase results and verify actual availability of Implementation Phase funding.

4.8   Refine the Implementation Phase tasks, schedule, and budget documents; plan the Implementation Phase. Include personnel assignments.

4.9   Verify that both your customer and your funding source will accept the Implementation Phase solution. Revise your solution as necessary.

4.10   Document the proposed project design and the reasons for its choice. Obtain Implementation Phase funding.

4.11   Describe how you would determine the optimum time to terminate the Design Phase. Terminate the Design Phase.

chapter **5**

1. What are the purpose and goal of the Implementation Phase of a project?

2. What tasks are involved in the Implementation Phase, and what are the activities or steps through which these tasks are performed?

3. How is money needed for projects typically obtained and delivered?

4. How are documents prepared during the Design Phase used in the Implementation Phase?

5. What tasks are typically part of the Implementation Phase, and how are they assigned?

6. What is the role of the project manager during the Implementation Phase?

7. Why are periodic meetings important during the Implementation Phase?

8. What are the common tasks that should be accomplished before actual implementation or manufacturing begins?

9. Why are prototypes developed?

10. What is the learning curve, and how does it relate to manufacturing production?

11. What documents should be prepared for the Implementation Phase and which should be delivered to the client?

12. What is "delivery" of a project, and what problems may occur at that stage?

13. What are supplier/manufacturer responsibilities and opportunities after the delivery of a product?

14. Why is having a review meeting at the end of a project important?

The reward of a thing well done is to have done it.
Ralph Waldo Emerson, 1844

The name for this phase—Implementation—implies that, after the three phases of conceiving, studying, and designing, it is time to construct and deliver your product or products. When this phase is complete, you will "have done it" (Graham, 1985).

SECTION 5.1

During the Implementation Phase, the design from the previous phases is converted into a finished product. Implementation costs are usually the greatest costs for the entire project.

IMPLEMENTATION PHASE PURPOSE AND GOAL

The **purpose** of the Implementation Phase is to provide the means, facilities, materials, and personnel for producing the end product. The **goal** of the Implementation Phase is to produce the completed design in accordance with the results of the previous phases. During this phase, you will continually review the product and its construction costs to ensure that they remain acceptable to the customer and the funding sources. Implementation costs are usually the greatest part of the costs for the entire project.

At the end of the Implementation Phase, you should know how to do the following:

- Review the Design Phase results after funding is received.
- Allocate tasks to team members and contractors as previously planned.
- Produce and control the quality of the previously designed product(s).
- Revise and prepare for delivery all documentation that will allow the client to operate and maintain the delivered product(s).
- Deliver the contracted product(s).
- Search for new work that will return a profit and enhance team skills.

Any changes offered during the Implementation Phase usually cause project delays and cost overruns. By now, no significant changes should be considered. You want to complete your project according to the specifications, on time, and within the money allotted.

As stated in chapters 1 and 2, the on-time completion of a project—according to specifications and within allotted funds—enhances the reputation of the manager, the team members, and the organization. This information quickly becomes known to those persons and groups who want quality work.

SECTION 5.2

IMPLEMENTATION PHASE ACTIVITIES

The activities for the Implementation Phase consist of the following:

Activity 1: Obtain Implementation Phase Funds

Activity 2: Review Design Phase Documents

Activity 3: Allocate Tasks to the Implementation Phase Team

    3A: Develop and monitor Implementation Phase details.

    3B: Organize the team into task groups.

    3C: Assign each group a set of tasks to perform.

Activity 4: Prepare to Produce the Designed Article

    4A: Define vendor schedules and deliveries.

    4B: Sign contracts with contractors and vendors.

4C: Obtain applicable construction permits.

4D: Provide temporary on-site facilities, tools, and equipment.

Activity 5: Produce and Evaluate Product

5A: Fabricate and evaluate prototype model (if necessary).

5B: Fabricate the designed article.

5C: Produce and evaluate items to be produced in quantities.

Activity 6: Revise, Review, and Deliver Final Documentation

6A: Correct Working and Detail Drawings.

6B: Deliver Implementation Phase documents.

6C: Deliver warranties and associated invoices.

6D: Deliver final product and instruction manuals.

Activity 7: Operate and Maintain Customer-Contracted Items

Activity 8: Review the Results of the Implementation Phase

Activity 9: Pursue New Projects

9A: Prepare public relations material.

9B: Offer presentations to prospective customers.

9C: Construct speculative products.

Activity 9 is included for those organizations that wish to pursue follow-on business.

As was true for the previous three phases, the purpose and goal for the Implementation Phase lead to defining the activities for that phase. The sequence of activities given below may change from one project to another. However, all of these activities must be accomplished before the Implementation Phase can be considered complete.

After the contract is signed with the funding source and before construction is initiated, the Implementation Phase team must be assembled, tools and materials purchased, and the work space prepared.

After the prime contract is signed with the funding source (activity 1) and before construction begins, the Implementation Phase team must be assembled (activity 3B), work space prepared (activity 4D), and tools and materials purchased (activity 4D). The project flow is indicated in figure 5.1.

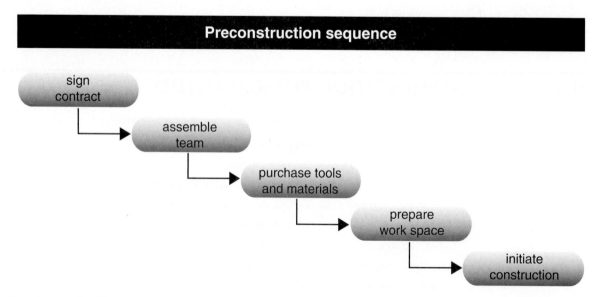

Figure 5.1   Preconstruction sequence

Activity 1: Obtain Implementation Phase Funds

Money is required to purchase parts and/or materials before construction starts. It can come from an advance payment provided by the customer or funding sources or from a loan given by a bank.

Money is required to purchase parts and/or materials before construction starts. If you do not receive an advance payment from the customer or funding sources, you may have to apply for a loan from a bank or other lending agency. Foundations usually donate all the necessary funds in advance of the Implementation Phase.

If the contract includes an advance payment, then you can deposit the money in a bank account to fund the cost of labor and the purchase of tools and materials. If the contract contains either a clause regarding **progress payments**—to be paid when a specified portion of the work is completed—or **payment upon completion,** then you may take the signed contract to a banker who will lend money against the contract. If a contract depends on a government or foundation grant, signing of the contract results in either a portion or all of the contract value being turned over to a bank or to the parent organization for the project. It then becomes the responsibility of a senior official in the government agency, foundation, or parent organization to monitor the progress of the contract and approve the disbursement of funds.

The signed contract may include or refer to the performance schedule and the specification. The project manager and each team leader should continually review these documents to ensure adherence to both costs and schedules.

Once the contract is signed, changes require extra time and effort. Team-initiated changes add to contract costs. These costs must be taken out of the contract profit, *if there is a profit.* A change initiated by the funding source must be paid for by the funding source. Such a change is known as a **change in** (contract) **scope.**

Unplanned changes that require additional money might occur during the Implementation Phase. There should be contingency funds to cover unplanned expenses.

Unplanned changes might occur during the Implementation Phase. There should be contingency funds to cover unplanned expenses. Banks, parent organizations, and foundations do not like being informed that more money is required to complete a project. Depending upon the wording of the contract, unused contingency funds may be either returned to the client, retained by the project, or included as a part of the project's profit.

Again, it becomes the responsibility of the project manager to analyze the effects of unplanned changes upon tasks, schedules, and budgets for an entire project and evaluate the trade-offs. The manager must select an appropriate course of action. The manager, in conjunction with a sales-oriented person, must convince the customer or funding source that contingency funds are important for flexible implementation. The customer or funding source should not have to be bothered each time an unplanned change occurs.

PROJECT EXAMPLE

The first meeting of the Implementation Phase team occurs on the afternoon of the first Monday in March. During the first part of this meeting, Professor Hulbert informs the team that the university has received the construction funds and has given him written authority to contract for the building foundation. The team can now order the materials based on the schedule previously devised. He reminds the team members that final exams occur during the third week in March. He also warns the team members that six months will pass rapidly. Roger schedules a meeting for Friday afternoon, at which he asks Alice, Joseph, and Manuel to contact vendors and obtain signed contracts within one week. (They may need to hand-carry paperwork in order to meet this schedule).

Activity 2: Review Design Phase Documents

Time may have elapsed while funding for the Implementation Phase was being approved. New team members need to be added and the selected contractors need to be informed and invited to participate. Each participant must now review the effects of any delay on the schedule.

IMPLEMENTATION

Both team members and contractors need to review the Design Phase documents so that they understand the tasks they are to accomplish, as well as cost and schedule constraints.

The schedules for delivery of work and materials may have to be revised. The selected contractors and subcontractors and specific members of the project team are assigned to perform the tasks that were carefully prepared during the Study Phase and revised during the Design Phase. However, because time has passed, some of the contractors and some members of the project team may no longer be available. Thus, assignments must be reviewed. Replacement individuals and companies must study the task descriptions and agree to their content. They must verify all of the following:

- What they are to accomplish (tasks)
- When they should start and finish each task (schedules)
- What their financial responsibilities are (budgets)

All team members and contractors should be given copies of the applicable task and schedule documents. Budgets of labor hours and materials costs should be accessible to each responsible team member. For small projects, *estimates* and *actuals* may be continually compared via wall charts. For larger projects, those persons in charge should be continually updated, perhaps by computer and Local Area Networks, to ensure that each group within the larger organization is staying within its budget and schedule as it performs the assigned tasks. As mentioned previously, the work may be coordinated by a separate group not directly involved in the construction (or fabrication).

Periodic project review meetings are often helpful. At these meetings, all those involved have the opportunity to meet and compare their ideas in detail on exactly how their individual tasks will be accomplished. The people involved must discuss and determine how various tasks are to be coordinated.

PROJECT EXAMPLE

It is now the first week of March. The ground in Bedford has not completely thawed. However, the foundation contractors assure Roger that this is not a problem: The foundation footing must be placed below the frost line.

The first meeting of the Implementation Phase team was on the afternoon of the first Monday in March. During the second part of that meeting, Professor Hulbert informs the team members that all orders for significant materials must be verified weekly to confirm that they will be delivered on schedule. He further reminded them that, with completion of the Design Phase the previous week, the activity center project is now scheduled to be completed in mid-September. The schedule cannot slip any further since classes for next year start the last week in September.

Activity 3: Allocate Tasks to the Implementation Phase Team

For the Implementation Phase, team members skilled in construction and manufacturing are usually added to the team.

The Implementation Phase normally adds team members who are skilled in construction and manufacturing. These performers are often referred to as blue-collar workers. These experienced individuals ensure that proper construction and manufacturing techniques are applied to the project. They are skilled in reading the Design Phase drawings and capable of implementing them.

Activity 3A: Develop and Monitor Implementation Phase Details

People with implementation experience enjoy building or manufacturing. They seldom need detailed guidance with regard to a particular task. However, since they may tend to focus on the details of their particular task, their efforts must be monitored to ensure that everyone's tasks are being implemented in the proper sequence and on a timely basis.

For all projects, implementation needs to be checked to verify that

1. Tasks are being accomplished properly

2. Schedules are being followed and achieved

3. Costs are being contained within their established upper limits

On small projects, the project manager is directly involved with day-to-day detailed activities and continually monitors the project's performance to verify that (1) tasks are being accomplished properly, (2) schedules are being followed and met, and (3) costs are being contained within their established upper limits. On larger projects, this function is performed by a person or group of persons in a project office. Monitoring and controlling a large project or program in great detail is a major effort.

Periodic review meetings are held to see if the project documents are being interpreted correctly. Changes may be considered during these meetings. Detailed documentation concerning any changes is prepared and distributed to all parties involved in the changes. Here again, it is the responsibility of the manager to approve, deny, or revise any proposed changes that will affect tasks, schedules, or budgets. No small detail can be neglected because it could affect the entire effort.

Before initiating activity 5 (Produce and Evaluate Product), the manager must initiate **management subtasks,** including the following:

- Assign project personnel to tasks

- Hire additional personnel as needed

- Hold project indoctrination meeting(s) for newly assigned personnel

- Sign contracts with selected contractors

- Notify materials vendors regarding start of contract

- Coordinate and obtain permits

- Acquire safety equipment required by OSHA:

    hard hats, safety ropes, safety glasses, and special tools

- Select and obtain work space furnishings, fixtures, and equipment

    provide first-aid kit

    obtain outdoor toilets

    rent or lease supervisor's trailer if necessary

- Purchase tools, construction supplies, and materials

- Occupy work space

Construction (or manufacturing) can now be started. Some planners prefer to identify the above set of management subtasks as a separate task. They include it as the first task on the Implementation Phase schedule prior to activity 5.

PROJECT EXAMPLE

At the Friday afternoon meeting, Roger describes the progress regarding site preparation. Roger states that he cannot assist directly in the initial construction effort, watch over implementation, and continue to achieve high academic grades. After a twenty-minute discussion, Alice is elected to become technical leader of the construction effort. Roger will continue to monitor the overall effort, including financing. Alice requests that each member note on the Implementation Phase schedule his or her assignment preferences. She gathers these notes and agrees to have initial assignments prepared by Saturday morning. Alice also agrees to visit the site and observe the start of the excavation. Ellery asks to go with her, and she accepts his offer.

Activity 3B: Organize the Team into Task Groups

The project manager must now accomplish the following:

- Hire semiskilled people to replace the creative people and the cost estimators.

- Discharge most of the creative people and some cost estimators, or pass them on to new projects. (See activity 9.)

- Conduct indoctrination meetings for all team members.

When construction personnel are involved, they should be treated as part of the team, even though they may be contractors or subcontractors.

On Saturday, Alice examines the implementation tasks. She tentatively assigns team members to appropriate construction tasks and requests their comments. She then interviews potential semiskilled workers recommended by the contractors and suppliers who will be involved in the construction work.

Activity 3C: Assign Each Group a Set of Tasks to Perform

The project manager, with the assistance of others, converts all the documentation developed during the Design Phase into tasks for each team and contractor. (This conversion could be done during the Design Phase.) The project manager is responsible for making sure that each group understands how its assigned tasks interact with the tasks assigned to other groups and the contractors.

It is the second Monday afternoon in March. Alice explains the assignments and schedule shown in figure 5.2. She notes that Ellery, Kim, and Joseph will need some support during the framing and plumbing tasks. The remainder of the team offers to take turns assisting the assigned personnel, based upon their class schedules and obtaining transportation to Bedford. A bus schedule is obtained and distributed.

Chart of construction assignments: first two months

month	March	April
prepare site		
Roger		
Alice		
excavate site		
Alice		
Roger		
Ellery		
erect & cap foundation		
Alice		
Roger		
Ellery		
erect rough framing & plumbing		
Ellery		
Alice		
Kim		
Joseph		

Figure 5.2   Bar chart of construction assignments: first two months

Activity 4: Prepare to Produce the Designed Article

The Implementation Phase has been initiated and funds are available that can now be committed. Vendors must be informed, and their delivery dates must be confirmed. Construction permits, requested in advance to allow the town committees to review and comment on them, must be obtained before the start of construction. On-site temporary facilities for the construction workers must be provided. Now construction and/or production can begin.

Activity 4A: Define Vendor Schedules and Deliveries

Types of vendors include these:

- Profit-making companies that are incorporated
- Groups and individuals "doing business as" (DBA) themselves
- Independent contractors who prefer not to incorporate but to work as sole proprietors
- Nonprofit organizations, such as a vocational school

Various state and local agencies and departments watch over each type of vendor to ensure that vendors perform only that type of work for which they are licensed.

Once implementation starts, vendors must be contacted to determine if they are still available at the price they bid.

Contractors providing labor, materials, and expertise must be contacted (by telephone, letter, fax, or e-mail) to determine if their bid is still in effect—and at their quoted price. Vendors providing supplies and services must be contacted to determine if they are still available at the price they bid. It is also vital that labor, materials, supplies, and services be provided on time and at the quoted prices so the project can be completed on schedule and within budget.

PROJECT EXAMPLE

At the end of the second Monday meeting, Alice asks Manuel to assist Joseph in verifying shipment of the framing lumber and plumbing supplies. Manuel and Joseph are also assigned to contact Jim Sullivan to verify timely assistance from his plumbing volunteers and Jim Stander to confirm assistance from the electrician volunteers. All team members leave a copy of their expected spring (April, May, and June) class schedules with Alice for consideration in later assignments.

Activity 4B: Sign Contracts with Contractors and Vendors

Contracts identify, in a legal manner, the participants in the project, and the respective responsibilities of those participants. The contractor and vendor contract or purchase order typically contains the following information:

- Responsible persons: their names, organizations with which they are affiliated, and addresses
- Contract costs and authorized signatures
- Applicable reference documents and warranties
- Material or services to be provided
- Schedule of performance and progress payments where applicable

The signatories to contracts include the funding source (optional), the prime contractor, and subcontractors. (See appendix D.) Vendors usually receive purchase orders from the prime contractor or a subcontractor.

PROJECT EXAMPLE

> It is the second Friday afternoon of the Implementation Phase. The Northeastern University treasurer meets with Professor Hulbert and those contractors and vendors who can attend. The participants sign, and are given copies of, their contracts. The lumber vendor brings sandwiches for all and invites them to tour the lumber yard. The vendors who could not attend this meeting mail their signed contracts. These arrive in the Monday mail.

Activity 4C: Obtain Applicable Construction Permits

For projects involving work on land and buildings, construction and other permits must be obtained in a timely manner so that they are available when construction is ready to start.

For projects involving work on land and buildings, construction and other permits must be obtained. The length of time required for processing applications for these permits must be known in advance because any delays will cause work slippage. Thus, the project manager or other team member assigned to the task must request applications from the appropriate licensing boards or other governmental agencies in a timely manner. In this way, the actual permits will be available when needed.

In some situations, the government officials involved must inspect the property prior to the issuance of permits. They must also inspect the work in progress and perform code inspections to certify that the work is being performed according to the applicable government rules and regulations and the information stated in the permits.

Many of these rules and regulations overlap or require interpretation. Thus, it is necessary for the project manager to coordinate the actions among the various government agencies because overlapping authority and disagreement may exist. At times, face-to-face meetings must occur. Then the various government representatives can agree on an acceptable solution to conflicting requirements, and the project can continue.

PROJECT EXAMPLE

> Fortunately, during the early days of the previous December, all of the permit forms required had been obtained by Alice and Jose. They were immediately prepared, verified in content, and submitted to the appropriate government agencies and licensing boards. The necessary application fees were paid at that time. Now the approved permits are issued.
>
> The Northeastern University treasurer had the checks prepared in advance for the permits so work could progress on the planned schedule. (The electrical and plumbing permits will be obtained later by Jim Stander and Jim Sullivan, who will be supervising and assisting in that work.)

Activity 4D: Provide Temporary On-Site Facilities, Tools, and Equipment

Temporary facilities, such as work space, office space, and storage space, must be provided at a new construction or manufacturing site.

Temporary facilities, such as work space, office space, and storage space, must be provided at a new construction or manufacturing site. Portable toilets and first-aid facilities must also be provided for the workers. Furnishings and fixtures for use by contractors, such as desks and chairs, are necessary, and they should be included as a part of the cost and schedule estimates developed during the Design Phase. OSHA-required safety equipment must be determined and purchased.

Also, tools and other supplies required by the project team must be ordered and purchased; these should be so noted in the task descriptions and accompanying budgets. Temporary telephones and electrical power connections must be provided via the local utility companies.

Decisions regarding renting, leasing, and purchasing the above items are a part of the Design Phase planning for the Implementation Phase. Any last-minute changes in these plans must be made before construction and manufacturing can begin.

Note: If management tasks and subtasks are extensive, then they should be inserted here. See page 127.

> Alice's uncle loans a small trailer-office to be used on-site for supervisory personnel. An electric power line is connected via a meter on a pole. The power line is connected to a circuit-breaker box with a disconnect switch and a pair of 115-volt, 60-Hertz outlets. The town provides a temporary water connection. A telephone is installed, and a portable toilet unit arrives.
>
> Roger verifies, via Alice, that all concerned have a copy of the tasks, schedules, budgets, and the Specification for the activity center (see appendix C). Ellery is assigned the responsibility for distributing drawings to the appropriate team members and contractors. The university loans a computer so that Jose and Kim can update the schedules and budgets on site.

Activity 5: Produce and Evaluate Product

For complicated devices and software, proof of performance may be accomplished by first constructing one item, known as a prototype.

Finally, the time has come to actually start construction. All of the planning must now result in a quality product, constructed in a timely manner, in accordance with the Design Specification, and within budget. Every project will be different; some of the problems encountered are included in the activity center example (see activity 5A below).

Manufacturing occurs when quantities of the same product are produced (Kaplan, 1993). For complicated devices and software, there are times when proof of performance must be accomplished by first constructing one item (activity 5B). That item is often referred to as a prototype of the production units that will be fabricated later, once tests of the prototype are successful.

After prototype construction, evaluation, and revision where necessary, production can begin. The first production models (activity 5C) are evaluated to ensure that all new production tooling and procedures are performing as designed. Larger production items are tested as sub-assemblies prior to final assembly.

Activity 5A: Fabricate and Evaluate Prototype Model (if necessary)

Prototypes may be constructed (1) to verify design assumptions or (2) to test production techniques.

Activities 5A and 5C apply to the fabrication and evaluation of several items of the same design. These activities do not apply to the activity center, unless the team decides to construct a scale model.

For production items, prototype construction may be required for either one or both of two major reasons:

1. Design assumptions and costs may need to be verified.
2. Production techniques may need to be tested.

Sometimes these two "proof via prototype" reasons occur sequentially (figure 5.3). When the costs of production tooling are excessive, then the production techniques are improved via the first production models, as discussed next and in chapter 9.

Prototype construction provides a model that allows for verification of the design drawings and accompanying specifications. Human factors—how humans and the product (hardware or software) interact—can also be tested. How the operators behave under stress or when they are tired can be determined by simulating problem situations and applying them in a sequence that causes operators to experience stress and fatigue.

Prototype units can also be tested in laboratories under simulated operating conditions to verify that they meet performance specifications. Environmental tests include shock and vibration, also known as "shake, rattle, and roll" testing. Temperature and humidity variations can also be simulated; salt-spray testing—to determine resistance to corrosion—may be performed.

Field conditions may be simulated by using the prototype unit in a location that closely approximates the environmental extremes to which the production units will be exposed. It is not possible to test for every variation that can occur. However, experienced professionals can often predict what may occur during extreme conditions by extrapolating from the test results.

Figure 5.3 Prototype development and evaluation

Prototype development and evaluation

select item → design prototype → construct sample unit → evaluate sample unit → accept / reject

Whenever possible, a production prototype is constructed using the same or similar techniques, equipment, and processes that will be used in final production.

Whenever possible, a production prototype is constructed using the same or similar techniques, equipment, and processes that will be used in final production. This approach may be expensive and/or time-consuming. Thus, decisions regarding the techniques, equipment, or processes to be used in final production require the advice of experienced manufacturing personnel.

Activity 5B: Fabricate the Designed Article

As the product is about to be fabricated, the physical conditions needed for efficient production must be reviewed.

Fabrication of a product may require preparing a site or building space. Room must be provided for the work about to be accomplished. Revisions to the existing site must occur before fabrication can begin. Environmental impact may need to be assessed, and measures to protect the environment may be required. Material storage areas may be needed. Security needs will have to be assessed to eliminate—or at least control—theft.

The workers involved on a project vary greatly in their need for supervision. Some workers have performed the same type of work so many times that they may need only general supervision. However, with the advent of monitoring environmental impact upon the location, additional training of these workers on environmental issues may be required.

As work progresses, the designated tasks are performed. Budgets and schedules are closely monitored to ensure that the Implementation Phase plans are either followed carefully or modified to fit the actual need.

PROJECT EXAMPLE

The site for the activity center has been prepared by town of Bedford employees, who have removed the topsoil and stored it locally. With the assistance of a third-year civil engineering student, Joseph and Manuel survey the foundation area, define the location of the foundation corners, and install the batter boards. (See appendix B.) Then the foundation contractor arrives with the excavation equipment and digs the hole for the foundation. Fortunately, no ledge is encountered.

The forms for the foundation spread footings are then constructed and braced; the concrete slump is tested; the footing is then poured. A few days later, the foundation and chimney forms are installed. The foundation concrete is slump-tested and then poured. Plastic drain pipe and pea stone arrive and are placed around the foundation footings. The pipes are then connected to an existing storm drain.

A few days later, the foundation forms are removed. Six inches of hay is firmly packed on top of the pea stone by Kim. After the foundation outer walls appear to be dry, two coats of asphalt emulsion are brushed onto the foundation by Laura; she creates a design that, sadly, disappears when the soil is returned to "backfill" around the foundation. It is compacted by Roger and Jose after school. The rough grading around the foundation is complete. Kim is also learning how to update the schedules and budget spreadsheets.

Alice observes that some of the town laborers assisting at the site exhibit crude manners, saying things and using language that offends the students. She discusses this problem with her Uncle Bill at Sunday dinner. He asks her, "Does the problem seem to be gender- or race-related?" Alice replies that it seems to be more a problem of blue-collar workers versus students. He comments that his workload in nearby Stoneham will not totally consume his days. He volunteers to visit the site most afternoons to review progress and handle problems. Alice and Bill call Roger and Professor Hulbert, who accept his offer.

Uncle Bill usually arrives in the late afternoon to inspect progress and answer questions regarding the next day's work. For example, the lally columns are late in arriving. A quick telephone call from Uncle Bill ensures their prompt delivery.

It is now early April. Most of the lumber arrives and is stored nearby. (The local police watch over it during nights and weekends.) The foundation cap is installed. The main carrying timbers are installed on the lally columns. The main floor joists are prepared and installed; the plywood subfloor is then installed by the team in one weekend.

The concrete trucks return; the floor slab is poured and leveled, and a floor drain is installed. Uncle Bill shows the students how to verify the level of the floor as it is poured. He privately talks to some of the laborers, explaining that the students are here to both work and learn. He encourages them to be understanding of these young students who are just now acquiring some practical experience. He also talks to the students about respecting the laborers, who are skilled in their occupations. He reminds both groups that they are all human beings who deserve to be treated with respect.

It is now mid-April and the construction is approximately one week behind schedule—partly because of weather and partly because of mid-term exams. Roger and Alice decide to ask members to work at least the next two weekends—weather permitting. The days are getting longer, daylight saving time has begun, and the delivered lumber is relatively dry. On the first weekend, Uncle Bill arrives with some special Italian food that he has prepared. He offers advice on how to install corner bracing. That day all of the team members learn much and eat well. The house is framed, which includes the construction of main floor timbers, rough flooring, wall studs, door and window openings, exterior wall plywood, ceiling joists, and roof rafters.

Laura is a little nervous regarding schedule slippage and cost control. On Monday, the team members meet and agree on how to increase their work output and how to save some money as well. Roger agrees to call those vendors who are late in delivering materials. They improve their deliveries so that work can gradually return to the original schedules.

Plumbing supplies are purchased from a distributor, thus saving a few hundred dollars when compared with the originally estimated retail prices. Rough plumbing is installed on the last weekend of April, when a licensed plumber (Jim Sullivan) can be there to both guide and assist the workers.

It is now the second week in May. The roof is framed and boarded with sheets of CDX exterior plywood. The roof and chimney are one week late being constructed—again because of weather. The brick mason agrees to work one weekend at no extra cost. She installs the chimney and roof flashing as part of constructing the chimney. Jose assists her by carrying the bricks to where she is working; Manuel assists by mixing the mortar under her guidance.

Kim is now looking for ways to get the project back on schedule. She chairs the next Monday meeting and offers her suggestions. The doors and windows are expected to arrive two weeks late. Alice and Joseph agree to contact the vendors to see if the delivery dates can be improved. They discover that, because of the slippage of another project, the windows and doors can now be delivered on schedule.

Uncle Bill arrives just in time to correct the team members' approach for installing the prehung windows and doors. He saves the team members a few days by assisting on the following weekend and, of course, by bringing some more excellent food. During lunch, he explains to them how work can be accomplished with less effort and performed more expertly. Laura decides to write a term paper that describes his suggestions. The exterior finish is installed; that effort is followed by the installation of the exterior siding, which consists of cedar shingles.

Jose now works with a local electrician (Greg Roberts, who is assisting Jim Stander). With Laura's help, they install the rough wiring in one week, including one weekend. The shingles are also coated with bleaching oil that same weekend. Now the project is back on schedule. Manuel is delighted and issues the corrected schedule.

The rough plumbing is installed with the help of one of Jim Sullivan's sons. The roof has to be penetrated for the bathroom and kitchen vent stacks. This work is accomplished on schedule.

It is the middle of June. The insulation and Sheetrock™ have arrived, and it is exam week. Thus, the materials are unloaded and stored within the center, since it can now be locked at night. Two additional staple guns and face masks are borrowed. Following exams, all team members work on installing insulation and Sheetrock™ so the schedule will not slip. When approximately one half of the insulation and Sheetrock™ is installed, the team is split into two groups. Jose plans to paint, so he is placed in charge of taping and spackling (covering the joints with compound) to provide smooth wall and ceiling surfaces. He then works and also supervises the sanding and interior painting. To stay on schedule, all team members work on the Fourth of July. They are invited to stay and enjoy the Bedford fireworks that evening. Much watermelon is consumed.

Roger and Alice have noted some friction among group members. Professor Hulbert reminds Roger and Alice that no one has had the opportunity to enjoy a week away from the effort; staggered vacations are then discussed and planned so everyone can leave for a week and return refreshed.

It is now mid-July. The flooring has arrived one week early; it is stored in the basement. The interior painting is begun, followed by installation of the flooring, room by room, after the paint has dried. This effort progresses slowly and is not complete until late August.

Roger discovers that the total charges are beginning to exceed the funding. He has to acquire an additional $2 000 quickly. The team decides to have a Labor Day open house for the townspeople. They leave a basket at the door and collect $1 850. Professor Hulbert, Bill D'Annolfo, and Jim Sullivan each contribute an additional $50 to the fund.

The first of September and Labor Day pass quickly. The electrical fixtures arrive on time and are installed on schedule. The plumbing fixtures are late in arriving, and their installation occurs after Labor Day, yet the installation is completed on schedule.

The New England weather has tuned cold early this year. Uncle Bill suggests that, to avoid further schedule slippage, the final landscaping should be initiated now. So, grass seed is sown and watered. Accomplishing this work becomes a problem because of preplanned vacation schedules.

It is now the middle of September. The beginning of the fall quarter of classes is only one week away. Professor Hulbert and Uncle Bill inspect the activity center to be certain that nothing has been forgotten. A few interior corners are discovered to have been painted poorly. Three of the siding shingles were not bleached. Some of the grass is not growing; those areas need to be reseeded. Alice calls on the few team members who have returned to school early to assist in performing the necessary work so a formal delivery date can be firmly established with the town officials. The corrections are completed during the next ten days.

Activity 5C: Produce and Evaluate Items to Be Produced in Quantities

The learning curve refers to the ability of operators to gain in productivity as they learn how to use tools more efficiently and as they gain dexterity.

The production of many identical items requires additional planning. The first few models require more time to manufacture; later ones benefit from the learning curve (figure 5.4). Production specialists are responsible for including learning-curve information in their Design Phase estimates of production costs.

A learning curve can be graphed as a curve of productivity versus time. When an individual is starting to learn to operate a machine or to perform an assembly operation, the level of performance is low at first until level A is reached. As the operator gains experience, the level of performance increases from level A to level B. This change is caused by increased experience and familiarity with the tooling and processes. Further experience gradually improves the rate of performance from level B to level C. This change is caused by increased dexterity. Additional experience will lead to a minimal improvement in performance from level C to level D. After level D, the improvement in performance is negligible. If greater productivity is desired, a change in manufacturing technique, procedure, or equipment is required. When prototypes are built, different manufacturing techniques can be tested and evaluated to determine the most productive ones.

The last tasks of a manufacturing plan involve inspection, testing, and shipping.

The last steps in manufacturing items involve inspecting, testing, and shipping them promptly.

1.   *Inspection* is usually done near the production facilities so that defective items can be quickly returned to the production group for correction and adjustment. For simple items, only selected samples are tested; however, for complex items, each manufactured example is thoroughly tested. The tolerances, which are the deviations allowed from the design-specified values, are established during the Design Phase. Measuring equipment must be available to check any variations from the tolerance values specified. The selection of inspection and test equipment is done by quality control specialists.

Figure 5.4   The learning curve

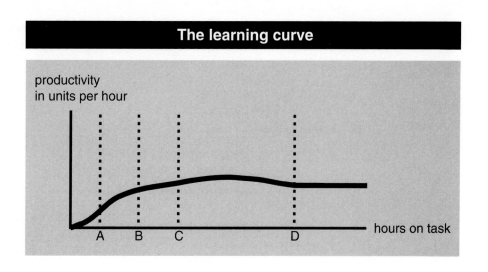

IMPLEMENTATION

2.   *Testing* may involve using equipment to verify that it meets all performance specifications. Pilot units may be used to establish that the manufacturing personnel correctly fabricate and assemble the equipment.

3.   *Shipping* is an additional factor to be considered in preparing products. For small, delicate items, shipping materials are available to protect them from being damaged in transit. For large, delicate items, crates are often used to protect the equipment. Recording devices can be installed in these crates to record the time and amount of shock and vibration so that the location where damage occurred can be established (since time can be converted to location).

The Implementation Phase may apply to units, devices, or systems and procedures. Where large-scale manufacturing is involved, the Implementation Phase is often divided into three subphases shown in figure 5.5:

1.   *Construction: Fabricate sample items and evaluate results.* Only one or a few items may be constructed. These items are normally referred to as prototype models or pilot runs.

2.   *Production: Manufacture a significant quantity of items.* Several or many items may be constructed. A manufacturing line may be designed and established to produce large quantities of the chosen item in order to apply the learning curve concept to cost and schedule efficiencies.

3.   *Employment: Operate and maintain items.* A simple example of equipment employment is a copier machine. The equipment manufacturer and/or copier seller perform both preventive and emergency maintenance. These machines may be leased or purchased from the manufacturer's or distributor's sales office.

Some engineering texts consider employment to be a separate phase following delivery. This makes sense because different parts of the company, or different companies, may provide the operation and maintenance services. (See activity 7.)

Production tooling is evaluated through exhaustive testing of a significant quantity of the first items off the production line. A balance must be achieved between the cost of this testing and the loss of reputation and business caused by products that do not meet specifications or customer expectations. The manufacturer may have placed higher expectations in the mind of the customer, via product marketing and advertising, than the product is able to deliver. Thus, there must be significant coordination between marketing and engineering if the customer is to receive what is advertised.

Automobile recalls are a result of insufficient product testing under very specific conditions. The incorporation of the technique known as "total quality control" greatly reduces manufacturing errors. The technique stresses the importance of doing things right the first time. Total quality control must be included at the beginning of the design process to reduce the occurrence of design and production deficiencies.

Figure 5.5 Implementation subphases for manufacturing

Implementation subphases for manufacturing

construction subphase
fabricate one or more items

production subphase
manufacture a quantity of items

employment subphase
utilize a product in a useful way

It is desirable to minimize the need for storing and maintaining large inventories. Large inventories require increased space and additional financial investment. A scheduling technique known as "Just-In-Time Performance" can be applied. This technique provides for shipping the needed components at a rate just equal to the rate of consumption. Only a very small inventory is required to continue the operation of the assembly line in a smooth and effective manner.

Activity 6: Revise, Review, and Deliver Final Documentation

During implementation, documentation corrections are often neglected. Sometimes changes are decided at the construction site and are approved verbally. People are busy and may neglect to prepare a formal change notice. However, any documentation to be delivered to the customer must represent the actual, final product. Therefore, all documentation should reflect the changes made at the site.

A portion of the delivery may contain material that has been purchased from a vendor and that is under warranty. That warranty must be passed on to the customer so that the customer can directly contact the vendor without bothering the project's parent organization.

Activity 6A: Correct Working and Detail Drawings

A Change Notice is prepared when changes are being made to the original design plans during implementation; these changes must be documented.

A Change Notice is prepared when changes are being made to the original design plans during implementation; these changes must be documented. This notice is sent to all those involved in design, construction, or manufacturing, and to the person or group in charge of documentation. It may be initiated by the design group, the construction organization, or the manufacturing organization. A meeting of all involved personnel may be necessary to explain the need for the change and to further explain how the change is to be implemented.

*All those involved should participate in the discussions about changes so each person (or group of persons) realizes the effect of changes upon the project. This is known as **bottom-up** management.*

During construction, changes may be required that could not be predicted in advance. Budgets may have to be changed; however, the total dollars should be kept close to or within the contracted amount. Tasks and schedules may have to be revised. These changes are the responsibility of the project manager and, in much larger projects and programs, the project control people. Whenever possible, all those involved should participate in discussions. In this way, all persons (or groups) realize the effect of changes upon their part of the project. This is known as **bottom-up** management, which is discussed in section 6.3.

PROJECT EXAMPLE

Ellery is assigned the task of documenting any changes to the various drawings as they occur. He quickly realizes that the changes need only be inserted into the drawings via the CAD program once or twice each week. He also discovers that sometimes a change may cause a previous change to be canceled. He informs all concerned individuals that a set of the most recent drawings is on display on a table in the loaned trailer. All proposed or processed change orders are available on a clipboard next to the set of up-to-date drawings.

Appendix E contains an example of a Contract Change Notice (CCN) developed specifically for the activity center project. The fifth change was requested after Robert Lanciani, an acquaintance of one of the students, happened to visit the construction site. As a trained and experienced firefighter, he noticed that the metal Simpson TP gusset was indicated on the drawings and in the Specification for the Activity Center (appendix C). At a recent fire where the heat (but not yet the fire) had reached the roof, the heated metal gussets fell out, causing the trusses to fail. From this experience, Lanciani pointed out that metal gussets and the associated trusses were a danger to firefighters. Therefore, at the activity center construction site, an informal conference occurred that led to a change order (noted in appendix E).

IMPLEMENTATION

Clients should receive documents that assist in the use of the product. These include instruction manuals and maintenance specifications.

Activity 6B: Deliver Implementation Phase Documents

For the Implementation Phase, the completed documents to be delivered to the clients for their use are (1) instruction manuals, (2) warranties, (3) maintenance specifications, and (4) As-Built Plans. The content of these documents is described in section 5.3.

A package of the corrected Working and Detail Drawings (activity 6A) has been gathered together. It must be accompanied with written material that (1) describes what changes occurred during construction (or manufacturing), and (2) explains why these changes occurred. Thus, both the client and the funding source(s) will have documentation that is correct and up-to-date. Included are explanations regarding the changes that occurred during the Implementation Phase.

Examine all change notices and incorporate information on the revisions in the documentation being prepared for delivery to the client and/or funding source(s). Review all construction or manufacturing drawings for changes that were not properly documented with change notices. Insert these changes into the proper place in the overall documentation. It may be necessary, during more formal and large projects or programs, to issue additional change notices upon construction completion to document all changes.

PROJECT EXAMPLE

Ellery has been given the assignment of noting changes to the specifications. As with the Working and Detail Drawings, he informs all concerned individuals that a corrected copy of the Specification for the Activity Center is on display on a table in the loaned trailer, next to the drawings.

Activity 6C: Deliver Warranties and Associated Invoices

PLANNING AHEAD

Promptly after receipt of goods, you must obtain warranties and copies of the applicable invoices that verify proof of purchase by you or your team. Thus, if an item that you have purchased fails, it can be repaired or replaced by the original source or manufacturer—usually without an extra cost to your team.

Once the product is delivered, manufacturers need to provide repair service. Sometimes even modifications are made to the product to ensure customer satisfaction.

For companies that look forward to "repeat business," as well as for good recommendations from their current customers to attract new customers, it is desirable to ensure customer satisfaction. This can be accomplished by trying to meet the following criteria:

•   Support warranties faithfully

•   Perform design revisions that improve the product

•   Prepare service contracts for product maintenance

A satisfied customer usually speaks well of the team who performed the work; that customer will recommend the team to others. If modifications to the equipment or software lead to more use of product and more flexibility in its use, follow-on contracts are likely to occur.

Many manufacturers provide servicing of products. This work may be covered by a service contract. Such a contract may cover both periodic and emergency maintenance and repair.

Warranties should be clear and specific. The equipment now belongs to a user who may not want to be concerned with its maintenance and repair. For continuous and reliable equipment performance, most users are willing to purchase a service contract from the manufacturer rather than having to maintain that equipment within their organization.

PROJECT EXAMPLE

As construction progresses, Kim is assigned the responsibility of gathering together all warranties and instruction manuals and filing them for later delivery to the town of Bedford. She soon learns to also obtain and copy the applicable invoices before they are sent to the university for payment. The invoice copies then become a part of the documentation package to be delivered to the town of Bedford.

Activity 6D: Deliver Final Product and Instruction Manuals

Delivery is considered to be an instant of time at the end of the Implementation Phase. There are three conditions associated with delivery:

1. Delivery may be refused by the customer until all questions and misunderstandings are resolved.

2. Delivery may be "conditional" while customer-requested revisions are being completed.

3. Delivery may occur with acceptance by the customer.

Delivery formally occurs when the applicable documents are signed. The associated paperwork transfers the responsibility for, and ownership of, the project to the customer for whom it was produced.

Delivery formally occurs when the applicable documents are signed. The associated paperwork transfers the responsibility for, and ownership of, the project to the customer for whom it was produced. This delivery and acceptance should include payment, or an agreement to pay, for the work satisfactorily accomplished.

Where manufactured products are involved, the customer may inspect the product at the customer's plant. This function is known as incoming inspection.

When the product is either large or complicated, then the customer may prefer to have a quality control inspector at the manufacturer's plant, as shown in figure 5.6. This is known as "inspection at the vendor's facility." Thus, necessary changes and/or repairs can be performed at the vendor's manufacturing facility without involving extra shipping costs and significant time delays.

It is very important to realize that the customer often accepts individual items or portions of a project as they are completed. Customer reviews may also have been a part of the design and development process. However, when it is time to deliver the product(s), the results may not be acceptable to the customer. Unplanned changes may be required to satisfy the customer.

A structure, equipment, or item of software often appears different once it is completed, even if the item accurately implements the drawings and specifications. Some people have a difficult time visualizing an outcome. They may have an idealistic picture in their mind regarding results—fantasy versus reality. For these customers, scale models and prototypes can be helpful.

PLANNING AHEAD

Those persons accepting delivery may believe they were going to receive something different from the item(s) constructed. The project manager must apply personal skills to convince the customers that they have received the items for which they contracted. The alternative is a legal battle that may consume considerable time and funds. This is another reason why it is important to continually involve the customer in the development of a project.

Figure 5.6   Delivery and acceptance

IMPLEMENTATION

Prior to asking a customer to accept a project, one or more team members must review the plans and specifications to ensure that the completed project actually complies with them. They must place themselves in the shoes of the customer. In this manner, the team is trying to avoid surprises when it requests customer acceptance. Persons who represent the customer may be involved because they will later be accepting responsibility for the finished product or project.

Delivery may have occurred satisfactorily. However, on initially working with the delivered project or items, the customer may decide that some portions are not performing as expected. Whether the contractor should assist in the desired (or even demanded) changes at no cost is a difficult decision. Some loss of profit may be less costly than an extended legal battle. There is also a possible loss of follow-on business as the result of a poor, even if undeserved, reputation for the project team.

Examine the following unfortunate example: The prime contractor for a military mobile digital computer system designed and tested the computer. Another company, under a separate government contract, designed and constructed the tape drive to be used with that computer and with other government computers. Contractually, the federal government accepted responsibility for the two separate specifications. However, when the computer and tape drive did not operate together properly, the federal government blamed the prime contractor. The prime contractor then had a very difficult time obtaining contracts to supply mobile computers to other federal agencies. The prime contractor was perceived to be at fault because of the failure of the computer and the tape drive to operate as one system. Thus, perception and reality may be in conflict. Someone must decide: Is the customer always right? and How will other potential customers perceive the problem?

Customer satisfaction can lead to more opportunities for an organization that wants to be profitable and grow in service and reputation.

Customer satisfaction can lead to more opportunities for an organization that wants to be profitable and grow in service and reputation. Recall that any project or program, from selection to delivery, consists of four relatively distinct phases: Conception, Study, Design, and Implementation. Note that, in each phase, documentation has been stressed. This helps to ensure that there are no unhappy surprises.

Lawyers are retained when people do not agree on the interpretation of documents. Therefore, it is vital to prepare brief, simple, yet complete documentation so that a project can be successful, satisfying all those involved. The funding sources, as well as those who will formally receive delivery of the project and its documentation, must especially be satisfied with the results.

PROJECT EXAMPLE

Mr. Williams, who is superintendent of the Department of Public Works (DPW) for the town of Bedford, visits the site of the activity center from time to time. Roger and Alice soon learn that at least one of them should be available to answer any of his questions. At each visit, he is shown the changes to the drawings and specifications so that the team is assured that they will be acceptable to him at "delivery time." He advises team members on how he would prefer delivery of the warranties and accompanying invoice copies for easy use by town employees.

It is late September. The activity center project is complete. Building inspectors perform the final inspections, verifying that the completed structure conforms with all applicable local, state, and national building codes. The team receives a verbal commendation from the inspectors for a job well done.

A plaque is designed with the names of the Northeastern University team members, the activity center benefactors, and the town officials. A friend of Ellery's offers to prepare the plaque in time for the formal activity center delivery. Mr. Williams is called and the date for formal delivery of the activity center is established.

Activity 7: Operate and Maintain Customer-Contracted Items

The responsibility for maintenance and repair of one item or product (such as an aircraft) or many items (such as copier machines) becomes an important income opportunity. If a group of students from a technical school, college, or university construct an item, then it must be agreed in advance that the educational organization will not be held responsible for maintenance and repair. (Why? Once the individual students have graduated, their skills and knowledge are no longer available.) For situations in which an existing company wishes to service its products, then a separate maintenance division or a separate service company may already exist or must be formed.

Maintenance is grouped in two categories:

1. Routine preventive maintenance, to ensure that the equipment operates as designed and that worn parts are replaced before they fail

2. Random maintenance, which cannot be predicted in advance but can be estimated on a statistical basis

A contractor can plan for both preventive maintenance and random maintenance, and it can estimate the number of employees and supervisors required.

A contractor can plan for both preventive maintenance and random maintenance, and it can estimate the number of employees and supervisors required. However, there will be times when two or more random failures will occur at the same time. A good reputation is earned when effective routine preventive maintenance prevents such simultaneous multiple random failures. This is *not* an easy assignment for a firm!

Activity 8: Review the Results of the Implementation Phase

*On completion of the work, all involved individuals should meet and review the work accomplished and the problems that arose during its implementation—known as **lessons learned.***

When people are busy working on a project, they may miss some important learning opportunities. "It is difficult to see the forest for the trees." On completion of the work, all involved individuals should meet and review the work accomplished and the problems that arose during its implementation—known as **lessons learned.** Such a meeting should not be an opportunity for individuals to blame others for the problems that had to be solved. Rather, the group should focus on what to do differently so the next project with which they are involved will flow more smoothly.

PROJECT EXAMPLE

On completion of the project and prior to formal delivery to the officials from the town of Bedford, Professor Hulbert conducts a meeting with all the team members present. He has each one describe what he or she has learned from working on the project. The list on the chalkboard grows, with some laughter as team members realize how different reality can be from theory. Northeastern's President Curry then arrives and presents each team member with a certificate of accomplishment from the university.

Sandwiches and soft drinks are served; the meeting is formally adjourned by Professor Hulbert as he reminds students to concentrate on their studies so they can graduate successfully four years from now. He reminds them to prepare resumes that include their work on the activity center and to hand-carry a copy to the Cooperative Education Department, which helps students obtain "co-op" jobs as part of the school's work/study curriculum.

PLANNING AHEAD ▶

Activity 9: Pursue New Projects

The pursuit of new projects applies to organizations interested in pursuing follow-on contracts.

IMPLEMENTATION

Activity 9A: Prepare Public Relations Material

Good public relations may be achieved if an open house or some kind of ceremony occurs to mark the formal delivery of the completed project.

Good public relations may be achieved if an open house or some kind of ceremony occurs to mark the formal delivery of the completed project. Speeches, ribbon cuttings, buffets, or even banquets are an opportunity to focus public attention on the completed project and to thank the workers, managers, and funding sources involved in project development. Photo opportunities may also be planned so a visual record of delivery and acceptance exists.

PROJECT EXAMPLE

An open house at the activity center is held to mark the formal transfer of the facility. Town officials, representatives from the funding sources, and supportive Northeastern faculty attend. A brief ceremony occurs where responsibility for the activity center is transferred from the team members to the town of Bedford. The document that transfers responsibility to the town is signed, and Roger delivers a box to Mr. Williams that contains these items:

- The warranties, appropriate invoices, and instruction manuals
- The most recent copy of the Production Specification
- A complete set of corrected current Working and Detail Drawings

A buffet—paid for out of the university's public relations budget—is provided for everyone to enjoy.

The students request Mr. William D'Annolfo to step forward. They present to him a certificate of appreciation that they have secretly prepared for "Uncle Bill." It expresses their thanks for his continuing advice, support, and encouragement during the entire project. He thanks them and reminds them that, thirty years ago, he was a student at Northeastern, majoring in chemistry and civil engineering. He tells them that, with persistence, good work, and a little luck, they can follow in his footsteps. He also informs them that he has one opening for a co-op student starting the following January. They all excitedly discuss who should apply to Uncle Bill's company for the assignment.

Activity 9B: Offer Presentations to Prospective Customers

Prior to completion of any current project, new customers are needed. Individuals who had been active in the Study and Design Phases and whose abilities could apply to similar projects can be transferred to a sales and marketing group so they can pursue new business opportunities together. Presentations are planned, rehearsed, and given to potential customers. These customers may sometimes want to examine previously completed projects. Permission should be requested from previous customers for site visits by the potential new customers.

Activity 9C: Construct Speculative Products

In some instances a contractor will build a structure without having an identified buyer. This is known as **building on speculation.** It means that

- The builder's business "contracts" with itself
- The builder defines what is to be built
- The builder obtains the financing

For example, software programs can be devised by individuals, groups, or companies on speculation. These programs can be demonstrated at conventions or seminars. Mailing lists may be purchased, and advertising literature prepared and sent to potential customers. Follow-up calls are then made to determine if potential customers are interested in purchasing the software. For more complicated software programs, demonstrations of software at a potential customer's location may be planned and made via a so-called road show.

| SECTION 5.3 | IMPLEMENTATION PHASE DOCUMENTS |

During the Implementation Phase, implementation or construction proceeds with the Production Specification and Working and Detail Drawings as a guide. Implementation, of course, never perfectly proceeds according to what is described in the above documents. Thus, Contract Change Notices (CCNs) and Engineering Change Notices (ECNs) are prepared, as approvals to modify the design or design approach are obtained. An example of a change is given in appendix E.

Although the project documents from the Design Phase define the project, implementation, of course, never perfectly proceeds according to what is described in them. Thus, Contract Change Notices (CCNs) and Engineering Change Notices (ECNs) are prepared, as approvals to modify the design are obtained.

The content of each of these documents is described below. The flow from the Conception Phase documents to the Implementation Phase documents is shown in figure 5.7.

As implementation progresses, the approved Contract Change Notices are gathered. The Working and Detail Drawings are modified to agree with these design changes. Instruction manuals are written to explain how to operate and maintain the equipment. More meetings are held to evaluate progress; more meeting reports (section 8.3) are written. These reports and modified drawings eventually lead to three Implementation Phase documents. At the end of the Implementation Phase, the completed documents are the following:

1. Instruction Manuals and Warranties
2. Maintenance Specifications
3. As-Built Plans

The content of each of these documents is described below:

During the Implementation Phase, documents need to be prepared to deliver to the client. Most important are instruction manuals, which describe how to use the product.

Here is how to prepare the **Instruction Manuals** and **Warranties:**

1.   Promptly after receipt of goods, instruction manuals must be obtained for each piece of equipment that is a part of the implementation. For the other portions of the implementation, typically those that the team developed as project-specific, the team must write its own system-oriented instruction manuals. These manuals might reference the manuals supplied by your vendors, including page and paragraph number. When a simpler set of instruction manuals is desired and all information is being gathered into one document, those parts of vendors' manuals that apply to the particular equipment or system can be extracted.

2.   Promptly after receipt of goods, warranties from vendors must be obtained, and warranties must be written for equipment the team developed. For equipment supplied by vendors, the team must provide to the client copies of the applicable vendor invoices that show proof of purchase. Thus, if an item that the project team purchased fails, it can be repaired or replaced at a client's location by the original source or manufacturer—usually at *no* cost to the project team's firm.

The **Maintenance Specifications** are prepared for large systems during the Implementation Phase. For small systems, maintenance information is delivered to the user in the form of one or more manuals.

1.   For large systems, a study is performed near the end of the Design Phase. It identifies potential single failures and potential multiple failures caused by the first (single) failure. This study then leads to the outline and preparation of one or more interrelated Maintenance Specifications. These specifications are often divided into routine preventive maintenance, which can be scheduled, and random maintenance whose need cannot be predicted in advance. (See appendix G.)

2.   For small systems, copies of vendor-supplied maintenance and troubleshooting manuals are provided to the user. The designers may prepare an overview document that guides the user to the proper vendor-supplied manuals and may also include interface information regarding

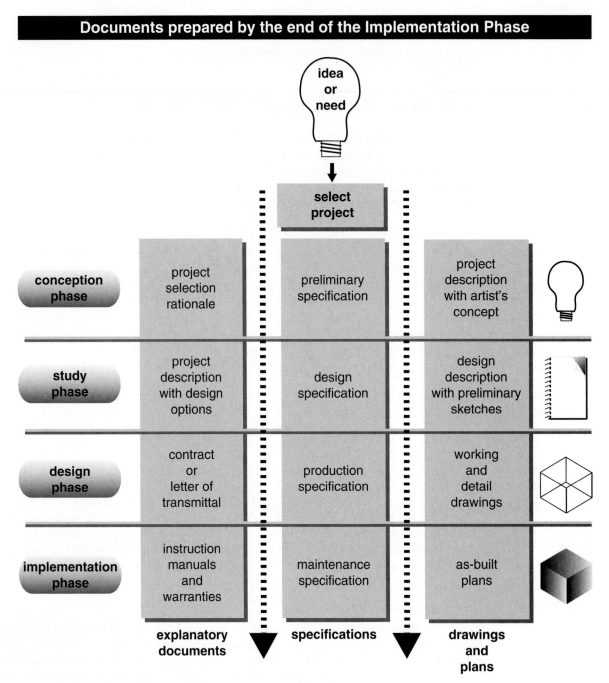

Documents prepared by the end of the Implementation Phase

Figure 5.7 Documents prepared by the end of the Implementation Phase

routine maintenance and random maintenance. This additional documentation ties together the small system parts.

The **As-Built Plans** are prepared as follows:

1. All change notices must be examined and these revisions included in the documentation being prepared for delivery to the client and/or funding source(s). All construction or manufacturing drawings containing changes that were not properly documented with change notices should be determined; descriptions of each change need to be inserted into their proper place in the overall documentation. For large projects or programs, it may be necessary to issue change notices for any undocumented changes. (People who are busy working often forget to document their changes.)

2. When a package of the corrected working and detail drawings has been gathered together, it must be accompanied with written material that describes the changes that have occurred during construction (or manufacturing). The written material must explain why these changes occurred. Thus, both the client and the funding source(s) will have documentation that is correct and up-to-date and that also includes explanations as to why the changes occurred during the Implementation Phase. Appendix H lists the content of the Student Activity Center As-Built Plans.

The As-Built Plans describe the project as it was actually completed, with all revisions to plans included. These plans and accompanying records are valuable to the client as help in using the product and to the group that performed the project.

Upon completion of a project, a final report should be prepared. It should contain a description of the project as it evolved and progressed. It should also include information regarding how the final design became the specific product that was implemented. The physical and electronic location of all related data and documents should be noted if it becomes necessary to refer to them at a later time.

SECTION 5.4   DEFINING PHASE COMPLETION

The Implementation Phase is considered complete when all of the following are accomplished:

- The documentation of the project implementation is complete.
- The customer has accepted the project.
- Final payment has been received for the project.

Now the project team can be disbanded. The team members can go on to a new project.

SECTION 5.5   ACCOMPLISHMENTS OF THE SYSTEMATIC APPROACH

As a review of chapters 2 through 5, a systems approach to a project requires that you accomplish the following:

- Formulate the problem versus its symptoms, recognizing the real versus perceived scope of the problem (Conception Phase)
- Analyze the data (Conception Phase)
- Search for alternatives (Conception Phase)
- Evaluate alternatives (Study Phase)
- Devise a solution (Design Phase)
- Implement the solution (Implementation Phase)
- Review the results (Implementation Phase)

Projects that operate by methodically applying a systematic approach will more likely achieve all three of the following desired outcomes:

- Complete all assigned tasks
- Remain on schedule
- Complete the project within budget

Projects are more successful when they are approached and performed in a systematic manner.

CHAPTER OBJECTIVES SUMMARY

Now that you have finished this chapter, you should be able to:

1. Define the purpose and goal of the Implementation Phase of a project.
2. Explain the tasks involved in the Implementation Phase of a project and the activities or steps through which these tasks are performed.

3. Describe ways in which money needed for projects is typically obtained and delivered.

4. Explain how documents prepared during the Design Phase are used in the Implementation Phase.

5. Describe tasks that are typically part of the Implementation Phase and how they are assigned.

6. Describe the role of the project manager during the Implementation Phase.

7. Explain why periodic meetings are important during the Implementation Phase of a project.

8. List common tasks that should be accomplished before actual implementation or manufacturing begins.

9. Describe what prototypes are and why they are developed.

10. Define the learning curve, and explain how it relates to manufacturing production.

11. Describe the documents that should be prepared for the Implementation Phase and which should be delivered to the client.

12. Define "delivery" of a project, and describe what problems may occur at that stage.

13. Outline the responsibilities and opportunities for a supplier/manufacturer after the delivery of a product.

14. Explain why a review meeting at the end of a project is important.

EXERCISES

5.1   Revise the Purpose and Goal statement given in section 5.1 to match each of your options for a class project.

5.2   Carefully examine the activities listed and described in section 5.2. Adapt them to each of your options for a class project.

5.3   Review the Design Phase effort with all team members. Develop any required additional Implementation Phase details with the assistance of all team members. Organize the team into task groups for the Implementation Phase, supported by personnel whose Implementation Phase skills are necessary. Assign each group a set of Implementation tasks to perform.

5.4   Develop an applicable CCN form and procedure for your project.

5.5   Contact selected vendors about exact schedule and delivery dates. Verify that all federal, state, and local requirements are being achieved. Sign contracts with all involved parties.

5.6   Document the Implementation Phase changes. Gather together and deliver warranties and applicable invoice copies. Review the results of the Implementation Phase.

5.7   Formally deliver the final product with its appropriate manuals and warranties. Terminate the Implementation Phase.

5.8   Describe how you would supervise contractor workers versus how you would supervise your other team members.

5.9   Describe how you would determine the optimum time to terminate the Implementation Phase.

5.10   Write a final report for your completed project.

5.11   Write a paper describing what you have learned from your project. Indicate how your effort has improved your technical and personal skills and how this effort has affected your choice of a professional career, if applicable. Revise your resume to reflect your newly acquired skills and experience and, if applicable, a change in your career direction.

chapter **6**

Project Management ▶

> **Management Functions**
> **Project Organizations**
> **Management Styles**
> **Project Staffing**
> **Project Reporting**
> **Gathering and Organizing Data**
> **Project and Program Control**

The Project Plan

Specifications and Reports

Modeling and System Design

1. What are the four key responsibilities of managers?

2. How do the role and responsibilities of a manager change over the phases of a project?

3. What is a typical organizational structure? What is the role of each group in the organization in project planning, performance, and implementation?

4. What are the two main styles of management, and how do they differ? What are the advantages and disadvantages of each?

5. How much should managers consider individual skills and interests in choosing people to assume certain roles in a project?

6. Why are performance reviews important, and what are the various ways in which people can be evaluated?

7. What are spreadsheets, and how can they be used by managers?

8. What are common databases, and how can they be used by businesses?

9. What are the responsibilities of project and program managers during the performance of a project or program? What is their role in controlling and reviewing the project or program?

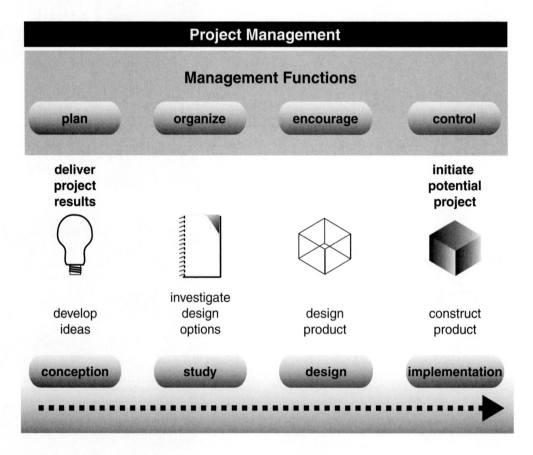

Nothing is impossible if you do not have to do it yourself.
Adapted from an A. H. Weiler New York Times *memo*

Individuals who possess a combination of management skills and technical knowledge are vital to the growth of business and industry, particularly for those organizations involved in highly technical fields.

This chapter focuses on the skills, requirements, and responsibilities associated with managing a project. The skills required to manage projects, programs, and people, combined with technical knowledge, are in great demand. Individuals who possess a combination of management skills and technical knowledge are vital to the growth of business and industry, particularly those organizations involved in highly technical fields. Much has been written on this subject (Archibald, 1992; Badiru, 1991; Badiru and Whitehouse, 1989; Chase, 1974; Farkas, 1970; Francks, Testa, and Winegardner, 1992; Lewis, 1991; Samaris and Czerwinski, 1971).

After you complete the study of this chapter, you should be able to accomplish the following:

- Identify management functions, organizations, and styles.
- Select people to staff a project.
- Read a spreadsheet.
- Gather and organize information necessary to monitor and control projects.
- Understand the components of project and program control.

Duncan (1996) observes that both leading and managing are required; one without the other is likely to produce poor results. Managing is primarily concerned with "consistently producing key results expected by stakeholders." That is, a successful manager contributes to the financial well-being of the organization. Leading, on the other hand, involves establishing direction, aligning, motivating and inspiring people—helping people to energize themselves to overcome barriers to change. Success requires the participation of all members of the team, but it remains the responsibility of managers to provide the resources needed for the team to succeed.

There are several important questions regarding management functions, organization, and styles. Each question will be presented below, with our opinion as to the answers. For each question, the general answer will be presented first, followed by a specific example from the activity center project (described in chapters 2 through 5) where this is applicable.

SECTION 6.1 MANAGEMENT FUNCTIONS

What is management, and what is the goal of management? These questions are discussed in this section.

*The group of people known as **managers** must plan projects, organize them, encourage workers, and control projects to ensure quality performance within the allotted time and budget.*

What Is Management? Management is the name given to the role of guiding and coordinating the activities of a project team. The group of people known as **managers** must plan projects, organize them, encourage workers, and control projects to ensure quality performance within the allotted time and budget. Here are some details of the four key management functions—plan, organize, encourage, and control:

Plan: Managers must ensure that a project moves smoothly and in its proper direction by planning the work to be accomplished and selecting the appropriate personnel to perform the work.

Organize: Managers must establish or enforce the use of standards for reporting and record-keeping in order to approve the purchase of materials, monitor contract performance, and control expenditures. Managers in an efficient organization need to examine reports and other records without expending a great amount of time and energy interpreting their content. Therefore, they need reports and other records presented in standard formats. If the formats are already established, managers merely have to enforce their use; but if these standards do not exist, the managers must develop them.

The manager of a well-organized project knows that written documentation is important. It is used to judge the status of a project as it develops. Managers must continually examine when to end a phase and when to initiate the next phase. They need to ask questions such as this: How much time should be allowed for project conception, study, design, and implementation? The longer the time a project requires—from conception through delivery—the higher the costs. Yet enough time must be allowed to correctly accomplish the requirements of each phase.

Managers must participate in the development of contractual documents because the final responsibility for fulfillment of the contract provisions falls upon them. Managers must also recognize their lack of knowledge in certain areas and so obtain the consulting services of specialists. Larger projects and programs often include an attorney and one or more technical advisors on their staff to help with legal and contractual issues.

It is the responsibility of managers to encourage team behavior on the part of their employees. They also need to promote training and growth on the part of employees.

Encourage: Employees work best when they work well together, and they need to feel that they are a part of the team. It is the responsibility of managers to encourage employees to perform as a team. Special courses are offered to technical managers to assist them in becoming more sensitive to the needs of employees and to guide them in a positive manner. Notice the use of the word *guide* rather than the word *direct*. As will be discussed in section 6.3, guiding workers is a more effective approach than directing workers. Brown (1992) offers the following suggestions for positive guidance:

- Treat people fairly and honestly.
- Give credit to those who assist you in any way.
- Be consistent—that is, let people know what to expect from you.
- Act in ways that avoid personal loss or embarrassment.
- Be a good listener.

It is generally agreed that the training and growth of employees has a positive effect on the growth of a company. However, there is a continuing debate in the field of management training regarding *how, when,* and *where* to encourage the growth potential of their employees. Some texts state that excellent technical specialists should be offered promotions that encourage them to increase their technical abilities. Other texts state that excellent technical persons can be trained to become good managers. The *how* can be accomplished by offering employees both technical and management courses. The *when* can occur during a formal performance review or during a meeting when the employee is reporting upon work status. The *where* may be company-sponsored training sessions at the office or company-paid courses at local colleges and universities.

Control: Managers monitor and control contract performance (tasks, schedules, and budgets) in order to see that the projects assigned to them are completed on time. They must also provide a quality product, perform within cost, and see that the people involved continue to work well and efficiently together.

Managers control expenditures, which include payments to subcontractors, project workers, and material suppliers. The manager of a project must know if actual expenditures exceed the estimated expenses and the effect of any budget overruns on the ability to complete the project. They must be able to judge the willingness and the ability of the lending or sponsoring financial institution to cover such additional expenses. The manager must continually compare the project expenditures with those funds allotted for the project accomplishment.

Managers approve the purchase of materials in order to ensure that any significant material purchase is at a price that agrees with the original estimates. Signature authority can be used to control these expenditures. It is necessary to decide when to insist on additional signatures and when that requirement leads to slowing down the project's progress. The decision as to the level of signature authority required may change as the project progresses from one phase to another.

The manager must become a skilled negotiator, as compromises are often necessary to achieve the overall project goals. In such situations, the manager may be acting more like a politician.

In order to guide the progress of a project, managers must have access to accurate and timely information, particularly regarding financial matters. The technology of today provides the capability for automated computation and revision of financial documents known as spreadsheets—the topic of section 6.5. Managers must verify the performance of previously authorized or approved labor, and they must obtain assurance that the material received from suppliers agrees with the description on the purchase order; that is, the received material is correct in quantity, cost, and quality. The manager must become a skilled negotiator, as compromises are often necessary to achieve the overall project goals. In such situations, the manager may be acting more like a politician.

What Is the Goal of Management?

The goal of management is to obtain the optimum quality output from individuals and groups by performing the four key management functions for the least investment of time, money, and other resources.

The emphasis placed on each of the four key management functions—plan, organize, encourage, control—shifts during the various phases of a project.

All four key management functions are important. However, the emphasis given to each of these functions may change from one phase of the project to another.

1.   The ideas created and the work accomplished during the Conception Phase will set the tone of the entire project. Thus, the manager must encourage all involved workers to be as creative as possible. Planning the remainder of this phase and the tasks, schedules, and budgets for the remaining three phases is also important but will be meaningless unless one or more creative solutions for the project are devised.

2.   The plans that evolve during the Study Phase will directly affect the direction and cost of the remainder of the project. Additional human and material resources are being applied at this time; more will be required later. Planning now becomes important so all tasks are accomplished and the project stays within budget and schedule. Encouragement is still important because new ideas often evolve during the Study Phase. Organizing for the next phase is growing in importance.

3.   The Design Phase must proceed as organized. A plan must be prepared for the Implementation Phase that is the most effective plan for the proposed design, even while the design details are being formulated. Control assumes greater importance because the cost of redesign will cause the cost of the project to increase greatly. Most designers need some supervision and encouragement so they will choose the optimum design details while not losing track of the goal of the entire project.

4.   Control is vital during the Implementation Phase. All theoretical work is now being converted to actual practice. This phase seldom proceeds smoothly without careful control of the tasks, schedules, and budgets being implemented. Workers must be encouraged to work within the plan or else promptly report any needed revisions to the manager. The manager must continually collect data and compare the results of the project work with the expected performance. When a difference between the planned or expected performance and the actual performance is detected, the manager must make the decision to modify the pattern of performance by adding or removing resources such as people, money, or equipment. Organizing now becomes reorganizing and should occur only when necessary. Additional planning should seldom occur except when a detail of the original plan proves to be impractical.

The following explanation shows how the key management functions were implemented for the activity center project, the example in chapters 2 through 5.

During the Conception Phase, Professor Hulbert encouraged the team and guided the initial planning. Organizing the team into small groups and controlling the time available were less important. The team members gradually took over the role of managing the project, with Professor Hulbert taking more of an advisory role as he realized that the team approach was operating successfully.

During the Study Phase, Professor Hulbert first emphasized planning, followed by encouraging the team members to focus upon potential designs. During the Design Phase, he tried to ensure that teams were effectively organized into groups capable of determining design details.

During the Implementation Phase, Professor Hulbert stressed the need to control the schedule and monitor costs carefully so the team would stay within the allotted time and budget. Much of the actual management was taken over by Roger, the project team leader. Later Roger was assisted by Alice, who oversaw the technical aspects of the activity center project.

Managing involves both people and paperwork. People prepare tasks, schedules, and budgets. Some people perform, other people evaluate, and other people ultimately accept the results—the final product. Much coordination is required, even for a project as small as the activity center.

SECTION 6.2   PROJECT ORGANIZATIONS

This section addresses the following three questions:

- How can people be organized to be productive and efficient?
- How are large projects and programs organized?
- How is a small project organized?

Organizations help managers fulfill the functions described in section 6.1. Organizations assist managers in handling personnel and organizing projects.

How Can People Be Organized to Be Productive and Efficient?   Any organization that expects to survive and grow after all its existing projects and programs are completed must consider the issue of preparing personnel for advancement. This is an important part of encouraging the personnel, who then will usually act as good team members and become both more productive and more efficient.

In many corporations, employees are organized into groupings known as **staff, line, and support.** *These categories describe whether the groups advise (staff), direct and perform (line), or provide support activities for other groups.*

For the organizational chart example shown in figure 6.1, Sales and Marketing (staff) advises the president and executive staff regarding customers and competition. The Program Office (staff) watches over programs being performed by the Research, Engineering, Manufacturing, and Quality Control (line) operations. Personnel and Purchasing (support) assist both the staff and line groups.

A firm can organize each one of their functional areas by product line, customer type, or some other type of grouping. For example, one major manufacturing firm is organized according

Figure 6.1 Typical organization chart showing staff, line, and support functions

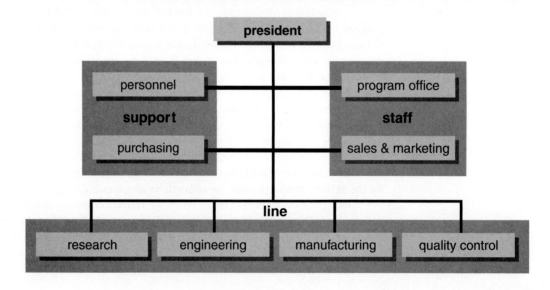

to type of product. It has a commercial division and a military or government division, each one of which has its own functional divisions (i.e., manufacturing, sales, marketing).

Projects can emerge from a firm's organizational structure or they may result from the good idea of a manager, worker, or consultant. Regardless of who was responsible for the initiation of a project, the project must be organized to encourage creativity and to promote the achievement of the goals and objectives of the firm. The next section discusses a range of organizational forms that are used for organizing projects and relating them to the parent organization.

How Are Large Projects and Programs Organized? The organization structure adopted for a particular project will depend upon the firm, the project goals, and the size of the project. Generally, it is recognized that there are three basic organizational forms for projects. Most projects are organized according to some variation of the standard organizational structures.

Stand-Alone Project Organization This type of project organization is sometimes referred to as a pure project structure. In the stand-alone organization, the project is organized similar to a small company. Figure 6.2 illustrates a program that consists of two projects organized according to the stand-alone configuration. In this organization structure, the project manager has full and total control of the project. Usually the project has a complete staff of workers. Therefore, it is unnecessary to "borrow" individuals from other projects or from the parent organization to complete the work. In small corporate organizations, the project manager for a stand-alone project will report directly to the highest level of management. Even in a large corporate environment, the manager of a stand-alone project will report at the vice president level. The organization of a stand-alone project is usually easy to understand—very flexible with decentralized decision making, and a strong sense of team spirit.

Some of the features that are considered to be benefits of the stand-alone organizational structure can become difficult to work within at some point in the life of a project. For example, the sense of team spirit is good at the beginning of a project, but can be a problem at the end of

Figure 6.2 Stand-alone project organization

a project's life. Why? The members of the team become so involved that they do not want to see the project end. Also, sometimes stand-alone projects result in overstaffing. The utilization of equipment that is already available in the parent firm is avoided; the project personnel "want" their own equipment.

Stand-alone projects are often focused on research with the intent of developing something new for the firm, such as a new product or a new production method. This project organizational structure is used by many large firms for writing proposals to potential customers. As an example, a major defense contractor rented a vacant building that had been a supermarket and assembled a team of several specialists to write a proposal to build a weapons system. The project was performed entirely "off site" (away from) the parent firm's buildings.

The Matrix Organization   Unlike the stand-alone project, the matrix organization is highly dependent upon the parent organization. The matrix organizational structure is a very popular form of configuration for firms wih many projects that have very similar labor requirements. Figure 6.3 illustrates the matrix form of project organization. Generally, in order to use this form of project organization effectively, there must be a project manager who is responsible for organizing and assisting in the implementation of the individual projects. Each project has its own project manager. The parent firm is organized in such a way that functional areas such as manufacturing, research, and engineering stand alone and provide a "home" for staff members who have the respective areas of expertise. The managers of the individual projects are provided with a budget to complete the work. It is the job of the project manager to negotiate with each functional area manager and obtain the type of expertise needed to complete the tasks on their project. For example, a project manager may estimate that she needs one thousand hours of software engineering work to complete the software development aspects of her project. The project manager would go to the Software Engineering Department manager and negotiate for one thousand hours of work from the functional manager. For each of the tasks a project manager needs completed, she will "buy time" (purchase services) from the appropriate functional group. At some point in time, it is possible in the matrix structure for the project manager to be the only full-time person working on the project.

Similar to the stand-alone project organization, the matrix organization has one individual who assumes the responsibility for completing the project on time and within budget, while

Figure 6.3 Matrix organization

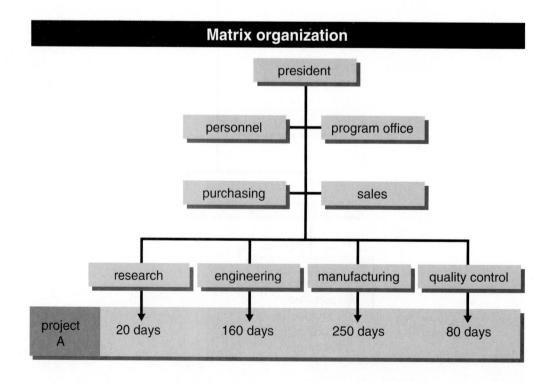

satisfying the customer requirements. The matrix organization has access to as many specialists and areas of expertise as the parent organization. From an overall corporate view, the matrix-management approach to managing projects allows the firm to realistically plan for and organize its resources.

There are some drawbacks in matrix-managed projects. The project manager is required to continually negotiate with functional managers in order to obtain the required personnel for a project. Individuals are not always available at exactly the time a project needs them. Scheduling is a major challenge in most matrix-managed projects. Project managers are sometimes competing for the same people, resulting in time-consuming politics and competition among the project managers.

The Embedded Project Organization   In some large organizations, it is common practice to integrate (embed) projects into the functional departments of the firm. For example, a project that involves some research may be assigned to the Vice President of Research and Development for completion. A project that has a focus on developing variations in existing products can be assigned to the Design Department. Projects organized according to their function are generally "picked up" (acquired) by the group that can provide the highest probability of successful completion. Generally, projects are embedded in the line functions. Figure 6.1 illustrates a typical organization chart.

Projects that are embedded in a functional organization can very easily draw upon the technical expertise of individuals employed within the organization. The biggest drawback to having a project embedded in a functional division is that corporate-assigned work generally takes precedence over the project tasks. Response to the client's needs may be less than enthusiastic within the organization. Most embedded projects are not in the mainstream of daily activity. On the other hand, when a project is very important to the corporation, embedding it in a functional division will ease the scheduling of necessary resources to get the work done on time. People with varying levels of expertise can focus on completing the work according to the customer's requirements.

Project Organization in Practice   It is a very rare instance in which a project is organized exactly as a stand-alone project, a matrix-organized project, or an embedded project. Most projects follow a mixed organizational format. Usually, well organized project managers adopt the features that promise successful completion of the project. For example, the manager of a project that requires substantial software development effort may employ ("bring on board") several software engineers for the life of the project. From the software development perspective, the project may appear to be organized as a stand-alone project. Other functions in the same project—such as manual writing and testing—may be performed by individuals whose time is negotiated with their functional manager. From the perspective of the manual-writing function, the project appears to be organized in a matrix format.

The president of a company must organize employees into efficient and effective groups and encourage the group managers to explore new paths for the corporation. The president must focus on the long-term goals of the corporation. The president should insist first on planning and must continually review plans to verify that they are either being followed or are being revised. Control is exercised only when a group does not meet its goals. This often leads to reorganizing, replacement of managers, or both. This management technique is known as **managing by exception.**

The president of a company and executive staff must focus on the long-term goals of the corporation and prepare long-range plans, as well as monitor whether current goals are being met.

Sales and Marketing personnel are responsible for moving the products into the marketplace, monitoring the marketplace, and investigating and planning new directions for the corporation. They must also encourage the line groups—particularly Research and Engineering—to investigate new technologies that will improve the corporation's position in the marketplace.

The Program Office personnel must plan, control, and verify the status of large projects and programs. They often support Sales and Marketing in the pursuit of new business opportunities.

The Personnel group, often known as Human Resources, retains employee records, including periodic evaluation of all employees. They can help employees no longer required on a project to find other work. They often provide employee guidance and encouragement in developing new skills via either in-plant seminars or local college and university courses and programs.

The Purchasing group buys needed materials, equipment, and supplies. Purchasing personnel should combine the purchase requisitions for common items needed across departments into a single purchase order. They can then negotiate the best price and delivery with suppliers and verify the receipt of the ordered material. They often monitor the Engineering and Manufacturing line groups to encourage the use of common items.

The line groups of Research, Engineering, Manufacturing, and Quality Control are responsible for the performance of day-to-day activities related to company projects. (Quality Control should report to the president to ensure top management attention.) Line managers organize, plan, encourage, and control their workers as the workers perform their assigned tasks.

Other support groups not shown on our simplified organization chart include Shipping and Receiving, Accounting, and the president's executive staff.

How Is a Small Project Organized?   The activity center project described in chapters 2 through 5 was a school project. It provides a good example of how a small project can be organized. See figure 6.4. The team leader reports to a teacher or dean who is responsible for encouraging, monitoring, and controlling the project as it develops. The teacher or dean is equivalent to a project office manager, whose role is to assure the school administrators that the project is progressing satisfactorily. The specialty consultants and construction company personnel support the involved student workers in the performance of the project. Such an organization is referred to as **project oriented.**

The activity center project team is organized as indicated in figure 6.5. The project team leader (Roger) has three types of groups reporting to him:

- Specialty consultants
- Student workers
- Construction companies

The specialty consultants include the following:

- Professional people who are registered to perform their profession within the state in which the work is to occur
- Tradespeople who are licensed with the state for their particular trade

Figure 6.4 Organizational chart for the activity center project

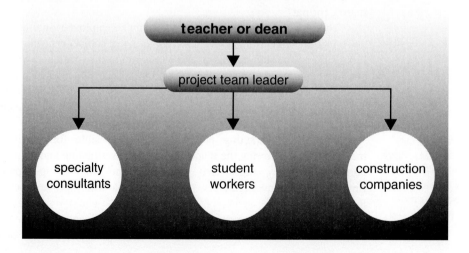

Organizational chart for the activity center project

teacher or dean

project team leader

specialty consultants

student workers

construction companies

Figure 6.5 Organizational details for the activity center project

Organizational details for the activity center project

```
                      ┌──────────────────┐
                      │ project team leader │
                      └──────────────────┘
         ┌────────────────┼────────────────┐
         ▼                ▼                ▼
    ┌─────────┐      ┌─────────┐      ┌─────────────┐
    │ specialty │      │ student │      │ construction │
    │ consultants │    │ workers │      │ companies │
    └─────────┘      └─────────┘      └─────────────┘
```

specialty consultants	student workers	construction companies
	surveyor's assistants	
	day laborers	
civil engineer*	carpenter's helpers	
environmental engineer*	electrician's helpers	construction equip. co.
licensed electrician	plumber's helpers	backhoe operator
licensed plumber	painter's helpers	tractor operator
licensed painter	floor installation workers	landscaping company
licensed rigger	masonry workers	gardeners
landscape designer	landscape workers	day laborers

*registered professional

They agree, via a contract, to assist the activity center team in those areas where their special skills and registrations or licenses are required.

The student workers are those personnel whose skills are required to perform the work scheduled. Most students are flexible enough to perform a variety of duties under the supervision of the professional people or tradespeople.

In this example, the construction companies consist of two separate organizations:

- The construction equipment company that provides

    Expertise in construction management

    Construction equipment

    Skilled workers who are capable of operating the construction equipment

- The landscaping company that provides

    Landscaping equipment

    Landscaping skills

    Skilled workers who are capable of implementing the landscaping design in a satisfactory manner

These companies are flexible enough to allow the students to perform many of the laborer duties under their supervision.

For the activity center project, the workers, laborers, and helpers are supplied from the student team wherever state and local laws allow. In this manner, students participating in the project gain experience in design, development, and construction.

SECTION 6.3   MANAGEMENT STYLES

How Do Managers Manage?   There are two different styles of management: **top-down management** and **bottom-up management.** Their advantages and disadvantages are described in this section. Most organizations apply a combination of these two styles.

In top-down management, a leader directs and gives orders; the result can be quick response to problems. In bottom-up management, all levels of workers participate in decision making; the result can be that all workers feel involved in the project.

1.   Top-down management is an organizational structure where the highest-ranking leader is personally involved in directing all other personnel. The leader directs through verbal orders and written directives. The leader does not expect or want to be challenged regarding decisions. This management approach can result in quick responses to information and to problems that occur. It is very effective on small projects where the workers report directly to the manager. However, on large projects, the leader may not be able to provide the level of attention needed and may lack enough detail to be efficient or effective. Workers' morale may often be poor because the workers do not feel involved.

2.   Bottom-up management is an organizational structure where the lowest level of personnel offers suggestions that are gathered by those individuals on the next level of hierarchy. This next level of managers examines the ideas of the workers, coordinates these ideas with other managers, inserts ideas of their own, and recommends these coordinated ideas to the next level of managers. This management approach is slow in response to information available. However, it may be more efficient and effective in the long run. Because the workers feel involved, morale is usually high and, as Brown indicates (1992), good human relations are crucial to change and improvement:

- Getting good information from people requires their cooperation
- Good ideas come from people who are properly motivated
- Receptivity to new ideas is more easily generated when people feel part of the decision-making process

For any style of management, managers must be excellent listeners. Managers must gather, absorb, and disseminate information in order to contribute to and control a project.

For any style of management, managers must be excellent listeners. Managers must gather, absorb, and disseminate information in order to contribute to and control a project. Managers need to work to reduce or eliminate dissension, strife, and perhaps even hostility among team members. Managers need to analyze significant differences of opinion to avoid alienating individuals and offer viable solution options. This technique is known as **conflict resolution.**

Conflicts may occur over the following issues:

- Specifications
- Schedules
- Budgets
- Tasks
- Activity priorities
- Resource allocation
- Goals
- Expectations
- Technical approach
- Personnel availability
- Personality differences
- Administrative procedures

Archibald (1992, p. 99) discusses the types of conflicts that must be resolved by the project manager:

1. Conflicts over project priorities
2. Conflicts over administrative procedures

3. Conflicts over technical opinions and performance trade-offs

4. Conflicts over people resources

5. Conflicts over costs

6. Conflicts over schedules

7. Personality conflicts

There may also be an issue regarding how much responsibility is assigned to the project manager, who may not have the authority to resolve a conflict. Such a problem must be resolved with those to whom the project manager reports.

Project managers can become diverted from their technical tasks when they must focus upon the supervision of people. Project managers must learn to continually weigh how much time they can invest in the technical details of a project and how much time they must allot to personnel problems.

One central role of the manager is to effectively resolve any conflicts that occur during the implementation of a project.

Managers can ignore the conflict for a while and see if it resolves itself. They can also force a resolution by insisting on a particular solution. One way of resolving conflicts that involves the team members is to perform the following actions:

• Request memos describing each point of view

• Convene a meeting

• Obtain an agreement for an acceptable compromise

This allows all involved some degree of recognition of their ideas.

During the conflict-resolution process, the manager must continually remind individuals that everyone is a member of the same team. The overall goal must be to effectively use the project's resources to complete the project on time and within the allocated budget. Another goal is to create an environment that results in all persons feeling like they have "won." (The socalled win-win situation is the best result possible.)

It is important to remember that there would be no conflict if the people involved did not care about the project. Conflicts can have their benefits if they are handled properly. As a result of successful conflict mediation, there may be a greater understanding of the project by everyone involved.

The activity center project was managed using primarily a bottom-up approach. Most of the time Roger discussed with the other students, in advance, the options for the project that he and Professor Hulbert had worked through together. Sometimes Roger would announce how the work should now proceed.

Note that the team was usually given the opportunity to react to Roger's decisions. In this manner, the team members felt involved and could better perceive the reasoning behind all major decisions. Team members also had a better view of how their work related to the work of others and to the overall project. This primarily bottom-up approach leads to a more efficient and effective result, except where personality clashes occur.

The effort of avoiding clashes and the large amount of responsibility given to one individual are reasons why many technically oriented persons prefer to avoid management responsibilities and concentrate on the technical effort. However, effective handling of conflicts is a key responsibility of managers.

SECTION 6.4 PROJECT STAFFING

This section focuses on how to staff a project for the most effective use of the available personnel and how the manager controls the assignment of staff members. Two questions are discussed:

• How are people selected to perform the work involved?

• How and when should people be evaluated?

Each of the four phases of a project needs a different combination or "mix" of skills on the part of the staff. The needs for creators, planners, performers, laborers, and administrators are also described in this section. Conflicts and their resolution are discussed in detail.

Managers are responsible for locating properly skilled personnel who are capable of assisting in the implementation of their project. Sometimes existing employees recommend friends or former colleagues. More often, a manager must either advertise for the personnel needed or use an employment agency. First the manager prepares a job description detailing the responsibilities and related skills needed. The job description may indicate the level of management to whom the future employee will report and the type of people the future employee may supervise. Resumes of potential employees' skills and interests are sent to the manager for review. Those people who appear most qualified based on their resumes are called in for a face-to-face interview. Based on these interviews, the manager makes a final selection.

In the assignment of tasks, the work preferences of individual personnel should be considered. However, to counterbalance this desirable goal, costs and schedules on a project must be controlled, and the required work must be performed and completed properly. All those working within an organization or working on a project must perform as members of a team rather than as individuals concerned with only their part in the effort. From time to time, the mix of skills of individuals within the organization will change; revising this mix will need to be managed effectively and on a continuing basis (Connor and Lake, 1994).

*Managers must be able to assess which people are best at what types of tasks and sense people whose skills can develop while working on the project. The manager must also be able to recognize how people will work together. These managerial capabilities are known as **people skills.***

The manager must be able to sense which people are best at what types of tasks and assess people whose skills are most likely to develop as the project planning, performance, and control progresses. The manager must also be able to recognize how personalities interact, and thus assign people so that they interact in a positive and constructive manner. These managerial capabilities are known as **people skills.** The development of the team starts with the manager and that manager's organizational abilities. (The issue of the role of the manager in resolving conflict was discussed in section 6.3.)

How Are People Selected to Perform the Work Involved?

People have different skills and interests. They may be creators, planners, performers, laborers, or administrators. Creators and planners are essential in the early phases of projects; performers, laborers, and administrators are instrumental in the later phases of projects.

How Are People Selected to Perform the Work Involved?   Each person has certain skills, capabilities, and interests. One person may like to build, another may prefer to plan, others like to negotiate, some enjoy organizing, and others prefer to supervise. People are selected based on how their training, skills, and interests fit with the needs of the project and which phase of the project is in progress—as noted in chapters 2 through 5.

Individuals may be grouped into a variety of categories according to skills and capabilities. Here are some of these categories:

- Creators
- Planners
- Performers
- Laborers
- Administrators

Each phase of a project requires a different combination of categories (see figure 6.6).

Creators: For the Conception Phase of a project, the necessary skills are those of imagination and vision. Creators or conceivers are people who can think about a problem and envision one or more solutions. Sometimes these people are also capable of developing the details of a concept. Other times, such people must transfer their ideas to the performers.

Planners: For the Study Phase, the most desirable of the proposed projects are to be developed into potential design projects. Planners are now very important to the eventual success of a project. Planners, such as cost estimators, like to work with numbers and analyze them. They enjoy planning the details of a proposed project and preparing and analyzing estimates.

Performers: For the Design and Implementation Phases, persons who enjoy working with details and coordinating a variety of activities are the key to success. Performers are often people who are very comfortable with developing and implementing the ideas of others.

Figure 6.6 Types of skills needed for each project phase

PPCP 6

They are usually people who enjoy the detail work. They are rewarded by observing the fruits of their efforts in the form of structures, equipment, software, or procedures.

Laborers: For the Implementation Phase, those persons who enjoy working with their hands and minds, while watching a project convert from paper to reality, are vital. Laborers are individuals who enjoy working primarily with their hands on physical activities.

Administrators: Monitoring and control of the overall project requires individuals who can visualize and remember the final goal. Administrators are often people who are excellent at judging performance and guiding the planners and performers. They are usually skilled at gathering records, evaluating results, and recognizing problems, thus sensing when corrective action is necessary. Working with the manager, they must carefully monitor the forward movement of a project from conception through implementation. They must simultaneously be able to compare the actual work being accomplished with the contracted tasks, schedules, and budgets, as discussed in section 7.5.

Which of these groups of persons is most important to a manager? At first, the creators are very important. In later phases, the planners and performers grow in importance. Once the Conception Phase is well underway, the administrators become very important. When there is work to be accomplished, the laborers are indispensable. Actually, this question is similar to asking, Which is more important—the heart, the brain, or the lungs? The answer is that all are needed and that they must work together as a team.

In some cases, managers have to be personnel developers to persuade individuals to accept different roles for a particular project. This way employees act to fulfill the needs of the team and, at the same time, they have the opportunity to develop new skills and become more flexible and more valuable to the company.

Where several projects are in progress at the same time, there should be a labor pool of employees—the team—that is maintained by a company to avoid continuous hiring and layoffs. A manager must examine the labor pool for the best combination of individuals to perform the tasks in progress or the tasks about to be initiated on a project. Sometimes it is necessary to convince employees of the importance of a team effort so they agree to work on tasks to promote the needs of a project, although the tasks may not match their immediate interest and skill levels. A manager who also enjoys being a personnel developer is often best at this effort. Acquiring new skills encourages employees to become more flexible, more valuable, and more enthusiastic.

Managers may need to obtain the services of vendors to assist when the team members do not have the necessary skills or qualifications to complete the project. Such vendors may be involved in the Design Phase and perhaps also in the Implementation Phase.

The vendors who are chosen to implement the project may not necessarily be the lowest bidders, although in many cases the lowest bidder is chosen.

1. There are times when the lowest bidder may not be the highest in quality and dependability.

2. The lowest bidders may have earned their way onto a bidder's list because they had established themselves as dependable and quality suppliers.

One or more members of a project team may be assigned to investigate potential vendors for their qualifications and recommend which should be used.

How and When Should People Be Evaluated?

Personnel are entitled to know how they are performing. Therefore, managers must evaluate their personnel at regular intervals, via performance reviews, so the employees have an opportunity to improve their performance, attitude, and self-image. In a similar way, managers are judged by their superiors; presidents are judged by the company stockholders.

Managers must evaluate their personnel at regular intervals, via performance reviews, so the employees have an opportunity to improve their performance, attitude, and self-image.

There are two types of performance reviews related to projects and programs: **contract performance reviews** and **personnel performance reviews**. The terms used vary from one company to another.

1.   A contract performance review involves those who are working on the contract and evaluates how satisfactorily they are fulfilling the terms of the contract and how well they are satisfying the customer. This type of review may be written by an individual who is responsible for the entire contract. Often such a review may result in a memorandum being placed in the personnel file of the involved management individuals. Such a memorandum may be one of congratulations for work well performed; it may be a reprimand for neglecting an important part of the contract or for offending a client.

2.   A personnel performance review involves each individual working for a company and that individual's supervisor. It is usually a formal document with a number of topics. The review may involve more than one contract and more than one supervisor. A separate review may be prepared by each of the involved supervisors, or these supervisors may condense their opinions into one document. Each person is judged on the basis of skills and on work as a team member. Personnel performance reviews normally occur regularly at three-, six-, or twelve-month intervals, and also when a significant change occurs in the individual's performance or status.

Pay increases for an individual are usually decided on the basis of performance as reported in both formal and informal reviews. They are recommended by the individual's immediate supervisor and usually require the approval of the personnel department.

People are usually offered promotions when an opening occurs that requires greater responsibility or use of skills on the part of the individual. A promotion may be accompanied by a pay increase or that increase may be withheld until the individual demonstrates the ability to perform in the new position.

One of the major drawbacks of using the matrix style of organization for a project is that the project manager does not evaluate the employees who are brought in from the functional areas. The manager of the functional area (i.e., marketing, engineering) generally evaluates the staff for raises and merit recognition. The employee works for one person, but is evaluated by another. This situation often results in unhappy employees who may look elsewhere for a job.

For projects such as the activity center, pay increases and promotions are not applicable. Students are learning to work together while they gain new skills—both technical and group-related.

SECTION 6.5   PROJECT REPORTING

Well-trained managers are those who have learned to sense when sufficient factors have changed to require project redirection. Information in reports allows managers to know when redirection may be necessary.

Managers need reports so they can choose effective directions for projects. They need accurate and timely information. Managers must realize that, as work on a project progresses, information may change. Well-trained managers are those who have learned to sense when sufficient factors have changed to require project redirection. Reports are often prepared and presented in the form of spreadsheets.

A spreadsheet is the presentation of an organized arrangement of data in matrix (tabular) form. Spreadsheets contain elements organized into rows (horizontal) and columns (vertical) of information. The individual elements or entries are known as cells. It is easy for people to revise the data

Figure 6.7 Spreadsheet with actual expenditures for six months

Spreadsheet with actual expenditures for six months

month category:	jan	feb	mar	apr	may	jun	totals by category
rent	70	70	70	70	70	70	420
utilities	26	28	29	24	18	15	140
auto	30	32	27	36	41	39	205
food	274	241	269	257	272	245	1558
totals by month	400	371	395	387	401	369	2323

when the spreadsheet is prepared on a computer, and computer programs can quickly manipulate and perform a variety of mathematical operations on those data (Shim and Siegel, 1984).

Expenses may be presented in tabular form. As an example, when a spreadsheet is constructed using a computer program, the rows can be added automatically across (horizontally). Also, the columns can be added automatically down (vertically). Thus, as an entry is changed in one or more data cells, new totals are available quickly and automatically. The updating of the spreadsheet cells must be accomplished on a regular and timely basis if spreadsheets are to be useful for project monitoring. Examine the spreadsheet in figure 6.7; it contains six months of information about actual expenditures.

On the example spreadsheet, the computer software computes the Totals by Month column information and Totals by Category row information. Thus, any changes entered into the data-entry cells cause all the Totals by Month and Totals by Category cells to be corrected to reflect the newly entered data.

This matrix of four rows and six columns contains 4 × 6, or 24 cells. One can quickly determine that $241 was spent on food during February and $29 was spent on utilities during March. Also, one can quickly determine that the total expenses for June were $369 and that the total cost of utilities for the six months was $140.

Computer spreadsheets are important tools for project managers. Spreadsheets summarize the financial status of a project. Computers allow spreadsheets to be updated quickly and easily. Results are easy to use and can be transferred instantaneously to all those involved in a project.

During the performance of a project, as actual information becomes available, this new information can be entered into the spreadsheet program, replacing the estimated information. As each item of information is entered, the computer software recomputes the spreadsheet and presents new column and row totals on the screen, providing an immediate and up-to-date review of the project status. This information may be printed by the computer equipment as hard copy and distributed to those who are concerned with the financial status of the project. If preferred, this information may be offered via such media as files transferred onto a local area network (LAN), e-mail, or Internet for appropriate personnel to display on their computer screens.

Properly organized information is easy to use, understand, and change. It is easy to examine entries and compare them with previously generated data. In the planning stages of a project, a tabulation of the estimated income and expenses for the project is prepared. This tabulation is known as a balance sheet. A balance sheet that consists of estimates can be automatically updated with actual information on income and expenses, as is discussed below.

Modern computers contain large amounts of memory, and computer programs are flexible. Most programs can be modified by technical personnel to fit the needs of a given company and project. For the activity center project, it was necessary for Manuel to devise a specialized spreadsheet program (Oberlender, 1993) in which data could be quickly entered and displayed, and the cost differentials immediately computed and displayed. Further, it was necessary for Manuel to obtain accurate data weekly from both the Northeastern University Treasurer's Office and from Accounting personnel. Normally, such data are supplied at the end of the month. For the activity center project, that would have been too late for the necessary cost-control requirements.

The problem with updating computer spreadsheets is typically obtaining accurate and up-to-date information to enter into the computer program.

The most frustrating problem for any project group is the need for up-to-date information to be entered into the spreadsheet. The problem is seldom one of computer time and availability. The problem is obtaining data and having the data approved before the information is entered on the spreadsheet. The "garbage in, garbage out" principle suggests that it is better to wait for verified, final information rather than to permit someone to enter interim information that might be incomplete and misleading.

Figure 6.8 A simplified "estimates versus actuals" spreadsheet

A simplified "estimates versus actuals" spreadsheet

		jan	feb	mar	apr	may	jun	totals by category:
				month category:				**totals by category:**
estimates:	rent	70	70	70	70	70	70	420
actuals:	rent	70	70	70	70	70	70	420
difference:	rent							0
estimates:	utilities	25	30	30	25	25	20	155
actuals:	utilities	26	28	29	24	18	15	140
difference:	utilities							−15
estimates:	auto	30	35	30	35	35	35	200
actuals:	auto	30	32	27	36	41	39	205
difference:	auto							+5
estimates:	food	275	240	270	260	270	245	1560
actuals:	food	274	241	269	257	272	245	1558
difference:	food							−2

	jan	feb	mar	apr	may	jun	totals by month:
estimates	400	375	400	390	400	370	2335
actuals	400	371	395	387	401	369	2323
differences							−12

As noted above, spreadsheets can also be designed to include both the estimated expenditures from the earlier (Conception, Study, and Design) phases, and the actual expenditures as they occur during the Implementation Phase. Figure 6.8 is an example spreadsheet where **estimates** are compared to **actuals**. (Note that estimated values often end in either a 5 or a 0.)

Managers monitoring "estimates versus actuals" can quickly determine if their budgets are within the limits acceptable to them. If there is concern that expenses are exceeding estimates, then the "estimates versus actuals" information can be monitored weekly instead of monthly.

Another solution for immediate expenditure information is to enter data that can be provided by those individuals who are incurring project expenses. These people may be the ones ordering the materials, receiving the materials, receiving the actual bills, or paying these bills. The entries, including labor expenditure entries, should be coordinated through one person and, if possible, coded to note the information source. Why? The answer is that expected costs may change once the vendor's bill arrives. No matter when and how data are entered, every effort must be made to ensure that the data are timely and, at least for the moment, provide enough information to allow for a general control of expenditures.

SECTION 6.6   GATHERING AND ORGANIZING DATA

In this section, application of spreadsheets to monitor and control a variety of data is discussed. Document formats may be standard or unique—that is, prepared especially for the project. The use of electronic databases is covered. Finally, an overview of both corporate and government reporting requirements is given. Additional details on these topics are available in chapters 7 and 8, and appendix F.

The use of a computer provides a fast and reliable method of processing different types of business documents, such as these:

- Personnel records
- Vendor data

- Purchase orders
- Invoices

There are also technical records, such as these:

- Engineering change orders (ECOs) and notices (ECNs)
- Equipment test and evaluation reports
- Development and evaluation procedures

Such documents may contain large amounts of written material—text. However, these documents also contain numerical data that might be extracted for other uses via spreadsheets.

Spreadsheets are valuable documents because a trained user can quickly view essential information. Therefore, many types of documents can be presented in spreadsheet format, such as these:

- Time sheets
- Payroll reports
- Profit-and-loss statements

Predetermined sets of software instructions can be written so that computer programs automatically insert the data entries from one type of spreadsheet into other types of spreadsheets.

Standard document formats may be purchased or a special document format may be developed. See appendix F. A standard document may be modified to suit the needs of a project. As an example, Manuel modified several spreadsheet programs for the activity center project.

Business operations require the preparation, review, and retention of various types of information that relate to individuals, company projects, and the company. Much of this information is available from existing databases, which are collections of related information.

Business operations require the preparation, review, and retention of various types of information that relate to individuals, company projects, and the company. Before computers became cost effective and user friendly, this information was prepared manually (by hand), forwarded to other parts of the company, and stored in several places. Revisions to such information were time-consuming and expensive. Often, changes in information were either not forwarded to the correct place or were not recorded. Reports were prepared that overlapped and often contained conflicting information because of the inaccuracy and age of the data.

Large quantities of both numeric data and text can now be stored and quickly accessed. Advances in both hardware and software capabilities have led to the design of an approach to information storage and retrieval known as a **database.** A database is a collection of related information that can be accessed by a variety of users and that can be updated—modified with later information—as required.

The cost of data storage is decreasing significantly every year so that the size and flexibility of databases continue to grow. A database can be accessed and revised—shared—by authorized individuals. Such a database is known as a **common database.** Reports can be prepared quickly via this common database.

There is information that government agencies insist must be established and retained, such as the following:

- Company income
- Payroll data
- Rent (occupancy) information
- Materials expenditures
- Travel data

These records are provided to government agencies on request or on a routine basis. The agencies may then verify the information by comparing it with the data supplied by others. As an example, the Internal Revenue Service (IRS) compares the company-supplied payroll data with an employee's personal income tax report data.

Figure 6.9 Typical
common database
content

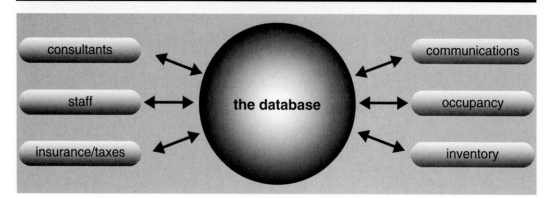

Also, there is information that the company may wish to retain for its own needs, such as the following:

- Evaluating the work that was accomplished
- Preparing cost and schedule estimates for later projects

Using this information, company executives are able to prepare more precise cost estimates and schedules based on the company's past experiences. These documents increase the company's chances of being awarded other contracts while remaining profitable. On the other hand, a bad experience on a certain kind of project may cause the executives to decide not to bid on a project that has similar characteristics.

The common database and related documents for a project might include information regarding the following (see figure 6.9):

- Consultants: individuals hired for brief periods of time for their specialized skills
- Staff: employees, who represent the continuing skills of the company
- Insurance/taxes: liability, workers' compensation, sales, and unemployment taxes
- Communications: mailings, telephone, and copying expenses
- Occupancy: rent, utilities, and maintenance
- Inventory: materials and supplies used while operating a business.

Other information such as the following may also be of value:

- Potential vendors: names of companies that offer skills that the team does not possess
- Office supply sources: names of companies that offer needed supplies at reasonable prices

It is customary to allow modification of the database to be performed by one person or by a very restricted group of persons. The reasoning is that these data should be changed only by someone who is able to verify that the entries are correct and appropriate. It is also customary to control access to the database so it can be used only by persons authorized by the team leader. Thus, it should be difficult for competitors to gain access to information.

A common database would have information useful for all departments in the corporation, such as personnel data or financial records. However, typically not all data can be accessed by all departments.

Leaders of a corporation must be able to extract data from a common database. They want the common database organized to provide appropriate data for the following groups in the corporation:

- Project-control personnel, to ensure that all contracts are profitable
- Accounting personnel, to monitor the project and corporate financial status
- Personnel in the Personnel Department, to maintain employee records

Figure 6.10 Typical structure of a corporate database

- Facilities personnel, to monitor the cost and usage of the buildings and grounds
- Purchasing personnel, to monitor vendors so they can evaluate their availability, cost, and performance

Records must be designed to provide corporate executives with data in a form that is of value to them.

Figure 6.10 examines how a corporate database could be constructed using the Personnel Department as an example. Note that each of the personnel records for the three people shown in figure 6.10 is identified by a unique number, in this case, their social security numbers. These records are protected by an **access code** so that only authorized personnel can extract information regarding employees. If the corporate officers do not wish their own personal records to be accessed by the authorized personnel, then their records can be further coded to allow access only by a specified corporate officer such as the head of the Personnel or Human Resources Department. Additional detail is given in appendix F.

Assume that Alfred T. Anderson is a salaried employee at a construction company and that he is working part of the time assisting Marketing in searching for new business and part of the time working on the activity center project. The supervisor responsible for the Marketing activity will approve Alfred's charges to his efforts for Marketing. The supervisor of the activity center project will examine Alfred's charges to that project. These two supervisors, or people working for them, must have access to a portion of the database for Alfred T. Anderson.

Employees usually submit work-related data weekly, either using a completed time sheet or time card. These hard-copy time data must be approved by someone—ordinarily by their immediate supervisor. Once approved, these data are entered into the common database.

Prior to the beginning of a project effort, numbers are assigned to each task in that project. These numbers are known as **charge numbers.** As individuals work on a specific task, they record the number of hours worked, along with its assigned charge number, on their weekly time card.

Alfred is issued one charge number for his work on the activity center project and another charge number for his work in Marketing in searching for new business. Because he is working on two unrelated projects, two different supervisors must approve his time charges before they are entered into the common database for automatic data processing.

In addition to the Marketing and activity center project groups, Accounting and Personnel both need access to Alfred's time charges. Accounting prepares his paycheck and Personnel must determine when he has used his allotted vacation or sick leave.

Although Accounting personnel must have access to the payroll portion of Alfred's record, they have no need to know about his personal nonpayroll data. Restricted access codes can be used to prevent unauthorized persons from gaining access to other files and items within

Figure 6.11 Information flow of time charges into database

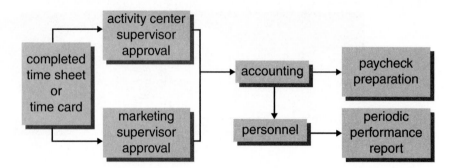

Information flow of time charges into database

Alfred's record. The Personnel Department normally has access to all of Alfred's record so it can maintain a continuous record of all aspects of his employment history and his contributions to the company. The time-charge information flow is shown in figure 6.11.

Additional details on various records and their interaction are given both in chapter 8 and in appendix F.

SECTION 6.7   PROJECT AND PROGRAM CONTROL

No matter what the status of the effort, or what the latest problems and changes being considered might be, it is the continuing responsibility of the manager to realize that any moment in time is but a small part of the overall work. The manager must continually consider how the present problems and plans affect the entire effort. The manager must not become so lost in the day-to-day work that the primary goals and objectives of the project are forgotten: If you are in a forest, you may not be able to see all the trees.

The manager must continually consider how the present problems and plans affect the entire effort. The manager must not become so lost in the day-to-day work that the primary goals and objectives of the project are forgotten.

On small projects, the manager is directly involved with controlling day-to-day activities and continually monitoring a project's performance.

On larger projects, a project office is established to oversee the proper completion of tasks, adherence to schedules, and performance within budgets. Some person, or group of persons, must be assigned to continually monitor and control project performance. For large projects and all programs, this group of people often has the title of program office. These people perform the following tasks:

- Gather data on task, schedule, and budget, and monitor the total effort

- Analyze and assess progress as compared with the projected schedule and budget

- Recommend the revision of plans where progress is unsatisfactory

- Identify special accomplishments that should be recognized publicly

The program office may also consist of a larger group of people that includes specialists who are responsible for judging the technical work of contributors. Typically, the program office has monitoring responsibility only, without the authority to direct or control the daily operations of the people performing the work. That authority is usually delegated to the line organizations performing the assigned work.

Note that a project office usually has more authority and control over small projects than does a program office. The extent of control given to either the project office or program office depends on the amount of authority and responsibility delegated by corporate management. It is the responsibility of management personnel (corporate, project office, or program office) to monitor and/or control the work that a group of people is to accomplish. It is the responsibility of workers to accomplish this work.

Figure 6.12 Monitoring and Control

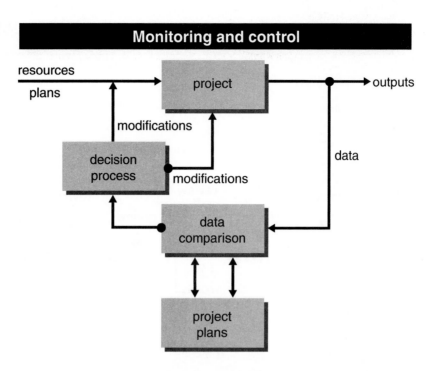

Control of a project or program is accomplished when the project managers or program managers issue instructions that ensure better understanding, coordination, and follow-through by the workers.

To ensure control, the project or program manager issues directives—orders. These orders are usually in the form of new and revised task descriptions, including staff, schedule, budget assignments, and charge numbers. Control of a project or program is accomplished when the project managers or program managers issue instructions that ensure better understanding, coordination, and follow-through by the workers.

The monitoring and control process can be viewed as an elementary control system. As illustrated in figure 6.12, the control process starts with collecting data from the project. The progress being made on the project, as reflected by the data, is then compared to a standard or a project plan. The results of these comparisons are evaluated by the project manager or assigned senior team members. A decision is made either to modify the work plan or leave it alone. If the decision is to modify the work plan, then the changes are recorded on the project plan so that, at the next review, the correct comparisons can be made.

The project initiation meeting is the name often given to the first meeting of those who will be involved with a project. This is the time to acquaint all of those persons on the project with where they fit into the overall effort. Written task descriptions (see section 7.2 and appendix B), schedules, budgets, and charge-number lists should be delivered to the invited participants prior to the meeting. The project plan and schedule must be presented so that all participants know where they will start and what is expected of them. Questions are often asked; not all of these questions will have immediate answers, however.

Managers typically review projects in portions, such as tasks and subtasks. Projects may be reviewed more frequently when the manager feels that such reviews are necessary.

Managers must review the total project or program periodically. Reviews for a large project may include only team leaders or supervisory personnel. These people then report the results of the meeting to their team members.

A project is typically reviewed in portions, such as tasks and subtasks. It may be reviewed more frequently when the manager feels that such reviews are necessary. Think of the changes in a project as small as the activity center project. During its performance, the amount of available money changed. Also, the sequence of the work to be accomplished had to be changed to match the schedules of contractors, suppliers, and student workers.

Reviews should begin during the Conception Phase, at that point when progress can be measured or when decisions must occur regarding changes in direction. Reviews should always occur at the end of a phase so that all persons involved in the next phase may become aware of what has been decided, what was accomplished, and what questions remain to be explored. Persons presenting information at these reviews must be well prepared to answer questions from the meeting attendees. These persons should be flexible in presenting their planned presentations;

Figure 6.13
Sequence for project
reviews

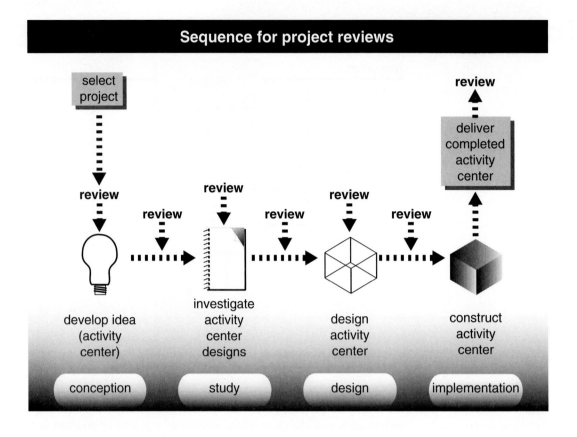

often a question may lead to an unexpected path of discussion. The project personnel participating in the review should speak in a neutral manner so that they will not appear defensive of their views but are willing to accept constructive criticism.

A typical project sequence, showing when reviews might occur for the activity center, is given in figure 6.13.

It is important to schedule a review after some milestone in a project has been achieved. Many companies schedule their project reviews according to the number of weeks after program start or according to some fixed time period such as the end of the month. Performing reviews at fixed time intervals is convenient for scheduling the review process, but it often leads to redundant reports and duplication of effort. Focus on the project deliverables. Schedule project reviews at points in the project where adjustment in resources may be required. This approach is much more effective than specifying a weekly, monthly, or quarterly review.

Managers have financial control of projects. They need to

- *Ensure that funds are available when needed*
- *Ensure that work is completed within the established budget*

The responsibility for the project or program finances is normally assigned to its manager. These responsibilities include the following:

- Ensure that funds are available when needed.
- Plan in advance so a budget surplus exists should extra funds be required later.
- Establish a cost center where cost control can be performed.
- Delegate financial responsibility for daily or weekly control to assigned personnel.
- Ensure that the work is completed on time and within the established budget.

Managers are judged by their ability to complete the effort on time, within budget, to the preagreed specifications, and to the satisfaction of the client. At the completion of a project, the manager must generate enough earnings or profit so that the company can survive to bid on other contracts.

When a project is nearing completion, there is a large amount of documentation, known as paperwork, that needs to be prepared, distributed, and filed for future reference. The project is not complete until the paperwork is finished.

Typical documentation includes the following:

- Engineering and manufacturing reports
- Test reports
- Instruction manuals
- Financial statements
- Cost/volume/profit analyses
- Overhead and borrowing costs distribution
- Return-on-investment report

These and other contracted reports or company-required reports must be prepared and reviewed by the manager's staff. Therefore, funds must be reserved to pay for the generation and review of this documentation. See chapters 7 and 8.

CHAPTER OBJECTIVES SUMMARY

Now that you have finished this chapter. you should be able to:

1. Explain the four key responsibilities of managers.
2. Discuss how the role of manager changes over the phases of a project.
3. Describe a typical organizational structure, which includes staff, line, and support personnel. Discuss the role of each group in the organization in project planning, performance, and implementation.
4. Describe the two main styles of management and the advantages and disadvantages of each.
5. Discuss ways managers consider skills and interests of individuals in choosing people to assume certain roles in a project.
6. Explain why performance reviews are important. Describe criteria on which people can be evaluated.
7. Define spreadsheets and explain how they are useful to managers.
8. Define common databases and explain how they are used by businesses.
9. Outline the responsibilities of project and program managers during the performance of a project and program. Describe how they can review and control the project and program.

EXERCISES

6.1   Talk to students who have performed technical work during the summer or while on a cooperative education assignment to determine why management is necessary. Determine how the organization is divided into staff and line groups, and how consultants are used. Ask them about and then list the positives and negatives regarding management at the locations where they were working. Also have them analyze how an improvement in management could have saved time and money.

6.2   Obtain or sketch an organization chart from the students interviewed in exercise 6.1 above. Identify the staff and line groups.

6.3   List any specialty consultants involved in exercise 6.1 above. Identify whether they were from within the organization or were hired as outside consultants. Identify their specialties.

6.4   From exercise 6.1, describe whether the management practiced top-down management, bottom-up management, or a combination of both. Note your opinion of the advantages and disadvantages of the management style applied as related to the work being managed.

6.5   Develop a performance review document that could be applied to evaluate the work of an employee. Also prepare three additional parts: one for a professional employee, one for a laborer, and another for a consultant.

6.6   Examine pay raises from the point of view of both the employee and management. For this exercise, ignore the effects of inflation. For a person who works for the same company for more than twenty years, calculate the salary of that employee at the end of that time, assuming annual 5 percent pay raises.

6.7   Discuss how you, as a manager, would react to an employee who had not taken advanced courses and yet expected a promotion or a significant pay increase. Also discuss how much more capability you would expect from an employee who had received 5 percent pay raises every year for twenty years.

6.8   Examine the skills of an entering technical employee. Discuss when you would consider that employee to have earned a promotion. For exercise 6.1 above, obtain a list of technical positions, their titles, and (if possible) a job description.

6.9   Examine at least two spreadsheet computer programs. Describe the advantages and disadvantages of each, particularly regarding how each spreadsheet is updated and how that updating affects the common database and presentation of estimates versus actuals.

6.10   Discuss how you would react to a project office or program office regarding how closely their members would want to control your daily work. Then discuss how you as a member of one of those offices would react if the daily work was not being accomplished on time and within budget.

6.11   Assume you are assigned the duties of a project manager. Develop a two-part plan to
   1. improve your managerial skills
   2. maintain your technical skills

Also realize that your assignment may require an extensive amount of your working day.

6.12   Assume you are assigned the duties of a project manager. The program manager in charge of your project directs you to focus on efficient and timely project completion. At the same time, your department manager directs you to apply your team members in such a manner that their technical skills increase. Develop a plan that will satisfy both of your managers.

6.13   Discuss your options for reassigning project personnel on completion of your project.

6.14   Write a paper describing what you have learned from your project work. Indicate how your involvement in this work has affected your choice of a professional career, if applicable. Revise your resume to reflect your newly acquired skills and experience and, if necessary, your career-change direction.

Project Management

The Project Plan

Specifications and Reports

Modeling and
System Design

1. Can you explain the importance of project planning?

2. Are you able to describe and develop a Work Breakdown Structure?

3. Have you ever created a Gantt chart for a project?

4. Can you establish who is responsible for project tasks and, with their assistance, create a responsibility matrix?

5. Can you build a network diagram for a project?

6. Are you able to analyze a network diagram and establish an acceptable schedule for the work?

7. Can you list the various kinds of costs that must be monitored in a budget?

8. Do you understand the schedule adjustment process and how to use software in making the adjustments?

What is conceived well is expressed well.

Nicolas Boileau, 1674

Planning, scheduling, and controlling is often referred to as the project management cycle. Each of these phases of the management cycle are closely linked together. One objective of this chapter is to illustrate approaches for developing schedules and budgets, and for monitoring and controlling a project.

One of the first of many challenges faced by a project manager is the development of a project plan. A project plan is not a single document. It consists of a Work Breakdown Structure, a responsibility chart, a schedule in the form of a bar chart and a network diagram, and supporting documentation describing costs and budgets.

The manager and the members of the project team prepare a project plan as a road map to provide them with direction and guidance from project kick-off to the day of delivery. The length and complexity of the project plan depend entirely on the type of project and the level of investment being made in it. For example, a real estate developer might only prepare a Work Breakdown Structure and a schedule of subcontractor due dates when building a single house. However, when the same contractor is building a 300-unit condominium complex, the work is broken down to a level of detail that will assist in developing detailed schedules and responsibility matrices.

After you complete the study of this chapter, you should know how to do the following:

- Participate in the preparation of written specifications.
    Subdivide a project into a hierarchy of tasks and work packages.
    Write clear task descriptions.

- Prepare a Work Breakdown Structure and the associated documentation.
- Create a responsibility matrix.
- Develop a Gantt chart for timing the project.
- Draw a network diagram for analyzing the project.
- Apply the Critical Path Method of analysis to develop a schedule for the project.
- Adjust a project schedule to match customer needs.
- Understand the budgeting process.
- Realize the complexities associated with the interaction of tasks, schedules, and budgets.
- Use a software package to organize data.

SECTION 7.1   THE WORK BREAKDOWN STRUCTURE

The Work Breakdown Structure (WBS) is often the first document developed as the project manager and project team formulate a project management plan and schedule. The schedule defines the sequence and duration of tasks that must be done to complete the project on time and within the cost guidelines established. Developing a Work Breakdown Structure is usually an iterative process. At each iteration new personnel get involved and more detail is developed about the activities, actions, processes, and operations that need to be performed to satisfy the customer's requirements.

Sometimes a company performs almost identical types of projects for every customer. Therefore, the project manager has an excellent grasp of the tasks required and the personnel who can perform these tasks. In these cases the Work Breakdown Structure may be nothing more than a standard form completed by the project manager. However, such a situation is very rare. Most projects are one-time occurrences, each with a unique set of characteristics that ultimately leads to a well-defined, but very individualized, set of results.

The purpose of the Work Breakdown Structure is to demonstrate clearly to all parties involved how each task is related to the whole project in terms of budgets, schedules, performance, and responsibility for the physical assets belonging to the project. Some project managers include enough detail so that the Work Breakdown Structure can be used as an instrument for scheduling, personnel assignments, resource allocations, monitoring project progress, and controlling how and when tasks are accomplished.

The objective of the Work Breakdown Structure is to partition the project into distinct work packages, each of which contains detailed work elements. The Work Breakdown Structure starts as a project task list, usually an indented list or a node tree, that shows the relationship of the tasks to each other. The indented list in figure 7.1 is a hierarchical list of tasks that must be performed to complete the project. The indented position of a task in the list indicates its position in the hierarchy of tasks. The more a task's position is indented, the further down it is in the hierarchy. The node tree shown in figure 7.2 is a hierarchical listing of the functional areas of the organization required to complete a project.

The Work Breakdown Structure can be developed by either the entire project team or a subset of the team. The composition of the team depends on the complexity of the project and the type of knowledge required. However, as the document is drafted, the following features must be included in the final package:

1. Each project task that forms an element of the Work Breakdown Structure should be big enough to be identified and assigned to an individual member of the project team.

2. Each task should be defined clearly enough that it can be viewed as a package of work to be accomplished by the project team.

Figure 7.1 Indented Work Breakdown Structure (WBS): partial task list

Indented Work Breakdown Structure (WBS): partial task list

```
1.0    purchase land (task)
       1.1    search for land (subtask)
       1.2    assess quality of land
       1.3    finalize purchase of land
2.0    prepare site (task)
       2.1    mark and stake lot lines
       2.2    cut and remove brush
       2.3    level lot
              2.3.1   bring in dirt
              2.3.2   grade lot
3.0    excavate site (task)
       3.1    stake foundation
       3.2    dig foundation hole
       3.3    stake position of footings
4.0    erect foundation (task)
       4.1    prepare footing frames
       4.2    pour footings
       4.3    install foundation forms
       4.4    pour concrete
       4.5    waterproof exterior walls
       4.6    allow foundation to dry
       4.7    backfill completed foundation
```

Figure 7.2 Node tree or tree diagram

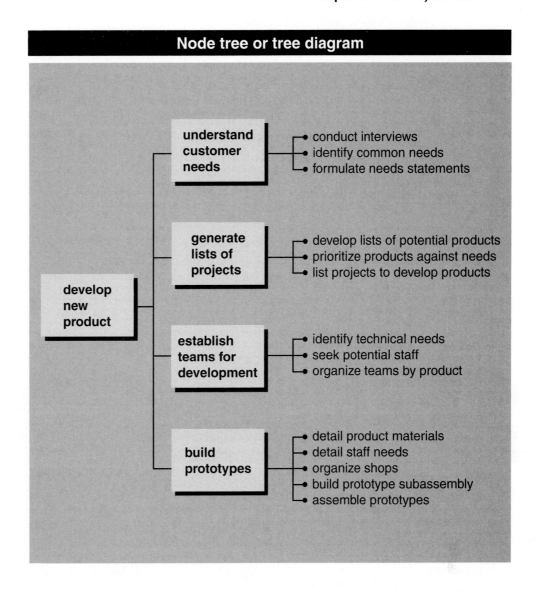

3. Each task should be described in such a way that it is possible to define each element of the task in terms of the money, labor, and resource materials required.

As the team develops the Work Breakdown Structure, it is vital for them to remember that this package of documents will form the foundation for all future work. After work has actually begun, it is frustrating to discover that an essential task has not been considered. Replanning a project and developing engineering change orders are both difficult and expensive. A careful and diligent effort to draft a comprehensive plan initially will reap major dividends. The project manager should never underestimate the value of developing a thorough understanding of the project right from the beginning.

As the Work Breakdown Structure evolves, a questioning attitude should prevail. Those involved should carefully consider not only *what* needs to be done, but also *why* it is necessary. "What" and "why" questions are critical elements in forcing the team to focus on the most important activities associated with project completion. This focus prevents distraction by those elements that may be unnecessary or even trivial to success. "Where" and "when" questions compel the team to identify those places where the work will take place and the optimum times during which it will be done. Defining who will do the work and asking how they will do it refines and drives an understanding of the tasks to a more precise level of detail.

A general set of steps to follow when preparing a Work Breakdown Structure is as follows:

1. Have the people who will be responsible for the tasks prepare a list of work units. Keep asking the questions: What needs to be done, and Why?

2. Organize the tasks in the order in which they must be completed and continue to break the tasks down into more precise levels of detail. Work hard at establishing the beginning and the ending points for each individual task. Remember that the task description must facilitate the following vital elements: scheduling, budgeting, monitoring, and controlling the project.

3. Organize the work packages into a hierarchy of tasks. This can generally be done with the aid of a node tree diagram. Complete the following steps for each work element:

    a. Write a work description that includes data inputs, materials requirements, contract requirements, and any unique features associated with completing the work.

    b. List the suppliers, vendors, and personnel associated with the tasks. To the extent possible, specifically identify individuals and vendors.

    c. Identify the tools required to perform the work. These include types of equipment, software packages, or unique skill sets requisite to personnel.

    d. Specify the output or the products of the task (activity) such as reports, design specifications, hardware, or other specific items.

    e. Develop a list of personnel who will be doing the work associated with each task.

4. Create an indented list of tasks including the task description, the inputs to the tasks, the outputs from the tasks, the mechanisms or tools required, and personnel responsible for the work. Figure 7.3 illustrates such a list.

Work Breakdown Structure with details				
activity	**responsible**	**input**	**output**	**time**
1.0 purchase land	team	listings	owned land	
1.1 search for land	Tom			5 wks
1.2 assess land quality	Tom, realtors			2 wks
1.3 finalize purchase of land	lawyers			2 wks
2.0 prepare site	surveyors	site topology	marked plan	
2.1 mark and stake lot lines	surveyors			1 wk
2.2 cut and remove brush	laborers			2 wks
2.3 level lot	excavator			2 wks
2.3.1 bring in fill dirt	excavator			1 wk
2.3.2 grade lot	excavator			2 wks
3.0 excavate site	excavator	equipment	prepared site	
3.1 stake foundation	surveyor			1 wk
3.2 dig foundation hole	excavator			2 wks
3.3 stake position of footings	surveyor			0.5 wk
4.0 erect foundation	concrete contractor	contracts	completed foundation	
4.1 prepare footing frames	laborer			0.5 wk
4.2 pour footings	concrete contractor			0.5 wk
4.3 install foundation forms	laborer			0.5 wk
4.4 pour concrete	concrete contractor			0.5 wk
4.5 waterproof exterior walls	contractor			0.5 wk
4.6 allow foundation to dry	none			3 wks
4.7 backfill completed foundation	excavator			1 wk

Figure 7.3 Work Breakdown Structure with details

SECTION 7.2 ESTABLISHING RESPONSIBILITY FOR TASKS

A major goal of project planning is assigning responsibility for the various elements of the project before the project is even started. The project manager who attempts to assign tasks as the project progresses is at serious risk of failure.

Each person who needs to see the work or bears responsibility for completion of the work must be identified in the project management plan. Although the plan may assign the performance of a task to a particular group of individuals, others will generally be involved to some degree. For example, a project to write a proposal for funding from a government agency may initially involve two or three members of a project team. Ultimately, however, the proposal may be checked and edited by the project manager, reviewed by the division director, and evaluated for approval by the vice president of research.

A responsibility matrix is a particularly useful technique for associating a list of individuals who will be involved in the project with the tasks that must be completed. Although there seem to be as many methods of presenting a responsibility matrix as there are project management consultants, all such matrices contain essentially the same information. The basic responsibility matrix is a grid whose left-hand column lists the tasks or work packages defined in the Work Breakdown Structure. Along the top of the grid, project team members, vendors, and others responsible for various tasks are identified by job title or name. The matrix is completed by inserting a code at the intersection of task and person that indicates the person's type and level of responsibility for that task. Table 7.1 illustrates a responsibility matrix for a small project.

A responsibility matrix can be time-consuming and expensive to prepare, but it is time and energy well invested. The matrix gives the project manager a clear indication of who will be responsible for the various tasks of the project. It identifies the levels of management that will be involved and their contribution to the work. If the project manager can obtain agreement from the individuals identified on the responsibility matrix, misunderstandings with respect to task assignments or task ownership can be avoided.

A secondary benefit is also derived from a responsibility matrix, because it highlights the workload assigned to each individual, group, or organization. The project manager can more easily pinpoint those who may compromise the success of the project because they are either overloaded or underutilized.

For a large involved project, the responsibility matrix can become quite complex. Meredith and Mantel (1995) provide illustrations of what they have named *linear responsibility charts*. One reference is a "verbal responsibility chart," which lists activities, actions, the action initiative, and the responsible individuals. In this illustration Meredith and Mantel mention that the original document is thirty pages in length and contains 116 major activities.

Table 7.1 Sample responsibility matrix

WBS Activity Task Listing	Responsibility for Task			
	Project Manager	Administration	Crew Chief	Contractor
1. Purchase land	5	1	5	0
2. Prepare site	2	3	1	0
3. Excavate site	2	4	2	1
4. Erect foundation	2	5	1	1

Key to Responsibilities
0 = None
1 = Accomplish
2 = Supervise
3 = Must be notified
4 = Final approval
5 = Consult for advice

SECTION 7.3   THE PROJECT SCHEDULE

The schedule defines specific points in a project when the project manager must bring in personnel and equipment resources to complete required tasks on time and within budget. Developing a schedule for a project involves deciding when each task and subtask listed in the indented Work Breakdown Structure should begin and how long it should last. The scheduling process translates the list of project tasks into a timetable of events or completion dates.

The scheduling process is similar to the development of a Work Breakdown Structure in that a high-level master schedule to provide a skeleton for the project is constructed and reviewed. High-level tasks that require a more detailed breakdown are selected, and detailed schedules are developed. The timing of these subschedules must fit within the time limits established by the master schedule.

The process of scheduling a project often involves trade-offs.

It is important to realize that the process of scheduling a project often involves making tradeoffs between the cost of personnel and equipment resources and the adjustment of task completion dates to satisfy customer requirements. For example, a project task's duration can be shortened by scheduling overtime work, but the additional labor cost may be too much for the budget to absorb.

Because a project schedule provides a visual representation of the relationships among the different pieces of a project, the method chosen to display these relationships is very important. It should be easy to follow and should not add complexity to an understanding of the project. The Gantt chart or bar chart and the network diagram are two commonly accepted methods for illustrating the relationships among the project elements. These methods result in two different types of graphical representations of the project and are very easy to understand once they are complete. Both of these graphical tools are important and should be used together when building a schedule for a project that goes beyond five or six activities.

The Gantt Chart

The Gantt chart or bar chart is the oldest and most frequently used chart for plotting work activities against a time line. Gantt charts show how long a project will take when tasks that are independent of each other are performed simultaneously.

The most common reason for using a Gantt chart is to monitor the progress of a project. Gantt charts provide an excellent method for comparing planned work activities with the actual progress made on a project. Note how information is organized on the Gantt chart shown in figure 7.4:

- The time in weeks is shown across the top.
- Each project activity is bracketed by inverted triangles (∇) that align with the week numbers of the activity start and complete dates.
- Solid lines connecting the inverted triangles show an activity's duration in time.
- Dashed lines improve the readability of the chart.

A Gantt chart similar to the one in figure 7.4 may be used as an overview for related schedules that include more detail. More detailed schedules would include the titles of the individual tasks and subtasks (Callahan, Quackenbush, and Rowings, 1992; Farkas, 1970).

Although it is better to remain with the original overall schedule and completion date, most schedules have to be revised as work on a project progresses. Noninverted (upright) triangles ($\triangle$) on the Gantt chart indicate new planned start and finish dates. If, for example, the designers of the project in figure 7.4 discover that an existing design from a previous project can be modified, they can shorten the "design product" task by one week. However, because of their experience with the previous design (the one being modified), the team members also realize that the construction phase will require an additional week. Therefore, they revise the schedule as shown in figure 7.5, and the triangles move to the left (earlier start or finish), remain where they are (no change), or move to the right (later start or finish).

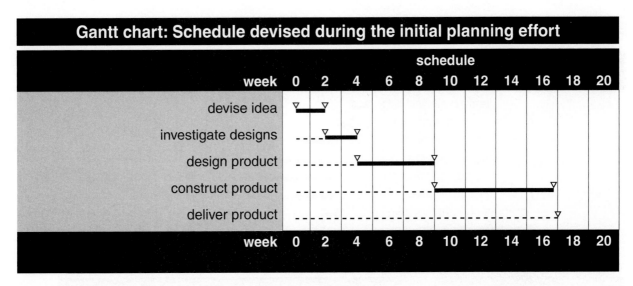

Figure 7.4 Gantt chart: Schedule devised during the initial planning effort

The schedule is modified using the upright triangle notation so that changes from the original schedule are readily apparent. If proposed revisions to the schedule are not accepted by the project manager or client, or if it is not possible to change the proposed schedule, the chart can be readily changed back to what it was before.

Gradually the schedule document will include more detail as the task descriptions are expanded to include information regarding materials and labor skills. For each approved task, rough costs are estimated and verified to the extent possible. An example of a more detailed schedule, a construction schedule, is given in figure 7.6.

Examine the tasks listed on the chart. Note that each task starts with an active verb (for example, *verify, prepare, inspect*) and that the schedule headings are the overall task titles from the Work Breakdown Structure, shortened where necessary. Task numbers may also be included. Several changes have been made to this detailed schedule, and the schedule scale has been enlarged so that calendar dates can be inserted if desired. Items that occur repeatedly, such as "inspect work in progress," are indicated as inverted triangles on a dashed line. The construction schedule now shows a number of tasks to be performed. Some tasks are listed in sequence; the schedule lines of others actually overlap.

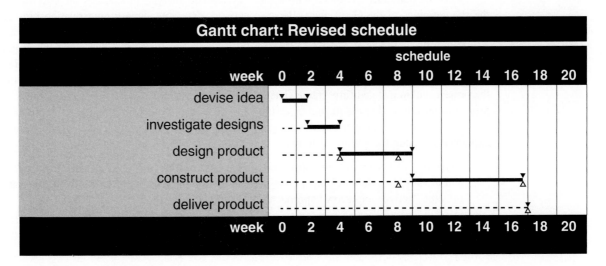

Figure 7.5 Gantt chart: Revised schedule

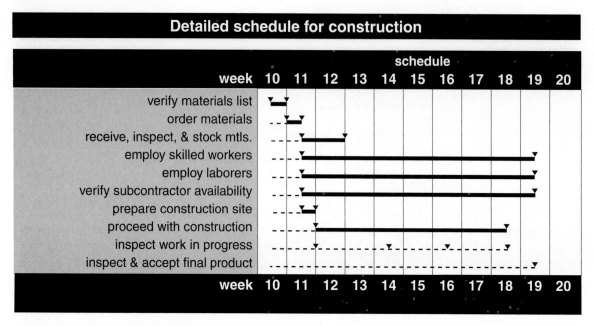

Figure 7.6   Detailed schedule for construction

The principal problem with the Gantt chart is that it does not provide enough information about how various tasks relate to each other. The Gantt Chart can be used by itself to create a master schedule for very small projects. Project managers encounter problems, however, when they try to create a schedule for a more complex project. Some of the following questions may arise:

- What parts of the tasks can be done at the same time?
- Is there any slack time or room for adjustment in the start times for the tasks?
- Are there precedent relationships for the whole task, or do they apply to just parts of the task?

Simply stated, bar charts are awkward to handle. When used in conjunction with a network diagram, however, the bar chart can be very useful.

The Network Diagram

Network diagrams combined with a set of systematic analysis procedures serve to remedy the shortcomings of the Gantt chart. Because network diagrams show timing relationships between various tasks on a project, they form an excellent framework for planning, scheduling, and monitoring the progress of a project. They are also communication tools that allow the project manager to show dependencies among tasks and prevent conflicts in timing. By using an algorithm, a project manager can calculate milestones and determine the probability of completing the project within a stated time frame. The manager can also experiment with starting dates for project tasks and predict the impact of certain start dates on the overall project completion date.

The concepts of network analysis and network representation of a project are more easily explained by using the following terms:

Activity: A task or job that forms a component of the project. Activities consume resources and always have definite start points and endings. This presentation of network diagrams uses the "activity-on-arrow" approach, that is, all activities will be shown as arrows.

Nodes or Events: The beginning and ending points of activities. A node cannot be realized (executed) until all activities entering it are complete. A node is shown as a circle with a label.

Merge Node: A node where more than one activity is completed.

Burst Node: A node where more than one activity is initiated.

Network: A graphical representation of a project plan with the activities shown as arrows that terminate at nodes.

Path: A series of activities joined together to form a distinct route between any two nodes in a network.

Critical Path: The limiting path(s) through the network that defines the duration of the project. Any reduction of the project duration must begin on the critical path.

Precedence Relationship: The order in which activities should be performed. For example, digging a hole for a foundation must precede the pouring of the foundation. There is a precedence relationship between the excavation and the cement-pouring tasks.

Dummy Activities: Fictitious activities that carry a zero time estimate and no cost are used to illustrate precedence requirements in a network diagram.

Time Duration: The total elapsed time of an activity from start to finish. The Critical Path Method (CPM) has one estimate of activity duration. The Program Evaluation and Review Technique (PERT) has three estimates of duration for each activity in the network.

In the activity-on-arrow representation of a project shown in figure 7.7, nodes (circles) are placed at the tip and tail of the activity arrow to identify the beginning and ending events for an activity. In the literature, authors often refer to the arrows as *arcs* and the nodes as *events*. Notice that a dummy activity has been inserted between nodes 3 and 5, showing the precedence requirement between activities B and G.

The following conventions must be observed when developing a network diagram for a project:

1. Each activity is represented by one and only one arrow.

2. All activities begin and end in events (nodes shown as circles on the diagrams).

3. The length of an arrow has no meaning with regard to the duration, cost, or importance of an activity.

4. Arrows originating at an event (node) can only begin after all activities terminating at the event have been completed or, as some authors state, the node has been realized.

5. The first node of the diagram and the last node of the diagram may have only output arrows and input arrows, respectively. All other nodes must have at least one input arrow and one output arrow.

6. No arrow can start and end at the same node.

7. If one activity takes precedence over another, but there are no activities relating them, a dummy activity can be used. The dummy activity will be shown as a dashed line arrow with no duration or cost. (See figure 7.7.)

Figure 7.7   Activity-on-arrow network

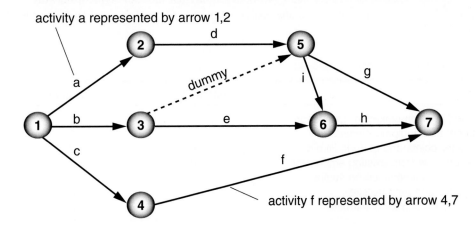

Activity-on-arrow network

activity a represented by arrow 1,2

activity f represented by arrow 4,7

Figure 7.8 Network
diagram for site preparation
project

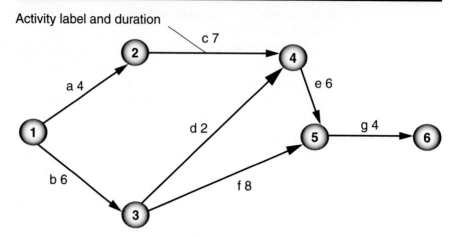

Network diagram for site preparation project

Figure 7.8 is an activity-on-arrow representation of the site preparation project described by the Work Breakdown Structure in table 7.2. (The **terminal node** is labeled: 6.) Notice that only high-level functions are modeled in the network diagram. Project managers very often develop a master schedule for the project from the high-level functions. Then they produce subschedules for the subactivities that fall within the timing established by the master schedule.

Follow these steps to develop a project network diagram:

1. Make a list of the activities that will drive the master schedule, that is, the activities on the Work Breakdown Structure that form major categories of work.

2. Label these activities (for example, A, B, etc.) so that the diagram is easy to read (see figures 7.7 and 7.8).

3. Determine or estimate the duration of the activity.

4. Note all precedence relationships and check that these relationships are correct.

5. Start with the initial node, label it node 1, and move forward, constructing the project network while continually checking the precedence relationships. For example, developing a network for the project described in table 7.2 will result in the diagram shown in figure 7.8.

The two network diagramming techniques to be discussed in this chapter are the Critical Path Method (CPM) and the Program Evaluation and Review Technique (PERT). CPM was developed by the industrial giant DuPont, Inc., for scheduling maintenance in their chemical plants. PERT was developed by the consulting firm Booz-Allen and Hamilton under contract to the U.S. Navy as part of the Polaris Program.

PERT and CPM both require that the same type of network diagrams be developed for a project before any analysis can be performed. Very often in the literature, the PERT and CPM

Table 7.2 Activities for site preparation project

Activity Description	Activity Label	Duration	Preceding Activities
Measure plot and position stakes for foundation	a	4	none
Identify personnel and equipment needs	b	6	none
Measure perimeter points and bring in fill dirt	c	7	a
Select and assign crew from existing employees	d	2	b
Secure and perform maintenance on equipment	e	8	b
Dig foundation hole and prepare site	f	6	c, d
Grade lot and prepare site for construction	g	4	e, f

techniques will be grouped under the single heading of "Critical Path Methods." The main difference between the two techniques is the method used for calculating task duration times. CPM requires that one fixed time-value estimate be provided for each task. The CPM analysis results in a single time-value estimate of the time to complete the entire project. PERT has been formulated to deal with uncertainties or probabilities of the type found in research-and-development projects. PERT uses three time estimates to calculate the duration of a task. The PERT analysis predicts the completion time of a project.

Before discussing each of the project planning tools in detail, it is important to mention that none of these tools is absolutely mandatory for a project manager to develop a good project management plan. Some companies and government agencies prescribe project management strategies that do not involve the development of responsibility charts or network diagrams. However, the diagramming and analysis tools that are presented in this chapter are used by a very wide range of project managers and companies. In their text titled *Analysis and Control of Production Systems,* Elsayed and Boucher (1985) cite a study that found as many as 80% of 400 construction firms were using the critical path method. In another study, a large percentage of the firms using quantitative methods were using PERT or CPM.

Many useful software packages have been developed to apply the PERT/CPM approaches to a project schedule. See Tapper (1998). Almost daily, software houses announce the availability of inexpensive, user-friendly personal computer (PC) based packages for managing projects. Each year *PC Magazine* reviews the project management software available, much of which is PERT/CPM based.

The Critical Path Method (CPM)

The critical path through a project network is the path that defines the duration of the project. The critical path is the limiting path or the longest path found when examining all potential routes from the initial (first) node to the terminal (last) node. The Critical Path Method (CPM) of project analysis and scheduling provides a stepwise procedure for combining times for activities that must be accomplished and for analyzing precedence relationships. In order to apply CPM, the following definitions must be established.

ES(X):   The Earliest Start time for activity X.

tx: Task (activity) duration time

EF(X):   The Earliest Finish time = the Earliest Start time plus the task duration time. For activity X with a duration tx, $EF(X) = ES(X) + tx$.

LS(X):   The Latest Start time for a task is the latest time that the activity can start without delaying the project.

LF(X):   The Latest Finish time for an activity that is started at the Latest Start time. For activity X, $LF(X) = LS(X) + tx$.

EOT: The Earliest Occurrence Time is the earliest time that an event (node) can be realized. When an event has only one preceding activity, the EOT for the event is equal to the earliest finish time for the single preceding activity. When more than one activity enters a node, all activities must be completed before the node is realized. The EOT is the longest time required for all paths leading to the node to be completed.

LOT: The Latest Occurrence Time is the latest time that an event can be realized without delaying the project. The LOT for an event is defined by the activities leaving a node.

To calculate the ES( ) and EF( ) activity times and the EOT event times, we perform what are referred to as **forward-pass calculations.** For these calculations the CPM algorithm assumes that node 1 represents time zero—that is, the beginning point for the project. The ES( ) time for any activity starting at the first node is zero. For the site preparation example illustrated in figure 7.8, ES(a) = ES(b) = 0, 0. The EF( ) for the activities starting at node 1 are calculated by adding the task duration to the earliest start times:

$$EF(a) = ES(a) + ta$$
$$EF(a) = 0 + ta = 0 + 4 = 4$$
$$EF(b) = 0 + tb = 0 + 6 = 6$$

Since node 2 can be realized at time 4, then the EOT for node 2 is 4. The earliest start ES(c) for activity c is 4 and the earliest finish EF(c) for activity c is calculated as $4 + 7 = 11$.

The EOT for node 4 is determined by calculating and comparing the earliest finish times for all activities entering the node. EOT cannot occur until all entering activities have finished. In this case, EOT for node 4 is 11 since that time is the longer of EF(c) and EF(d). This relationship is expressed as:

$$EOT \text{ for node } 4 = \max\left[EF(c), EF(d)\right]$$

where

$$ES(c) = 4 \text{ and } EF(c) = 4 + 7 = 11$$
$$ES(d) = 6 \text{ and } EF(d) = 6 + 2 = 8$$
$$EOT \text{ for node } 4 = \max\{11, 8\} = 11$$

$$ES(e) = 11, \text{ resulting in the following:}$$
$$EF(e) = 11 + 6 = 17$$
$$EF(f) = 6 + 8 = 14$$
$$EOT \text{ for node } 5 = \max\{17, 14\} = 17$$

Therefore

$$ES(g) = 17$$
$$EF(g) = 17 + 4 = 21$$

The final duration for the network is 21 time units with an EOT for node 5 of 17 time units and an EOT for node 6 of 21 time units. Recall that the critical path is the longest path through the network and defines the duration of the project. The critical path for this example consists of activities a, c, e, and g.

In order to calculate the LS( ) and LF( ) activity times and the LOT event times, you must know the duration of the network. The terminal node of the network will define the latest finish time for activities ending at that node. To calculate the times for LS( ), LF( ), and LOT we perform **backward-pass calculations.**

The backward-pass calculations are required to determine the values of the latest start, LS, and the latest finish, LF, times for the project activities. The latest occurrence time, LOT, for the nodes is similarly calculated.

The relationship between the LF and the LS is

$$LF = LS + t$$

Therefore, for our example, the latest finish for activity g and the finish time for the project is 21 time units. Therefore

$$LS(g) = LF(g) - t$$
$$LS(g) = 21 - 4 = 17$$

The LOT for node 5 is equal to 17 since the latest that node 5 could occur and still not delay the project is time 17.

Moving backward through the network:

$$LF(e) \text{ and } LF(f) = 17$$

Table 7.3 CPM calculations for site preparation project activities

Activity	Duration (t)	ES	LS	EF (ES + t)	LF (LS + t)	Slack
a	4	0	0	4	4	0
b	6	0	3	6	9	3
c	7	4	4	11	11	0
d	2	6	9	8	11	3
e	6	11	11	17	17	0
f	8	6	9	14	17	3
g	4	17	17	21	21	0

$$LS(e) = LF(e) - t$$
$$LS(e) = 17 - 6 = 11$$
$$LS(f) = LF(f) - t$$
$$LS(f) = 17 - 8 = 9$$

To obtain the LOT for a node we must obtain the LS for all activities leaving the node. The minimum activity LS value will define the value at which the node is realized (LOT) and, in turn, the LF for all activities entering the node. For node 4 the LS(e) = 11 and the LOT for 4 is 11 time units. In the case of node 3:

$$LS(d) = 11 - 2 = 9 \text{ and } LS(f) = 9.$$

Therefore

$$LF(b) = 9$$

since

$$LF(b) = \min \{LS(d); LS(f)\} = \min \{9, 9\}$$
The LOT for node 3 is 9.

$$LS(b) = LF(b) - t$$
$$LS(b) = 9 - 6 = 3$$

$$LS(a) = LF(a) - t$$
$$LS(a) = 4 - 4 = 0$$

Therefore, the node 1 LOT becomes $\min \{LS(b), LS(a)\} = \min \{3, 0\} = 0$

Table 7.3 and table 7.4 illustrate the results of the calculations made. Note that many of the calculations can be done within the tables.

Table 7.4 CPM calculations for site preparation project events

Event (node)	EOT	LOT	Slack
1	0	0	0
2	4	4	0
3	6	9	3
4	11	11	0
5	17	17	0
6	21	21	0

The results of the forward and backward calculations allow the project manager to gain an understanding of the schedule with the activity duration times originally assigned. Any changes made to the activity times along the critical path affect the project duration times. For activities outside the critical path, changes in duration and start time can be made when certain conditions exist. If an activity is to be extended in time, then the activities to be changed must have slack time associated with them or the overall project duration will change. The activity slack time identifies the range of time that is available to start an activity without delaying the completion date of the project. The slack time for activities can be found by taking the difference between the latest start time, LS, for an activity and the earliest start time, ES, for an activity. Likewise, the event slack (see table 7.4) provides the project manager with an understanding of how much time the realization of an event can be delayed without affecting the project completion time. Note that activities on a critical path do not have any slack associated with them. Any changes to activities on a critical path will change the project completion time.

The Program Evaluation and Review Technique (PERT)

In principle the Program Evaluation and Review Technique (PERT) and the Critical Path Method (CPM) are very similar. The overall objective of both of these approaches is to derive a workable schedule for a project. Once an estimate of each task time has been established, the basic PERT procedure for estimating the times for milestone points in the project network is the same as the CPM approach. The forward-pass calculations and the backward-pass calculations are the same for PERT and CPM.

A fundamental difference between PERT and CPM is the approach used for estimating the times for the project tasks. The CPM method assumes that the project manager's single estimate of task times is good enough for estimating the project schedule. PERT takes the calculation of project completion times to a higher level of mathematical sophistication. The PERT techniques of analysis use the theories of probability and statistics to evaluate project uncertainties. Since this book does not require the reader to have a background in the mathematics of probability and statistics, we will not attempt a detailed discussion of the many features of PERT. The reader interested in mathematically based scheduling techniques should refer to El-sayed and Boucher (1985) or Meredith and Mantel (1995).

In PERT the task times are calculated using a formula based on three time estimates provided by the project manager or the project team. The three required estimates of the time to complete the project are the most optimistic estimate, the most pessimistic estimate, and the most likely time estimate. The early developers of the PERT technique found that by making some assumptions regarding the probability distribution associated with predicting the task times, a good single value estimate could be made using these three estimates. The benefit of this approach is that the derived estimating procedure results in a task time estimate that takes uncertainty into account.

Figure 7.9 illustrates the concept of three time estimates for a task time. The most optimistic task time (a) might be described as a duration that would occur with a frequency of one

Figure 7.9 Task time estimates for PERT

in one hundred. The most pessimistic time (b) might also be a time with a duration that would occur one time in one hundred. The most likely time (m) is the estimated time that the task will most often take. Figure 7.9 demonstrates that the optimistic time "a" is less than time "m," the most likely time. Thus "m" is less than "b."

The formula that the early PERT researchers developed for calculating the single time estimate (T_e) for the task is given as:

T_e = PERT time estimate for a task

$$T_e = \frac{(a + 4m + b)}{6}$$

where

a = most optimistic task time estimate

b = most pessimistic task time estimate

m = most likely task time estimate

See Meredith and Mantel (1995).

Another statistical measure that is an indicator of the variability of the estimate made using T_e is the variance (Var), which can be calculated as follows:

$$Var = \left(\frac{b - a}{6}\right)^2$$

Figure 7.10 presents a hypothetical network with associated task times. The next step in arriving at an estimate for the project schedule would be to perform the forward-pass and the backward-pass calculations using the T_e values calculated for each task as the estimates of task times.

Figure 7.10 PERT network with time estimates

PERT network with time estimates

activity	time estimates			T_e
	a	m	b	
a	1	2	3	2.00
b	2	3	6	3.33
c	4	5	6	5.00
d	3	3	3	3.00
e	3	4	8	4.50
f	1	2	3	2.00
g	4	5	6	5.00
h	3	4	7	4.33

SECTION 7.4   REFINING AND ADJUSTING THE SCHEDULE

The CPM and PERT methods of project analysis can give a project manager considerable insight into the project tasks' start and complete times. However, there is more to scheduling than calculating milestones. The project Gantt chart, responsibility chart, and network diagram provide the project manager with the tools to think beyond just getting the project done and to focus on finishing the project efficiently and according to specifications. The CPM analysis shows how the project can be completed in the time specified by the critical path if task times remain as they were estimated. If the estimated project completion time is later than the time desired by the customer, adjustments must be made.

The project completion date can only be advanced by reducing the duration of one or more of the tasks that make up the critical path. This can be done by bringing in new people, equipment, or other resources. Shortening the duration of an activity that is not on the critical path will not reduce the overall time it takes to complete the project. Reducing the critical path time is tricky and must be done very systematically. Each task has to be examined to determine how much each unit of time reduction will cost in terms of the resources required to achieve the lower time value. The project manager must be aware of the relationship between the time it takes to perform a task and its cost.

When a project time must be reduced, the project manager should select the task on the critical path that will cost the least to shorten and then reduce that task by one time unit. Since the overall project duration will be one time unit less as a result of the task reduction process, it is possible that one or more other paths on the network have become critical. If a new critical path has emerged, the tasks on that new path must also be considered in the time reduction process. The overall project duration can be iteratively reduced one task at a time until either customer requirements are met or the tasks have reached their limits of reduction. Every task has a **limit of reduction,** a point at which the addition of one more worker or another piece of equipment has no positive effect on the task completion time. To successfully reduce the critical path, the project manager must evaluate every unit of time reduction with respect to cost, new critical paths, personnel needs, and equipment needs.

During a CPM analysis, very little thought is usually given to the skill levels required by the workers involved. It is during the post-CPM analysis that the project manager must perform a skills assessment. A problem arises when more of the same type of skilled worker is needed than the system can realistically provide. When too many of a particular class of worker are needed, the work schedule must be adjusted to accommodate the availability of workers. This workload leveling is an important part of the scheduling process.

The Gantt chart is a good tool for assessing the number and type of personnel needed for a project. At any point on the time line of the Gantt chart, draw a vertical line extending upward through the project tasks. For each task that the line passes through, determine the type of workers required to do the work. A tally of the required number of workers provides a count of the people involved with the project at that point in time.

Adjustments and refinements made to the project schedule can be very costly if they are not properly assessed and conscientiously implemented. Rushing through a schedule evaluation can be very costly in the long run if all of the significant variables are not considered.

SECTION 7.5   COSTS AND BUDGETS

A major concern on every project is the ability to control time and costs, because time, money, and resources are directly related. Here are some of the issues that affect costs:

1. The *amount* of time that is charged to the entire effort by the workers
2. The *duration* of time from start to completion

3. The *time* lost due to
   a. factors that are within the control of management
   b. factors that are beyond the control of management
4. The *resources* required to perform the project

Costs and Costing

During the beginning phases of a project, the project manager often prepares initial estimates for the time and costs needed to complete a given item within a project. The assumptions involved in the estimate are noted.

An estimate, which is an educated guess, usually takes into account additional time and money that may be needed to cover unexpected delays, worker inefficiency, and other factors beyond the control of management. Including such amounts in estimates is the responsibility of management.

As noted previously, time and money are directly related. However, never assume that the cost of a task is reduced if that task is completed sooner. Also, it costs less to do a task right the first time than to do it over again. All those involved in the project should continually search for the most efficient amount of time that requires the least expenditure of money.

When complicated projects and programs are initially devised, managers and designers plan for some modest changes. It should be noted that specific changes may not be known at the time that planning occurs. The planners hope that these modest changes will not significantly affect tasks, schedules, or costs, and that the client will observe no overall change in the project plan or performance.

Changes may irritate higher-level managers and clients. They are often more interested in controlling schedules and costs than in knowing how well the work is performed. It is the responsibility of the team to perform quality work, as well as to adhere to the allotted tasks, schedules, and budgets.

The activity center project provides an excellent example of the interaction of time and costs. During the Study Phase, the activity center size and content were determined. When more detailed information was obtained during the Design Phase, changes in the overall plan were made. If the type of lumber originally selected was no longer readily available, its lack of availability would delay the project schedule and would cause the activity center costs to increase beyond budget. Therefore, the related portion of the specifications would be changed via a Contract Change Notice (appendix E), and the schedule would also be changed to reflect the new design.

Costs are normally subdivided into a variety of categories. Two of these categories are **fixed costs** and **variable costs.**

1. Fixed costs include rent, loan payments, and property taxes. The exact amount of these costs can be estimated in advance for a year or more.

2. Variable costs include labor and employer-paid social security taxes, utilities, travel expenses, telephone calls, freight charges, and sales taxes. Costs can also vary when the amount of work contracted or the effort applied to obtain work (Sales and Marketing) changes from the original estimate. Such costs can also be controlled by applying limits (ceilings) beyond which managerial permission must be obtained for further expenditures.

For estimating purposes, these costs are usually divided into different categories, such as the following:

Direct Costs: Labor (salary and hourly) and Materials

Overhead Costs and Rates: Indirect Costs, Facilities, Taxes and Insurance

The overhead costs can be subdivided as follows:

Indirect Costs: Benefits, purchasing, sales and marketing, management, travel, entertainment, education and training (in-house, conference attendance, and courses at schools, colleges, and universities)

Figure 7.11 Break-even
analysis graph

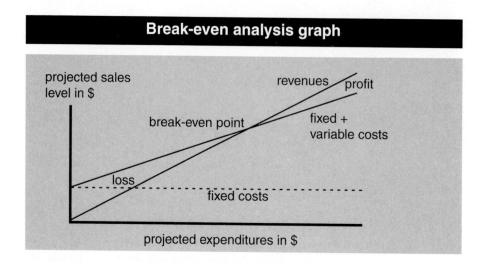

Facilities: Rent, lease, or ownership; building maintenance and grounds maintenance

Taxes and Insurance: Federal (social security, personal income, corporate income, and unemployment); state (unemployment and workers compensation); local (property taxes and city sales taxes)

These categories will also appear on the appropriate spreadsheets.

Accountants who wish to estimate corporate costs for one or more fiscal years prefer to use computer programs that convert the above categories into fixed and variable costs. Accountants who are analyzing and projecting costs for one or more fiscal years also develop charts, such as the one shown in figure 7.11, that present a pictorial description of these relationships.

The lines on figure 7.11 represent an accountant's summary of sales versus expenditures. The fixed costs, described earlier, are shown as a horizontal line because they change minimally during a given fiscal year. The variable costs increase as more money is spent; they are related to the amount of money spent for developing projects. The **break-even point** indicates where the corporate income changes from a loss to a profit as the income from sales exceeds the costs incurred.

The comparison of project income versus project expenditures is referred to by business and industry executives as the **bottom line.** Executives are judged by how much profit is derived from a project—the amount the income exceeds the expenditures. These executives are judged less by whether the project is performed on time and to the exact specifications. No matter how well a project is performed and no matter how fast it is completed, if the project expenditures exceed costs, that fact is most remembered by corporate executives.

Sometimes a project is stopped (killed) because it becomes clear that the project is going to exceed its originally estimated costs. If additional money is not available, then all the effort and money expended to this point will have been wasted. Most project financial failures can be avoided if costs are estimated carefully at the beginning, during the Conception Phase, and fine-tuned during the Study and Design Phases. Costs need to be monitored and carefully controlled while the actual work is in progress, during the Study, Design, and Implementation Phases.

Budgets

A budget is a plan that describes the authorized expenses for a specified period of time. The word *budget* used as a verb means "to prepare a plan of expected income and expenditures." A budget is based upon an estimate of the income expected so that related expenses can be projected or controlled and remain within a preagreed limit or ceiling (Carrithers and Weinwurm, 1967).

Budget estimates, developed by a technical group within a corporation, are prepared with the assistance of Purchasing Department personnel. The technical people describe the items desired, often with an approximate price included. The purchasing personnel negotiate with vendors to obtain the best price for those items.

Technical personnel are usually required to estimate only the amount of labor required (such as hours or days by labor category) and the approximate cost of materials needed to perform the anticipated project. Accounting personnel then extend those estimates by including the applicable dollar amounts and overhead costs. These two sets of budget estimates are then reviewed by management personnel, who may require that the estimates be revised. It is the responsibility of the technical personnel to indicate when downward revisions would harm the quality of work, or require a change in the specifications.

The budget categories described in the previous Costs and Costing section of this chapter are the ones that are to be used in the cost-estimating effort. Cost estimating for a project is best performed by the designers who have decided on the labor categories to be involved and who have selected the materials needed. If the project is large, then some technical personnel will be assigned to assist the Purchasing personnel in the materials estimation process.

Once the design direction has been selected, it may be worthwhile to compare both labor and materials estimates. If labor category estimates can be combined, then efficiencies result. For example, where needed skills are similar on several tasks, fewer employees may be needed to work on the project, thus reducing administrative and management costs. If common materials for several parts of the project are selected, lower prices can result from buying larger quantities. These efficiencies are best achieved by those designers who have developed the design being estimated. Thus, looking for efficient solutions requires a team approach.

The selection of vendors is critical. Costs can increase if vendors are not dependable in delivering ordered items or if the quality of delivered items is poor. Also the decision to construct items, rather than purchase preassembled items, is critical. This decision involves comparing the costs of labor, overhead, and materials for constructing an item to the total cost of a purchased preassembled item.

The activity center project provides an example of a make-or-buy decision concerning a set of steps. Refer to chapter 4 and figure 7.12.

Make: Students design the stairs, purchase the lumber, and construct the stairs.

Buy: Students (school) purchase a prefabricated set of stairs from a lumber supplier.

The totality of labor and materials costs, convenience, and availability must be compared in a make-or-buy decision. If the cost differential is small, it may not be worth the effort for the company to build the set of stairs. Also, the availability of personnel (when it is time to construct the stairs) is crucial. It is important not to invest more time, and therefore, dollars reaching a decision than will be saved by purchasing the set of stairs from a lumber supplier.

Figure 7.12 Steps comparing make-versus-buy budgets

Steps comparing make-versus-buy budgets			
make		**buy**	
design stairs	$200	select standard design	$100
purchase lumber	$100	purchase prefabricated stairs	$350
construct stairs	$400	install stairs	$100
totals	$700	totals	$550

The estimates versus actuals spreadsheets are used to monitor the financial progress of projects as well as corporations. They can be updated weekly, monthly, or quarterly. The choice of updating periods depends upon how rapidly projected costs are expected to change and how significantly these costs are affecting the bottom line of the corporation. A typical estimates versus actuals spreadsheet is described in section 6.5 and shown in figure 6.6.

As indicated previously, charge numbers can be used to coordinate tasks, schedules, costs, and budgets. A number or coding system—such as a system that is a combination of letters and numbers (alphanumeric)—can be used for project planning, monitoring, and control (Samaris and Czerwinski, 1971).

An example of a numbering system is given below:

XX,YY,6.2.1

This simplified example of a numbering system consists, from left to right, of two letters followed by a comma (XX,), two more letters also followed by a comma (YY,), and numbers separated by periods (6.2.1), where

XX identifies the alphanumerics as either a bid effort or an awarded contract

YY identifies the type of document, such as

ET for estimated task

ES for estimated schedule

EC for estimated costs

EB for estimated budget

AT for actual tasks

AS for actual schedule

AC for actual costs

6.2.1 identifies the related tasks, schedules, costs, and budgets

The number sets are separated by periods. This allows a large project or program to increase the number of digits for a given set of tasks without having to modify previously numbered items.

The numbering system can, for example, be used to identify computer files that contain the related information, such as the document for actual costs. The use of such an alphanumeric system allows those involved to do the following:

- Quickly access task, schedule, cost, and budget documents
- Modify these documents as necessary

Computer programs can "link" documents so that changes made to one document will result in the same changes automatically occurring in related documents. If an individual is not authorized to change a document, that person is notified by a computer-displayed warning. In this way, the data are protected from unauthorized changes.

A trial document is a document devised to resolve an uncertainty. Computers permit rapid preparation of trial task, schedule, and budget documents for management examination and decision making. These trial documents can be manipulated without disturbing the original estimates of tasks, schedules, and budgets. When trial documents are accepted and approved, they can become the applicable set of documents by merely changing their code to replace the original documents.

Sometimes information stored from previously completed work will be similar to that being bid. Data available in computer storage can be accessed to save the time and effort of preparing new estimates. However, it is necessary to verify the labor, overhead, and materials portions of the costs because they may have changed since the earlier effort was completed. Once these verifications and modifications are done, the code on the document may be changed to automatically insert that document into the work being bid. It now becomes an integral part of the proposal.

Tasks, schedules, costs, and budgets are closely related. They are a key part of project planning; they become an important part of project control once implementation is initiated. Experience and teamwork in establishing them and monitoring them are invaluable.

SECTION 7.6   MONITORING AND CONTROLLING A PROJECT

To effectively control a project, the project manager must monitor each task and compare its actual results to the expected results. A good method for monitoring a project is to plot actual progress on the Gantt chart for the entire project. Color coding is very helpful for making comparisons. For example, black blocks can illustrate the planned activity, while green blocks illustrate actual progress. To understand how project resources are being used, the project manager must calculate the difference between planned or budgeted expenditures and the actual expenditures. Cost overruns need to be identified early in the project.

When the progress or costs do not agree with the expectations (plans), it is the manager's responsibility to provide guidance and support in terms of advice and resources. How much action to take is a tough management decision. It depends upon the type of project and the size of the problem. A "loose" style of project management can result in a project getting so much out of control that it fails due to cost overruns and perhaps missed deadlines, also. At the other extreme, overreaction can bring a project to a standstill, and controlling a project too "tightly" makes team members nervous. They then tend to follow the project requirements and budgets so closely that they do not try new ideas or attempt to be creative. This situation is the opposite of what any good project manager wants to accomplish. Monitoring and controlling a project must be done very carefully.

SECTION 7.7   SOFTWARE SUPPORT FOR PROJECT MANAGEMENT

Planning, monitoring, and controlling even a reasonably sized project requires the organization of large amounts of data. For the small projects used to illustrate the concepts throughout this book, the data can be easily organized. However, in the real world most projects consist of more than forty tasks. Each task has to be monitored, and comparisons must be made between the planned time and cost and the actual performance of the task. Reports have to be written; the progress of the project requires documentation.

The project manager must have data available for decision making on a timely basis. When the customer calls and asks for the status on a certain phase of a project, the project manager needs accurate data to quickly prepare a satisfactory answer.

The project-management data manipulation and calculations required can be prepared by available computer software. For this reason, several good project management software packages have been developed. Today's desktop computers use software that was designed for personal computers, and they can handle very large projects that contain large amounts of data to be processed. Surveys by some private marketing groups and a professional society indicate that Microsoft Project is a very popular project management software package; it is applied by many project managers. Microsoft Project provides the tools to graphically display a project via a Gantt chart or PERT format. Microsoft Project also offers the project manager a good report-writing capability. To illustrate the usefulness of a software package for planning, monitoring, and controlling a project, the application of Microsoft Project will be demonstrated in this section.

Before we provide an illustration of the application of software to the challenges of project management, it is important for the reader to understand that software is only as good as the data provided by the project manager. The use of software to document and support the project-management function can save the project manager many hours of analysis. However, the manager must be careful to continually check the reasonableness of every calculation performed

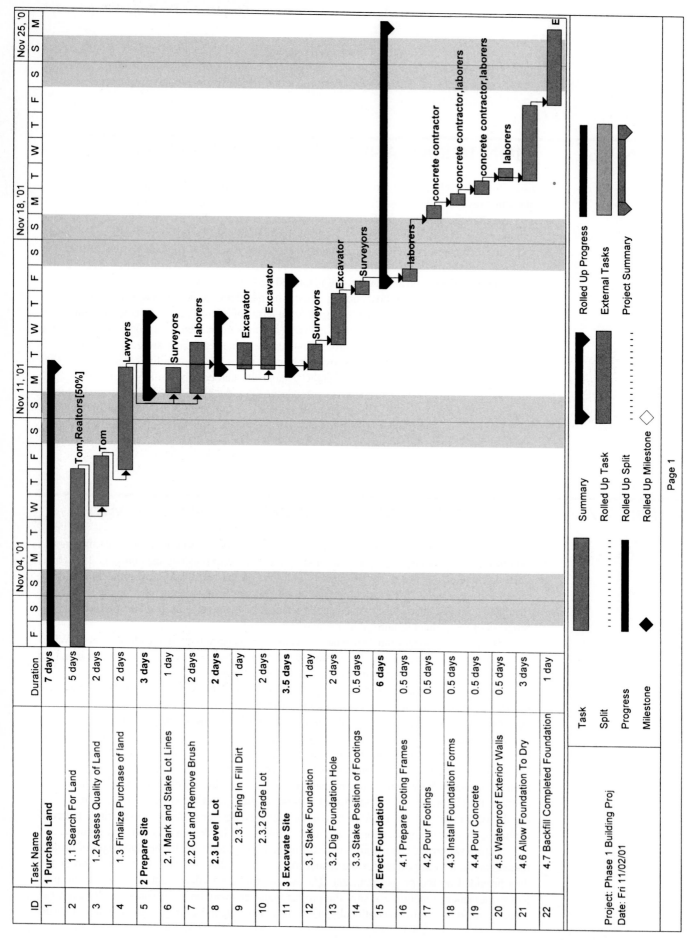

Figure 7.13 Gantt chart from Microsoft Project

Phase 1 Building Proj								
ID	❶	Resource Name	Initials	Group	Max. Units	Std. Rate	Ovt. Rate	Cost/Use
1		Surveyor	S		100%	$50.00/hr	$70.00/hr	$0.00
2		Realtors	R		100%	$0.00/hr	$0.00/hr	$0.00
3		Lawyers	L		100%	$100.00/hr	$200.00/hr	$0.00
4		Surveyors	S		100%	$80.00/hr	$100.00/hr	$0.00
5		laborers	l		100%	$25.00/hr	$30.00/hr	$0.00
6	◈	**Excavator**	E		**100%**	**$100.00/hr**	**$200.00/hr**	**$0.00**
7		concrete contractor	c		100%	$100.00/hr	$100.00/hr	$0.00

Figure 7.14   Phase I building project resource data

by the software. A simple human error, such as the transposition of two numbers, can cause erroneous results that can destroy a project. The software will accept any data provided and it will perform the designated calculations whether the data are correct or incorrect.

The greatest benefit of using a software package (such as Microsoft Project) is the ability to manipulate, modify, and graphically display project schedules. Figure 7.13 illustrates the results of entering the data from the Student Activity Center project, shown in figure 7.3, into Microsoft Project. Data regarding each task on the Work Breakdown Structure can be entered into Microsoft Project using data templates. Figure 7.14 illustrates the set of data stored in the student project database regarding the resources used to accomplish the project. The data must be entered by the project manager or by a knowledgeable assistant. Once the project manager provides the project database with a work breakdown structure, task precedence relationships, duration of tasks, resources required and the cost of those resources, and any fixed dates the project must satisfy, most commercially available software can generate a full range of reports. Figure 7.13 is a Gantt chart for the Phase I Student Activity Center project prepared via Microsoft Project. All of the resources used are shown as labels on the bars of the chart. The precedence relationships that exist between activities are shown by arrows on the chart.

Within Microsoft Project is the built-in capability to prepare a wide range of reports and charts. Figure 7.15 is an illustration of a resource utilization chart. This chart outlines, for all resources used on the project, the number of time units each resource will apply to the project and to which tasks the named resource will be assigned.

In figure 7.16 there is a demonstration of how Microsoft Project can overlay a project schedule on a calendar. Further, figure 7.17 is a Gantt chart in which the Critical Path has been identified and coded. It should be noted that the graphics applied by a particular software package may require some analysis on the part of the user.

Microsoft Project and other software packages offer capabilities beyond the ones illustrated in this section. In many of the packages, the features allow a project manager to devise a PERT chart, to perform resource leveling, and to track a project as it is being completed. For large projects, the project manager must rely on software for planning, monitoring, and controlling the work.

CHAPTER OBJECTIVES AND SUMMARY

Now that you have finished this chapter, you should be able to:

1. Explain the importance of project planning.
2. Describe and develop a Work Breakdown Structure.
3. Create a Gantt chart for a project.
4. Establish who is responsible for project tasks and create a responsibility matrix.
5. Build a network diagram for a project.
6. Analyze the network diagram and establish an acceptable schedule of the work.
7. List the various kinds of costs that must be monitored in a budget.
8. Understand the schedule adjustment process and use software to make the adjustments.

Phase 1 Building Proj

Week of Nov 04, '01 covers columns S–S; week of Nov 11, '01 covers columns S–W.

ID	ⓘ	Resource Name	Work	Details	F	S	S	M	T	W	T	F	S	S	M	T	W
		Unassigned	0 hrs	Work													
		Allow Foundatio	0 hrs	Work													
1		Surveyor	36 hrs	Work													
		Search For Lan	20 hrs	Work	8h			8h	4h	4h	4h	4h					
		Assess Quality	16 hrs	Work	8h			8h	4h	4h	8h						
2		Realtors	20 hrs	Work	4h			4h	4h	4h	4h						
		Search For Lan	20 hrs	Work	4h			4h	4h	4h	4h						
3		Lawyers	16 hrs	Work				8h				8h					
		Finalize Purcha	16 hrs	Work				8h				8h					
4		Surveyors	20 hrs	Work											8h	8h	
		Mark and Stake	8 hrs	Work											8h	8h	
		Stake Foundatio	8 hrs	Work											8h	8h	
		Stake Position a	4 hrs	Work													
5		laborers	32 hrs	Work											8h	8h	
		Cut and Remov	16 hrs	Work											8h	8h	
		Prepare Footing	4 hrs	Work													
		Install Foundatio	4 hrs	Work													
		Pour Concrete	4 hrs	Work													
		Waterproof Exte	4 hrs	Work													
6	◇	Excavator	48 hrs	Work												16h	16h
		Bring In Fill Dirt	8 hrs	Work												8h	8h
		Grade Lot	16 hrs	Work												8h	8h
		Dig Foundation	16 hrs	Work												8h	8h
		Backfill Comple	8 hrs	Work													
7		concrete contractor	12 hrs	Work													
		Pour Footings	4 hrs	Work													
		Install Foundatio	4 hrs	Work													
		Pour Concrete	4 hrs	Work													

Figure 7.15 Resource utilization chart

November 2001

Sunday	Monday	Tuesday	Wednesday	Thursday	Friday	Saturday
10/28				01	02	03
	04	05	06	07	08	09
11/04						10
	11	12	13	14	15	16
11/11						17
	18	19	20	21	22	23
11/18						24
	25	26	27	28	29	30
11/25						

Search For Land, 5 days

Finalize Purchase of land, 2 days

Assess Quality of Land, 2 days

Stake Position Prepare Foo

Dig Foundation Hole, 2 days

Stake Foundation, 1 day

Finalize Purchase of land, 2 days

Mark and Stake Lot Lines,

Cut and Remove Brush, 2 days

Bring In Fill Dirt, 1 day

Grade Lot, 2 days

Allow Foundation To Dry, 3 days

Waterproof E

Pour Concrete, 1 day

Pour Footings Install Foundation Forms,

Allow Foundation To Dry, 3 days

Backfill Completed Founda

Figure 7.16 Project overlays on calendar

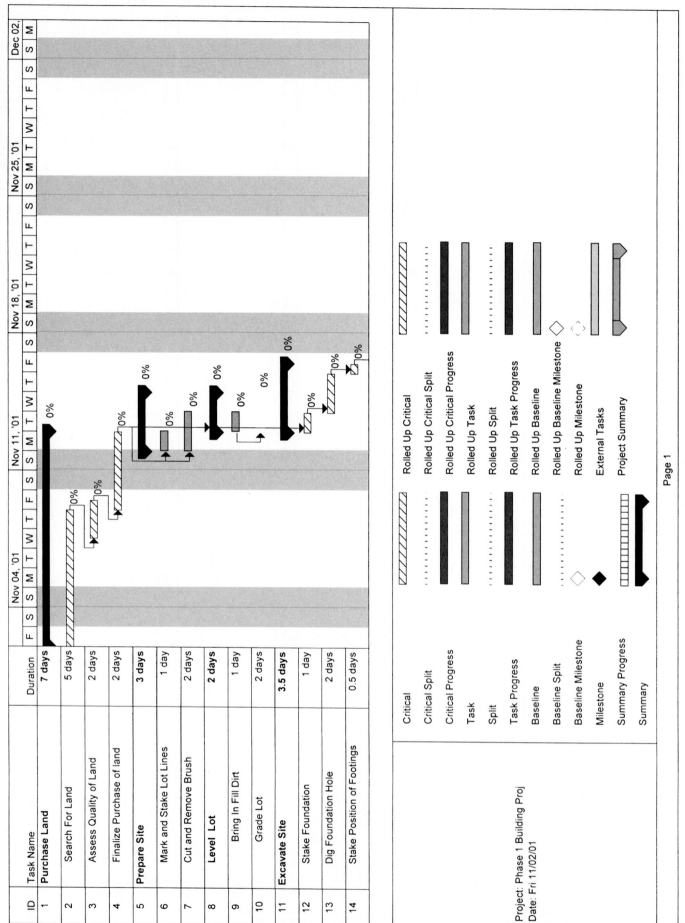

Figure 7.17 Critical Path analysis and coding

EXERCISES

7.1   Write a task description for the work that you are going to do today. Be very specific as to how you will identify the beginning and ending points for the task.

7.2   Preparing a meal can be a very challenging project. Develop a Work Breakdown Structure for the preparation of a specific meal, such as a backyard cookout.

7.3   Prepare the tasks, schedules, and budgets for an instructor-assigned project.

7.4   Develop a network diagram and perform the CPM forward-pass calculations and the backward-pass calculations to arrive at a schedule for the project assigned in exercise 7.3.

7.5   Describe how you would recommend monitoring the progress of a project utilizing the Work Breakdown Structure, the Gantt chart, the responsibility chart, and the network diagram.

7.6   Consider the situation where a member of your family (or yourself) is considering starting a mail-order business from your home. List all of the fixed and variable costs associated with such a venture.

Project Management

The Project Plan

Specifications and Reports

Modeling and
System Design

Project Management

The Project Plan

Specifications and Reports

Preparing Specifications
Contracts and Change Notices
Trip and Meeting Reports
Periodic Project Reports
Government Reports

Modeling and System Design

1. How are specifications developed through the phases of a project?

2. Why are trip and meeting reports useful, and what do they typically contain?

3. What are the types of contracts for projects?

4. What are periodic reports for projects? What are their contents? For whom are they intended?

5. What kinds of reports are prepared for government projects, and what are their typical contents?

6. What are the goals of ISO standards?

Specifications and Reports

Progress imposes not only new possibilities for the future but new restrictions.

Norbert Weiner (1954)

During the last fifty years, project documentation has evolved into several standard documents, such as specifications, contracts and change notices, meeting reports, periodic project reports, and government reports. Each of these documents, or groups of documents, is discussed in this chapter.

Documentation of the individual project phases has been described at the end of each of the project phase chapters. The present chapter includes a more in-depth description of the contents of project specifications and the way in which specifications change during the Conception, Study, and Design Phases. In the Implementation Phase, specifications become critical to the writing of contracts and change notices.

Specification descriptions become more detailed with each phase. The type of information and level of detail required for meeting and project reports remain fairly constant, however, regardless of the specific phase in which the reports are prepared. Government reports are many and varied. Often, different types of government reports are associated with different phases of a project.

After you complete the study of this chapter, you should know how to do the following:

- Participate in the preparation of a specification.
- Understand the content of contracts and change notices.
- Write meeting reports.
- Contribute to periodic project reports.
- Provide information to be included in appropriate government reports.

SECTION 8.1   PREPARING SPECIFICATIONS

At the beginning of the planning process, an overview of the entire sequence of a project is devised. That overview consists of the following documents:

- Description of the expected final product

- Approximate schedule that leads to the final product

- Estimate of total costs that will lead to the final product

- Initial list of the work that will eventually lead to the desired product

The simplest and most direct way of moving forward from this initial effort is to assign team members to write individual task descriptions representing work that will lead to the final product. These descriptions are trial documents that are circulated among the team members. As they are revised, they become part of the Conception Phase documentation (see Section 2.3). However, it is not possible to write detailed task descriptions without reference to standards of design and workmanship that help to define the final product.

Specifications (specs) are documents that supply those standards. Specifications describe the desired end result of the work to be accomplished. They contain requirements that are the conditions to be fulfilled in order to complete a task or project. In addition, specifications typically describe desired features for the project. The sequence of specification development is given in figure 8.1.

Conception, Study, and Design Phase Specifications

During the Conception Phase of a project, a Preliminary Specification is prepared. The content of this specification depends upon the type of projects being considered. Notes are included that identify entire standards or specific paragraphs to be referenced.

During the Study Phase, the Design Specification is written to define both design requirements and design limitations or constraints. Although these specifications place constraints upon the designers, they should *not* define design methods unless the method is a regulatory requirement. The designer needs as much flexibility as possible.

Figure 8.1 Specification
development

The object of the Design Specification is to stimulate the designer's imagination. An example of a design-stimulation statement is the following:

The selected project is an activity center to be used by children from ages four through ten.

This information is a general guide to the designers.

At the same time, the Design Specification should note any constraints that must be considered. An example of a constraint is

The cost of the activity center shall not exceed $20 000.

Depending upon the available land, constraints include: local building-code restrictions, environmental guidelines, and activity center-site physical conditions.

During the Design Phase, the Design Specification is expanded to include sufficient detail to build or manufacture the product. The resulting Production Specification defines the design requirements and design limitations or constraints. It should not, however, define manufacturing methods. This effort is the responsibility of the manufacturing personnel.

Any questions or options remaining from the Study or Design Phases must be resolved prior to the start of the Implementation (or Production) Phase. Thus the specifications to be used during this last phase of the project are now final.

The object of the Production Specification is to guide the manufacturing (or construction) personnel and, at the same time, note any constraints that must be considered. An example of a construction specification statement that allows for flexibility is the following:

The type of lumber may be spruce, white pine, or fir.

An example of a constraint would be the following:

The wall and roof sheathing shall be 5/8" CDX (X for exterior-glue) plywood.

The Production Specification is the defining document for the entire technical portion of a project. This specification must be detailed and precise so that once the project is complete, the finished product will meet the specification. This specification may also contain tests, or references to tests, that will verify product acceptability.

The Production Specification and the documents that are referenced in it form the technical portion of a contract. A precise specification ensures that two or more groups bidding on the same project will be fulfilling the same requirements. This is often referred to as comparing apples to apples, rather than apples to oranges. Where a particular equipment or device is desired, specifications may include a brand-name reference or references along with the phrase "or equivalent." Then it is the responsibility of the bidders to propose an equivalent replacement for that specified item if they so desire and if they can show that the replacement is equal to or better than the brand name(s) referenced.

Specification Content

The organization and content of a typical specification are summarized in figure 8.2. The terms in figure 8.2 are explained in the following list.

Scope of Specification typically contains a Specification Descriptive Title and a brief narrative description of the specification content.

Applicable Documents reference those documents that are to be considered a part of the specification. This listing eliminates the need to repeat all the standard requirements already contained in these documents, which are often referred to as "boilerplate." (The term originates from the boiler design of a steam engine, which requires the use of strong material.) These boilerplate documents have been standard reference documents for many decades.

Requirements consist of many paragraphs that describe the following:

System Definition is a general description that includes the purpose of the specification, a system diagram, interface definitions, and, if government sponsored, the Government Furnished Property List.

System Characteristics describe the system's physical and performance characteristics, which include: reliability, maintainability, availability, system effectiveness models, environmental conditions, and transportability where applicable.

Design and Construction includes: materials, processes, and parts; nameplates and product markings; workmanship; interchangeability; safety; and human performance/human engineering information.

Figure 8.2 Hierarchy of specification content

Hierarchy of specification content

scope of specification

applicable documents

requirements
  system definition
  system characteristics
  design and construction
  documentation
  logistics
  personnel and training
  precedence

quality assurance provisions

preparation for delivery

notes and appendixes

Documentation refers to the complete sets of drawings, instruction manuals, performance and acceptance test reports, and scale models (if they have been constructed).

Logistics lists maintenance and supply facilities, and facility equipment for use with the implemented system.

Personnel and Training describes employee skills, training requirements, training facilities, and instructors with their instructional material necessary to prepare those people who will operate and maintain the system.

Precedence references those documents that will take precedence over another should any two or more referenced documents conflict.

Quality Assurance Provisions include specifications for tests and procedures to verify that the equipment and/or system has been designed and constructed to meet the quality-level requirements.

The "general" paragraphs assign responsibility for all tests. They reference any tests and examinations required by the specification.

Quality Conformance Inspections include on-site inspection of test facilities, test procedures, and test personnel by qualified inspectors appointed by the client or the government.

Preparation for Delivery includes specifications for acceptable packaging and shipping methods.

Notes and Appendixes typically include any comments that apply to the various paragraphs within the specification.

Drawings are used where words are insufficient. Three-dimensional scale models may be constructed. Thus, more complicated devices and systems can be examined visually and understood by nontechnical personnel who may not be capable of interpreting technical drawings.

Levels and Types of Specifications

There are various *levels* of specifications (see figure 8.3). The system-level specification is an overview of the project in terms of its overall performance or function. Design specifications are more detailed and can be further subdivided into component or device, performance, installation (such as National Electrical Code), and environmental specifications.

Maintenance information is often either noted or referenced at the design, device (or subassembly), performance, and installation levels (see section 5.3). For large systems or projects, however, a separate maintenance specification or plan may be prepared. This plan, at a minimum, should contain the following (where applicable):

Figure 8.3 Specification hierarchy

- Class, or level, of maintenance involved
- Suggested schedules for maintenance and parts replacement
- Mechanical parameters, including

  Inspection and cleaning

  Testing and lubrication

  Measurement locations and tolerance factors

  Alignment and adjustment recommendations

  Related mechanical, assembly, and part-layout drawings, block diagrams and flowcharts, electrical and/or electronic schematics, and troubleshooting trees

- Electronic test and calibration equipment specifications, including recommended

  Specific corrective maintenance activities, as required performance procedures

Include in the maintenance plan, where appropriate, all precautionary information regarding radio frequency, electromagnetic, or LASER radiation interference. Ensure that instructions never violate OSHA standards for personnel safety during plan activities. Where standards do not exist, follow related MIL-SPEC and MIL-STD practices. These are industry accepted and must be followed for government contracts. If not part of the maintenance plan, include vendor documentation as a separate package along with warranty and other related information.

There are also various *types* of specifications:

- Commercial
- Industrial
- Government

  Local

  State (DOR)

  Federal

  NIST—National Institute of Standards and Technology

  GSA—General Services Administration (similar to commercial, and industrial)

  DOT—Department of Transportation (including the Coast Guard)

  DoD (Department of Defense—military)—Army, Navy, Air Force, and Marines

  NASA—National Aeronautics and Space Administration

Applicable codes, often published by national associations, are usually referenced within a specification. For example, the National Electrical Code (NEC) for wiring is published by the National Fire Protection Association. Military specifications (MIL-SPECs) often contain references to military standards (MIL-STDs) for various standard components, devices, and subsystems.

Government specifications are the most complex because they are used for wide and diverse applications. Industrial specifications are usually much simpler because they are directed to more specific applications. The construction industry often follows a format offered by the Construction Specifications Institute (1998).

Specifications are the most important documents of the family of documents described in this chapter. They provide the overall and specific guidelines to the designer and to the management monitoring-and-control team.

SECTION 8.2   CONTRACTS AND CHANGE NOTICES

A contract is an agreement between two or more parties regarding the nature of the product to be delivered, the delivery schedule, and the product cost. See Section 4.3. The contract may be as simple as a Letter of Transmittal or it may be a multipage document prepared by a team of lawyers. Specifications and cost and schedule documents must be referenced within the contract.

There are several types of contractual agreements, such as

- Fixed-price contracts
- Cost-plus-fixed-fee (CPFF) contracts
- Incentive contracts

Each contract type has its unique benefits. These are discussed in more detail in Horgan and Roulston (1989). Typical terms are defined in the appendixes of their book.

A **fixed-price contract** is used where the work to be accomplished can be completely specified in advance. Potential contractors use the supplied documentation to determine the prices for all materials, equipment, and labor. They then prepare and submit a bid and will be paid the prices specified in the contract upon completion of various portions of the project. These payments are known as progress payments. Alternately, the total price of the contract may be withheld until the entire project is satisfactorily completed. If specifications are considered final as a result of careful and complete work during the Design Phase, then a fixed-price contract may be awarded.

A **cost-plus-fixed-fee (CPPF) contract** contains two significant groupings of designs—those designs that will not change and those designs that are incomplete. (The incomplete designs occur because more technical data and experimentation are necessary before the design stabilizes.) The contractor is paid for expenses incurred in performing the work, receiving a previously established fee instead of a percentage of the estimated contract cost at various intervals. A contract for work to be done during the Study Phase or the Design Phase is often a CPFF contract.

An **incentive contract** is one in which the contractor is rewarded with extra money for completing the work within a preagreed time or for less cost than originally estimated. The incentive contract is very valuable to the awarding organization when the contract is one of many interrelated contracts. Failure of one contractor to complete a contract on time may cause very expensive overruns because the other contractors cannot depend upon their start date. Typical contract content is given in the activity center example of appendix D.

Production specifications are seldom perfect. Thus, an Engineering Change Notice (ECN) or Contract Change Notice (CCN) is usually necessary. The wording and content of a typical CCN for the activity center is given in appendix E. The wording and content of a typical ECN is similar.

SECTION 8.3   TRIP AND MEETING REPORTS

When a project is first conceived, it is necessary to gather information and exchange ideas if progress is to be made. Both of these activities usually involve trips and meetings. Visits to libraries, to potential clients, and to other persons or groups must be documented in the form of a Trip Report. In order to cover any type of visit, a simplified form, known as a Contact Report Form, is often used. That form typically contains the following information:

How the contact was made (trip, visit, telephone, or other)

Name and address of the organization visited

Purpose and date of the contact and the person reporting

Name, title, and telephone numbers of persons contacted

Summary of any discussions

How the contact was initiated, the source of the "lead"

Materials collected and where they are filed

Action items and person(s) responsible for taking action

Distribution list of persons who should receive a copy of this Contact Report Form

A sample Contact Report Form is shown in figure 8.4. (The name on the right-hand edge is for hard-copy filing purposes.)

Figure 8.4 Contact Report
Form

CONTACT REPORT FORM

Contact was made by: trip ☐ , visit ☐ , telephone ☐ , or _____

Organization Name _____

Address_____ City_____State_____Zip_____

Purpose of Contact: _____

_____ Person Reporting:_____Date_____

Persons Contacted	Title	Telephone
_____	_____	_____
_____	_____	_____
_____	_____	_____
_____	_____	_____

Summary of Discussion: _____
_____
_____
_____
_____
_____
_____
_____

Purpose of Visits: _____

Source of Lead: _____

Materials Collected	Where Filed
_____	_____
_____	_____
_____	_____

Action Items	Person(s) to Take Action
_____	_____
_____	_____
_____	_____
_____	_____
_____	_____
_____	_____

Report Recipients: _____ _____ _____ _____
_____ _____ _____ _____
_____ _____ _____ _____
_____ _____ _____ _____

PROJECT NUMBER

PPCP 8

Project progress also requires comparisons; comparisons require examining trade-offs. Ideas are discussed and debated during group meetings of team members, sponsors, and leaders. As shown in figure 8.5, the project team together examines the project concept. The team then studies the various ideas offered and compares them by developing trade-off information. The conclusion is the selected project.

People can spend many hours at meetings arguing about how to proceed and which way to proceed. A **meeting report** records the **minutes** of each meeting. Copies of the minutes are distributed to each participant and to other involved persons. If no one records the discussions and the decision-making process, then the same arguments may be repeated later and meeting time will be wasted. On the positive side, these documented arguments may become valuable resources. If new information becomes available that changes the basis for previous decisions, then these decisions may be modified.

Typical contents for a meeting report include the following:

- Names of meeting attendees
- Topics discussed

Figure 8.5   Project selection

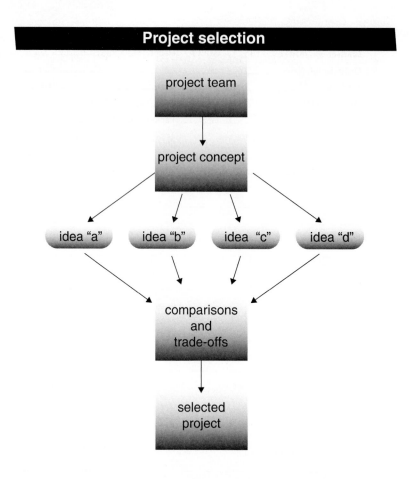

Project selection

project team

project concept

idea "a"   idea "b"   idea "c"   idea "d"

comparisons and trade-offs

selected project

Sample meeting report

Subject: Material Selection Meeting for Activity Center Project   cc: F. Eagle
Date: 1995 June 3   J. James
From: W. Jones   T. Marsh
To: J. Jewett–Manager; Dept 21

Attendees: F. Eagle
              J. James
              W. Jones
              T. Marsh

A meeting was held in Conference Room B to discuss the selection of materials for painting the interior of the Activity Center. It was decided that all ceilings will be painted with one coat of primer and two coats of flat white. The game room walls will be painted with Sunny Peach on the wall above the chair rail, and Desert Sand below the chair rail. The kitchen walls will be painted pale yellow. The colors for the remaining rooms will be decided at our next meeting on June 7.

    Action items
        Purchase 2 gallons of Desert Sand epoxy paint   F. Eagle
        Purchase 1 gallon of Sunny Peach epoxy paint   F. Eagle

Figure 8.6   Sample meeting report

Figure 8.7
Summary of typical
action items

Summary of typical action items		
action item	responsible person	completion date
prepare minutes of meeting	W. Jones	June 3
order floor tile material	R. Wells	June 8
select colors and order paint for each room	F. Eagle	June 8
select and order game room equipment	T. Marsh	June 13
install floor material	R. Wells	July 5
complete painting of walls and ceiling	F. Eagle	July 13

- Progress achieved
- Directions chosen
- Decisions agreed upon or made
- Action items to be performed

The document shown in figure 8.6 is considered to be a meeting report.

Action items are very important. They not only describe actions to be taken, they also identify the persons assigned the responsibility for performing the specified action. Thus project progress is ensured. The list of action items in figure 8.7 includes the persons responsible for implementing the items and the required completion dates.

Written words contribute to progress. They can be read when the meeting is over. They can lead to ideas not considered during these meetings. A meeting report is a record of the ideas and progress of the group.

SECTION 8.4   PERIODIC PROJECT REPORTS

Documentation of work on a project includes periodic reports such as daily charges, weekly expenditures, monthly progress reports, and quarterly and annual summary reports. Additional documentation is required at the end of each phase as described in section 3 of chapters 2 through 5. The types of the periodic reports may vary greatly; typical report titles are provided as a list in figure 8.8.

Periodic reports are grouped into three categories:

- Financial reports
- Technical reports
- Managerial reports

Figure 8.8 Typical titles of periodic reports

Typical titles of periodic reports
daily charges
weekly expenditures
monthly progress
quarterly summary
annual summary

Figure 8.9 Managerial
report content and follow-up

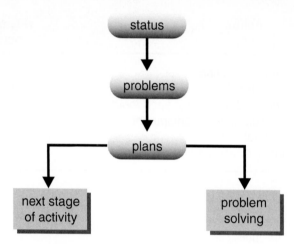

Managerial report content and follow-up

PLANNING AHEAD

Such reports can be prepared on a computer and are often transmitted over a network to the persons or groups who have an interest in their content.

Financial reports are primarily spreadsheets of detailed data. Where appropriate, this information may be preceded by a summary that compares the original cost estimates to the actual financial data. These spreadsheets contain such items as daily charges and weekly expenditures. Attachments may include explanatory statements where necessary.

Technical reports combine words, diagrams, and drawings. These reports are of greatest interest to the technical manager, whether that manager is part of the design team or part of a Project or Program Office.

Managerial reports combine words, graphics, and summary financial spreadsheets. Managers may not be technical experts and may therefore be more interested in the overall progress of the project and its adherence to schedules and budgets. The content of managerial reports, summarized in figure 8.9, is typically the following:

- *Status:* Work accomplished during the reporting period
- *Problems:* Problems and their proposed solutions
- *Plans:* Work to be accomplished during the next reporting period

When the planning portion of a managerial report is being prepared, an assessment of any risks involved should be included. As noted, managerial reports either include or refer to the applicable financial reports. Often, summaries of those financial reports are included in the managerial reports.

SECTION 8.5   GOVERNMENT REPORTS

Most projects, even those involving only private companies, require some type of government reporting. Each level of government requires the submission of reports or other documents and, where applicable, accompanying money. These levels of government are

1. Local (including towns, cities, counties, or parishes)
2. State
3. Federal
4. International

Documents and financial payments must be prepared and submitted in a timely manner to satisfy government requirements. Typical contents of these reports are described below.

The reports for local town, city, and county—or, in Louisiana, parish—typically include information regarding compliance with building, sanitary, and environmental codes. Other reports indicate the payment of personal property taxes, real estate taxes, and local income taxes, where applicable.

State reports may include information regarding compliance with hazardous waste disposal. They also typically contain payroll, sales, or purchasing information for the payment of state income, sales, unemployment, and other taxes.

Federal reports may include information regarding compliance with OSHA (Occupational Safety and Health Act), ADA (Americans with Disabilities Act), and many other acts that have been passed by Congress. The federal government also has appointed the IRS (Internal Revenue Service) to collect the federal portion of the national unemployment tax, the federal portion of the withheld income tax, and the Social Security and Medicare taxes (FICA and OASDI or FICA-HI).

International reports may include information regarding compliance with standards developed and distributed by ISO (International Standards Organization). Their headquarters in Geneva, Switzerland, is a consortium of 130 contributing countries whose goal is to promote quality standards on a global basis, and to improve the exchange of quality and environmentally acceptable goods and services. These standards contain guidelines prepared by the standards organizations of the contributing countries. The international reports required of companies who sell outside their country are based upon ISO9000 and ISO14000.

Duncan (1996, p. 24) excerpts two ISO definitions that distinguish between a standard and a regulation.

> A **standard** [such as the size of computer disks] is a document developed by a recognized professional body. A standard promotes common and repeated use by providing rules, guidelines, or characteristics for products, processes, or services. Compliance with a standard is not mandatory. A **regulation** [such as a building code] is a document that lays down product, process, or service characteristics including the applicable administrative provisions. Compliance with a regulation is mandatory.

ISO9001 and ISO9002 focus on manufacturing and quality control. Companies must prove they employ an effective quality management system to attain product uniformity and predictability. Any company that manufactures a product falling within a specified industry category must certify that its quality system meets the appropriate ISO standard. Such certification reduces or eliminates customer quality audits. This compliance requirement is part of the product safety laws of many European countries and is being considered for inclusion in other countries around the world. ISO14000 is a similar series of international standards that concentrate on the protection, preservation, improvement, and reconstruction of the environment. To comply with this standard, products must meet the following requirements.

- Material selection should be based on the following criteria to reduce waste:

    Minimize toxic waste content

    Incorporate recycled and recyclable materials

    Use more durable materials

    Reduce total material use

- Production standards and procedures should have the following effects:

    Reduce process waste

    Reduce energy consumption

    Reduce use of toxic materials

- Designs for recycling and reuse should include these features:

    Incorporate recyclable materials

    Disassemble easily

    Reduce materials diversity

    Include labeled parts

    Use standard material types

- Designs that extend the useful life of products and components should include the following features:

  Design for remanufacture

  Design to permit upgrades

  Designs that make maintenance and repair techniques and procedures easier

  Designs that incorporate reconditioned parts and assemblies

- Designs should describe end-of-life safe-disposal techniques.

There are two aspects of the ISO14000 series. The first aspect is the organizational element that addresses environmental management systems. The second aspect addresses product-oriented issues. ISO14001 describes environmental management systems; ISO14010 is the guideline for environmental auditing.

CHAPTER OBJECTIVES SUMMARY

Now that you have finished this chapter, you should be able to:

1. Describe how specifications are developed through the phases of a project.
2. Describe the types of contracts for projects.
3. Explain the importance of trip and meeting reports, and describe the typical contents of these reports.
4. Name the categories of periodic reports and describe their contents. Identify who receives them.
5. Name the various levels of government for which reports are prepared. Describe the typical contents of these reports.
6. Describe the goals of ISO standards.

EXERCISES

8.1   Write a meeting report based upon a group of your peers who have worked together and have met to describe that work. Identify the action items that are to be accomplished before they meet again.

8.2   Develop a change notice form that would be applicable to the work with which you are involved.

8.3   Write a project report describing your monthly accomplishments for either a project or for this course.

8.4   Develop the outline of a specification for a project to which you have been assigned that describes and constrains that project. Indicate how that specification could be modified to become the final specification.

8.5   From your previous work, develop a set of documents that describes your work. Describe how it could be presented to future employees so they can improve their contributions based upon your experiences.

Project Management

The Project Plan

Specifications and Reports

Modeling and System Design

Project Management

The Project Plan

Specifications and Reports

Modeling and System Design

1. What are models, and why are they used in the development of designs?

2. What kinds of models are typically used in the development of designs, and what are examples of each?

3. Why is it important to decide early in a project what to model?

4. What criteria should a model meet?

5. What are modules, and why is it advantageous for models to be designed as modules?

6. What are block diagrams and flow diagrams, and how can they be useful in preparing models for projects?

7. What kinds of activities are performed in relation to models during the four phases of a project?

8. What is the study of human factors, and why is it important in design?

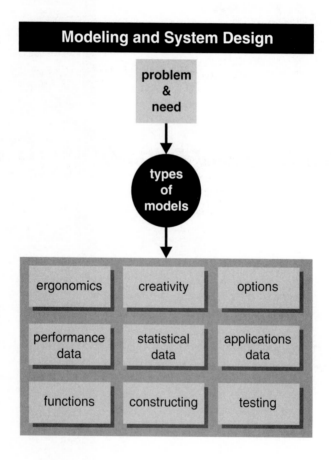

What is false in the science of facts may be true in the science of values.

George Santayana, 1900

Simulation models may be used to replicate a portion of a proposed or existing system. They may also be used to replicate an entire system. The selection of appropriate models for a project occurs as part of the system development process.

This chapter focuses on the values and uses of modeling as related to a system design. Simulation models may be used to replicate a portion of a proposed or existing system. They may even be used to replicate an entire system.

After you complete the study of this chapter, you should know how to do the following:

- Realize when the use of a model would be advantageous.
- Determine where a simulation would be helpful during design.
- Develop a system block diagram that can be used for a model design.
- Examine the applicability of a model to design needs.
- Understand how various models can be interconnected and tested simultaneously.
- Comprehend how modeling can be applied throughout the phases of a project.
- Learn when to apply human factors techniques and guidelines to either a model or to the actual device or system

Rechtin (1997) defines a model as a representation of selected features of a system. It may be a physical scale model of a proposed structure, it may be a defining set of equations, or it may be an operating prototype of a product.

When do we stop modeling and start building our product? Modeling often lasts for the entire life of the project! The initial model is gradually improved until it closely simulates the final product. Models help identify those characteristics that are not immediately evident to the designers. The decision about how much modeling is needed as a part of the system development process must be considered by all designers. See Reutlinger (1970) and section 9.7 in this chapter.

SECTION 9.1   THE NEED FOR MODELS

Modeling is similar to a miniature project to be performed within the overall project. Models are used when there is a significant concern regarding the feasibility of all or a part of the design approach being considered. Modeling a proposed design should be considered when the cost in labor, time, and materials involved in designing and implementing the model is significantly less than that of constructing the actual product. The usefulness of the model in testing the effectiveness of a design must be proportional to the costs involved.

A model is both an abstraction and a simplification of an event or function in the so-called real world. The purpose of a model is to simulate the actual system—or a portion of that system—in an effective and efficient manner. A model must represent the key system characteristics as closely as possible.

Since the purpose of a model is to simulate the actual system—or a portion of that system—in an effective and efficient manner, a model must represent the key system characteristics as closely as possible.

The model is *not* the actual system, nor a portion of that system. Models are simplifications of events and functions in the real world. However, a model that is too simple may lead to incorrect or incomplete results because it does not accurately reflect the real-world situation. Such results would then guide the designers improperly. Therefore, it is mandatory to evaluate the limitations of a proposed model before using the information gained from the study of the model.

Figure 9.1 Types of models

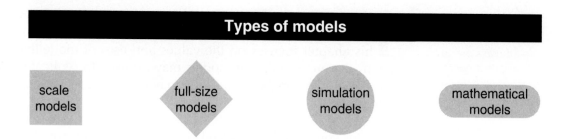

Modeling often occurs during a feasibility study. Studying the operation of a model can lead to ideas that improve a system design. These designs can then be tested before being applied to a project. Some benefits of a model are these:

- Models can demonstrate that a design is unsatisfactory, which can prevent waste of design and implementation costs on products that would not be acceptable.
- Design direction can be obtained from the data gathered from testing the model.

Models can be devised for items as varied as metalworking, insurance policies, chemical processes, and transportation systems. For each area of application, specialized expertise is needed to design a model.

Models can be devised for items as varied as metalworking, insurance policies, chemical processes, and transportation systems. For each area of application, specialized expertise is needed to design a model.

The purpose of a model is to simulate the actual system, or portion of that system, in an effective and efficient manner. There are four types of models (see figure 9.1):

- Scale (reduced-size) models: both static and dynamic
- Full-size models or mock-ups: for technique and process evaluation
- Simulation models: for design, evaluation, and training purposes
- Mathematical models: for test and evaluation via computers

For each type of model, many options exist. Each model typically offers special features, which may be more suited to particular applications. Also, note that a prototype is a type of model. It is a sample of the production version. Prototypes are used to test system and equipment functions. They may not look like the final production version; for example, they might be constructed with different materials.

Here are examples of each type of model:

- Scale model of a radar, for evaluation of radar beam patterns
- Full-size model of the same radar, for evaluation of construction techniques and materials
- Simulation model, for evaluating how many radars are needed to ensure adequate coverage of the specified surface area or volume
- Mathematical models, for analysis of risk (Raferty, 1994) and for data analysis via computer simulations

In addition, design-deficiency monitoring and evaluation models can be used for data gathering and analysis, for example, for studying automotive vehicle safety. Each model should be as modular as possible so it can later be adapted and applied to other design situations.

It is the responsibility of the team leader or manager to decide which modeling approach to apply, for example, weighing the effects of relying totally on a computer simulation rather than constructing a prototype model. The trade-offs include time and money. An inaccurate or poorly designed model may ultimately result in the canceling of the entire project.

During the Conception and Study Phases, models can be developed and manipulated to predict performance outcomes. These outcomes can be used to guide the work of the Design Phase.

Figure 9.2 A typical model

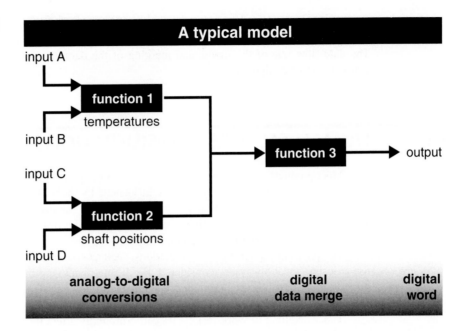

In figure 9.2, Function 1 combines and modifies input A and input B. Function 2 combines and modifies input C and input D. Function 3 modifies inputs from function 1 and function 2. Here is a more specific explanation:

- The inputs to function 1 (input A and input B) might be the outputs of two sensors that are monitoring temperature.

- The inputs to function 2 (input C and input D) might be the outputs of two shaft-to-position transducers.

- Functions 1 and 2 subsystems calibrate the input data and convert these data to digital information.

- Function 3 would then merge or multiplex the digital data into one digital word that will become the output of function 3.

A computer or physical simulation of this subsystem (see figure 9.3) would include the characteristics of a variety of sensors and transducers to ensure that the design works and to

Figure 9.3 A model showing data merging

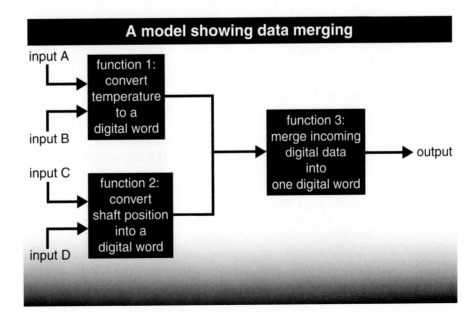

establish the effects of error on the remainder of the system. In this example the temperature sensors, shaft-to-position transducers, and digital-word-merging (multiplexer) are simulated. The data flow rate of the inputs and merging of the data can now be studied without actual construction of equipment.

SECTION 9.2   # HUMAN FACTORS CONSIDERATIONS

*A product will be more efficient and safer to use if the characteristics and limitations of the users are considered in its design. The application of knowledge about human beings to the design of products is variously referred to as **human factors** or **ergonomics**.*

Most products will interact in some way with people. People may operate them, maintain them, be served by them, or be otherwise influenced by them. A product will be more efficient and safer to use if the characteristics and limitations of the users are considered in its design. The application of knowledge about human beings to the design of products is variously referred to as **human factors** or **ergonomics.**

The physical capabilities and limitations, such as size and strength of the people who will use a design, must always be considered. For lifting or moving heavy objects, people may require training in using the optimum procedures to do so. People may require assistance in the form of devices such as mechanical levers or powered lifts.

The scheduling of work-rest cycles can profoundly affect the performance and well-being of workers. For example, much attention has been given to determining optimum rest and exercise periods in jobs that require continuous operation of computer keyboards.

The operation of human senses needs to be considered in designs. For display information—relating to sense of sight—size, shape, brightness, color, and more legible written characters can all be used to improve transfer of information.

In many applications, the meaning of color codes has been standardized. Here are some examples:

$$green = safe$$

$$amber \ or \ yellow = caution \ or \ warning$$

$$red = danger$$

$$white = status \ (\textbf{ON, STANDBY})$$

Critical elements should be coded in other ways also, since some people are color-blind.

Aircraft pilots and navigators complain about the color coding used in cars. Imagine the nervousness experienced by these aircraft-cockpit-oriented persons when they are driving a car in which red lights are used as merely indicators, rather than as warnings!

Information may be conveyed to senses other than sight. Vision works only when an operator is looking at a display; audible alarms can attract attention no matter where the operator is looking. Odor-producing substances are added to odorless toxic gases so that the gases can be detected. Attention has also been given to coding items through touch and vibration so that they can be distinguished.

In Western cultures, people learn to read from left to right and from the top to the bottom of a page. Thus, people from these cultures tend to scan computer displays or meters, dials and knobs, the controls, and readouts in the same way. Such items should be designed to exploit this manner of scanning. For example, the most frequently used or most basic information might be located at the upper left. Similarly, controls should match expectations. For example, controls should move to the right or up for **ON** and to the left or down for **OFF.** Moving elements in displays should move in the same direction as the controls that activate them.

Controls must be designed and located to be compatible with the size and strength of expected users. Often, requirements must be developed for the selection and training of personnel. This ensures that they have the skills and knowledge needed for safe and effective operation of products and systems.

The environment needs to be designed so those persons controlling system processes, operating important equipment, or monitoring systems are able to concentrate their attention on their assigned tasks. Distracting noises and colors should be avoided wherever possible. However, the environment must be neither so quiet nor so monotonous that an operator falls asleep.

Considerable attention has been devoted recently to problems arising from long hours spent at computer work stations. These include back and neck problems that might be alleviated by improved design of seats to provide adequate support; carpal tunnel syndrome (arm pains, hand numbness) from inadequate support of wrists during continuous operation of keyboards; and headaches resulting from glare spots and inadequate character size and contrast on display screens.

To the extent that the environment affects people, it will also affect design. Workspace design should consider amount of space, illumination, accessibility of work and maintenance areas, temperature, humidity, noise, and vibration. For example, some manual controls may be inoperable by gloved or cold hands.

These analyses are intended to determine how best to design equipment so that it will accommodate the operators expected to use it. The purpose is to disover how to make the equipment "user friendly", easy to use, and "idiot-proof." For example, a large amount of human factors analysis is applied in the design of aircraft, submarine, and NASA cockpits, not so much to make them comfortable for the pilots, but to make information instantly available to them when they need it. Whatever the specific intent, the general intent is to determine methods that improve human performance.

Specialists who apply knowledge about human behavior to design are known as human factors or ergonomics specialists. They are generally educated in both psychology and engineering and are often additionally educated in anthropometry, physiology, sociology, medicine, or other human-related sciences. Human factors specialists help to design products and systems that can be operated and maintained more accurately and easily and, hence, more efficiently and effectively. These specialists also strive to ensure users' safety and comfort in operating products and systems, as well as to prevent long-term deleterious effects on the user's well-being.

Very large systems or project teams have their own human factors groups. Smaller efforts may employ one or more temporary consultants. Engineers on small projects may have to do their own designing and evaluating. They can refer to textbooks and handbooks that describe human factors or ergonomics. However, they should have a consultant review and critique their efforts.

Representative textbooks in human factors include Dinsmore (1990) and Sanders and McCormick (1992). Two sources for data related to human factors are Karwowski (2000) and Salvendy (1997).

SECTION 9.3

PLANNING AHEAD ▶

During the Conception Phase, areas are identified in the proposed design that may cost too much to implement or that might even cause the design to fail. If such areas are modeled and tested early in a project, the results can be a workable—or even improved— end product.

TO MODEL OR NOT TO MODEL

Examine figure 9.4. The Conception Phase requires planning the Study, Design, and Implementation Phases of a project. At this time, areas within the proposed design that may cost too much to implement or that might even cause the design to fail are identified. If such areas can be modeled and tested and if useful and accurate results are obtained, then the Study and Design Phases—and thus the entire project—will benefit.

During the Conception Phase, any questionable system characteristics, poorly defined variables, unusual design conditions, and vague assumptions need to be identified. The value of using a model is examined early in the project. Why? Modifications at later stages are more costly because they usually affect work already done. In fact, the project may even be delayed as the modifications to the design are studied and implemented. The system specifications must also be revised to reflect the results of the modeling.

When past experience is not considered a sufficient guide to a new design, then feasibility studies should be performed that include modeling. A trade-off must occur between the cost of designing and evaluating an **exact replica** of a portion of the system to be studied versus studying a less expensive **equivalent model.** The word *equivalent* is the key word. The Conception Phase team must continually compare the cost of a more accurate model versus the expected savings in time, money, and design complexity that a less accurate model could offer.

Figure 9.4 Modeling sequence

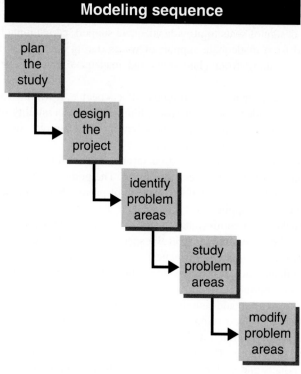

The Conception Phase team must continually compare the cost of accurate modeling versus the expected savings in time, money, and design complexity that a more accurate model could offer.

Any model to be considered must be worth the investment of time, money, and designer talent. An appropriate model should meet most of the following criteria:

- It should be relevant to the system design.
- The output from building and testing the model should result in useful and accurate predictions.
- Realistic relations should exist among the various system components.
- There should be a minimum of complexity.
- The format of the model should be flexible and simple to change.
- The model results should be easy to compare with real-world observations.
- Devising and applying the model should cost significantly less than construction of the actual device.
- The result of using the model should lead to cost reductions in system design.
- The result of using the model should lead to improved performance of the system.

Modeling can be applied to research, management, education and training, plant layout, production facilities, equipment design, and equipment operation.

SECTION 9.4   MODELING APPLICATIONS

A desirable feature in models is that they be modular. Models that are modular can be tested and validated for the current project, as well as be available for use in future projects.

A company or team that expects to continue its existence beyond the present project will develop models that are modular. Why? The module—or the information obtained from designing the module—can be carried to other projects or systems.

In the field of computer programming, for example, the concept of modularity has led to object-oriented modular programs. These modular programs are designed to be used over and over again as parts of different programs. The modular programs can be used flexibly, and they can be adapted for use in other more extensive and sophisticated programs.

Radar design can only be accurately evaluated by scale models or full-size models. For large airports where a number of radar systems may be operating simultaneously, computer simulations of their interaction continue to be too approximate. Scale models of radar equipment are still used to more accurately simulate expected airport conditions. The data gathered are then compared with measurements taken after the full-size radar equipment is constructed and installed. Then the value and accuracy of the scale models can be evaluated and revised to be more accurate for the next simulation.

In the area of building construction, different types of materials, such as woods, metals, and plastics, are used. Some buildings are constructed, monitored, and evaluated over a number of years. For example, for buildings constructed in desert climates or at shoreline locations, the effect of the climate on different materials can be studied. Data regarding temperature, sun exposure, humidity, salt spray, and other variables are gathered. The materials and construction techniques used are then evaluated for the purpose of determining the most appropriate materials and of developing better construction materials and techniques.

Mathematical models lend themselves to computer implementation and analysis. The continually decreasing cost of computer use allows many designers to consider computer simulation for more rapid and less costly evaluations of proposed designs. Computer simulation can be very flexible and is often quickly adapted to new concepts, such as the following:

- Wind tunnel testing of skyscraper scale models
- Architects' $\frac{1}{100}$ scale model presentation via models of buildings
- Process plant piping layout
- ASTME-119 standard fire resistance rating tests
- Failure mode and effect analysis (Pugh, 1993, p. 208)

The general limitations regarding computer modeling are these:

- The amount of computer Random Access Memory (RAM) available
- The computational speed of the computer

The continually decreasing cost of computers and their increasing use allows many designers to consider computer simulation for more rapid and less costly evaluations of proposed designs for automobiles and aircraft.

Also, if a computer model is extremely complicated, then it may be very slow and difficult to operate.

Where a design requires repetitive use (figure 9.5), such as a program for analyzing the output of an assembly line that produces semiconductors, the statistics gathered on wafer size, conductivity, response time, and so on, can be presented in a tabular format. The statistical tables can then be activated by the programmer or operator to analyze the performance and trends of the existing production line. Thus, corrective action can be taken before the semiconductor output no longer meets the design specifications.

Automotive vehicles are similarly monitored. The U.S. federal government has developed an evaluation and "recall" procedure. This procedure assures the driving public that noted vehicle

Figure 9.5 Production line data analysis

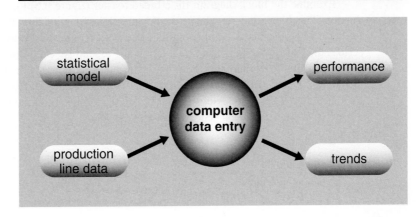

deficiencies are corrected once the problem has been identified and evaluated. Corrective parts and replacement procedures are developed and distributed to local repair stations. The public is then notified to bring in their vehicles for correction. (The federal government has become involved because of the harmful effect of vehicle malfunction on a large portion of society.)

Pugh (1993, p. 208) suggests asking the following general question: What area, if improved, would likely yield the greatest reduction in severity of failure and the frequency of its occurrence, and would also increase failure detectability? Brown (1992, p. 36) offers the following nine specific questions:

1. Can the design be changed to eliminate parts?
2. Can the present design be purchased at lower cost?
3. Can a standard part, or a modified standard part, be used?
4. If the part is to improve appearance, is its use justified?
5. Can the design be changed to simplify it?
6. Can standard inspection equipment be used?
7. Can a part designed for other equipment be used?
8. Can a less expensive, or newly developed, material be used?
9. Can the design be modified to permit manufacture on automated equipment?

Cross (1944, pp. 24–32) warns that the "real" problems must be identified prior to performing a value analysis. It is not always easy to identify the real problems until the design is partially complete.

SECTION 9.5   BLOCK DIAGRAMS

Prior to deciding what portion of a proposed design is to be modeled, the entire design should be translated into a block diagram. Such a diagram defines the input to each block, the functions of the block, and the output from the block. Each block represents a part of the product. The interconnections of the various blocks indicate the relationships among the parts of the product.

Block diagrams are useful in visually dividing a product into its component parts. The blocks can be analyzed to see whether new models should be developed and tested or whether models that have been developed for other projects can be used or adapted.

The Conception Phase team can now ask such questions as these:

- Which blocks within the design are well known and understood?
- Are there blocks that have been used elsewhere in a similar fashion?
- Which blocks consist of newly proposed designs?
- Are the blocks interconnected in a manner previously used?

Based on the answers to these questions, the Conception Phase team may decide that some design issues need to be further explored. Research into existing similar designs may need to be performed.

Examine the block diagram for a bread toaster (figure 9.6) that is to be designed for production. This block diagram shows the designers the functional relationship of each part of the toaster to the other parts. Manufacturing, however, requires a different diagram—one that describes the flow of the toaster's construction and assembly. This flow is illustrated in figure 9.7.

From this flow diagram, the manufacturing functions of purchasing (make-or-buy decisions), tooling, fabrication, assembly, inspection, and testing may be planned.

First, the **ideal system solution** is proposed. For the above manufacturing functions, models are devised. The typical sequence is as follows:

Define the problem

Identify potential solutions

Evaluate alternatives

Select one solution

Figure 9.6   Toaster block diagram

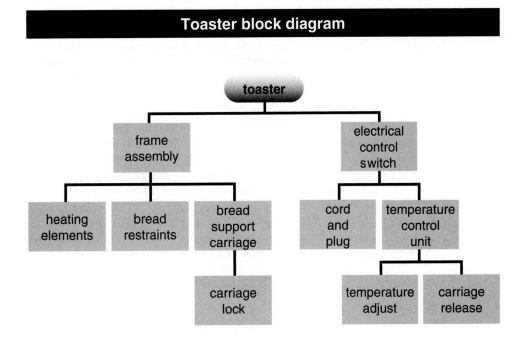

Figure 9.7   Toaster construction and assembly flow diagram

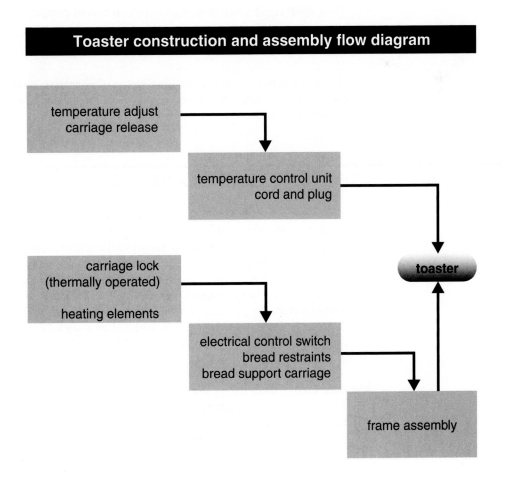

Designers can develop block diagrams that show the flow for manufacturing a product. Such diagrams are useful in planning the manufacturing functions of purchasing (make-or-buy decisions), tooling, fabrication, assembly, inspection, and testing.

Designers can develop block diagrams that show the flow for manufacturing a product. Such diagrams are useful in planning the manufacturing functions of purchasing (make-or-buy decisions), tooling, fabrication, assembly, inspection, and testing.

Creativity is needed in developing solutions for the various parts of the manufacturing process. If large quantities of toasters are to be manufactured, then less expensive and more reliable assembly line and quality control techniques are investigated and trade-offs examined.

Manufacturers are willing to invest money in research and planning because the results of the studies and plans will provide worthwhile savings. The large savings obtained in the production of thousands of toasters can provide money for further studies and savings. Accountants amortize the cost of research and planning across all of the toasters produced. The money saved by designing more efficient and reliable production facilities lowers the production cost of each toaster. Thus, the selling price of each toaster may be decreased.

The toaster construction and assembly flow diagram (figure 9.7 on p. 227) becomes the production flow diagram. It identifies the individual steps required for efficient and reliable production. Such a diagram shows the sequence of assembly line relationships. Pugh (1993, p. 211) provides another example that involves a car door.

The production-line designers next commit to paper their ideas regarding the following:

- Who (workers or subcontractors) will produce which parts of the process?
- What is to be accomplished at each work station of the production line?
- When is the incoming material needed?
- Where will the incoming materials, partial assemblies, and final product be stored?
- Why should a new toaster design be considered?
- How can a new design meet consumer needs?
- How can a new design eliminate current production problems?
- How much could a new design contribute to overall company profits?

These questions—who, what, when, where, why, and how—are used to guide the investigators in a manner that will direct their work along productive paths.

The above questions may be used as a means of examining nearly any situation where several choices are available. The answers then provide the justification for investing money in the development and production of a new product.

SECTION 9.6   EXPANDING THE MODELING

This section continues the example of the use of block diagrams to help in effective design throughout the phases of a project. During the Conception Phase, the overall product or system block diagram is developed, as shown in the toaster example in section 9.5. The Conception Phase team may have devised a new approach to the solution. Sometimes, more than one block diagram is developed. Those diagrams are then expanded and evaluated during the Study Phase. From a block diagram, task lists, schedules, and cost data can be prepared.

Portions of the block diagram may be in question. Each questionable portion of the solution needs to be investigated before it is accepted as a workable solution. Whenever possible, the questionable portion of the solution should be either simulated and evaluated, or actually constructed and tested.

At the beginning of the Study Phase, information is gathered regarding existing models, which are used or modified for use whenever possible. For those portions of the block diagram where no existing models can be easily modified, new simulations or prototype models must be devised. The models are then used or tested and data are gathered. For models that were newly devised, data are often gathered over the life of the project during field trials of new units and during equipment and system operation. The information gathered can lead to

Modeling is very important in the Study Phase. Models are prepared and results from tests of models guide the development of the design.

modifications in later stages of the project and can be useful in preparing new designs of similar equipment.

The Design Phase takes advantage of the knowledge gained during the Study Phase modeling. The modeling results now point in the direction of the preferred design. If the design direction is still not clear, then the prototype of the entire system may need to be constructed. In this case, the remaining portions of the modeled system may then be constructed. They are connected to the partial-system prototypes previously constructed and evaluated. Additional data can now be gathered and examined for the entire system. Last-minute design changes may be needed prior to system construction.

As computers become more sophisticated and can simulate real-world situations more accurately, the need for prototype models decreases. However, it would be incorrect to assume that all prototype models are unnecessary. First, most production tooling cannot be evaluated without the construction of a production prototype. Second, human-machine interaction that accurately reflects the effects of human boredom or tiredness upon the system cannot yet be simulated. Third, computer models are often not as accurate or all-encompassing as their designers may claim.

The Implementation Phase involves constructing and proving the actual system. Verification of the design for quantity production units may lead to some changes when the first production units reach the field. These changes are usually sent out to the users in "kit" form. More complicated changes to products may require field-service technicians to implement them.

There are times when it is necessary to run a simulation in real time. Such a simulation is connected to a portion of the prototype system. It must function at a speed that is at least as fast as the connected prototype. It must also be an accurate simulation; otherwise there will be GIGO (garbage in, garbage out). As an example, imagine a computer program for weather forecasting that operates so slowly that the actual weather has occurred by the time the weather predictions become available from the computer simulation.

Human beings have a wide variety of skills, abilities, and limitations. Machines with which humans interact must be designed with attention paid to these skills, abilities, and limitations.

Training can improve many of the skills and abilities of machine operators. Simulated emergencies can test and evaluate improvement in skills. Simulation of seldom-occurring problems can be helpful in further improving an operator's skills.

People react differently when rested, when tired, and when under stress. These three situations require study and, where possible, simulation, test, and evaluation.

According to Nadler (1970, p. 327), " . . . human agents represent any human resources used in or between any steps of the sequence or as part of the environment that aid in converting the inputs into . . . outputs without becoming part of the outputs." He identified the following typical human agents in a system:

Machine Operator	Tool and Die Maker	Fork Lift Truck Operator
Secretary	Computer Programmer	Janitor
Teacher	Nurse	Telephone Operator
Vice President	Supervisor	Engineer
Doctor	Clerk	Attorney

SECTION 9.7   MODEL INTERCONNECTING AND TESTING

When large systems are being modeled, initially subsystems may be devised separately. After each subsystem model is designed, constructed, debugged, and tested, then the subsystems must be interconnected—preferably two at a time.

Prior to designing the individual subsystem models, agreement must be reached on how they will eventually be interconnected. These interconnections are often referred to as **interfaces.** (Interfaces are the mechanical and electrical boundary for two or more pieces of equipment; cables, connectors, transmitting and receiving circuits, signal-line descriptions, and timing and control information are included.) Interfaces contain information related to electrical, mechanical, hydraulic, thermal, and environmental parameters. (The dynamic portion of these interfaces is known as **handshaking.**)

The individual subsystems are tested separately. Once the models are revised to reflect the final product as closely as possible, then it is time to interconnect the subsystems—two at a time. First the overall test information is gathered. Then the results are compared with the initially determined individual test results. When any deviation is noted, the models must be modified to reflect the corrections. The interfaces are now considered verified.

Now additional subsystems can be connected with the tested pair of subsystems. The procedure is repeated until all of the modeled subsystems are connected into the entire system, if this is feasible.

These subsystems are developed in a modular manner so they can be used later with other system designs with or without modification. Many people devote their professional careers to subsystem modeling and testing.

SECTION 9.8 MODELING THROUGHOUT THE PROJECT PHASES

A summary and sequence of the application of models is given below, by project phase. The flow is further summarized in figure 9.8.

Figure 9.8 Sequence of Modeling

Sequence of Modeling

conception phase
devise & develop new system
identify, simulate, & test subsystems
investigate applicable model types
establish performance goals

study phase
select old models or design new models
interconnect, test, & evaluate models
modify design specifications & standards

design phase
design new subsystems
compare subsystem to design
revise specifications & drawings

implementation phase
construct subsystem prototype
incorporate new subsystems
compare constructed system to model
improve models

Conception Phase

1. Devise and develop the system block diagram.

    Use old blocks where possible; devise new blocks where needed.

    Select or devise new models for newly devised subsystem blocks.

2. Identify critical subsystem blocks that could cause system failure.

    Devise and expand critical-block solutions.

    simulate and evaluate

    construct and test

3. Investigate model types that would apply to identified blocks.

4. Establish system and subsystem performance goals.

Study Phase

1. Select old models that apply to the identified blocks.

    Gather information from existing models.

    simulate prototype

    construct prototype

2. Design new models that are needed.

3. Examine the effect upon the system of each model individually.

4. Interconnect models; test and evaluate model interactions.

5. Modify design specification based upon modeling results.

6. Establish system performance standards within that specification.

Design Phase

1. Design actual contents of each subsystem block.

    Construct and test new subsystem designs.

    Evaluate subsystem test results.

    Revise designs as necessary.

2. Compare subsystem design performance to design specification.

3. Revise Production Specification as necessary.

4. Revise Working and Detail Drawings as necessary.

Implementation Phase

1. Construct prototype of new subsystem designs.

2. Incorporate new subsystems into original system.

3. Compare total system performance with modeling results.

4. Improve the models so they are more realistic when used again.

As computers and the companion software become faster, more powerful, and more flexible, the application of simulations to modeling will increase. Therefore, it is advisable for persons interested in technical careers to learn one or more programming languages and become familiar with the capabilities of a wide variety of application programs.

Since it is not granted us to live long, let us transmit to posterity some memorial that we have at least lived.

Pliny the Younger (61 to 114 A.D.)

CHAPTER OBJECTIVES SUMMARY

Now that you have finished this chapter, you should be able to:

1. Define models and tell why they are used in development of designs.
2. List the kinds of models that are typically used in development of designs and give an example of each.
3. Explain why it is important to decide early in a project what to model.
4. Describe the criteria that a model should meet.
5. Define modules and tell why it is advantageous for models to be designed as modules.
6. Define block diagrams and flow diagrams and tell how they might be useful in preparing models for projects.
7. Describe what kinds of activities are appropriate in relation to models during the four phases of a project.
8. Define the study of human factors and tell why it is important in the design of projects.

EXERCISES

9.1   Describe the inputs, processes (functions), and outputs for a model assigned by your instructor.

9.2   Develop a modeling sequence that describes, in more detail, the applicable sequence by applying or adapting the blocks shown in figure 9.3 for a project assigned by your instructor.

9.3   Indicate which of the models indicated in figure 9.1 applies to your assignment for exercise 9.2 above.

9.4   Develop a flow diagram and/or block diagram for exercise 9.2 above.

9.5   Discuss how you would interconnect your model with those of other students involved in other parts of the same project. Note how the overall interconnection could be tested.

9.6   Write a paper describing how you could apply human factors considerations to your project.

9.7   Write a paper describing what you have learned from this text. Indicate how this text has improved your technical and personal skills, and how this text has affected your choice of a professional career, if applicable. Revise your resume to reflect your newly acquired skills and experience and, if necessary, your career-change direction.

APPENDIX A
Value Analysis and Engineering

HISTORY

Lawrence D. Miles developed value engineering in 1949 at General Electric. Materials were scarce because of the War effort. Thus, other materials were substituted to produce essential products. Informal analysis indicated that substitutes often performed better than the specified materials. From these findings, Miles organized and established the procedure, method, or approach known as **Value Analysis/Engineering (VA/E).**

The main focus of this method is to identify the functions of the product, design, or service under consideration. Alternate ways to fulfill each function are brainstormed. (See chapter 2.) Cost reduction is achieved through critical evaluation to find the best alternative (and least expensive way) for meeting those functions. Because the goal is to provide the essential functions at low cost while maintaining or increasing user acceptance and acceptable quality, the target of the Value Analysis effort is not fixed. In traditional cost reduction programs, the focus is merely on substituting less expensive parts into a product, without changing the basic configuration (Miles, 1972). Therefore, the objective of a Value Analysis study is to achieve the function with increased user acceptance and higher quality at a lower cost. This would be equivalent to increasing the ratio of function at a higher quality and greater user acceptability to the cost. An equation representing value can be expressed as

$$\text{Value} = \frac{\text{Function} + \text{Greater User Acceptance} + \text{Acceptable Quality}}{\text{Cost}}$$

In the 1960s, the Department of Defense embraced the Value Analysis concept and inserted incentive clauses into all government contracts. Programs meeting the guidelines and achieving savings on the contracts received extra money. Companies established new departments. Civilian projects in the private sector followed the military approach and established the process in the manufacturing and construction area (Dell'Isola, 1982).

As the military programs ended following the Korean and Vietnam conflicts, Value Analysis programs were scaled down or eliminated. However, as with all worthwhile techniques and ideas, the programs came back in all sectors of the economy, including manufacturing (both civilian and military businesses), service, financial, and construction. Reengineering and Concurrent Engineering concepts and programs brought back Value Analysis. The process starts at the beginning and continues throughout the design cycle. This replaced a design review after the product, process, or system was nearing completion or in production.

The term *Value Analysis* will be used in the rest of this appendix to describe the *process.* It employs teams, with three to seven people on each team. Mixed groups are composed of people from different departments. Individuals familiar with the problems and others with no previous background appear to be the most successful team members. Initial communications barriers may exist. An experienced leader is essential. The total procedure, with examples, is included in the following paragraphs.

THE VALUE ANALYSIS PROCESS

Poor value is designed into a product when functions are not analyzed. This occurs because individuals follow tradition. They lack information or make the wrong assumptions or do not think creatively. Value Analysis does not accept a designed part, process, or system; it stresses cost reduction by defining the **function.** A product or service increases in value when its basic functions, as well as its secondary functions, perform better than those of competing products or services. Value analysis answers the following questions (Brown, 1992):

- What are the parts, processes, or pieces?
- What does it do?
- What does it cost?
- What else will do the job?
- What will that cost?

Value Analysis has been successfully used in all engineering disciplines and specialties, and in organizations within the human and social services fields. The process is a structured sequential plan or strategy that consists of four phases: the information phase, the speculation phase, the evaluation and analysis phase, and the implementation phase (Miles, 1972; Fasal, 1972; and Mudge, 1971). It is best taught and learned by limited lecturing and with many exercises, demonstrations, and projects. Each of these phases will be discussed in more detail.

THE INFORMATION PHASE

In creative problem solving, the emphasis is on the creative thinking activities: idea generation and evaluation of creative ideas. In Value Analysis, as in any design process, the first (and the hardest) step is problem formulation or definition. The four tasks of the information phase are as follows:

1. Data collection
2. Function identification
3. Cost analysis
4. User reaction surveys

Task 1.   *Data collection* focuses on identifying accurate user data about the product, part, object, or service. These words will be used in different situations but will apply to all problems. Market surveys on consumer satisfaction and attitudes, user expectations and experiences, customer wants and needs, as well as competitive comparisons are very important in obtaining complete and accurate information. Three distinct groups of users must be consulted:

1. Consumers, customers, or clients who have experience with the product
2. Managers or administrators who are involved in supervising the production or acquisition of the product
3. People who are directly involved in the manufacture or execution of the product.

Task 2. *Function identification* is a difficult and time-consuming task. The primary rule is:

ALL FUNCTIONS ARE EXPRESSED IN TWO-WORD (VERB-NOUN) PHRASES.

Functional analysis is similar to the development of task descriptions for projects such as those described in chapter 7. All functions that the product does or is expected to do are expressed in verb-noun phrases in Value Analysis studies. Verbs are action words (see appendix B). Nouns are measurable and must be used in primary functions. Nonmeasurable nouns represent basic or supporting functions.

First, the primary function must be identified. This function is the reason for all other basic and supporting functions. For example, the primary function of a pencil is to make marks; the primary function of a lawn mower is to cut grass; the primary function of an engine is to supply power; the primary function of a window is to provide light.

Next, basic and supporting functions must be identified. This activity is surprisingly difficult and requires a lot of brainstorming by the teams. Basic functions are critical to the performance of the primary function. Supporting functions are subordinate to the basic functions. In many products, these are "perks" added to increase buyer appeal. However, they can add significantly to the cost of the product. Basic and supportive functions are then subdivided into secondary and tertiary (third level) groupings. In brainstorming, combining ideas is encouraged. In function identification, separation is the goal.

A chart is prepared that shows how the different functions are connected. It is known as the **FAST (Function Analysis System Technique) diagram** and is organized horizontally. Each phrase branches to answer *how* the function directly adjacent to it is to be performed; each phrase along the chart answers *why*. For example, in figure A.1 "scribe arc" is the primary function of the compass. To perform that function, the secondary functions of "position" and "rotate the marker" must be accomplished. To position marker, we must "have marker," "hold marker," "separate legs," and "anchor center" (tertiary functions).

This chart can be developed as a group activity. Each phrase is written on a small card. These cards are moved around and new phrases are added. The group must be satisfied that all the functions of the product have been identified and organized in their correct relationship on the chart.

For example, the primary function of a pencil is to make marks. Several secondary functions are identified. One of these is to contain advertising and another is to correct mistakes; an eraser is included. Tertiary functions are not necessary in a design as basic as a pencil. A completed FAST diagram—figure A.1—shows a sketch of a compass, all its functions, and the boundary conditions (scope) of this study (Salvendy, 1992).

Let's look at another example. The primary function of a window is to provide daylight. Secondary functions are to allow air circulation, provide security, and keep out undesired weather. A tertiary function would be to repel insects.

Task 3. *Cost analysis* is very detailed and analytical, and it can be tedious and boring. Various strategies and costing procedures are available for this task. The most appropriate or easiest one should be used to yield a reasonable allocation of cost to each item in the function tree. Labor, material, design, and overhead costs must be included. Other factors may be involved as well. Accounting specialists use a variety of equations to allocate costs. Accounting functions within the organizations should be consulted. The use and allocation of the data, however, must be relevant to the function. All costs must be tabulated and included under the appropriate function.

Task 4. *User reaction surveys* are a diagnostic tool. When the function tree has been completed, the team must determine which of the functions are most important to product performance and customer or client acceptance. Feedback should be obtained from all stakeholder groups. Functions that are relatively high in cost but are judged unimportant by

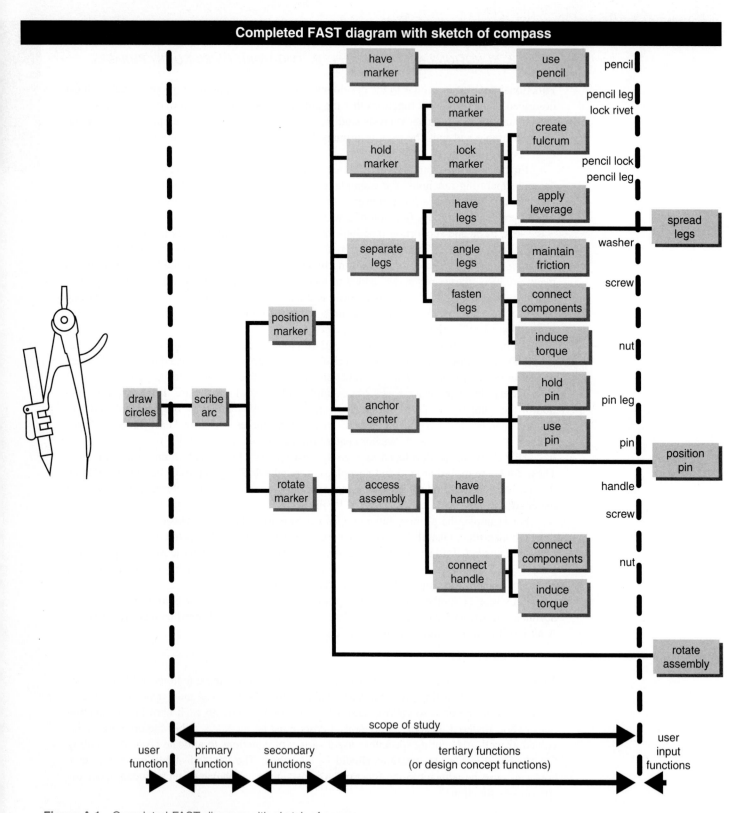

Figure A.1 Completed FAST diagram with sketch of compass

Salvendy, G., *Handbook of Industrial Engineering,* © 1992. Reprinted by permission of John Wiley & Sons, Inc.

stakeholders are prime candidates for cost reduction. This identification of high, low, and indifferent acceptance (or A, B, C classification) of function categories is essential to the next phase. Development of user-desired product criteria is an activity that requires creative thinking and data analysis.

SPECULATION OR SEARCH PHASE

Brainstorming is used to generate ideas. The questions to be answered about each function are:

- What else could do the job?
- In what other ways can each function be performed?

Great emphasis is placed on deferred judgment; the group members are not allowed to assess, evaluate, or criticize. Individuals are encouraged to note their ideas before verbal brainstorming begins. All ideas are recorded. These ideas are shared, additional ideas are generated, and all ideas are written on large charts for all to see. (Refer to chapter 2 for additional guidance on brainstorming.)

EVALUATION AND ANALYSIS PHASE

Brainstormed ideas are evaluated in terms of cost, feasibility, and other relevant criteria. The key objective for this phase is to improve ideas. Ideas are only eliminated if a better solution is developed. Although critical judgment is used, people are encouraged to maintain a positive attitude. The cost figures and the importance ratings developed earlier are very useful for focusing this effort. This phase is very important for those functions that have a high acceptance or a high cost.

IMPLEMENTATION PHASE

The objective of this phase is to sell the recommended improvements to stakeholders for the product resulting from the Value Analysis study. A proposal is prepared that demonstrates that the proposed changes are technically feasible and meet the management objectives. Substantial cost savings are also documented. Schedules and budgets for implementation need to be prepared, as well as an assessment of the new skills and employee training that will be required. Long-range and short-range feedback and monitoring plans must be established to evaluate the results of the effort. The proposal presentation is then made to management and administrators using good presentation techniques and visual aids. The "sales" presentation should be brief and should focus on the highlights.

Implementation of creative problem solving through value analysis requires support from top management. Cooperation and teamwork among departments make it a multidisciplinary approach. Value Analysis requires the allocation of necessary resources. A variety of forms, data collection and analysis procedures, and computer programs can be developed so the process will be more efficient (Brown, 1992).

ADDITIONAL THOUGHTS AND IDEAS

Some supporters of Value Analysis recommend that the Implementation Phase be split into three phases:

1. Program Planning involves summarizing additional sources of ideas or solutions from plant personnel and vendors.
2. Execution involves preparing and evaluating additional proposals.
3. Summary and Conclusion is when the formal report and presentations are given.

Training employees in creative thinking and problem solving is effective and productive only when top management is committed to these activities and provides a supportive environment. Special techniques are available to make you become a better problem solver without having to develop a new procedure for your work. See Allen (1962), Lumsdaine, E. & M. (1990), Pugh (1993), and von Oech (1993).

SUMMARY

The following techniques or phrases are used in any Value Analysis study. Use them in your studies as a checklist.

- Set up the Value Analysis job plan.
- Practice creative thinking to overcome roadblocks; then refine the new functions.
- Evaluate each function by comparison.
- Get data and facts from the best sources using actual costs and standards.
- Put dollar signs on the main idea and key tolerances.
- Use specialty products, materials, and processes.
- Spend company money as you would your own.
- Work on specifics, not generalities.
- Use your own judgment with good human relations.

The Value Analysis process is simple and organized. Implementing it will lead to an improved design at a lower cost.

APPENDIX B
Objectives, Task Descriptions, and Active Verbs

WRITING OBJECTIVES FOR TASKS

Written objectives are used to guide a project. Some describe activities that have been accomplished many times previously. If this is the case, then the previously written and used objectives may be applied directly or modified to suit the current project. Also, written objectives may describe a new, unique, and untried activity to be undertaken. It may be uncertain that the goals of the activity can be met without a further, more precise description.

The written-objective technique was devised under the direction of the late Admiral Rickover. He was assigned responsibility for the design, development, construction, and testing of nuclear-powered submarines. At approximately the same time, Robert Mager developed the written-objective technique for education.

Many school systems use the written-objective technique to define the material to be taught and learned. At the end of the school term or year, special exams are given to determine both the new abilities and specific shortcomings of individual students. These exams also evaluate the instructor's success in teaching the material.

In business and industry, written objectives are prepared to describe the intended outcome, or result, of the work to be performed. They describe what the results should look like, or act like, when the tasks have been completed successfully. They are included either within a Specification document or in a separate Project Task Description document.

The work to be performed is divided into tasks that are included in the Project Task Description. Today, objectives are a key portion of each task in a project. Many objectives are written with the measurable goals to be achieved clearly stated. Results are judged by how closely the design agrees with the numbers that are a part of a measurable objective. The use of numbers permits persons contracting for the construction of equipment and systems to evaluate the progress of the engineering and management team performing the design. There are, therefore, fewer lawsuits when objectives are defined and negotiated in advance.

An objective describes the destination, or end result, of a task. Task analysis documents describe the details, such as: when the task is to begin (the origin), the work to be performed (the route), and the end result (the destination). An objective indicates the direction to be pursued without restricting the designer to a specific final result. An objective may also mention related goals. Thus, all persons involved can verify that the documented goals have been achieved.

The Mager Six-Pack (1996) is an excellent guide to writing objectives. It contains both instructions and examples, with built-in feedback.

Note that a written objective contains the following descriptions:

- The conditions under which the task will be performed
- What you want someone to be able to do (the necessary skills)
- The criteria that describe successful performance; the definition of the *measurable* final result(s)

The objective within a task should allow evaluation of the end result. All persons involved will know when the documented goals have been achieved because the objective is written in a clear manner.

Three Types of Objectives

behavioral objectives
qualitative goals
active verbs

performance objectives
quantitative goals
active verbs

technical objectives
quantitative goals
active verbs

There are three types of written objectives (figure B.1):

1. Behavioral objectives broadly describe the goals of a project or portion of a project and cannot be measured with numbers.

2. Performance objectives describe the goals of a project or portion of a project by means of numbers. All persons involved agree that the goals can be measured with numbers to determine that they have been satisfactorily achieved.

3. Technical objectives precisely describe, in technical terms, the work to be accomplished. They can be measured with numbers.

An objective that describes the desired end result is a **terminal** objective.

Behavioral objectives provide the qualitative goals for a project. An example of a behavioral objective for the activity center would be the following:

Design an activity center for children that provides a pleasant atmosphere leading to friendly interactions with their companions and their adult supervisors.

Performance objectives should be key portions of a task description. Equipment and procedures are judged by how closely their design agrees with the numbers that are a part of each performance objective. They permit persons contracting for equipment and systems to evaluate the progress of the engineering and management team performing the design. Therefore, there should be fewer recriminations, hard feelings, and lawsuits when objectives are defined in advance: Everyone agrees in advance on what the outcomes should be. For the activity center, an example of a performance objective would be the following:

There shall be a minimum of 1' clearance between the exterior walls of the foundation and the interior walls of the excavation.

The specifications for projects contain many technical objectives. (See figure B.2.) Terms are used that are meaningful to those professional persons involved in achieving those objectives. Designers have flexibility of choice within the broad constraints provided by the technical design criteria.

For the activity center, here is an example of the evolution of a technical objective through the various phases of a project. For the Conception Phase, the wording is often most general:

Select flooring whose cost is less than 50¢ per square foot.

Figure B.2   Development in the content of objectives through the project phases

For the Study Phase, the technical objective should not include a conclusion or result.

Wrong:
Construct the floor with ³/₄-inch CDX plywood.

Right:
Select the least expensive flooring whose cost is less than 50¢ per square foot and has a life expectancy of at least 10 years.

With the more general objective, during the Study Phase, designers should evaluate only those types of flooring that will be within the price and life-expectancy limits given in the Design Specification being developed.

The "wrong" Study Phase technical objective provides both the direction and the result or conclusion. The "correct" Study Phase technical objective indicates only the direction toward a conclusion.

The Study Phase "wrong" objective now represents the correct wording for the Design and Implementation Phases:

Construct the floor with ³/₄-inch CDX plywood.

An objective is written as an instruction. An objective starts with an active verb and is a complete (standalone) sentence. Words that are used in an objective should be understandable to all persons assigned to study, design, or implement the design product, process, or procedure. A list of active verbs appears at the end of this appendix. These active verbs are used in the writing of behavioral, performance and technical objectives.

WRITING TASK DESCRIPTIONS

A task description focuses upon *what* is to be accomplished. As an example, the activity center foundation is to be constructed according to the foundation portion of the Production Specification. The Project Task Description describes in writing how the foundation work is to be accomplished (appendix C gives the final specification). A well-written task description leaves no question regarding what work is to be performed and how that work is to be performed.

Why have task descriptions? Because there are more wrong ways to do something than right ways. Verbal instructions are sometimes given for work to be performed. However, such verbal instructions may be vague, which in turn may lead to misunderstandings and incorrect performance of work. Once a project is initiated, someone must decide what work is to be done, who is to do it, when it is complete, and whether it has been performed satisfactorily.

A task is a small part of a project. Therefore, a task will have many of the attributes of a project. It may be considered a miniature project. The work to be performed must be defined in sufficient detail to allow the workers to complete the task with a minimum need for further instructions.

A task description will contain the following:

- The name and objective of the task
- The relation of the task to the overall project
- A description of the work to be done
- The specifications relating to the materials and quality of work
- A schedule for the performance of the task

Two examples of the *technical* content for a task description for the activity center are given below.

Prepare Site

The site shall be surveyed, by Registered Land Surveyors or Civil Engineers, to establish grade levels of the basement floor. A stake shall be placed at each corner of the foundation with "depth of cut" noted on each stake. Batter boards shall be installed for each corner and marked with the location for each foundation wall. See figure B.3.

Excavate Site

The excavation of the basement and foundation footings is to be performed next. There shall be a minimum of 1' clearance between the exterior walls of the foundation and the interior walls of the excavation. If ledge outcroppings are discovered, then they are to be drilled and blasted to remove the ledge.

The above paragraphs give a **technical** description of the work to be accomplished. Next, let's expand the latter paragraph to include all the information required of a total task description.

Figure B.3 Foundation wall positioning technique

Excavate Site

   —*This is the name and objective of the task.*

Site excavation shall follow completion of site preparation and precede the erection and capping of the foundation.

   —*This describes the relation of the task to the overall project.*

The excavation of the basement and foundation footings is to be performed next. There shall be a minimum of 1′ clearance between the exterior walls of the foundation and the interior walls of the excavation. If ledge outcroppings are discovered, then they are to be drilled and blasted to remove the ledge. (See the specification in Appendix C, Cast-in-Place Concrete, paragraph G.)

   —*This is a description of the work to be done, and it includes a reference to the paragraph in the specification relating to the materials and quality of work.*

Site excavation shall be initiated during the first week of the project and shall be completed prior to the end of the second week of the project.

   —*This is a schedule for the performance of the task.*

Note that the first task described above (Prepare Site) directly leads to the second task (Excavate Site). All other tasks connect to at least one previous task and lead to at least one other task. Once the last task is completed, the inspection would be performed according to the final criteria for the project. (Other inspections may be required during project performance.)

When people are assigned to work on a project, each person is given oral and written instructions describing the work to be performed. All participants should be given enough information so that they understand how their work contributes to the completion of the overall project. Then they will realize the importance of their contribution to the total project and will be motivated to do their best work. Verbal instructions are often used for this purpose. However, it is better to also provide written instructions so that each worker may refer to them as needed to be certain that the work is being completed in accordance with the contract.

The Project Task Description should be brief and concise. It describes work that is extensive and complicated enough to require the coordinated efforts of several people. Work to be performed, as described within the task description, must be measurable.

Many engineers and technologists write poorly. Employers complain bitterly that their technical employees cannot communicate effectively and in writing, considering the salaries they are paid. This communication problem includes both their technical supervisors and their higher-level nontechnical executives. The U.S. Accrediting Board for Engineering and Technology (ABET) has indicated that correcting this communication deficiency is one of its top priorities.

A LIST OF ACTIVE VERBS

Objectives start with active verbs and are a complete (stand-alone) sentence. Words that are used in an objective should be understandable to all persons assigned to study, design, or implement the design.

Below is a list of active verbs that might be used in task descriptions. It is considered neither perfect nor complete. Add to this list any new active verbs that you "discover."

absorb	accept	access	accommodate
accompany	accomplish	achieve	acquaint
acquire	activate	adapt	add
adhere	adjoin	adjust	advance
advise	advocate	affect	agree

align	allot	allow	alter
amortize	analyze	announce	appear
apply	appraise	appropriate	approve
approximate	arrive	ascertain	assemble
assign	assist	associate	assume
assure	attain	authorize	avail
avoid	award		
backfill	balance	base	become
begin	believe	bend	bid
bind	blast	block	boil
boot	bore	bounce	brace
break	budget	build	
calculate	catch	cause	certify
change	charge	chart	choose
collect	combine	commit	communicate
compare	compensate	complain	complete
comply	comprehend	compute	conceive
concentrate	concern	condense	conduct
confer	configure	confirm	conflict
connect	consider	constrain	construct
contact	contain	continue	contract
contribute	control	convert	convince
coordinate	correct	correlate	cost
create	cut		
debate	decide	decrease	define
delay	delegate	deliver	demonstrate
deny	depend	derive	describe
design	designate	desire	determine
develop	devise	differentiate	direct
discover	discuss	display	disseminate
distinguish	distribute	disturb	divide
do	document	draft	drill
earn	edit	effect	elect
elevate	elicit	eliminate	employ
empty	emulate	enable	enclose
encourage	engrave	enhance	enjoy
enlarge	enlist	enroll	ensure
enter	equip	erase	erect
escape	establish	estimate	evaluate
evoke	evolve	examine	excavate
exceed	excel	exchange	excite
exempt	exercise	exert	exhibit
expand	expect	expel	expend
experiment	explain	explore	expose
extend	extract		
fabricate	feel	finish	fit
focus	forecast	form	formulate
forward	frustrate	fulfill	function
gain	gather	generate	give
graph	grow	guess	guide
hire			
identify	ignore	illustrate	implement
improve	include	incorporate	increase

indicate	inform	initiate	insert
inspect	install	instruct	integrate
interact	interconnect	interest	interpret
intertwine	invest	investigate	invite
involve	irritate	issue	
jack	jam	join	judge
justify			
keep	kick	kill	know
label	lace	lay	lead
learn	leave	lend	lengthen
let	level	license	lift
light	limit	list	loan
locate	lock	lower	
mail	maintain	make	manage
manipulate	manufacture	map	match
mate	measure	meet	memorize
mend	merge	minimize	miss
mix	model	modify	monitor
mop	motivate	mount	move
mow	multiplex	multiply	
need	neglect	negotiate	note
notify	number		
observe	obtain	occur	offend
offer	operate	order	organize
originate	outline	overlap	oversee
paint	participate	pay	perceive
perform	permit	place	plan
precede	predict	prefer	prepare
present	preserve	prevent	proceed
process	produce	progress	project
promote	propose	protect	prove
provide	purchase		
react	read	realize	recall
receive	recognize	recommend	recompute
reconstruct	record	reduce	refer
reference	refine	reflect	regard
register	reinforce	relate	remain
remember	remove	repair	repeat
replace	report	represent	reproduce
require	reschedule	research	reserve
resolve	respond	retain	review
revise	reward		
satisfy	save	scan	schedule
search	select	sell	separate
share	shorten	sign	simplify
simulate	sketch	solder	solve
specify	stabilize	standardize	start
state	stop	store	structure
study	subdivide	submit	substitute
subtract	summarize	supervise	supply
support	synthesize		

take	telephone	terminate	test
trace	train	transfer	transform
understand	unite	update	use
utilize			
vanish	vary	verify	visualize
want	waste	watch	waterproof
win	wish	withdraw	withhold
work	write		

APPENDIX C

Specification for the Town of Bedford, Massachusetts: "An Activity Center"

GENERAL SPECIFICATIONS

For the purposes of the contract and this specification, the following terms shall have the meanings set forth below.

Both organizations and individuals are identified since both are considered responsible should legal action be required.

A.   The term "client" refers to Town of Bedford, in Massachusetts, whose principal Town Office address is 44 Mudge Way, Bedford, MA 01730. The authorized representative for the Town of Bedford is James T. Williams, Superintendent of Public Works.

B.   The term "contractor" refers to the corporation, identified as such in the contract, responsible for execution of the work contracted for by the client. The contractor is Northeastern University, whose principal address is 360 Huntington Avenue, Room 467, Snell Engineering, Boston, MA 02115-5096. The authorized representative for Northeastern University is Thomas E. Hulbert, Professor of Industrial Engineering.

The contractor is responsible for all subcontractors.

C.   The term "subcontractor" means, without limitation, any firm or person working directly or indirectly for this contractor, whether or not pursuant to a formal subcontract, that furnishes or performs a portion of the work, labor, or material, according to the drawings and specifications.

The contract will refer to several documents, including this specification. These documents interact with one another. Therefore, for legal reasons, their interrelation needs to be described.

D.   The term "contract" means the construction agreement signed by the client and the contractor, which includes this specification and all other documents listed as contract documents.

E.   The term "work" includes all labor necessary to produce the construction required by the contract, all materials and equipment incorporated or to be incorporated in such construction, and other items necessary to produce the construction required by the contract.

GENERAL REQUIREMENTS

The contractor and subcontractor must carefully study all applicable documents.

A.   The contractor warrants and represents that it has carefully examined all of the plans and specifications, and has satisfied itself as to the conditions and difficulties likely to be encountered in the construction of the work. The contractor agrees that any conditions or difficulties that may be encountered in the execution of the work, which should have reasonably been discovered upon such examination, will not constitute a cause for modification in the contract amount, or a termination hereof.

Public agency rules and regulations indicate which permits are the responsibility of the client and which rules and regulations are the responsibility of the contractor.

B.   The contractor shall obtain and pay for all permits (except for building and subsurface wastewater disposal system permits), licenses, certifications, tap charges, construction easements, inspections, and other approvals required, both temporary and permanent, to commence and complete the work. No additional cost to the client shall be made because of this requirement.

C.   In the event of nonacceptance of the work by any regulating authority, the contractor shall perform the additional work required to bring the work into a condition of acceptance, and such additional work shall be performed by the contractor without any further cost to the client.

D.   The contractor shall protect the work and all nearby property from loss or damage resulting from its operations, and in the event of such loss or damage, shall make such replacements or repairs as required by the client without additional cost to the client.

The withholding of money is sometimes used by the client or other funding agencies to ensure the completion of work on time and according to the applicable documents.

E.   The contractor shall furnish the client any permits and warranties required or obtained before final payment shall be due to the contractor. All work shall comply with applicable state and local codes and ordinances.

F.   All work shall be performed in a good workmanlike manner, using accepted engineering practices and accepted construction methods.

G.   All materials and products are to be installed with strict adherence to manufacturers' instructions in order to validate warranties.

Contractors must have some flexibility because some materials and equipment may not be available at the time that actual purchase is attempted.

H.   The contractor shall have the option to use material or equipment equal to or better than materials specified in these documents. Samples shall be submitted to the client for approval before any substitutions are made.

INTENT OF CONTRACT DOCUMENTS

As stated previously, the contractor and subcontractors carefully study all applicable documents because they are held responsible for their content—even if errors exist in these documents.

A.   The agreement and each of the contract documents are complementary, and they shall be interpreted so that what is called for on one shall be binding as if called for by all. Should the contractor observe any conflicts within the contract documents, it shall bring them promptly to the client's attention for decision and revision.

B.   The contract documents will describe the scope of work for the project. A duplication of work is not intended by the contract documents. Duplications specified shall not become a basis for extra cost to the client.

SUBCONTRACTORS

The client does not want to be involved in a disagreement between the (prime) contractor and its subcontractors. Management of subcontractors is, in this contract, the contractor's responsibility.

A.   The contractor, at its discretion, may elect to have certain portions of the work required to be performed by others under subcontract.

B.   No provisions of the contract, nor of any contract between the contractor and subcontractors, shall be construed as an agreement between the client and the subcontractors.

C.   The contractor shall be fully responsible to the client for the acts and omissions of the subcontractor, as it is for the acts and omissions of its own employees.

PROJECT MEETINGS

Interaction among individuals and groups is vital in order to achieve technical understanding. English is not a precise language. Thus, to avoid misunderstandings, it is necessary to communicate verbally as well as via paper documents. The importance of such meetings includes identifying problems and agreeing upon the action that must be taken. See chapter 8.

A.   Periodic project meetings during construction will be scheduled and administered by the contractor with the client to review work progress, note field observations and problems, and coordinate projected progress. Written minutes of each meeting shall be prepared by the client. They shall be distributed to all attendees within five (5) working days of the meeting, documenting all decisions and action items agreed upon during that meeting.

CLEANING

A.   The contractor shall at all times keep the premises free from accumulation of waste materials or rubbish caused by its employees, contractors, or their work. At the completion of the work, the contractor shall remove from the building and site all rubbish (including damaged trees and any other stumps), tools, and surplus materials, and shall leave the workplace "broom clean" unless otherwise specified.

WORKERS' COMPENSATION AND INSURANCE

A.   The contractor shall, at its own expense, comply with all the provisions of the Workers' Compensation laws of the Commonwealth of Massachusetts and shall supply the client with documentation verifying same prior to commencing work.

B.   Before commencing work, the contractor shall deliver to the client an insurance policy whose form and company are satisfactory to the client.

PROJECT CLOSEOUT

Formal documents are often necessary to "prove" that the contractor is the responsible party and the client is only responsible for receiving (accepting) the results and paying for the associated services.

A.   The contractor will be required to deliver to the client affidavits of payment of debts, release of liens for final payment, and all maintenance and operating manuals, warranties, and guarantees, if any are available or required.

GENERAL SITE WORK

Now the more technical wording begins!

A.   The contractor shall excavate as indicated on the drawings. Earth banks shall be braced against caving in the work area. The bottoms of all footing excavations shall be level, and on solid undisturbed earth or rock ledge. Excavations are to be kept free of standing water.

B.   All obstructions to the progress of work area are to be removed. Obstructions include: two trees next to the road and a significant portion of a lilac bush. These obstructions will be marked by the client with white cloth and orange spray paint.

C.   Property damaged during construction shall be repaired by the contractor. Any damage to adjacent property is to be repaired at the expense of the contractor.

D.   All disturbed topsoil in the building area and for a distance of 10′ beyond the outside walls of the building is to be stockpiled on the lot.

E.   Demolition and removal of any existing dwelling shall be included in the contract price.

EARTHWORK

A.   All excavating, filling, backfilling, and grading required to bring the entire project to the finish grades shown on the drawings shall be performed using the stockpiled topsoil and other material.

B.   Fill shall be free from debris, large stones (over 6″ in diameter) and perishable, toxic, or combustible materials.

C.   A minimum of 6″ of crushed stones or graded gravel shall be provided as an underlayment under all exterior slabs on grade, compacted to 90%.

D.   All rocks and boulders greater than 1 cubic yard shall be buried a minimum distance of 8′ from the structure or removed from the site. If there is not room to bury the rocks and boulders nearby, then they must be removed to another location. A state environmental permit may be required. Responsibility for these costs should be determined prior to contract initiation.

E.   Backfill around exterior foundation walls shall consist of clean and well-compacted material with stones that do not exceed 4″ in any dimension.

F.   Remainder of site shall be graded to ensure drainage of surface water away from building.

G.   Any excess soil is to be removed from the site upon completion of work.

This is a qualitative statement. The radius of the slope curve will have to be determined when the grading is in progress.

H.   Grades not otherwise indicated on the plans shall be uniform levels or slopes between points. Changes in slopes shall be well rounded.

LANDSCAPING

A.   Topsoil shall be provided and spread to a minimum depth of 4″ in areas to be seeded.

B.   All areas not paved, planted, or occupied by buildings shall be seeded with grass. Seeding, fertilizing, and liming shall be carried out according to standard practices. Seed shall be supplied by the client. The seeded area shall contain a minimum of 4″ of topsoil.

SITE UTILITIES

A.   The contractor shall furnish all materials, labor, tools, and related items to complete the construction in every detail and leave in working order all utilities as called for herein and/or shown on the construction documents. This includes, but is not limited to, sewer connection, water service, natural gas, electric service, and telephone.

CONCRETE FORMWORK

A.   The contractor shall provide all labor, material, and equipment required to complete all the concrete work. All walls shall be plumb and level.

B.   Formwork for concrete shall conform to the shape, lines, and dimensions as specified for the foundations, walls, and footings, and shall be sufficiently tight to prevent mortar leakage.

C.   All forms shall be adequately braced to maintain their positions during pouring operations.

CAST-IN-PLACE CONCRETE

A.   Foundation walls and concrete footings are to be of sizes shown below:

1.   Foundation footings—18" × 10" placed and poured at one time
2.   Lally column footings—36" × 36" × 12" to carry the load of the center partition
3.   Chimney footing—pour simultaneously with foundation footing
4.   Foundation walls—8" thick with two rows of rebars, with a clear basement height of 8'0" from top of basement floor to bottom of floor joist
5.   Insulate interior of concrete basement walls using 2" R-10 styrofoam

B.   The basement slab on grade shall be 5" thick, nonreinforced, and troweled to a hard, smooth finish. The basement floor shall be installed prior to commencement of wall framing—depending upon the external air temperature. The slab grade is to be set to ensure a level floor that does not deviate more than $\frac{1}{4}$" in 10'. A 4" floor drain shall be installed as shown on the plan.

C.   Footing concrete shall be Type I and have a minimum 28-day compressive strength of 2500 psi.

D.   Foundation and floor slab concrete shall be Type I and have a minimum of 28-day compressive strength of 3000 psi.

E.   The foundation footing shall be installed below the depth of frost penetration, and shall be coated with a mastic sealant. Insulation shall also be installed on the interior of the foundation walls, having a minimum "R" factor of "8," and applied with a mastic or nails to hold it in place.

There are times when the reasons for technical information, such as the 4" slump, are explained. This usually occurs when the contractor may want flexibility and needs to know why the 4" slump was specified.

F.   Footing and foundation concrete shall be poured with a 4" slump. This is a fairly stiff mixture and will require a vibrator. The vibrator, if not used properly, would defeat the use of a 4" slump and cause segregation. An alternate solution would be to add plasticizer to concrete that would increase the slump to a range from 3" to 8" and not reduce the strength of concrete. The purpose of a 4" slump is to obtain a uniform mixture of concrete and create a tight wall that will resist leakage.

If the cost of ledge removal is not acceptable to the client, then an alternative approach (such as omission of the basement) may be necessary. This is normally decided "in the field," which means at the construction site.

G.   If ledge is encountered during footing preparation, the foundation and/or footings may be anchored to solid ledge. Ledge removal is not part of this contract. The cost of ledge removal shall be borne by the client, with that cost determined prior to performance of work.

H.   Sill plates are to be secured to the foundation with $\frac{1}{2}$" diameter, 12" long anchor bolts, embedded no less than 8" into the concrete and secured with washers and nuts.

DAMPPROOFING

A.   Provide a 6-mil polyethylene vapor barrier under the floor slab, extending the barrier to cover the top of the interior footing.

B.   Break all form ties; seal with hydraulic cement.

C.   To prevent capillary action of the concrete foundation with the soil, apply a generous coating of asphalt (bituminous) emulsion to the outside of the foundation below grade. The emulsion may be applied hot or cold, and brushed, sprayed, or troweled onto the foundation.

Trade names for materials are often selected because of the material's reputation for long-term, high-quality performance.

D.   Place polyethylene sheeting over the emulsion for the entire foundation. Trade names of acceptable cross-laminated polyethylene wraps are Tu-Tuff, Super Sampson, Griffolyn, and Cross-Tuff. Extend the emulsion to the top and side of the exterior footing, and extend the polyethylene to cover the top and side of the footing.

SUBSURFACE DRAINAGE SYSTEM

A.   Around the exterior footing, install 4″ perforated plastic pipe embedded in $^3/_4$″ or 1″ stone. The pipe must be 4″ below the bottom of the basement slab and pitched downward, toward the outside wall, at a minimum slope of at least 1″ in 10′. Place 6″ of stone under and around the pipe; cover the pipe with 3″ of pea stone. Cover the pea stone with 6″ of straw or hay, firmly packed, or use an external synthetic fabric drainage envelope filter sleeve. (This sleeve is produced by American Drainage System and is known as ADS Drain Guard or ADS Sock. It comes with a drain envelope/filter installed and requires only a few inches of stone on which to lay the pipe.) Extend and pitch the pipe so the water will drain away from the basement for a distance of at least 50′.

B.   In the interior of the basement area, install 4″ of perforated plastic pipe around the perimeter of the foundation footing. Extend the pipe through the footing to connect to the pipe installed on the exterior side of the footing. Fill the basement subfloor with a minimum of 6″ of $^3/_4$″ or 1″ process stone.

FRAMING AND CARPENTRY

A.   The sills should not be installed unless the foundation does not deviate more than $^1/_2$″ on any plane. Install the sill seals underneath the 2″ × 6″ pressure-treated sill. The sills are to be pressure treated with chromated copper arsenate (CCA) and are to have a 15-year warranty life.

Correction of nonvertical or nonhorizontal foundations is very expensive and complicated. Therefore, contractors are very careful when installing the foundation forms. Consult a specialized text on this matter.

B.   All structural members shall be kiln-dried construction grade spruce or fir. The following dimensioned lumber shall be used as specified:

1.   Floor joists—2″ × 10″

2.   Ceiling joists—2″ × 8″

3.   Roof rafters—2″ × 8″

4.   Exterior wall studs—2″ × 6″

5.   Interior studs—2″ × 4″; where plumbing is to pass vertically, use 2″ × 6″ studs

6.   Carrying beams—4 each 2″ × 10″, bolted together every 48″, with nails in between

7.   Door and window headers—2″ × 10″

C.   All subfloor, wall, and roof sheathing shall be as specified:

1.   Subfloor sheathing—$\frac{3}{4}$" T&G exterior-glue U.L. plywood
2.   Wall and roof sheathing—$\frac{1}{2}$" CDX exterior-glue plywood

CDX panels are not designed to withstand prolonged exposure to weather and the elements; they lack A-grade or B-grade veneers. They should be covered as soon as possible to prevent excessive moisture absorption. The moisture raises the grain and causes checking and other minor surface problems.

D.   Fasten the subfloor sheathing with an adhesive and 8-penny annular-ring nails spaced 12" on center, except for the butt ends. (The butt ends are to be fastened every 8".) When fastening the subfloor sheathing, leave a $\frac{1}{8}$" space at all edges and end joints. Important: Do not hammer the sheathing to close the joints. Cut the end of an adhesive caulking gun at a 45-degree angle and position the gun perpendicular to the joist. Apply a $\frac{3}{16}$" bead in a continuous line except where the butt ends of the plywood meet. Apply two beads for each butt end. (The adhesive prevents squeaky floors.) Recommended adhesive manufacturers are H. B. Fuller Company; DAP, Inc.; and Miracle Adhesive Company.

E.   Bridging will be required. It shall consist of either commercial metal bridging or strapping cut to length and toenailed to the joists.

F.   Wall sheathing shall be fastened with 6- or 8-penny common nails, 8" on center, except for the butt ends. The butt ends are to be fastened every 6".

G.   For 2" × 6" exterior wall openings for door and window headers, use box beams, prefabricated and formed by gluing and nailing plywood web to the headers.

H.   All rooms are to be strapped with 1" × 3" strapping, placed 16" on center, each secured with two 6-penny or 8-penny nails.

I.   The ridge boards are 2" × 10". At the ridge, leave 1.5" air space between the ridge boards and the last sheet of plywood, both sides of the ridge, to provide an opening for the ridge vent.

J.   Nails for installation of doors, window, and trim shall be as follows:

1.   Exterior door frames shall be installed with 10-penny galvanized finish nails, countersunk $\frac{1}{8}$", the heads covered with oil-based putty.
2.   All window units shall be installed with 8-penny galvanized finish nails, set and puttied.
3.   All exterior trim shall be installed with 8-penny galvanized finish nails, set and puttied.
4.   All interior door frames and trim shall be installed with 8-penny finish nails, set and puttied.

The shoe is a horizontal timber, to which the vertical wall timbers are fastened.

K.   The shoe for the 2" × 4" basement-carrying partition shall be pressure treated. It is to be installed on 15# asphalt saturated felt, secured 6" up on both sides. (The wood will be less apt to absorb dampness.)

Note that ramps are specified. This allows access by all people, whether or not they are physically handicapped.

L.   All lumber used for the ramps and porches shall be pressure treated with chromated copper arsenate (CCA), sealed and/or stained. All nails for the ramps and porches shall be galvanized.

ROOF

A.   Roof shingles shall be GAF Timberline Series shingles, 30-year Timberline in "Pewter Grey" blend, Class A. The ridge vent shall be the Shinglevent II as manufactured by Air Vent, Inc., or an equal vent system.

B.   Roof sheathing is to be installed in accordance with the manufacturer's recommendation, leaving $\frac{1}{8}$" between each butt end, with 8-penny common nails at 12" on center, except at the butt ends. The butt ends are to be fastened every 8".

Each roof sheathing manufacturer recommends a different application technique that depends upon temperature, wetness, and lumber treatment.

C.   The roof covering is to be installed within seven (7) working days after installation of the roof sheathing. When fastening the sheathing, leave a $\frac{1}{8}$" space at all edges and end joints. Important: Do not hammer the sheathing to close the joints.

D.   Install roofing as soon as practical to prevent roof sheathing from absorbing moisture, or being affected by rain or sun. Install the roof system in conformance with the Asphalt Roofing Manufacturers Association (ARMA) recommendations that require $\frac{1}{8}$" spacing at edges of all plywood and 15-pound asphalt paper conforming to ASTM specification D4869 or D226. Their specified installation sequence is as follows:

1.   Install the eave drip edge first.
2.   Install the ice-and-water shield over the drip edge at the eaves and up the roof 3' above the exterior wall line of the building.
3.   Attach the 15# asphalt saturated felt to the entire roof, overlapping the ice-and-water shield a minimum of 6". Apply roof cement between the ice-and-water shield and the asphalt felt.
4.   Install the drip edge over the asphalt felt.
5.   Use aluminum nails with an aluminum drip edge, or galvanized nails with a galvanized drip edge.

Snow collects on a roof during an extended period of continuous below-freezing, snowy weather. The heat from the interior of the house, combined with sunshine, causes the snow on the upper part of the roof to melt. The cold water runs down the roof. This cold water, now on the lower part (overhang) of the roof, freezes and causes an ice dam. Additional cold water that is running down and is not yet frozen is blocked by the ice dam. It works up under the shingles and into the interior of the building, causing ceiling and wall damage.

E.   When roof shingles are installed, nails must be located below the adhesive line. (Nails located above the adhesive line affect the shingle wind resistance, allowing snow or roof ice to be driven under the shingles, thus causing water backup.)

WINDOW AND DOOR SCHEDULE

A.   Windows and doors shall be installed in accordance with the manufacturer's recommendation. Fifteen-pound asphalt saturated felt shall be installed under all windows, and extend 4" beyond the window. (Typar® wrap may be used; it will eliminate the need for the asphalt felt.) A $\frac{3}{4}$" space shall be left between the sides and tops of the door and window frames, and the studs and headers, for eventual insulating-foam application. (This is because $\frac{1}{2}$" is too tight. It is easier to fill the $\frac{3}{4}$" space with the nozzle of a standard insulation gun.) Install aluminum header flashing above all exterior doors and windows.

B.   Door and window wood surfaces shall be stained with client's choice of stain; finished with two coats of (nonpetroleum-based) polyurethane. Exterior doors shall be finished with color of client's choice.

C.   The window schedule is as follows (all windows and doors shall include extension jams and screens):

Andersen, 4 each of #2442

Andersen, 1 each of #5042

Andersen, 6 each of #3042

Andersen, 1 each of #CR23

Andersen, 1 each of #3032

Door widths were selected to provide wheelchair access.

D.   The door schedule is as follows:

Exterior Pre-Hung Doors—3'0" × 6'8" frame opening

  1.   Two Brosco BE-70 Steel Doors, steel-insulated, with foam-insulated cores

  2.   Hardware: double-cylinder dead-bolt locks, brass handles, and key-in knobs

Interior (Pre-Hung) Doors—3 each, 3'0" × 6'8" Morgan six-panel pine, sealed on all six sides (two coats) to reduce moisture absorption

EXTERIOR TRIM AND SIDING

A.   The entire house shall be enveloped with Typar®, manufactured by W. R. Grace.

B.   The exterior house trim—rakeboard, fascia, and plancia—shall be covered with prefinished vinyl or aluminum trim cover. A continuous white aluminum/vinyl louver shall be installed on the plancia board, approximately 2" from the fascia board.

Suppliers of caulking may no longer offer 50-year-life; "or equivalent" is often specified.

C.   The exterior siding shall be 16" S&R (squared & rebutted) white cedar shingles, installed 5" to weather. The corner board shall be of rough white cedar or fir to match the shingles. The shingles and corner board are to be coated with bleaching oil supplied by the client. At the areas where the shingles butt against the windows, the doors and rakeboard shall be caulked with a 50-year-life white caulking. The shingles shall be installed with 5-penny galvanized box nails. The contractor shall provide an extra bundle of shingles to the client for future repair purposes.

PLUMBING AND HEATING

Internal plumbing is within internal walls to decrease the possibility of pipes freezing.

A.   The water line from the water main to the meter within the activity center will include a repeater. It is to be purchased and installed by the contractor. The Bedford Municipal Water Company contact (Mr. Alfred Horch) requests that the contractor contact him before any digging commences and before any materials are purchased in order to ensure compatibility with the water-main materials. At the water-line entrance to the house, there are to be a shutoff valve, the water meter, and a back-flow prevention device, in that sequence. The pipe from the water main to the house must be buried at a depth and in a manner acceptable to the water company. The materials costs are to be included in the contract.

B.   The sewer line is to be installed according to the attached document titled: Town of Bedford Sewer Tie-In Application. The pitch of the sewer line from the house to the town sewer line is to be at least $1/4$" per foot.

C.   Internal plumbing is to be installed in conformance with the requirements of the Town of Bedford code. Waste lines are to consist of 4" PVC pipe. All internal water lines are to be installed with type L copper. All plumbing is to be pressure-treated and examined by the Town of Bedford plumbing inspector prior to approval. All valves are to be tagged, stating their purpose (function).

D.   The following bathroom fixtures are to be purchased and installed by the contractor unless otherwise noted:

  1.   Toilet: Kohler, Wellworth Lite, 1.5-gallon flush, K-3420-EB; color—Heron blue

  2.   Toilet Seat Cover: Kohler Lustra

  3.   Bathroom Sink:

       Panel Vanity—Merrilat Industries, Model #782430; 30" × 21"; 1" door, 2 drawers

       Vitreous China Top and Drop-In Lavoratory—Merrilat Industries, Model #4638; 31" × 22'1$1/2$"—white

4. Contemporary Mirrored Medicine Cabinet—Merrilat Industries, Model #7714305; 30″ × 26″

5. Faucet for Bathroom Sink—UPC#0-34449-00663: Delta Chrome Model 575PHDF with (single) lever handle and pop-up drain

E.   The following kitchenette fixtures shall be purchased and installed by the contractor:

1. Sink, Kohler; K3228, 18-gauge insulated undercoat

2. Faucet, Kohler; K15170AP plus basket strainer Kohler K8801-PC

F.   The contractor shall install a standard 2′ × 6′ countertop for the kitchenette sink. The contractor shall cut a hole in the countertop suitable for installing the sink and shall install the kitchen sink.

G.   All waste lines and water lines are to be installed with a pitch to permit the water to drain to the basement without entrapment of any water in the lines for winter-season drainage.

Paragraph G is included should the town of Bedford later decide that the activity center is not to be used during the winter months.

H.   Two exterior freeze-resistant sill cocks are to be installed. These sill cocks shall be pitched to drain to the outside. One is to be located on the south side of the center and one is to be located on the north side near the door in locations satisfactory to the client.

I.   The contractor is to purchase and install an energy-efficient 40-gallon electric hot-water heater with a hand-operated shutoff valve and having a ten-year warranty. A brick support is to be constructed to raise the water heater 4″ above the floor. The drain in the basement floor is to be under the faucet of the water heater so it will remove water from seasonal tank drainage, accidental spills, or leaks from the water heater.

J.   The contractor is to install the Boston Gas–donated hot-water, gas-fired furnace and associated radiators under the guidance of Boston Gas Company personnel.

ELECTRICAL

The distribution panel must contain a lock because children will be present. It must also be low enough so an attendant in a wheelchair can access the panel.

A.   The contractor is to supply and install an electric service to be 100A @ 230V with one lockable distribution panel on the main floor to be provided by the contractor. The distribution panel is to contain a master circuit breaker and space for 20 other circuit breakers. Power-distribution panels: the bottom edge is to be 42″ from the floor. The electric power is to enter the house via an underground-feed (conduit) service entrance on the south side—2′ from the southwest corner. The KWHR meter is to be installed externally.

B.   The contractor is to supply and install the following fixtures for the main floor bathroom:

1. Radiant Wall Heater, NuTone—Model #9358

2. Fan/Light NuTone—Model #9965; 4″ duct required

WALLS, FLOORS, AND CEILINGS
Bathroom

This interior insulation provides a bathroom that is quiet.

A.   Install ½″ moisture-resistant Sheetrock™ on the bathroom walls and ceiling. Insulation for the interior walls shall be R-19 fiberglass with a kraft-based or foil-based vapor barrier.

B.   The wall covering for the bathroom shall be American Olean Crystalline Azure Blue 4.25″ × 4.25″ ceramic tile. The tile is to be installed from the floor to a height of 46″ to 48″.

The area above the tile shall be wallpaper: Breakfast in the Country Book, Lorraine Stripe #2382718, price code B, Fashion.

C.   The floor covering for the bathroom shall be Armstrong Sundial Solarian #66174.

D.   The bathroom ceiling shall be a suspended ceiling with 12″ × 12″ Armstrong Vinyl-coated Temlok Ceiling Tile; #225 Glenwood.

Remainder of Activity Center

E.   Insulation for all exterior walls shall be R-19 fiberglass with a kraft-based or foil-based vapor barrier.

F.   Ceilings shall consist of $\frac{3}{8}$″ Sheetrock™ with a haircoat of plaster and a glazed finished coat.

G.   Walls shall consist of $\frac{3}{8}$″ Sheetrock™ with taped and coated joints, sanded to a smooth finish. The walls shall be covered with one coat of primer and two coats of wall paint to be selected and supplied by the client.

H.   Floors shall consist of $\frac{5}{8}$″ CD plywood covered with 12″ square linoleum tile. The tile is to be supplied by the client.

I.   Window, door trim, and baseboards will consist of soft pine with a natural finish. The pine will be supplied by the client.

LOCKS

The volunteers who manage the activity center will be able to enter via the handset locks. The dead-bolt locks permit a town employee responsible for the building to prevent entry during unauthorized times.

A.   All internal-door lock sets are to be provided by the client and installed by the contractor.

B.   The two lock sets in the exterior doors will each consist of a dead-bolt lock and a handset lock. The two dead-bolt locks are to be keyed alike. The two handset locks are to be keyed alike. The dead-bolt locks are to be keyed differently from the handset locks.

LANDSCAPING, DRIVEWAY, RAMP, AND WALKS

Gutters and downspouts are thereby eliminated, reducing maintenance requirements.

A.   The area from the foundation, out to 3′ from the foundation on the north and south (drip edge) sides, is to be excavated to a depth of $5\frac{1}{2}$″. Pressure-treated 2″ × 6″ lumber shall be installed on the north and south sides of the foundation, parallel to the foundation at the edge of the excavated area and level with the ground. (See the document "Finish Grade Information.") The lumber is to be secured by stakes in the ground. The remaining excavated volume is to be filled with processed gravel.

B.   An approximately 25′ × 26′ parking area shall be constructed in an area 10′ from the street and 10′ from the north property line via an 8′-wide driveway from the street. The size of the grassed-over parking area is to be approximately 25′ from north to south and 26′ from east to west, with its north edge approximately starting along the line of the south side of the activity center. Pressure-treated 2″ × 4″ lumber (or 6″ × 8″ railroad ties), secured by stakes, shall be installed around the three nonroad sides of the rectangle to contain the grassed-over parking area. Client shall supply the grass seed.

C.   A 3′-wide walk shall be installed from the parking area to the ramp using either processed gravel or granite dust. The ramp is described in the drawings.

APPENDIX D
Bedford Activity Center Contract

This contract represents an agreement between the client (who is acting for the selectmen of the Town of Bedford, Massachusetts)

James T. Williams, Superintendent of Public Works
Town of Bedford
44 Mudge Way
Bedford, MA 01730

and the contractor (who is acting for Northeastern University)

Thomas E. Hulbert, Associate Professor of Industrial Engineering
Northeastern University
360 Huntington Avenue, Room 467 Snell Engineering
Boston, MA 02115-5096.

The project consists of constructing an activity center and landscaping the associated grounds within thirty (30) feet of the activity center at

The Bedford Common, Southwest Corner
The Great Road
Bedford, Massachusetts 01730.

Normally, the client supplies drawings via an architect to the contractor.

The contractor shall supply to the client one (1) set of reproducible drawings of the activity center (sepias, also known as brownlines) within seven (7) days of contract signing.

During construction and landscaping of the new structure, the contractor will supply promptly (as appropriate) either videotapes or photographs (that the client will retain) of the status of site preparation, new-structure construction, changes that circumstances may require, and landscaping.

Cost of This Contract is: $20 000, fixed price.

Signed and Accepted: _____; date: _____
    (James T. Williams, client's representative)

The remaining pages are initialed by the client and contractor.

Signed and Accepted: _____; date: _____
    (Thomas E. Hulbert, contractor's representative)

A list of contract documents is given on page 2 of this contract.

Client's Initials: _____; Date: _____; Contractor's Initials: _____; Date: _____

Contract—page 2 of 3

Contract Documents

1 each Specification for the Town of Bedford, Massachusetts: "An Activity Center," dated June 6, 1996

1 each Finish-Grade information, dated May 17, 1996

1 each Grade Information (enlarged), dated May 28, 1996

1 each Town of Bedford Sewer Tie-In Application dated 11-7-95 and permit dated 2/12/96

1 each building permit, dated March 7, 1996

and

1 each Task Description for Construction of Bedford Activity Center

1 each set of drawings, dated 1996 June 11, titled: Bedford Activity Center, consisting of

A1 — Site Plan

A2 — Foundation Plan

A3 — Basement Plan

A4 — Main Floor Plan

A5 — Cross-Section

A6 — Long Section

A7 — East Elevation & West Elevation

A8 — North Elevation & South Elevation

A9 — Door & Window Schedules

Any agreed-upon Contract Change Notice to these attachments shall be endorsed by both the client's representative and the contractor's representative.

Warranties

In addition to warranties given by vendors, the contractor warrants the construction and materials for a minimum of one year.

Client's Initials: _____; Date: _____; Contractor's Initials: _____; Date: _____

Contract—page 3 of 3

Schedule of Performance and Progress Payments

The "start" date is: 1996 March 1

- completion of foundation forms prior to pouring of concrete
  payment: 10% on completion, expected date: 1996 April 1

- pouring of foundation concrete (James T. Williams will witness slump test)
  payment: 10% on completion, expected date: 1996 April 8

- framing, roof, and "boarding in" prior to shingling
  payment: 15% on completion, expected date: 1996 April 29

- pouring of basement-floor concrete (Mr. Williams will witness slump test)
  payment: 5% on completion, expected date: 1996 May 6

- shingling of roof and sides, and installing exterior trim
  payment: 15% on completion, expected date: 1996 May 20

- installation of water, natural gas, electricity, and telephone connections
  payment: 5% on completion, expected date: 1996 June 17

- completion of tie-in to Town of Bedford water and sewer system
  payment: 5% on completion, expected date: 1996 July 15

- completion of bathroom and kitchenette plumbing
  payment: 5% on completion, expected date: 1996 August 19

- completion of interior finish (ceilings, walls, and floors)
  payment: 10% on completion, expected date: 1996 September 3

- completion of exterior landscaping and parking area
  payment: 10% on completion, expected date: 1996 September 9

- final inspection and acceptance
  payment 10% on completion, expected date: 1996 September 16

A penalty of $2 000 will be assessed the contractor if work is not completed by 1996 September 23rd.

Compensation in the form of a check shall be mailed to the contractor upon completion of work, or agreed-to partial work, within seven calendar days from receipt of an approved invoice/bill.

Progress and funds shall be monitored by two selectmen of the Town of Bedford and funds released only by checks signed by them.

Client's Initials: _____; Date: _____; Contractor's Initials: _____; Date: _____

For the case study, total payment occurred on 1996 March 1; the school's internal release of funds is noted here.

APPENDIX E
Bedford Activity Center Contract Change Notice (CCN)

The following is an example of a change notice used to communicate, in writing, the desired changes to a contract. The contract is assumed to be already signed and, therefore, in effect. Many companies display the sign "AVOID VERBAL ORDERS" to remind their employees to document changes in writing in order to protect all involved parties from later misunderstandings.

1996 July 14

TODAY'S DATE	CONTRACT CHANGES	PRICE INCREASE	PRICE DECREASE
96 July 03	Spec page 242 ¶ C. & Drawing page A11, Window Schedule: change Anderson Double Hung #B, D, E, H, L, M, N, O, P from #3042 to #DC3042 (tilt-in feature)	$400	
96 July 03	Spec page 239, Cast-in-Place Concrete ¶ B & Drawings, pages A2, A3, A6, A7, A11: change 5" thick nonreinforced to 4" thick reinforced with fiberglass mesh		$200
96 July 03	Drawing page A6: Change Simpson TP gussets to plywood-scrap gussets on both sides of all inner trusses		no charge
96 July 03	Spec page 238 ¶ A—Site Utilities— include a spare pipe for cable TV	$20	

Signed: _____; _____
              Contractor   Client

        Date: _____   Date: _____

APPENDIX F
Records and Their Interactions

The goal of this appendix is to introduce the reader to record design and maintenance. This appendix will also focus upon the content of records, how they interrelate, and how they are initiated, maintained, and accessed via a computer. Specialized texts are available for readers who are interested in learning more about records—their content and design. Sources include Carrithers and Weinwurm (1967), Graham (1982), Isaak (1994), and Kaimann (1973).

Recordkeeping started more than 4000 years ago. Records were initially kept on stone, then on parchment, and later on paper.

Paper records are known as hard copy. They require large amounts of space in storage cabinets and file drawers. As the cost of computer memory decreased and the speed of computer processing increased, more records were both generated and stored in computer memory. The cost of recordkeeping decreased and the ease of access increased.

As programming became more sophisticated, the concept of records changed. Computer speed, memory costs, records access, and computation flexibility have allowed for greater record interaction. This appendix is an overview of the progress achieved in records and their design.

As projects became larger and more complex, it was necessary to provide information regarding a project's initial estimates, its latest status, and the present plans. In the past, documents of this type were prepared and maintained manually—by hand. Today, with the assistance of inexpensive and flexible computers, these documents are prepared and maintained via computers that use special programs.

SECTION F.1   TYPES OF COMPUTER RECORDS

The word **record** has two meanings. It is the name of a document that contains information worth developing, distributing, and maintaining. It is also the name of a portion of a computer file. A computer record is information that is stored electronically. This record may contain many **fields** of information—a concept that will be discussed later. A record or field may be structured (fixed) or unstructured (open ended).

A **structured record or field** is a set of categories of related data. Every set of fields is identical in content, arrangement, and length. For a structured field, the maximum length of each item within that field must be defined in advance. For example, a structured field that can be used for both generation of mailing labels and quick access to a person's telephone number might contain a total of four items. See figure F.1.

IDENTIFICATION ITEM—9 characters

These nine characters are allotted for each individual's social security number, which is a unique descriptor assigned by the U.S. federal government. The Federal Privacy Act, many states, and some other organizations prefer to develop their own numbering system rather than use social security numbers.

Figure F.1 Structured field
within a record

NAME ITEM—25 characters

These twenty-five characters were determined from an extensive study of name lengths. Longer family names are often truncated (shortened); exceptions may be stored in a separate, unstructured file whose location then becomes part of this structured file.

ADDRESS ITEM, LINE #A—27 characters

These twenty-seven characters were determined by the length of a given mailing label. Mailing labels are available in many lengths and widths.

ADDRESS ITEM, LINE #B—27 characters

These twenty-seven characters were also determined by the length of the mailing label.

TELEPHONE ITEM—14 characters

For the United States, whose telephone number formats were established by AT&T many years ago, the fourteen characters are allotted to

> area code—3 characters
>
> telephone exchange—3 characters
>
> person's number within that exchange—4 characters
>
> extension number if applicable—4 characters maximum

Figure F.2 Unstructured
field within a record

Within a structured field, all items are in the same location with respect to the start of the field. Therefore, programs can be written that search a given portion of that field. They can compare and prepare a document that, as examples, lists all persons with the same street address, zip code, or telephone number.

Sometimes three-digit country codes are included. Thus, the maximum number of characters for this entire record is 102 or 105. Memory space is allotted for the maximum number of structured records (or fields) to be stored for later use.

An unstructured information record or field is a set of categories of data related to one another. Every item within each field may be different in content, arrangement, and length. For an unstructured field, the maximum length of the total field must be defined in advance in order that memory locations and size may be allotted. Unstructured fields vary in length because some descriptors will require more storage space than others. Unstructured fields are searched using key words, phrases, or numbers. The use of unstructured records and fields allows for greater record-design flexibility. An example of an unstructured field would be the resume of Alfred T. Anderson, shown in figure F.2.

Structured fields are usually of the same length. Such records may be inefficient because fields may contain blank spaces to allow for the longest acceptable word or number. However, because the location of the beginning of each item occurs at the same position within its field, that particular item may be quickly accessed and used for other purposes.

SECTION F.2   RECORD INTERRELATIONS

We have been examining the interrelation of various items and fields within a record. A **database** is a group of interrelated records.

Databases are only as accurate as the data submitted to them. The phrase "garbage in, garbage out" aptly describes the relationship of input and output when inaccurate data are included in a database. Financial auditors periodically examine the contents and historical records of a database. They want to assure corporate executives that the information entered from the hard copy is the same as the data within the database and that the database has not been altered without proper authorization.

Here are some basic definitions relating to databases, using personnel information as an example:

- Database—a group of records that describes several persons, places, or things

    Personnel example: the persons who work for the company

- Record—a group of fields that describes one person, place, or thing

    Personnel example: employment history, attendance reports

- Field—a group of items that contains information regarding one person, place, or thing

    Personnel example: (full) name, address, and telephone number

- Item—a piece of information that is to be stored for later processing

    Personnel example: last name, first name, middle initial

The database hierarchy is outlined in figure F.3.

Thus, a database consists of many records, as displayed in figure F.3. A record consists of many fields. A field consists of many items. An item consists of many characters or digits. A character or digit consists of many computer bits.

Figure F.3 Typical hierarchy of an electronic database

Typical hierarchy of an electronic database

database–(most significant level)
    record
        field
            item
                character or digit
                    computer bit (least significant level)

Figure F.4 Information flow of time charges into database

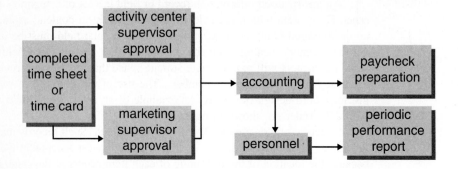

Information flow of time charges into database

Memory sizes are grouped into **bytes.** One byte consists of eight bits. The quantity of computer bytes is now used to describe the size of a computer memory. As an example, a 3.5″ (9 cm) floppy computer disk can store 1.3 million bytes of usable data, expressed as 1.3 megabytes.

The content of a record depends on both the intended use of that information and the design of the forms used for record entry and display. The display may be on a computer screen display or through a printed hard copy.

Examine the information flow for the time charges of Alfred T. Anderson. Assume that Alfred T. Anderson is a salaried employee. He is working part of the time assisting Marketing in searching for new business and part of the time working on the activity center project. Alfred is issued two charge numbers—one by Marketing and the other by the manager of the activity center project. The typical flow of this information, whether hard copy or computer data, is shown in figure F.4.

All employees usually submit attendance data weekly, either using a time sheet if salaried or via a time-clock-generated card if hourly. For each different project upon which Alfred worked, he provides the time that he worked on that project on his time sheet or card. He has two entries. Each is identified with the assigned charge number and the number of hours worked for each is noted. This hard-copy information is then approved by the appropriate supervisor(s) and entered into the appropriate parts of the database.

Alfred is working part of the time on the activity center project. The head of that project will want to examine and verify Alfred's charges to the project. Alfred is working part of the time searching for new business for the Marketing Department. The person responsible for that activity will want to examine and approve Alfred's charges to this effort.

A supervisor may sign the approval via a computer "pad." This saves hard-copy paperwork and allows others to verify the signature at a later time.

Note that two other departments have a special need for Alfred's time charges:

- Accounting, so that it may record his time charges and prepare a paycheck for him
- Personnel, so that they may determine if he has used his vacation or sick leave and also so that they may accumulate data for his periodic performance report

Accounting personnel must have access to the payroll portion of Alfred's record. However, they have no need to know about his personal nonpayroll data. Thus, restricted access codes are used to prevent unauthorized persons from gaining access to other files and items within Alfred's record.

The Personnel Department will want to receive, monitor, and retain information regarding Alfred's time charges and performance. Members of the Personnel Department are often responsible for obtaining all performance inputs so Alfred may be evaluated for a merit raise and/or promotion.

The Marketing Department will need to know how much time and money is being charged to its budget. Alfred's time sheet or time card provides this information. Alfred's information is entered into the database, and data information from the files of Alfred and all others who have assisted the Marketing Department can be extracted from the database.

The activity center manager, Roger, will want to know how much time and money is being charged against his effort. Manuel will have prepared the form for presenting the data desired by Roger. Those persons completing this document must have access to the files of Alfred and all others who have assisted in this project.

Figure F.5 Typical structure of a relational database

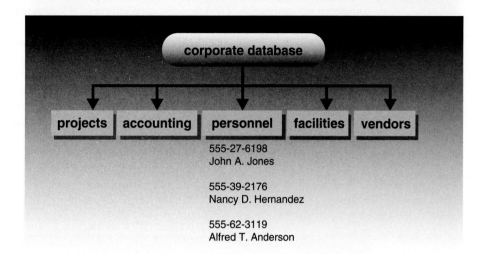

The database may be a relational or interrelated database. Therefore it can be shared by several groups or organizations, such as shown in figure F.5.

Each group or organization may have total access or limited access to data, depending on its needs. Modification of the database must be further restricted to avoid improper alteration of records.

Database activities include data gathering, manipulation, storage, and retrieval. An interrelated database (figure F.5) may consist of the following types of records:

Projects

    External (such as activity center)

    Internal (such as research)

Accounting

    Project Costs

    Payables and Receivables

    Department Costs

    Balance Sheets

    Profit and Loss Statements

Personnel

    Employees

    Job Descriptions

    Employment Agencies

Facilities

    Buildings

    Furnishings and Fixtures

    Paved Areas

    Landscaped Areas

    Maintenance

Vendors

    Office Supplies

    Electronic Parts

    Computer Hardware and Software

    Machine Tools

    Assembly Equipment

    Security

Within the storage medium of a computer, there is an index of key words or groups of digits. These words or digits are used to locate records, such as personnel records.

As an example, a new personnel record may be initiated from hard copy, such as from a completed job application. The job application information is arranged in a form so that the data can be readily processed by and stored within a computer.

Data storage sizing involves estimating the number of records and the length of each record. Data retrieval requires knowing how each type of record has been designed so access to that record is simple and easy to comprehend. The computer data storage subsystem is indexed so records, or portions of records, may be easily accessed by authorized departments. Also, each record, whether structured or unstructured, must contain locations that always contain the same type of information. Figure F.6 indicates a flow of information related to the preparation of a paycheck and the associated payroll data.

Figure F.6   Flow of payroll information

Flow of payroll information

employee
  work hours as requested   time sheet
department
  receive hours worked
personnel
  establish pay rate
payroll
  compute gross pay
  determine deductions
      federal withholding tax
      state withholding tax
      health insurance
      credit union
                                    paycheck
  prepare paycheck
bank
  deduct paycheck value from   bank record
  corporate bank account
accounting
  allot time charges to
      department   department report
      personnel   personnel report
      project   project report
historical records
  store historical data
accounting   government quarterly report
  prepare government quarterly
  reports from historical records

A database is designed so that the data contained can be used to formulate a variety of documents. Thus, interrelated information can be extracted and turned into documents. Each document will have a standard format and layout that allows information to be transported from the database into the correct portion of that document. Typical documents include the following:

Current and Potential Vendors: capability and prices

Office Supply Sources: supplies and prices

Personnel: staff and consultants

Occupancy: rent, utilities, and maintenance

Insurance and Taxes

   Business Liability Insurance

   Workers' Compensation Insurance

   Unemployment Taxes

Communications

   Telephone

   Copying

   Fax

Travel

   Transportation

   Lodging

   Meals

Inventory

   Construction Materials

   Office Supplies

   Furnishings and Fixtures

   Equipment

Typical information to be accessed includes the following:

Per Person (This also includes information for Payroll.)

   Labor Rate

   FICA Rate

   Federal (IRS) Tax Rate

   State (DOR) Tax Rate

   Local Tax Rate

   Fringe Benefits, such as health insurance

Per Project

   Tasks versus Months Schedule

   Labor versus Months Schedule, and Labor Rates for

      Foreman

      Carpenter

      Masons

      Electrical

For the Corporation

    Cost Control Records

        Estimates versus Actuals

        Payroll: salaries and wages

        Inventory

            Materials

            Supplies

            Furniture

            Equipment

        Taxes

            Federal

            State

            Local

These categories will vary from one corporation to another, and from one database to another. They may be displayed on a computer screen or converted to hard copy.

SECTION F.3 · DOCUMENT DESIGN

Computer programs can be designed by a programmer to extract information from an interrelated database and place it into documents. See figure F.7. The programmer designs a Payroll document and also designs a Project Report document. The programmer writes a program for the Payroll Department that indicates the following: FICA information is in location 002, Hourly Rate is in location 003, Hours Worked is in location 004, and Gross Pay is in location 005. The program will automatically extract this information from an employee's record, such as Alfred's record.

For the Activity Center Project Report, the programmer writes a program that indicates the following:

1. FICA information is in location 002 of an employee's record.
2. (Activity Center) Hours Worked is in location 006.
3. (Activity Center) Gross Pay is in location 008.

The program will automatically extract this information from Alfred's record. For Nancy Hernandez, John A. Jones, and others, the same program can be repeated to extract the same information.

In practice, the record for Alfred T. Anderson and all other employees will contain many more items and fields than are shown in figure F.7. As an example, at the time each employee is hired, entries and fields might be the following:

Employment Application

Interviewer's Critique

Reference Checks

    Payroll Authorization and Deductions

    Gross Pay (hourly or salary)

    FICA (Federal Insurance Contributions Act), more commonly known as social security

    Withholding: federal, state, and perhaps local

    Health Insurance: medical and dental

Figure F.7 Use of an interrelated database

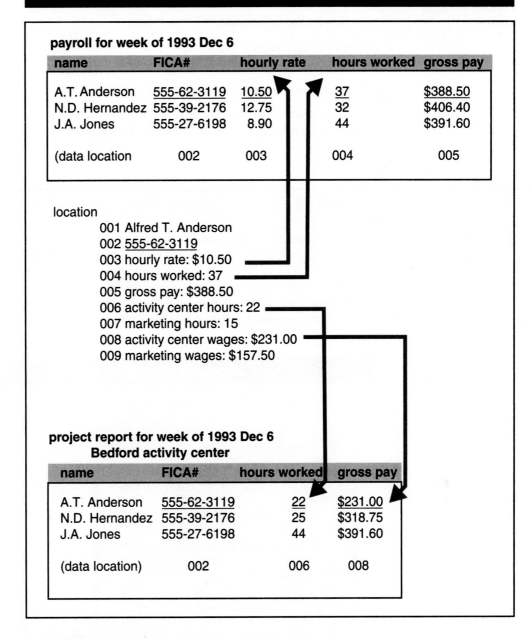

During their employment, the records might be the following:

    Periodic Evaluations: performance reviews

    Attendance Information

        Time Clock or Sheet (date, hours worked, project or task number)

        Vacation Days

        Personal Days

        Other Time Off: with and without pay (direct and indirect charges)

    Salary and Salary Change Data

        Payroll Change Notice (including deduction changes)

           Withholding: number of exemptions

           Credit union: deposits

           Health benefit changes

Accident Report

Medical Report

Termination Information

When Alfred leaves the company, there may be the following:

1. A report from the department head or supervisor to the Personnel Department
2. A closure notice to the Payroll Department and to Alfred's department head

Project managers often need to access portions of the above information. Their access may be direct, via a computer network, or through the Personnel Department, depending upon company policy.

SECTION F.4   CORPORATE DATABASE REQUIREMENTS

An interactive corporate database requires the ability to retrieve and manipulate data from the company's customers, vendors, and its own corporate departments. These data (shown in figure F.8) will be in identified locations similar to those in the previous personnel example.

The overall corporate storage requirements include all those records developed and kept by the departments indicated in figure F.9. As mentioned earlier, access is limited to those persons who are authorized to both view and modify these records.

Figure F.8 Corporate interactive storage

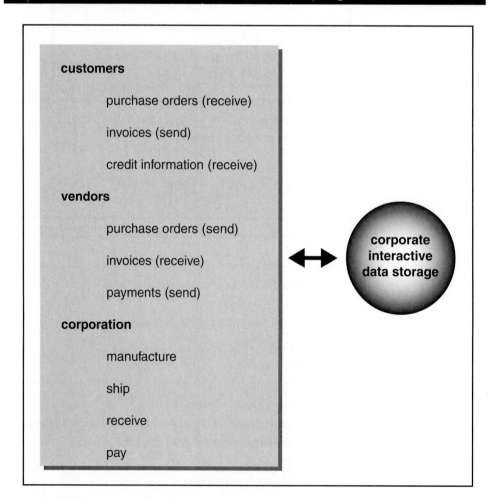

Corporate interactive storage

customers

purchase orders (receive)

invoices (send)

credit information (receive)

vendors

purchase orders (send)

invoices (receive)

payments (send)

corporation

manufacture

ship

receive

pay

corporate interactive data storage

Figure F.9 Corporate overall storage requirements

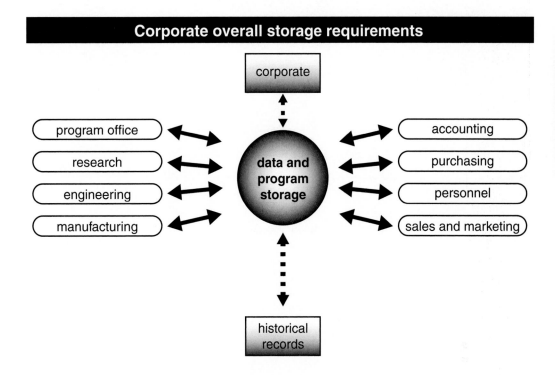

Note that historical records—archives—are also kept and cannot be modified: They can only be retrieved. A well-trained auditor can also determine if someone has altered records in an inappropriate manner. This auditor can often trace the alteration to the computer terminal on which the alteration was entered.

Computer records can be disseminated to various locations within a corporation and to other corporations with which the corporation interacts. Within a given building or adjacent building, Local Area Networks (LANs), such as Ethernet, Token Ring, and FDDI, can be utilized. Where the locations are far apart, the Wide Area Networks (WANs), such as X.25, SDLC, SMDS, B-ISDN, and ATM, can be utilized. Popular protocols that allow database interaction include FDDI, X.25, and X.400.

A National Information Infrastructure (NII), referred to in the nontechnical press as the Information Superhighway, is being designed and tested. This infrastructure will span a multitude of standards-development organizations on a worldwide basis. The challenge is to work together at all levels to provide a coherent environment for the NII. The standards that are incorporated into the NII will eventually link every household and desktop in the nation and, later, in the world.

APPENDIX G
System-Level Specifications

GENERAL

The general content and hierarchy of a system-level specification is given in section 8.1, figure 8.2, and is repeated here.

- Scope of Specification
- Applicable Documents
- Requirements

  System Definition

  System Characteristics

  Design and Construction

  Documentation

  Logistics

  Personnel and Training

  Precedence

- Quality Assurance Provisions
- Preparation for Delivery
- Notes and Appendixes

This appendix will focus on the "System Definition" and "System Characteristics" sections within the Requirements paragraph. This section is the more technical portion of a system-level specification. Typical content of these sections is given below for each of the following fields of interest:

Aeronautical

Architectural

Biomedical and Biotechnology

Chemical

Civil

Communications

Computer

Electrical and Electronic

Environmental

Hazardous Waste

Industrial

Manufacturing

Marine and Marine Science

Materials

Mechanical

Nuclear

Optics

Systems

AERONAUTICAL

System Definition

System Characteristics

ARCHITECTURAL

System Definition

For a given piece of land, devise a compatible and attractive family of buildings containing no more than five floors. Design one structure for use by retail stores, a second structure as an office building, and a third structure as a warehouse. Include in the design a parking area and landscaping that causes the entire family of buildings to look pleasing to a passing observer.

System Characteristics

The dimensions of each building shall not exceed: 50′ in height, 60′ in width, and 30′ from the front to the rear of the building. Local building codes will apply with regard to frontage requirements.

The first structure shall contain second-floor-and-above private apartments. The first-floor retail stores shall be modular in construction so there could be

1. three stores with a 20′ front,
2. two stores with a 30′ front, or
3. one store with a 20′ front and a second store with a 40′ front

Each store will have a separate and controllable access to its portion of the basement. Each store and private apartment shall have its own entrance and rear exit, heating, ventilation and air conditioning system, metered electrical power, communications, natural gas, water, and sewage. A common elevator shall be provided for both freight and passenger use. There shall be two stairways for each floor of apartments. Those stairways shall be on opposite ends of the building for fire-exit purposes. A hallway shall be provided for each private apartment.

The second structure shall contain only offices and shall be modular in construction. Each office shall have its own entrance, heating, ventilation and air conditioning system, metered electrical power, communications, natural gas, water, and sewage. There shall be two stairways for each floor of offices. Those stairways shall be on opposite ends of the building for fire-exit purposes. A hallway shall be provided for access to all offices on the second floor and above. A common elevator shall be provided for both freight and passenger use.

The third structure shall contain warehoused materials that are separated into either two or three modular sections. Each warehouse section shall have its own entrance and rear exit, heating, ventilation and air conditioning system, metered electrical power, communications, natural gas, water, and sewage. Each loading-dock entrance shall be large enough to accept materials that are at least 10′ wide and 6′ high. If additional floors are included in the design, then separate elevators shall be provided for freight and passenger use. (The size of the freight elevator and the floor loading characteristics shall be determined as a part of the design process.)

Separate elevators shall be provided for freight and passenger use. There shall be two stairways for each floor of the warehouses. Those stairways shall be on opposite ends of the building for fire-exit purposes. A hallway shall be provided for each warehouse.

All three buildings will be provided with electrical power, communications, gas, water, and sewage connections.

BIOMEDICAL AND BIOTECHNOLOGY

CHEMICAL

CIVIL

System Definition

Identify one or more abutting properties that can be surveyed and designed for multiple use as housing and industrial subdivisions, with perhaps a small airport. Survey the identified property(s). Prepare plot plans and topographic plans. Determine existing zoning constraints such as setbacks and permitted usage of the land. Establish vehicular access that coordinates with adjacent properties.

System Characteristics

Devise a layout of the property(s) subdivided into

1. wildlife refuges and wetlands,
2. agricultural,
3. residential,
4. commercial, and
5. industrial.

Consider the need for buffer zones, roadways, bridges, drainage, electrical power, natural gas, and sewage installations that take advantage of the land contours, trees, rock outcroppings, and waterways. Describe any constraints regarding future structure location, size, style, and exterior finish.

COMMUNICATIONS

System Definition
System Characteristics

COMPUTER

System Definition

Devise a portable computer that shall be compatible with a variety of accessory and communication devices. It is to be easy to transport, set up, use, and store and shall operate and/or be chargeable from a variety of external power sources. It shall be operable in an environment suitable to an ungloved operator operating in a safe manner. The processing abilities and cost of the total package and its accessories shall be competitive to those expected to be marketed within the same time frame as this portable computer. That time frame is to be within eighteen months from concept initiation. The useful lifetime of this computer and its accessories shall be at least three years.

System Characteristics

The portable computer shall consist of a data processor and controller, keyboard, mouse or equivalent pointing device, monitor, 8.9 cm (3.5″) floppy disk drive, and power supply. Connections shall be provided for its use with an external monitor, CD-ROM drive, printer, optical character reader, and communications devices. An optional carrying case is to be either selected from one already in stock or designed as a new accessory. When the computer is removed from the carrying case, its maximum base dimensions shall permit its use on a small portion of a standard desk top. It shall contain no exposed sharp edges. There shall be no access by the user to internal electrical power.

The data processor and controller shall utilize standard components. These components are to be compatible with the manufacturing and repair-parts market availability during the four and one-half years from computer conception through its expected lifetime.

The keyboard and mouse or equivalent pointing device shall be designed ergonomically to minimize long-term physical stress such as carpal tunnel syndrome. The monitor shall be designed to minimize eye strain. The locations of the keyboard, mouse or equivalent pointing device, monitor, and any other related controls shall be compatible with each other and with the intended user.

The 8.9 cm (3.5″) floppy disk drive shall be able to receive disks formatted for either Macintosh or PC applications. The portable computer shall be able to both read from and write to disks contained within the floppy disk drive. The drive shall automatically protect itself when not in use.

The external power source shall be either 115 V, 50 to 60 Hz, or a car cigarette lighter socket. An internal power supply, possibly a combination line rectifier and battery, shall provide internal power, line surge filtering, and external power regulation. A combined audible and visual signal shall be provided to warn the user that the energy being supplied from the internal power source is within a few minutes of being unable to permit computer operation.

Connections for use with an external monitor, CD-ROM drive, printer, optical character reader, and communications devices shall meet IEEE Standard #XXX.X. Communications devices shall include infrared computer-to-computer links and hard-wired standard telephone jacks. Any required modem shall be contained within the portable computer.

The optional carrying case should contain at least one pocket that can store up to ten disks and another pocket that can store a pad of paper that is no more than 22 cm by 28 cm (8.5″ by 11″). When closed, the case shall resist the penetration of rain and snow. When stored, the case shall protect the computer from damage due to industrial-level shock, vibration, temperature, and humidity conditions.

ELECTRICAL AND ELECTRONIC

System Definition

System Characteristics

Describe system concept—attributes, functions, and features

Attributes—comfort, portability, durability

Functions—to be determined later

Features—safety, cost, and speed

Provide bounds and/or goals for system performance

What the system must do; not what it must be

Indicate design boundaries (constraints), both technical and economic
Identify system and subsystem functions

ENVIRONMENTAL

System Definition
System Characteristics

HAZARDOUS WASTE

INDUSTRIAL

MANUFACTURING

MARINE AND MARINE SCIENCE

MATERIALS

MECHANICAL

NUCLEAR

OPTICS

System Definition
System Characteristics

SYSTEMS

System Definition

Devise a system that can sense, display, and activate existing and planned remote analog and digital devices. The system shall be designed to

1. sense and store information in a digital format,
2. transmit digital information to one or more remote locations, and
3. receive, store, and implement digital instructions.

The system shall consist of a family of compatible sensors, transducers, data entry devices, controllers, recorders, displays, transmit/receive devices, and their necessary power subsystems.

Human factors considerations shall be an important part of the design. Problems related to operation during quiet times and when the operators are being stressed by either or both the system and the environment are to be considered.

Each device within the system shall be designed for both commercial and industrial purposes. The format and data content shall be programmable so as to lend itself to a variety of applications.

Parameters to be monitored and controlled can be as simple as temperature, humidity, and water levels. They can also be as sophisticated as identifying out-of-specification parameters of a process or a security system so alarms can be automatically transmitted to other locations.

Initiate a design that approximates the system characteristics described below. Then perform a marketing study to determine competitive existing and expected systems. Also determine the preferences of potential customers regarding flexibility, cost, and maintenance and repair expectations. Estimate the size of each market studied.

System Characteristics

The sensors and transducers shall have the ability to measure the parameters for which they were designed. They shall provide their information in a digital format to be determined later. The sensors shall provide that information to a controller when they are interrogated. The digital communication technique will be determined as a part of the design.

Parameters to be monitored and controlled shall include temperature, humidity, wind speed and direction, and any other parameters that can be presented in a digital format. Controls, such as on/off functions, shall also be available. The range of parameters to be monitored and controlled shall depend upon a study of the potential market.

The data entry devices shall be keyed by a human being or by previously recorded data that are entered based upon clock time. This information will be stored by one or more of the applicable recorders.

The controllers are the heart of the system. Each controller shall perform at least the following functions:

1. Exercise control over a minimum of four parametric functions and a maximum that is to be determined during a market study.

2. Provide power to all active devices.

3. Provide timing signals to all connected devices.

4. Transmit and receive data between units as programmed.

5. Provide data location, data value, and time-clock information to the connected recorders and to backup recorders.

6. Connect to a keyboard.

7. Contain computational circuitry that can provide data for each connected display in the format described for that display.

8. Accept preprogrammed ROM circuitry designed for a specific application that includes the quantity and type of input, output, and transmit/receive devices and information that describes those given parameters that are out of specification. The preprogrammed ROM parameters shall be retained within the controller in such a way that an authorized operator can modify them. The controller will transmit the identification of the authorized operator and the time of parameter modification to the appropriate recorder and its backup recorder.

9. Identify out-of-specification parameters, select one or more preidentified telephone numbers from a recorder, activate one or more calls until a human being responds, and verify that the person who has received that emergency notification has responded with a correct identification code.

The recorders shall store all data delivered to them from either the controllers or the data entry devices. That data shall be stored in a common format for each sensor, transducer, and data entry device. The data shall be coded with respect to time of information arrival.

The displays shall consist of at least two types—one small portable display and one desktop display.

1. The smaller display shall provide, as a minimum, eight alphanumeric characters per row for two rows. The first row shall indicate the source and type of data; the second row shall indicate the value of that data. The smaller display shall also provide for alphanumeric keyboard entry.

2. The larger display shall provide, as a minimum, the ability to present information in both alphanumeric and graphical format. The graphical format shall provide a vertical axis labelled with the parameter numeric data, including the appropriate units and a horizontal axis labelled as a "time" axis with the appropriate units. The vertical axis shall be convertible from metric units to U.S. common units upon command. The larger display shall also provide for alphanumeric keyboard entry.

The presentation of both displays shall be controllable by a properly identified operator using a connected data entry device.

The transmit/receive devices shall contain a slow-speed modem and shall operate via existing analog and digital

(a)   telephone lines and

(b)   vehicular communications systems.

In the field where there may be no controller, the transmit/receive device shall have the ability to interrogate existing sensors and transducers. Whenever a controller is present, the devices shall be slaved to that controller. It may be desirable to develop two or more separate transmit/receive devices, depending upon information gathered during a study of the potential market.

The power subsystem shall consist of at least three units:

1. A power-storage unit that can remain in the field and can be charged by solar and/or wind power.

2. A vehicular power-supply unit that can operate from the 12 Vdc of that vehicle or from conversion from that vehicle's 12 Vdc to whatever voltage or voltages are required by the equipment being powered. The power supply shall have the ability to be connected to a receptacle such as a cigarette lighter or other receptacle associated with vehicular communications.

3. A power supply that is operated from a 115/230 V, 50 Hz to 60 Hz source of electrical power.

APPENDIX H
Student Activity Center
As-Built Plans

GENERAL

The As-Built Plans for the Student Activity Center consist of eleven drawings:

    Topographical Plan of Property
    Site Plan
    Foundation Plan
    Basement Plan
    First Floor Plan
    Attic Crawl Space Plan
    Cross Section
    Long Section
    End Elevations
    Long Elevations
    Door and Window Schedule

Their content is given below.

TOPOGRAPHICAL PLAN OF PROPERTY

    Property Line Dimensions and Directions (as magnetic or GPS bearings)
    Final Grades and Lot Drainage

SITE PLAN
(SHOWING STUDENT ACTIVITY CENTER LOCATION)

    Utility Connections
        Water
        Sewer
        Natural Gas
        Electricity
        Telephone
        Cable Television

FOUNDATION PLAN

Floor Drain Piping

Foundation Wall Footings

Chimney Footings

Lally Column Bases

Furnace Base

BASEMENT PLAN

Floor Drains

Basement Floor

Utilities Entrances and Exit (water and sewer)

Stairway

Furnace Location

Water Heater Location

Lavatory Content and Piping Locations

Partitions

Door(s)

FIRST FLOOR PLAN

Stairway

Windows and Doors Locations

Partitions

Heat and Duct Layout and Locations

Lavatory Content and Piping Locations

Kitchen Content, Layout, and Locations

Storage Shelves Locations

ATTIC CRAWL-SPACE PLAN

Entrance Hole

Ventilation Louver Locations

CROSS SECTION (END VIEW)

Footings and Applicable Walls

Chimney

Trusses

Ridge Vent

Doorways where applicable

LONG SECTION (SIDE VIEW)

Footings and Applicable Walls

Floors

Stairways

Rafters

Chimney

END ELEVATIONS

Entrance Ways

Windows

Chimney

Typical Exterior Finish

LONG ELEVATIONS

Entrance Ways

Windows

Chimney

Typical Exterior Finish

DOOR AND WINDOW SCHEDULE

Type

Quantity

Location

Glossary of Terms

GENERAL

This glossary contains a brief definition of both technical and nontechnical terms. These definitions focus on how the words are used in this text.

Access code.   A software security code that is used to control access to a database.

Action item.   Work identified during a meeting that requires immediate effort to correct or modify the budget, task, or schedule of performance.

Activity.   A process such as searching, learning, doing, or writing, that involves the application of both a mental and a physical operation; an expenditure of work or energy is required. An action or pursuit that relates to the planning or performance of a project or program.

Actuals.   The record of the expenditures of a project or organization. It is a record of the monies spent during a defined timeframe. *See also* estimates.

Administrators.   Persons who monitor and control an overall project and who can visualize the final goal of that project. They judge performance and guide the project team.

Analysis.   The gathering of data. The separating or breaking up of the whole into its parts so as to determine their nature, proportion, and function. The solving of problems. The process of logical reasoning that leads from stated premises to the conclusion concerning specific capabilities of equipment or software and its adequacy for a particular application. The process of listing all design requirements and the reduction of those requirements to a complete set of logically related performance specifications.

Applied research.   From "search again." A careful, patient, systematic, diligent, and organized inquiry or examination in a field of knowledge. It is undertaken to establish facts or principles. It is a laborious and continued search after truth or information. Its goal is to convert an idea into a practical plan.

Archival documents.   Documents retained for reference and historical purposes.

Bionics.   An abbreviation for *biology-electronics.* It is the application of biological principles to the study and design of engineering systems that often involve animals and plants. It is also known as *nature analysis.*

Block diagram.   A diagram of interconnected rectangles known as "blocks." The input to a block, the function(s) of that block, and the output from that block must be specified; each block represents a part of the product; the interconnections of various blocks indicate the relationships among the parts.

Budget.   A plan that describes the types and amounts of authorized expenses for a specified period of time.

Brainstorming.   The unrestrained offering of ideas and suggestions by all members of a group during a meeting that typically focuses on a predetermined range of items. During a brainstorming session, no one is allowed to comment with negative remarks. Instead they are encouraged to expand and enlarge on ideas as they are presented.

Byte.   A unit of computer memory. Eight computer bits.

CPM.   *See* Critical Path Method

Charge numbers.   Numerics or alphanumerics used to uniquely identify a task or subtask.

Charges, time.   *See* time charges.

Code, access.   *See* access code.

Component.   A portion of a device that normally performs a useful function only when used within that device.

Conceivers.   *See* creators.

Concurrent engineering.   A systematic approach that integrates the initial idea for a project with its applied research, design, development, marketing, production, sales, and distribution. It leads to a more efficient and shorter design cycle while maintaining or improving product quality and reliability.

Conflict resolution.   The work of executive personnel to reduce or eliminate dissension, strife, and perhaps hostility among team members.

Construction.   *See* production.

Control(ling) of a project.   The act of seeing that the project proceeds according to a well-prepared plan.

Costs, direct.   *See* direct costs.

Costs, fixed.   *See* fixed costs.

Costs, indirect.   *See* indirect costs.

Costs, variable.   *See* variable costs.

Creativity.   The art of devising new ideas that may be ingenious, inventive, or innovative.

Creators.   Persons who have the skills of imagination and vision and can think about a problem and devise one or more solutions.

Critical Path Method (CPM).   A means for indicating which task sequence will have the greatest effect on schedule performance.

Database.   A collection of related information associated with a specific organization or project.

Database, common.   A collection of related information. It can be accessed by a variety of users and can be updated (modified with later information) as required.

Deliverables.   Tangible, verifiable products such as a feasibility study, a detailed design, or a working prototype. The conclusion of a project phase is generally marked by a review of deliverables (such as end-of-phase documents) and project status. Deliverables include both equipment and documents that are provided to a client.

Delphi (approach to selecting a problem solution).   Applies numeric measures to potential problem solutions.

Design.   Refers to the conversion of an idea into a plan for a product, process, or procedure by arranging the parts of a system via drawings or computer models so that the part will perform the desired function when converted to an actual product.

Design options.   Choices that are offered to a client or to the managers in order that they may participate in the selection process.

Desire.   Similar to a wish, it is a longing for something that promises enjoyment or satisfaction. A desire is not a need. A strong desire may eventually become a need; a weak desire may be considered a luxury.

Deterministic.   Each activity is determined by a sequence of events over which no one has control. A foundation must be constructed prior to building the walls, for example.

Development.   The activity of modifying a design, product, process, or procedure.

Device.   The portion of a subsystem that can perform an identifiable function either alone or with other parts of that subsystem.

Direct costs.   Labor and material costs that are part of a cost package.

Distribution.   The process of transporting completed products to warehouses, customers, or retail outlets.

Document, trial.   *See* trial document.

Documentation.   The records developed to describe a planned or performed effort. It includes words, figures, drawings, tables, and/or graphs.

Documents, archival.   *See* archival documents.

Ergonomics.   *See* human factors.

Estimates.   The record of the planned expenditures of a project or organization.

Evaluation.   Determining the accuracy with which alternative designs fulfill performance requirements for operation, manufacture, and sales before the final design is selected.

Field.   A group of items that contains information regarding a person, place, or thing.

Fixed costs.   Costs whose amount can be determined and will remain unchanged for an extended time. Costs that are independent of the amount of engineering or production.

Form.   The shape, outline, or solution that results from the definition of a function or system function. "Form follows function."

Function.   The act or operation expected of a person or thing. The ability of an individual, process, device, or equipment to perform in a given manner. It is sometimes provided as a system function.

Gantt chart.   A technique for presenting related schedule information in the form of a graph.

Goal.   An object of desire or intent. That which a person sets as an objective to be reached or accomplished. The end or final purpose. An ambition, aim, mark, objective, or target.

GPS (Global Positioning System).   A satellite-based system that precisely locates (within a few meters) a position on our earth.

Ground rules.   Rules that govern all conduct, procedures, and aspects of the proposed project output. They are typically established during the latter part of the Conception Phase or during the Study Phase.

Hierarchy.   A group of persons or things that are arranged in a predetermined order of rank, grade, or class.

Human factors.   The application of knowledge regarding human beings through the design of products or procedures.

Idea.   A concept first formulated in the mind of one or more persons. It may be a concept that can be designed or developed immediately, or it may require further study.

Indirect costs.   Costs that are not directly related to the design or production of an item or service. All costs that are not direct costs.

Interface.   The mechanical and electrical boundary for two or more equipments. Cables, connectors, transmitting and receiving circuits, signal-line descriptions, timing, and control information are included.

Item.   A piece of information that is to be stored for later processing.

Item, action.   *See* action item.

Iterative.   Said or performed repeatedly until the result or product is acceptable.

Just-in-time.   The timing determined so that materials will be delivered or work will be performed no sooner than is necessary to meet schedule requirements.

Laborers.   Persons who work primarily with their hands on physical activities.

Letter contract.   A brief document that contains both legal and technical information. It defines the work to be accomplished, its schedule, and its price. It is used where the work is simple in nature and does not require a lengthy contract with applicable attachments.

Letter of transmittal.   A letter that contains both legal and technical information. It accompanies a contract of significant length and refers to that contract and its applicable attachments.

Life cycle (of a project plan).   Starts with the initial idea for a project and continues through applied research, design, development, marketing, production, sales distribution, and, in some cases, maintenance, disassembly, and salvage or disposal.

Logistics.   From the beginning to the end of the supply chain, the procurement of raw materials and components. The acquisition, storage, movement, and distribution of subassemblies and finished products.

Luxury.   The best and most costly thing that offers the most physical, intellectual, or emotional comfort, pleasure, and satisfaction.

Make-or-buy decision.   The option that relates to that portion of a design that will be fabricated within the organization (make) or will be purchased from vendors (buy).

Management, bottom-up.   An organized structure where the lowest level of personnel offers suggestions that are gathered, coordinated, and acted upon by the next higher level of personnel.

Management by exception.   The monitoring of an activity or project. Control is exercised only when a person or group does not meet its assigned goals.

Management, top-down.   An organized structure where the highest ranking leader is personally involved in directing all other personnel via verbal orders and written directives.

Manager.   One who holds an administrative, executive, or managerial position. Normally one who directs the performance of a supervisor.

Market Research.   The process of determining the need for a new product, process, or procedure, and the amount of money that potential customers are willing to invest. Market research must also determine if it will sell in sufficient quantities to meet the total project costs as well as earn a profit.

Marketing.   The process of selling a given product, and determining its selling price and selling potential.

Model.   An abstraction and simplification of an actual event or function. It simulates the actual system, or portion of that system, in an effective and efficient manner. A representation of selected features of a system. It may be a physical scale model of a proposed structure, it may be a defining set of equations, or it may be an operating prototype of a product.

Monitor.   To advise, warn, or caution a person, activity, or project.

Nature Analysis.   *See* bionics.

Need.   Something that is considered necessary or essential. There is a hierarchy of needs. (*See* page 23 of the text.)

Objective.   Describes the work to be performed. It is included within a Specification document or in a separate Project Task Description document. It is analogous to a road map in that it indicates the direction to be pursued without restricting the designer to a specific result.

Optimum.   The best or most favorable degree, condition, or amount of a design that is not necessarily the best for each individual item, but is the best for the overall design. (Many common design problems have multiple local optima, as well as false optima, that make conventional optimization schemes risky.) *Optimum* is a technical term that infers a mathematical, quantitative context.

Organization.   Any unified, consolidated body of persons working together for a specific purpose.

Organize.   To plan in a methodical manner. To bring about an orderly disposition of individuals, units, or elements. To assemble resources and prepare for their use.

Part.   *See* component.

Perform.   To do what is required to achieve a desired goal. To fulfill or complete a process, product, or procedure to a successful conclusion.

Performance reviews, contract.   A document, used in conjunction with a face-to-face interview, that evaluates the activities of those individuals working on a given contract. It offers both positive evaluation and constructive criticism.

Performance reviews, personnel.   A document, used in conjunction with a face-to-face interview, that evaluates the activities and behavior of an individual who works with other persons. It offers both positive evaluation and constructive criticism.

Performers.   Persons who enjoy working with details, who are comfortable with developing and implementing the ideas of others, and receive satisfaction from coordinating a variety of activities.

PERT chart.   A technique for presenting related schedule information in the form of a graph. The precedence of each activity is indicated by means of linking arrows.

Plan.   The document that describes the conversion of ideas into a product, process, or procedure. It typically consists of budgets, tasks, and schedules accompanied by a description of what is to be accomplished.

Planners.   Persons who prepare the details of a project and analyze estimates.

Process.   A series of actions that leads to a result.

Production.   The act of fabricating numerous, identical copies of an item.

Program.   A group of related projects.

Project.   An organized effort to accomplish something useful or attain a useful end result. It is sometimes referred to as a plan, venture, or enterprise.

Purpose.   That which one proposes to accomplish or perform. The reason that one wants to accomplish something. An aim, intention, design, or plan.

Rationale.   A statement of causes or motives. An explanation, justification, or reason.

Record.   The name of a document that contains information worth developing, distributing, and maintaining. It is also the name of a portion of a computer file that contains more than one field of data.

Record, structured.   A set of categories of related data that is identical in content, arrangement, and length containing more than one field of data.

Record, unstructured.   A set of categories of data related to one another. Every item within each field may be different in content, arrangement, and length that contains more than one field of data.

Recycling.   Stripping into pieces. Also known as *deManufacturing* (tearing apart). Recycling should be planned during the Conception Phase.

Return on investment.   The percent of money earned based upon the amount of money loaned.

Sales.   Identifying and contacting customers to convince them to purchase an item.

Slack time.   The extra time available in a schedule to allow for unplanned changes that may occur during the performance of one or more related tasks.

Specification.   A document that describes the work to be accomplished, including the conditions (requirements) that must be fulfilled in order to complete a task or project.

Spreadsheet.   The presentation of an organized arrangement of data in matrix (tabular) form.

Stakeholder.   A person or organization that has a financial investment (stake) in a project or product. A person or organization that monitors its performance to ensure that their investment is efficiently and successfully applied.

Structured record.   *See* record, structured.

Subsystem.   A portion of a system that performs one or more functions that can, alone or in a system, operate separately.

Synthesis.   The putting together of separate parts or elements so as to form a connected whole. It is a qualitative process and is the opposite of analysis.

Synthesize.   The bringing together of separate parts into a coordinated unit.

System.   A combination of things that actively work together to serve a common purpose. They are composed of combinations of parts, people, and procedures.

Systematic approach.   An orderly and methodical way of working when conceiving, studying, designing, and implementing a project.

Task.   An undertaking or portion of work assigned to be accomplished. Sometimes known as a job.

Task description.   A record that describes the name and objective of a task, the relation of that task to other tasks, a description of the work to be performed, the specification(s) relating to any materials designated, an explanation of the expected quality of work, and a schedule for the performance of that task.

Time charges.   Information related to the number of hours that each individual has worked on a given task or project.

Trade-off.   The exchange of one benefit or advantage to gain another benefit or advantage that is considered to be more desirable.

Trial document.   A document devised to resolve an uncertainty. It is not considered an official document until the appropriate managers review and approve it.

Unstructured record.   *See* record, unstructured.

Variable costs.   Costs that will change depending upon the production level of an item or the amount of service provided to a customer.

Warranty.   A document that indicates the extent to which the provider of parts and procedures is responsible for their performance.

Bibliography

Allen, M. S. *Morphological Creativity: The Miracle of Your Hidden Brain Power.* Upper Saddle River, NJ: Prentice-Hall, 1962.

American Institute of Architects (AIA) and Associated General Contractors of America (AGCA). *Abbreviated Form of Agreement between Owner and Contractor with Instruction Sheet.* AIA Document 107. 9th ed. Washington DC: American Institute of Architects (AIA) and Associated General Contractors of America (AGCA), 1987.

American Institute of Architects (AIA) and Associated General Contractors of America (AGCA). *Recommended Guide for Competitive Bidding Procedures and Contract Awards for Building Construction.* Washington, DC: American Institute of Architects (AIA) and Associated General Contractors of America (AGCA), 1980.

Archer, L. B. *Systematic Method for Designers.* Chichester, U.K.: Wiley, 1984.

Archibald, R. D. *Managing High-Technology Programs and Projects.* New York: John Wiley & Sons, 1992. ISBN 0-471-51327-X.

Badiru, A. B. *Project Management Tools for Engineering and Management Professionals.* Norcross, GA: Institute of Industrial Engineers, 1991. ISBN 0-89806-114-8.

Badiru, A. B., and Whitehouse, G. E. *Computer Tools, Models, and Techniques for Project Management.* Blue Ridge Summit, PA: TAB Books, 1989. ISBN 0-88906-3200-X.

Banios, E. W. "An Engineering Practices Course." *IEEE Transactions on Education,* 35, no. 4 (November 1992): 286–293.

Boff, K. R., and Lincoln, J. E., eds. *Engineering Data Compendium: Human Perception and Performance.* Wright-Patterson Air Force Base, OH: Henry G. Armstrong Aerospace Medical Laboratory, 1988.

Bransford, J. D., and Stein, B. S. *The Ideal Problem Solver.* New York: W. H. Freeman, 1993. ISBN 0-7167-2204-6.

Brown, J. *Value Engineering—A Blueprint.* New York: Industrial Press Inc., 1992.

Callahan, M. T., Quackenbush, D. J., and Rowings, J. E. *Construction Project Scheduling.* New York: McGraw-Hill, 1992. ISBN 0-07-009701-1.

Carrithers, W. M., and Weinwurm, E. H. *Business Information and Accounting Systems.* Columbus, OH: Charles E. Merrill, 1967. ISBN 675-09749-5.

Chase, W. P. *Management of System Engineering.* New York: John Wiley & Sons, 1974. ISBN 0-89874-682-5.

Clark, C. H. *Brainstorming: How to Create Successful Ideas.* North Hollywood, CA: Wilshire Book Company, 1958.

Clawson, R. H. *Value Engineering for Management.* Princeton: Auerbach Publishers, Inc., 1970.

Connor, P. E., and Lake, L. K. *Managing Organizational Change.* Westport, CT: Praeger, 1994. ISBN 0-275-94652-5.

Construction Specifications Institute, P.O. Box 85080, Richmond, VA 23285-4236, 1998.

Cross, N. *Engineering Design Methods.* Chichester, U.K.: John Wiley & Sons, 1944.

Dell'Isola, A. J. *Value Engineering in the Construction Industry.* New York: Van Nostrand Reinhold, 1982.

Dinsmore, P. C. *Human Factors in Project Management.* New York: American Management, 1990. ISBN 0-8144-5003-2.

Duncan, W. R. *A Guide to the Project Management Body of Knowledge.* Project Management Institute, 130 South State Road, Upper Darby, PA 19082, 1996.

East, E. W., and Kirby, J. G. *A Guide to Computerized Project Scheduling.* New York: Van Nostrand, Reinhold Co., 1990. ISBN 0-442-23802-9.

Elsayed, E. A., and Boucher, T. O. *Analysis and Control of Production Systems.* Upper Saddle River, NJ: Prentice Hall, 1985.

Farkas, L. L. *Management of Technical Field Operations.* New York: McGraw-Hill, 1970. L.O.C. 76-107289.

Fasal, J. H. *Practical Value Analysis Methods.* New York: Hayden Book Co., 1972.

Fisk, E. R. *Construction Project Administration.* 4th ed. Englewood Cliffs, NJ: Prentice Hall, 1992. ISBN 0-13-174137-3.

Francks, P. L., Testa, S. M., and Winegardner, D. L. *Principles of Technical Consulting and Project Management.* Chelsea, MI: Lewis Publishers, 1992.

Goode, H. H., and Machol, R. E. *System Engineering.* New York: McGraw-Hill, 1957.

Graham, N. *Introduction to Computer Science: A Structural Approach.* St. Paul, MN: West Publishing Company, 1982. ISBN 0-314-64968-9.

Graham, R. J. *Project Management: Combining Technical and Behavioral Approaches for Effective Implementation.* New York: Van Nostrand Reinhold Co., 1985. ISBN 0-442-23018-4.

Heyne, P. *The Economic Way of Thinking.* 6th ed. Toronto: Macmillan Publishing Company, 1991. ISBN 0-02-354181-4.

Horgan, M. O'C., and Roulston, F. R. *The Foundations of Engineering Contracts*. 1989. ISBN 0-419-14940-6.

Hosny, O. A., Benjamin, C. O., and Omurtag, Y. "An AI-based Decision Support System for Planning Housing Construction Projects." *Journal of Engineering Technology*, Fall 1994: 12–19.

IEEE *Standard Dictionary of Electrical & Electronics Terms*. New York: Wiley Interscience, 1984.

Isaak, J. "Standards for the Information Infrastructure." *IEEE Standards Bearer*, July 1994: 10.

Jones, J. C. *A Method of Systematic Design*. Chichester, U.K.: Wiley, 1984.

Kaimann, R. A. *Structured Information Files*. Los Angeles: Melville Publishing Company, 1973. ISBN 0-471-45483-4.

Kaplan, G. "Manufacturing, Á La Carte." *IEEE Spectrum*, September 1993: 24–85.

Karwowski, W., ed. *International Encyclopedia of Ergonomics & Human Factors*. Taylor & Francis, 2000. ISBN 0-7484-0847-9.

Kim, S. H. *Essence of Creativity*. New York: Oxford University Press, 1990. ISBN 0-19-506017-2.

Lewis, J. P. *Project Planning, Scheduling, and Control*. Chicago: Probus Publishing Company, 1991. L.O.C. 91-60939. ISBN 0-9631886-0-7.

Lumsdaine, E., and Lumsdaine, M. *Creative Problem Solving*. New York: McGraw-Hill, 1990. ISBN 0-07-039087-8.

Mager, R. F. *The New Mager Six-Pack*, Belmont, CA: Lake Publishers, 1996. ISBN 1-879-61801-X.

March, L. J. *The Logic of Design*. Chichester, U.K.: Wiley, 1984.

Metedith, J. R., and Mantel, S. J. *Project Management: A Managerial Approach*. New York: John Wiley and Sons, 1995. ISBN 0-471-01626-8.

Miles, L. D. *Techniques of Value Analysis and Engineering*. New York: McGraw-Hill Book Company, 1972.

Mudge, A. E. *Value Engineering: A Systematic Approach*. McGraw Hill, New York: 1971.

Muller, E. J., Fausett, J. G., and Grau, P. A. *Architectural Drawing and Light Construction*. 5th ed. Upper Saddle River, NJ: Prentice Hall, 1998. ISBN 0-13-520529-8.

Nadler, G. *Work Design: A Systems Concept*. Homewood, IL: Richard D. Irwin, 1970. L.O.C. 70-110417.

Nicholas, J. M. *Managing Business and Engineering Projects*. Englewood Cliffs, NJ: Prentice Hall, 1990. ISBN 0-13-551854-7.

Oberlender, G. D. *Project Management for Engineering and Construction*. New York: McGraw-Hill, 1993. ISBN 0-07-048150-4.

Osborn, A. *Applied Imagination—The Principles and Problems of Creative Problem Solving*. 3rd ed. New York: Charles Scribner's Sons, 1963.

Pahl, G., and Beitz, W. *Engineering Design*. London: Design Council, 1984.

Priest, J. W., Bodensteiner, W., and Muir, N. K. "A Survey of Educational and Training Needs for Transition of a Product from Development to Manufacturing." *IEEE Transactions on Education*, 37, no. 1 (February 1994): 13–22.

Pugh, S. *Total Design: Integrated Methods for Successful Product Engineering*. Reading, MA: Addison-Wesley Publishing Company, 1993.

Raferty, J. *Risk Analysis and Project Management*. London: E & FN, 1994. ISBN 0-419-18420-1.

Rechtin, E. "The Synthesis of Complex Systems." *IEEE Spectrum*, July 1997: 51–55.

Reutlinger, S. *Techniques for Project Appraisal under Uncertainty*. Baltimore: Johns Hopkins Press, 1970. ISBN 0-8018-1154-6.

Roze, M., and Maxwell, S. *Technical Communications in the Age of the Internet*. Upper Saddle River, NJ: Prentice Hall, 2002. ISBN 0-13-020574-5.

Salvendy, G. *Handbook of Human Factors and Ergonomics*, 2nd ed. New York: John Wiley & Sons, 1997. ISBN 0-471-11690-4.

Samaris, T. T., and Czerwinski, F. L. *Fundamentals of Configuration Management*. New York: Wiley Interscience, 1971. ISBN 0-471-75100-6.

Sanders, M. S., and McCormick, E. J. *Human Factors in Engineering and Design*. 7th ed. New York: McGraw-Hill, 1992. ISBN 0-07-054901-X.

Shepherd, J. M. *How to Contract the Building of Your New Home*. 3rd ed. Williamsburg, VA: Shepherd Publishers, 1991. ISBN 0-9607308-7-7.

Shim, J. K., and Siegel, J. G. *Theory and Problems of Managerial Accounting*. Schaum's Outline Series. New York: McGraw-Hill, 1984. ISBN 0-07-057305-0.

Smith, R. P. "Teaching Design for Assembly Using Product Disassembly." *IEEE Transactions on Education, 41*, no. 1 (February 1998): 50–53.

Steiner, C. J. "Educating for Innovation and Management: The Engineering Educators' Dilemma." *IEEE Transactions on Education, 41*, no. 1 (February 1998): 1–7.

Stolarski, T. A. *Analytical Techniques*. Elsevier Science B.V., 1995 Edition.

Tapper, J. *Evaluating Project Management Software: How, Why, and What*. jtapper@coe.neu.edu, 1998.

Texas Instruments, Inc. *Working with Suppliers*. TI-29503.

Turner, W. C., Mize, J. H., and Case, K. E. *Introduction to Industrial and Systems Engineering*. Upper Saddle River, N.J.: Prentice Hall, 1987.

Van Cott, H. P., and Kinkade, R. G. *Human Engineering Guide to Equipment Design*. Washington, DC: American Institutes for Research, Superintendent of Documents, U.S. Government Printing Office, 1972. (Includes an extensive bibliography.)

Verein Deutscher Ingenieure (VDI). *VDI-Guidelines*. VDI 2221, *Systematic Approach to the Design of Technical Systems and Products*. Germany Professional Engineers' body.

von Oech, R. *A Whack on the Side of the Head*. New York: Warner Books, 1993. ISBN 0-446-77808-7.

Wilde, D. J. *Globally Optimal Design*. New York: John Wiley & Sons, 1978.

Index

PART 2

Taken from
Essentials: Microsoft Office Project 2003
by Dawn Parrish Wood and Mary E. Pascarella

305

Table of Contents

Introduction

Essentials courseware from Prentice Hall Information Technology is anchored in the practical and professional needs of all types of students.

The *Essentials* series is conceived around a learning-by-doing approach that encourages you to grasp application-related concepts as you expand your skills through hands-on tutorials. As such, it consists of modular lessons that are built around a series of numbered, step-by-step procedures that are clear, concise, and easy to review.

The end-of-project exercises have likewise been carefully constructed, from the routine Checking Concepts and Terms to creative tasks in the Discovery Zone that prod you into extending what you've learned into areas beyond the explicit scope of the lessons proper.

How to Use This Book

Typically, each *Essentials* book is divided into eight projects. A project covers one area (or a few closely related areas) of application functionality. Each project consists of six to nine lessons that are related to that topic. Each lesson presents a specific task or closely related set of tasks in a manageable chunk that is easy to assimilate and retain.

Each element in the *Essentials* book is designed to maximize your learning experience. A list of the *Essentials* project elements and a description of how each element can help you follows. To find out more about the rationale behind each book element and how to use each to your maximum benefit, take the following walk-through.

Essentials Series 2003 Walk-Through

Project Objectives. Starting with an objective gives you short-term, attainable goals. At the beginning of each project are objectives that closely match the titles of the step-by-step tutorials. ▶

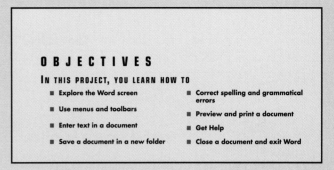

OBJECTIVES

IN THIS PROJECT, YOU LEARN HOW TO

- Explore the Word screen
- Use menus and toolbars
- Enter text in a document
- Save a document in a new folder
- Correct spelling and grammatical errors
- Preview and print a document
- Get Help
- Close a document and exit Word

◀ **Why Would I Do This?** Introductory material at the beginning of each project provides an overview of why these tasks and procedures are important.

Visual Summary. An illustrated introductory ▲ feature graphically presents the concepts and features you will learn, including the final results of completing the project.

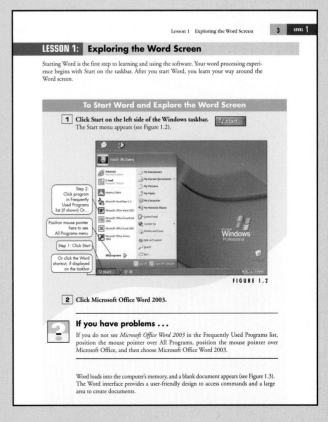

Step-by-Step Tutorials. Hands-on tutorials let you "learn by doing" and include numbered, bold, step-by-step instructions. ▶

◀ **If You Have Problems.** These short troubleshooting notes help you anticipate or solve common problems quickly and effectively.

◀ **To Extend Your Knowledge.** These features at the end of most lessons provide extra tips, shortcuts, alternative ways to complete a process, and special hints about using the software.

◀ **Creative Solution Exercises.** Special icons mark selected end-of-project exercises. The creative solution exercises enable you to make choices that result in a unique solution.

End-of-Project Exercises. Extensive end-of-project exercises emphasize hands-on skill development. You'll find three levels of reinforcement: Skill Drill, Challenge, and Discovery Zone. Accompanying data files eliminate unnecessary typing. ▶

SKILL DRILL

Skill Drill exercises reinforce project skills. Each skill reinforced is the same, or nearly the same, as a skill presented in the project. Detailed instructions are provided in a step-by-step format.

Work through exercises 3, 4, and 5 in sequential order. You can work through the rest of the Skill Drill exercises in any order. Close open documents and exit Word at the end of your work session.

1. Exploring Menus and ScreenTips

You want to study Word's menus. The more you study the screen components, the more you understand the structure and logic of using Word. You want to use the keyboard to select menu options. You also want to display keyboard shortcuts in the ScreenTips until you learn them.

1. Start Word, if necessary.
2. Press Alt+A to display the Table menu. (You press A because *a* is underlined in Table.)
3. Click the Expand arrows, if necessary, to display the full Table menu.
4. Try choosing Table Properties.

   Nothing happens because the option is dimmed. It is available only when you perform a specific task first.
5. Press Alt once to close the Table menu without choosing any options.
6. Choose Tools from the menu bar, and choose Customize from the Tools menu.
7. Click the Options tab, if needed.
8. Look at the *Show shortcut keys in ScreenTips* option. If it is selected, click Close. Otherwise, click the *Show shortcut keys in ScreenTips* check box to select it and then click Close.

3. Click Show All; then click the Microsoft Access Help window Maximize button.
4. Scroll through and read the information about data access pages.
5. Click Close on the Microsoft Access Help window title bar to close the Help window.
6. Click Close on the Search Results task pane to close the task pane.
7. Click Close on the Microsoft Access window title bar to exit Access.

CHALLENGE

Challenge exercises expand on or are somewhat related to skills presented in the lessons. Each exercise provides a brief narrative introduction, followed by instructions in a numbered-step format that are not as detailed as those in the Skill Drill section.

Complete Project 1 Challenge exercise 1 first. Then work through the remaining exercises in any order.

1. Opening and Backing Up a Database and Editing Fields in a Table

Aggie Travel has developed a new coding system for tracking travel schedules in its database by client. After adding fields to the database and coding the travel schedules using the new coding system, another field from the database table is no longer required. As a result, you need to remove the field from the *Scheduled Travel* table design. To preserve the original file, you make a backup of the file prior to editing the table structure and make the changes using the backup file. When you have completed the edits, the table appears as shown in Figure 1.42.

DISCOVERY ZONE

Discovery Zone exercises require advanced knowledge of topics presented in *Essentials* lessons, application of skills from multiple lessons, or self-directed learning of new skills. Each exercise is independent of the others, so you may complete the exercises in any order.

1. Training on Access

Microsoft Office Online has set up a series of training lessons at its online Web site. You can access these training sessions from the Microsoft Access Help task pane and Office Online through the links starting on the task pane and Office Online available on George Washington or a figure who was prominent in your field of study. For example, if you are ics they currently offer for Access. Review the *Introduction to Databases* training session to see if you believe it rates five stars.

2. Using Databases on the Internet

In this project, you learned that the main purpose of a database is to store related data in such a way that retrieving the specific information you want is more efficient. The Internet comprises a treasure trove of data stored in online databases that contain data and information about many topics. Each time you search for Web sites containing information in much the same way as Access database tables are related. Explore the depth of Web information available on George Washington or a figure who was prominent in your field of study. For example, if you are studying to become a scientist, search for information about Galileo or Einstein. If you are studying to become a football coach, search for information about Bear Bryant. Record the different types of Web sites listed as you move deeper into the Web. Print samples of the information you discover.

INTEGRATING P R O J E C T S

Essentials 2003: Microsoft Excel

The Integrating Projects exercises are designed to provide additional hands-on practice in working with Excel. Each exercise requires the application of skills from multiple projects; a cross-reference by each exercise title tells you which projects introduced the skills applied in the exercise. The exercises are independent and can be worked in any order.

You follow a checklist as you create and enhance each complete end product. Many of the exercises include opportunities to make decisions about the best approach and features to use in a particular situation.

1 CREATING A TARGET HEART RATE CALCULATOR

Based on Projects 2, 3, and 4

You are beginning an intensive workout program in preparation for a backpacking trip on the Appalachian Trail. You want to train effectively, and you have started an Excel worksheet that computes target heart rates for several activity levels. Now you want to add remaining content, make sure that the worksheet calculates correctly, and add formatting to enhance appearance. Figure EIP.1 illustrates your plans for the completed worksheet. Save your work periodically as you make your changes.

FIGURE EIP.1

FILE GUIDES

Guide to Files in Essentials: Microsoft Word 2003

Word	Original Student File	Student File Saved As	Related Solution Notes
Project 1			
P1-L1 and L2			No files; explore Word screen, menus, and toolbars
P1-L3 thru L8	New document	Class_Introduction.doc	Create folder and rename it as Project_1_Documents; save file in this folder
P1-SD1 and SD2			No files; explore Word screen, menus, and toolbars
P1-SD3			Create three folders: Project_2_Documents, Project_3_Documents, and Project_4_Documents
P1-SD4 and SD5	New document	Turner_Note.doc Baxter_Note.doc	Baxter_Note.doc is a slight revision of Turner_Note.doc
P1-SD6			No files; explore Help topics
P1-CH1	New document	Introduction_Letter.doc	Creative Solution exercise
P1-CH2	New document	Project_1_Study_Guide.doc	
P1-CH3			No files; explore Help topics
P1-CH4		Keyboard_Shortcut_Practice.doc	Download a keyboard practice document from Microsoft's Web site
P1-DZ1		Password_Information.doc	Copy a Help topic and save it with the password tOP sECreT
P1-DZ2	New document	Committee_Meeting.doc	
P1-DZ3		Introduction_Letter_and_Envelope.doc	Create an envelope for the letter saved in CH1 as Introduction_Letter.doc
Project 2			
P2-L1 thru L9	EW1_0201.doc	Basic_Document_Formats.doc	
P2-SD1-SD5	EW1_0202.doc	Fun_with_Graphics.doc	

P = Project   L = Lesson   SD = Skill Drill   CH = Challenge   DZ = Discovery Zone   IP = Integrating Projects

Creative Solution exercises permit individual choices that produce unique solutions

MICROSOFT WORD 2003 TASK GUIDE

A book in the *Essentials* series is designed to be kept as a handy reference beside your computer even after you have completed all the projects and exercises. Any time you have difficulty recalling the sequence of steps or a shortcut needed to achieve a result, look up the general category in the alphabetized listing that follows, and then quickly find your task. If you have difficulty performing a task, turn to the page number listed in the second column to locate the step-by-step exercise or other detailed description. Additional entries without page numbers describe tasks that are closely related to those presented in the projects.

Word Task	Page	Mouse	Menu Bar	Shortcut Menu	Shortcut Keys
AutoComplete, entering date	124				Type first few letters of current month and (←Enter)
AutoCorrect options	257		Tools | AutoCorrect Options | select options		
Bold	198	on Formatting toolbar	Format | Font | Bold		Ctrl+B
Bulleted list, create	169	on Formatting toolbar	Format | Bullets and Numbering	Select text, right-click, Bullets and Numbering	
Change case	245		Format | Change Case		⇧Shift+F3
Character spacing	206		Format | Font, Character Spacing tab	Right-click text, Font, Character Spacing tab	
Close document	141		File | Close		Ctrl+F4
Copy	249	on Standard toolbar	Edit | Copy	Right-click selected text, Copy	Ctrl+C
Create new folder (in Open, Save As, or Insert Picture dialog box)	128	within dialog box			
Cut	248	on Standard toolbar	Edit | Cut	Right-click selected text, Cut	Ctrl+X
Date Field	241		Insert | Date and Time		Alt+⇧Shift+D
Delete, rest of word	166				Ctrl+Del
Delete, word on left side of insertion point	165				Ctrl+⬅Backspace

Typeface Conventions Used in This Book

Essentials Microsoft Office 2003 uses the following typeface conventions to make it easier for you to understand the material.

Key terms appear in ***italic and bold*** the first time they are defined in a project.

Monospace type appears frequently and `looks like this`. It is used to indicate text that you are instructed to key in.

Italic text indicates text that appears onscreen as (1) warnings, confirmation, or general information; (2) the name of a file to be used in a lesson or exercise; and (3) text from a menu or dialog box that is referenced within a sentence, when that sentence might appear awkward if it were not set off.

Hotkeys are indicated by underline. Hotkeys are the underlined letters in menus, toolbars, and dialog boxes that activate commands and options, and are a quick way to choose frequently used commands and options. Hotkeys look like this: <u>F</u>ile, <u>S</u>ave.

Student Resources

Companion Web Site (www.prenhall.com/essentials). This text-specific Web site provides students with additional information and exercises to reinforce their learning. Features include: additional end-of-project reinforcement material; online Study Guide; easy access to *all* project data files; and much, much more!

Accessing Student Data Files. The data files that students need to work through the projects can be downloaded from the Companion Web site (www.prenhall.com/essentials). Data files are provided for each project. The filenames correspond to the filenames called for in this book. The files are named in the following manner: The first character indicates the book series (E = *Essentials*), the second character denotes the application (W = Word, E = Excel, etc.), and the third character indicates the level (1 = Level 1, 2 = Level 2, and 3 = Level 3). The last four digits indicate the project number and the file number within the project. For example, the first file used in Project 3 would be 0301. Therefore, the complete name for the first file in Project 3 in the *Word Level 1* book is *EW1_0301*. The complete name for the third file in Project 7 in the *Excel Level 2* book is *EE2_0703*.

Instructor's Resources

Customize Your Book (www.prenhall.com/customphit). The Prentice Hall Information Technology Custom PHIT Program gives professors the power to control and customize their books to suit their course needs. The best part is that it is done completely online using a simple interface.

Professors choose exactly what projects they need in the *Essentials Microsoft Office 2003* series, and in what order they appear. The program also enables professors to add their own material anywhere in the text's presentation, and the final product will arrive at each professor's bookstore as a professionally formatted text.

To learn more about this new system for creating the perfect textbook, go to www.prenhall.com/customphit, where the online walk-through demonstrates how to create a book.

Instructor's Resource CD-ROM. This CD-ROM includes the entire Instructor's Manual for each application in Microsoft Word format. Student data files and completed solutions files are also on this CD-ROM. The Instructor's Manual contains a reference guide of these files for the instructor's convenience. PowerPoint slides, which give more information about each project, are also available for classroom use.

Companion Web Site (www.prenhall.com/essentials). Instructors will find all of the resources available on the Instructor's Resource CD-ROM available for download from the Companion Web site.

TestGen Software. TestGen is a test generator program that lets you view and easily edit test bank questions, transfer them to tests, and print the tests in a variety of formats suitable to your teaching situation. The program also offers many options for organizing and displaying test banks and tests. A built-in random number and text generator makes it ideal for creating multiple versions of tests. Powerful search and sort functions let you easily locate questions and arrange them in the order you prefer.

QuizMaster, also included in this package, enables students to take tests created with TestGen on a local area network. The QuizMaster utility built into TestGen lets instructors view student records and print a variety of reports. Building tests is easy with TestGen, and exams can be easily uploaded into WebCT, Blackboard, and CourseCompass.

Prentice Hall has formed close alliances with each of the leading online platform providers: WebCT, Blackboard, and our own Pearson CourseCompass.

WebCT and Blackboard. Each of these custom-built distance-learning course features exercises, sample quizzes, and tests in a course management system that provides class administration tools as well as the ability to customize this material at the instructor's discretion.

www.blackboard.com

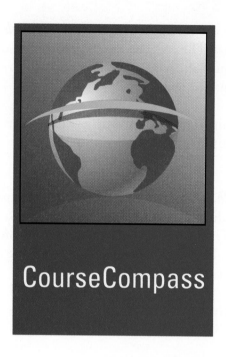

CourseCompass.   CourseCompass is a dynamic, interactive online course management tool powered by Blackboard. It lets professors create their own courses in 15 minutes or less with preloaded quality content that can include quizzes, tests, lecture materials, and interactive exercises.

Performance-Based Training and Assessment: Train & Assess IT.   Prentice Hall offers performance-based training and assessment in one product—Train & Assess IT.

The Training component offers computer-based instruction that a student can use to preview, learn, and review Microsoft Office application skills. Delivered via Web or CD-ROM, Train IT offers interactive multimedia, computer-based training to augment classroom learning. Built-in prescriptive testing suggests a study path based not only on student test results but also on the specific textbook chosen for the course.

The Assessment component offers computer-based testing that shares the same user interface as Train IT and is used to evaluate a student's knowledge about specific topics in Word, Excel, Access, PowerPoint, Windows, Outlook, and the Internet. It does this in a task-oriented, performance-based environment to demonstrate students' proficiency and comprehension of the topics. More extensive than the testing in Train IT, Assess IT offers more administrative features for the instructor and additional questions for the student. Assess IT also enables professors to test students out of a course, place students in appropriate courses, and evaluate skill sets.

TAKING A TOUR OF PROJECT 2003

OBJECTIVES

IN THIS PROJECT, YOU LEARN HOW TO

- **Start Microsoft Project, open a project, and save a project**

- **Explore the Project window**

- **Understand the task table**

- **Understand the timeline in Gantt Chart view**

- **Preview and print a standard report**

- **Get Help**

- **Close a project and exit Microsoft Project**

WHY WOULD I DO THIS?

Microsoft Project is a project management program used by project and resource managers to collaborate, administer, track, and analyze project information. Managers use projects primarily for organizing and analyzing the details involved with achieving a specific goal or objective. With little effort, you can manage an advertising campaign, introduce a new inventory system in a production plant, balance caseloads in a law firm, and much more.

A *project* is a self-contained group of tasks performed to achieve a specific objective. Projects are temporary, lasting only until a specific goal is met. Some projects, such as planning a birthday party, are simple and require only a few tasks. Some projects are complex, such as building a house, preparing a legal case, or creating a new software application. Simple projects may require only one person, while projects that are more complex require a team of people or even several departments or companies. Regardless of the complexity, every project has a definite start and finish date. Although few businesspersons would classify themselves as project managers, in reality many professionals are informal project managers. A *project manager* is simply one who oversees all stages of a project plan. Many professions—such as construction, engineering, architecture, and law—are project-based.

A project is comprised of a series of *tasks*—specific activities that have a start date, duration, and completion time. Time, resources, and cost usually limit each project. A *resource* is anything needed to complete the task, and each task has at least one resource. For example, a resource may be an employee, a vendor, a conference room, a building, or equipment. Finally, the project manager must consider the overall expenditure of a project.

Microsoft Project is a powerful organizing tool for project management. Microsoft Project stores the details of the project plan in its database. Then, it uses the information you provide to calculate and maintain the project plan's schedule and costs. As you make changes to individual tasks, Microsoft Project adjusts the schedule, resources, and costs accordingly. There are two versions of Microsoft Project: Project Standard and Project Professional. This book and its figures are based on Microsoft Project 2003 Standard. Microsoft templates are the basis for some of the project plans used in this book. A *template* is a model providing generic tasks and resources, which you can then modify to suit your individual project plan specifications. The lesson files used in this book are designed to be fun and smaller in scale, outlining projects the average person might encounter so as to demonstrate the usefulness, benefits, and features of Microsoft Project.

This initial project in your text illustrates how Microsoft Project organizes and assists the user in managing a project. After you start Microsoft Project and open a sample project—the development of a marketing brochure—you explore the elements that comprise the project environment as well as the main features of the program. You view the tasks involved in the brochure project, view the schedule, and print a report. You also learn how to use Help to access more information about Microsoft Project.

V I S U A L   S U M M A R Y

Unless you change the original settings, a project file displays in Gantt Chart view when you open it in Microsoft Project. *Gantt Chart view* contains the task table and the Gantt chart for a project file. A *Gantt chart* is a project management tool that can be used to represent the timing of tasks required to finish a project and to measure the progress toward completing the tasks. Gantt charts were developed by Henry Laurence Gantt (1861–1919), a mechanical engineer, as a visual tool to show scheduled and actual progress of large-scale engineering projects.

In Microsoft Project, the Gantt Chart view has two main areas. A list of tasks, called the *task table*, displays on the left side of the window. Each column of data in the task table represents a *field* of data for each task in the project, such as task name, start date, and finish date. The Gantt chart displays on the right side of the window and has two parts: the timeline and timescale (see Figure 1.1). The *timescale*, which in the sample is the calendar month and day, appears across the top of the Gantt chart. The *timeline* is the horizontal bar graph.

FIGURE 1.1

In this initial text project, you open the brochure project shown in Figure 1.1. You glimpse the power of the Microsoft Project program as you explore this predesigned project. You view the schedule, the timeline, and a sample report. You also print the report and use Help.

LESSON 1: Starting Microsoft Project, Opening a Project, and Saving a Project

To understand the planning phase of a project, you must first grasp the fundamentals of a simple project plan. Project plans must clearly state a specific and measurable goal. Generally, project plans are measured in time and money. How long will it take, and how much will it cost? Once a project is defined, the planning stage ensues. The planning stage involves laying the groundwork for the project. Usually a project manager is put in place; a project manager oversees all aspects of a project, including the assignment of tasks, resources, and budgeting. During the planning stage of a project, the project manager and/or project team lay out an approximation of the costs, identify *stakeholders* (key players), and state the project deliverables. Planning is crucial so that stakeholders do not make unrealistic assumptions or assign unavailable resources. A *constraint* is a condition that you cannot overlook or ignore for a task's completion. If the project manager identifies all constraints and potential obstacles from the outset, the project has a greater chance of finishing on time and within budget.

The project manager is responsible for coordinating tasks and resources and must manage the budget and time constraints. The project manager must also communicate all deliverables, inform project stakeholders of the overall progress, and coordinate any changes to the plan.

Once you complete the planning phase, you can begin creating your project file in Microsoft Project. It contains the tools and utilities to track and manage all aspects of the three critical components of a project plan: budget, time, and scope. Project managers refer to these constraints as the *constraint triangle.* The *budget* is the amount of money slated to finance the project. It is what the business unit deems the project plan's result is worth. The *time constraint* refers to the deadline of the overall project plan as well as how much time each individual task requires. Finally, the *scope* of the project plan encompasses the performance expectations (quality). It defines the minimum quality level that is acceptable and is the product of how much time and money is spent.

Once you create a project file by using Microsoft Project, you should save it so you can later reopen the project file and resume working with its data. You can also open and use a project file that someone else developed by using Microsoft Project. If you want to keep revisions, you must save the project file.

Microsoft Project provides a variety of ways to open a file. For example, the New Project task pane includes an Open button (see Figure 1.2). A *task pane* provides quick access to related tasks. If the file you want to open displays in a list of recently opened files, just click its name to open it. Otherwise, you can start the process by clicking the Open button in the Getting Started task pane, clicking the Open button on the Standard toolbar, or selecting File, Open on the menu bar. Those actions open the Open dialog box, in which you specify the name and location of the file you want to use.

FIGURE 1.2

You save a previously named file under the same name by clicking the Save button on the Standard toolbar or by selecting File, Save on the menu bar. If you are saving a project for the first time, or if you want to save an existing project under a new name and/or location, choose the File, Save As command sequence. The Save As dialog box has the same layout as the Open dialog box.

In this lesson, you open the student data file shown in the Visual Summary (refer to Figure 1.1). You then save the file under another name, thus creating a copy of the original. Throughout this book, you work on copies of original data files so that you can restart any lesson or exercise if desired.

To Start Project 2003 and Open a Project

1 **Move the mouse pointer to the Start button; then click the left mouse button.**
The Start button's popup menu displays.

2 **Move the mouse pointer to the *All Programs* menu item.**
You see a listing of available programs on your system.

3 **Move the mouse pointer to the Microsoft Office folder and then to Microsoft Project 2003; then click the left mouse button.**
Microsoft Project loads into the computer's memory and a blank project displays (refer to Figure 1.2).

4 **Locate the toolbar area below the menu bar on your screen (refer to Figure 1.2).**
The *menu bar* contains common menu names that, when activated, display a list of related commands. A *toolbar* is a set of buttons. Each button provides a shortcut to a frequently used command. Your screen may display the default setting of a single toolbar comprised of only the most commonly used Standard and Formatting buttons. In this context, *default* refers to a setting that a program uses unless you specify another setting. The *Standard toolbar* provides shortcuts to common tasks including Save, Print, Cut/Paste (Move), and Copy/Paste. The *Formatting toolbar* provides shortcuts to frequently used commands for changing the appearance of field contents.

5 **Click the Toolbar Options button at the right end of the Standard toolbar.**
A drop-down list opens.

6 **Click *Show Buttons on Two Rows.***
Separate Standard and Formatting toolbars display below the menu bar—the view reflected in the text figures and hands-on instructions.

7 **Close the Getting Started task pane, if necessary.**

8 **Choose File on the menu bar.**
The File menu opens to display a number of commands.

9 **Choose the Open command.**
The Open dialog box opens.

10 **Click the drop-down arrow at the right end of the *Look in* box, and select the drive and folder containing the student files for this text (see the sample location in Figure 1.3).**

FIGURE 1.3

The *Look in* drop-down list reflects the drives, folders, or files on a specific computer. The drives, folders, and files on your system may be different, depending on the software and hardware on the computer.

If you have problems . . .

Do not be concerned if you see a different arrangement of information from that shown in Figure 1.3. Figures in this text display file extensions, such as .mpp (which indicates a Microsoft Project project). The presence or absence of extensions is a function of a Windows setting specified from the Control Panel. You can use the Views button in either the Open or the Save As dialog box to select one of eight file displays. The icon for the current view displays with a color background and border. Selecting a view is a matter of personal preference; you can apply each option one at a time to see which view you prefer. The figures in this book reflect List view.

11 | **Click the *EPr1_0101* filename or its icon within the list of files.**
EPr1_0101 displays with blue highlighting.

12 | **Click the <u>O</u>pen button in the lower-right corner of the Open dialog box.**
The apartment brochure project shown in Figure 1.4 opens, and *EPr1_0101* displays in the title bar. The ***title bar*** displays the name of the software and the name of the active project—either a default name, such as Project1, or a user-determined filename. It also includes buttons at the right end of the bar that you can click to change window size or close the window.

FIGURE 1.4

When you name a file, the filename that you specify must comply with the Windows file-naming rules. You can include numbers, upper- and lowercase letters, spaces, and selected characters such as dashes and underscores. Microsoft Project automatically stores the file in the default file format, adding the .mpp (Microsoft Project project) file extension.

To Save a Copy of a Project

1 **Choose the File menu again; then choose the Save As command.**
The Save As dialog box opens.

2 **In the *File name* text box, type `Apartment_Brochure` to replace *EPr1_0101*.**

3 **From the *Save in* drop-down list, select the appropriate drive and folder for saving the new file (see the sample location in Figure 1.5).**

FIGURE 1.5

4 **Click Save in the dialog box.**
The Save As dialog box closes. Microsoft Project saves a copy of the *EPr1_0101* project as *Apartment_Brochure* and adds the extension *.mpp* to the filename. The new filename displays in the title bar at the top of the screen. Throughout this book, you modify copies of student data files. Each original file remains intact in case you want to rework a project.

Keep the *Apartment_Brochure* project file open and continue with the next lesson. If you prefer to complete the project later, close the file and exit Microsoft Project.

TO EXTEND YOUR KNOWLEDGE . . .

OPENING A FILE
To open a file quickly from the Open dialog box, double-click the file's name, or the icon that precedes its name, in the list of files. You can also display the Open dialog box by clicking the Open button in the Getting Started task pane or clicking the Open button on the Standard toolbar (refer to Figure 1.2).

LESSON 2:   Exploring the Project Window

The project window consists of a title bar and six additional sections: the menu bar, one or more toolbars, the Project Guide (or one of five task panes), the entry bar, task table, and Gantt chart. At times a task pane, rather than the Project Guide, displays at the right side of the screen. These elements form the Project work environment (see Figure 1.6).

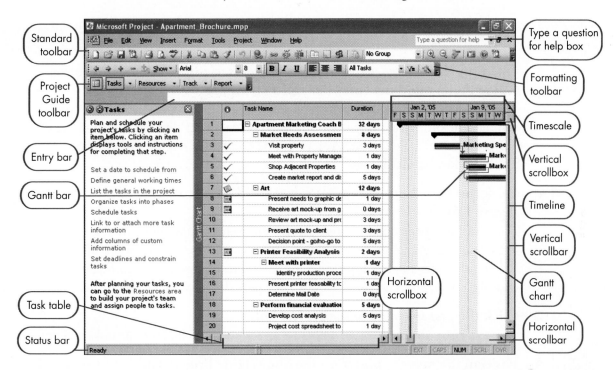

FIGURE 1.6

Table 1.1 explains other elements shown in Figure 1.6 that relate specifically to Microsoft Project.

TABLE 1.1 SELECTED PROJECT-RELATED ELEMENTS

SCREEN ELEMENT	DESCRIPTION
Entry bar	A bar that displays the contents of the current field.
Project Guide toolbar	A toolbar that provides access to step-by-step instructions and wizards in four different goal areas: task creation, resource assignment, task tracking, and project reporting.
Timescale	The time period legend appearing across the top of the Gantt chart.
Timeline	The graph area of a Gantt chart.
Gantt bar	A horizontal bar within a Gantt chart showing task information, due date, and task dependencies.

M'SOFT 1

Microsoft Project features easy access to onscreen Help. For example, the ***Type a question for help box*** near the right end of the menu bar enables you to specify a new Help topic or redisplay a previous Help topic. You learn how to access Help in a variety of ways in Lesson 6.

For a quick start to learning the power of Microsoft Project, launch the program and explore the work environment. The following steps guide you through the process.

To Identify Parts of a Project

1 **Open the *Apartment_Brochure* file, if necessary; then locate the Project Guide toolbar and the entry bar (refer to Figure 1.6).**

The Project Guide toolbar helps you learn, explore, and use features as you work through the project management process. The entry bar displays the contents of the current (active) field. If the Project Guide toolbar is not onscreen, choose <u>V</u>iew, <u>T</u>oolbars, Project Guide.

2 **Click the Tasks button on the Project Guide toolbar (refer to Figure 1.6).**

The Tasks side pane opens. A ***side pane*** is an overall project guide that appears to the left side of the Microsoft Project window when you click the corresponding button on the Project Guide toolbar. It provides links to topics that guide you through the steps of creating a basic project. The Tasks side pane provides assistance with task-related steps.

3 **Click the *List the tasks in the project* link.**

The List Tasks content displays. There are several methods for entering tasks in a project.

4 **Position the mouse pointer on the Show/Hide Project Guide button on the Project Guide toolbar.**

The name of the button displays in a ScreenTip (see Figure 1.7).

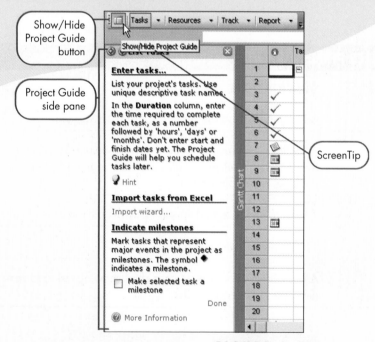

FIGURE 1.7

5 **Click the Show/Hide Project Guide button.**
The side pane closes. The project window extends to both sides of the screen.

6 **Locate the status bar near the bottom of the screen (refer to Figure 1.6).**
The *status bar* provides information about the current actions or settings. For example, NUM indicates that the Num Lock setting on the keyboard is active.

7 **Move to various project locations of your choice, using scrollbar features.**
The *scrollbar* enables you to move the project window vertically and horizontally so that you can see other parts of the work area. Notice that there are two horizontal scrollbars—one for the task table area and one for the Gantt chart. However, there is only one vertical scrollbar, which controls the task table and the Gantt chart movements simultaneously. A *scrollbox* is an object within a horizontal or vertical scrollbar that you can drag. Dragging the scrollbox quickly shifts the display within a window in the direction that you drag the scrollbox. You can also scroll by clicking and holding down the arrow at either end of a scrollbar or by clicking once either above or below the scrollbox to move a page at a time.

8 **Press** Ctrl + Home.
Pressing Home while holding down Ctrl moves you quickly to the beginning of the task table.

Keep the *Apartment_Brochure* project file open and continue with the next lesson. If you prefer to complete the project later, close the file and exit Microsoft Project.

TO EXTEND YOUR KNOWLEDGE . . .

DISPLAYING THE PROJECT GUIDE OPTIONS WITHOUT DISPLAYING THE SIDE PANE
You can display the list of options for the Project Guide without displaying the Project Guide side pane by clicking the arrows on the Project Guide toolbar buttons (Tasks, Resources, Track, Report) rather than the buttons themselves.

M'SOFT 1

LESSON 3:   Understanding the Task Table

Individual tasks are listed in the task table, one component of the Gantt Chart view. A *task table* is a table containing fields that relate to tasks. Microsoft Project contains many predefined tables and also allows the creation of custom tables. The default task table is the *entry table,* which is used to enter and edit tasks. The task table resembles an Excel worksheet, arranging data in a row and column format. Each row is numbered and that number comprises the *Task ID.* Columns represent a category of information called a *field.* By default, the entry table contains the following fields: Indicator, Task Name, Duration, Start Date, Finish Date, Predecessors, and Resource Names. Rows contain one complete record of information, in this case a task.

In this lesson, you explore the *Apartment_Brochure* project. This project file is comprised of many levels of tasks needed to create a marketing brochure for an apartment complex. Several tasks belong to more than one resource. Some tasks are partially completed while others are complete.

To View Individual Tasks

1 Open the *Apartment_Brochure* file, if necessary; then in the task table area of the Gantt Chart view, point the mouse pointer to the first column of Task 3 (*Visit property*).

The first column in the Gantt chart task table has a letter *i* within a blue circle as the column header. This column is the **indicator column,** which displays icons, where appropriate, to provide general information about a task. When you point to an icon next to a particular task, a ScreenTip appears with information about task completion (see Figure 1.8). Task 3 is complete.

	o	Task Name	Duration	Start	Finish	Predece:
1		⊟ Apartment Marketing Coach B	32 days	Sat 1/1/05	Tue 2/15/05	
2		⊟ Market Needs Assessmen	8 days	Wed 1/5/05	Fri 1/14/05	
3	✓	Visit property	3 days	Wed 1/5/05	Fri 1/7/05	
4	✓	This task was completed on Fri 1/7/05.	1 day	Sat 1/8/05	Mon 1/10/05	3
5	✓		1 day	Sun 1/9/05	Mon 1/10/05	4
6	✓	Create market report and dis	5 days	Sun 1/9/05	Fri 1/14/05	5
7	✐	⊟ Art	12 days	Thu 1/20/05	Fri 2/4/05	
8	📝	Present needs to graphic de	1 day	Thu 1/20/05	Thu 1/20/05	6
9	📝	Receive art mock-up from g	0 days	Thu 1/20/05	Thu 1/20/05	8
10		Review art mock-up and pro	3 days	Fri 1/21/05	Tue 1/25/05	9
11		Present quote to client	3 days	Wed 1/26/05	Fri 1/28/05	8,10
12		Decision point - go/no-go to	5 days	Mon 1/31/05	Fri 2/4/05	8,11
13	📝	⊟ Printer Feasibility Analysis	2 days	Mon 2/7/05	Tue 2/8/05	
14		⊟ Meet with printer	1 day	Mon 2/7/05	Mon 2/7/05	12
15		Identify production proce	1 day	Mon 2/7/05	Mon 2/7/05	
16		Present printer feasibility to	1 day	Tue 2/8/05	Tue 2/8/05	15
17		Determine Mail Date	0 days	Tue 2/8/05	Tue 2/8/05	16SS
18		⊟ Perform financial evaluation	5 days	Wed 2/9/05	Tue 2/15/05	16,17
19		Develop cost analysis	5 days	Wed 2/9/05	Tue 2/15/05	
20		Project cost spreadsheet to	1 day	Wed 2/9/05	Wed 2/9/05	

Indicator column · *Field names* · *ScreenTip about Task 3* · *Task IDs* · *Gantt Chart*

FIGURE 1.8

If you have problems . . .

ScreenTips appear for only a short time. If the ScreenTip disappears and you want to redisplay it, move the mouse pointer away and then back again, and the ScreenTip reappears.

2 Move your mouse pointer to the Task Name field for Task 8 (*Present needs to graphic designer*).

A ScreenTip displays the entire task name. Because of the width of the column, the task name is not fully visible.

3 Point the mouse pointer to the indicator column for Task 7 (*Art*) and pause on the icon.

A ScreenTip appears with a note (see Figure 1.9).

	①	Task Name	Duration	Start	Finish	Predece:
1		⊟ Apartment Marketing Coach B	32 days	Sat 1/1/05	Tue 2/15/05	
2		⊟ Market Needs Assessmen	8 days	Wed 1/5/05	Fri 1/14/05	
3	✓	Visit property	3 days	Wed 1/5/05	Fri 1/7/05	
4	✓	Meet with Property Manager	1 day	Sat 1/8/05	Mon 1/10/05	3
5	✓	Shop Adjacent Properties	1 day	Sun 1/9/05	Mon 1/10/05	4
6	✓	Create market report and di:	5 days	Sun 1/9/05	Fri 1/14/05	5
7	📝	⊟ Art	12 days	Thu 1/20/05	Fri 2/4/05	
8		Notes: 'Graphic designer has new	1 day	Thu 1/20/05	Thu 1/20/05	6
9		glossy paper they want to try. Get	0 days	Thu 1/20/05	Thu 1/20/05	8
10		specs on how it will feed through high-speed presses.'	3 days	Fri 1/21/05	Tue 1/25/05	9
11		Present quote to client	3 days	Wed 1/26/05	Fri 1/28/05	8,10
12		Decision point - go/no-go to	5 days	Mon 1/31/05	Fri 2/4/05	8,11
13		⊟ Printer Feasibility Analysis	2 days	Mon 2/7/05	Tue 2/8/05	
14		⊟ Meet with printer	1 day	Mon 2/7/05	Mon 2/7/05	12
15		Identify production proce	1 day	Mon 2/7/05	Mon 2/7/05	
16		Present printer feasibility to	1 day	Tue 2/8/05	Tue 2/8/05	15
17		Determine Mail Date	0 days	Tue 2/8/05	Tue 2/8/05	16SS
18		⊟ Perform financial evaluatio	5 days	Wed 2/9/05	Tue 2/15/05	16,17
19		Develop cost analysis	5 days	Wed 2/9/05	Tue 2/15/05	
20		Project cost spreadsheet to	1 day	Wed 2/9/05	Wed 2/9/05	

Indicator column

Notes icon

ScreenTip

FIGURE 1.9

4 | **Click the right-pointing arrow on the horizontal scrollbar of the task table until the last column displays.**

The Resource Names column displays. Notice the various departments that are responsible for various tasks within this project.

5 | **Scroll back to the left and position the mouse pointer in the indicator column for Task 9 (*Receive art mock-up from graphic team*).**

The ScreenTip indicates that this task has a constraint—there is a certain condition that cannot be ignored for this task's completion. Also, notice that the duration for this task is zero days. This task is a ***milestone*** task, meaning that it marks the completion of one or more tasks yet has no duration of its own. ***Duration*** is the length of time needed for task completion as well as the completion of the overall project.

6 | **Double-click anywhere in the Task 9 row.**

The Task Information dialog box opens (see Figure 1.10). This dialog box shows detailed information about a task, and you can use it to alter the properties of a task.

M'SOFT 1

FIGURE 1.10

7   **Click the Advanced tab.**

Notice the details of the task (see Figure 1.11). The Advanced tab shows supplemental data about a task, such as any constraints (deadlines) or any special calendar applied to that task.

FIGURE 1.11

8   **Click Cancel and then press** Ctrl + Home .

Keep the *Apartment_Brochure* project file open and continue with the next lesson. If you prefer to complete the project later, close the file and exit Microsoft Project.

TO EXTEND YOUR KNOWLEDGE . . .

HIDING A COLUMN IN THE TASK TABLE

At some time, you may need to hide a column in the task table. For example, you may want to print a copy of the task table, but you do not need the predecessor column. To hide a column, right-click within that column and select *Hide Column*. To unhide the column, right-click within the task table headings and select *Insert Column*. Then choose the column name from the drop-down list and click *Best fit* to ensure the column width is readable. The new column is inserted to the left of the selected column.

LESSON 4: Understanding the Timeline in Gantt Chart View

The default view for Microsoft project is Gantt Chart view, which includes the task table and the Gantt chart. A Gantt bar represents the duration for each task in the timeline of the Gantt chart.. Gantt charts also display *task links* (or *task dependencies*), indicating when the start or finish of one task depends upon the start or completion of another task.

The Gantt chart includes a timescale in the top portion of the chart. The timescale includes dates and the days of the week. Gantt bars represent each task in the timeline. Gantt bars are shown in the appropriate time window for the task duration. The Gantt bar style indicates the task type of the task.

In this lesson, you explore the timeline and identify a task type by its Gantt bar.

To Use the Gantt Chart

1 Open the Apartment_Brochure file, if necessary; then move the mouse pointer to the split bar separating the task table and the Gantt chart.
The mouse changes to a resizing shape (see Figure 1.12).

Mouse icon used to resize the window

FIGURE 1.12

2 Drag the border to the left until the Gantt chart takes up about ⅔ of the window.
Now you can see more of the Gantt chart and less of the task table.

3 Use the horizontal scrollbar in the Gantt chart to display Tasks 3–6 and point to the second summary task bar above them, if necessary (see Figure 1.13).

M'SOFT 1

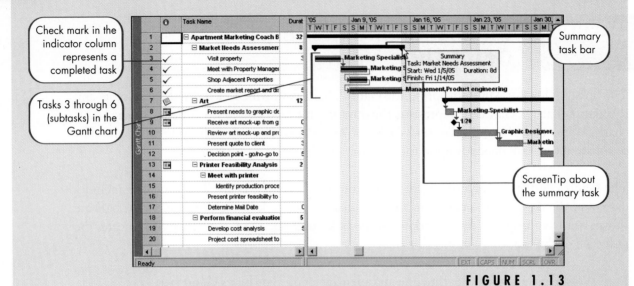

Check mark in the indicator column represents a completed task

Tasks 3 through 6 (subtasks) in the Gantt chart

Summary task bar

ScreenTip about the summary task

FIGURE 1.13

A ScreenTip with the task name, task type, start date, finish date, and duration appears (refer to Figure 1.13). A *summary task* is a task that consists of additional tasks called *subtasks* (mini-tasks) indented and listed below it.

Summary tasks appear bold in the task table. Each summary task can be expanded to view the subtasks below it or collapsed so that the subtasks are not visible. You expand or collapse a summary task by clicking on the plus or minus sign that appears to the left of the task name in the task table. To complete a summary task, you must complete all subtasks. A summary task is represented by a solid black Gantt bar expanding across all subtask Gantt bars in the Gantt chart. Notice that Gantt bars for Tasks 3–6 have black lines through them. The black line indicates the percent of completion of a task. When the black line is the length of the Gantt bar, it indicates a completed task, just like a check mark in the indicator column in the task table.

4   **Point to the blue line between Task 6 (*Create market report and distribute*) and Task 8 (*Present needs to graphic designer*).**

A ScreenTip about the task relationship appears (see Figure 1.14). The blue arrow linking Tasks 6 and 8 designates a task link, which defines a dependency between the start and finish dates of two tasks. In other words, Task 8 cannot begin until Task 6 is complete.

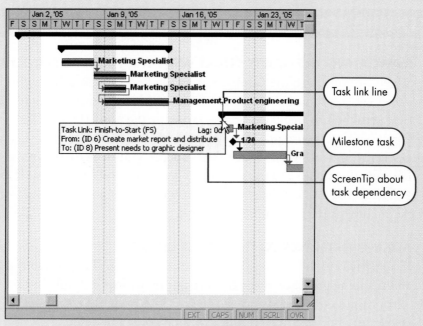

FIGURE 1.14

---

5 **Point to the black diamond beside Task 9 (*Receive art mock-up from graphic team*).**

A ScreenTip about the task appears (see Figure 1.15). The black diamond beside Task 9 indicates that this task is a milestone. Remember, a milestone task is a task that has no duration but is essential for project completion.

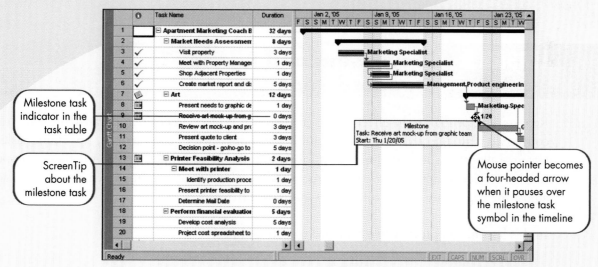

FIGURE 1.15

---

6 **Scroll through the rest of the chart to view other tasks and Gantt bars. When finished, return to the top-left position on the timeline.**

Keep the *Apartment_Brochure* project file open and continue with the next lesson. If you prefer to complete the project later, close the file and exit Microsoft Project.

TO EXTEND YOUR KNOWLEDGE . . .

NAVIGATING THE GANTT CHART WITH THE VERTICAL SCROLLBAR
When working with the Gantt chart, it can be a bit confusing to find the specific Gantt bar you want to view. You can click and hold down your mouse on the vertical scrollbox to display a ScreenTip with the Task ID and Task Name of the Gantt bar that is currently in view. To move to a particular Task ID, you can scroll vertically and both the Task table and the Gantt chart move simultaneously. Pointing the mouse and pausing on a Gantt bar displays the Task ID and the Task Name as well and can help you orient yourself. In addition, clicking on a Gantt bar highlights the task in the task table.

ADDING GRIDLINES TO THE GANTT CHART
If you have trouble seeing the correlation between the task table and the Gantt chart, adding gridlines in the Gantt chart may prove helpful. To do so, right-click within the Gantt chart and select *Gridlines*. Select *Gantt Rows* in the *Line to change* list and select the gridline type and color you desire.

USING THE VIEW BAR IN MICROSOFT PROJECT
Gantt Chart view is the default view in Microsoft Project, but there are many other helpful views. You can change the view using the View Bar. To utilize the View Bar, choose <u>V</u>iew, <u>V</u>iew Bar. A task pane displays that lists all the view types available, and the current view has a yellow square behind it. Click the name of the view you wish to see.

LESSON 5: Previewing and Printing a Standard Report

Reports are essential to the effective use of Microsoft Project. Reports summarize the activities concerned with a project. They are useful for keeping track of completions, upcoming tasks, resource allocation, and other needed information. Before printing a report, it is always a good idea to preview onscreen the way the report will look when it is printed. That way, you can adjust the page setup before you print—and save a tree as well.

In this lesson, you preview two standard reports and print one.

To Use Buttons to Preview and Print

1 Open the *Apartment_Brochure* file, if necessary; then select <u>V</u>iew and then **<u>R</u>eports from the menu.**
The Reports dialog box opens (see Figure 1.16). There are six report categories: Overview, Current Activities, Costs, Assignments, Workload, and Custom. Within each category are more specific report types.

FIGURE 1.16

2 | **Click the <u>A</u>ssignments button and then click <u>S</u>elect.**
The Assignment Reports dialog box opens. More specific report options are now available.

3 | **Click <u>W</u>ho Does What, if necessary, and then click <u>S</u>elect.**
A preview of the report displays (see Figure 1.17).

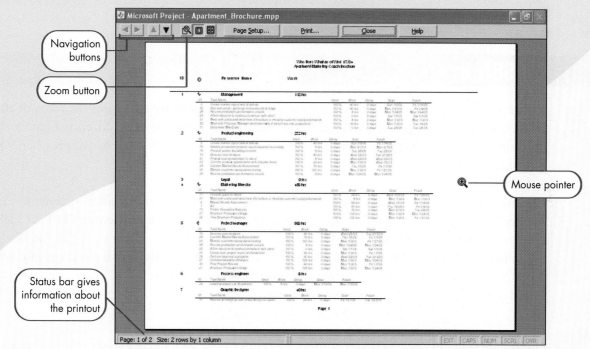

FIGURE 1.17

4 | **Click the Zoom button; then scroll through the window to view the report.**

5 | **Click inside the report preview area.**
The report returns to full screen view.

6 | **Click <u>P</u>rint on the toolbar.**
The Print dialog box opens.

M'SOFT 1

7 | **Click OK (or click Close if you do not want to print at this time).**
Microsoft Project sends the report to the default printer (or cancels printing).

8 | **Click Close and then click Close again.**
The Reports dialog box closes.

Keep the *Apartment_Brochure* project file open and continue with the next lesson. If you prefer to complete the project later, close the file and exit Microsoft Project.

TO EXTEND YOUR KNOWLEDGE . . .

PRINTING THE INFORMATION IN THE GANTT CHART VIEW
You can print a copy of the project window by simply choosing File, Print or by clicking the Print button on the Standard toolbar.

LESSON 6:   Getting Help

In just five lessons, you learned to execute quite a few actions by following the steps in this text—open and save a project, view tasks, use the Gantt Chart, preview and print a report. As you continue to use the program on your own, there likely will be many occasions when you don't know the steps to produce a desired result.

Extensive help is built into all Office programs. The Microsoft Project window includes several methods for accessing Help: the Help option on the menu bar, the Microsoft Project Help button on the Standard toolbar, and the *Type a question for help* box near the right end of the menu bar (see Figure 1.18). Figure 1.19, in the exercise steps that follow, shows the results of a Help topic search. Because Microsoft continually updates online Help, the results of your searches may vary from the figures in this book.

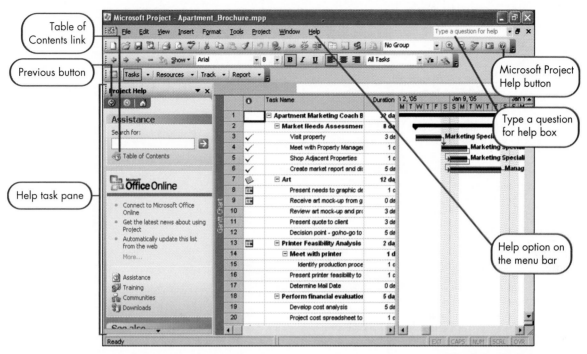

FIGURE 1.18

To get information quickly about a specific topic, you can type a descriptive word or phrase in the *Type a question for help* box and press ⏎Enter). You do not have to type your request in the form of a question.

The *Type a question for help* box and the Help task pane are likely to be your primary means to get information. You use both of these resources in the following steps. Opportunities to use these and other Help features are also provided throughout the text.

Microsoft's Help support is so extensive that some of its content can be accessed only if you have an Internet connection. The following steps are written as though your Internet connection is active. Additional steps on your part might be necessary to activate a connection as needed.

To Get Help

1 Type **project guide** in the *Type a question for help* box (refer to Figure 1.18); then press ⏎Enter).
After the search is complete, the Search Results task pane opens (see Figure 1.19).

M'SOFT 1

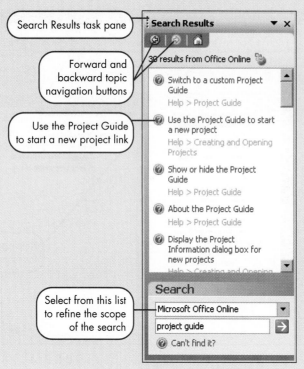

FIGURE 1.19

2 **Click *Use the Project Guide to start a new project* in the Search Results list.**
The Microsoft Project Help window opens in Auto Tile mode (see Figure 1.20). The
Help task pane may appear on the left or the right side of the screen, depending on
the last location from which it was closed.

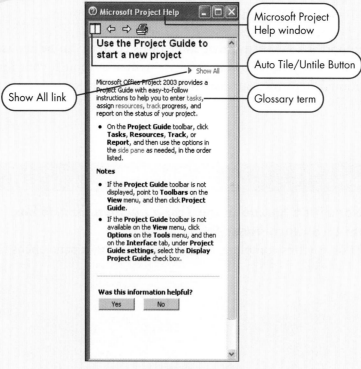

FIGURE 1.20

3 **Click *Show All* at the top of the Microsoft Project Help window.**
The entire topic expands. Each blue word represents a glossary term, which expands and displays its definition in green type.

4 **Click *Hide All* to hide the definitions.**
The entire topic collapses, including the glossary definitions.

5 **Close the Microsoft Project Help window; then close the Search Results task pane.**

6 **Click Microsoft Project Help on the Standard toolbar.**
The Project Help task pane displays. You can also press F1, choose Help from the menu bar, or click the arrow in the task pane title and select Help to display the task pane.

7 **Click the *Table of Contents* link below the *Search For* text box.**
The Table of Contents displays (see Figure 1.21). Topics display with closed or open book icons, depending on which topics were recently reviewed. Clicking a closed book icon expands the level of detail in the table of contents. Clicking an open book icon collapses the level of detail. The Table of Contents is available both online and offline.

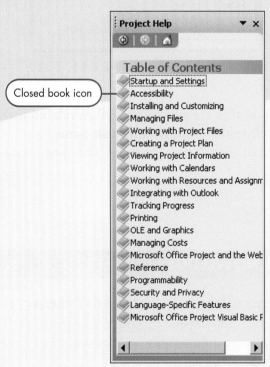

FIGURE 1.21

8 **Click the *Startup and Settings* book.**
Project displays subtopics related to general Office 2003 information.

M'SOFT 1

9 Click *What's new in Microsoft Office Project 2003.*
The Microsoft Project Help window displays with hyperlinks to topics about new software features for Project 2003 (see Figure 1.22). You can resize the Help window by clicking the Auto Tile button or by dragging any of the window borders.

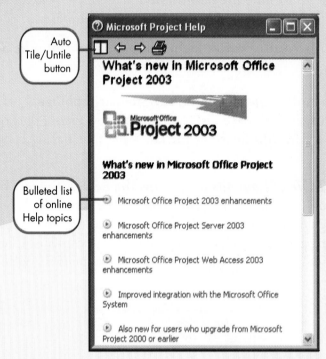

FIGURE 1.22

10 **Read the information on this Help page as well as related links at the bottom, as desired; then close the window and task pane.**
Project restores a full-screen view of the *Apartment_Brochure* project.

Continue to the last lesson, in which you close the file and exit Microsoft Project.

TO EXTEND YOUR KNOWLEDGE . . .

ALTERNATIVE WAY TO DISPLAY THE MICROSOFT PROJECT HELP TASK PANE
If another task pane is already open, clicking the arrow to the right of that task pane's name displays a list of available task panes. Click Help to display the Microsoft Project Help task pane.

DISPLAYING THE VERSION OF PROJECT
To display the version number of the Project software you are using, choose Help, About Microsoft Project.

USING WEB-BASED HELP
If you have an online connection, the Microsoft Project task pane provides access to broad Web-based support for all Office applications (refer to the *Office online* section in Figure 1.18). For example, you can click *Training* to access a *Browse Courses* area and select among 30- to 60-minute interactive tutorials on selected features in Word, Excel, Access, Visio, Outlook, FrontPage, InfoPath, Project, Publisher, PowerPoint, and Project.

LESSON 7: Closing a Project and Exiting Microsoft Project

The steps you take to close a project depend on whether you also plan to exit Project. If you have finished working in Project, use an Exit command. If you want to close the current project but continue working in Project, use a Close command.

You can perform Close and Exit operations by using buttons or menu options (see Figure 1.23). Whichever command you choose, Project provides a warning if changes to a project have not been saved.

FIGURE 1.23

In the following steps, you close the project, saving your changes. If you do not plan to continue with end-of-project exercises, you can complete an optional step to exit Project.

To Close a File and Exit Project

1 | **Click the Close button for the *Apartment_Brochure* window.**
This action closes the open project and leaves you with the main Project window open. If you made changes to the file but did not save them, Microsoft Project warns you of unsaved changes. To save those changes, click Yes. To close the file without saving changes, click No. To cancel the close and leave the project file open, click Cancel.

2 | **Click Yes, if necessary.**
If you want to continue exploring Microsoft Project, you can work through one or more exercises at the end of this project, or begin a new project in this text. If you want to exit Microsoft Project, complete the next step.

3 | **Click the Close Microsoft Project button.**
Microsoft Project closes.

S U M M A R Y

In this initial project in your text, you first learned definitions related to project management in general and the Microsoft Project software. You then explored the Microsoft Project work environment by opening an .mpp extension file for a project that tracks the steps for creating a marketing brochure for an apartment complex. Navigation in the project file and recognition of the various components in the Microsoft Project window are essential, as you learned through practice. After you looked at the individual tasks both in the task table and in the Gantt chart, you viewed a standard report and printed it. Assistance is sometimes necessary when learning a new program, so you accessed Microsoft Help button on the Standard toolbar. Finally, you closed and saved the project and exited Microsoft Project.

You can extend your learning by reviewing concepts and terms and by practicing variations of skills presented in the lessons. Use the following table as a guide to the numbered questions and exercises in the end-of-project learning opportunities.

LESSON	MULTIPLE CHOICE	DISCUSSION	SKILL DRILL	CHALLENGE	DISCOVERY ZONE
Starting Microsoft Project, Opening a Project, and Saving a Project	5	1, 3	1	1, 4	2
Exploring the Project Window	10		2	2, 3	
Understanding the Task Table	2, 4, 6	2	2	2	
Understanding the Timeline in Gantt Chart View	1, 7		3	2	
Previewing and Printing a Standard Report	9		4	4	
Getting Help	3		5	2	1, 2
Closing a Project and Exiting Microsoft Project	8		4	3, 4	

K E Y   T E R M S

budget	entry table	indicator column
constraint	field	menu bar
constraint triangle	Formatting toolbar	milestone
default	Gantt bar	project
duration	Gantt chart	Project Guide
entry bar	Gantt Chart view	project manager

resource	subtask	template
scope	summary task	time constraint
scrollbar	Task ID	timeline
scrollbox	task links (task dependencies)	timescale
side pane		title bar
stakeholders	task pane	toolbar
Standard toolbar	task table	*Type a question for help* box
status bar	tasks	

CHECKING CONCEPTS AND TERMS

SCREEN ID

Label each element of the project window shown in Figure 1.24. [L2]

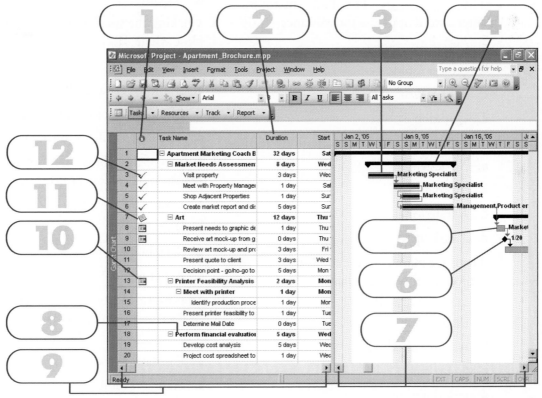

FIGURE 1.24

A. Gantt bar	**G.** Task table
B. Completed task	**H.** Indicator column
C. Summary task Gantt bar	**I.** Task with a constraint
D. Summary task	**J.** Task dependency (link line)
E. Time needed to complete a task	**K.** Gantt chart
F. Note about the task	**L.** Milestone task

M'SOFT 1

MULTIPLE CHOICE

Circle the letter of the correct answer for each of the following.

1. A graphical illustration of a project is called a _____. [L4]

   a. bar chart

   b. Gantt chart

   c. task pane

   d. scrollbar

2. What is a single activity or action that has a duration? [L3]

   a. Task

   b. Project

   c. Gantt chart

   d. Gantt bar

3. The _____ box allows you to enter a word or phrase for assistance. [L6]

   a. Office Assistant

   b. Project Guide

   c. *Type a question for help*

   d. Question

4. Which type of task has no duration? [L3]

   a. An activity

   b. A project

   c. A milestone

   d. A task tip

5. The three main considerations of a project are time, scope, and _____. [L1]

   a. budget

   b. resource allocation

   c. Gantt bar

   d. task duration

6. A(n) _____ could be a person, group of people, piece of equipment, or even a building. [L3]

   a. task

   b. activity

   c. project manager

   d. resource

7. What is the term for the amount of time it takes to complete a task? [L4]

   a. Gantt bar

   b. Duration

   c. Cost

   d. Baseline

8. Clicking the smaller close button will close what? [L7]

   a. Windows

   b. Both Project and all open files

   c. Microsoft Project application

   d. The Project file in the active window

9. Which of the following is not a standard report in Microsoft Project? [L5]

   a. Costs

   b. Workload

   c. Stakeholders

   d. Assignments

10. Step-by-step instructions for creating a project are provided by the _____. [L2]

    a. Formatting toolbar

    b. Standard toolbar

    c. Task pane

    d. Project Guide toolbar

DISCUSSION

1. Imagine that you are responsible for planning a surprise party. According to project management fundamentals, there are three main constraints when completing tasks in a project: time, budget, and scope. What happens to the other constraints when one of them changes? For example, suppose you decide to have a formal party rather than a luau (change in scope). How does this affect time and budget? Consider changing the time and the budget as well, and discuss the implications for the project. [L1]

2. Suppose you are the editor of the school newspaper. When publishing any newspaper, what resources would you need to utilize (consider both persons and equipment)? Which resources would be used with every paper, and which ones would be used only occasionally? [L3, Why Would I?]

3. Make a list of potential responsibilities for a project manager. Consider various types of projects when compiling the list. [L1]

SKILL DRILL

Skill Drill exercises reinforce project skills. Each skill reinforced is the same, or nearly the same, as a skill presented in the project. Detailed instructions are provided in a step-by-step format.

You should complete exercises 1–4 in sequence. Skill Drill exercise 5 is independent of the others and can be worked at any time.

1. Open a Project and Save It with a New Name

You are the project manager for the development and implementation of a new software package. The project includes planning, designing, testing, documenting, training, piloting, implementing, and reviewing the software. Every phase is your responsibility, although you have assigned various resources to complete each phase and task. To manage this project as effectively as possible, you are using Microsoft Project. Your assistant has entered the information into a file and has given it to you for review.

To open a project and save it with a new name, follow these steps:

1. From the File menu, select Open.
2. Click the drop-down arrow at the right end of the *Look in* box, and select the drive and folder containing the student files for this project.
3. Select *EPr1_0102* and then click Open.
4. Close the Getting Started task pane, if necessary.
5. Choose the File menu, and select Save As.
6. Select the folder in which you are storing your solutions.
7. Type **Software_Deployment** in the *File name* box.
8. Click Save and leave *Software_Deployment* open for the next exercise.

2. View the Tasks and Project Information

Now that you have the project open, you want to take a few minutes to orient yourself with the various tasks and the layout. There are 12 summary tasks in this project, including 86 tasks. You look at the tasks to make sure they are correct and inclusive for this project.

To view several tasks in the task table, follow these steps:

1. Open *Software_Deployment*, if necessary; select *Project* and then *Project Information* from the menu.

   The Project Information dialog box opens.

2. Read the general project parameters and then click Cancel.

3. Drag the split line between the task table and the timeline to the right to widen the task table as shown in Figure 1.25.

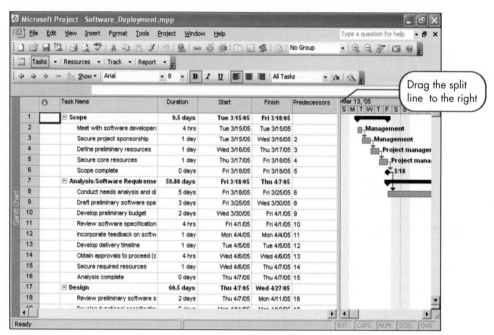

FIGURE 1.25

4. Locate Task 8 (*Conduct needs analysis and . . .*) and pause your mouse pointer on it.

   Read the ScreenTip to see the complete task name.

5. Point to the vertical column header border between Task Name and Duration; then drag to widen the column enough to see the complete task name.

6. Locate Task 33 (*Develop unit test plans using product specifications*).

   Notice that the predecessor for this task is Task 24 (*Design complete*).

7. Double-click the task and preview each tab in the dialog box; click Cancel when finished.

8. Save *Software_Deployment* and leave it open for the next exercise.

3. Explore the Gantt Chart

Now you need to familiarize yourself with the timeline. This visual representation of the tasks shows you the time period in which the project and each task must be accomplished as well as how tasks link to one another.

To view the Gantt chart, follow these steps:

1. Open *Software_Deployment*, if necessary, and drag the split line between the task table and the timeline to the left to widen the timeline.

2. Press Ctrl+Home, and then point to Task 1 (*Scope*) in the Gantt chart.

   Task 1 is a summary task for Tasks 2–6.

3. Point to Task 6 (*Scope complete*) in the Gantt chart area.

   Task 6 is a milestone task. If you have difficulty locating Task 6 in the Gantt chart, hover the mouse over the bar to read the task information. You can also turn on the gridlines.

4. Scroll to Task 78 (*Train Support Staff*) in the Gantt chart and hover the mouse over the bar to read the task information.

5. Point to the line linking Task 78 to Task 77.

   Task 77 must be complete in order to begin Task 78.

6. Navigate back to Task 1 (*Scope*) in the task table and in the Gantt chart.

7. Save *Software_Deployment* and leave it open for the next exercise.

4. Print a Report

The project is finally under way. Microsoft Project is proving to be a useful tool. Just to make sure that you stay on task, you would like a list of the tasks that are specifically your responsibility. Luckily, there is a standard report to do just that.

To print a report, follow these steps:

1. Open *Software_Deployment*, if necessary, and choose View, Reports.

2. Select *Assignments* and then click Select.

3. Select *To-do List* and then click Select.

4. From the drop-down list in the Using Resource dialog box, select *Project manager* and then click OK.

   A To Do List report displays in Print Preview.

5. Click the Page Setup button.

6. Click the *Adjust to* down spinner until the number is 80 (otherwise the report prints on two pages). Click OK.

7. Click Print and then click OK.

8. Click Close on the Reports dialog box; then save and close *Software_ Deployment*.

5. Use Help to Learn About Templates

Before creating a project from scratch, it may be useful to preview the templates that come packaged with Microsoft Project. Help is a great place to start, and the quickest and easiest form of Help is the *Type a question for help* box. Use it now to learn about templates and how to use them. (Note: You need an Internet connection to complete this exercise.)

To learn about templates, follow these steps:

1. Click in the *Type a question for help* box and type **template**. Press ↵Enter.
2. Click the *How templates are used in Microsoft Office Project 2003* link in the *Search Results* box.

   Your Web browser opens and the Microsoft Online Help window displays.

3. Read the information; then click the *What's the function of templates in Project?* link.
4. Read this information. Also read the *What type of templates does Project provide?* and *How do I use a template file?* topics. Close the browser window.
5. Click the *Available templates* link in the Search Results task pane.
6. Click several template names to display information about those particular templates. Read the information, and then close the Help window.

CHALLENGE

Challenge exercises expand on or are somewhat related to skills presented in the lessons. Each exercise provides a brief narrative introduction, followed by instructions in a numbered-step format that are not as detailed as those in the Skill Drill section.

Exercises 1–3 should be worked in order. Challenge exercise 4 is independent of the others and can be worked at any time.

1. Use a Template to Create a Project

You have decided to start your own business and you want to use Microsoft Project to track the tasks involved in preparing a business plan. Before you take the time to create the project, you want to look at the templates provided by Microsoft Project to see if one fits your needs, such as the New Business template.

To preview several templates and save the New Business template as the starting point for a project, complete the following steps:

1. Take a look at several of the templates located on your computer under *Project templates* in the New Project task pane.
2. Select the New Business template located on your computer under *Project templates.*
3. Scroll through the task table and Gantt chart to learn about the tasks and durations.
4. Click the collapse button (minus sign) beside the first summary task (Task 1); then collapse all other summary tasks.

5. Compare the Predecessor column information with the link lines in the Gantt chart.

6. Save the template as a project named **New_Business**, and leave it open for the next exercise.

2. View Project Information and Tasks in a Project Gantt Chart

Now you need to review the template so that you can later customize it to fit your schedule. To do so, you need to know what tasks are included, their durations, and overall project information. For starters, the dates given for the project and all tasks are old dates. You need to identify the tasks that you do not need, as well as areas where you will need to add new tasks.

1. Open *New_Business*, if necessary, and drag the split line between the task table and the timeline to the left.

2. View Task 8 (*Interview owners of similar businesses*).

   Notice that Task 6 must be complete before starting Task 8.

3. In the task table, double-click Task 8.

   Notice that the Task Information window appears; read through the options in this window.

4. Locate the Resources tab in the Task Information window, click on it, and read through the options. Click Cancel.

5. In the timeline, locate the first milestone (Task 25) and click on it. Notice that the task is highlighted in the task table as well. See if you can locate an additional three milestone tasks in this project file.

6. Move to Task 1 (*Phase 1 - Strategic Plan*).

7. Save *New_Business* and leave it open for the next exercise.

3. Preview Various Views in a Project

Gantt Chart view is just one of many views you can use in Project. Other views are helpful in different circumstances. Take a few minutes now to look at the other views in Project.

1. Open *New_Business*, if necessary, and then select View, View Bar.

2. Click the Calendar button and then click the Print Preview button to see how many months are necessary to complete this project. Then, close the preview.

3. Scroll down the list, select the Resource Sheet button, and review the various resources assigned in this project as well as the types of resources.

4. Preview other views.

5. Return to Gantt Chart view and turn off the View Bar.

6. Save and close *New_Business*.

4. Preview a Costs Report

As a manager of a software company, you handle many new software developments. You are beginning a new project that is very similar to a project you did in 2004. To plan better, you want to look at the cost information from that project to predict more accurately the budget for this project. You print a report to do so.

M'SOFT 1

1. Open the *EPr1_0103* file and save it as **Software**.

2. Open the Reports dialog box and select *Costs Report.* Then select *Budget.*

3. Zoom in on Task 39 (*Conduct marketing/technical review*). The total cost of this task was $34,592.

4. Before printing, access Page Setup and modify the header and footer. The header should be **Budget Report for 2005 Project** on the top line and *your name* on the second line.

5. Modify the footer to include the page number printed on the right side.

6. Change the page setup so that the report fits on two pages. Print it.

7. Save and close *Software.*

DISCOVERY ZONE

Discovery Zone exercises require advanced knowledge of topics presented in *Essentials* lessons, application of skills from multiple lessons, or self-directed learning of new skills. Each exercise is independent of the others, so you may complete them in any order.

1. Using Interactive Help

It is always important to fully understand the scope of a venture before beginning. In this case, you should have a basic understanding of projects and how to effectively plan and manage one. Microsoft Project 2003 provides several options for learning through interactive means, including the tutorials. The Project Map walks the user through building a project plan, tracking the project's progress, and communicating project information with others.

Access the Project Map (refer to online Help if necessary) and read as much information about the building process as possible. Keep notes on what you learn for future reference. Create an outline of steps. Then, go online to find additional information about three of the topics on which you took notes.

2. Researching Project Management

To better understand the role of a project manager, it would be useful to research some of the responsibilities, expectations, and lingo of project management. Project management differs from typical management in that it is shorter-lived by comparison. In other words, management in a company is required as long as there is a company, but project management is necessary only as long as there is a project—whether the duration of the project is 2 weeks or 20 years.

Visit the Project Management Institute Web site (www.pmi.org). PMI is the leading authority on project management. Using this Web site, research the overall project management role and its responsibilities. Be sure to learn about the profession as well as project management standards in particular. Use links listed on the Web site to learn about project management from other sources as well. Write a short paper about what you discover. Be sure to cite your sources.

SPECIFYING OVERALL PROJECT SETTINGS

OBJECTIVES

IN THIS PROJECT, YOU LEARN HOW TO

- Create a new project and assign the start date

- Create a project calendar

- View and modify project options

- Modify calendar working time options

- Print the Working Days calendar

- Create a project from a template

WHY WOULD I DO THIS?

After you complete the initial project planning phase, you create your project file in Microsoft Project. You may either use an existing template or create one from a blank file. One of the many benefits of using Microsoft templates is that you can start with a model project, with tasks and resources already entered, and then you modify those tasks and resources to suit your individual project plan. Upon first creating a project file, you must enter the preliminary data, including the start and finish dates of the project. Most projects are created from the *project start date,* with the finish date automatically calculated as you enter tasks and their durations.

You also create the overall project calendar. The *project calendar* includes the working days and hours, the number of hours in a given week, and any *nonworking time* such as holidays or vacation time. Besides maintaining the working times and days off for the entire project, the project calendar dictates when tasks are scheduled and when resources are scheduled to work on assigned tasks. The project calendar forms the basis for the overall project.

 VISUAL SUMMARY

In Lessons 1–4, you create a project file by using a new blank file. You specify the start date, create a project calendar, modify project options, and modify working times. Tasks are scheduled based on the default working times created in the project calendar, and resources are assigned individual calendars based on the project calendar. In Lesson 5 you print a calendar that shows the working and nonworking days (see Figure 2.1).

FIGURE 2.1

Lesson 6 provides an alternative method of creating a project file. You create a project file by using a template. Creating a project by using both methods allows you to compare the two processes and determine which method is best for a given situation.

The instructions in this project reflect entering or revising project dates in March 2005, which might already be in the past when you work through this text. You should follow the directions given so that dates associated with tasks are consistent with those shown in the figures. For your own projects, of course, the dates that you view and enter will be current or in the future.

LESSON 1:   Creating a New Project and Assigning the Start Date

After you define the project objectives, scope, and constraints, it is time to create your project file. You can create a new project in several ways: from another project file saved with a new name, from a template located on your computer or from Microsoft Online, or from a blank template. The first step, after creating the project file, is setting the start date. Later, as you develop the project plan, Microsoft Project uses this start date to compute the finish date based on the task deadlines you assign. The finish date of a project is equal to the finish date of the last task in the project plan and is fluid so it continually changes as you add tasks and modify durations.

In Project 2, you and a coworker create a project file for tracking the orientation process for new employees. In this lesson, you use the Project Guide to create a project file named *New_Hires* and provide the start date for the orientation. The Project Guide provides instructions and wizards to guide you through the process of creating and managing a project. A ***wizard*** is a feature of Microsoft Office programs that walks you step-by-step through an activity.

To Create a New Project and Assign a Start Date

1 **Start Microsoft Office Project 2003.**

2 **Close the Getting Started task pane.**
The Tasks side pane displays (see Figure 2.2).

FIGURE 2.2

If you have problems . . .

If you do not see the Project Guide toolbar, choose <u>V</u>iew, <u>T</u>oolbars, Project Guide. If you accidentally close the Project Guide side pane, reopen it by clicking Tasks on the Project Guide toolbar.

3   **Click the *Set a date to schedule from* link.**
The *Set a date to schedule from* wizard displays.

4   **Click the drop-down arrow next to the estimated date text box in the side pane.**
A calendar displays (see Figure 2.3). You may select the date from this calendar, or you may type the date into the text box.

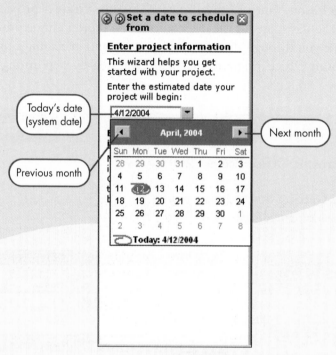

FIGURE 2.3

5   **Click a Next or Previous arrow in the calendar title bar as needed to display March 2005.**

6   **Click *1* in the calendar to select March 1, 2005.**
Once the start date is set, you are ready to define the project base calendar.

7   **Click Done at the bottom of the side pane.**

8   **Choose <u>F</u>ile, Save <u>A</u>s.**

9 From the *Save in* drop-down list, select the appropriate drive and folder for saving the file.

10 In the *File name* text box, type `New_Hires`, and then click **Save**.

11 Close the *New_Hires* project file.

You have created a new project file and assigned a start date for the project plan. If you prefer to complete the project later, exit Microsoft Project.

TO EXTEND YOUR KNOWLEDGE . . .

USING THE PROJECT INFORMATION DIALOG BOX

You can also set the **Start** date by using the Project Information window. Choose **Project**, **Project Information**. Enter the start date by using the drop-down calendar or type in the date manually.

LESSON 2:   Creating a Project Calendar

After you set the start date, you need to define the working days and times for the project. The ***working times*** may be the typical 8:00 A.M. to 5:00 P.M. time frame, but it can also include holidays and other nonworking times, such as evenings and weekends.

Microsoft Project provides three default base calendars: Standard, 24 Hours, and Night Shift. A ***base calendar*** is a project and task calendar that specifies default working and nonworking times. These times are used for task and resources scheduling. You can modify a base calendar to create your own unique project calendar. The Standard base calendar defines a work day as 8:00 A.M. to 5:00 P.M., Monday through Friday, with a one-hour lunch from noon to 1:00 P.M. The 24 Hours base calendar has no nonworking hours. The Night Shift base calendar defines a work day as midnight to 8:00 A.M., Tuesday through Saturday, with a one-hour lunch.

In this lesson, you create a project calendar to schedule task constraints. Your coworker has already added some tasks for the project but you must alter the project calendar to avoid having task deadlines falling on a nonworking day. While working through this project, the start date of the tasks changes as the project calendar changes.

To Create a Project Calendar

1 Open the *EPr1_0201* file.

2 Save the file as New_Hire_Orientation.

3 View Task 7 (*COBRA*) and notice that the start date is listed as *Thu 3/17/05*.

4 Click Tasks on the Project Guide toolbar, if necessary, and then click the *Define general working times* link in the Tasks side pane.
The *Project Working Times – Define the project's general working hours* wizard displays in a side pane on the left, and the Preview Working Time window displays on the right (see Figure 2.4).

FIGURE 2.4

5 Click the drop-down arrow in the *Select a calendar template* box.
There are three base calendars to choose from: Standard, 24 Hours, and Night Shift (see Figure 2.5). For this project, the Standard calendar template is most appropriate.

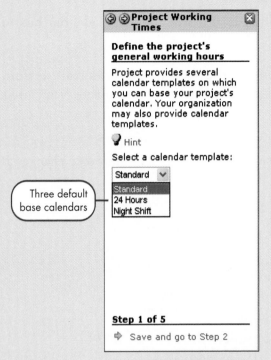

FIGURE 2.5

6 | Select the Standard calendar template, if necessary; then click *Save and go to Step 2.*
The *Define the work week* side pane displays. The *I'll use the hours shown in the preview on the right* option is the default option, which you accept.

7 | Click *Save and go to Step 3.*
The *Set Holidays and Days Off* side pane displays.

8 | Click *Change Working Time.*
The Change Working Time dialog box opens (see Figure 2.6).

FIGURE 2.6

9 Use the vertical scrollbar in the *Select Date(s)* calendar box to locate March 2005; then click *17.*

10 Select *Nonworking time* in the Set selected dates (to): section.

March 17, 2005, has just been set aside for a company picnic; thus it is a nonworking day.

11 Click OK. View Task 7 again.

Notice the start date is now *Fri 3/18/05.* The start date changes as specified by the project calendar.

12 Click *Save and go to Step 4.*

The *Define time units* side pane displays (see Figure 2.7).

Project Working Times

Define time units

When scheduling, Project changes all time units to hours. However, you can define the number of hours that make up a day and a week and the number of days that make up a month for your project. For example, if you specify that 8 hours make a day, the Project calculates a two-day task as 16 hours.

It is recommended that you set the settings below to match the working times you entered in the previous step:

Hours per day: 8

Hours per week: 40

Days per month: 20

Step 4 of 5

➡ Save and go to Step 5
⬅ Go back to Step 3

FIGURE 2.7

13 Accept the default settings of 8 hours per day, 40 hours per week, and 20 days per month. Click *Save and go to Step 5.*

The project calendar is complete.

14 Click *Save and Finish;* then click Save on the Standard toolbar.

You have added the project calendar for this project.

Keep the *New_Hire_Orientation* project file open and continue with the next lesson. If you prefer to complete the project later, close the file and exit Microsoft Project.

TO EXTEND YOUR KNOWLEDGE ...

CREATING A NEW BASE CALENDAR

If you use the same modified calendar on a regular basis, you can create a custom calendar so you do not have to re-create it with each new project. To do so, choose Tools, Change Working Time. Click the New button. Type a calendar name in the *Name* box. Select the *Make a copy of (base) calendar* arrow and select the base calendar you need. Click OK and set the working times as necessary. The calendar that you create becomes a calendar template that you can then choose when setting project working times.

LESSON 3: Viewing and Modifying Project Options

The Project Information dialog box contains the basic properties of a project at a glance. It contains the start, finish, current, and status dates as well as the base calendar on which the project calendar was created. The ***current date*** is the system date, the date provided by your computer. It can be used as an optional start date for new tasks rather than the project start date, which is the default setting.

The ***status date*** is used when both recording and reporting progress information for individual tasks as well as the entire project plan. The status date is also used for calculating earned value totals. ***Earned value*** is the cost of work up to the status date. The status date can also be modified if you are reporting actual work remaining. For example, if you receive actual data on a Friday but do not enter the data until the following week, the status date would be incorrect. By modifying the status date you can avoid this pitfall. You may also set the status date to *NA*. If you do, Microsoft Project uses the current date as the status date.

Priority is a numeric setting between 0 and 1000 and is used when leveling resources across multiple project files. A higher number indicates a higher priority project. The default setting is 500. The Project Information dialog box also shows whether the tasks are scheduled according to the start or finish date. You can assign a priority to the project when working with multiple projects that share resources.

In the following steps, you open the Project Information dialog box. You also change the settings for the current date and the status date.

To View and Modify Project Options

1   **Open the *New_Hire_Orientation* file, if necessary; then choose Project, Project Information.**

The Project Information for 'New_Hire_Orientation.mpp' dialog box opens (see Figure 2.8).

FIGURE 2.8

2   **Click the *Current date* drop-down arrow.**

A calendar displays. You need to change the current date to March 2, 2005, which falls within the begin and end dates of the project.

3   **Use the arrows in the calendar toolbar to locate March 2005; then click *2*.**

In the ***Current date*** text box, ***Wed 3/2/05*** displays.

4   **Click the *Status date* down arrow and change it to *Thu 3/17/05*.**

All dates are now set (see Figure 2.9).

FIGURE 2.9

5   **Click OK; then click Save on the Standard toolbar.**

Keep the *New_Hire_Orientation* project file open and continue with the next lesson. If you prefer to complete the project later, close the file and exit Microsoft Project.

TO EXTEND YOUR KNOWLEDGE . . .

SCHEDULING FROM THE PROJECT FINISH DATE

The Project Guide provides the option to create a schedule from a known starting date. This option provides the greatest flexibility. However, you can also create a schedule from a finish date by applying the ***project finish date*** setting. To do so, select Project, Project Information. Change the *Schedule from* option to *Project Finish Date.* Select the finish date.

If you define a project plan based on the finish date, Microsoft Project calculates the start date rather than the finish date and assigns the default constraint of *As Late As Possible (ALAP)* to existing tasks.

CHANGING THE DEFAULT START DATE FOR NEW TASKS

For projects scheduled from a finish date, it may make more sense that any new tasks you enter into the project plan use the current date as their default start date, rather than the project's finish date. To change this option, select Tools, Options and click the Schedule tab. Click the *New Tasks* drop-down arrow and choose *Start on Current Date.*

LESSON 4: Modifying Calendar Working Time Options

Generally speaking, the base calendar templates provide the dates and times necessary to create a project calendar. However, at times there are exceptions to the "normal" working times.

The **default working time** reflects the hours the team works on a project. For example, office hours may be 9:00 A.M. to 5:00 P.M. **Nondefault working time** refers to the work day hours that are not available for the project. Use this option when you need to change a day or a selection of days to nonworking time (such as Thanksgiving Day) or to change the working hours (such as closing early on Christmas Eve). You can also designate a particular time as nonworking time, such as a lunch hour from noon to 1:00 P.M.

In this lesson, you change March 17 back to a working day. The company has rescheduled the picnic, but the new date is not known yet. You also change the working times for Fridays.

To Modify Calendar Working Time Options

1 **Open the *New_Hire_Orientation* file, if necessary; then select Tools, Change Working Time.**
The Change Working Time dialog box opens.

2 **Scroll to March 2005 in the *Select Date(s)* calendar.**
Notice that the date of March 17, 2005, is bold and underlined (see Figure 2.10). This date is set in the project calendar as a nonworking day for a company picnic. However, the company has changed the date of the picnic.

M'SOFT 2

FIGURE 2.10

3 Select March 17, 2005; then click *Use default* in the *Set selected date(s) to* section.

March 17 is now a working day again.

4 Click the column heading for Friday (refer to Figure 2.10) and then click the option *Nondefault working time* in the *Set selected date(s) to* section.

On Fridays, this office is open only from 8:00 A.M. to 2:00 P.M.

5 Click in the first *To* text box (*12:00 PM*), delete the current text, and then type **2:00 PM.**

Now the working time is six hours without a break (see Figure 2.11).

FIGURE 2.11

6 Press Tab⇆ to move to the second *From* text box.

7 Press Del to delete *1:00 PM;* press Tab⇆ to move to the *To* text box; press Del; and then click OK.

You updated the project calendar for the current project file and adjusted the working time for Fridays. You have also adjusted the overall hours for a work week from 40 to 38.

If you have problems . . .

A warning box appears if you did not delete the second *From* and *To* hours. One period must end before another begins. If the starting time for the next period is earlier than the end of the previous period, you cannot save the change. Make the correction, and then click OK.

---

8 **Look at Task 7 (*COBRA*).**

Notice the start date for this task is March 17, 2005. You just found out that the human resource technician assigned to this task is taking vacation time that day, so you need to change March 17 to a nonworking day.

9 **Choose Tools, Change Working Time.**

10 **Scroll to March 2005 in the *Select Date(s)* calendar, and then select *17*.**

The calendar shows which dates are typical working hours, which are nonworking days, and which have edited working hours (see Figure 2.12).

FIGURE 2.12

11 **Select the *Nonworking time* option and click OK; then click Save on the Standard toolbar.**

12 **Look at Task 7 again.**

The start date for the task is now March 18.

13 **Save *New_Hire_Orientation*.**

Keep the *New_Hire_Orientation* project file open and continue with the next lesson. If you prefer to complete the project later, close the file and exit Microsoft Project.

TO EXTEND YOUR KNOWLEDGE . . .

RESOLVING WORK WEEK CONFLICTS
If you adjust the overall hours on the base calendar (as in this lesson) from a 40-hour work week to a 38-hour work week, scheduling a task over a week assigns a 40-hour work week when in reality it is a 38-hour work week. To resolve this problem, adjust the formula that Microsoft Project uses to convert task duration into time amounts. Choose Tools, Options, and then click the Calendar Tab. Change the *Hours per week* option to **38**.

LESSON 5:   Printing the Working Days Calendar

After you create the project calendar by specifying the working times, you may need to print it for distribution to key players in the project or for your own reference. Microsoft Project provides a report for printing a project's calendar, called the **Working Days report.** This report displays the working days and times and any exceptions (the nonworking days).

In the following steps, you open a dialog box that lists the available reports. You view how the Working Days report will look when printed, and you learn the methods to print or to close without printing.

To Preview a Report and View Print Options

1 Open the *New_Hire_Orientation* file, if necessary; and then select View, Reports.
The Reports dialog box opens.

2 Click the *Overview* option, if necessary; then click *Select*.
The Overview Reports dialog box opens.

3 Click the *Working Days* option and click *Select;* then click within the top of the report to zoom it.
You see an onscreen display of the Working Days report, showing which base calendar was used to create it (see Figure 2.13). This is a preview of what the printed output would look like.

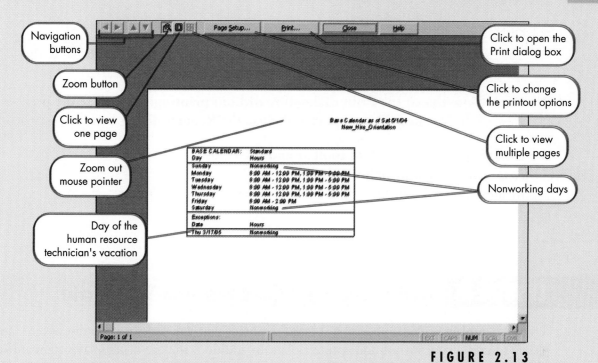

FIGURE 2.13

4 **Click the Page Setup button from the Print Preview toolbar (refer to Figure 2.13).**

The Page Setup – Base Calendar dialog box opens.

5 **Click the Header tab, and then click the Right tab in the *Alignment* area.**

There are three sections in the header: left, center, and right (see Figure 2.14). You want to add your name to the right side of the header.

FIGURE 2.14

6 **Click in the white text box and type your first and last name; then click OK.**

Your name now appears in the header of the report.

7 Click **Print** from the **Print Preview toolbar.**

The Print dialog box opens. Selecting OK at this point would send the output to the specified printer. For now, forego printing to conserve paper.

8 Click **Close to exit the Print dialog box without printing; then close the preview of the Working Days report and close the Reports dialog box.**

9 Click **Save on the Standard toolbar and then close the** **New_Hire_Orientation** project file.

If you prefer to complete the final lesson later, exit Microsoft Project.

LESSON 6:   Creating a Project from a Template

Using a template provides generic tasks and resources that you can then modify, add to, and delete to create your own unique project plan. In addition, the use of templates standardizes the look, feel, and usage of project files within a team or organization. Even if you create a new blank project, a global template named *global.mpt* is invoked. The **global template** is a collection of default settings controlling everything from startup view options to how Microsoft Project calculates formulas. When you use a template, you can still modify the project file options such as the working time, as discussed in previous lessons.

Microsoft Project installs some templates on your computer and makes others available online. In the following steps, you open one of the templates on your computer, save it under its default name, and explore its contents.

To Create a Project from a Template

1 Select **File, New.**

The New Project task pane opens.

2 In the *Templates* section, click *On my computer.*

The Templates dialog opens.

3 Click the **Project Templates tab, if necessary.**

There are many templates installed with Microsoft Project to make project creation easier (see Figure 2.15). There are also many more on Microsoft's Web site.

FIGURE 2.15

4 **Select the *Office Move* template; then click OK.**
A copy of the template loads and the Tasks side pane displays (see Figure 2.16).

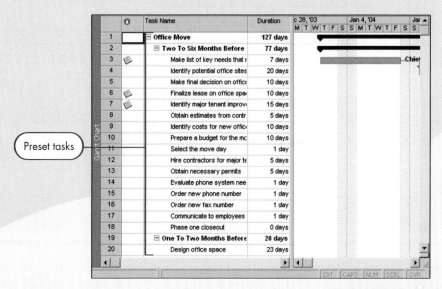

FIGURE 2.16

5 **Select File, Save As.**

6 **From the *Save in* drop-down list, select the appropriate drive and folder for saving the file.**

7 **Accept the default filename of *OFFMOVE*, and click Save.**

8 **Click the Close button on the Tasks side pane and navigate through the *OFFMOVE* project file.**
Notice that preset tasks are in the file along with resource allocations (see Figure 2.17). In later lessons, you learn how to modify these preset entries.

M'SOFT 2

FIGURE 2.17

9 | Close the *OFFMOVE* file.

Leave Microsoft Project open if you plan to continue with the end-of-project exercises or another project; otherwise, exit Microsoft Project.

SUMMARY

In this project you experienced creating a project from scratch (Lessons 1–5) and by using one of the templates available on your computer (Lesson 6). To create a project from scratch, you must first create a new project and a project calendar, using the Project Guide toolbar and the step-by-step wizards to set the working times. You also modified the working times, start date, and current date from the Tools menu and set up printing for the Working Days report. Finally, you created a project from the *Office Move* template and viewed the default entries.

You can extend your learning by reviewing concepts and terms and by practicing variations of skills presented in the lessons. Use the following table as a guide to the numbered questions and exercises in the end-of-project learning opportunities.

LESSON	MULTIPLE CHOICE	DISCUSSION	SKILL DRILL	CHALLENGE	DISCOVERY ZONE
Creating a New Project and Assigning the Start Date	1, 3	1	1	1, 4	
Creating a Project Calendar	2, 5	2	2	2, 4	1
Viewing and Modifying Project Options	6, 9, 10	1		1, 4	
Modifying Calendar Working Time Options	4	2	3, 4	3	
Printing the Working Days Calendar	7			4	2
Creating a Project from a Template	8	3		4	2

KEY TERMS

base calendar	nonworking time	status date
current date	priority	wizard
default working time	project calendar	Working Days report
earned value	project finish date	working time
global template	project start date	
nondefault working time		

M'SOFT 2

CHECKING CONCEPTS AND TERMS

MULTIPLE CHOICE

Circle the letter of the correct answer for each of the following.

1. The pane shown below the Standard and Formatting toolbars that displays step-by-step instructions on how to create a new project file is the
_____. [L1]

   a. task pane

   b. guide bar

   c. Project Guide

   d. wizard

2. Which of the following is provided as a guide to help you create a project calendar? [L2]

   a. Base calendars

   b. Tasks lists

   c. Project information

   d. Standard templates

3. What is the date you enter to designate when the project starts? [L1]

   a. Begin date

   b. Start From date

   c. Working date

   d. Schedule From date

4. Which option in the Change Working Time dialog box modifies the working times in the project calendar for a selected group of dates? [L4]

   a. Default work time

   b. Begin and end time

   c. Nonworking time

   d. Nondefault working time

5. When using the Standard base calendar, what are the default work day times? [L2]

   a. 9:00 A.M. to 5:00 P.M.

   b. Work day times are not set. You specify them.

   c. 8:30 A.M. to 5:30 P.M., Sunday through Friday, with a one-hour lunch break

   d. Monday through Friday, 8:00 A.M. to 5:00 P.M., with noon to 1:00 P.M. for lunch

6. What does the earned value calculation indicate? [L3]

   a. The current cost of work, up to the status date

   b. How much time it will take to complete the project

   c. How much money you will earn while working on the project

   d. How much extra time you will earn

7. To print the project calendar, you would choose which report category? [L5]

   a. Reports

   b. Current Activities

   c. Overview

   d. Page Setup

8. Which of the following is a generic project plan that you can modify to your own specifications? [L6]

   a. Project plan

   b. File

   c. Template

   d. Office Online

9. Which date, by default, reflects the date and time set by your computer but can be modified to match your project plan? [L3]

   a. Start date

   b. Finish date

   c. Earned value

   d. Current date

10. Which date is used to report earned value? [L3]

   a. Start date

   b. Status date

   c. Current date

   d. Finish date

DISCUSSION

1. Imagine that you are assigned to manage a project. Your supervisor does not know when the actual work will come in but does know that the project must be completed before the end of the current business quarter. You are provided a basic set of tasks and resources and told to start creating the project even though you don't know when you will actually begin work on it. With this agenda, would you schedule your project with a begin date or an end date? Discuss which option you would choose and why. [L1, L3]

2. You create the project calendar by specifying the begin and end dates of the work week and the begin and end times of each work day. This project calendar then makes up the calendar that each resource uses when working on the project. You can create additional project calendars and utilize multiple calendars in one project file. Discuss some reasons why you would do this and how it would be useful. [L2, L4]

3. Take a look at some of the templates available for use in Microsoft Project, both on your computer and online. Which template or templates could you use if you were going to upgrade the software used in your office to a new version? [L6]

SKILL DRILL

Skill Drill exercises reinforce project skills. Each skill reinforced is the same, or nearly the same, as a skill presented in the project. Detailed instructions are provided in a step-by-step format.

You should complete exercises 1 and 2 in sequence. Skill Drill exercises 3 and 4 are independent of the others and can be worked at any time.

1. Creating a New Blank Project for New Member Orientation

You are the office manager for a large real estate board. Many real estate agents who are new to the area join this nonprofit association. Bylaws require the board to provide each new member with a very specific orientation, including the services offered and the rules and regulations of the governing body. To ensure that you do not forget a piece of information and possibly jeopardize the nonprofit status of the board, you decide to create a simple project plan to help you with this new member orientation.

To create a new project plan, follow these steps:

1. Choose File, New; then click the *Blank Project* link in the New Project task pane.
2. Click the *Set a date to schedule from* link in the Tasks side pane.
3. Click in the *Project will begin* text box and type **1/1/2006**.
4. Click Done.
5. Choose File, Save As.
6. Select the appropriate drive and folder for saving the file.
7. In the *File name* text box, type **Board_New_Member.**
8. Then click Save; and leave *Board_New_Member* open for the next exercise.

2. Modifying the Working Times in the New Member Orientation Project

Now that you have created the *Board_New_Member* project plan file, you need to specify the *Schedule from* date and the project working times to coincide with the time frame of your project.

To create the project calendar, follow these steps:

1. Open *Board_New_Member*, if necessary, and in the Tasks side pane, click *Define general working times.*

2. Select the Standard calendar template, if necessary, and then click *Save and go to Step 2.*

3. Click the *I'll use the hours shown in the preview on the right* option, if necessary; then click *Save and go to Step 3.*

4. Click *Save and go to Step 4.*

5. Click in the *Hours per day* text box and type **7**. Press ⇥ to move to the *Hours per week* text box and type **35**. Click *Save and go to Step 5.*

6. Click *Save and Finish;* then click Save on the Standard toolbar.

7. Close the *Board_New_Member* project file.

3. Modifying Project Working Times in a Forms Project

Another responsibility of the real estate board is processing forms. You have a project file that assists you in completing this portion of the orientation. To customize an existing project plan, you modify the project calendar working times.

To modify working time, follow these steps:

1. Start Microsoft Project, if necessary, and open the *EPr1_0202* project file; then save it as **Forms_Procedures**.

2. Click Tasks on the Project Guide toolbar, if necessary; then click *Define general working times* in the Tasks side pane.

3. Click *Save and go to Step 2.*

4. Click the *I want to adjust the working hours shown for one or more days of the week* option.

5. Scroll down in the task pane so you can view the *Hours for, From,* and *To* text boxes.

6. Click the first *From* drop-down arrow and select *8:30 AM.*

7. Click the last *To* drop-down arrow and select *5:30 PM.*

8. Click *Apply to All Days* and then click *Save and go to Step 3.*

9. Click *Save and go to Step 4.* Click *Save and go to Step 5.*

10. Click *Save and Finish;* then click Save on the Standard toolbar.

11. Close the *Forms_Procedures* project file.

4. Scheduling Holiday Time in a Purchase Order Processing Project

As the accounts payable manager for a college, you keep track of all purchase orders used in the school. The college is being audited and you are required to track and take notes of all the things you do when purchase orders are processed. You decide to create a project file to ensure that you document each step of the process. Now, you need to mark nonworking days in the project calendar.

To schedule nonworking times, follow these steps:

1. Start Microsoft Project, if necessary; and open *EPr1_0203* and save it as **PO_Routing**.

2. Close the Tasks side pane, if necessary. Notice that the start date for Task 3 (*Review inbox*) is *Tue 7/4/06.*

3. Choose <u>T</u>ools, <u>C</u>hange Working Time.

4. Scroll to July 2006.

5. Click the calendar square for July 4, 2006; then click *Nonworking time,* and click OK. Notice that the start date for Task 3 (*Review inbox*) is now *Wed 7/5/06,* rather than *Tues 7/4/06.*

6. Click Save on the Standard toolbar.

7. Save and close *PO_Routing.*

CHALLENGE

Challenge exercises expand on or are somewhat related to skills presented in the lessons. Each exercise provides a brief narrative introduction, followed by instructions in a numbered-step format that are not as detailed as those in the Skill Drill section.

Exercises 1–2 should be worked in order. Challenge exercises 3–4 are independent of the others and can be worked at any time.

1. Scheduling a Project from the Finish Date

You are a technical writer for a small software company. You work in a team of four writers and an editor. For every new software program created or current software updated, you write and format the software documentation. You use the same procedures for creating each manual. The project completion date is the key to scheduling; the company predicts the software distribution date, and the software manual must be ready to accompany it. So you take the distribution deadline and set your schedule accordingly.

To set your schedule, follow these steps:

1. Open *EPr1_0204* and save it as **Manual_Schedule**.

2. Close the Tasks side pane if necessary; and then review the tasks in this project.

   This project takes 30 days to complete.

3. Open the Project Information dialog box; then set the current date to April 6, 2005.

4. Change the *Schedule from* option to *Project Finish Date.*

5. Change the finish date to December 1, 2005, and click OK. Close the Project Information dialog box.

6. Scroll through the Gantt chart and see when the project must begin in order to be completed on schedule.

7. Save *Manual_Schedule* and leave it open for the next exercise.

2. Creating a Custom Base Calendar

The software company has two shifts of technical support representatives, so your working hours differ from the typical 8-to-5 work day. In the three-week period prior to software release, the company requires all employees involved in software testing, programming, and documentation to work two Saturdays. To project the schedule correctly, you need to create a custom base calendar. Your calendar must account for legal holidays as well as those two working Saturdays.

To create a custom base calendar that accounts for legal holidays as well as the two working Saturdays, follow these steps:

1. Open *Manual_Schedule*, if necessary, and then open the Change Working Time dialog box.

2. Create a new calendar called **Writers** based on the Standard base calendar.

3. Change the Monday through Thursday working times of the new *Writers* calendar you created to 9:00 A.M. to 6:00 P.M., with an hour for lunch.

4. Change Friday's *Start* and *From* schedule to 9:00 A.M. to 1:00 P.M. removing any other times.

5. Change November 12 and 19, 2005, to working days, 9:00 A.M. to 4:00 P.M., with one hour for lunch.

6. Mark all legal holidays on the calendar, such as Columbus Day, Veterans Day, and Thanksgiving.

7. Apply the Writers calendar to the entire project.

8. Save and close *Manual_Schedule*.

3. Resolving a Work Week Conflict

Your work week is only 36 hours rather than the typical 40 hours. However, the base calendar is for a 40-hour week. You need to resolve the conflict so that any tasks that span more than 40 hours have correctly calculated finish dates.

To resolve the calendar conflict by correcting the number of hours in the work week, follow these steps:

1. Open *EPr1_0205* and save it as **Magazine_Article**.

2. Open the Change Working Time dialog box and view the nondefault working time options.

   Notice that for this project, the working day begins at 8:00 A.M. and ends at 2:30 P.M., with a 30-minute lunch. It is a 6-hour working day.

3. Look through this project file and notice that the summary tasks (tasks in bold) are calculated in days while the subtasks are calculated in hours.

   Notice also that the summary task calculations are incorrect and do not reflect a 6-hour work day.

4. In the Change Working Time dialog box, use the Options button to change the hours per day to 6 and the work week to 30 hours.

5. Review the project file again and notice that for the entire project plan, the summary tasks now calculate correctly with the adjustment of the hours per day and per week.

6. Save and close *Magazine_Article*.

4. Modifying a Template's Calendar and Working Times

You are an assistant to a general contractor for residential housing. The stages of building a house are constant for all jobs. You need to create a project file, and Microsoft Project provides a template that you decide to use. The template contains the basic tasks you need as well as a few custom project calendars.

To create a project file for your firm that reflects the stages of building a house, follow these steps:

1. Open a new project file, access the templates on your computer, and click the Project Templates tab.

2. Open the *Residential Construction* template and save it as **Building_Plan**.

3. Set June 1, 2006, as the start date for the project.

   Notice the finish date for the project. You may need to move the split bar between the task table and the Gantt chart.

4. Access the Change Working Times dialog box and look at all the available calendars.

5. Change the working times for the general contractor as follows: Monday through Friday, 7:00 A.M. to 7:00 P.M., with a one-hour lunch. Make sure this change is applied to all days.

6. Mark all major holidays for the 2006 year.

7. Save and close the *Building_Plan* project.

DISCOVERY ZONE

Discovery Zone exercises require advanced knowledge of topics presented in *Essentials* lessons, application of skills from multiple lessons, or self-directed learning of new skills. Each exercise is independent of the others, so you may complete them in any order.

1. Creating a Project with Multiple Calendars

You are the production manager for a chocolate factory. One of the year's busiest production times is Valentine's Day, when the company generally produces 100% more than during the rest of the year. You hire two temporary crews in addition to your usual employees to meet this

CREATIVE SOLUTION

demand. Your employees will work a total of three shifts during the month of January to ensure that your company produces enough chocolate to fulfill future orders. This will include weekend shifts as well.

Create a new project and save it as **Production**. Set the *Schedule from* date for January 3, 2005. Create three project calendars for this time period. First shift works 7:00 A.M. to 3:00 P.M., second shift works 3:00 P.M. to 11:00 P.M., and third shift works 11:00 P.M. to 7:00 A.M. Each shift has a one-hour break to eat. You can base the first shift calendar on the Standard calendar and the third shift on the Night Shift base calendar. Also create a project calendar for management personnel, who work 8:00 A.M. to 5:00 P.M.

Use the Tasks side pane to view the new calendars in the *Calendars* drop-down list.

Note: When creating the third shift calendar, remember that the finish time of the shift must be later than the start time. See the If You Have Problems feature in Lesson 4. Also, note that you cannot use the 24 Hours calendar when creating a three-shift work day.

2. Creating a Template

Microsoft Project provides many useful templates, but at times you need a unique template. You can create a template of your own. Use Help to learn how to create a template and have it display on the Project Templates tab in the Templates dialog box. Use one of the project files in this project to create a template. Close the file; then open the template from the New Project task pane.

ENTERING TASKS AND CREATING A PROJECT SCHEDULE

OBJECTIVES

IN THIS PROJECT, YOU LEARN HOW TO

- Enter tasks and specify duration

- Organize tasks

- Create milestone and recurring tasks

- Link tasks by specifying task predecessors

- Use outline features and view Work Breakdown Structure (WBS) codes

- Apply a calendar to a task

- Set constraints

WHY WOULD I DO THIS?

One of the difficult aspects of creating a project plan is finding the right words to convey your thoughts about all of the work that needs to be completed. There are several actions you can take to help ensure that tasks are not overlooked. Collaborate with team members and ask them for their "to-do" lists on similar projects they have worked on in the past. Research related projects, both within your organization and on the Internet. Remember to consult with the stakeholders involved with the project plan—the ones who are not directly associated with working on the project but are affected by its outcome. Chances are they may have some insight into the proposed project. If there is a written document describing the scope of the project plan, it too can be a source of valuable information. Finally, as you identify the tasks to include in the project plan, you may find it helpful to create a large list of tasks in a word-processed document, not worrying about anything but entering the names of the tasks. Then you can further refine this list—combining, deleting, and reorganizing the tasks until you form a cohesive project plan.

Once the project planning phase is complete and the project calendar is in place, you should launch Microsoft Project and begin entering the tasks necessary to complete the project plan. If you are working with a template or a copy of another project plan, you can modify the tasks already in place and add to the plan as needed.

Besides entering tasks, you also create phases by using the outline features. A *phase* is a major step, or a group of related tasks, in a project plan and phases are present throughout the project life cycle, much like the beginning, middle, and end of a story. You also enter *deliverables,* which are the tangible and measurable results you get from completing a task or series of tasks.

 VISUAL SUMMARY

You are one of many key people working on a large regional sales conference. Now that the tasks involved in planning this event have been identified, it is your responsibility to begin setting up the overall project file by using Microsoft Project.

Your efforts include entering tasks and their duration, organizing those tasks into a logical order, creating milestones and recurring tasks, applying a calendar to certain tasks, and setting constraints. The Gantt chart in Figure 3.1 illustrates the results of those efforts.

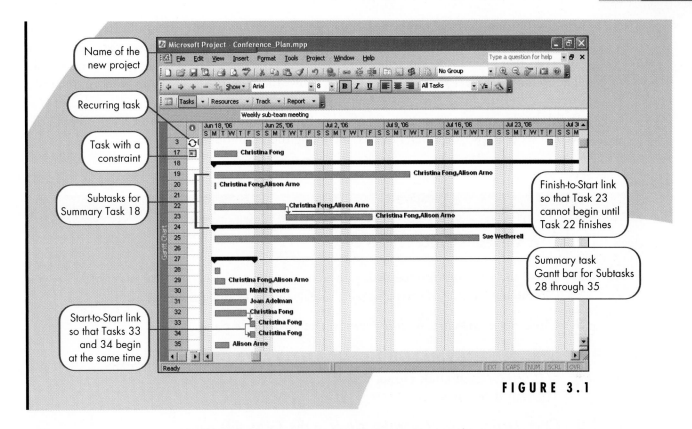

FIGURE 3.1

LESSON 1:   Entering Tasks and Specifying Duration

A project file is comprised of tasks. Each task is one piece of the project puzzle. Each task has a start date, duration, and finish date. Most tasks are assigned to a resource. Once the project calendar is in place, it is time to enter tasks.

There are several ways to enter a task. You can enter them by using the Gantt chart, by using the task table, or by importing data. Microsoft Project allows up to 1 million tasks in a single project file, far more than a personal computer can hold or an individual can manage.

Before entering tasks, an understanding of the fields in the task table is essential. The task table, by default, contains eight fields: ID, Indicator, Task Name, Duration, Start, Finish, Predecessors, and Resource Names. The **_ID field_** is a number automatically assigned by Microsoft Project that is used as a unique identifier for each task. You cannot input this ID or edit it, and it is automatically updated when a task moves to another location.

The Indicator field is used to display icons that signal there is additional information about a task—such as notes, constraints, and finish status. The **_Task Name field_** describes the task and can contain up to 255 characters. Unlike the Task ID, the Task Name does not have to be unique.

The Duration field is perhaps the most important field in the task table, because it specifies how long it takes to complete a task. In many cases, the duration is an estimate that can be entered in increments of months, weeks, days, or hours, with the default duration being days. The **_Start field_** and the **_Finish field_** show the calendar date of when the task starts and when the task finishes, as based on the task duration. Typically, you want Microsoft Project to calculate these dates to allow for the most flexibility in the schedule. The **_Predecessors field_** shows any tasks that must be considered before calculating the start or finish date of the current task. The **_Resource Names field_** in the task table shows the resources assigned to work on the task.

In this lesson, you complete two sets of steps. You begin by creating the project calendar. In the second set of steps, you enter 11 tasks, including their durations.

To Create the Project Calendar

1 **Start Microsoft Office Project 2003.**

2 **Close the Getting Started task pane.**
Closing the Getting Started task pane reveals the Tasks side pane beneath it.

3 **Click _Set a date to schedule from_ in the Tasks side pane.**

4 **In the _Enter the estimated date your project will begin_ text box, select _6/19/2006;_ then click Done.**
The start date is now set.

5 **Click _Define general working times_ in the Tasks side pane.**
A wizard opens to help you set up the wroking times for the resources of this project plan.

6 **In the _Define the project's general working hours_ side pane, click _Save and go to Step 2._**
This action accepts the default Standard calendar template.

7 **Click _I want to adjust the working hours shown for one or more days of the week;_ then change the working hours to 9:00 A.M.–12:30 P.M. and 1:30 P.M.–6:00 P.M.**

8 **Click _Apply to All Days;_ then click _Save and go to Step 3._**
This modifies the working hours of the project calendar.

9 **Click _Change Working Time_ in the Set Holidays and Days Off side pane.**

10 **Set July 4 and September 4, 2006, as <u>N</u>onworking time and click OK; then click _Save and go to Step 4._**

11 **Click _Save and go to Step 5;_ then click _Save and Finish._**
The working times and nonworking times for this calendar are set.

12 **Drag the border of the task table to display the Start column.**

You completed defining the project base calendar. The next set of steps involves entering tasks and specifying the associated durations for those tasks.

To Enter Tasks and Specify Durations

1 Click *List the tasks in the project* in the Tasks side pane.
The List Tasks side pane displays.

2 Click in the Task Name box of Row 1, type `Planning meetings and con-`
`ference calls`, and press `⏎Enter`.
Notice that a start date for Task 1 automatically displays in the Start column as *Mon 6/19/06*, and a default duration of *1 day?* appears in the Duration column (see Figure 3.2). The question mark indicates that the duration is an estimate.

FIGURE 3.2

If you have problems . . .

The entire task name may not appear after you enter it. To widen the Task Name column to show more of the contents, point to the right border of the column header and drag it to the right, or double-click the right border of the column header to AutoFit the contents of the Task Name column.

3 Type `Schedule bi-weekly status meetings` in the Task Name box in Row 2.

4 Press `Tab↹` to move to the Duration column; type `2?`; and then press `⏎Enter`.
2? expands to *2days* because "days" is the default duration type.

5 Enter the remaining tasks and durations as shown in the table below.

Task Name	Duration
Arrange core-team site visit	3d?
Budget funding and tuition	1d?
Develop budget	16d?
Determine tuition	0.5d?
Review status with sub-team leaders	1d?
Network group management review	1.5d?
Determine billing process	6.5d?
Budget reconciliation process	7d?
Identify all vendors	22d?

If you have problems . . .

Overflow markers are crosshatch characters (###) that indicate the entry in a field is too wide to fit within the column. These markers may appear in your Duration column as you enter tasks. To resolve this problem, move your mouse to the gridline between the Duration and Start column headers, and drag the gridline to the right to increase the width of the Duration column. You can also double-click the column border in the column header to allow AutoFit to resize the column to fit the data.

6 Click Done in the List Tasks side pane.

7 Click Save on the Standard toolbar, and then save the file as `Conference_Preplanning`.

8 Close the file.

You have added the project calendar for this project and entered tasks. If you prefer to complete the project later, exit Microsoft Project.

TO EXTEND YOUR KNOWLEDGE . . .

SETTING TASK DURATIONS

The default duration type is days (d), and it is an estimated time as indicated by the question mark that appears next to it. You can also specify durations as minutes (m), hours (h), weeks (w), or months (mo). Likewise, you do not have to use estimated time. To change the duration type, type in the duration, using the correct ending. For example, if a task will take 2 hours, type **2h**.

CHANGING THE DEFAULT DURATION

You can modify the default duration type by selecting Tools, Options and clicking the Schedule tab. Click the *Duration is Entered in* list box and choose the desired duration type.

EDITING A TASK

You can edit a task in the task table by selecting the task and pressing F2 or clicking in the entry bar, then making corrections. Alternatively, you can simply click twice in the field that needs to be changed and make your corrections.

USING UNDO

In Microsoft Project, you can undo only the last operation. Click the Undo button on the Standard toolbar or press Ctrl+Z.

LESSON 2:   Organizing Tasks

In a perfect world, you would enter tasks in the correct order as you type them the first time. However, that is not usually the case. If you are creating a project from scratch, you may need to combine, delete, and reorganize the master list of tasks you created to form a cohesive project plan. If you are using a template or an existing spreadsheet or project file, you may need to add and/or delete tasks so that the project plan reflects the current work at hand. Once you have created a basic project plan, you need to group the tasks into phases and organize the project tasks into a more logical order.

In this lesson, you use cut-and-paste method to reorganize tasks in a project to plan a conference.

To Organize Tasks

1 **Start Microsoft Project and then close any open side panes, if necessary.**

2 **Open *EPr1_0301* and save it as `Conference_Plan`.**
This file is the same as the one you created in the previous lesson. However, there are 32 additional tasks added at the end of the file.

3 **Click within Task 11 (*Identify all vendors*).**
You need to insert an additional task above row 11.

4 **Choose Insert, New task; add the task name `Vendor support`; and then press ↵Enter.**
Microsoft Project automatically adds an estimated duration of *1 day?* (see Figure 3.3).

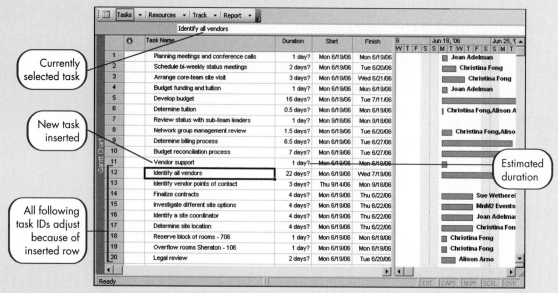

FIGURE 3.3

5 | **Click within Task 15 (*Investigate different site options*); then press** Insert.
Insert also inserts a new row above the selected task. All of the subsequent task IDs adjust when the new task is inserted.

6 | **Type** Site/hotel **as the task name, and then press** Enter.

7 | **Insert a row above Task 24 (*Make arrangements for receipt and storage of shipments*), type** General issues **as the task name, and then press** Enter.

8 | **Click the ID field for Task 8 (*Network group management review*), and then choose Edit, Cut Task.**
The previous Task 9 becomes Task 8 when the task is cut (see Figure 3.4).

FIGURE 3.4

9 | **Now click the row heading for Task 15 (*Investigate different site options*); then choose Edit, Paste.**
The previous Task 8 (*Network group management review*) is pasted above the original Task 15 and becomes the new Task 15. All tasks following have new task IDs.

If you have problems . . .

Note that there are two *Network group management review* tasks; one is in row 15 and the other in row 23. For this project, that particular task must be duplicated.

---

10 **Scroll down and select Tasks 24 (*General issues*) through 33 (*Presenter check-in*) by clicking Task 24's ID field and dragging to Task 33's ID field.**

All 10 tasks are selected (see Figure 3.5). Any action taken affects all selected tasks.

FIGURE 3.5

If you have problems . . .

If not all tasks in the group are visible before selecting, dragging the pointer toward the bottom of the screen as you are selecting may cause the tasks to scroll on the screen too quickly. To avoid this problem, scroll down to display all tasks to be selected before selecting them.

When dragging to select, be careful not to move the tasks. If you select the wrong task, click within any task to deselect and try again.

---

 11 **Choose Cut on the Standard toolbar.**

A warning box opens (see Figure 3.6). The message appears because several of the tasks have a value entered in the % Complete field.

FIGURE 3.6

12	**Click Yes.**

13	**Click anywhere in the first blank row after Task 36 (*Provide information to communications team for web page*); then click Paste on the Standard toolbar.** The tasks are moved to the new location.

14	**Save *Conference_Plan*.** You have successfully reorganized the *Conference_Plan* project file. Keep the project open and continue with the next lesson, or close the file and exit Microsoft Project.

LESSON 3: Creating Milestone and Recurring Tasks

Recall that a *milestone task* is one that has no duration but instead marks a significant point in the project plan. You should create milestones for stages you want to monitor closely in a project plan. Specific deliverables that occur after a group of tasks has been completed are often milestones. For example, if you were printing a newsletter, a milestone might be *Printing complete,* which marks that one set of tasks has been completed and another set of tasks—such as collating and distributing the newsletter—are ready to start.

A *recurring task* is one that repeats with some pattern, such as weekly, monthly, or bi-weekly. The most common use of a recurring task is for status meetings. Other uses are quality reviews, risk assessments, and weekly/monthly workers' meetings. The effort toward the project plan is captured, but there are no real work-related tasks involved. A recurring task is placed in the task list as a summary task, with each occurrence as a subtask. A summary task is a task that appears in bold type with several related tasks indented and listed below it. Microsoft Project calculates the duration of the recurring task by using the start of the first subtask and the finish of the last subtask. The summary task uses roll-up formatting; in the Gantt chart, each subtask shows short segments for the scheduled times rather than one large Gantt bar. If you have a task that recurs but has no pattern, schedule it as several individual tasks instead.

In this lesson, you create a recurring task for the weekly sub-team meeting for the conference. You also change Task 60 (*Conference begins*) and Task 49 (*Approve transportation plan*) to milestones because they mark the completion of a set of tasks.

To Create a Recurring Task and a Milestone Task

1	**Open the *Conference_Plan* project file, if necessary, and then click Task 3 (*Arrange core-team site visit*).**

2	**Choose Insert, Recurring Task.** The Recurring Task Information dialog box opens (see Figure 3.7).

FIGURE 3.7

3 Type `Weekly sub-team meeting` in the *Task Name* text box.

4 Select *Weekly* under *Recurrence pattern,* if necessary; then check *Friday* and click OK.

A warning box appears (see Figure 3.8). Because you are inserting a new recurring task into a Microsoft Project file with existing tasks, there are start date conflicts that need to be resolved.

FIGURE 3.8

5 Click Yes to allow Microsoft Project to reschedule the conflicts.

A new recurring task is entered into row 3 with an icon in the Indicator column signifying that it repeats (see Figure 3.9). This recurring meeting must occur on a scheduled day each week. Each occurrence automatically has a *Start No Earlier Than* constraint applied to it, which means that the task must start on or after the specified date for each meeting occurrence.

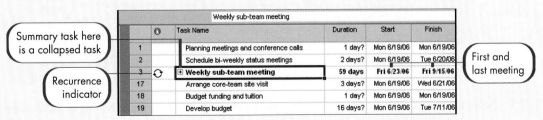

FIGURE 3.9

6 Click in the first blank row after Task 60 (*Presenter check-in*), and then type
Conference begins.

7 Press Tab⇆ to move to the Duration field, type **0**, and then press ↵Enter.
Entering a zero duration marks a task as a milestone, as indicated by the symbol on
the Gantt chart (see Figure 3.10).

	ⓘ	Task Name	Duration	Start	Finish
54	✓	Arrange for onsite fax machines	2 days?	Thu 8/10/06	Fri 8/11/06
55	✓	Arrange for onsite printers	2 days?	Thu 8/10/06	Fri 8/11/06
56		Set up schedule for security requirements	2 days?	Thu 8/10/06	Fri 8/11/06
57		Create/order message board (for attendees)	2 days?	Fri 9/15/06	Mon 9/18/06
58		Hotel rooms and cross check	3 days?	Thu 9/14/06	Mon 9/18/06
59		Registration	3 days?	Thu 9/14/06	Mon 9/18/06
60		Presenter check-in	3 days?	Thu 9/14/06	Mon 9/18/06
61		Conference begins	0 days	Mon 6/19/06	Mon 6/19/06

Duration of 0 signifies a milestone

Milestone symbol

6/19

FIGURE 3.10

8 Click in the Duration column of Task 49 (*Approve transportation plan*), type
0, and then press ↵Enter.
A small green flag appears in the upper-left corner of the cell, indicating a note (see
Figure 3.11). Microsoft Project requires additional information about this duration
change for Task 49.

Green flag

47		Determine shuttle services to/from airport	2 days?	Mon 6/19/06	Tue 6/20/06
48		Determine any special needs given conference	2 days?	Mon 6/19/06	Tue 6/20/06
49		Approve transportation plan	0 days	Mon 6/19/06	Mon 6/19/06
50		Provide information to communications team fo	2 days?	Mon 6/19/06	Tue 6/20/06
51		General issues	1 day?	Mon 6/19/06	Mon 6/19/06
52		Make arrangements for receipt and storage of	2 days?	Thu 8/10/06	Fri 8/11/06
53		Conduct walk-through site visit	2 days?	Mon 6/19/06	Tue 6/20/06

FIGURE 3.11

9 Move the mouse to the green flag and pause.
A smart tag appears. Smart tags appear whenever a change is made that requires additional information.

10 Point to the smart tag, and then click the down arrow when it appears.
A list of choices displays (see Figure 3.12).

Smart tag

Resolution choices

48		Determine any special needs given conference	2 days?	Mon 6/19/06	Tue 6/20/06		MnM2 Events
49		Approve transportation plan	0 days	Mon 6/19/06	Mon 6/19/06		6/19
50		Provide information to communications t					
51		General issues					
52		Make arrangements for receipt and st					
53		Conduct walk-through site visit					

You just decreased the duration of this task. Is it because the:
○ Work (person-hours) required to do this task has decreased, so it will take less time.
○ Resources will work more hours per day, so the task will take less time to complete.
Show me more details.

Reason the green flag appeared

FIGURE 3.12

11 Select *Work (person-hours) required to do this task decreased, so it will take*
less time.
The first option is the default action Microsoft Project uses if no action is taken with
the smart tag.

12 Save *Conference_Plan.*

You have successfully created a recurring task and specified milestones in the *Conference_Plan* project file.

Keep it open and continue with the next lesson, or close the file and exit Microsoft Project.

LESSON 4:   Linking Tasks by Specifying Task Predecessors

Some tasks work hand-in-hand with other tasks in the project file. For example, Task 1 may need to be completed before you start Task 2. When you link a task, you specify a *predecessor task* (the first task in the link) and a *successor task* (the dependent or linked task). A task link—also referred to as task dependency—sets the field for working with lag and lead time. *Lead time* is an overlap of time between two dependent tasks, while *lag time* is a delay between two tasks. The advantage to using links in a task list is clear when changes in scheduling become necessary. If the schedule for the predecessor task changes, Microsoft Project automatically reschedules the dependent tasks and recalculates the schedule for you.

When referring to a task dependency, you name the linked date of the predecessor task first and then the linked date of the successor task. The most common and default type of task dependency is *Finish-to-Start (FS).* An FS link means that the successor task cannot begin until the previous task, or predecessor, is complete.

You can also create a *Finish-to-Finish (FF)* dependency, which mandates that when a predecessor task finishes, the successor task also finishes. A *Start-to-Start (SS)* dependency means that both the predecessor and successor tasks start at the same time. This type of link is employed when several related tasks must begin at the same time. There is also a *Start-to-Finish (SF)* dependency in which, as soon as a predecessor task starts, the successor task can finish. This type of relationship is used less frequently than the other types.

In this lesson, you create a variety of task links by specifying task predecessors. You begin by creating multiple FS (Finish-to-Start) task links. You also create FF (Finish-to-Finish) and SS (Start-to-Start) task links.

To Link Tasks by Specifying Task Predecessors

1 Open the *Conference_Plan* file, if necessary; then drag the split bar between the Task table and the Gantt chart to the right until you can see some of the Predecessors column.

The mouse pointer becomes a resizing pointer when positioned on the split bar (see Figure 3.13). The task table now occupies approximately ¾ of the screen.

FIGURE 3.13

---

2   **Click in Task 19 (*Develop budget*).**

Notice that the task has a start date of *Mon 6/19/06* and a finish date of *Tue 7/11/06*. This task cannot begin until you identify the source for the budget funding and tuition monies specified in Task 18.

3   **Click in the Predecessors column for Task 19, type 18, and press ⏎Enter.**

A Finish-to-Start link between Tasks 18 and 19 appears on the Gantt chart (see Figure 3.14). The link line begins at the end of the first task's Gantt bar and ends at the start of the second task's Gantt bar. Notice that both the start and finish dates for Task 19 have been increased by one day—the duration it will take to complete Task 18.

FIGURE 3.14

---

4   **Select Tasks 22 (*Determine billing process*) and 23 (*Budget reconciliation process*).**

If you have problems . . .

To select adjacent tasks, click the first task's ID field and drag to the last task's ID field. To select two or more nonadjacent tasks, click the first task's ID field, press Ctrl, and click the other tasks' ID fields.

---

5 **Click Link Tasks.**

The number *22* is inserted in the Predecessors column in Task 23, creating an FS link, and the start and finish dates for Task 23 adjust (see Figure 3.15).

FIGURE 3.15

6 **Select Tasks 47 (*Determine shuttle services to/from airport*) through 50 (*Provide information to communications team for web page*), and then click Link Tasks.**

Each successor has the previous task as the predecessor. Microsoft Project assigns predecessors for a group of tasks in sequential order.

7 **Select Tasks 53 (*Conduct walk through site visit*) through 61 (*Conference begins*), and then click Link Tasks.**

8 **Click in the Predecessors column for Task 42 (*Menus for welcome and executive sessions and special evening event*), type 40, and then press ↵Enter.**

A ***noncontiguous link*** joins tasks that are not directly adjacent. In this case, a default FS link between Task 42 and Task 40 (*Recommend am/pm break menus*) is created because both tasks deal with the selection of menus for breaks and special sessions.

9 **Press Ctrl+Home.**

Tasks 1 and 2 are so closely linked that both must be completed at the same time.

10 **Click anywhere in Task 2 (*Schedule bi-weekly status meetings*).**

11 **Choose Project, Task Information; and then click the Predecessors tab.**

12 **Click in the Task Name column, and then click the drop-down arrow.**

A list of all tasks entered into the Project plan, except the selected task, appears (see Figure 3.16).

M'SOFT 3

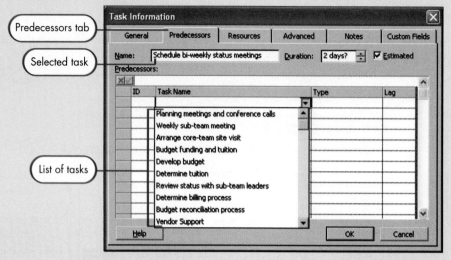

FIGURE 3.16

13 Choose the first task (*Planning meetings and conference calls*).

14 Click in the Type column, click the drop-down arrow, choose *Finish-to-Finish (FF)*, and then click OK.

The Predecessors column shows *1FF*, indicating the Finish-to-Finish link with Task 1. A join line has been added from the end of the Task 1 Gantt bar to the end of the Task 2 Gantt bar (see Figure 3.17). Notice also that this type of relationship does not affect the finish date for Task 2.

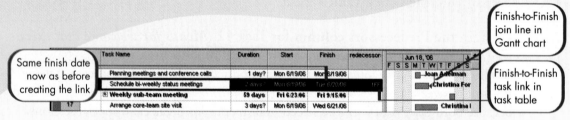

FIGURE 3.17

15 Locate Task 33 (*Reserve block of rooms - 706*); then click in the Predecessors column, type 32, and press ⏎Enter.

A default FS link to Task 32 (*Determine site location*) is created, adjusting the start date from *Mon 6/19/06* to *Fri 6/23/06*.

16 Double-click Task 34 (*Overflow rooms Sheraton - 106*), and then click the Predecessors tab, if necessary.

17 In the Task Name column, type **Res**; then click the drop-down arrow and choose *Reserve block of rooms - 706*.

As you type letters in the *Task Name* text box, Microsoft Project automatically searches in the task names for a match. When you click the drop-down arrow, the list displays the first match as the selected task name.

18 Choose *Start-to-Start (SS)* in the Type column and click OK.

The Predecessors column shows *33SS,* indicating the Start-to-Start link with Task 33. A join line has been added from the beginning of the Task 33 Gantt bar to the beginning of the Task 34 Gantt bar (see Figure 3.18). In addition, the start date is adjusted to match that of Task 33.

32	Determine site location	4 days?	Mon 6/19/06	Thu 6/22/06		Christi
33	Reserve block of rooms - 706	1 day?	Fri 6/23/06	Fri 6/23/06	32	Chri
34	Overflow rooms Sheraton - 106	1 day?	Fri 6/23/06	Fri 6/23/06	33SS	Chri
35	Legal review	2 days?	Mon 6/19/06	Tue 6/20/06		Alison Arno
36	Approve contract with hotel	10 days?	Mon 6/19/06	Fri 6/30/06		

Start-to-Start task link in task table

Start-to-Start join line in Gantt chart

FIGURE 3.18

19 Save *Conference_Plan.*

You created links between the various tasks in your project plan and specified dependencies and predecessors. Keep the *Conference_Plan* file open and continue with the next lesson, or close the file and exit Microsoft Project.

TO EXTEND YOUR KNOWLEDGE . . .

CHOOSING THE DEPENDENT TASK

If you have equal scheduling control over two related tasks, make the task that must be completed first the predecessor and the later task the successor. If you do not have control, make the more flexible task the successor, regardless of which task actually comes first.

M'SOFT 3

LESSON 5: Using Outline Features and Viewing Work Breakdown Structure (WBS) Codes

The outline features provided with Microsoft Project enable you to visually identify the phases of a project and to group related tasks. When you use outlining, major topics are called summary tasks, which appear in bold type in the task table, and subordinate tasks that represent the details of a summary task are called subtasks. Subtasks are indented below the corresponding summary task. The duration of a summary task is the combined durations of the subtasks below it.

To make a task a subtask, you demote the task by using the Indent button on the Formatting toolbar. The summary task occurs as a result of having tasks demoted below it. When you create a summary task, Microsoft Project calculates the duration, using the start date of the first subtask and the finish date of the last subtask. You cannot edit the duration of a summary task.

When you utilize the outline features, Microsoft Project automatically assigns **Work Breakdown Structure (WBS) codes.** These codes are the default outline numbers automatically assigned to each task that identify its hierarchical position within your project plan.

Once a project plan has been outlined, you can use the Show features—the plus (+) or minus (–) symbol—to collapse and expand the tasks that you want to view. This feature can be especially handy for creating a quick report for a stakeholder or manager who is not interested in the fine details of a project.

In this lesson, you create summary tasks in the Conference_Plan project file by utilizing outlining techniques. You also view the WBS codes of several tasks that have been assigned by Microsoft Project.

To Use Outline Features

1   Open *Conference_Plan,* if necessary; then select Tasks 2 (*Schedule bi-weekly status meetings*) through 17 (*Arrange core-team site visit*).

➡ **2**   Click Indent on the Formatting toolbar.
Task 1 (*Planning meetings and conference calls*) becomes a summary task, while Tasks 2 through 17 become subtasks (see Figure 3.19).

FIGURE 3.19

3   Select Tasks 19 (*Develop budget*) through 23 (*Budget reconciliation process*); and then click Indent.

4   Select Tasks 25 (*Identify all vendors*) through 27 (*Finalize contracts*) and indent these tasks as well.

5   Select Tasks 28 (*Site/hotel*) through 35 (*Legal review*) and then click Indent two times.
Task 27 (*Finalize contracts*) becomes a summary task for Tasks 28 through 35, while it also remains a subtask of Task 24 *Vendor support* (see Figure 3.20). Task 24 starts a phase within a phase.

FIGURE 3.20

6 Select Tasks 36 (*Approve contract with hotel*) and 37 (*Network group management review*), and then click Indent.

7 Finish outlining the project plan, beginning with Task 39 (*Determine special dietary needs of participants*), as shown in the table below.

Tasks	Indentation
Tasks 39–42	Indent once
Tasks 44–58	Indent once
Tasks 59–60	Indent twice

The outlining of the project is complete. There are now eight summary tasks. Recurring tasks are displayed as summary tasks, but in the Gantt chart, individual Gantt bars are displayed rather than one summary task.

8 Press Ctrl + Home, click **S**how on the Formatting Toolbar, and then choose *Outline Level 1*.

This view displays only the level 1 summary tasks you created (see Figure 3.21). Note that Task 81 (*Conference begins*) is not a summary task; however, it is a level 1 task thus it is included in this view.

FIGURE 3.21

9 Click **S**how, **A**ll Subtasks.

Notice that Task 3 is the recurring task and all its subtasks (meetings) are displayed, which is not necessary.

10 Click the minus sign on the left of the Task Name field Task 3.

The task collapses. To expand it again, click the plus sign.

11 Double-click Task 1 (*Planning meetings and conference calls*) and then click the Advanced tab.

Notice that the WBS code of *1* is automatically applied to the task (see Figure 3.22).

M'SOFT 3

FIGURE 3.22

12 **View the WBS codes for Task 2 (*Schedule bi-weekly status meetings*) and Task 28 (*Site/hotel*).**

The WBS code for Task 2 is 1.1, and the WBS code for Task 28 is 3.3.1 (see Figure 3.23). Each code is assigned a sequential outline number indicating the hierarchical position the task holds within the overall project plan. WBS codes cannot be modified unless the entire scheme is changed.

FIGURE 3.23

13 **Click OK to close the Task Information dialog box, and save the file.**

You have successfully created an outline to visually identify the various phases of the project.

Keep the *Conference_Plan* project file open and continue with the next lesson, or close the file and exit Microsoft Project.

TO EXTEND YOUR KNOWLEDGE . . .

WORKING WITH THE OUTLINE FEATURES

There are several other ways to outline a task list besides using the Formatting toolbar. You can use the Project Guide, which is a good idea if you are new to using the program. You can use the mouse to drag the task left or right. To do so, place the mouse over the first letters of the task name until it appears as a double arrow. Drag the pointer to the left or right to change the indent or outdent level of the task. Alternatively, choose Project, Outline, Indent or Outdent; or press Alt+Shift+→ to indent or Alt+Shift+← to outdent.

SETTING UP CUSTOM WBS CODES

By default, WBS codes are created like outline numbers. Some companies rely heavily on WBS codes and have created custom schemes tailored to the specific needs of the organization. To modify the default scenario created by Microsoft, select Project, WBS, Define code. Enter any prefix used in front of the code in the Project Code Prefix box, and then specify whether the sequence is a letter or number, specify the length of this level of code, and the type of separator between this level and the next. Repeat this process for each level of the hierarchical structure for the custom WBS codes until all codes are created.

LESSON 6:   Applying a Calendar to a Task

In addition to creating a project base calendar, you can also specify unique calendars for individual tasks. By default, all tasks use the project base calendar you create; however, if there are tasks that are independent of the project calendar, you can apply an additional calendar to them. Task calendars provide control over the schedule for particular tasks and do not affect the overall project calendar. Assigning a task calendar to a recurring task affects all occurrences of the task. Assigning a task calendar has the potential to affect the schedule of related predecessor or successor tasks as well as a summary tasks. However, assigning a task calendar to a summary task does not affect the schedule for subtasks nor does it change the schedule for the summary task.

In this lesson, you apply a different calendar to the meeting tasks because some of your team members are in Bangkok. Your team meetings must be at 9:00 P.M. EST to accommodate the time difference.

To Apply a Calendar to a Task

1 Open *Conference_Plan,* if necessary; then double-click Task 3 (*Weekly sub-team meeting*) and click the Calendar drop-down arrow.
A list of calendars in the project file open in the Recurring Task Information dialog box (see Figure 3.24).

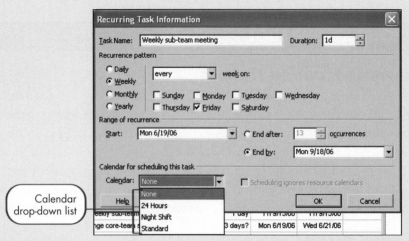

FIGURE 3.24

2 Choose *24 Hours* and then click OK.

3 Click the plus sign to the left of the Task 3 Task Name to expand the group, and then point your mouse in the Indicator column of Task 4.

A *constraint icon* appears in the Indicator field next to each occurrence, showing that a scheduling constraint has been applied. Notice that the summary task as well as all the subtasks utilize the 24 Hours calendar (see Figure 3.25).

3		⊟ **Weekly sub-team meeting**	253 days	Fri 6/23/06	Fri 9/15/06	
4		Weekly sub-team meeting 1	1 day	Fri 6/23/06	Fri 6/23/06	
5		This task has a 'Start No Earlier Than' constraint on Fri 6/23/06.	1 day	Fri 6/30/06	Fri 6/30/06	
6			1 day	Fri 7/7/06	Fri 7/7/06	
7		The calendar '24 Hours' is assigned to the task.	1 day	Fri 7/14/06	Fri 7/14/06	
8		Weekly sub-team meeting 5	1 day	Fri 7/21/06	Fri 7/21/06	
9		Weekly sub-team meeting 6	1 day	Fri 7/28/06	Fri 7/28/06	
10		Weekly sub-team meeting 7	1 day	Fri 8/4/06	Fri 8/4/06	
11		Weekly sub-team meeting 8	1 day	Fri 8/11/06	Fri 8/11/06	
12		Weekly sub-team meeting 9	1 day	Fri 8/18/06	Fri 8/18/06	
13		Weekly sub-team meeting 10	1 day	Fri 8/25/06	Fri 8/25/06	
14		Weekly sub-team meeting 11	1 day	Fri 9/1/06	Fri 9/1/06	
15		Weekly sub-team meeting 12	1 day	Fri 9/8/06	Fri 9/8/06	
16		Weekly sub-team meeting 13	1 day	Fri 9/15/06	Fri 9/15/06	

Note about the constraint and task calendar

Constraint icon

Task calendar icon

FIGURE 3.25

4 Select Tasks 59 (*Registration*) and 60 (*Presenter check-in*).

5 Click Task Information on the Standard toolbar and then click the Advanced tab.

6 Choose *24 Hours* in the Calendar list box and then click OK.

The calendar is applied to both selected tasks.

7 Save *Conference_Plan*.

You have added individual calendars to a recurring summary task and to multiple tasks.

Keep the *Conference_Plan* project file open and continue with the next lesson. If you prefer to complete the project later, close the file and exit Microsoft Project.

TO EXTEND YOUR KNOWLEDGE . . .

USING BASE CALENDARS VERSUS TASK CALENDARS

To distinguish the task calendars from the base calendars, it is a good idea to name each calendar with some identifier, such as a prefix. Doing so makes it easier to find the calendar you need when assigning calendars.

CREATING A CUSTOM CALENDAR FOR A TASK

You can create a custom task calendar for individual tasks. To do so, choose Tools, Change Working Time. Click New and name your calendar. Click *Create new base calendar,* then click OK. Make your changes, just as you did to create your project calendar.

LESSON 7:   Setting Constraints

Constraints are restrictions applied to the start or finish date of a task. *Flexible constraints* are not tied to a task on a specific date. There are four flexible constraints. The *As Soon As Possible (ASAP)* constraint allows you to start a task as soon as possible in relation to the scheduled start date. By default, Project assigns an ASAP constraint to all tasks in project files that are scheduled from the start date, because it is the most flexible constraint. The opposite of ASAP is the *As Late As Possible (ALAP)* constraint, which allows you to start a task as near as possible to the scheduled project finish date. By default, Project assigns an ALAP constraint to all tasks in projects that are scheduled from the finish date, because it is the most flexible constraint for this type of project file. The *Finish No Earlier Than (FNET)* constraint requires that a task finish on or after a specific date. *Finish No Later Than (FNLT)* schedules a task to finish on or before a specified date. All flexible constraints take into account other task dependencies and constraints. Tasks with flexible constraints display a blue dot in the constraint icon in the Indicator column.

Inflexible constraints tie a task to a specific date. They are generally applied to tasks controlled by external or outside factors. External factors might include drop-dead deadlines or availability of an asset, such as a crane. There are four inflexible constraints. *Must Finish On (MFO)* has an associated date that controls when a task finishes. *Must Start On (MSO)* has an associated date that controls when a task starts. Start No Earlier Than (SNET) schedules the task to start on or after a specified date. *Start No Later Than (SNLT)* schedules the task to start on or before a specified date. Tasks with inflexible constraints display a red dot in the constraint icon in the Indicator column.

In the event that a constraint and a task link conflict, Microsoft Project honors the constraint and ignores the link.

In this lesson, you assign constraints to those tasks that have specific scheduling restrictions not addressed by the automatic scheduling utilized in Microsoft Project.

M'SOFT 3

To Set Constraints

1 **Open *Conference_Plan,* if necessary; then double-click Task 17 (*Arrange core-team site visit*).**

Because this task involves a business trip and is the starting point for many of the other tasks in the project plan, you apply a flexible constraint indicating that the task must be completed by June 21, 2006.

2 **Click the Advanced tab, if necessary, then click the *Constraint type* drop-down arrow.**

A list of constraint types displays (see Figure 3.26).

List of constraint options

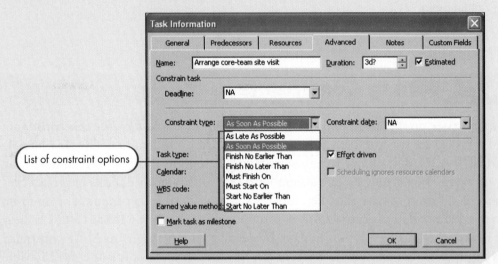

FIGURE 3.26

3 **Choose *Finish No Later Than,* click OK, and then deselect the task.**

A calendar icon appears in the Indicator column, signifying the task constraint.

4 **Double-click Task 17 again.**

Notice that the entry in the *Constraint date* text box has been completed for you (see Figure 3.27). When using flexible constraints, Microsoft Project automatically applies the correct date as based on the current project plan's estimated task duration. Recall that a red dot in the constraint icon represents an inflexible constraint.

FIGURE 3.27

5 | Click Cancel to close the dialog box.

6 | Double-click Task 36 (*Approve contract with hotel*) and then apply the Must Finish On constraint.

7 | Click in the Duration column for Task 36 and change the duration to *11 days;* then press ↵Enter).
The Planning Wizard dialog box appears because of the constraint applied to this task (see Figure 3.28).

FIGURE 3.28

8 | Click the first option and then click OK.
Because of the constraint, the finish date of the task is not modified; instead, the task's start date is changed to June 16, 2006, which is earlier than the project's start date of June 19. This does not make sense.

9 | Click Undo on the Standard toolbar to return the duration of Task 36 to 10 days, and then click Save.
Leave Microsoft Project open if you plan to continue with the end-of-project exercises; otherwise, exit Microsoft Project.

TO EXTEND YOUR KNOWLEDGE . . .

CHANGING THE SCHEDULE TO A FIXED FINISH DATE
If you want to change scheduling for a project from a fixed start date to a fixed finish date, you may also desire to change the default constraint type. To do so, use the Replace feature. Choose Edit, Replace. Type **As Soon As Possible** in the *Find what* box, and then type **As Late As Possible** in the *Replace with* box. Select *Constraint Type* in the *Look in* Field drop-down list and select *equals* in the Test box.

DOCUMENTING A CONSTRAINT
Because constraints can create conflicts in the schedule, you should use the Note field in the Task Information dialog box to document the purpose of a constraint. Notes are especially helpful in alleviating confusion if you are sharing the project file or if someone else assumes the responsibility of the project.

SUMMARY

In this project, you entered tasks into the task table and specified task durations. Your actions included organizing tasks by inserting new blank rows and cutting and pasting tasks into different locations within the project file, creating a recurring task, and specifying two milestone tasks. Task links provided the next area of focus. You learned to specify predecessors to create links between related tasks, and you observed how this modified the start and finish dates of linked tasks. Microsoft Project's outline features enabled you to create summary tasks and subtasks to visually organize the project file. After viewing the WBS codes assigned by Microsoft Project, you learned how to assign unique calendars to a task and how to set scheduling constraints.

You can extend your learning by reviewing concepts and terms and by practicing variations of skills presented in the lessons. Use the following table as a guide to the numbered questions and exercises in the end-of-project learning opportunities.

LESSON	MULTIPLE CHOICE	DISCUSSION	SKILL DRILL	CHALLENGE	DISCOVERY ZONE
Entering Tasks and Specifying Durations	1, 6	1	1	1	1
Organizing Tasks	2		2		1
Creating Milestone and Recurring Tasks	3, 9		3	1	1
Linking Tasks by Specifying Task Predecessors	5, 10	3	4	3	1
Using Outline Features and Viewing Work Breakdown Structure (WBS) Codes	7	2	2	2	1
Applying a Calendar to a Task	8		5	4	1
Setting Constraints	4		5	4	2

KEY TERMS

As Late As Possible (ALAP)

As Soon As Possible (ASAP)

constraint icon

deliverables

Finish field

Finish No Earlier Than (FNET)

Finish No Later Than (FNLT)

Finish-to-Finish (FF)

Finish-to-Start (FS)

flexible constraints

ID field

inflexible constraints

lag time

lead time

Must Finish On (MFO)

Must Start On (MSO)

noncontiguous link

overflow markers

phase

predecessor task

Predecessors field

recurring task

Resource Names field

Start field

Start No Earlier Than (SNET)

Start No Later Than (SNLT)

Start-to-Finish (SF)

Start-to-Start (SS)

successor task

Task Name field

Work Breakdown Structure (WBS) codes

M'SOFT 3

CHECKING CONCEPTS AND TERMS

SCREEN ID

Label each element of the Project screen shown in Figure 3.29 [L1–L7]

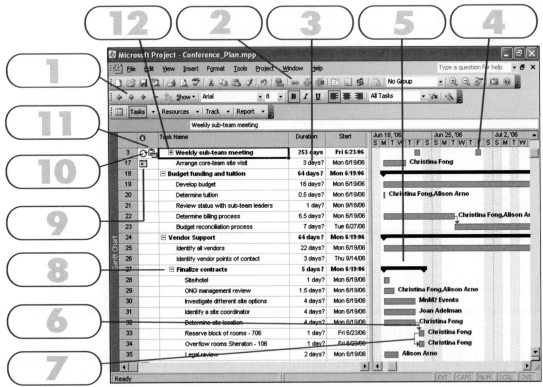

FIGURE 3.29

A. Recurring task symbol

B. Collapsed phase

C. FS link

D. Summary task Gantt bar

E. Indent button

F. Estimated duration

G. Constraint symbol

H. Task calendar symbol

I. SS link

J. Recurring task in Gantt chart

K. Expanded phase

L. Link Tasks button

MULTIPLE CHOICE

Circle the letter of the correct answer for each of the following.

1. Which of the following does not designate a task duration type? [L1]

  a. d

  b. mo

  c. w

  d. y

2. What happens when you try to paste a task into a row with existing data? [L2]

  a. The existing task is deleted automatically.

  b. A new row is inserted and the task being moved is placed in that row.

  c. A warning box appears concerning the deletion of existing data.

  d. You cannot paste a task in a row with existing data.

3. Which task type has no duration? [L3]

  a. Recurring

  b. Summary

  c. Milestone

  d. Subtasks

4. What is the default constraint type for new tasks? [L7]

  a. ALAP

  b. ASAP

  c. FNET

  d. FNLT

5. Which task is the first in a task link? [L4]

  a. Milestone

  b. Summary

  c. Successor

  d. Predecessor

6. Which of the following is not a default field in the task table? [L1]

  a. Budget

  b. Predecessor

  c. Task Name

  d. Duration

7. Which field cannot be modified in a summary task? [L5]

  a. Task Name

  b. Duration

  c. Resource

  d. Predecessor

8. Which of the following is true of a task calendar? [L6]

  a. It affects the schedule of all occurrences in a recurring task.

  b. It affects the schedule of all subtasks when applied to a summary task.

  c. It affects the schedule of all summary tasks in the project file.

  d. It never affects any task other than the selected task.

9. Which task below would be most appropriately formatted as a recurring task? [L3]

  a. Risk assessment

  b. Job interviews

  c. Holidays

  d. Company picnic

10. Suppose your project file includes the tasks for painting a house. Task 1 is painting the first coat and Task 2 is painting the second coat. Which type of link should you use? [L4]

  a. Finish-to-Start

  b. Finish-to-Finish

  c. Start-to-Finish

  d. Start-to-Start

M'SOFT 3

DISCUSSION

1. The duration of a task can be measured in minutes, hours, days, weeks, or months. Give one example of how to use each different duration type. [L1]

2. Some project managers develop a project plan by creating phases and then determining the detailed subtasks. Other project managers do the reverse—meaning they group the tasks after they are created. Discuss the advantages and disadvantages of each method. [L5]

3. Suppose you are building a home, and you are contracting the work yourself. You decide to use Microsoft Project to help you keep track of the various activities. Give an example of each task link type (FS, FF, SF, SS). [L4]

SKILL DRILL

Skill Drill exercises reinforce project skills. Each skill reinforced is the same, or nearly the same, as a skill presented in the project. Detailed instructions are provided in a step-by-step format.

You should complete exercises 2–5 in sequence. Skill Drill exercise 1 is independent of the others and can be worked at any time.

While working with the Skill Drill exercises, a Planning Wizard dialog box may appear suggesting a faster method to perform the current action. You can close this dialog box by clicking OK.

1. Entering Tasks

You and your spouse are members of a social club. The social club is planning to take a cruise as a group. You have been asked to organize the club's efforts in finding a cruise, booking it, and making other necessary arrangements. You are considering becoming a cruise specialist for a travel agency and decide to use Microsoft Project to determine if it is the right tool for managing cruises for clientele.

To create a new project and enter tasks, follow these steps:

1. Start Microsoft Office Project 2003, close any open side panes, and then open a new project file.

2. Choose P̲roject, P̲roject Information.

3. Select *Thu 12/1/05* as the Start d̲ate and then click OK.

4. Click in the first row in the Task Name column and type **Research cruises online**.

5. Press (Tab↹), and type **1w**.

6. Click in the Task Name box in row 2 and type **Consult travel agent**.

7. Press (Tab↹), and type **3h**.

8. Complete typing the remaining tasks and durations as shown in the following table.

Task Name	Duration
`Choose travel dates`	`1wk`
`Choose the cruise`	`1d?`
`Downpayment on cruise`	`1d?`
`Obtain birth certificate`	`6wks`
`Choose onshore excursions`	`4d`
`Book transportation/hotel to port`	`1d?`
`Pack for the cruise`	`2d`
`Bon Voyage`	`1d?`

9. Save the file as **`Cruise_Planning`** and then close it.

2. Organizing Tasks

As the committee leader for the cruise planning committee, you have created a project file to track the progress of the cruise preparations you created in the previous exercise. During the last committee meeting, the members made some suggestions for other tasks that need to be added to the plan. They also pointed out where some tasks were in the wrong location.

To organize and outline tasks, follow these steps:

1. Start Microsoft Project, if necessary.

2. Open *EPr1_0302* and save it as **`Club_Cruise`**, and then close any open side panes.

3. Click Task 1 and choose <u>I</u>nsert, <u>N</u>ew task.

4. Type **`Research`** as the task name.

5. Click within Task 7 (*Choose travel dates*); then press (Insert).

6. Type **`Narrow cruise choices to 2 - 3 cruises`** as the task name.

7. Press (Tab↹) and type **`3d?`**.

8. Insert a row above Task 14 (*Obtain birth certificate*), and then type **`Obtain necessary paperwork`** as the task name using the default duration.

9. Click the row heading for Task 12 (*Choose the cruise*), and choose <u>E</u>dit, Cut Task.

10. Click the row heading for Task 9 (*Compare prices of cabins*), and then choose <u>E</u>dit, <u>P</u>aste.

11. Select Task 14 (*Obtain necessary paperwork*) through Task 16 (*Obtain passport*).

12. Click Cu<u>t</u> Task on the Standard toolbar.

13. Click in Task 7 (*Narrow cruise choices to 2 - 3 choices*) and click Paste on the Standard toolbar.

14. Save *Club_Cruise*, and leave it open for the next exercise.

3. Outlining Tasks

Now that you have a complete list of tasks for the cruise committee, you need to outline the tasks into summary tasks and subtasks.

To outline tasks, follow these steps:

1. Open *Club_Cruise,* if necessary, and then highlight Task 2 (*Research cruises online*) through Task 5 (*Choose departure port*) and click Indent on the Formatting toolbar.

2. Select Task 8 (*Obtain birth certificate*) and Task 9 (*Obtain passport*), and then click Indent.

3. Select Task 14 (*Choose type of cabin*) and Task 15 (*Choose deck of cabin*), and then click Indent.

4. Select Task 18 (*Book onshore excursions*) and click Indent.

5. Select Task 20 (*Purchase any clothing or necessities*) and click Indent.

6. Click <u>S</u>how on the Standard Toolbar and choose *Outline Level 1*.

7. Click <u>S</u>how and then <u>A</u>ll subtasks.

8. Click the minus sign to the left of Task 1 (*Research*).

9. Double-click Task 14 (*Choose type of cabin*); then click the Advanced tab, if necessary, look at the WBS code, and close the dialog box.

10. Save *Club_Cruise,* and leave it open for the next exercise.

4. Assigning Recurring Tasks and Milestones

As you work with the cruise plan and the project file, you realize you need to add two different recurring meetings to the plan: the regular club meeting once a month and the cruise committee's bi-weekly meetings. You also realize that two of the listed tasks do not actually include work; they are milestones.

To create recurring tasks and milestones, follow these steps:

1. Open *Club_Cruise*, if necessary.

2. Click Task 1 (Research).

3. Choose <u>I</u>nsert, <u>R</u>ecurring Task; then type **Cruise Committee meeting** in the <u>T</u>ask Name text box.

4. Under Recurrence pattern, select <u>W</u>eekly, if necessary; then check *T<u>u</u>esday,* and choose *every other* from the drop-down list above the days of the week.

5. Choose February 28, 2006, as the *End <u>b</u>y* date and then click OK.

6. Click <u>I</u>nsert, <u>R</u>ecurring Task; then type **Club meetings** in the <u>T</u>ask Name text box.

7. Under *Recurrence pattern,* select *Mont<u>h</u>ly* and then select *The first Monday of every month.*

8. Choose February 6, 2006, as the *End <u>b</u>y* date, and then click OK.

9. Click in the Duration column of Task 24 (*Choose the cruise*), type **0** to change this task to a milestone, and then press ⏎Enter.

10. Make Task 36 (*Bon Voyage*) a milestone task by changing the duration to zero.

11. Save *Club_Cruise,* and leave it open for the next exercise.

5. Setting Constraints and Linking Tasks

The project file for the cruise is almost finished. Now, you just need to create links to make sure the timing of the tasks is correct. The downpayment for the cruise is due 60 days before the cruise departure date. The departure date is also inflexible. Both of these tasks need constraints.

To set constraints and link selected tasks, follow these steps:

1. Open *Club_Cruise*, if necessary, and drag the split bar between the Task table and the Gantt chart to the right so that you can see the Predecessors column.

2. Click in the Predecessors column for Task 15 (*Choose cruise line*), type **14**, and then press ⏎Enter.

3. Continue creating links as listed in the table below (all are Finish-to-Start links).

   Link between:

Task	Predecessor
Task 18	Task 17
Task 21	Task 20
Task 22	Task 18
Task 24	Task 23
Task 26	Task 22
Task 27	Task 22
Task 30	Task 28
Task 33	Task 28
Task 36	Task 35

4. Click anywhere on Task 16 (*Choose travel route*); choose <u>P</u>roject, Task Information, and then click the Predecessors tab.

5. Click in the Task Name column, and then click the drop-down arrow.

6. Choose the *Choose cruise line* task.

7. Click the Type column drop-down arrow, choose *Start-to-Start (SS),* and then click OK.

8. Locate Task 17 (*Choose departure port*), click in the Predecessors column, type **16SS**, and then press ⏎Enter.

9. Double-click Task 23 (*Choose travel dates*) to view the Task Information dialog box and click the Predecessors tab, if necessary.

10. In the Task Name column, click the drop-down arrow and then choose *Narrow cruise choices to 2 - 3 cruises.*

11. Choose *Start-to-Start (SS)* as the task type, and then click OK.

12. Create an SF link between Tasks 34 (*Pack for the cruise*) and 36 (*Bon Voyage*), using Task 34 as the predecessor task.

13. Double-click Task 36 (*Bon Voyage*), and click the Advanced tab.

14. Click the *Constraint type* drop-down arrow, choose *Must Finish On,* select *Mon 3/6/06* in the *Constraint date* box, and then click OK.

15. Choose *Continue* in the warning box, and then click OK.

16. Double-click Task 20 (*Obtain birth certificate*), and then apply the Finish No Later Than constraint type with a date of January 11, 2006.

17. Double-click Task 28 (*Downpayment on cruise*), and then apply the Must Finish On constraint with a constraint date of January 6, 2006.

18. Save the *Club_Cruise* file and close it.

CHALLENGE

Challenge exercises expand on or are somewhat related to skills presented in the lessons. Each exercise provides a brief narrative introduction, followed by instructions in a numbered-step format that are not as detailed as those in the Skill Drill section.

Exercises 2–3 should be worked in order. Exercises 1 and 4 are independent of the others and can be worked at any time.

While working with the Challenge exercises, a Planning Wizard dialog box may appear onscreen, suggesting a faster method to perform the current action. You are encouraged to read the suggestion and then try suggested method.

1. Creating a New Project File and Entering Tasks and Milestones

You are a graphic designer assigned to create several brochures, banners, and a variety of give-away gifts, such as T-shirts and coffee mugs, for a new apartment complex opening in your community. This apartment complex is targeted toward the university in your city, and the promotional items you are creating need to be available prior to the start of the new school year.

To create a new project plan to manage the many aspects of this ongoing project, follow these steps:

1. Create a new project file and save it as **Signs_Graphics**.

2. Specify May 2, 2005, as the date to schedule from, and create a project base calendar using the Standard calendar template.

3. Define the general working times to begin at 9:00 A.M. and to end at 5:30 P.M., with a 30-minute lunch and a standard 8-hour day.

4. Add Memorial Day, July 4th, and Labor Day as nonworking days.

5. Enter the following tasks and durations into the plan, using estimated duration:

ID	Task Name	Duration
1	Develop overall look and style	15d
2	Develop logo and slogan	15d
3	Design stationery	10d
4	Provide mock-up to marketing director	1d
5	Receive feedback and make changes	2d
6	Receive green light	1d
7	Provide logo to web designer	1d
8	Design opening banner for bldg 1	10d

9	Design community event banner	10d
10	Provide all banners to printer	1d
11	Leasing office sign	2d
12	Provide leasing materials to print shop	1d
13	Select giveaways	5d
14	Marketing director approval	5d

6. Change Task 6 (*Receive green light*) to a milestone.

7. Insert a new milestone task at the bottom of the plan called **Community Lease-up**.

8. Change the start date of the new milestone task to August 1, 2005. (If a smart tag appears, accept the constraint.)

9. Insert a new recurring task after Task 1 and name it **Weekly Meeting**, to occur each Tuesday starting on May 3, 2005, and ending by July 29, 2005.

10. Click Yes in response to the dialog box that warns there are some nonworking holidays in the plan and some of the meetings will need to be rescheduled.

11. Save *Signs_Graphics* and close it.

2. Creating Summary Tasks and Using the Outline Features

Your work on the apartment complex lease-up has grown, and additional tasks and responsibilities have been entered into the plan. To further refine the project, you want to insert new summary tasks to create phases and then use the outline features in your plan.

To insert new summary tasks and use the outline features in your plan, follow these steps:

1. Open *EPr1_0303* and save it as **Apartment_Artwork**.

2. Insert the following new summary tasks:

   Insert a new Task 1 with the name **Templates and graphics**.

   Insert a new task above Task 23 (*Design opening banner for bldg 1*) with the name **Signs and banners**.

   Insert a new task above Task 27 (*Leasing office sign*) with the name **Leasing materials**.

   Insert a new task above Task 41 (*Provide leasing materials to print shop*) with the name **Giveaways**.

3. Now use Microsoft Project's outline features to demote the appropriate groups of tasks listed below the summary tasks you inserted, to create an outline showing the different phases of your project plan.

   You should end up with four groups of tasks demoted below each summary task, and then the final task, which is a milestone and should not be demoted.

4. Save *Apartment_Artwork* and leave it open for the next exercise.

3. Linking Tasks

Now that you've outlined your *Apartment_Artwork* project plan, you need to create links between those tasks that have dependencies so that the task durations will calculate correctly.

M'SOFT 3

To link tasks, follow these steps:

1. Open *Apartment_Artwork*, if necessary, and widen the task table to display the Predecessors column.

2. Link Task 2 (*Develop overall look and style*) and Task 17 (*Develop logo and slogan*) with the default Finish-to-Start link.

3. Link the following tasks, all with the Finish-to-Start link type, using the first task listed as the predecessor task:

   Task 17 (*Develop logo and slogan*) to Task 19 (*Provide mock-up to marketing director*)

   Task 19 (*Provide mock-up to Marketing Director*) to Task 20 (*Receive feedback and make changes*)

   Task 20 (*Receive feedback and make changes*) to Task 21 (*Receive green light*)

   Task 21 (*Receive green light*) to Task 22 (*Provide mogo to Web Designer*)

   Task 24 (*Design opening banner for Bldg 1*) to Task 25 (*Design Community Event banner*)

   Task 25 (*Design Community Event banner*) to Task 26 (*Provide all banners to printer*)

   Task 33 (*Community information sheet*) to Task 34 (*Notes on our community*)

   Task 34 (*Notes on our community*) to Task 35 (*Map of community*)

   Task 35 (*Map of community*) to Task 36 (*Sheet with local listings*)

   Task 36 (*Sheet with local listings*) to Task 42 (*Provide leasing materials to print shop*)

   Task 43 (*Select giveaways*) to Task 44 (*Marketing Director approval*)

4. View the Task Information dialog box for Task 25 (*Design Community Event banner*) and create a Start-to-Start link with Task 24 (*Design opening banner for Bldg 1*).

5. Create a Finish-to-Finish link for Task 28 (*Leasing office sign*) with Task 26 (*Provide all banners to printer*).

6. Save and close *Apartment_Artwork*.

4. Setting Constraints and Assigning Task Calendars

You are on a team developing a new internal training Web portal where employees of your company can go to download product information papers and listen to streamed media or recordings of engineers discussing the technical specifications for their products that can be played via the Internet. You will work on this project file by adding constraints and assigning task calendars.

To set constraints and assign task calendars:

1. Open *EPr1_0304* and save it as **Training_Portal**.

2. View the task information for Task 15 (*Showcase booth with test prep site*) and set a Start No Earlier Than constraint for this task so that it does not begin until November 8, 2005.

3. View the task information for Task 3 (*Review logos and identify favorite two*) and set a Finish No Later Than constraint with a date of September 13, 2005.

4. Assign a 24 Hours calendar to Task 6 (*Insert mouse overs*), Task 12 (*Document where existing links go for new UI*), and Task 13 (*Hook-up system with existing items*).

5. Enter a query in the *Type a question for help* box on creating a new task calendar, and read the Help instructions.

6. For Tasks 20 (*Determine query requirements*) through 26 (*Deliver final query solution*), create a new calendar.

   You need a task calendar that encompasses the testing and production team hours of 11:00 A.M. to 9:00 P.M. with a 1-hour lunch.

7. Save and close `Training_Portal`.

DISCOVERY ZONE

Discovery Zone exercises require advanced knowledge of topics presented in *Essentials* lessons, application of skills from multiple lessons, or self-directed learning of new skills. Each exercise is independent of the others, so you may complete the exercises in any order.

1. Creating a New Software Implementation Project File from a Template

You have the ability to deal with highly technical programmers while still being able to relate to nontechnical end users. With this unique ability, you are the perfect choice to work on the development of a new accounting software package that will allow the employees of your company to process business expense reports online. You are working with the programming team to document this new software program, provide an online training tutorial, and establish ongoing end user support as the software is rolled out in your company.

Create a new project from the Software Development template located on your computer and save it as `Accounting_Software`. Modify the start date of the schedule, to begin February 7, 2005. Because the software has already been determined as needed, there will be no analysis, design, or software requirement investigations. Remove those tasks in the template that are not necessary. Remove any additional tasks that are not representative of the scope of this project.

Add a recurring task that involves a bi-weekly meeting with the Accounting Management team. Modify existing tasks and add new tasks to cover creating an online training manual. Create links between these tasks as you see fit.

Review the Predecessors column and explore the links between the tasks as created by the template. Add additional links where needed, and remove any that do not belong.

2. Working with Task Constraints

Create a new project from any existing template located either online or on your computer and save it as `Constraint`. Use the *Type a question for help* box to research information on constraints and read about the eight different types of task constraints that are available. Using the *Constraint* project that you created, apply each constraint to eight individual tasks and modify the durations of these eight tasks to see how the constraint affects the task finish date and the overall project plan.

P R O J E C T 4

SCHEDULING RESOURCES AND ASSIGNING COSTS

O B J E C T I V E S

IN THIS PROJECT, YOU LEARN HOW TO

- View and set up resources
- Enter resource information
- Enter fixed costs
- Assign resources to tasks
- View and modify resource assignments
- Print resource allocations and project costs

WHY WOULD I DO THIS?

When creating a project plan, you must consider what resources are necessary to complete the project. These resources may include personnel, materials, equipment, outside contractors, and other assets. You may already have some resources in mind, and as you create tasks and durations, identifying resources becomes more clear. Once you assign resources, you can then review the project file to ensure that the resulting schedule meets the target date. However, part of the project management process is to handle those things that come up that affect or alter the schedule. Employees take days off, equipment breaks down, or materials are unavailable. Managing resource allocation and task durations becomes critical. Even for simple projects, assigning resources to tasks allows you to record the cost of materials and equipment and the hours allocated to each person, and you can then check for overallocations. Using resources also allows you to take advantage of the many ways you can keep track of the overall budget.

Resources and costs work hand in hand in a project plan. Each resource has the potential to have a cost attached to it. If you include the cost information for each resource, Microsoft Project automatically calculates the cost of each task. These calculations aid the project manager in figuring a budget for the entire project plan.

◉ VISUAL SUMMARY

In this project, you use Microsoft Project to set up, assign, and monitor the resources needed to create a business plan—resources needed to perform a comparative market analysis to ensure that your business idea is viable, to determine start-up expenses including management and staffing salaries as required by the loan officer at the bank, and so forth. After you make adjustments to the project file, your resource allocation should resemble the data in Figure 4.1 below.

FIGURE 4.1

When you assign resources to a task, Microsoft Project considers the duration of the task as well as the working time available by the resource. At times, these two do not match. There are several views you can use to correct any conflicts that occur.

LESSON 1: Viewing and Setting Up Resources

When creating resources for a project file, you can manually add them or import resources from another file. A list of available resources for a project plan is called the ***resource pool***. A resource pool can be created either before or after tasks are defined. The resource pool contains a list of people, equipment, and materials that are available to be assigned to a task.

Resources can be either of two types: work resources or material resources. A ***work resource*** such as personnel or machinery performs work to accomplish a task. Facilities such as conference rooms are also considered work resources. A ***material resource*** is a consumable material used to complete the work required by a task. For example, if a task includes printing a newsletter, paper is a material resource. In addition, both resource types can be individuals or single items, or they can be groups of people or things. An ***individual resource*** is a single unit such as a person or a single asset such as a piece of raw material or equipment. A ***group resource***—or ***consolidated resource***—represents multiple interchangeable resources, such as a group of engineers with the same knowledge and skills concerning this project plan. When using a group resource, it is not important which specific resource within the group performs the task.

The Resource Sheet view is the easiest method to manually create resources for a project file. After you enter the resource name, Microsoft Project automatically supplies default values for many of the other fields in the table. Alternately, you can use the Resource Information dialog box to create or edit resources, or you can type in the name of a resource in the Resource Names column in Gantt Chart view or several other views. However, these options do not allow you to enter additional information such as cost data; therefore, Resource Sheet view is the preferred view for entry (see Figure 4.2).

	ⓘ	Resource Name	Type	Material Label	Initials	Group	Max. Units	Std. Rate	Ovt. Rate	Cost/Use	Ac
3	◈	Accountant	Work		AP		25%	$75.00/hr	$0.00/hr	$0.00	Pr
2		Advisor	Work		MEP		100%	$75.00/hr	$0.00/hr	$0.00	Pr
9	📝	Amit Patel	Work		AP	Accounting	100%	$75.00/hr	$0.00/hr	$0.00	Pr
6		Brent Fosdal	Work		BF	Marketing	100%	$125.00/hr	$0.00/hr	$0.00	Pr
1		Business Owner	Work		DEW	Office	100%	$0.00/hr	$0.00/hr	$0.00	Pr
5	◈	Hilda Alvarez	Work		HA	Accountin	100%	$0.00/hr	$0.00/hr	$0.00	Pr
8		Marketing Group	Work		Mktg	Marketing	100%	$0.00/hr	$0.00/hr	$0.00	Pr
11		Mary Marshall	Work		M		100%	$0.00/hr	$0.00/hr	$0.00	Pr
4		OfficeMax Copy Shop	Material	sheet	Off			$0.05		$0.05	Pr
7		Shaneika Jones	Work		SJ	Office	100%	$0.00/hr	$0.00/hr	$0.00	Pr
10		UPS Store Overnight	Material		UPS	UPS		$0.00		$0.00	Pr

FIGURE 4.2

The resource sheet provides a variety of information about each resource assigned to a project plan. Recall from Project 3 that the *ID field* contains automatically supplied numbers—which cannot be edited—that are used to identify a resource. ID numbers appear down the left margin of the resource sheet much like the row numbers of a spreadsheet. The *Indicator field* displays icons that provide information about an assignment, resource, or task. For example, there is an indicator to signal that a task is completed and another to indicate that a note is attached. Look for an icon in the column headed by the single letter *i* inside a blue circle. The *Resource*

M'SOFT 4

Name field in the resource sheet provides a descriptive name for each resource; most users prefer this field to the nondescript ID field. Microsoft Project does not require that resource names be unique; however, it is best to make each resource name unique and easily identifiable. You use the ***Type field*** to distinguish between work and material resources. The default Type field entry is *Work.* The resource type assigned to a resource can affect the schedule for a task. For instance, a Work resource can be linked to the Resource calendar, whereas a Material resource cannot be linked.

Use the ***Material Label field*** to define the unit of measure for material resources. Units of measure are the familiar measurements such as quarts, boxes, or yards. Although the Resource Name field provides a description of a resource, the ***Initials field*** provides a brief name used in Gantt Chart view or Network Diagram view. You can use the ***Group field*** to add a keyword, such as the department name, to a resource. Group fields are extremely useful for sorting, filtering, and grouping resources. Use the ***Max. Units field*** to enter the maximum availability of a resource. It is a percentage that indicates the availability of a resource. The default entry is *100%;* however, if a person is assigned to the project and can work on the task for only half of the day, the person's max units would be 50%.

Four of the resource fields are currency fields that deal with the costs of using the resource. Use the ***Std. Rate (Standard Rate) field*** to assign the charge per unit of normal working time for a resource. The ***Ovt. Rate (Overtime Rate) field*** is used to assign charges per unit of overtime work for a resource. A ***Cost/Use field*** assigns a flat rate, such as one-time usage fees, per use of a resource. This field is generally associated with material resources. For example, one box of printer paper might be $25. The ***Accrue At field*** defines how and when resource costs are incurred and when actual costs are charged to a project. Accrue At can be either Start, End, or Prorated. By default, it is set at the start of a project plan.

Recall that a base calendar controls a group of resources. In contrast, a ***Resource calendar*** is assigned to each resource to reflect unique scheduling considerations such as the type of work day and vacation schedules. The calendar is based on either the Standard 8-hour work day calendar, the 24 Hours calendar, or the 8-hour Night Shift calendar. In addition, you can apply any special project calendars that you created. For example, if you have a group of resources that are available only 20 hours a week instead of the standard 40-hour work week, you would specify that calendar in this field. The ***Code field*** can be used to add any unique data that you want to use to identify resources. For example, if you want to include additional information about a resource such as his or employee ID or account number, you could enter it in this field. If you choose to utilize the Code field, be sure to include an entry for every resource, to correctly sort and organize your resources.

In this lesson, you work with a partially completed resource sheet related to creating a business plan. These resources support conducting a market analysis survey and determining start-up expenses that include management and staffing salaries—data needed by the loan officer at the bank to show the planned business is viable. For now, your task is to create a resource pool for this project file.

To View the Resource Sheet and Set Up Resources

1 Open the *EPr1_0401* file and save it as `Business_Model`; then close any open side panes.

2 Drag the split bar between the task table and Gantt chart to the right until the last column, Resource Names, is visible.

Some tasks already contain resource assignments. Although you can view and create new resources from the Gantt Chart view, the Resource Sheet shows much more information.

3 Choose <u>V</u>iew, Resource <u>S</u>heet.

A grid showing resource names, resource type, resource costs, and other resource information displays (see Figure 4.3).

FIGURE 4.3

There are four types of information icons that can appear in the Indicator column for resources: overallocation, note, hyperlink, and response pending. An ***overallocation icon*** indicates that the resource has too much work assigned to it for the time frame involved or has been assigned to two tasks at once. A ***note icon*** provides text about the resource that the user added. A ***hyperlink icon*** associates a link to a resource or a Web page or document. A ***response pending icon*** indicates that the resource has not responded to an e-mail notification about task assignment.

4 Pause the mouse pointer over the information icon for Resource 3 (*Accountant*).

A ScreenTip appears. This resource appears in red because it is overallocated. Notice that the base calendar for the Accountant resource is the Standard calendar. The calendar has the default 8-hour work day and 40-hour work week. The Accountant works only 2 hours per day on this project, as indicated by the 25% Max. Units field.

5 Click in the first blank row after Resource 4 (*OfficeMax Copy Shop*) in the Resource Name column, type `Hilda Alvarez`, and then press Tab.

Pressing Tab enters the data and moves the insertion point to the next column in the resource sheet (see Figure 4.4). Default entries appear in the other resource fields.

FIGURE 4.4

M'SOFT 4

6 Accept the *Work* type by pressing ⭾Tab to move to the next field.

7 Press ⭾Tab again, type **HA** in the Initials column, and then press ⏎Enter.

8 Continue entering the remaining resources listed below.

Resource Name	Type	Initials
Brent Fosdal	Work	BF
Shaneika Jones	Work	SJ
Marketing Group	Work	Mktg
Amit Patel	Work	AP
UPS Store Overnight	Material	UPS

Now that you have entered resource names, you can sort them. Sorting makes it easier to locate resources in the list.

9 Choose **P**roject, **S**ort, by **N**ame.
The list reorganizes in alphabetical order by the resource name (see Figure 4.5). Notice, however, the resource IDs do not change.

	ⓘ	Resource Name	Type	Material Label	Initials	Group	Max. Units	Std. Rate	Ovt. Rate	Cost/Use	Ac
3	◈	Accountant	Work		Act		25%	$75.00/hr	$0.00/hr	$0.00	Pr
2		Advisor	Work		MEP		100%	$75.00/hr	$0.00/hr	$0.00	Pr
9		Amit Patel	Work		AP		100%	$0.00/hr	$0.00/hr	$0.00	Pr
6		Brent Fosdal	Work		BF		100%	$0.00/hr	$0.00/hr	$0.00	Pr
1		Business Owner	Work		DEW		100%	$0.00/hr	$0.00/hr	$0.00	Pr
5		Hilda Alvarez	Work		HA		100%	$0.00/hr	$0.00/hr	$0.00	Pr
8		Marketing Group	Work		Mktg		100%	$0.00/hr	$0.00/hr	$0.00	Pr
4		OfficeMax Copy Shop	Material		Off Max			$0.00		$0.00	Pr
7		Shaneika Jones	Work		SJ		100%	$0.00/hr	$0.00/hr	$0.00	Pr
10		UPS Store Overnight	Material		UPS			$0.00		$0.00	Pr

IDs remain the same

FIGURE 4.5

10 Save your changes to the *Business_Model* file.
Your project file now contains 10 resources. Keep the *Business_Model* project file open and continue with the next lesson. If you prefer to complete the project later, close the file and exit Microsoft Project.

TO EXTEND YOUR KNOWLEDGE . . .

MAKING A SORT PERMANENT
When sorting resources, you can make the sort permanent by reassigning the resource IDs. Choose **P**roject, **S**ort, **S**ort by. In the Sort dialog box, choose the field you want to sort the resources by, such as Name. Check the *Permanently renumber resources* check box and then click S**o**rt.

ADDING RESOURCES BY USING THE PROJECT GUIDE
You can also use the Project Guide when adding resources, which is especially helpful if you are adding resources from a company address book or importing

them from another external source. From Gantt Chart view, click Resources on the Project Guide and then click the *Specify people and equipment for the project* link. In the Specify Resources side pane, click the option that indicates where you are getting the resources from, and then follow the directions to complete the process.

CREATING A RESOURCE TEMPLATE

If you use a common group of resources repeatedly, it is useful to create a project template. To begin, create a blank project file; then enter the names of the resources that make up the resource pool. Choose File, Save As. Click the *Save as type* drop-down arrow and choose *Template (mpt)*.

LESSON 2:   Entering Resource Information

There are several types of costs involved in a project plan. A ***resource cost,*** the most common type of cost, is incurred due to the expense associated with using a resource. Resource costs are represented by the dollar amount entered in the Std. Rate field, the Ovt. Rate field, or the Cost/Use field (as shown in the Resource Sheet view). Microsoft Project uses resource costs in conjunction with the task duration to calculate the expense associated with a task. The cost of a material resource is based on the dollar amount entered in the Cost/Use column and the unit specified in the Material Label column. For example, if you want to track the cost of each ream of paper used in project plan, you would enter **$2.50** in the Cost/Use column and specify **Ream** in the Material Label column.

Microsoft Project calculates resource costs for a work resource by multiplying the cost per unit (i.e., hourly cost) for the resource by the amount of time the resource spends on the task (time × Std. Rate and/or Ovt. Rate). On the other hand, material resource costs are calculated solely on the number of units consumed or used up by the task. In other words, the calculation is the number of units of the resource multiplied by the per unit cost of the resource (units × Cost/Use).

In this lesson, you assign costs to each resource in the resource pool and assign groups. Additionally, you update resource information, using the Resource Information dialog box.

M'SOFT 4

To Enter Resource Costs and Additional Resource Information

1 Open *Business_Model,* and choose View, Resource Sheet, if necessary.

2 Click in the Group column for Amit Patel and type **Accounting**.

3 Press Tab⇄ two times to move to the Std. Rate column; type 75 and then press ↵Enter.
Amit Patel is now a member of the Accounting group and costs $75.00 per hour as a resource (see Figure 4.6).

	ⓘ	Resource Name	Type	Material Label	Initials	Group	Max. Units	Std. Rate	Ovt. Rate	Cost/Use	Ac ▲
3	◇	Accountant	Work		Act		25%	$75.00/hr	$0.00/hr	$0.00	Pr
2		Advisor	Work		MEP		100%	$75.00/hr	$0.00/hr	$0.00	Pr
9		Amit Patel	Work		AP	Accounting	100%	$75.00/hr	$0.00/hr	$0.00	Pr
6		Brent Fosdal	Work		BF		100%	$0.00/hr	$0.00/hr	$0.00	Pr
1		Business Owner	Work		DEW		100%	$0.00/hr	$0.00/hr	$0.00	Pr
5		Hilda Alvarez	Work		HA		100%	$0.00/hr	$0.00/hr	$0.00	Pr
8		Marketing Group	Work		Mktg		100%	$0.00/hr	$0.00/hr	$0.00	Pr
4		OfficeMax Copy Shop	Material		Off Max			$0.00		$0.00	Pr
7		Shaneika Jones	Work		SJ		100%	$0.00/hr	$0.00/hr	$0.00	Pr
10		UPS Store Overnight	Material		UPS			$0.00		$0.00	Pr

New group

Hourly cost

FIGURE 4.6

4 Click in the Group column for Brent Fosdal and type `Marketing`.

5 Press Tab⇄ two times; type 125 and then press ↵Enter.
Brent Fosdal is a member of the Marketing group at a rate of $125 per hour.

6 Enter the remaining group and rate information as shown in the table below.

Resource	Group	Rate/Hr
Business Owner	Office	$0.00/h
Hilda Alvarez	Accounting	$75.00/h
Marketing Group	Marketing	$250/h
Shaneika Jones	Office	$0.00/h
UPS Store Overnight	UPS	

7 Click in the Material Label column for OfficeMax Copy Shop and type `Sheet`.

8 Click in the Cost/Use column and type `.05`.
The cost of each sheet of paper copied is 5 cents. You have added the resource costs and groups to your resource pool.

9 Double-click the Amit Patel resource.
The Resource Information dialog box opens (see Figure 4.7).

FIGURE 4.7

10 Click the Notes tab and then click in the text box.

11 Type `Promoted into Accounting department 1/06` and then click OK.
A note icon in the Indicator column signifies that a note pertaining to Amit's status on the project is in the resource information.

12 Point to the note icon.
A ScreenTip appears, showing you the note text.

13 Save your changes to the *Business_Model* file.
You have added the necessary resource information. Keep the *Business_Model* project file open and continue with the next lesson. If you prefer to complete the project later, close the file and exit Microsoft Project.

M'SOFT 4

LESSON 3:   Entering Fixed Costs

A *fixed cost* is a cost that is not specifically related to any one resource. It does not accrue based on work hours but is instead tied to the task to which it applies. Fixed costs are often one-time expenses, such as shipping. Fixed costs are entered into the task table as a lump sum. The sum of all resource costs and fixed costs is the *total cost* of the project plan.

In this lesson, you enter fixed costs for material resources.

To Add Fixed Costs

1 Open *Business_Model,* if necessary, and then switch to Gantt Chart view.

2 Select Task 10 (*Overnight to Advisor*) and then choose **V**iew, Ta**b**le: Entry, and **C**ost.

The column headings change to display the cost fields (see Figure 4.8).

FIGURE 4.8

3 In the Fixed Cost column, type **5.50** and then press ↵**Enter**.

This amount is the cost to overnight a letter pack.

4 Click in the Fixed Cost column for Task 20 (*Update plan & overnight to Bus. Own*); type **6.75** and then press ↵**Enter**.

The fixed costs are complete (see Figure 4.9).

FIGURE 4.9

5 **Choose View, Table: Cost, and Entry.**
The view changes back to the Table Entry view, which is the default.

6 **Save your changes to the *Business_Model* file.**
You have now specified fixed costs in your project file. Keep the *Business_Model* project file open and continue with the next lesson. If you prefer to complete the project later, close the file and exit Microsoft Project.

LESSON 4:   Assigning Resources to Tasks

You now know that the first step in working with Microsoft Project is to create the project base calendar by specifying the start date for the entire project plan as well as outlining the actual work hours. You also know the second step is to enter tasks and how long you think each task should take (the task duration). When you assign a resource to a task, Microsoft Project uses a **scheduling formula** that schedules the task according to the formula *Duration = Work / Units*. **Work** is what is assigned to a resource and also represents the total labor required to complete a task. The duration of a task can be affected by a resource assignment if the maximum units for a resource are not 100%. For example, if a resource is assigned to work 100% on a task with a 1-day duration, the work unit is 8 hours. If the work resource is working only 25%, the work unit is 2 hours.

In addition, not only do work units calculate automatically, but the overall duration for a task also automatically updates when you start assigning more than one resource. For example, if you assign two resources to a task with a duration of 1 day, each resource is assigned 4 hours of work and that task duration reduces to 1/2 day. Likewise, if you assign two resources to work on a task with a 1-day duration, each working 100%, the total work involved is 200%.

In this lesson, you assign resources to specific tasks. Then you alter the durations and resource assignments to create a schedule that allocates all resources more effectively.

To Assign Resources to Tasks

1 **Open *Business_Model*, if necessary.**

2 **In Gantt Chart view, click in the Resource Names column for Task 2 (*Access available information*).**

3 **Click the drop-down arrow and choose Brent Fosdal from the list; then press ⏎Enter.**
Brent Fosdal appears in the Resource Names column and to the right of the Gantt bar in the Gantt chart (see Figure 4.10).

FIGURE 4.10

4   In the Resource Names column for Task 3 (*Create market analysis plan*), choose Brent Fosdal; then press ⏎Enter.

5   In the Resource Names column for Task 4 (*Implement market analysis plan*), choose Marketing Group, and then type , (Note: Do not press space).
You can use a comma as a separator character to add multiple resources to a task.

If you have problems . . .

If you mistakenly pressed ⏎Enter at this point, click in the cell again and press F2 to edit the field.

6   Click the Resource Names drop-down arrow again.

7   Choose Brent Fosdal, and then press ⏎Enter.
Two resources are assigned to the task (see Figure 4.11).

		Task Name	Duration	Start	Finish	Predecessors	Resource Names	Feb 19, '06
								S M T W T F S S
1		⊟ Business market analysis	16 days?	Mon 2/20/06	Mon 3/13/06		**Business Owner**	
2		Access available information	1 day?	Mon 2/20/06	Mon 2/20/06		Brent Fosdal	Brent Fosdal
3		Create market analysis plan	2 days?	Tue 2/21/06	Wed 2/22/06	2	Brent Fosdal	Brent Fosdal
4		Implement market analysis pl	5 days?	Thu 2/23/06	Wed 3/1/06	3	ing Group,Brent Fosdal	Brent Fo
5		Identify competition	2 days?	Thu 3/2/06	Fri 3/3/06	4		
6		Summarize the market	2 days?	Mon 3/6/06	Tue 3/7/06	5		

Two resources to assigned to one task

FIGURE 4.11

8   In the Resource Names column for Task 5 (*Identify competition*), type `Mary Marshall` and then press ⏎Enter.
Mary Marshall is a new resource that did not exist in the resource pool. By simply typing the name of the resource in the Resource Names column, you add a new resource directly from Gantt Chart view.

If you have problems . . .

Be careful when adding a resource by typing a name in the Resource Names column in Gantt Chart view. If you duplicate an existing resource with only a change in spelling, you have two resource entries representing the same resource due to the spelling error, and the resource allocations are skewed.

You can assign resources to summary tasks, but be aware that there may be misleading information that requires explanation. For example, if you assign a manager to a summary task to show his or her ownership for that part of the project plan, that manager has the sum total for all the subtask durations, work hours, and costs rolled up and assigned to him. This may be confusing for those not closely involved with the project.

9 Complete the remaining resource assignments as shown in the following table.

Task ID	Task Name	Resource Name
6	Summarize the market	*Marketing Group, Brent Fosdal*
7	Identify target market niche	*Marketing Group, Brent Fosdal*
8	Type up plan	*Shaneika Jones*
10	Overnight to Advisor	*UPS Store Overnight*
11	Identify needed materials and supplies	*Business Owner*
12	Select a business approach	*Accountant*
13	Identify management staff resources	*Business Owner*
15	Identify staffing requirements	*Business Owner*
20	Update plan & overnight to Bus. Own	*UPS Store Overnight*

Now that you have added resources to individual tasks, let's take a look at the Assign Resources dialog box. You can use this dialog box to add or remove a resource assignment as well as alter the work units of each resource.

To Create Work Resource Assignments

1 **Highlight Tasks 17 (*Identify needed raw materials*) and 18 (*Identify needed utilities*).**
Notice that the duration for each of these tasks is approximately 2 days. You have two resources who share the work on these tasks.

 2 **Click Assign Resources on the Standard Toolbar.**
The Assign Resources dialog box opens (see Figure 4.12).

FIGURE 4.12

3 | Click *Amit Patel* and then click **Assign.**

4 | Click *Hilda Alvarez* and then click **Assign.**
Hilda Alvarez moves below Amit Patel. Check marks appear next to each assigned resource (see Figure 4.13).

FIGURE 4.13

If you have problems . . .

If you do not want the duration to be reduced because more than one resource is assigned to a task, start by assigning just one resource. Then assign the additional resources in a separate operation.

---

5 | Click **Close.**
Amit Patel and Hilda Alvarez are assigned to Tasks 17 and 18. The duration for these tasks reduces to approximately 1 day each (8 hours of work). If assigned resources work at 100%, Microsoft Project divides the duration by the number of resources assigned to the task. So, when 16 hours of work is split between two resources, the duration is reduced by half and each resource is assigned 50% (see Figure 4.14).

	14		Target monies for manage	5 days?	Thu 3/16/06	Wed 3/22/06		Accountant[25%]
	15	⊟ Identify staffing requiren	5 days?	Thu 3/16/06	Wed 3/22/06	14SS	Business Owner
	16		Target monies for staff	days?	Thu 3/16/06	Wed 3/22/06		Accountant[25%]
	17		Identify needed raw material	1 day?	Thu 3/23/06	Thu 3/23/06	16	Amit Patel,Hilda Alvarez
	18		Identify needed utilities	1 day?	Fri 3/24/06	Fri 3/24/06	17	Amit Patel,Hilda Alvarez
	19		Summarize operating expens	1 day?	Mon 3/27/06	Mon 3/27/06	18	Accountant[25%]
	20		Update plan & overnight to B	1 day?	Tue 3/28/06	Tue 3/28/06	19	UPS Store Overnight[1]
	21	⊟ Evaluate potential risks and	10 days?	Wed 3/29/06	Tue 4/11/06		

Altered duration (callout pointing to row 15/16)

Multiple resources assigned to task (callout pointing to rows 17–18)

FIGURE 4.14

6 Select Tasks 22 (*Assess market size and stability*) and 23 (*Access needed resources availability*), and then click Assign Resources.

7 Assign Amit Patel and Hilda Alvarez to the tasks, and then click Close.
Hilda Alvarez and Amit Patel are assigned to Tasks 22 and 23. The duration for these tasks reduces from approximately 2 days to 1 day each, because the total work hours to complete the task were evenly distributed between the two resources and required a shorter duration.

8 Save your changes to the *Business_Model* file.
Now you have added resources to most tasks within the project file. Keep the *Business_Model* project file open and continue with the next lesson. If you prefer to complete the project later, close the file and exit Microsoft Project.

TO EXTEND YOUR KNOWLEDGE . . .

ASSIGNING RESOURCES BY USING THE PROJECT GUIDE

You can also assign resources to tasks by using the Project Guide, which displays current resource assignment information, something that can be quite helpful if you have questions regarding how task durations are translated to work hours for a resource. To use the Project Guide, first select the task to which you want to assign a resource; then click the Resources drop-down arrow on the Project Guide toolbar and click *Assign people and equipment to tasks*. The Assign Resources side pane displays, where you select the *Assign resources* link. Follow the numbered steps in the side pane. In *Step 4 Review information*, you can view resource assignments for a selected task.

ASSIGNING RESOURCES BYUSING THE ASSIGN RESOURCES DIALOG BOX

Resources can also be created from within the Assign Resources dialog box. To add a resource by using this method, click in the next blank row, type the resource name, and press ↵Enter. To assign the new resource, select the name you just created and click <u>A</u>ssign.

VIEWING RESOURCE INITIALS ON THE GANTT CHART

You may find that the Gantt chart becomes cluttered when the full resource name is shown next to each Gantt bar. You can format the Gantt chart to display resource initials instead. In Gantt Chart view, choose F<u>o</u>rmat, <u>B</u>ar Styles, and click the Bar Text tab. Click in the row where you see resource names, and then click the drop-down arrow and choose *Resource Initials*. The default position of the resource name in relation to the Gantt bar is Right. Notice also that you can alter the position to Left, Top, Inside, or Bottom, if you prefer.

M'SOFT 4

LESSON 5: Viewing and Modifying Resource Assignments

As defined in Lesson 4, *work* is what is assigned to a resource and also represents the total labor required to complete a task. The ***work unit*** is the amount of time it should take a resource to complete a task. It is automatically calculated by Microsoft Project when the task duration is translated into a unit of work for the resource. By default, Microsoft Project translates the duration of a task into hours, as indicated by the abbreviation *hrs* seen in the Resource Usage sheet and other views. Work units are the measurement of the duration (usually in hours) and are helpful in project planning, like knowing how much you weigh upon starting a diet.

For this information to calculate correctly and make sense to you, it is important that you have a good understanding of the project calendar. For example, if you created a project base calendar using the default business day from 9:00 A.M. to 5:00 P.M. with a 1-hour lunch, this translates to an 8-hour work day. So remember that when you enter estimated task durations, a duration of 1 day equals 8 hours of work in this scenario. When you assign a resource to a task with a 1-day duration, the duration translates to 8 hours of work for this resource.

In this lesson, you view resource assignments and make modifications to make a sound work schedule for the project plan.

To View Resource Assignments and Make Modifications

1 Open *Business_Model,* if necessary; then choose **V**iew, Resource **U**sage.
The view changes to Resource Usage view. This view contains a table with work hours assigned to each task by resource name and a corresponding ***timephased*** bar graph that displays work across time (see Figure 4.15).

FIGURE 4.15

If you have problems . . .

If necessary, you may need to drag the split bar between the table and the timephased graph to the right to view the Work column. Also, you may need to click once on the scrollbox in the horizontal scrollbar of the timephased bar graph to view the starting date of the project in the bar graph.

Notice that the Business Owner has been assigned 320 hours of work. This is because the Business Owner is assigned to several summary tasks, which can display misleading information.

2 | **Choose** <u>V</u>**iew,** <u>G</u>**antt Chart.**

3 | **Click in the Resource Names column for Task 1 (*Business market analysis*) and then press** Del.
The Business Owner is removed from Task 1.

4 | **Select Task 11 (*Identify needed materials and supplies*) and click *Assign Resources*.**
The Assign Resources dialog box opens.

5 | **In the Assign Resources dialog box, select *Business Owner*.**

6 | **Click** <u>R</u>**emove and then click Close.**
The Business Owner is removed from Task 11.

7 | **Remove the Business Owner from Task 13 (*Identify management staff resources*) and Task 15 (*Identify staffing requirements*).**

8 | **Choose** <u>V</u>**iew, Resource** <u>U</u>**sage.**
Notice that the Business Owner is now assigned a more reasonable 24 hours of work in the project plan (see Figure 4.16).

	O	Resource Name	Work
1		⊟ Business Owner	24 hrs
		Revise plan	*8 hrs*
		Submitt to bank	*8 hrs*
		Confirm decisio	*8 hrs*
2		Advisor	0 hrs

Reduced work hours

FIGURE 4.16

In the next set of steps, you take a further look at analyzing the project plan and making modifications to the expenses generated by task assignments and methods to resolve overallocations. You use the Assignment Information dialog box to change the assignment units for several resources.

M'SOFT 4

To Fix Resource Assignment Errors

1 **In the Indicator column, point to the overallocation icon for the Accountant resource.**

A ScreenTip appears concerning the overallocation. Too many work hours have been generated by the task assignments for the Accountant resource, and Microsoft Project recommends that you level the resource. *Leveling* refers to an automatic feature whereby Microsoft Project balances the workload for a resource by adding delays and splits in the project plan. Rather than utilizing the automatic leveling feature, however, you can adjust the resource assignments by adding additional resources to adjust task duration and overall work hours.

2 **Double-click the second task for the Accountant resource, *Target monies for management staff.***

The Assignment Information dialog box opens (see Figure 4.17).

FIGURE 4.17

Recall that the original work unit was 10 hours. Since the Accountant only works 25% of an 8-hour work day on this project, he/she works just 2 hours per day, which translates to a 5 day duration (2 hours × 5 days = 10 hours work). The percentage of a resource's time allocated to a task is called *assignment units.* Assignment units differ from max. units in that max. units represents the resource's total availability on the project whereas assignment units represents a resource's units on an individual task assignment. The Business Owner is paying $75 per hour for each hour the Accountant works, currently making the cost of this task $750. You change the assignment units from 25% to 100%.

If you have problems . . .

If you are unable to view enough of the task name listed below each resource, double-click the column separator between the Resource Name and Work columns in the gray header to the right. You may also need to drag the split bar between the Resource Usage table and the bar graph to the right as well.

---

3 | Under *Units* in the Assignment Information dialog box, increase the percentage to **100%** and then click **OK**.
A green flag appears in the left corner of the task, indicating further action is required (see Figure 4.18).

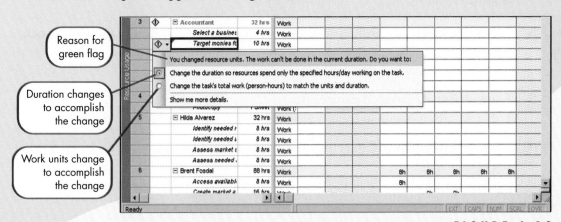

FIGURE 4.18

4 | In the Indicator column, click the smart tag.
A list of options appears (see Figure 4.19).

FIGURE 4.19

The first option decreases the task duration of the task to 1.25 days because the resource can now spend 100%, or the full work day of 8 hours, on this task. The second option does not change the task duration but instead increases the work hours to 40.

5 | Select the second option, *Change the task's total work (person-hours) to match the units and duration.*
The work now translates to 40 hours.

6 | Double-click *Target monies for management staff* again.
Notice that the overall cost for this task is now $3,000 if the Accountant applies 100% of his or her time to a 5-day task (see Figure 4.20).

M'SOFT 4

FIGURE 4.20

7 **Change *Units* back to 25% and then click OK.**
Another green flag appears beside the task.

8 **Click the smart tag and choose the second option to change the total work hours back to 10.**
The duration is now 5 days and the work is 2 hours per day.

9 **Click *Hilda Alvarez* (Resource 5).**
Hilda Alvarez has only four tasks assigned to her, equaling 32 work hours.

10 **Choose <u>V</u>iew, <u>G</u>antt Chart and then select Task 14 (*Target monies for management staff*).**
Notice that the duration of this task is approximately 5 days (see Figure 4.21).

11	⊟ Identify needed materials a	11 days?	Tue 3/14/06	Tue 3/28/06	7	
12	Select a business approach	2 days?	Tue 3/14/06	Wed 3/15/06	2SS,10	Accountant[25%]
13	⊟ Identify management sta	5 days?	Thu 3/16/06	Wed 3/22/06	12	
14	Target monies for manag	5 days?	Thu 3/16/06	Wed 3/22/06		Accountant[25%]
15	⊟ Identify staffing requiren	5 days?	Thu 3/16/06	Wed 3/22/06	14SS	

Estimated duration

FIGURE 4.21

Currently this task is assigned to the Accountant, but the task responsibility can be shared with Hilda Alvarez.

11 **Click *Assign Resources;* then select *Hilda Alvarez* and click <u>A</u>ssign.**

12 **Click Close and then click the smart tag beside the task.**
A list of options appears (see Figure 4.22).

Same work, less duration

Same duration, more work

Reason for green flag

Work and duration constant but hours decreased

FIGURE 4.22

13 Choose the first option, *Reduce duration so the task ends sooner, but requires the same amount of work (person-hours).*

By choosing the first option, Microsoft Project divides the task duration between the two assigned resources according to their individual assignment units and recalculates the work hours. The Accountant receives a 2 hour assignment (25% of an 8-hour day), and Hilda Alvarez, who works 100% of her time on this project, receives an 8 hour assignment. The combination of the resource assignments equals 10 hours of work, thus the work can be accomplished in one day by utilizing these two resources.

14 Choose <u>V</u>iew, Tas<u>k</u> Usage, and locate Task 14 (*Target monies for management staff*).

The grid on the left shows the tasks with the specific resource assignments listed beneath them (see Figure 4.23).

Task 14 has total work units of 10 hours

Hilda works 8 hours (100%)

Accountant works 2 hours (25%)

FIGURE 4.23

The Task Usage view is almost identical to the Resource Usage view. This view allows you to work with resource assignment organized by task rather than by resource, and it also provides a Duration column so that you can see work hours by task as well as task duration.

Recall that with the addition of a second resource, the task duration was reduced to 1 day. The original work unit was 10 hours, which Microsoft Project translated to 2 hours of work per day for 5 days.

Normally the work hours are split equally among the two resources so each resource would be assigned 5 hours of work. However, the accountant works only 25% of the work day on this project.

M'SOFT 4

15 Choose <u>V</u>iew, <u>G</u>antt Chart, and then select Task 16 (*Target monies for staff*).

16 Click *Assign Resources,* assign Hilda Alvarez to the task, and then close the dialog box.

17 Click the smart tag and choose the first option, *Reduce duration so the task ends sooner but requires the same amount of work (person-hours).*

18 Save your changes to the *Business_Model* file.

You looked at resource assignments and made modifications to level resource usage. Keep the *Business_Model* project file open and continue with the next lesson. If you prefer to complete the project later, close the file and exit Microsoft Project.

TO EXTEND YOUR KNOWLEDGE . . .

SMART TAG OPTIONS WHEN RESOURCE ASSIGNMENTS CHANGE
When you add or remove resources from a task, a smart tag appears, prompting you to reschedule the task as a result of the assignment change. You are provided three choices. The first choice, which is the default, reduces the duration of the task but keeps the amount of work units (hours) the same. The second option keeps the duration the same but increases the amount of work hours. The third option keeps the duration the same but reduces the amount of hours worked per day.

LESSON 6: Printing Resource Allocations and Project Costs

Resource allocations and project costs represent two key areas of the project triangle, and there are many reports devoted to these areas. The **Resource Usage report** is designed to provide assignment hours for each resource by week and is very similar to the Resource Usage view. There is also a **To-do List report** that provides a particular resource with his or her assigned tasks and also provides the week the task begins and the start date of the task. There are several cost reports and each provides a different means of tracking cost issues. The **Budget report** lists all project tasks and sorts them in descending order by total cost.

In this lesson, you preview these three reports. On your own, you can also print the reports, if desired.

To Preview Resource Allocations and Project Costs

1 **Open** *Business_Model,* **if necessary; then choose** <u>V</u>**iew,** <u>R</u>**eports.**
The Reports dialog box opens (see Figure 4.24).

FIGURE 4.24

2 **Click** <u>W</u>**orkload and then click** <u>S</u>**elect.**
A list of workload-related reports displays in the Workload Reports dialog box.

3 **Choose** <u>R</u>**esource Usage and then click** <u>S</u>**elect.**
A preview of a report appears, containing a list of tasks, by date, with Resource and work hours.

4 **Click in the report to magnify it.**
The report lists all tasks for the project file (see Figure 4.25). The tasks are organized by date and the total time involved in each task.

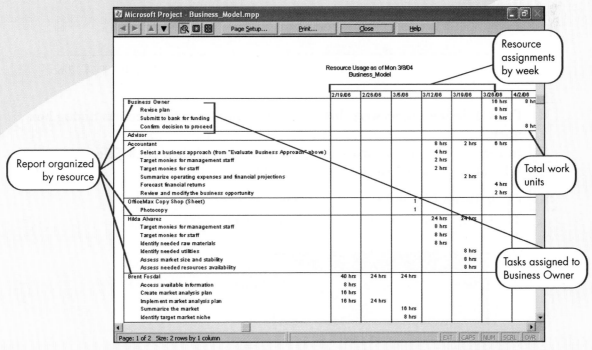

FIGURE 4.25

5 Click **C**lose to exit without printing. (If you prefer to print, you can click the Page **S**etup button to first modify print settings, or you can click the Print button to immediately start the print process at default settings.)
The report closes and the Reports dialog box displays again.

6 In the Reports dialog box, click Cos**t**s and then **S**elect.
A list of cost-related reports displays.

7 Click **B**udget and then click **S**elect.
The report includes the cost of each task as well as total costs. Look at the report more closely to see the predicted costs of the project plan (see Figure 4.26).

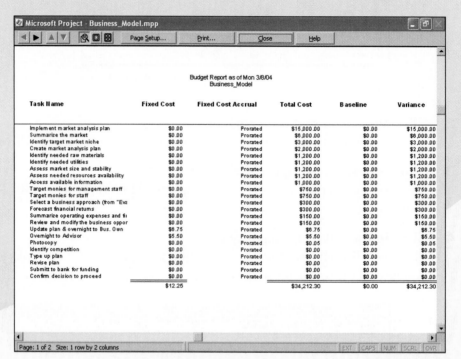

FIGURE 4.26

8 Print if desired; otherwise close the report and leave the Reports dialog box open.

9 In the Reports dialog box, select **A**ssignments and then click **S**elect.
A list of assignment-related reports is available.

10 Click **T**o-do List and then click **S**elect.
The Using Resource dialog box displays (see Figure 4.27).

FIGURE 4.27

11 **Click the drop-down arrow and choose *Business Owner;* then click OK.**
A report with a list of tasks assigned to the Business Owner as well as the start dates displays (see Figure 4.28).

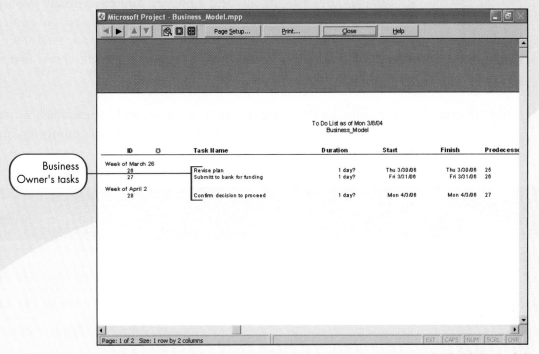

FIGURE 4.28

12 **Print if desired; otherwise close the preview window and then close the Reports dialog box.**

13 **Save your changes to the *Business_Model* file and close it.**

TO EXTEND YOUR KNOWLEDGE . . .

VIEWING RESOURCE ALLOCATION FROM THE PROJECT GUIDE

You can view resource allocation and task duration information in the Resources side pane. Click the Resources drop-down arrow on the Project Guide and choose *Assign people and equipment to tasks.* Click on the task whose information you want to view. The Resources side pane displays duration and work hours under *4) Review Information.*

SUMMARY

In this project you learned that adding resources enables you to work with many crucial areas of the project, including resource assignments and a budget. You created new resources and assigned them to tasks. You learned how to view resource allocations, analyze the result of your task assignments, and make modifications. By modifying resource task assignments, you affected both task duration and task cost. Finally, you looked at several reports that support resource task assignment and cost issues.

You can extend your learning by reviewing concepts and terms and by practicing variations of skills presented in the lessons. Use the following table as a guide to the numbered questions and exercises in the end-of-project learning opportunities.

LESSON	MULTIPLE CHOICE	DISCUSSION	SKILL DRILL	CHALLENGE	DISCOVERY ZONE
Viewing and Setting Up Resources	1, 2, 3, 8	1, 2, 3	1	1	1
Entering Resource Information	1	3	1	2	1, 2
Entering Fixed Costs	8	3		2	2
Assigning Resources to Tasks	4, 6, 8	2, 3	2	3	
Viewing and Modifying Resource Assignments	7, 9	2, 3	3, 4	4	
Printing Resource Allocations and Project Costs	10	2	5	4	

KEY TERMS

Accrue At field	leveling	response pending icon
assignment units	Material Label field	scheduling formula
Budget report	material resource	Std. Rate field
Code field	Max. Units field	timephased
consolidated resource	note icon	To-do List report
Cost/Use field	overallocation icon	total cost
fixed cost	Ovt. Rate field	Type field
Group field	resource assignment	work
group resource	Resource calendar	work resource
hyperlink icon	resource cost	work unit
individual resource	resource pool	
Initials field	Resource Usage report	

CHECKING CONCEPTS AND TERMS

MULTIPLE CHOICE

Circle the letter of the correct answer for each of the following.

1. Which view is used to enter resource information? [L1, L2]

   a. Resource Usage view

   b. Resource Sheet view

   c. Gantt Chart view

   d. Task Usage view

2. What is it called when a resource has too much work assigned? [L1]

   a. Overallocating

   b. Overscheduling

   c. Leveling

   d. Any of the above

3. Which of the following does *not* represent a valid work resource? [L1]

   a. Personnel

   b. Facilities

   c. Equipment

   d. Time

4. Which of the following best explains what a work unit is? [L5]

   a. The amount of time it takes to complete a task

   b. How long the resource actually spends completing a task

   c. A calculation that converts task duration to work hours when a resource is assigned to it

   d. A measurement expressed in hours

5. A cost that is not specifically related to any one resource is referred to as which of the following? [L3]

   a. Cost

   b. Resource cost

   c. Prorated cost

   d. Fixed cost

6. The amount of time a resource spends on assigned tasks is called what? [L4]

   a. Resource hours

   b. Work

   c. Assignment units

   d. Task duration

7. Which view shows a table displaying work hours assigned to each task by resource name, with a corresponding bar graph that displays work across time? [L5]

   a. Resource Usage view

   b. Gantt Chart view

   c. Resource Sheet view

   d. Task Usage view

8. Which of the following is *not* a method used to add a new resource? [L1, L4]

   a. Type the resource name in the resource sheet.

   b. Type the resource name in the Resource Names column in Gantt Chart view.

   c. Type the resource name in the Assign Resources dialog box.

   d. Type the resource name in the Gantt bar chart.

9. The amount of effort to complete a task is referred to as what? [L4, L5]

   a. Duration

   b. Work

   c. Assignment unit

   d. Force

10. Which report provides a list of costs by task and a total project cost? [L6]

    a. Task Usage report

    b. Workload report

    c. Budget report

    d. Costs report

M'SOFT 4

DISCUSSION

1. There are three types of resources that work can be assigned to: people, equipment, and materials. Describe how you would determine which resource type to use for various tasks, and why. [L1]

2. With the addition of resources, tracking the progress and determining the overall accuracy of the project schedule is improved. Describe some of the things you are able to track and record when you add resources and assign them to tasks. [L1, L4-L6]

3. Take a look at the following three views in Microsoft Project: Resource Sheet, Task Usage, and Resource Usage. Describe what each of these three views shows you and the differences between them. [L1-L5]

SKILL DRILL

Skill Drill exercises reinforce project skills. Each skill reinforced is the same, or nearly the same, as a skill presented in the project. Detailed instructions are provided in a step-by-step format. The exercises relate to a single file, and you should work the exercises in order.

1. Creating Resources

The company you work at recently experienced a severe virus attack that has damaged the e-mail servers, the network, and several employee workstations. In anticipation of any recurrence, your company has created a virus recovery program that includes a project plan. Your job is to communicate the status of the clean-up operation to upper management, and to ensure that each step in your virus recovery plan is complete. You must assign tasks to the appropriate team member from the Information Systems department and track the cost of the clean-up operation.

To create a resource pool, complete the following steps:

1. Open *EPr1_0402* and save it as **Virus_Recovery**.
2. Choose View, Resource Sheet.
3. Enter the following resource data:

Name	Type	Material Label	Initials	Group	Max Units	Std. Rate	Cost/Use
Jackie DeDios	Work		JD	IS	100%	$45	
Joe Belson	Work		JB	IS	100%	$45	
Rich Betters	Work		RB	HR	100%	$45	
Virus Software Update	Material		V	Virus			$5.00
Network downtime	Material		Net	Network			$2000.00
Recovery Manuals	Material	Dozen	Man	Virus			$120.00

4. Double-click *Network downtime* and then click the Notes tab.

5. Type `This cost per hour represents approximate cost of having the network down during virus clean-up.` Then click OK.

6. Save *Virus_Recovery* and leave it open for the next exercise.

2. Assigning Resources to Tasks

You have created the resource sheet specifying both material and nonmaterial resources in the *Virus_Recovery* project. Now, you want to assign resources to the appropriate tasks.

To assign resources, complete the following steps:

1. Open *Virus_Recovery*, if necessary, and choose <u>V</u>iew, <u>G</u>antt Chart.

2. Select Task 2 (*Virus, worm, or Trojan*) and click *Assign Resources*.

3. From the Assign Resources dialog box, select *Joe Belson* and then click the Assign button.

4. Select Task 3 (*Check Web for operating system fixes*) and click *Assign Resources*.

5. From the Assign Resources dialog box, select *Rich Betters* and then click the Assign button.

6. Complete the remaining resource assignments, as listed in the table below.

ID	Task Name	Resource Name
4	Check for virus patch	*Rich Betters*
5	Communicate with end users	*Jackie DeDios, Recovery manuals*
6	Identify affected computers	*Jackie DeDios*
8	Bring down e-mail server	*Joe Belson, Network downtime*
9	Bring down the network	*Joe Belson, Network downtime*
10	Clean server and network	*Rich Betters, Network downtime*
12	Clean-up virus	*Joe Belson*
13	Scan for virus	*Rich Betters*
14	Recover damaged mailboxes	*Joe Belson*
15	Repair damaged workstations	*Jackie DeDios*
17	Analyze affected computers	*Joe Belson*
18	Identify where the attack came from	*Joe Belson, Rich Betters*
19	Communicate with upper level	*Jackie DeDios*
20	Educate end users	*Jackie DeDios*

7. Save *Virus_Recovery* and leave it open for the next exercise.

3. Reviewing Resource Allocations

You have entered resource assignments. The next step is to take a look at the overall project and analyze the results. Then, you can make necessary changes.

To review resource allocations, complete the following steps:

1. Open *Virus_Recovery*, if necessary, and choose <u>V</u>iew, Resource <u>U</u>sage.

Notice that the names of Joe Belson and Rich Betters are in red because they are overallocated.

2. Point to the warning icon for Jackie DeDios, Joe Belson, and read the message.

3. Under Jackie DeDios, double-click the *Repair damaged workstations* task.

   This task requires 32 hours of work and costs $1,440. The amount of time calculated is not reasonable for this resource.

4. Under Joe Belson, double-click the *Analyze affected computers* task.

   Notice that the cost of this task is also $1,440. You need to reduce the cost of this task.

5. Click Cancel to close the Assignment Information dialog box.

6. Choose View, Gantt Chart and then drag the split bar between the task table and the Gantt chart to the right until you can view the Resource Names column.

7. View Task 15 (*Repair damaged workstations*) and note that this task has a 4-day estimated duration.

8. Choose Project, Project Information and note that the project base calendar is the Standard project calendar; click Cancel.

   Using the Standard project base calendar and the 100% maximum units of the resources, Task 15 translates to 8 hours of work each day for Jackie DeDios and requires a total of 32 hours of work. The amount of time calculated is not reasonable for this resource, given the other tasks already assigned to her.

9. Save *Virus_Recovery* and leave it open for the next exercise.

4. Leveling Resources

You have looked at your resource allocations and realize that some resources are overallocated in the virus recovery process. You need to manually level these resources to make the workloads more reasonable.

To level resource allocations, complete the following steps:

1. Open *Virus_Recovery*, if necessary, and select Task 17 (*Analyze affected computers*); then click *Assign Resources.*

2. Click in the first blank row in the Assign Resources dialog box, type **Ashish Mehta**, and then press ⏎Enter.

3. Press Up Arrow to select *Ashish Mehta*, click Assign, and then click Close.

4. Click the smart tag and choose the first option, *Reduce duration so task ends sooner, but requires the same amount of work (person-hours).*

5. Select Task 18 (*Identify where the attack came from*) and then click *Assign Resources.*

6. Select *Joe Belson,* and then click Remove.

7. Select *Ashish Mehta,* click Assign, and then click Close.

8. Click the smart tag and choose the first option in the list.

9. Select Task 15 (*Repair damaged workstations*) and click *Assign Resources.*

10. Click in the first blank row in the Assign Resources dialog box, type **Anita McKay**, and then press ⏎Enter.

11. Press Up Arrow to select *Anita McKay,* click Assign, and then click Close.

12. Click the smart tag and choose the first option in the list.

13. Choose Yiew, Resource Usage.

　　Although resources are still overallocated, the work hours are more reasonable than before. Jackie DeDios is now scheduled to work 16 hours on the *Repair damaged workstations* task, rather than 32 hours; the duration is also reduced from 4 days to 2. Joe Belson is now scheduled to work 16 hours on the *Analyze affected computers* task, rather than 32 hours. Half the work on these tasks went to Ashish Mehta and Anita McKay.

14. Save *Virus_Recovery* and leave it open for the next exercise.

5. Printing Resource Allocation and Cost Reports

You have adjusted the plan the best you know how. You want to provide the creators of the virus recovery plan some reports to review. They need to see how the Information Systems department has been dispatched to handle this problem as well as review the overall costs associated with this project.

To print resource allocations and a cost report, complete the following steps:

1. Open *Virus_Recovery,* if necessary, and choose Yiew, Reports.

2. Click Workload and then click Select.

3. Under *Workload Reports,* click *Resource Usage* and then click Select.

4. Click Print on the toolbar and then click OK.

5. In the Reports dialog box, click Costs and then click Select.

6. Under *Cost Reports,* click *Budget* and then click Select.

7. Click Print on the toolbar, click OK, and then click Close.

8. Save *Virus_Recovery* and then close it.

CHALLENGE

Challenge exercises expand on or are somewhat related to skills presented in the lessons. Each exercise provides a brief narrative introduction, followed by instructions in a numbered-step format that are not as detailed as those in the Skill Drill section.

These Challenge exercises relate to a single file and should be worked in order.

1. Adding Resources By Using the Resource Information Dialog Box

You work at a company that recently spun off a division that provides temporary employees for businesses that require extra office workers for a short period of time. Your first client requires 50 temporary employees for a huge car dealership that is being built in your area. You have received more than 500 resumes and must review these resumes for potential candidates. For legal purposes, you must verify each resume and potential candidate and conduct interviews for the group you choose. You plan to use the project plan provided by Human Resources to help you.

To add resources, complete the following steps:

1. Open the *EPr1_0403* file and save it as **Temps_Hiring_Plan**.

2. Switch to the Resource Sheet view.

3. Double-click the first empty resource row, and click the General tab, if necessary.

4. Add the resources listed in the table below. (Click OK after each resource entry and double-click the next blank row.)

Resource Name	Initials	Group	Type	E-Mail
Corporate Law	Law	Lawyers	Work	law@jkedwards.com
Dante Peeples	DP	Review Team	Work	d.peeples@tempsplus.com
Jackie Gibson	JG	HR	Work	j.gibson@tempsplus.com
Joy Ti	JT	Review Team	Work	j.ti@tempsplus.com
Letterhead paper	Letterhead	Supplies	Material	
Postage	Postage	Correspondence	Material	
Renee Thibodeaux	RT	Review Team	Work	r.thibodeaux@tempsplus.com
Saul Jeffers	SJ	Review Team	Work	s.jeffers@tempsplus.com
Testing Vendor	Vendor	Vendor	Work	kewood@questions.com
Tim Daniels	TD	HR	Work	t.daniels@tempsplus.com
UPS Overnight Store	UPS	Correspondence	Material	
Victoria Hunter	VH	HR	Work	v.hunter@tempsplus.com

5. Double-click the Corporate Law resource, and then click the Help button to learn how to use the Resource Availability table.

6. Make the Corporate Law resource available only from February 22, 2006, through March 2, 2006, and from April 3, 2006, through April 6, 2006.

7. Add a note to remind yourself that Corporate Law is involved in arbitration and other legal proceedings and will be available only on the dates specified.

8. Edit the Tim Daniels and Corporate Law resources to have a max unit of 25% each.

9. Save *Temps_Hiring_Plan* and leave it open for the next exercise.

2. Adding Costs to Material and Work Resources

Now that your resource pool is complete, you need to assign the costs to each resource. The testing vendor has quoted a set price for his services. Some resources have an hourly rate attached, while others have a per unit fee.

To add resource costs, complete the following steps:

1. Open *Temps_Hiring_Plan,* if necessary, and switch to Resource Sheet view.

2. Enter the following resource costs:

Resource Name	Std. Cost	Ovt. Cost	Cost/Use
Corporate Law	$250.00	$375.00	
Dante Peeples	$16.50	$24.75	
Jackie Gibson	$8.50	$12.75	
Joy Ti	$16.50	$24.75	
Letterhead paper			$6.50
Postage			$0.37

Renee Thibodeaux	**$16.50**	**$24.75**
Saul Jeffers	**$16.50**	**$24.75**
Tim Daniels	**$20.00**	
UPS Overnight Store		**$12.75**
Victoria Hunter	**$16.00**	

3. Double-click the *Letterhead paper* resource and add **Box** as the material label.

4. Switch to Gantt Chart view, and then change the Table: Entry view to the Table: Cost view.

5. Add **$2500** as the fixed cost for Task 18 (Contact testing vendor).

6. Switch back to the Table: Entry view.

7. Save *Temps_Hiring_Plan* and leave it open for the next exercise.

3. Assigning Tasks to Resources

Now that your resource pool is complete, you need to assign specific tasks to each resource. To assign resources to tasks, complete the following steps:

1. Open *Temps_Hiring_Plan,* if necessary, and click Resources from the Project Guide toolbar.

2. Click the *Assign people and equipment to task* link, and assign the following resources to the tasks. To modify the resource's assignment units, double-click a name in the Assign Resources dialog box and specify the percentage in the Units cell:

ID	Task Name	Resource/Units
2	Organize Candidate Review team	Victoria Hunter - 50%; Tim Daniels - 25%
3	Review	Victoria Hunter - 100%; Dante Peeples, Joy Ti, Renee Thibodeaux, Saul Jeffers - 80%
4	Contact candidates	Jackie Gibson - 25%; Letterhead (3); Postage (100)
6	Complete worker validity form	Victoria Hunter - 50%
7	Verify all certification and education data	Victoria Hunter - 25%
8	Receive copies of transcripts and certificates	Jackie Gibson - 10%
9	Complete education validity form	Jackie Gibson - 25%
10	Contact references	Victoria Hunter - 50%; Tim Daniels - 50%
12	Narrow down selections	Victoria Hunter - 75%; Tim Daniels - 75%
13	Provide policy and procedures	Victoria Hunter - 100%
14	Review legal issues	Corporate Law - 25%
15	Distribute candidate resumes to Review team	Victoria Hunter - 100%

16	Identify interviewing team members	Dante Peeples, Joy Ti, Renee Thibodeaux, Saul Jeffers - 100%; Victoria Hunter - 100%; Tim Daniels - 100%
17	Identify interview questions	Dante Peeples, Joy Ti, Renee Thibodeaux, Saul Jeffers - 100%; Victoria Hunter - 100%; Tim Daniels - 100%
18	Contact testing vendor	Tim Daniels -100%; UPS (1)
19	Review test questions	Dante Peeples, Joy Ti, Renee Thibodeaux, Saul Jeffers - 100%; Victoria Hunter - 100%; Tim Daniels - 100%
20	Perform 1st round interviews	Victoria Hunter - 75%; Tim Daniels - 25%
22	Meet with Review team to discuss	Dante Peeples, Joy Ti, Renee Thibodeaux, Saul Jeffers - 100%; Victoria Hunter - 100%; Tim Daniels - 100%
23	Perform 2nd round interviews	Victoria Hunter
25	Meet with Review team to discuss	Dante Peeples, Joy Ti, Renee Thibodeaux, Saul Jeffers - 100%; Victoria Hunter - 100%; Tim Daniels - 100%
27	Candidate start date	Victoria Hunter
28	Confirm with manager	Jackie Gibson
29	Confirm with candidate	Victoria Hunter

3. Select <u>V</u>iew, Tas<u>k</u> Usage.

   This view shows each task and how the work involved is distributed to the assigned resources.

4. Select <u>V</u>iew, Resource <u>U</u>sage to check for overallocations.

   Several resources are overallocated—namely, being assigned too much work for 1 day.

5. Save *Temps_Hiring_Plan* and leave it open for the next exercise.

4. Leveling Resource Assignments

As you know, several resources are overallocated. You need to level the resources to fit within normal working hours. Remember that the Corporate Law and Tim Daniels (the Human Resources manager) resources have a maximum unit of 25%.

To level resources, complete the following steps:

1. Open *Temps_Hiring_Plan,* if necessary, and scroll down to the Tim Daniels resource.

2. Using the timephased bar graph, look for the days on which Tim is scheduled to work for more than 2 hours.

3. Change the units for any task necessary to level Tim's time.

Remember that at times it is okay to assign more hours.

4. Respond to any smart tags by changing the work to fit the change.

5. Level all other resources as you see fit.

6. Save *Temps_Hiring_Plan* and leave it open for the next exercise.

5. Changing Text in the Gantt Chart

As you look at the Gantt chart, you see how cluttered it appears. You need to shorten the text shown beside the Gantt bar. You try several options to determine which is best for you.

To change Gantt chart text, complete the following steps:

1. Open *Temps_Hiring_Plan,* if necessary, and switch to Gantt Chart view and widen the Gantt chart area.

2. Double-click the name beside the Task 10 Gantt bar.

3. Click the Text tab in the Bar Styles dialog box.

4. Click in the Right text box and then click the drop-down arrow.

5. Select *Resource initials* and close the dialog box.

6. Double-click the Gantt bar and change the bar text to *Resource Group*.

7. Save *Temps_Hire_Plan* and close it.

DISCOVERY ZONE

Discovery Zone exercises require advanced knowledge of topics presented in *Essentials* lessons, application of skills from multiple lessons, or self-directed learning of new skills. Each exercise is independent of the others, so you may complete them in any order.

1. Creating a Template with a Standard Resource Pool

Assume that you are a member of a fraternity/sorority or a civic organization. These organizations continually work on projects. To make the input easier, you can create a template that contains only a common resource pool. Decide which organization you want to use in this exercise. Create a new project and create a resource pool with at least 10 resources. Save the project file as a template. If necessary, consult Microsoft Project's Help.

2. Working with Costs

There are many different costs involved in a project, including fixed costs, variable costs, and budgets. Take some time to research costs using all available Help sources. Then add, edit, or remove costs within an existing project. Save the updated project as a separate file.

5

MODIFYING TASK INFORMATION

OBJECTIVES

IN THIS PROJECT, YOU LEARN HOW TO

- Edit and replace task information and check spelling

- Save a baseline

- Enter percent complete

- View percent complete

- Enter actuals

- Specify lead and lag time

- Resolve constraint conflicts and set a task deadline

5

WHY WOULD I DO THIS?

When tracking progress, you must decide ahead of time how you want to receive updates from your team members and how often you want to receive them. There are several levels of detail for incorporating progress, from the simple to the complex. Tracking progress at the task level is the most simple. An example of task-level progress is noting that a task is 50% complete. Assignment-level progress provides more tracking details, but it can be used only if you have assigned resources to tasks. An example of assignment-level tracking is noting how many resources are assigned to a task and the cost and work values associated with each resource. If you track progress by time period, you are interested in the progress of an assignment relative to work hours. An example of tracking progress by time period is noting the time a resource worked on a task each day or in a given week.

Once you decide on your tracking method, there are many different options for viewing progress. **_Progress bars_** appear in each task's Gantt bar, giving you an at-a-glance view of each task's overall status. You can view the Percent Complete column or use any of the several table views that can be applied to the Gantt Chart view so you can see additional columns of data.

VISUAL SUMMARY

As you design a project plan, modifications are necessary. After fine-tuning the project file, you save the **_baseline,_** a "snapshot in time" that includes all the project's original start, finish, duration, and cost estimates. Then as you begin tracking progress, you can compare baseline data against actual data. For example, you can note when you estimate a task to begin and when it actually began, or you can track the estimated work hours a resource should spend completing a task compared to the actual amount of time the resource spent completing the task. Figure 5.1 provides an example of a baseline within a project file, which you create in this project.

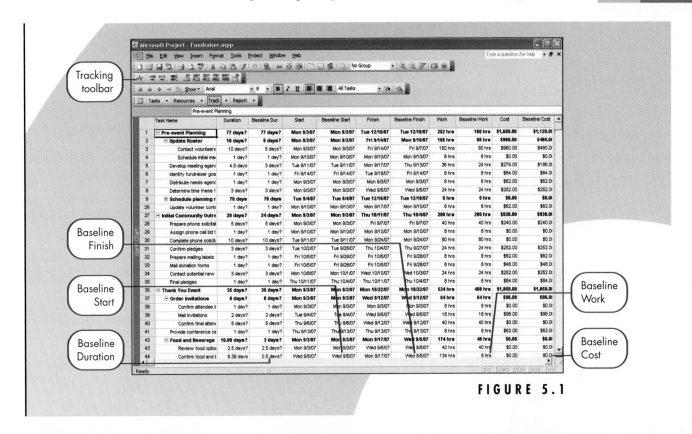

FIGURE 5.1

LESSON 1: Editing and Replacing Task Information and Checking Spelling

Microsoft Project utilizes *effort-driven scheduling* to lengthen or shorten the duration of a task based on the resources assigned to the task. The total amount of work for the task is not changed. Effort-driven scheduling is a default feature that can be turned off on a task-by-task basis for those instances in which you cannot predict the amount of work a task will generate.

Fine-tuning a project plan involves analyzing estimated task duration and how it affects the overall project completion date. You can adjust resource assignments, resource assignment units, and estimated task durations to modify task duration and thus the overall project completion date. You can check spelling and use Find and Replace features to edit language and grammar.

In this lesson, you are part of a team managing an annual fundraiser for your community's downtown events program. You are managing the tasks assigned to a group of volunteers and full-time city employees. In the first set of steps, you adjust the resources for one of the tasks to see the effect of effort-driven scheduling. In the second set of steps, you use Replace to make a global change to a word used in task descriptions, and you use the Spelling feature to find and correct spelling errors.

To Edit and Replace Task Information

1 Open the *EPr1_0501* file and save it as Fundraiser; then close any open side panes, if necessary.

2 Choose **View**, **Task Usage**; then drag the split bar between the Task Usage table and the bar chart to the right until the Finish column appears.

3 Select Task 3 (*Contact volunteers*).

Task 3 has a 10-day estimated duration that results in 80 hours of work for the Student Work Study Aides resource (see Figure 5.2). However, the Student Work Study Aids resource is actually two students, not one, so the assignment units need modifying.

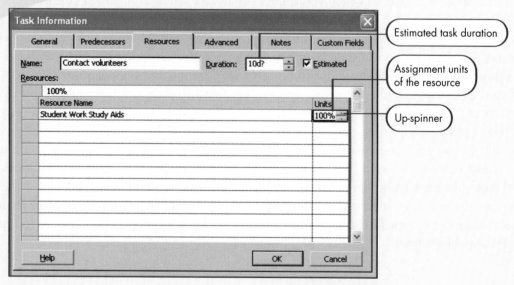

	ℹ	Task Name	Work	Duration	Start	Finish
1		⊟ Pre-event Planning	160 hrs	77 days?	Mon 9/3/07	Tue 12/18/07
2		⊟ Update Roster	88 hrs	11 days?	Mon 9/3/07	Mon 9/17/07
3		⊟ Contact volunteers	80 hrs	10 days?	Mon 9/3/07	Fri 9/14/07
		Student Work S	*80 hrs*		*Mon 9/3/07*	*Fri 9/14/07*
4		⊟ Schedule initial meet	8 hrs	1 day?	Mon 9/17/07	Mon 9/17/07
		Gail Green	*8 hrs*		*Mon 9/17/07*	*Mon 9/17/07*

Work units in hours showing the resource assignment

Resource for Task 3

Estimated duration of the task

FIGURE 5.2

4 Double-click Task 3 (*Contact volunteers*).

The Task Information dialog box opens.

5 Click the Resources tab, and then click in the first Units cell.

You set the assignment units for a resource on the Resources tab in the Task Information dialog box (see Figure 5.3). To show more than one resource at 100% usage, you multiply the number of resources by 100%: 200% represents the work of the two students.

Estimated task duration

Assignment units of the resource

Up-spinner

FIGURE 5.3

6 Click the up-spinner until *200%* displays; then click OK.

A smart tag appears in the Indicator column for Task 3 (see Figure 5.4).

FIGURE 5.4

7 Click the smart tag down arrow and select the first option.

Recall that the first option is the default and reduces the duration of the task by half because each resource is assigned 40 hours of work. By ignoring the smart tag, you automatically apply the first option. The second option would increase the work hours to 160 and assign 80 hours of work to each resource, thus keeping the task duration constant at 10 days.

8 Save your changes to the *Fundraiser* file.

In addition to modifying task information, basic text editing tools such as Find and Replace and spell-check are available. In the next set of steps, you modify the project file by replacing "employee" with "volunteer" and then check the spelling in the file.

Using Find and Replace and Checking Spelling

1 Choose <u>V</u>iew, <u>G</u>antt Chart.

2 Drag the column separator between the Task Name and Duration columns to the right until you can see all of the Task Name information.

Widening the Task Name column enables the display of full names. You can also double-click the separator line in the headings to automatically size a column to display the longest entry.

3 Choose <u>E</u>dit, <u>R</u>eplace.

The Replace dialog box opens (see Figure 5.5).

FIGURE 5.5

4 **In the *Find what* text box, type `employee`.**

You plan to replace the word "employee" in the Task Name column with the word "volunteer" because the human resources in this project plan are actually volunteers.

5 **In the *Replace with* text box, type `volunteer`.**

After specifying the *Find what* and *Replace with* criteria, you have several options. You can click Replace to change the current selection only, click Replace All to change all occurrences, or click Find Next to skip the current selection and locate the next occurrence.

6 **Click Replace All.**

An information box appears letting you know that Microsoft Project replaced three occurrences (see Figure 5.6).

FIGURE 5.6

7 **Click OK and then click Close.**

8 **Click Spelling on the Standard toolbar.**

The Spelling dialog box opens. The Spelling tool checks content and lists as a spelling error any word not found in its dictionary. The first spelling error is "solicitaton" (see Figure 5.7). The first suggestion in the *Suggestions* list is the correct spelling.

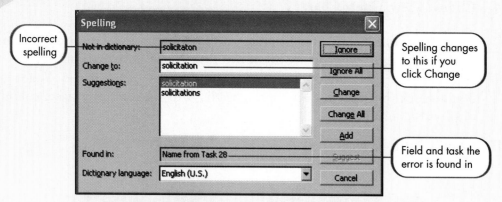

FIGURE 5.7

9 **Click Change.**

The second spelling error is the word *pic* in Task 50. This spelling error is not actually an error because it is an abbreviation for *picture*.

10 **Click Ignore.**

The third spelling error is a plural term that is not generally plural. In this case, the word *actuals* is a term used by managers to describe actual work and is correct. (Actuals will be discussed in more detail in Lesson 5.)

11 **Click Ignore.**

The last spelling error is *Merriweather*, the last name of a work resource.

12 **Click Ignore.**

An information box appears, telling you that the Spelling program finds no more errors (see Figure 5.8).

FIGURE 5.8

13 **Click OK.**

14 **Save your changes to the *Fundraiser* file.**

You modified task information and checked for spelling errors in this project file. Keep the *Fundraiser* project file open and continue with the next lesson. If you prefer to complete the project later, close the file and exit Microsoft Project.

TO EXTEND YOUR KNOWLEDGE . . .

FINDING AND REPLACING A RESOURCE

Occasionally you may find that a resource is replaced by another resource or that you inadvertently added the same resource twice because you spelled the name differently. To resolve this problem, select the task in Gantt Chart view, and then click the Assign Resources button on the Standard toolbar. In the Resource Name column, select the resource you want to replace and then click Replace. In the Replace Resource dialog box, click the resource that is the replacement, and then click OK.

LESSON 2:   Saving a Baseline

Think of a baseline as your ideal project scenario. As explained in the Visual Summary, a baseline is your original project plan and shows the project teams' best estimations as to how long their tasks should take, the approximate cost, and the overall finish date of the entire project. You should save a baseline after you have created your project plan, assigned resources, and made all the necessary adjustments. This fine-tuned project plan becomes a "snapshot in time" and the basis with which you can view variances.

A baseline allows you to analyze key data, such as estimated task duration with actual task duration or estimated costs with actual costs. Imagine that your project plan is the rollout of a new product for a customer. Knowing the overall cost of the rollout and the product's delivery date can give other teams, such as marketing and accounting, a clear directive for putting together the budget, processing payables, and developing the advertising campaign. This information can then be used to put together much more accurate project plans in the future.

When you save a baseline, Microsoft Project copies 20 pieces of information in the background about task, resource, assignment schedules, and cost data into new columns of fields that you can view. In addition, you can save up to 11 baselines within one project file. Typically, multiple baselines are used only in very long projects or in projects that have strayed so far from the original baseline that it is no longer relevant and a new baseline is warranted. A baseline is an optional component of project planning and is used only if you plan to compare estimated project data with actual project data.

In this lesson, you save a baseline for the fundraiser project file that you fine-tuned in the last project. You also view a baseline table to see what data have been recorded.

To Save a Baseline

1 **Open *Fundraiser*, if necessary, and then press** Ctrl + Home.
The cursor moves to the upper-left area of the task table.

2 **Click Track on the Project Guide toolbar.** Track ▾
The Track side pane appears (see Figure 5.9).

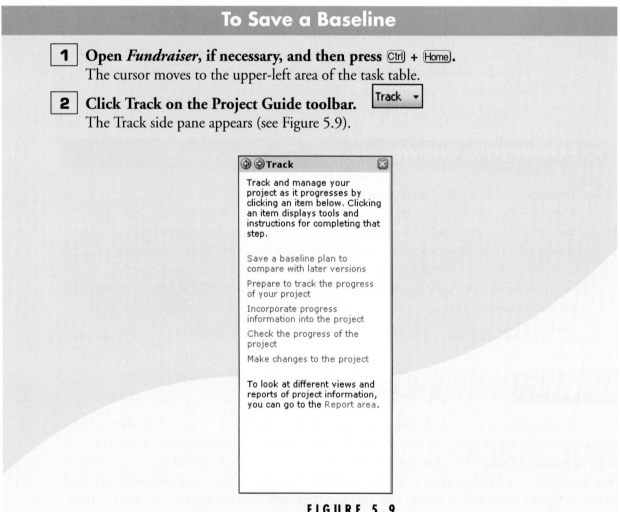

FIGURE 5.9

3 Click the first link, *Save a baseline plan to compare with later versions.*

4 Click Save Baseline. Save Baseline
The side pane shows the date and time you saved the baseline (see Figure 5.10).

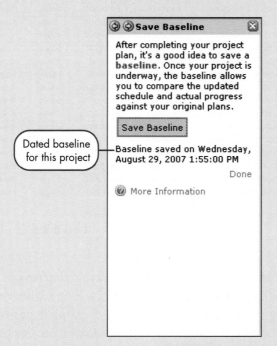

Dated baseline for this project

FIGURE 5.10

5 Click Done.
In the background, Microsoft Project has copied the data into a set of identical baseline fields that are used for comparison purposes.

6 Close the Track side pane.

7 Choose View, Tracking Gantt.
The Tracking Gantt view displays.

8 Choose View, Table: Entry, Variance.
The Variance view appears, enabling you to view the differences between the baseline data and the actual data.

9 Drag the split bar between the task table and the Gantt chart to the right until the last column, Finish Var. (Finish Variance), displays .
The Gantt chart is not visible (see Figure 5.11). By hiding the Gantt chart portion from view, you can print only the variance table and have a copy of the baseline data upon its initial creation.

	Task Name	Start	Finish	Baseline Start	Baseline Finish	Start Var.	Finish Var.
1	⊟ Pre-event Planning	Mon 9/3/07	Tue 12/18/07	Mon 9/3/07	Tue 12/18/07	**0 days**	**0 days**
2	⊟ Update Roster	Mon 9/3/07	Mon 9/10/07	Mon 9/3/07	Mon 9/10/07	**0 days**	**0 days**
3	Contact volunte	Mon 9/3/07	Fri 9/7/07	Mon 9/3/07	Fri 9/7/07	0 days	0 days
	Schedule initial	Mon 9/10/07	Mon 9/10/07	Mon 9/10/07	Mon 9/10/07	0 days	0 days
	Develop meeting a	Tue 9/11/07	Thu 9/13/07	Tue 9/11/07	Thu 9/13/07	0 days	0 days
	Identify fundraiser	Fri 9/14/07	Fri 9/14/07	Fri 9/14/07	Fri 9/14/07	0 days	0 days
7	Distribute needs a	Mon 9/3/07	Mon 9/3/07	Mon 9/3/07	Mon 9/3/07	0 days	0 days
8	Determine time fra	Mon 9/3/07	Wed 9/5/07	Mon 9/3/07	Wed 9/5/07	0 days	0 days
9	⊞ Schedule planni	Tue 9/4/07	Tue 12/18/07	Tue 9/4/07	Tue 12/18/07	**0 days**	**0 days**
26	Update volunteer c	Mon 9/10/07	Mon 9/10/07	Mon 9/10/07	Mon 9/10/07	0 days	0 days
27	⊟ Initial Community (	Mon 9/3/07	Thu 10/4/07	Mon 9/3/07	Thu 10/4/07	**0 days**	**0 days**
28	Prepare phone sol	Mon 9/3/07	Fri 9/7/07	Mon 9/3/07	Fri 9/7/07	0 days	0 days
29	Assign phone call	Mon 9/10/07	Mon 9/10/07	Mon 9/10/07	Mon 9/10/07	0 days	0 days
30	Complete phone s(	Tue 9/11/07	Mon 9/24/07	Tue 9/11/07	Mon 9/24/07	0 days	0 days
31	Confirm pledges	Tue 9/25/07	Thu 9/27/07	Tue 9/25/07	Thu 9/27/07	0 days	0 days
32	Prepare mailing lat	Fri 9/28/07	Fri 9/28/07	Fri 9/28/07	Fri 9/28/07	0 days	0 days
33	Mail donation form:	Fri 9/28/07	Fri 9/28/07	Fri 9/28/07	Fri 9/28/07	0 days	0 days
34	Contact potential n	Mon 10/1/07	Wed 10/3/07	Mon 10/1/07	Wed 10/3/07	0 days	0 days
35	Final pledges	Thu 10/4/07	Thu 10/4/07	Thu 10/4/07	Thu 10/4/07	0 days	0 days
36	⊟ Thank You Event	Mon 9/3/07	Mon 10/22/07	Mon 9/3/07	Mon 10/22/07	**0 days**	**0 days**

Actual finish date of tasks

Variance between actual and baseline finish dates

Baseline finish date of tasks

FIGURE 5.11

 10 **Click Print on the Standard toolbar and then save *Fundraiser*.**

You have created a baseline and have looked at the Tracking Gantt view. You are now ready to begin tracking project progress. Keep the *Fundraiser* project file open and continue with the next lesson. If you prefer to complete the project later, close the file and exit Microsoft Project.

TO EXTEND YOUR KNOWLEDGE . . .

ALTERNATIVE WAY TO SAVE A BASELINE

In this lesson you used a link on the Track side pane to save a baseline. You can also save a baseline by choosing Tools, Tracking, Save Baseline.

SAVING AN ADDITIONAL BASELINE

You can save up to 11 baselines in a project file. To save an additional Baseline, click Track on the Project Guide toolbar, and then click the first link, *Save a baseline plan to compare with later versions*. From the Save a Baseline side pane, click the first option, *Save a new baseline*, and then click Done.

LESSON 3: Entering Percent Complete

In Microsoft Project, the ***percent complete*** value shows how much of a task has been completed and is a percentage of the whole duration. For instance, if you complete half of a task, the percent complete is 50%. Microsoft Project calculates the percentage of work for a summary task based on the progress of its subtasks. Entering percent complete is the simplest way to monitor overall task progress.

In this lesson, you complete two sets of hands-on steps. In the first set, you enter the percent complete for several tasks by using the Task Information dialog box. In the second set, you use the *Tracking toolbar* to enter the percent complete for another task and view the % Complete column.

To Enter Percent Complete by Using the Task Information Dialog Box

1 Open *Fundraiser*, if necessary; then choose <u>V</u>iew, <u>G</u>antt Chart.

2 Double-click Task 3 (*Contact volunteers*), and then click the General tab.
You can enter the percent complete in the Task Information dialog box (see Figure 5.12).

FIGURE 5.12

3 Click the *Percent complete* up-spinner until *100%* displays.

4 Click OK.
A check mark appears in the Task 3 Indicator column, and a black line runs through the corresponding Gantt bar (see Figure 5.13).

FIGURE 5.13

Task 2 is the summary task for Tasks 3 and 4. Task 3 has a 5-day duration, which is 40 hours of work. Task 4 has a 1-day duration, which is 8 hours of work.

5 Double-click Task 2 (*Update Roster*).
Note that the percent complete is now 83% to reflect the total of the subtasks below it. Because Task 3 is complete, 40 hours of work out of 48 total hours are complete.

6 Click OK.

7 Double-click Task 4 (*Schedule initial meeting with volunteer*); change the percent complete to *100%* and click OK.

Notice that Microsoft Project marks the summary task for Tasks 3 and 4 (Task 2) complete as well (see Figure 5.14).

FIGURE 5.14

8 Enter the remaining percent complete values as shown in the following table:

Task ID	Task Name	% Complete
5	Develop meeting agenda	50%
7	Distribute needs agenda and review	100%
8	Determine time frame for planning meetings	100%
26	Update volunteer contact info	25%
28	Prepare phone solicitation list	10%

9 Save your changes to the *Fundraiser* file.

You can use the Tracking toolbar to update and view project information. For example, you can click one of the predefined percentage buttons (0%, 25%, 50%, 75%, and 100%) to change the percent complete value for a task (see Figure 5.15).

FIGURE 5.15

You can also use the Update Tasks button to manage additional functions, such as rescheduling work. Clicking the Project Statistics button opens the Project Statistics dialog box in which you can view the current project start data, project baseline data, the project finish date, and the duration, work, and cost of the overall project.

In the following steps, you use the Tracking toolbar to change the percent complete for multiple tasks.

To Enter Percent Complete by Using the Tracking Toolbar

1 Choose <u>V</u>iew, <u>T</u>oolbars, Tracking.
The Tracking toolbar appears (refer to Figure 5.15).

2 **Scroll down to show Task 42 at the top of the screen.**

3 Select Tasks 43 (*Review food options*) and 44 (*Confirm food and beverage choices*), and then click 75% Complete on the Tracking toolbar.

4 Click Task 46 (*Confirm MC*), and then hold Ctrl while clicking Tasks 49 (*Review AV with conference center*) and 51 (*Hire photographer*).

5 Click 100% Complete.

6 Select Task 47 (*Confirm speakers*) and then click 25% Complete.

7 Double-click Task 45 (*Speakers and MC*).
Task 45 is the summary task for Tasks 46 through 49. The estimated duration is 21 days and 14% of Task 45 is complete. This computation is automatic and reflects the 100% completion of tasks 46 (1 day) and 49 (1 day), and the marking of Task 47 as 25% complete (1 day). Thus, 3 days out of 21 days are complete, equalling 14%. The percent complete of a summary task is derived from the task duration and the percent complete of its subtasks.

8 Click OK.

9 Choose <u>V</u>iew, <u>T</u>oolbars, Tracking.
You turned off the Tracking toolbar.

10 Save your changes to the *Fundraiser* file.
Keep the *Fundraiser* project file open and continue with the next lesson. If you prefer to complete the project later, close the file and exit Microsoft Project.

TO EXTEND YOUR KNOWLEDGE . . .

MARKING RECURRING TASK OCCURRENCES COMPLETE

In the *Fundraiser* project file, Task 9 (*Schedule planning meetings*) is a recurring meeting. With tasks like this, it is important to mark each meeting as 100% complete once it has passed. Although these types of tasks have no work units associated with them, they do affect the overall percent complete for the entire project.

LESSON 4: Viewing Percent Complete

The two easiest methods for viewing percent complete are by using the Gantt chart and by adding the percent complete column to the task table. When using the Gantt chart, pointing to a progress bar on a Gantt bar with the mouse displays a Progress information dialog box containing additional task information, including the full task name, the actual start date, and the task duration.

In addition, once you enter values in the % Complete field, Microsoft Project performs several calculations in the background to help you better track the overall progress of your project. First, **actual duration** is automatically calculated when you enter a value in the percent complete column by using the formula *Actual Duration = Duration * Percent Complete*. Another calculation is **remaining duration,** which uses the formula *Remaining Duration = Duration − (Duration * Percent Complete)*.

In this lesson, you examine the task to contact volunteers and take a closer look at viewing percent complete information in the Gantt chart. You also expand the task table by adding the percent complete column.

To View Percent Complete

1 Open *Fundraiser*, if necessary; then select the task name of Task 3 (*Contact volunteers*).

2 Scroll to view the Task 3 Gantt bar, if necessary.
A horizontal black bar appears within the Gantt bar (see Figure 5.16). This is a progress bar and shows the percent complete for a task. This task is 100% complete because the bar runs completely from left to right.

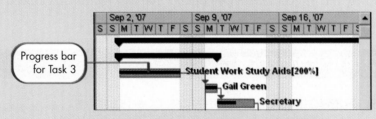

FIGURE 5.16

3 Point to the progress bar in the Task 3 Gantt bar.
A ScreenTip appears with Progress information (see Figure 5.17).

FIGURE 5.17

If you have problems . . .

To see Progress information, you must point to the black progress bar within the Gantt bar. If you point to a Gantt bar rather than the progress bar, the ScreenTip displays Task information instead.

---

4 **Choose Insert, Column.**
The Column Definition dialog box opens (see Figure 5.18).

FIGURE 5.18

5 **Click the *Field name* drop-down arrow.**

6 **Scroll to the top of the list and select *% Complete*.**
The % Complete column appears at the top of the field list because it starts with a symbol.

7 **Click OK.**
You inserted the % Complete column to the left of the Task Name column (see Figure 5.19).

M'SOFT 5

FIGURE 5.19

8 Click in the % Complete column for Task 6 (*Identify fundraiser goals*); click the up-spinner to *15%* and then press ⏎Enter.

9 Click in the % Complete column for Task 38 (*Confirm attendee list*); click the up-spinner to *5%* and then press ⏎Enter.

10 Save your changes to the *Fundraiser* file.

Keep the *Fundraiser* project file open and continue with the next lesson. If you prefer to complete the project later, close the file and exit Microsoft Project.

LESSON 5: Entering Actuals

As defined in Project 4, "Scheduling Resources and Assigning Costs," *work* is the total labor required to complete a task. Microsoft Project allows you to track work progress very simply by entering the percent complete. You can also track progress in more complex ways by tracking actual work that a resource has applied to a task or by specifying the date on which the resource should finish the task and the actual work durations. Whichever method you choose, the related fields automatically update as you enter data. By simply entering the percent complete, you are able to track remaining work, remaining task duration, and the start and finish dates of a task. *Actual work,* sometimes referred to as *actuals,* is the amount of work already completed by the resources assigned to the task. Once actual work is reported for a task, Microsoft Project calculates remaining work by using the formula *Remaining Work = Work − Actual Work.* The *actual start* is the date that work on a task begins, and the *actual finish* is the date when work on a task ends. *Remaining work* is the amount of hours still required to complete the task. Although percent complete is the most common means of charting progress, there are several other fields from which to choose.

There are management considerations related to the flow of project information that need to be addressed. First, you need to determine how to gather actual progress information from team members. This can be challenging. It is best to determine what kind of actual progress you need to monitor and create a form or specify a format that you can then distribute to your project team. Another important consideration that needs to be communicated to the project team is how you receive that information and its frequency. Do you want to meet face-to-face, or would you prefer receiving an e-mail update? Do you want to receive updates daily, weekly, or as they occur? Finally, it is important that you inform the team members of remaining work on the tasks that have been assigned to them once you have incorporated their progress.

In this lesson, you enter actual data into the project file, including actual duration, work, and date data. You also view the Tracking Gantt again to compare project progress against the baseline.

To Enter Actuals

1 | **Open *Fundraiser*, if necessary; then choose <u>V</u>iew, <u>M</u>ore Views.**
The More Views dialog box opens (see Figure 5.20).

FIGURE 5.20

2 | **Scroll down and select *Task Sheet* and then click Apply.**
The task sheet displays (see Figure 5.21). Only the tasks are shown, without a Gantt chart.

FIGURE 5.21

3 **Choose View, Table: Entry, and Tracking.**

This view is used for entering tracking data for tasks. There are additional fields concerning actuals, including start date, finish date, duration, percent complete, cost, and work.

4 **Right-click the Act. Dur. (Actual Duration) heading; then choose Insert Column.**

5 **Click the *Field name* drop-down arrow; scroll up and select *Duration* and then click OK.**

The Duration column displays to the left of the Actual Duration (Act. Dur.) column (see Figure 5.22).

FIGURE 5.22

If you have problems . . .

There may be Duration fields with a number following them (e.g., Duration1, Duration2, and so on), which can be confusing. The Duration field that you want to use is the field without any number following it, and it is the first one in that part of the list.

---

6 | **Select Task 5 (*Develop meeting agenda*) and view the Duration, Actual Duration, and Remaining Duration fields.**
A resource has informed you that they will need more than the 1.5 days shown in the remaining duration field to complete this task.

7 | **Click in the Rem. Dur. (Remaining Duration) column, and then click the up-spinner to *3 days* and press ⏎Enter.**
Notice that the % Complete decreases from 50% to 33% for Task 5 and the Duration increases from 1.5 days to 4.5 days as a result of rescheduling the meeting from Friday to Monday (see Figure 5.23).

	Task Name	Act. Start	Act. Finish	% Comp.	Phys. % Comp.	Duration	Act. Dur.	Rem. Dur.	Act. Cost	Act. Work
1	⊟ Pre-event Planning	Mon 9/3/07	NA	37%	0%	77 days?	########	########	$915.10	135.2 hrs
2	⊟ Update Roster	Mon 9/3/07	Mon 9/10/07	100%	0%	6 days?	6 days	0 days?	$480.00	88 hrs
3	Contact volunte	Mon 9/3/07	Fri 9/7/07	100%	0%	5 days?	5 days	0 days?	$480.00	80 hrs
4	Schedule initial	Mon 9/10/07	Mon 9/10/07	100%	0%	1 day?	1 day	0 days?	$0.00	8 hrs
5	Develop meeting a	Tue 9/11/07	NA	33%	0%	4.5 days	1.5 days	3 days	$93.00	12 hrs
6	Identify fundraiser	Fri 9/14/07	NA	15%	0%	1 day?	0.15 days	0.85 day	$12.60	1.2 hrs

Decreased % Complete

Increased Duration

FIGURE 5.23

8 | **Click in the Rem. Dur. column for Task 44 (*Confirm food and beverage choices*).**
Assume that this task will not be completed in the time remaining and the resource requires 8 additional days.

9 | **Use the up-spinner to specify *8 days* and press ⏎Enter.**
The % Complete decreases from 75% to 4% and the Duration increases from .5 days to 8.38 days.

10 | **View Task 3 (*Contact volunteers*) and notice that this task is already completed.**
The resource informs you that although the task was reported as complete, they continued working on the volunteer list and therefore worked longer than they said.

11 | **Click the drop-down arrow in the Act. Finish (Actual Finish) column for Task 3 and select *Fri 9/14/07* on the drop-down calendar.**
Notice that the Duration and the Actual Duration increase from 5 days to 10 days, the Actual Work increases from 80 to 160 hours, and the Actual Cost changes from $480 to $960 (see Figure 5.24).

M'SOFT 5

FIGURE 5.24

12 **Click in the Act. Work column for Task 6 (*Identify fundraiser goals*).**
The current Actual Work is 1.2 hours.

13 **Use the up-spinner to specify *4 hrs* and press ⏎Enter.**
Notice that the % Complete changes from 15% to 50%, the Actual Duration changes from .15 days to .5 days, the Remaining Duration from .85 days to .5 days, and Actual Cost from $12.60 to $42.

14 **Click the Act. Start (Actual Start) column drop-down arrow for Task 26 (*Update volunteer contact info*); change the date to *Wed 9/12/07* and press ⏎Enter.**

15 **Choose View, Tracking Gantt.**

16 **Select Task 3 (*Contact volunteers*) and compare the Baseline Finish and Finish dates.**
The baseline finish date is Fri 9/7/07, but the actual finish date is Fri 9/14/07. This task, if you recall, took an additional week.

17 **View the Finish Var. (Finish Variance) column for Task 3.**
Notice the variance value of *5 days* (see Figure 5.25). One week is equal to 5 days when using the default Standard calendar.

FIGURE 5.25

18 **View the Start Var. (Start Variance) column for Task 26 (*Update volunteer contact info*).**
Notice the variance of *2 days*. This task did not start on Mon 9/10/07 but rather on Wed 9/12/07 instead.

19 **Save your changes to the *Fundraiser* file.**
Keep the *Fundraiser* project file open and continue with the next lesson. If you prefer to complete the project later, close the file and exit Microsoft Project.

TO EXTEND YOUR KNOWLEDGE . . .

MODIFYING ACTUALS

When modifying Actual Work, Actual Start, Actual Finish, and Actual Duration for tasks that are not 100% complete, you create a split task, which is discussed in the next project. Split tasks appear as two Gantt bars separated by a dotted line in the Gantt chart.

LESSON 6:   Specifying Lead and Lag Time

Lead time, as you learned in Project 3, is an overlap between one task and another. For example, you can have a task that cannot begin until its predecessor is completed (finish-to-start dependency), but you later realize that the predecessor task need only be partially complete before you start the dependent task. You can specify a lead time in days in this type of scenario. To show lead time in a project, you enter a negative number because you are allowing extra time to begin a task.

Recall that *lag time* is generally time that needs to occur between two tasks but is not another task. For example, you may need a 2-day span of time between tasks due to some external delay, such as shipping or waiting for an approval or response on a deliverable. To show lag time, you enter a positive number.

In this lesson, you create lead time for two tasks and lag time for one.

To Create Lags and Lead Time

1 Open *Fundraiser,* if necessary, and then choose <u>V</u>iew, <u>G</u>antt Chart.

2 Shorten the Task Name column, and then drag the split bar between the task table and Gantt chart until the Predecessors column displays.

3 Double-click Task 29 (*Assign phone call list to volunteer*), and then click the Predecessors tab.
You enter both lag and lead time in the Lag column (see Figure 5.26). Lead time is entered as a negative number in the Lag column.

FIGURE 5.26

4 **Click in the Lag column; type -2 and then click OK.**

You can also specify lag time by clicking the down-spinner until *-2* displays. By entering a lead time of 2 days, you are specifying that the task can start earlier. Notice that the start date changes from Mon 9/10/07 to Thu 9/6/07 (see Figure 5.27). When Microsoft Project calculates the lead time, it ignores nonworking days.

8	✓	100%	Determine time frame for planning	3 days?	Mon 9/3/07	Wed 9/5/07	7SS	James Merriweather
9	○	0%	⊞ Schedule planning meetings	76 days	Tue 9/4/07	Tue 12/18/07		
26		25%	Update volunteer contact info	1 day?	Mon 9/10/07	Mon 9/17/07	3	
27		2%	⊟ Initial Community Outreach	17 days?	Mon 9/?/07	Tue 9/25/07		
28		10%	Prepare phone solicitation list	5 days?	Mon 9/3/07	Fri 9/7/07		Student Work Stu
29		0%	Assign phone call list to volunteer	1 day?	Thu 9/6/07	Thu 9/6/07	28FS-:	Gail Green
30		0%	Complete phone solicitations	10 days?	Fri 9/7/07	Thu 9/20/07	29	
31		0%	Confirm pledges	3 days?	Fri 9/14/07	Tue 9/18/07	30FS-:	
32		0%	Prepare mailing labels	1 day?	Wed 9/19/07	Wed 9/19/07	31	
33		0%	Mail donation forms	1 day?	Wed 9/19/07	Wed 9/19/07	32SS	

Start date changes to Thu 9/6/07

Lead time shown in the Predecessors column

FIGURE 5.27

5 **Scroll in the Gantt chart to see the Task 29 Gantt bar, then click Undo on the Standard toolbar.**

Notice the shift in position of the Task 29 Gantt bar.

6 **Click Redo on the Standard toolbar.**

Notice the lead time line in the Gantt bar (see Figure 5.28).

8	✓	100%	Determine time frame for planning	3 days?	Mon 9/3/07	Wed 9/5/07	7SS	James Merriweather
9	○	0%	⊞ Schedule planning meetings	76 days	Tue 9/4/07	Tue 12/18/07		
26		25%	Update volunteer contact info	1 day?	Mon 9/10/07	Mon 9/17/07	3	
27		2%	⊟ Initial Community Outreach	17 days?	Mon 9/3/07	Tue 9/25/07		
28		10%	Prepare phone solicitation list	5 days?	Mon 9/3/07	Fri 9/7/07		Student Work Stu
29		0%	Assign phone call list to volunteer	1 day?	Thu 9/6/07	Thu 9/6/07	28FS-:	Gail Green
30		0%	Complete phone solicitations	10 days?	Fri 9/7/07	Thu 9/20/07	29	
31		0%	Confirm pledges	3 days?	Fri 9/14/07	Tue 9/18/07	30FS-:	
32		0%	Prepare mailing labels	1 day?	Wed 9/19/07	Wed 9/19/07	31	
33		0%	Mail donation forms	1 day?	Wed 9/19/07	Wed 9/19/07	32SS	
34		0%	Contact potential new charitable c	3 days?	Thu 9/20/07	Mon 9/24/07	33	

Lead time shown in Gantt bar

FIGURE 5.28

7 | **Scroll to view Task 31 (*Confirm pledges*) in the task table and the Gantt chart.**
Notice that Task 31 (*Complete phone solicitations*) starts the day after Task 30 (*Confirm pledges*) ends (see Figure 5.29).

FIGURE 5.29

8 | **Double-click Task 31, type -5 in the Lag column, and click OK.**
This action creates a lead time of 5 days. Notice that the Gantt bar for Task 31 shifts to the left 5 days, as do its successors.

9 | **Point to the join line between Tasks 30 and 31 in the Gantt chart.**
A Task Link ScreenTip appears (see Figure 5.30). The lead time is noted.

FIGURE 5.30

10 | **Use the horizontal scrollbar below the Gantt chart to find Task 56 (*Post pictures on conference Web site*) and select it in the task table.**
Notice that Task 56 starts on Monday. You want to allow 3 extra days for the pictures to be developed, so you create lag time.

11 | **Double-click Task 56, type 3 in the Lag column, and click OK.**
Notice that the Predecessors column updates to reflect this change (see Figure 5.31). The Gantt bar also moves the right, moving the start of the bar 3 days later. Now the task begins on Thursday.

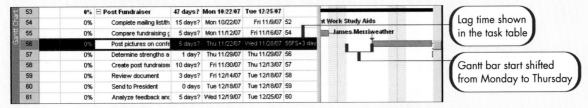

FIGURE 5.31

12 **Point to the join line between Tasks 55 and 56 in the Gantt chart.**
A ScreenTip appears, and the lag time is noted.

13 **Save your changes to *Fundraiser* and close the file.**
Continue with the final lesson. If you prefer to complete the project later, exit
Microsoft Project.

LESSON 7: Resolving Constraint Conflicts and Setting a Task Deadline

In Project 3, "Entering Tasks and Creating a Project Schedule," you learned to make changes
to constraints one task at a time. However, there are times when constraints need to be
reviewed, modified, or removed on a larger basis than task-by-task. For example, if you have a
due date for the project that you are not meeting, the first place to gain improvements is to
adjust or remove date constraints. When this involves more than one task, multiple changes
can be made at one time.

A ***deadline*** is a target date indicating when you want a task to be completed. If the deadline date
passes and the task is not completed, Microsoft Project displays an icon in the Indicator column.

In this lesson, you complete two sets of steps. In the first set, you resolve problems with date
constraints. In the second set, you set a deadline for a task.

To Correct Constraint Conflicts

1 **Open *EPr1_0502* and save the file as `Programming`.**

2 **Point to the note icon for Task 2 (*Identify presenter database fields*).**
Notice that it has a *Start No Earlier Than* constraint for Thu 6/29/00 (see
Figure 5.32).

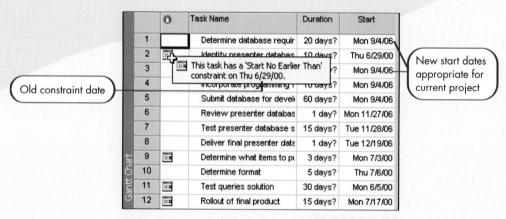

FIGURE 5.32

3   Choose <u>V</u>iew, Ta<u>b</u>le: Entry, <u>M</u>ore Tables.

4   Select Constraint Dates, and then click App<u>l</u>y.
The view shows both the constraint type and date for all tasks (see Figure 5.33), which gives you an at-a-glance tool for reviewing the constraints for all the tasks at once.

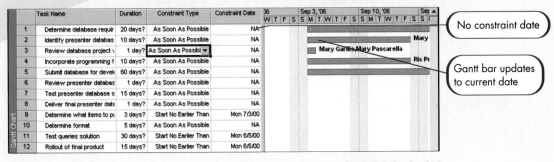

	Task Name	Duration	Constraint Type	Constraint Date
1	Determine database requir	20 days?	As Soon As Possible	NA
2	Identify presenter databas	10 days?	Start No Earlier Than	Thu 6/29/00
3	Review database project \	1 day?	As Soon As Possible	NA
4	Incorporate programming f	10 days?	As Soon As Possible	NA
5	Submit database for devel	60 days?	As Soon As Possible	NA
6	Review presenter databas	1 day?	As Soon As Possible	NA
7	Test presenter database s	15 days?	As Soon As Possible	NA
8	Deliver final presenter date	1 day?	As Soon As Possible	NA
9	Determine what items to pt	3 days?	Start No Earlier Than	Mon 7/3/00
10	Determine format	5 days?	As Soon As Possible	NA
11	Test queries solution	30 days?	Start No Earlier Than	Mon 6/5/00
12	Rollout of final product	15 days?	Start No Earlier Than	Mon 6/5/00

Specified constraint date

FIGURE 5.33

5   Click in the Constraint Type column for Task 2 (*Identify presenter database fields*).

6   Click the drop-down arrow; then choose *As Soon As Possible* and press (↵Enter).
Recall that with projects scheduled from the start date, the default constraint is As Soon As Possible, as in Task 1 (*Determine database requirements*). By changing the constraint type to the default, you also remove the constraint date (see Figure 5.34).

	Task Name	Duration	Constraint Type	Constraint Date
1	Determine database requir	20 days?	As Soon As Possible	NA
2	Identify presenter databas	10 days?	As Soon As Possible	NA
3	Review database project \	1 day?	As Soon As Possibl ▾	NA
4	Incorporate programming f	10 days?	As Soon As Possible	NA
5	Submit database for devel	60 days?	As Soon As Possible	NA
6	Review presenter databas	1 day?	As Soon As Possible	NA
7	Test presenter database s	15 days?	As Soon As Possible	NA
8	Deliver final presenter date	1 day?	As Soon As Possible	NA
9	Determine what items to pt	3 days?	Start No Earlier Than	Mon 7/3/00
10	Determine format	5 days?	As Soon As Possible	NA
11	Test queries solution	30 days?	Start No Earlier Than	Mon 6/5/00
12	Rollout of final product	15 days?	Start No Earlier Than	Mon 6/5/00

No constraint date

Gantt bar updates to current date

FIGURE 5.34

7   Select Tasks 9 (*Determine what items to put on Web site*) through 12 (*Rollout of final product*), and then click Task Information on the Standard toolbar.

8   Click the Advanced Tab.

9   Click the *Constraint type* drop-down arrow; then choose *As Soon As Possible* and click OK.
The remaining tasks are reset to the default and the constraint dates are removed.

M'SOFT 5

Now all tasks contain dates that are more current. You can now set an appropriate deadline for a specific task.

To Set a Deadline

1 Choose <u>V</u>iew, Ta<u>b</u>le: Constraint Dates, <u>E</u>ntry.

2 Double-click Task 1 (*Determine database requirements*), and then select the Advanced tab, if necessary.

3 Under *Constrain task,* click the *Dead<u>l</u>ine* drop-down arrow.

4 Select *Fri 9/29/06,* and then click OK.

5 Click the horizontal scroll arrow to view the entire Gantt bar for Task 1.
Notice the green arrow that appears indicating the deadline you applied to this task (See Figure 5.35).

	ⓘ	Task Name	Duration	Start	Finish
1		Determine database requir	20 days?	Mon 9/4/06	Fri 9/29/C
2		Identify presenter databas	10 days?	Mon 9/4/06	Fri 9/15/C
3		Review database project \	1 day?	Mon 9/4/06	Mon 9/4/C
4		Incorporate programming f	10 days?	Mon 9/4/06	Fri 9/15/C
5		Submit database for devel	60 days?	Mon 9/4/06	Fri 11/24/C
6		Review presenter databas	1 day?	Mon 11/27/06	Mon 11/27/C
7		Test presenter database s	15 days?	Tue 11/28/06	Mon 12/18/C
8		Deliver final presenter date	1 day?	Tue 12/19/06	Tue 12/19/C
9		Determine what items to pt	3 days?	Mon 9/4/06	Wed 9/6/C
10		Determine format	5 days?	Thu 9/7/06	Wed 9/13/C
11		Test queries solution	30 days?	Mon 9/4/06	Fri 10/13/C
12		Rollout of final product	15 days?	Mon 10/16/06	Fri 11/3/C

Deadline for Task 1 as well as finish date

FIGURE 5.35

6 Save your changes to *Programming* and close the file.

SUMMARY

This project focused on ways to modify task information and view results. Initial activities included changing a resource allocation, replacing multiple occurrences of a word in task descriptions, checking spelling, and creating a baseline. You learned to track project progress by entering percent complete values for individual tasks and by using actual progress data. Adding a column of data to the task table facilitated the tracking of project progress. After learning about lead and lag time, you worked with global methods to resolve constraint conflicts.

You can extend your learning by reviewing concepts and terms and by practicing variations of skills presented in the lessons. Use the following table as a guide to the numbered questions and exercises in the end-of-project learning opportunities.

LESSON	MULTIPLE CHOICE	DISCUSSION	SKILL DRILL	CHALLENGE	DISCOVERY ZONE
Editing and Replacing Task Information and Checking Spelling	4, 8, 10		2, 3	1, 2	
Saving a Baseline	5	1	3	2	
Entering Percent Complete	1	3	4	3	
Viewing Percent Complete	9		4	3	2
Entering Actuals	3	3	5	4	1
Specifying Lead and Lag Time	2, 7	2	6	3	
Resolving Constraint Conflicts and Setting a Task Deadline	6		1		

KEY TERMS

actual duration	**actual work**	**percent complete**
actual finish	**baseline**	**remaining duration**
actual start	**deadline**	**remaining work**
actuals	**effort-driven scheduling**	**Tracking toolbar**

CHECKING CONCEPTS AND TERMS

MULTIPLE CHOICE

Circle the letter of the correct answer for each of the following.

1. Suppose a summary task has two subtasks each with one resource assigned at 100% max. units. The first subtask has 12 hours of work and is 50% complete. The other subtask has 6 hours of work and is 25% complete. What is the summary task's percent complete value? [L3]

   a. 40%

   b. 42%

   c. 45%

   d. 50%

2. Which of the following represents a lag time between two tasks? [L6]

   a. -2d

   b. 0d

   c. +3d

   d. <4d

3. Which term describes true data in a project plan? [L5]

   a. Actuals

   b. Baseline

   c. Work

   d. Lead time

4. Which field does Microsoft Project change to adjust for new or removed resources assigned to a task? [L1]

   a. Work

   b. Cost

   c. Duration

   d. Start date

5. What is the original, fine-tuned project plan called? [L2]

   a. Gantt chart

   b. Task table

   c. Baseline

   d. Duration

6. What happens if a task goes beyond its deadline? [L7]

   a. The task is automatically deleted.

   b. An e-mail notification is sent to the resource.

   c. A notice icon appears in the Indicator column.

   d. A popup note appears on the screen.

7. What do you add between two tasks if their duration can overlap? [L6]

   a. Lead time

   b. Lag

   c. Baseline

   d. Actuals

8. Which of the following values represents the work units for three resources working full-time on one task? [L1]

   a. 3%

   b. 33%

   c. 100%

   d. 300%

9. Which of the following formulas does Microsoft Project use to figure remaining duration? [L4]

   a. *Duration * Percent Complete*

   b. *Percent Complete * Duration*

   c. *Work - Actual Duration*

   d. *Duration - (Duration * Percent Complete)*

10. If you add a second resource to a task with a 4-day duration, which of the following should happen? [L1]

   a. Duration increases

   b. Duration reduces by half

   c. Work decreases

   d. Task splits

DISCUSSION

1. Considering a baseline, what type of analyses might you be able to perform when comparing the baseline to actual data? [L2]

2. Suppose you are working with a project to plan a wedding. Describe a few tasks that would allow lead time as well as a few that would allow lag time. [L6]

3. Discuss several methods to collect actual data from resources. [L3, L5]

SKILL DRILL

Skill Drill exercises reinforce project skills. Each skill reinforced is the same, or nearly the same, as a skill presented in the project. Detailed instructions are provided in a step-by-step format.

You should complete the six exercises in sequence.

1. Setting Constraints

As a project manager for a software company, you coordinate all software releases, including programming, distribution, manual compilation, printing, and testing of the software and the accompanying manual. Currently, you are coordinating a new software package to be distributed in September 2006. To ensure that the software and manual are both ready, you need to set some constraints. The programming, testing, and editorial staff must have 6 weeks to work on each beta of the software.

To set constraints, complete the following steps:

1. Open *EPr1_0503* and save the file as **Software_Manual**.
2. Double-click Task 9 (*Second beta software available*), and then select the Advanced tab.
3. Under *Constrain task,* click the *Deadline* drop-down arrow.
4. Select *June 30, 2006,* and then click OK.
5. Select Task 15 (*Final software available*) and click Task Information on the Standard toolbar.
6. Set the Deadline date to *Tues 8/1/06,* and then click OK.
7. Save *Software_Manual* and leave it open for the next exercise.

2. Modifying Task Information

As you look over your project file, you realize that the resource information needs modification. Specifically, the Programmers resource represents five programmers, the Technical Writers resource represents two writers, and the Software Testers resource represents three testers. The work shown is inaccurate. You must change the assignment units to correctly reflect the work.

To modify task information, complete the following steps:

1. Open **Software_Manual**, *if necessary.*
2. Choose View, Task Usage; then drag the split bar between the Task Usage table and the bar chart to the right until the Finish column is displayed.
3. Double-click Task 3 (*Software tested*).
4. Click the Resources tab and then click in the first Units cell.
5. Click the up-spinner until *300%* displays; then click OK.
6. Click the smart tag drop-down arrow and select the second option.

7. Continue editing the assignment units as follows (leave the duration constant):

Task ID	Task Name	Resource	Unit
4	Make changes in software	Programmers	500%
7	Walk-through of software	Technical Writers	200%
11	Verify steps in draft manual	Technical Writers	200%
16	Final run-through of steps	Technical Writers;	200%
		Technical Editor	50%

8. Save *Software_Manual* and leave it open for the next exercise.

3. Checking Spelling and Saving a Baseline

Now the project file is almost complete. You just need to check the spelling in the tasks and save a baseline for future reference.

To check spelling and save a baseline, complete the following steps:

1. Open *Software_Manual*, if necessary, and then choose View, Gantt Chart.

2. Press Ctrl+Home and then choose Tools, Spelling.

   The first error is the word *Distribue* in Task 25.

3. Click Change.

   The next error is *Readme* in Task 28, which is not actually an error.

4. Click Ignore.

5. Click Track on the Project Guide toolbar.

6. Click the first link, *Save a baseline plan to compare with later versions.*

7. Click Save Baseline and then click Done.

8. Close the Track side pane, save *Software_Manual,* and leave it open for the next exercise.

4. Entering Percent Complete

Now, the project is under way. Some of the tasks have been partially completed. You need to enter the appropriate data to track the progress of the project.

To enter percent complete, work through the following steps:

1. Open *Software_Manual*, if necessary.

2. Double-click Task 2 (*Distribute beta to writers and testers*), and then click the General tab.

3. Click the *Percent complete* up-spinner until *100%* displays, and then click OK.

4. Double-click Task 1 (*Software beta available*) to see the percent complete, and then click OK.

5. Select the task name for Task 3 (*Software tested*), and then choose Insert, Column.

6. Click the *Field name* drop-down arrow.

7. Scroll to the top of the list and select *% Complete*.

8. Click OK.

9. Click in the % Complete column for Task 3 (*Software tested*); then click the up-spinner to *30%* and press ↵Enter.

10. Complete the remaining percent complete values as shown in the following table:

TaskID	Task Name	% Complete
4	Make changes in software	25%
6	Read through programmers' notes	66%
7	Walk-through of software	66%

11. Save *Software_Manual* and leave it open for the next exercise.

5. Entering Actuals

With the project under way, it is time to enter actual data. Management has decided to reduce the amount of time allotted for testing the software to be sure the programmers have the time necessary to update the software. Also, during the first week of updates, there were only four programmers working on the task rather than five.

To enter actuals, complete the following steps:

1. Open *Software_Manual*, if necessary.

2. Select Task 3 (*Software tested*), and then point to the progress bar in the Task 3 Gantt bar to see the progress of the task.

3. Choose View, More Views.

4. Scroll down and select *Task Sheet* and then click Apply.

5. Choose View, Table: Entry, and Tracking.

6. Right-click the Rem. Dur. (Remaining Duration) heading, and then choose *Insert Column*.

7. Click the *Field name* drop-down arrow; then select *Duration* and click OK.

8. Click in the Duration column of Task 3; click the down-spinner to *5 weeks* and press ↵Enter.

   The remaining duration and actual duration values adjust to reflect the new Duration.

9. Click on the smart tag and select the first option.

10. Click in the Act. Work (Actual Work) column for Task 4 (*Make changes to software*).

11. Type **260** and press ↵Enter.

   The Actual Cost amount adjusts for the change in work.

12. Save *Software_Manual* and leave it open for the next exercise.

6. Specifying Lead and Lag Times

When programming or updating software, flexibility is essential at particular junctions. The software manual schedule must be flexible at points as well. A few tasks in your project plan are flexible in their links. You need to add lead and lag times to these tasks.

To create lead and lag times, complete the following steps:

1. Open *Software_Manual,* if necessary; then choose <u>V</u>iew, <u>G</u>antt Chart.

2. Shorten the Task Name column; then drag the split bar between the task table and Gantt chart until the Predecessors column displays.

3. Double-click Task 21 (*Choose three prototypes for manual cover*), and then click the Predecessors tab.

4. Click in the Lag column; type **6** and then click OK.

5. Double-click Task 27 (*Hyperlink on web page to manual*); type **7** in the Lag column and then click OK.

6. Double-click Task 28 (*Create Readme file for any update*); type **-3** in the Lag column and then click OK.

7. Save *Software_Manual* and close the file.

CHALLENGE

Challenge exercises expand on or are somewhat related to skills presented in the lessons. Each exercise provides a brief narrative introduction, followed by instructions in a numbered-step format that are not as detailed as those in the Skill Drill section.

You should complete the four exercises in sequence.

1. Using Spell Check and Replacing a Resource

You are managing a direct mail marketing campaign and are utilizing a template from the online Microsoft Template Gallery for the project. You have modified the tasks to fit the overall project at your own company and have set up the basic project information. Your job is to take this existing plan and finalize everything in it so that you can begin tracking overall project progress, some of which has already begun.

To check spelling and replace a resource, complete the following steps:

1. Open *EPr1_0504* and save it as **Direct_Market**; then close any open side panes.

2. Spell-check and correct any spelling errors in the project file. Note: Do not change the words *marcom* and *Ardis.*

    A few of the tasks list a person's name for the Resource Name rather than the position title, which you need to correct.

3. Use Find and look in the Name field to locate all instances of the name *Patty Ardis,* writing down the Task ID # for each instance.

4. Open the Assign Resources dialog box and for each task assigned to Patty Ardis, replace *Patty Ardis* with **Media Planner**.

5. Use Replace and look in the Name field to locate all instances of the word *vertical* and replace it with nothing (to delete the word).

6. Save *Direct_Market* and leave it open for the next exercise.

2. Changing Resource Assignment Units and Saving and Viewing the Baseline

Now that you have cleaned up the tasks in your project, you need to work on the resources. Next, you need to save and print the project file baseline.

To change resources assignment units and save a baseline, complete the following steps:

1. Open *Direct_Market* if necessary, and then close any open side panes.

2. Switch to Task Usage view and select Task 32 (*Determine sales monies and calculate ROI*).

3. Change the Resource units to reflect two people working full-time on this task.

4. Choose the smart tag option to reduce the duration to 2.5 days.

5. Change the Resource Units value for Task 33 (*Compile final counts and summaries*) to reflect two people working full-time on this task, and choose the smart tag option to reduce the duration to 5 days.

6. Switch to Gantt Chart view and save a baseline for the file.

7. Use Help to learn how to view the baseline; then display the baseline and print it for future reference.

8. Save *Direct_Market* and leave it open for the next exercise.

3. Specifying Lag and Lead Time and Entering Percent Complete

Now that you have a basically sound project file, you can update the file with the progress reports that you have been receiving from the team members assigned to the project.

To specify lag and lead time and enter percent complete, complete the following steps:

1. Open *Direct_Market*, if necessary, and specify a 3-day lag for Task 13 (*Review first article samples, artwork, and drafts*).

2. Specify a 2-day lag for Task 17 (*Review and approve direct mail piece*).

3. Specify a 1-day lead for Task 4 (*Segment by industry or market*).

4. Using the Tracking toolbar, update the following tasks with the appropriate percent complete:

Task ID	Task Name	Percent Complete
3	Establish targeted markets	75%
4	Segment by industry or market	100%
5	Quantify total available market	50%
6	Define served available market	50%
10	Solicit designs from marcom vendors	25%
11	Select vendor and design	50%
12	Make format, quantity, and cost decisions for media	50%
20	Select initial markets	50%

5. Print a Current Activities report that shows tasks in progress.

6. Save *Direct_Market* and leave it open for the next exercise.

4. Entering Actual Progress Data

Once resources have been assigned to their tasks, you will need to track their progress.

To enter task progress, complete the following steps:

1. Open *Direct_Market* if necessary, and switch to Task Sheet view.

2. Switch from the Entry table to the Tracking table.

3. For Task 4 (*Segment by industry or market*), update the actual duration to 4 days.

4. For Task 5 (*Quantify total available market*), you received an update from the resources assigned to it, informing you that it will require 2 days to complete this task, not half a day. Update Task 5 to make the Actual duration 2 days .

5. You received another update from the resources assigned to Task 10 (*Solicit designs from marcom vendors*), informing you that this task is complete. Update Task 10 to reflect its completion.

6. You received an e-mail from the resource assigned to Task 20 (*Select initial markets*) stating, "Market survey data is not progressing as planned, due to a software upgrade delay. This job will require 3 more days to accurately compute the survey results." Update Task 20 to add 3 more days to the actual duration.

7. You received an e-mail from the resource assigned to Task 25 (*Enter prospects into customer relationship management database*), stating, "Shelly is no longer working on this project and it has been assigned to someone else. Please allow transition time for our new recruit." Update Task 25 to show a total of 15 days in the remaining column.

8. Switch to Gantt Chart view, and then print a Project Summary overview report.

9. Save *Direct_Market* and then close the file.

DISCOVERY ZONE

Discovery Zone exercises require advanced knowledge of topics presented in *Essentials* lessons, application of skills from multiple lessons, or self-directed learning of new skills. The exercises are independent of each other, so you may complete them in any order.

1. Learning About Project Tracking Online

Now that you have established basic proficiency in using Microsoft Project, you should explore more topics about tracking as well as creating progress reports for the different team members working on a project.

From the Help menu, choose Microsoft Project Help and then click the *Get the latest news about using Project* hyperlink. From the Microsoft Project 2003 Web page, locate the Tracking Progress topic and click on the *Updating Actuals* hyperlink. Read the various topics by clicking on each of the article hyperlinks.

2. Working with Views

Create a new project from any existing template located either online or on your computer, and save it as **View_Options**. Take a closer look at the View, More View options and apply each view to the project file you created. Explore the Table views in conjunction with the different views. Create a view using both view options that will show the tasks assigned to each resource and the amount of completed work and the amount of remaining work by task. Print the table.

MODIFYING TASKS USING THE GANTT CHART

OBJECTIVES

IN THIS PROJECT, YOU LEARN HOW TO

- **Add a progress line to a Gantt chart**

- **Remove task dependencies**

- **Reschedule uncompleted work**

- **Modify and remove a split**

- **Use Tracking Gantt view to analyze the critical path**

- **Check overall project progress**

WHY WOULD I DO THIS?

When working with a project plan, you must constantly check the overall status of the project. Recall from Project 1 the project triangle, which consists of the three main elements of a project: time, budget, and scope. Once your project is under way, you need to periodically check that the project goals (especially the final finish date for the entire project) are attainable, that the budget is within limits, what tasks are in progress, what tasks are not yet started, and what tasks are complete. Microsoft Project provides several tools that enable critical analysis as well as several views that provide project summary data. Once you have looked at this information, you can then decide on whatever actions are needed to adjust the project plan. You can also determine which specific tasks impact the project finish date so you can reschedule uncompleted work if necessary. In addition, there are summary reports that provide general statistics regarding the project triangle so you can distribute this information to the project team.

VISUAL SUMMARY

In this project, you are initiating an advertising campaign for the apartment complex you manage. It involves print advertising in several trade journals as well as several popular apartment advertising Web sites. You have created a project plan for this campaign to help you keep track of deliverables required for each periodical. Several of the lessons in this project involve using the Gantt chart to examine the project plan. In addition, you use several methods to adjust the Gantt bars to reschedule work.

To track the progress of your project, you view Project Statistics, print a Project Summary Report and view the critical tasks as shown in Figure 6.1. A ***critical task*** is one that, in combination with its predecessors, drives the overall finish date for the entire project.

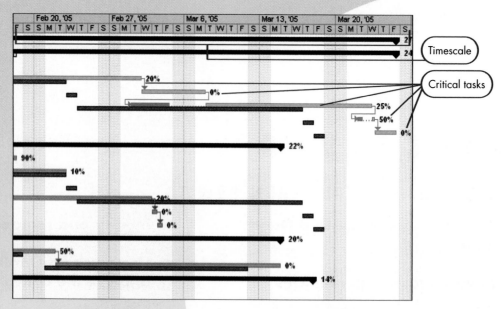

FIGURE 6.1

LESSON 1: Adding a Progress Line to a Gantt Chart

A *progress line* is a vertical line added to the Gantt chart on a particular date of interest. It is a visual representation of the status of your project plan at that time. The intention is to draw your eyes quickly to those tasks that are either behind or ahead of schedule.

A progress line is set for a specific date (the *progress date*), which can be the current date (computer clock) or the status date and is user-specified in the Progress Information dialog box. The progress line appears in red and runs vertically from the timescale at the top of the Gantt chart. It contains spikes for tasks behind or ahead of schedule (see Figure 6.2). You can read the direction of the spikes to gauge the approximate status of work. Spikes that run to the left indicate work that is behind schedule, and spikes that run to the right indicate work that is ahead of schedule. Recall that work is the number of hours required by a resource to complete a task, not the task duration. Note that all tasks that are behind or ahead of schedule in relation to the status date are marked with a red diamond inside a circle.

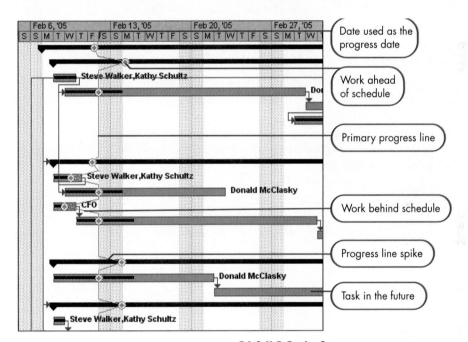

FIGURE 6.2

The distance from the primary progress line to the spike indicates the degree to which the task is ahead or behind schedule as of the specified date. For example, if a task is incomplete and behind schedule, the progress line connects to the end of the progress bar in that task's Gantt bar. Remember, the progress bar is the black bar located within each task Gantt bar that represents the percent complete. If a task with a start date in the past has no work completed, the progress line connects to the task start date. If a task is ahead of schedule, the progress line spikes on the summary task Gantt bar for that subtask, not on the actual task Gantt bar itself. The progress line ignores any past tasks that are complete or any future tasks that have not begun. Therefore, the progress line solely points out the tasks that are behind or ahead of schedule. Also, you can add multiple progress lines to a Gantt chart. The primary progress line appears in red and additional progress lines appear in black.

Summary tasks are also included in the progress line spikes. When considering progress lines in relation to summary tasks, keep in mind that progress lines are drawn down the Gantt chart based on a task's cumulative percent complete up to the date you specify. Summary tasks show the overall percent complete of the group of subtasks demoted beneath it; thus a spike may be drawn to a summary Gantt bar if any of its subtasks are ahead or behind schedule.

In this lesson, you are working to initiate an apartment advertising campaign that utilizes several trade journals and a couple of popular advertising Web sites. You add a progress line to the Gantt chart to determine which tasks are falling behind and which are ahead of schedule.

To Add Progress Lines to a Gantt Chart

1 Open the *EPr1_0601* file and save it as **Ad_Campaign**; then close any open side panes.

2 Drag the split bar between the task table and the Gantt chart to the left until only the Task Name column displays in the task table.

3 Choose <u>P</u>roject, <u>P</u>roject Information.
The Project Information dialog box opens (see Figure 6.3). Notice that the Status Date is *Fri 2/11/05*. You use this date to track progress of the project to date.

FIGURE 6.3

4 Click Cancel.

5 Choose <u>T</u>ools, <u>O</u>ptions, and click the Calculation tab.

6 Under Calculation options for, check the Edits to total task % <u>c</u>omplete will be spread to the status date check box, and then click OK.
Setting this option causes the progress line to denote specific tasks that are ahead of schedule, not just summary tasks, when the percent complete is updated.

7 Choose <u>T</u>ools, Trac<u>k</u>ing, Progress <u>L</u>ines.
The Progress Lines dialog box opens (see Figure 6.4).

8 On the Dates and Intervals tab, check the *Always display cu<u>r</u>rent progress line* check box.
The two date options become active. You can create a progress line to compare the current status of the project to either the current date or a status date. In this case, you want to compare progress to the status date.

FIGURE 6.4

9 Verify that the *At project status date* option is active; then look at the two options near the lower-right corner of the dialog box (refer to Figure 6.4).
You can compare the progress of the project to the actual data or to the baseline.

10 Under the *Display progress lines in relation to* section, select *Actual plan*, if necessary, and then click OK.
A vertical red progress line displays on the Gantt chart located on the date Feb 11,'05, the project status date (see Figure 6.5). If necessary to help visualize the progress, draw an imaginary line down the chart between Friday and Saturday where the primary progress line pivots or shows the spikes running to the left or to the right.

The left-pointing spikes denote specific tasks that are behind schedule; however, subtasks that are ahead of schedule are denoted by the right-pointing spike on the corresponding summary task Gantt bar. Spikes do not appear on subtasks that are ahead of schedule until you update the percent complete field for that specific task. Notice a diamond within a circle shape on the summary task that automatically marks the progress of the subtasks below.

M'SOFT 6

FIGURE 6.5

If you have problems . . .

You may need to use the horizontal scrollbar to display Feb 11, '05.

---

11   **View the progress line at Task 12 (*Sign contract*).**
Notice that the progress line is angled to the left from the original progress line, indicating work that is behind schedule (refer to Figure 6.5).

12   **View the progress line at Task 16 (*Fall 2006 covers submitted*).**
Notice that the progress line is angled to the right, indicating work that is ahead of schedule. Recall that this is a summary task, and the fact that it is ahead of schedule indicates at least some subtasks below it are ahead of schedule as well (refer to Figure 6.5).

13   **In the Gantt chart, click the Task 11 (*Determine contract*) Gantt bar, and then click Task Information.**
The Task Information dialog box opens (see Figure 6.6). The task is currently 30% complete.

FIGURE 6.6

14 **In the *Percent complete* box, change the number to *50%* and click OK.**
Notice that the relatively straight line is now angled to the right, indicating the task is ahead of schedule (see Figure 6.7).

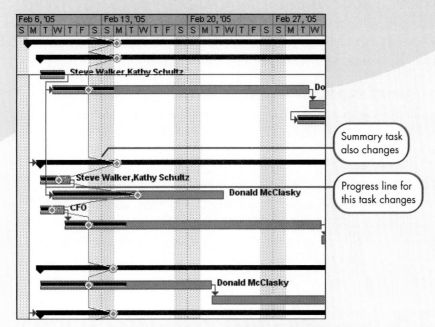

FIGURE 6.7

15 **Click Undo to view the change in the progress line; then click Redo to change the task completion back to 50%.**

16 **Choose Tools, Tracking, Progress Lines.**
The Progress Lines dialog box opens.

M'SOFT 6

17 Clear the *Always display current progress lines* check box, and then click **OK**.
The red progress line disappears from the Gantt chart and is hidden from view.

18 Save *Ad_Campaign*.
Keep the *Ad_Campaign* project file open and continue with the next lesson. If you prefer to complete the project later, close the file and exit Microsoft Project.

TO EXTEND YOUR KNOWLEDGE . . .

CREATING A PROGRESS LINE BY USING THE TRACKING TOOLBAR
You can also add progress lines to your Gantt chart from the Tracking toolbar. Click Add Progress Line on the Tracking toolbar. A popup displays and your mouse pointer displays as a progress line icon. Then click on the date for comparison. You can add multiple progress lines as well.

DISPLAYING PROGRESS LINES AT REGULAR INTERVALS
You may desire to track the progress of a project plan at regular intervals. To do so, select Tools, Tracking, Progress Lines. Check *Display progress lines at recurring intervals*. Then select the type of occurrence or specific date.

TRACKING PROGRESS IN THE TASK TABLE
You can also add the Status field to the task table to see which tasks are on schedule, behind schedule, or complete. To add the status field to the task table, choose Insert, Column and select Status from the *Field name* list box.

COMPARING PROGRESS TO THE BASELINE
You can also compare the progress of the project to the baseline if you have saved one. To do so, choose Tools, Tracking, Progress Lines. Select *Baseline plan* as the data to compare to.

DELETING PROGRESS LINES
To remove additional progress lines that you have added to the file, choose Tools, Tracking, Progress Lines. Select the Dates and Intervals tab. In the *Progress Line Dates* area, select the progress line you want to delete and click Delete; then click OK.

LESSON 2: Removing Task Dependencies

At times, you may determine that a link between two or more tasks is no longer necessary. For example, in the *Ad_Campaign* project file you may find that the *Front cover submission* task is not necessarily dependent upon the completion of the *Standard Insertion Ad Full Color* task. If you decide that a task dependency is unnecessary, you can **unlink** (or remove) the dependency. When you unlink a task, the start date of the task is no longer dependent upon another task's start or finish date; therefore, the task's start date becomes the same as the project start date.

Making this type of an adjustment to your project plan can have positive results on the overall finish date for the project.

In this lesson, you remove task dependencies for several tasks that do not depend on one another for task completion. The *Determine contract* task is not necessarily dependent upon the *Standard Insertion Ad Full Color* task for both trade magazines, so you remove the task link. Likewise, there should be no link between the *Contract* task and the *Platinum property package* task. All of these links are removed by using the Unlink Tasks button or the Predecessors column in the task table.

To Remove Task Dependencies

1 **Open *Ad_Campaign*, if necessary, and scroll to the right until you can view the Task 8 (*Front cover submission*) Gantt bar and click on it.**
Clicking on a task bar is not necessary to remove a dependency but is helpful to visually locate the task with which you are working.

2 **With your mouse pointer, pause on the Gantt bar for Task 8 and view the Task ScreenTip.**
Note the start date of Wed 3/23/05. Also note that there are two join lines coming to Task 8 (see Figure 6.8).

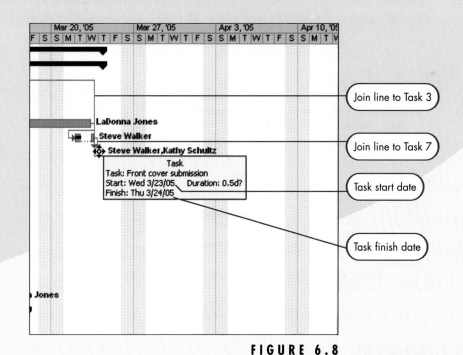

FIGURE 6.8

3 **Pause the mouse pointer on each join line to view the Link ScreenTip.**
There are Finish-to-Start links with Tasks 3 (*Standard Insertion Ad Full Color*) and 7 (*Photo page submission*) (see Figure 6.9), implying that Task 8 cannot start until these

tasks are completed. It is not necessary, however, to wait for both tasks to be completed before beginning work on this task, so you change the dependency.

FIGURE 6.9

 4 **Click Unlink Tasks on the Standard Toolbar.**
Notice that the join lines are removed from the Gantt chart and Task 8 is no longer visible in the area of the Gantt chart you are viewing.

5 **Scroll left until you locate Task 8 and read the Task ScreenTip.**
Task 8 is no longer linked to Task 3 or Task 7 (see Figure 6.10). The start date changes from Wed 3/23/05 to Mon 2/7/05, which is the project start date. Using the Unlink Tasks button removes all links to a task. However, this is not what you want to happen. A link is necessary to Task 7, but not to Task 3.

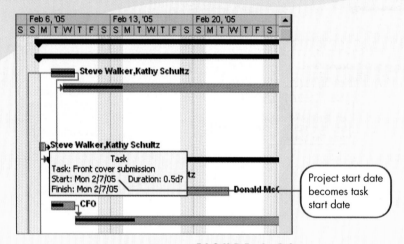

FIGURE 6.10

6 **Click Undo.**
Task 8 is once again linked to both Tasks 3 and 7.

7 **Click Task Information on the Standard Toolbar, and then click the Predecessors tab.**
The two links to Task 8 are listed (see Figure 6.11). To unlink only one task rather than all tasks, you must use the Task Information dialog box instead.

FIGURE 6.11

8 Click on Task 3 in the *Predecessors* list; press Del and then click OK.
Task 8 remains linked to Task 7, but the link to Task 3 is removed.

9 Point to the Task 11 (*Determine contract*) Gantt bar and read the Task ScreenTip.

If you have problems . . .

Be sure to point to the portion of the Gantt bar that does not contain the progress bar, which appears as a black bar within the blue Gantt bar, to successfully view the Task ScreenTip. When working with a Gantt bar, two ScreenTips can be viewed; the Progress ScreenTip appears when you point at the progress bar, and the Task ScreenTip appears when you point at any part of the Gantt bar except the progress bar.

---

10 Point to the join line and read the ScreenTip.
The join to Task 3 (*Standard Insertion Ad Full Color*) and Task 10 (*Standard Insertion Ad Full Color*) must be removed.

11 Click the Task 11 Gantt bar and then click Unlink Tasks.
The links to Tasks 3 and 10 are gone.

12 Save *Ad_Campaign.*
Keep the *Ad_Campaign* project file open and continue with the next lesson. If you prefer to complete the project later, close the file and exit Microsoft Project.

ALTER TASK DEPENDENCIES IN THE GANTT CHART

Task dependencies are also easily removed from the Gantt chart. To remove a task dependency or modify it, double-click the join line between two tasks on the Gantt chart. The Task Dependency dialog box opens. You can choose a different type of dependency or select None to remove the task dependency.

LESSON 3:   Rescheduling Uncompleted Work

Sometimes another task becomes more critical and resources must be reassigned temporarily. Rescheduling uncompleted work is also useful for those times when a resource cannot complete a task as scheduled or when other interruptions occur and you want to have as little impact on the overall finish date of the project as possible. For example, suppose a resource is working on a task when a business trip becomes necessary. That resource cannot work on the task during the business trip and thus there is a delay in task completion. The task can be split to allow completion around the business trip.

One alternative to rescheduling work is to literally create two tasks from the existing task, tracking each task individually. However, keep in mind that by creating two tasks, you have an additional item to track and monitor in the plan. A *split* task is one that has a time delay within it, therefore creating two or more segments. Splitting a task is the same as rescheduling work. To reschedule work in the Gantt chart, you right-click at the beginning of the incomplete portion of the task displayed in the Gantt bar, and follow onscreen instructions to split the task.

When rescheduling work, the task is split at the point where the completed portion of the task stops and the incomplete portion begins. You specify the date on which you want to resume work on the unfinished portion of the task. Splitting a task does not extend the duration but does change the finish date. A task can be split as many times as needed. Once a task is split, you can modify its duration, start date, and finish date. Even though a task is split into two or more bars, it still appears as one line item in the task table. The new start date for the rescheduled portion of a task is the ***resume date.*** The length of the split depends on the timescale used in the project file. If the timescale is days, a split is equal to one day. If the timescale is in hours, the split is equal to one hour. The length of the split is one unit by default, whether days or hours, but it can be lengthened, if necessary. The assigned resume date depends on whether you use the manual or automatic method for rescheduling work. Using the automatic rescheduling feature, the resume date is one unit (day, in most costs) after the status date. However, when manually rescheduling work, the resume date is specified by the user.

In this lesson, you first reschedule uncompleted work for Task 4 (*Determine contract*) because the resource requires additional days to negotiate the contract. You use the Split Task button on the Standard toolbar to complete this action. Next, you reschedule uncompleted work using the Reschedule Work button on the Tracking Toolbar.

To Manually Reschedule Uncompleted Work

1 Open *Ad_Campaign,* if necessary.

2 On the Gantt chart, point to the Task 4 (*Determine contract*) Gantt bar.
The Task ScreenTip appears. Note the start date of Wed 2/9/05 and the finish date of Tue 3/1/05. The duration is 15 days.

3 Click the Task 4 Gantt bar.
Clicking on the Task 4 bar is not necessary to reschedule work but is helpful to visually locate the task with which you are working.

4 Click Split Task on the Standard toolbar.
The Split Task information box displays, and the mouse appears as a split task pointer shape.

5 Point to the end of the progress bar in the Gantt bar.
The date in the ScreenTip is Mon 2/14/05 (see Figure 6.12).

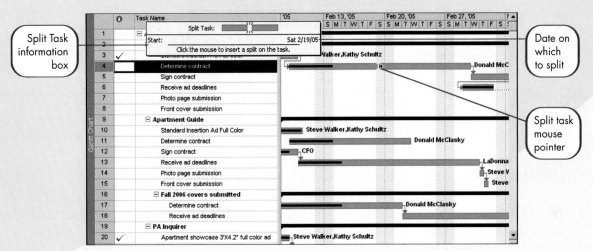

FIGURE 6.12

6 Move the mouse to the right 1/8″ on the Gantt bar.
Notice that the date in the Split Task information box changes. As you move your mouse horizontally on the Gantt bar, the date in the Split Task information box changes according to the location on the Gantt bar. The date shown in the Split Task information box is one unit (in this case, one day) prior than the proposed resume date.

7 Move the mouse on the Gantt bar until Wed *2/16/05* displays, and then click the Gantt bar.
The task is now split on Wed 2/16/05, with a dotted line linking the two Gantt bars (see Figure 6.13). Wednesday becomes a pause in work for this task, and a portion of the task is rescheduled to begin on Thursday.

M'SOFT 6

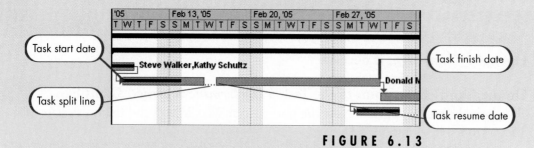

FIGURE 6.13

8 **Point to the split line to read the Split ScreenTip.**

The split (pause in work) begins on Tue 2/15/05 and ends on Thu 2/17/05, thus there is a one day pause in work: Wednesday.

9 **Point to the left-most Gantt bar for Task 4.**

Read the Task ScreenTip and note that the resume date of Wed 2/9/05 remains the same as before, but the finish date is now Tue 2/15/05 for this segment of the task (see Figure 6.14).

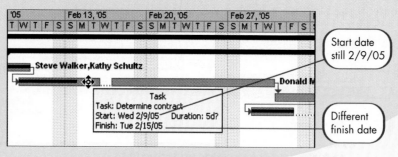

FIGURE 6.14

10 **Pause the mouse on the right-most Gantt bar for Task 4.**

The Task ScreenTip appears (see Figure 6.15). Notice that the resume date is Thu 2/17/05 and the finish date is Wed 3/2/05, which is one day later than the original finish date of Tue 3/1/05. There is now a one day pause in work for the completion of this task.

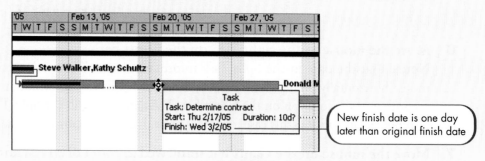

FIGURE 6.15

In addition to manually rescheduling uncompleted work, you can also use the Tracking toolbar and Microsoft Project automatically reschedules uncompleted work for a task. This feature automatically sets the resume date of the unfinished portion of the task to one day (unit) past the status date, making the status date where the pause in work occurs.

To Automatically Reschedule Uncompleted Work

1 Choose <u>V</u>iew, <u>T</u>oolbars, Tracking.

2 Point to the Task 10 (*Standard Insertion Ad Full Color*) Gantt bar and read the Task ScreenTip.

Notice the start date of Tue 2/8/05, the finish date of Thu 2/10/05, and the duration of 2.5 days (see Figure 6.16). Recall that the status date is Fri 2/11/05.

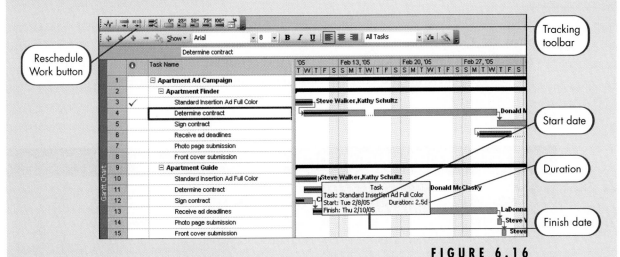

FIGURE 6.16

3 Click the Task 10 Gantt bar.

4 Click Reschedule Work on the Tracking toolbar.

The task automatically splits, adding one working day to the duration (see Figure 6.17).

FIGURE 6.17

5 Pause the mouse on the second Gantt bar for Task 10.

The Task ScreenTip appears (see Figure 6.18). Notice the new finish date of Mon 2/14/05. When using the automatic rescheduling feature, Microsoft Project selects the day after the status date as the resume date. Because the status date is a Friday, the next day is nonworking time. Monday 2/14/05 is the next working day, thus the resume date.

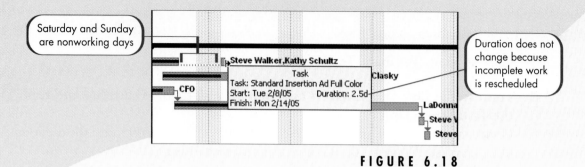

Saturday and Sunday are nonworking days

Steve Walker,Kathy Schultz

Task
Task: Standard Insertion Ad Full Color
Start: Tue 2/8/05   Duration: 2.5d
Finish: Mon 2/14/05

Clasky

CFO

LaDonna

Steve

Steve

Duration does not change because incomplete work is rescheduled

FIGURE 6.18

6 **Save** *Ad_Campaign.*

Keep the *Ad_Campaign* project file open and continue with the next lesson. If you prefer to complete the project later, close the file and exit Microsoft Project.

TO EXTEND YOUR KNOWLEDGE . . .

RESCHEDULING UNCOMPLETED WORK FOR THE ENTIRE PROJECT

Choose <u>T</u>ools, Trac<u>k</u>ing, Update <u>P</u>roject. Click *Reschedule uncompleted work to start after* and then type or select the date after which you want to reschedule all remaining work. Select the *En<u>t</u>ire project* option button and then click OK.

LESSON 4:   Modifying and Removing a Split

Sometimes, the schedule of a task alters so that it is no longer necessary to reschedule uncompleted work. For example, you may split a task because of an unexpected business trip that is removing the resource assigned to that task, but then the trip gets canceled. You may also simply find that rescheduling the uncompleted work does not have the results that you prefer. In either case, you can easily remove the split.

When you add a split to a task, Microsoft Project adds one unit to the task duration. In other words, if the project file utilizes Days in the timescale, splitting a task adds one day to the task schedule. However, there are times when you need to add more than one day between the complete and remaining work of a task that has been split. Microsoft Project provides a simple way to make changes and even remove a split from a task. You can check the resume date for the uncompleted part of the task by inserting the Resume field in the table portion of the Gantt chart, or you can drag the end of the uncompleted task Gantt bar to extend the duration.

In this lesson, you remove the split that you added to Task 4 (*Determine contract*) because it is no longer necessary. Then, you increase the delay of one day between the completed and uncompleted portions of Task 10 (*Standard Insertion Ad Full Color*) to provide additional time for the resource to resume work on Task 10.

To Modify and Remove a Split

1 Open *Ad_Campaign*, if necessary.

2 Click the left-most edge of the second Gantt bar of Task 4 (*Determine contract*).
The mouse becomes a four-way sizing arrow (see Figure 6.19).

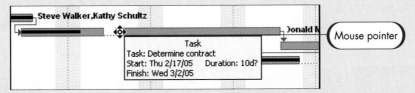

FIGURE 6.19

3 Drag the left edge of the Gantt bar until it is flush with the right-most edge of the first Gantt bar for Task 4.
The split is removed from this task (see Figure 6.20).

FIGURE 6.20

4 Point to the Task 4 Gantt bar and read the Task ScreenTip.
Microsoft Project removes the split on Task 4 and the finish date is now Tue 3/1/05, which was the original date (see Figure 6.21).

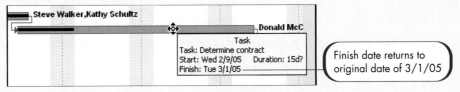

FIGURE 6.21

5 Locate Task 10, point to the second Gantt bar, and read the Task ScreenTip.

6 With the four-way arrow, drag the left-most edge of the second Gantt bar to the right until *Fri 2/18/05* appears in the popup.
The resume date for the second portion of Task 10 changes to Fri 2/18/05.

7 Save *Ad_Campaign*.
Keep the *Ad_Campaign* project file open and continue with the next lesson. If you prefer to complete the project later, close the file and exit Microsoft Project.

M'SOFT 6

TO EXTEND YOUR KNOWLEDGE . . .

ADDING THE RESUME FIELD TO THE TASK TABLE
You can check the resume date for the uncompleted part of a split task by inserting the Resume field in the table portion of the Gantt Chart. To insert the Resume field, choose <u>I</u>nsert, <u>C</u>olumn and select *Resume* from the *Field <u>N</u>ame* list box and then click OK.

LESSON 5: Using Tracking Gantt View to Analyze the Critical Path

The *critical path* represents a task and all of its predecessors as indicated by join lines on the Gantt chart (or even a single task) that dictate the overall finish date of your project plan. Each task that comprises the critical path is called a *critical task*. The terms can be a bit misleading because the critical path and its critical tasks do not necessarily represent the most important tasks in your project plan. Instead, Microsoft Project automatically chooses one task because it has a finish date that is the same as the project finish date. The finish date of this task, along with any of its predecessors, determines the critical tasks and thus the critical path. When the last task in the critical path is complete, the project is complete. It is useful to know which tasks comprise the critical path, as this lets you determine which tasks can affect your project's finish date and whether your project finishes on time.

As you know, Microsoft Project provides various views that can be customized to help keep track of the various components of a project plan. Critical tasks are best viewed in the *Tracking Gantt view,* which displays a baseline Gantt bar beneath the current Gantt bar and highlights the critical tasks by displaying them in red. The Tracking Gantt view allows the user to compare actuals to baseline data and thus differs from the usual Gantt chart you have seen. The baseline Gantt bars are gray, while the task Gantt bars display in color.

In this lesson, you use the Tracking Gantt view along with the Variance task table view to compare the baseline to actuals. You also see the critical path of this project plan and modify the duration of one critical task to extend the project finish date.

To Analyze the Critical Path

1 Open *Ad_Campaign,* if necessary.

2 Select <u>V</u>iew, Tracking Ga<u>n</u>tt.

If you have problems . . .

If you do not see Gantt bars in the Tracking Gantt view, use the horizontal scrollbar to scroll to the right until *Feb 6, '05* appears in the timescale.

3 **Select <u>V</u>iew, Ta<u>b</u>le: Entry, <u>V</u>ariance.**

The Tracking Gantt chart displays (see Figure 6.22).

FIGURE 6.22

4 **Point to the Task 1 (*Apartment Ad Campaign*) Gantt bar.**

A Summary ScreenTip appears. This task is the summary task for all the tasks in the plan, and it has a finish date of Thu 3/24/05 (see Figure 6.23).

FIGURE 6.23

5 **Point to the right side of the red Task 4 (*Determine contract*) Gantt bar.**

The Critical ScreenTip appears (see Figure 6.24). The Gantt bar is red, indicating this task is a critical task.

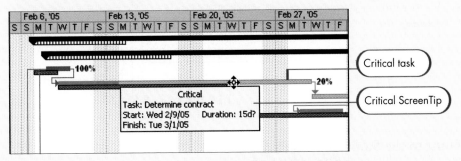

FIGURE 6.24

6 **Scroll horizontally to the right until *Mar 20, '05* is visible on the timescale.**

7 **Point to the red Task 8 (*Front cover submission*) Gantt bar.**
The Critical ScreenTip appears (see Figure 6.25). Notice that this is the last task in the critical path and it has a finish date of Thu 3/24/05, which is the same as the project finish date.

FIGURE 6.25

8 **Click the Task 8 Gantt bar and then click Task Information.**

9 **Click the General tab, and then click the *Duration* up arrow to *2 days*.**

10 **Check the *Estimated* check box, and then click OK.**
The Gantt bar lengthens and the finish date for Task 8 is now Fri 3/25/05 (see Figure 6.26).

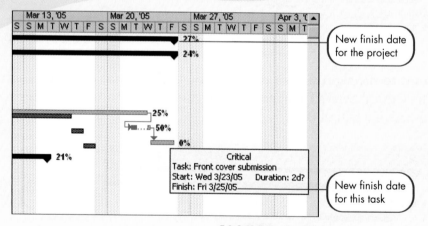

FIGURE 6.26

11 **Point to the Summary Task 1 Gantt bar.**
The Summary ScreenTip appears (see Figure 6.27). Notice the finish date for the entire project now matches the new finish date for Task 8: Fri 3/25/05.

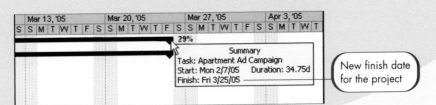

FIGURE 6.27

12 **Save** *Ad_Campaign.*

Keep the *Ad_Campaign* project file open and continue with the next lesson. If you prefer to complete the project later, close the file and exit Microsoft Project.

TO EXTEND YOUR KNOWLEDGE . . .

FILTER TASKS TO VIEW THE CRITICAL TASKS

If you want to see only the critical tasks in a project, you can filter the tasks. Click the Filter button on the Formatting toolbar and select the filter you want to apply (Critical). Alternatively, select Project, Filtered For, Critical.

LESSON 6:   Checking Overall Project Progress

At anytime, you can review the overall status and well-being of your project and compare the baseline to the actual project plan. *Project statistics* provide up-to-the-minute statistics for the overall project plan, using actual and baseline data. These data include start and finish dates, task duration, work, cost, and percent complete. You cannot make any modifications to the data here; you can only view and print it.

The *Project Summary report* outlines actual and baseline data for the overall project plan. It is good for basic project analysis and displays the most critical project information on one page. It includes the finish dates of your project plan for both the actual plan and the baseline. The report also shows task and cost data summaries and a summary of task and resource status.

Finally, the Tracking Gantt view enables you to see task progress bars compared to baseline progress bars, with the critical path appearing in red. Some of the same statistics that are in the Project Summary report also appear in the Project Statistics dialog box; however, the report is more comprehensive and includes additional detail.

In this lesson, you view the project statistics to check the progress of the project to-date. Then, you open Project Summary report to see where the project stands concerning dates, duration, work, costs, task status, and resource status. Finally, you use ScreenTips on task Gantt bars and baseline Gantt bars to check the progress of specific tasks.

To Check Overall Project Progress

1 **Open *Ad_Campaign*, if necessary, and click Project Statistics on the Tracking toolbar.**

The Project Statistics for 'Ad_Campaign.mpp' dialog box displays (see Figure 6.28). Take a moment to look at the statistics.

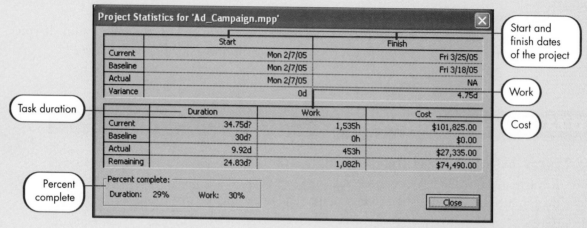

Task duration

Percent complete

Start and finish dates of the project

Work

Cost

	Start	Finish
Current	Mon 2/7/05	Fri 3/25/05
Baseline	Mon 2/7/05	Fri 3/18/05
Actual	Mon 2/7/05	NA
Variance	0d	4.75d

	Duration	Work	Cost
Current	34.75d?	1,535h	$101,825.00
Baseline	30d?	0h	$0.00
Actual	9.92d	453h	$27,335.00
Remaining	24.83d?	1,082h	$74,490.00

Percent complete:
Duration: 29%   Work: 30%

Close

FIGURE 6.28

2 **Click Close.**

You can also view and print the Project Summary report for distribution.

3 **Choose View, Reports.**

4 **Select Overview, and then click Select.**

5 **Select Project Summary, and then click Select.**

The Project Summary report opens in Print Preview (see Figure 6.29).

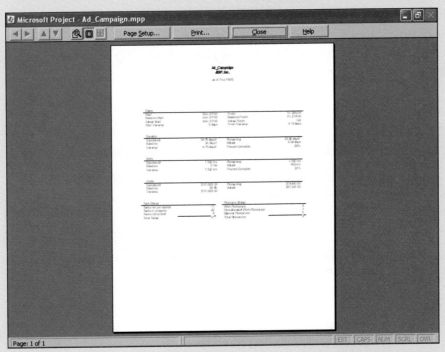

FIGURE 6.29

6 **Click in the report to magnify it.**
The report has six sections: Dates, Duration, Work, Costs, Task Status, and Resource Status (see Figure 6.30).

FIGURE 6.30

7 **Click Close on the toolbar, and then click Close in the Reports dialog box.**
The report closes and you can see the project file again.

Now that you have checked the project's progress overall, you look at individual task progress. By pointing to a Gantt bar, you can read important information about a task through a ScreenTip. In the next set of steps, you view a ScreenTip for a task Gantt bar and then compare it to the baseline Gantt bar ScreenTip.

To Check Individual Task Progress

1 **View the Task 36 (*Contract: Jan 2005-March 2006*) Gantt bar.**
Notice that it is in line with the baseline bar located below it (see Figure 6.31).

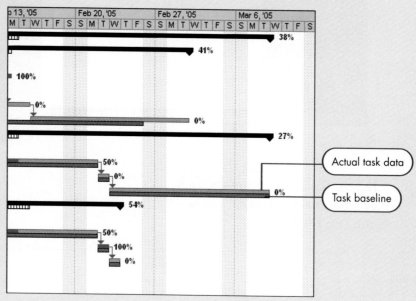

FIGURE 6.31

2 **Point to the Task 36 Gantt bar and read the Task ScreenTip.**
The start date is Wed 2/23/05, the finish date is Tue 3/8/05, and the duration is 10 days.

3 **Point to the Task 36 baseline bar and read the Baseline ScreenTip.**
The start and finish dates for both the task and the baseline are the same.

4 **View the Task 13 (*Receive ad deadlines*) Gantt bar.**
Notice that it started sooner than the baseline (see Figure 6.32).

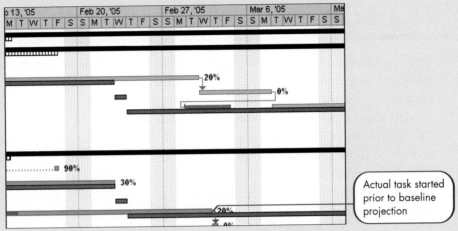

FIGURE 6.32

5 **Point to the Task 13 Gantt bar and read the Task ScreenTip.**
The start date is Thu 2/10/05, the finish date is Wed 3/2/05, and the duration is 15 days.

6 **Point to the Task 13 baseline bar and read the Baseline ScreenTip.**
The task actually started on Thu 2/10/05, while the baseline shows the taks scheduled to start on Thu 2/24/05.

7 **Point to the Task 17 Gantt bar (*Determine contract*) and read the Task ScreenTip.**
Notice that it started later than the baseline plan (see Figure 6.33).

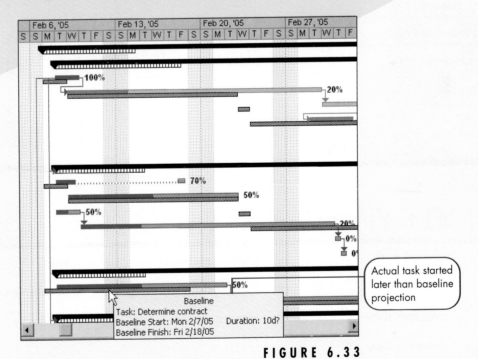

FIGURE 6.33

8 **Point to the Task 17 baseline bar and read the Baseline ScreenTip.**
Task 17 was supposed to start on Mon 2/7/05 but it actually started on Tue 2/8/05.

9 **Save the *Ad_Campaign* file, and then close it.**

SUMMARY

In this project, progress lines were added to the Gantt chart to view the overall status of those tasks that were either behind or ahead of schedule. The Gantt chart was critically analyzed to examine task dependencies, and you removed those that were no longer needed. You also learned about rescheduling uncompleted work in a task and used the manual and automatic split task features to reschedule uncompleted work. You viewed the critical path of a project and noted those tasks that comprise the critical path and drive the overall project finish date. The Project Statistics dialog box was opened, and the Project Summary report was previewed to check the overall status of the project. Finally, you learned about the Tracking Gantt view and how it is designed to enable you to check individual task status against the baseline.

You can extend your learning by reviewing concepts and terms and by practicing variations of skills presented in the lessons. Use the following table as a guide to the numbered questions and exercises in the end-of-project learning opportunities.

LESSON	MULTIPLE CHOICE	DISCUSSION	SKILL DRILL	CHALLENGE	DISCOVERY ZONE
Adding a Progress Line to a Gantt Chart	1, 3	1	1	1, 4	1
Removing Task Dependencies	5		2	2	
Rescheduling Uncompleted Work	2, 4	3	3	2	
Modifying and Removing a Split		3	3	2	
Using Tracking Gantt View to Analyze the Critical Path	6, 7	2	4	3	
Checking Overall Project Progress	8, 9, 10		4		2

KEY TERMS

critical path

critical task

progress date

progress line

project statistics

Project Summary report

resume date

split

Tracking Gantt view

unlink

CHECKING CONCEPTS AND TERMS

MULTIPLE CHOICE

Circle the letter of the correct answer for each of the following.

1. Progress lines can be added to a Gantt chart and shown in relation to what types of plans? [L1]

   a. The project status date plan

   b. The actual plan or the base plan

   c. The critical path plan

   d. All of the above

2. Where are split task actions performed? [L3]

   a. On the task table

   b. From the Task Information dialog box

   c. On the Gantt chart

   d. From the Progress Lines dialog box

3. What are progress lines? [L1]

   a. Vertical lines added to the Gantt chart that show overall project progress for a particular date

   b. Horizontal black bars that display within the Gantt bars shown in the Gantt chart

   c. Red bars that display on the Gantt chart showing the most important tasks in the project plan

   d. Horizontal lines added to the Gantt chart that show overall project progress for a particular date

4. What is the difference between modifying the finish date and splitting a task? [L3]

   a. Nothing

   b. Modifying the finish date of a task extends the finish date, while splitting a task does not modify the finish date.

   c. Splitting a task breaks the task into two or more tasks that list as one item on the task sheet but are viewed as separate bars on the Gantt chart, while modifying the finish date of a task only changes the finish date of the task.

   d. None of the above

5. When you unlink a task, what happens to the task's start date? [L2]

   a. It stays the same.

   b. It returns to the project start date.

   c. A smart tag appears and you can specify whether you want to keep the start date the same or have it reset to the project start date.

   d. It changes to the total duration subtracted from the task finish date.

M'SOFT 6

6. What is the critical path? [L5]

   a. The most important tasks in the overall project plan that comprise the majority of work

   b. Vertical red lines added to the Gantt chart to show progress for a particular date

   c. A task and all of its predecessors that dictate the overall finish date of a project

   d. The finish date of the project plan

7. What are critical tasks? [L5]

   a. The most important tasks in the overall project plan in terms of work and cost

   b. Each task that comprises the critical path

   c. The tasks that are falling behind schedule

   d. The tasks that appear in red because there is a scheduling problem

8. What type of data is viewed in the Project Statistics popup? [L6]

   a. The overall start and finish date of the project plan

   b. The start and finish date of the baseline

   c. Current duration work and cost

   d. All of the above

9. How are project statistics viewed? [L6]

   a. In the Project Information dialog box

   b. By clicking Project Statistics from the Tracking toolbar

   c. By selecting the Project Summary report

   d. Both b and c

10. Which option is *not* a valid section on the Project Summary report? [L6]

    a. Baseline

    b. Dates

    c. Duration

    d. Resource Status

DISCUSSION

1. What type of information can you obtain by viewing progress lines on the Gantt chart, and who on the project team would be interested in it? [L1]

2. Why is it important to periodically view the critical path and the individual tasks that comprise the critical path? What type of information can you obtain from the critical path, and how can it help you manage a project? [L5]

3. When rescheduling work (splitting a task), what often happens to the finish date of a split task? How could this impact the overall finish date of the entire project, and why is that important? [L3]

SKILL DRILL

Skill Drill exercises reinforce project skills. Each skill reinforced is the same, or nearly the same, as a skill presented in the project. Detailed instructions are provided in a step-by-step format. The exercises relate to a single file, and you should work them in order.

1. Adding Progress Lines

The company you work for utilizes a great many contractors. Part of your job is to study all bids and distribute the requests for proposals in a timely manner for project completion. You have a current construction bid process you are working on. You have customized your project file, and now you want to add a progress line.

To add a progress line, complete the following steps:

1. Open the *EPr1_0602* file and save it as **Request_For_Proposal**.
2. Drag the split bar between the task table and the Gantt chart to the left until only the Task Name column is displayed in the task table.
3. Choose Tools, Tracking, Progress Lines.
4. In the Progress Lines dialog box, click the Dates and Intervals tab.
5. Check the *Always display current progress lines* check box, and then select the *At project status date* option button.
6. Under *Display progress lines in relation to*, select *Actual plan* and then click OK.
7. View the progress line for Task 6 (*Define requirements*).
8. Turn off the progress lines for choosing Tools, Tracking, Progress Lines and then uncheck the *Always display current progress line* check box.
9. Click OK, save *Request_For_Proposal*, and leave it open for the next exercise.

2. Unlinking Task Dependencies

Now that you have viewed the overall project status in the *Request_For_Proposal* project plan, you modify the plan further by removing unnecessary task dependencies.

To unlink a task dependency, complete the following steps:

1. Open *Request_For_Proposal*, if necessary.
2. Select the Gantt bar for Task 5 (*Presolicitation Process*) and click Unlink Tasks on the Standard Toolbar.
3. Select the Gantt bar for Task 19 (*Receive oral and written proposals*) and click Task Information on the Standard Toolbar.
4. Select the Predecessors tab and click on Task 17 (Release RFP to industry) in the *Predecessors* list.
5. Press Del and then click OK.
6. Select the Gantt bar for Task 31 (*Debrief unsuccessful bidders*) and click Task Information on the Standard toolbar.
7. Select the Predecessors tab, if necessary; click on Task 28 (Debrief unsuccessful bidders) in the Predecessors list, press Del, and then click OK.
8. Save *Request_For_Proposal* and leave it open for the next exercise.

3. Split a Task and Modify a Split

Now, you work on tasks that are falling behind by rescheduling uncompleted work to allow extra time for delays that have come up.

To create and modify a split task, complete the following steps:

1. Open *Request_For_Proposal,* if necessary.

2. Click the Task 6 (*Define requirements*) Gantt bar and then click Split Task on the Standard Toolbar.

3. When you see the date of Mon 3/21/05 in the Split Task information box, click the Gantt bar to split the task.

   Note that the timescale unit is one week; thus, the new split is equal to one week (one unit).

4. From the Gantt chart, pause on the Task 14 (*Draft RFP*) Gantt bar, avoiding the black progress bar (your mouse becomes a four-way directional arrow) and read the Task ScreenTip.

   Note the start date of Mon 3/28/05 and the finish date of Mon 4/4/05.

5. Click the Task 14 Gantt bar and then click Split Task.

6. When you see the date of Wed 3/30/05 in the Split Task information box, click the Gantt bar to split the task.

7. Pause on the second Gantt bar for Task 14 and read the Task ScreenTip.

   Note the start date is Wed 4/6/05 and the finish date is Mon 4/11/05.

8. Drag the right edge of the second Gantt bar for Task 14 to the right until the finish date of Wed 4/13/05 appears.

9. Save *Request_For_Proposal* and leave it open for the next exercise.

4. View the Critical Path and Check Overall Project Progress

Now that you have made modifications to the project plan, you want to view the tasks that are driving the overall finish date of the project. You look at the critical path to determine the project finish date.

To view the critical path and check the overall progress of the project plan, complete the following steps:

1. Open *Request_For_Proposal,* if necessary, and then view Task 1 (*Request For Proposal Plan*).

   Notice that this is a summary task for all the tasks in the plan and that it has a finish date of Wed 6/1/05.

2. Choose View, Tracking Gantt.

3. Choose View, Table: Entry, Variance.

4. Scroll horizontally to the right until *Mar 20, '05* is visible on the timescale.

5. Locate the first critical task in the Gantt chart, which is Task 19 (Receive oral and written proposals).

6. Locate the last critical task in the Gantt chart, which is Task 31 (*Debrief unsuccessful bidders*), and read the Critical ScreenTip.

7. Choose View, Toolbars, Tracking, if necessary, to display the Tracking toolbar.

8. Click Project Statistics on the Tracking toolbar.

9. Click Close after viewing the project statistics.

10. Choose <u>V</u>iew, <u>R</u>eports, <u>O</u>verview, <u>P</u>roject Summary.

    The Project Summary report loads in Print Preview.

11. Click <u>P</u>rint, and then click OK, and then click Close.

12. If you prefer not to print, click Close on the Print Preview toolbar and then click Close again to return to Gantt chart view.

13. Save and close *Request_For_Proposal.*

CHALLENGE

Challenge exercises expand on or are somewhat related to skills presented in the lessons. Each exercise provides a brief narrative introduction, followed by instructions in a numbered-step format that are not as detailed as those in the Skill Drill section. The exercises relate to a single file, and you should work them in order.

1. Tracking Progress Against the Baseline

You are the human resources technician for a Fortune 500 bakery. Because of the vastness of the company, you have a project file that you use when orienting new employees. The orientation takes approximately two months to completely cover all issues. You have several new employees starting work in the next month, so you have updated your project file. The file has a baseline saved and you have already begun working on the orientation. Now, you need to compare what work you have done to the baseline you projected.

To track progress against baseline data, complete the following steps:

1. Open *EPr1_0603* and save it as **Orientation**; then close any open side panes.

2. Open the Project Information dialog box and note the status date.

3. Add a % Complete column in the task table and enter the percentages shown in the following table:

Task ID	Task Name	% Complete
2	New Hire Application form	100
3	Verify OPS employment form	100
4	401K savings plan	100
5	Complete 941	50
6	Emergency contact info	100
7	COBRA	50
8	Personnel Action Form	100
12	Review PPO and HMO Plans	100
13	Receive completed pkg choices	35
14	Review then submit to Benefits	50

16	Enter new hire in PeopleSoft	50
17	Update AP Dept code	90
22	Review Annual Report	20
23	Sign and return Code of Ethics	100

4. Switch to Tracking Gantt view and then choose View, Table: Entry, Variance.

5. Change the start date for Task 12 (*Review PPO and HMO plans*) to 5/23/06.

6. Choose Tools, Tracking, Progress Lines.

7. Select the option to display the progress line and to use the baseline plan for comparison.

8. Look at the progress line; then change to view the progress line using actual data.

9. View the actual progress line.

10. Turn off all progress lines.

11. Save *Orientation* and leave it open for the next exercise.

2. Modifying Task Links and Task Information

As you work with the project file, you realize that some of the tasks have dependencies that are not accurate or are not necessary. You also need to modify the schedule to allow for the Comp & Benefits Rep's one-week vacation. The vacation date is the week of June 18.

To modify a task link and task information, complete the following steps:

1. Open Orientation, if necessary, and then switch to Gantt Chart view.

2. From the Gantt chart, double-click the join line between Task 10 (*Submit the OPS PAAR form to Human Resources*) and Task 9 (*Provide copies to employee*).

3. Change the join type to Start-to-Start and close the dialog box.

4. Read the join line ScreenTip to verify the change.

5. Double-click the join line between Task 24 (*Run corporate video*) and Task 23 (*Sign and return Code of Ethics*), and then select *None* as the join type.

6. Remove the join between Task 25 (*Corporate Qtr Meeting attendance*) and Task 24 (*Run corporate video*).

7. Split Task 13 at 6/20/06 (resume date of 6/21/06), and then modify the split to resume the task on 6/26/06.

    Notice the new finish date of 7/12/06.

8. Save *Orientation* and leave it open for the next exercise.

3. Filtering Critical Tasks

Sometimes it is necessary just to view the crucial tasks in a project. You can quickly do so in Microsoft Project by filtering the tasks.

To filter critical tasks, complete the following steps:

1. Open *Orientation* and then close any open side panes, if necessary.

2. Switch to Tracking Gantt view to view the critical path.

3. Switch back to Gantt Chart view.

4. Click the Filter button on the Formatting toolbar.

5. Select *Critical* on the drop-down list.

Only the critical tasks for this project are listed now.

6. Click the Filter button again and select *All Tasks*.

7. Save *Orientation* and leave it open for the next exercise.

4. Tracking Status in the Task Table

Although the Tracking Gantt view provides a quick way to see where task progress is, you may want to see it in the task table. There are two fields that you can use to see the progress of your tasks quickly: Status and Status Indicator.

To track the status of a project by using the task table, complete the following steps:

1. Open *Orientation* and then close any open side panes, if necessary.

2. Insert the Status column to the right of the Task Name column.

3. Scroll through the tasks to read the Status field for each.

4. Add another column but use Status Indicator as the new field.

5. Look at the icons in the Status Indicator column and compare them to the text in the Status column.

6. Save *Orientation* and then close the file.

DISCOVERY ZONE

Discovery Zone exercises require advanced knowledge of topics presented in *Essentials* lessons, application of skills from multiple lessons, or self-directed learning of new skills. Each exercise is independent of the other, so you may complete them in any order.

1. Using Multiple Progress Lines

At times, you may need to check the progress of a project compared to more than one date. Microsoft Project allows you to include multiple progress lines. Use Help to learn more about progress lines, particularly using the Add Progress Line button and viewing progress lines at regular intervals. Then, open one of the project files from this lesson and add at least three progress lines at a regular interval, such as every Tuesday for the first three weeks of the project.

2. Viewing Other Progress Reports

You have looked at the Project Summary report and project statistics. There are other reports that help you in tracking the progress of your project. Open one of the project files from this project and open the Reports dialog box. Look through the reports to see what reports are available. Then, open each of the following reports and view the details within each: Overview Reports – Critical Tasks and Project Summary; Current Activities – Should Have Started Tasks and Slipping Tasks.

CUSTOMIZING MICROSOFT PROJECT AND SHARING INFORMATION

O B J E C T I V E S

IN THIS PROJECT, YOU LEARN HOW TO

- Customize the timescale

- Create a custom field

- Create a custom view

- Create a custom report

- Use the Organizer to share custom views, reports, and calendars

- E-mail a project file

- Route a project file

- Send a schedule note message

WHY WOULD I DO THIS?

Microsoft Project enables you to create custom views and reports that fit the specifics of the project plan you are managing. Depending on the needs of your organization and project plan, you can track information and create views and reports that support specific information in which you are interested. In addition, Microsoft Project provides a tool that helps you copy these views and reports to the global template so that they are available to all project files.

Communicating information with the project team and other stakeholders in a timely and relevant manner is critical for a successful project plan. Microsoft Project supports various methods of communication to enable collaboration among members of the project team as well as individuals outside of the project team who have a vested interest, such as stakeholders. You can e-mail the entire project file, send note messages to members of the project team, or route the project file. ***Routing*** is a way to send the project file to one or more individuals for comments and modifications and have the file returned to you after the routing recipients have reviewed the project.

VISUAL SUMMARY

In this project, you are one of two business owners who would like to obtain approval for a plan to remodel an existing building in your historic downtown to become a restaurant. The project plan outlines the tasks you need to complete for submitting a food service operation plan prior to beginning construction.

In the first four lessons, you modify the timescale to make viewing your project plan more meaningful, and then you create a custom field, custom view, and custom report. In Lesson 5, you use the Organizer to share these customized elements. The ***Organizer*** is a tool that allows you to copy Microsoft Project elements such as views, reports, and project base calendars between the open file and the global template file (see Figure 7.1). Finally, you communicate the project plan by using three different methods.

FIGURE 7.1

LESSON 1:   Customizing the Timescale

The timescale runs across the top of many views, such as the Gantt Chart, Task Usage, and Resource Graph views. You can modify the timescale to better view work within the time period that you specify. For example, you can see work within periods ranging from one minute to one year depending on the scope of the project. You may find that the timescale default setting (weeks and days) is inappropriate for a project that is entered in hours, necessitating a change to the timescale time unit format. The timescale contains three main parts: the ***top tier*** (top level of the timescale), the ***middle tier*** (middle level of the timescale), and the ***bottom tier*** (bottom level of the timescale). The default setting shows only the middle and bottom tiers. Besides modifying the time unit, you can also change the date label to appear with any or all tiers of the timescale and the ***count,*** which is the unit that appears between labels. For example, entering **3** with a time unit of *weeks* would specify that the scale is separated into 3-week segments.

In this lesson, you modify the formatting features of the timescale across the top of the Task Usage view. Then, you complete another set of steps to modify the view to include additional data and make a formatting change.

To Customize a Timescale

1 Open the *EPr1_0701* file, save it as `Restaurant`, and then close any open side panes.

2 Choose <u>V</u>iew, <u>V</u>iew Bar.
A toolbar containing the most common views appears on the left side of the screen (see Figure 7.2).

FIGURE 7.2

3 **Scroll down the View Bar, and then click *Resource Usage.***
The project displays in Resource Usage view.

4 **Click once on the scroll button on the horizontal scroll bar in the timephased bar graph window.**
The bar graph now shows *May 14, '06* in the timescale (see Figure 7.3).

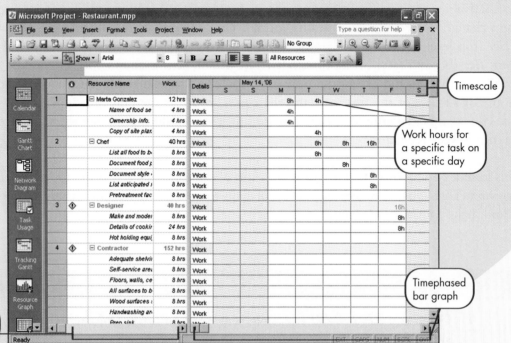

FIGURE 7.3

5 **Choose F̲ormat, Timescale.**
The Timescale dialog box opens (see Figure 7.4). The timescale shows two tiers: middle and bottom. By default, the Middle Tier tab is on top, with the units set to *Weeks.*

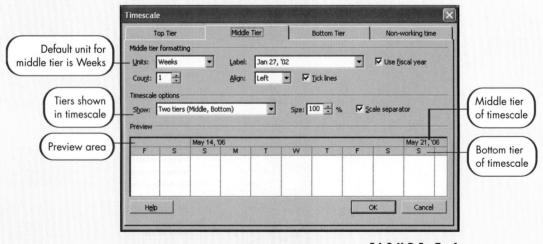

FIGURE 7.4

6 **Under *Middle tier formatting*, click the U̲nits drop-down arrow and select *Days.***
In the *Preview* area, you can see the changes to the timescale, showing days on the top line (the middle tier) (see Figure 7.5).

Preview area shows
Days in middle tier

FIGURE 7.5

7   **Click the Bottom Tier tab.**

The same options are available for all three tiers. The default setting is *Days*.

8   **Click the *Units* drop-down arrow and select *Hours*.**

The *Preview* area displays the change (see Figure 7.6). Notice that all hours for one day do not fit under the day label in the middle tier.

Hours shown
in the bottom tier

FIGURE 7.6

9   **Click the *Label* drop-down arrow, choose the first option (*Mon Jan 28, 11 AM*), and then click OK.**

The timescale in the bar graph portion of Resource Usage view changes to show days and hours rather than weeks and days (see Figure 7.7). Each column represents a date and an hour.

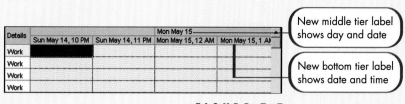

New middle tier label
shows day and date

New bottom tier label
shows date and time

FIGURE 7.7

10 Use the horizontal scroll bar to view *Mon May 15, 9 AM,* and then use the vertical scroll bar to view the *City* resource.

The summary of work allocations for the City resource are shown (see Figure 7.8).

		Smoking design.	8 hrs	Work					
		Plan fee	8 hrs	Work					
		Approval letter re	240 hrs	Work					
6	⊟ Fire Dept		8 hrs	Work					
		Maximum capac	8 hrs	Work					
7	⊟ City		40 hrs	Work		1h		1h	1h
		Plan reviewed	40 hrs	Work		1h		1h	1h
		Public health ins	0 hrs	Work					
				Work					
				Work					
				Work					

Summary task accounts for all work during the hour block

Work by the hour, not just by day

FIGURE 7.8

If you have problems . . .

Using the scrolling arrows may be a slow process when looking for a specific date. It may be easier and quicker to drag the horizontal scroll button to view the date you need. The date appears as a ScreenTip as you drag.

In addition to modifying the timescale, you can modify the appearance of details within a view to better match the project plan you have created. For example, the project may be defined by using hours rather than days; thus the timescale would be more appropriate if displayed as days and hours. Other projects might require quarters and months in the timescale. In the next set of steps, you add additional columns of data to the Resource Usage view and change the color of the Work row.

To Modify Resource Usage View

1 Choose F**o**rmat, Detail **S**tyles.

The Detail Styles dialog box opens (see Figure 7.9). The Usage Details tab displays on top.

FIGURE 7.9

2 In the *Show these fields* list, click *Work*, if necessary.

3 Click the *Cell background* drop-down arrow and choose the seventh color, *Blue*.
The Work field should display in the bar graph with a blue background.

Show ▾ **4** In the *Available fields* list, select *Baseline Cost*, and then click the **Sho**w
button.
The Baseline Cost field is now added to the *Show these fields* list (see Figure 7.10).
The cell background should be yellow for the Baseline Cost field.

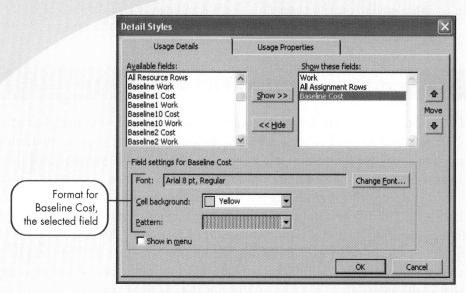

FIGURE 7.10

5 | **Click OK.**

You can see the formatting changes and the additional Baseline Cost field that you added (see Figure 7.11). Notice the Baseline Cost rows are yellow, and the Work rows are blue. All nonworking time slots are gray.

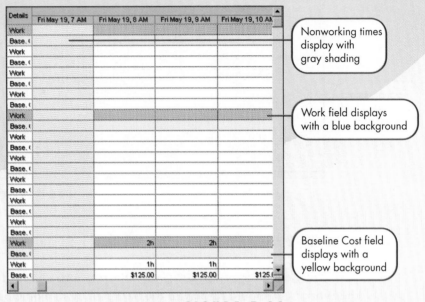

Nonworking times display with gray shading

Work field displays with a blue background

Baseline Cost field displays with a yellow background

FIGURE 7.11

6 | **Save your changes to the *Restaurant* file.**

You modified the timescale for Resource Usage view and changed the formatting of certain fields. Keep the *Restaurant* project file open and continue with the next lesson. If you prefer to complete the project later, close the file and exit Microsoft Project.

LESSON 2:   Creating a Custom Field

A *custom field* is used to store unique data that can be any number, cost, text string, date, or even formula. Custom fields are used to track information that Microsoft Project, by default, does not monitor. You could, for example, create a field named *Order Date* that tracks the date certain materials are ordered and then go on to create another field named *Received* that indicates whether or not you received the materials you ordered. You can add up to 10 cost fields, 10 additional date fields, 10 additional finish date fields, 20 flag fields (which are Yes/No fields that indicate a status requiring further action or some sort of function), 20 number fields, 10 outline codes fields (which are often used for Work Breakdown Structure [WBS] codes), 10 additional start date fields, and 30 additional text fields. Custom fields can be added to any *sheet view,* which is the spreadsheet-like presentation of data such as the task table. Gantt Chart view is the most common sheet view and a likely place where you might want to add custom fields.

In this lesson, you create a custom field to display fixture prices in your remodeling project. After creating the new field, you add it to Gantt Chart view.

To Create a Custom Field

1 Open *Restaurant*, if necessary, and click *Gantt Chart* on the View Bar.

2 Choose **T**ools, **C**ustomize, Fiel**d**s.
The Customize Fields dialog box opens (see Figure 7.12). The Custom Fields tab displays on top by default.

Change the type of custom fields you want to work with

Click to import a field from another project file

Click to create a formula

FIGURE 7.12

3 Click *Cost1* and then click the Rena**m**e button.
The Rename Field dialog box opens (see Figure 7.13).

FIGURE 7.13

4 Type **Fixture Price** and then click OK.
The field now has the new name you specified but also maintains the *Cost1* name in parentheses for reference (see Figure 7.14).

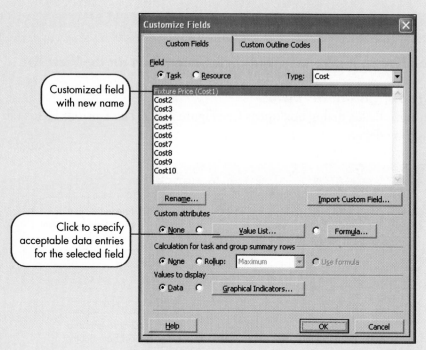

Customized field
with new name

Click to specify
acceptable data entries
for the selected field

FIGURE 7.14

5   **Click the Value List button.**

The Value List for "Fixture Price" dialog box opens (see Figure 7.15). Here you specify the acceptable values for this field.

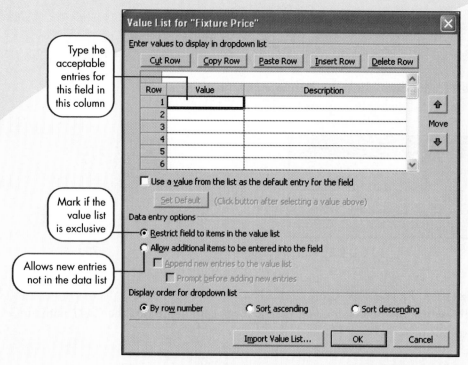

Type the
acceptable
entries for
this field in
this column

Mark if the
value list
is exclusive

Allows new entries
not in the data list

FIGURE 7.15

6   **Click in Row 1 in the Value column, type 100, and then press ↵Enter.**

7 Enter the following numbers, one in each cell in the column:

150

200

300

You have created the acceptable entries for this field.

8 Select the *Allow additional items to be entered into the field* option.
This option lets you enter data that are not already entered in the value list.

9 Check the *Append new entries to the value list* option, and then check the *Prompt before adding new entries* option.
The first option gives you the choice to add a new entry to the value list without opening this dialog box. Microsoft Project prompts you with a confirmation dialog box before adding the entry to the value list if you check the second option.

10 Click OK, and then click OK again in the Customize Fields dialog box.

11 Right-click the Indicator column heading, and choose Insert Column.
The Column Definition dialog box opens.

12 Click the *Field name* drop-down arrow, select *Cost 1 (Fixture Price)*, and then click OK.
The Fixture Price column appears on the left side of the task table (see Figure 7.16).

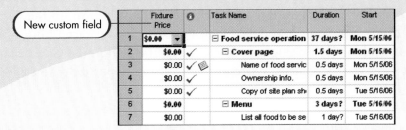

FIGURE 7.16

13 Scroll to Task 28 (*Prep sink*), and then click in the Fixture Price cell.

14 Click the Fixture Price drop-down arrow, choose *$150*, and press ⏎Enter.
The amount is accepted.

15 Click in the Fixture Price field for Task 29 (*3 compartment sink*), type **250**, and press ⏎Enter.
A dialog box opens, asking if you want to add the entry to the value list (see Figure 7.17).

FIGURE 7.17

16 Click **No.**

The entry is accepted in this field, but the amount is not added to the value list.

17 Specify a Fixture Price of *$100* for Task 30 (*Mop sink*) and *$300* for Task 31 (*3 compartment sink for bar*).

18 Save your changes to the *Restaurant* file.

You created a custom field in this lesson and inserted it into the task table of the Gantt Chart view. Keep the *Restaurant* project file open and continue with the next lesson. If you prefer to complete the project later, close the file and exit Microsoft Project.

TO EXTEND YOUR KNOWLEDGE . . .

CREATING A CALCULATED FIELD

You can use predefined functions—such as sum or average—and comparison operators—such as greater than or less than symbols—to create a custom field that involves a calculation. For example, you could create a calculated field that displays a warning message for each task that has a cost over a certain dollar amount.

To create a calculated field, select Tools, Customize, Fields. Select the field type from the *Type* drop-down list, and click the Formula button. In the Formula for Field dialog box, you can use the Field, Function and character buttons to create the calculation. After doing so, you can insert the field in the Gantt chart or any other sheet view. Challenge Exercise 1 provides an opportunity to create a calculated field.

LESSON 3:   Creating a Custom View

In addition to the number of views already available in Microsoft Project, you can also modify an existing view to create your own unique view option or use the View Definition dialog box to create an entirely new view. Project managers can better understand and manage a project plan when using a view designed to meet their specific needs. They can better see relationships between elements, analyze costs, and identify potential problems before they become serious.

There are different options in the View Definition dialog box depending on whether you are creating a single or combination view. A *single view* is a view such as the Gantt chart or Network diagram, while a *combination view* has one view in the top half of the screen and another view in the bottom half of the screen. For example, a combination view might have the Task Usage view in the top half of the window and the Task Details Form in the bottom half.

In a single view, you identify several elements or *controls* that comprise the view. The *screen control* becomes the underlying structure for the entire view. Resource Sheet view or Gantt

Chart view are just two different types of screens. The ***table control*** is the list of fields you want in the view and is determined by the screen that you choose. For example, if you choose Gantt chart as the screen, you could select Baseline as the table and the fields from the Baseline table become the columns that comprise the view. The ***group control*** is a way to categorize the view. For example, you could group tasks by priority. The ***filter control*** either limits or highlights those tasks that fit the criteria. For example, you could filter the view to show only critical tasks.

In this lesson, you create a custom view to highlight tasks that are currently in progress. Then, you apply it in the *Restaurant* project file.

To Create a Custom View

1 Open *Restaurant*, and close any open side panes, if necessary.

2 Click *More Views* on the View Bar.

3 In the More Views dialog box, click Gantt Chart and then click <u>N</u>ew.
The Define New View dialog box opens (see Figure 7.18).

FIGURE 7.18

4 Click *Single view*, if necessary, and then click OK.
The View Definition in 'Restaurant.mpp' dialog box opens. Here you select options to set up the custom view.

5 Specify the options for this view as shown in the following table:

<u>N</u>ame:	`Summary in Progress`
S<u>c</u>reen:	Gantt Chart
<u>T</u>able:	Summary
<u>G</u>roup:	No Group
<u>F</u>ilter:	In Progress Tasks
<u>H</u>ighlight filter:	Checked

6 Click OK.
The More Views dialog box reappears, and the new Summary in Progress view is selected in the list of available views.

7 Click Appl<u>y</u> in the More Views dialog box.
The Summary in Progress view displays (see Figure 7.19). Notice some tasks are blue text because a filter is applied to tasks that are in progress and you have checked the *Highlight filter* check box.

MSOFT 7

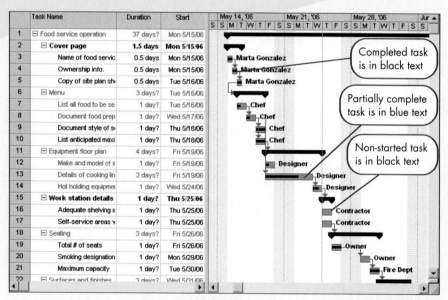

FIGURE 7.19

8 | **Scroll in the Gantt chart to see the Gantt bars.**

The Gantt bars with partial progress bars correspond to the tasks in blue text (see Figure 7.20). Notice the tasks that are 100% are not formatted in blue, nor are the tasks that have not begun.

FIGURE 7.20

9 | **Save your changes to the *Restaurant* file.**

You created a custom view and applied it to the *Restaurant* project file. Keep the project file open and continue with the next lesson. If you prefer to complete the project later, close the file and exit Microsoft Project.

LESSON 4:   Creating a Custom Report

Microsoft Project provides 29 predefined reports. If the information in these reports does not meet your needs, you can create your own unique report using one of the existing reports as a template. You can create custom task or resource reports, a unique monthly calendar report, or a custom crosstab report. A ***crosstab report*** is one in which the data are presented in column and row format with totals that can be applied to the column, row, or both, like a spreadsheet.

To create a custom report, you first specify the type by choosing Task, Resource, Monthly Calendar, or Crosstab and then selecting the elements it should contain. Reports are grouped into these four categories as each category requires slightly different options in the ensuing dialog boxes. When you create a custom report, you specify the table on which it is based and any filters you would like to apply. The Task and Resource reports allow you to specify a period or time frame, such as the entire project or just weeks or hours. You also have options to modify the text used for the entire report or for particular items on the report. For example, you may want to highlight critical tasks by applying bold and red text. Finally, you have the ability to sort the tasks and add elements such as borders and gridlines.

In this lesson, you create a unique, customized task usage report that allows you to filter tasks for a specific resource. You create a *Tasks and Work by Resource* report to display all tasks assigned to a specific resource, including assignment units, task durations, start and finish dates, percent complete, cost, and work (baseline, actual work, and remaining work). You then preview the report. When prompted, you select the Contractor resource and then print the report. A report displaying the tasks and work for the Contractor resource is the result of your efforts.

To Create a Custom Report

1 Open *Restaurant*, if necessary, and close any open side panes.

2 Choose **V**iew, **R**eports.

3 Click C**u**stom, and then click **S**elect.
The Custom Reports dialog box opens (see Figure 7.21).

FIGURE 7.21

4 **Click the New button.**

The Define New Report dialog box opens (see Figure 7.22). There are four report types available: Task, Resource, Monthly Calendar, and Crosstab.

FIGURE 7.22

5 **Select Task, if necessary, and then click OK.**

The Task Report dialog box opens (see Figure 7.23). The Definition tab allows you to specify the table containing the field listing you want as well as a time period for the report and any filters you would like to apply.

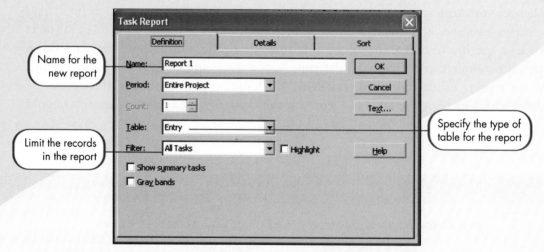

FIGURE 7.23

6 **Specify the options for this report on the Definitions tab as shown in the following table:**

Name:	**Tasks and Work by Resource**
Period:	Entire Project
Table:	Summary
Filter:	Using Resource...

7 **Click the Details tab.**

You can use the Details tab to specify additional fields you would like to include, such as *Notes* or *Predecessors*, as well as any borders or gridlines (Figure 7.24).

FIGURE 7.24

8 Under *Assignment*, check the <u>Work</u> check box, and then click OK.

The Custom Reports dialog box reappears and the new Task and Work by Resource report is selected in the list of available reports.

9 Click the Pre<u>v</u>iew button.

The Using Resource dialog box opens (see Figure 7.25). Here you select the resource you want for the report.

FIGURE 7.25

10 Click the drop-down arrow, choose *Contractor*, and then click OK.

The new report opens (see Figure 7.26). Your report shows tasks for the contractor resource and includes work units.

FIGURE 7.26

11 Click the Page Setup button on the Print Preview toolbar.

> Page Setup...

12 Click the Margins tab, change the left and right margins to 0.5", and then click OK.

13 Click within the report and view the data.

14 Click Close to exit without printing. (If you prefer to print, you can click the Print button to immediately start the print process at default settings.)
After you print or close Print Preview, the Custom Reports dialog box reappears.

15 Click Close and then click Close in the Reports dialog box.

16 Save your changes to the *Restaurant* file.
You created and viewed a custom report in this lesson. Keep the *Restaurant* project file open and continue with the next lesson. If you prefer to complete the project later, close the file and exit Microsoft Project.

LESSON 5: Using the Organizer to Share Custom Views, Reports, and Calendars

The Organizer is a tool that allows you to copy certain project elements—such as fields, groups, calendars, toolbars, views, and reports—between the current project file and the global template. In addition to copying, you can rename and delete these elements as well. There are 11 tabs in the Organizer dialog box, with each tab representing an element that you can manage: Views, Reports, **Modules** (pieces of programming code that you create to perform an action),

Forms, Tables, Filters, Calendars, Toolbars, *Maps* (formats that are used when importing and exporting data between programs), Fields, and Groups.

The global file (Global.mpt) is a Microsoft Project file that contains default settings that are applied to all new project files. The global file includes settings that control the view displayed at startup, the unit in which work is displayed (hours, days, or weeks), and whether schedule calculations are manual or automatic. A *schedule calculation* is a value that Microsoft Project calculates as based on other data. For example, work units are a calculation of task duration. Once you copy custom elements to the *Global.mpt* file, they become available to all new blank project files and can also be copied to existing files. In addition to being able to copy project elements, you can use the Organizer to delete and rename elements from both the global file and the current file.

If you should alter the global file, do so with extreme caution. Changes made to the global file affect any other projects or users that utilize the Microsoft Project program. Many corporations that use Microsoft Project on a server provide policies and procedures concerning alterations to the global file. Many do not allow access to the global file except to specific users. It is best to make a copy of the global file prior to making any changes to it in case a restoration is necessary.

In this lesson, you use the Organizer to perform two sets of steps. First, you copy the Summary in Progress view, the Work by Resource report, and the Contractor calendar to the global template. Then, you verify the existence of these items in the global file by opening a new project file. Finally, you remove the custom items from the global file.

To Use the Organizer

1 **Open *Restaurant* and then choose <u>T</u>ools, Organizer.**
The Organizer dialog box opens (see Figure 7.27). Organizer allows you to copy, move, or delete views between the open project file (*Restaurant.mpp*) and the global template (*Global.mpt*).

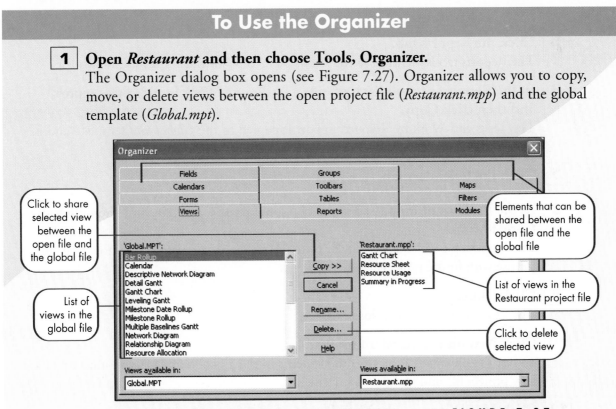

FIGURE 7.27

M'SOFT 7

2 | Click the Views tab, if necessary.

3 | In the *'Restaurant.mpp'* list box, select the Summary in Progress view, and then click the Copy button.

4 | Scroll through the *'Global.MPT'* list to verify that Summary in Progress view is listed.

The Summary in Progress view copies to the *Global.mpt* file (see Figure 7.28).

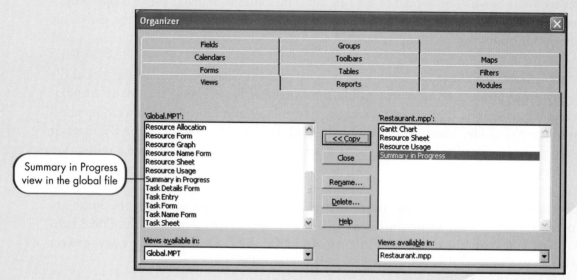

FIGURE 7.28

5 | Click the Reports tab.

The Reports tab is identical to the Views tab except for the entries in the two lists.

6 | In the Restaurant.mpp list box, select Tasks and Work by Resource report, and then click Copy.

The Tasks and Work by Resource report is copied to the *Global.mpt* template and is now available for use with future projects.

7 | Click the Calendars tab.

8 | In the Restaurant.mpp list box, click Contractor Calendar, and then click the Copy button.

The Contractor Calendar is copied to the *Global.mpt* template and is now available for use with future projects.

9 | Click Close.

The Organizer dialog box closes.

10 | Click New on the Standard toolbar.

To test the presence of the custom elements in the global template, you must open a new project file and look for that element.

11 | Click More Views on the View Bar.

12 **Scroll through the Views list and verify that Summary in Progress is listed.**
The view is available in the new file (see Figure 7.29).

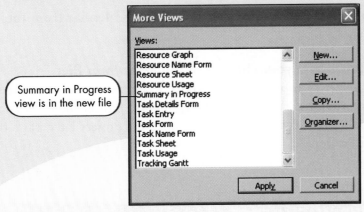

Summary in Progress
view is in the new file

FIGURE 7.29

13 **Click Cancel, and then close the new project without saving changes.**
You have now made your unique custom view, report, and calendar available for each
new blank project file and can be added to any existing project file.

Sometimes you may want to remove a customized element from the global file. In this case,
you need to remove the custom view, report, and calendar you added in the previous set of
steps so they are not available on the lab computer.

To Remove Items from the Global Template

1 **Choose Tools, Organizer and then click the Views tab, if necessary.**
The Organizer dialog box opens.

2 **In the 'Global.MPT' list box, select Summary in Progress and then click Delete.**
A warning appears (see Figure 7.30).

FIGURE 7.30

3 **Click Yes.**
The Summary in Progress view is removed from the global file but remains a part of
the *Restaurant* project file.

4 **Click the Reports tab.**

5 **In the 'Global.MPT' list box, select Tasks and Work by Resource and then
click Delete.**
A warning dialog box opens.

6 | **Click Yes in the warning box.**
The Tasks and Work by Resource report is removed from the global file.

7 | **Click the Calendars tab and remove the Contractor Calendar from the 'Global.MPT' list.**

8 | **Click Close, and then save your changes to the *Restaurant* file.**
You used the Organizer to copy a custom report, calendar, and view to the global template. Then you removed them. Keep the *Restaurant* project file open and continue with the next lesson. If you prefer to complete the project later, close the file and exit Microsoft Project.

TO EXTEND YOUR KNOWLEDGE . . .

RENAMING ITEMS IN THE ORGANIZER

You can also use the Organizer to rename project elements. Select the element you want to rename and click the Rename button. Type a new name and click OK; then close the dialog box.

RESETTING THE GLOBAL FILE

The global template file (*Global.mpt*) itself cannot be opened in Microsoft Project, as it is merely a collection of settings that are applied to all new projects. To preserve the global file, you should copy the template to a safe location. To replace/overwrite a changed global file, restore the backup of the original global file.

LESSON 6:   E-Mailing a Project File

Microsoft Project has several integrated MAPI-compliant e-mail features that allow you to e-mail project plans directly from Microsoft Project by using Outlook or another MAPI e-mail program. ***MAPI*** (Messaging Application Programming Interface) is the standard programming interface supported by Microsoft for accessing electronic messaging.

You are able to e-mail a project file to others by using Outlook or any MAPI compliant e-mail system. E-mailing a project file is the simplest method of sharing your project with other people. E-mailing a project file can be done from within Microsoft Project and involves sending the open file to a recipient. A ***recipient*** is simply the person to whom you are addressing the e-mail. The open project file is sent as an ***attachment,*** which is a file that is included with an e-mail but is not part of the e-mail message.

In this lesson, you explore using the *Send-to* feature on the File menu. You perform the setup needed to e-mail the project file as an attachment.

To Set Up E-Mailing a Project File

1 Open *Restaurant*, if necessary, and close any open side panes.

2 Choose **F**ile, Sen**d** To, M**ai**l Recipient (as Attachment).
Your e-mail application launches and a new e-mail message form displays, showing your project file as an attachment. A subject line displays the name of the project file (see Figure 7.31).

FIGURE 7.31

If you have problems . . .

Depending on the e-mail program you are using and the settings or virus protection programs in use, you may receive warning dialog boxes stating something similar to *A program is trying to access e-mail addresses you have stored in Outlook. Do you want to allow this? If this is unexpected, it may be a virus and you should choose 'No'.* Proceed by clicking Yes or as directed.

3 In the *To* text box, enter the e-mail address of a recipient.

4 In the message area, type `Attached please find the latest copy of the Restaurant project plan`.
You completed the specifications to send the current project file as an e-mail attachment. At this point, clicking Send would complete the process. Instead, you close without sending.

5 Click Close and do not save your changes to the e-mail form.
The e-mail form closes.

6 Save your changes to the *Restaurant* file.
You explored how to send the open project file as an attachment. Keep the *Restaurant* project file open and continue with the next lesson. If you prefer to complete the project later, close the file and exit.

LESSON 7:   Routing a Project File

Routing a project file means sending the file to specific individuals for feedback. For example, you may require information from the designer concerning certain equipment for the kitchen, which also requires input from the contractor regarding installation feasibility. Routing sends your project plan through e-mail to a list of people—and you can specify that each individual receives the file one at a time in sequence, or you can send the file to everyone simultaneously, creating multiple copies of the project file. In general, sequential routing is ideal for review and evaluation, as each e-mail recipient can edit the project file, provide comments, and then send it along to the next recipient. Upon completion, the file is returned to you, where you can review one file (as opposed to multiple copies) and then incorporate comments and changes to it. When you receive the completed routed file, it will have a number appearing after the name to preserve the original copy of the project file. When you route a file, you complete a *routing slip* that contains e-mail address information along with instructions and message text for the e-mail recipients.

In this lesson, you create a routing slip to forward the *Restaurant* project file to two recipients. Please note that this exercise includes instructions on how to route a file but does not include steps on viewing and forwarding a routed project file.

To Route a Project File

1 Open *Restaurant*, if necessary, and close any open side panes.

2 Choose **File, Send To, Routing Recipient.**
The Routing Slip dialog box opens (see Figure 7.32).

FIGURE 7.32

If you have problems . . .

Depending on the e-mail program you are using and the settings or virus protection programs in use, you may receive warning dialog boxes stating something similar to *A program is trying to access e-mail addresses you have stored in Outlook. Do you want to allow this? If this is unexpected, it may be a virus and you should choose 'No'.* Proceed by clicking Yes or as directed.

3 **Click A̲ddress.**
The Address Book dialog box opens.

4 **Select the first e-mail recipient from the list of names and click the *To* button.**

5 **Click the second e-mail recipient from the list of names, click the *To* button, and then click OK.**

6 In the *M̲essage text* box, type `Please review Tasks 11-14 concerning equipment floor plan and update the attached file with your progress. Include a note regarding the status of this equipment installation.`

7 Under *Route to recipients*, click *O̲ne after another*, if necessary.

8 Check the *Return w̲hen done* and *Trac̲k status* check boxes (see Figure 7.33).

9 **Click A̲dd Slip.**
You completed the specifications to route the current project file. At this point, clicking R̲oute rather than A̲dd Slip would add a routing slip and forward the project file simultaneously. Instead, you close without sending. The project file is ready to be routed to the first e-mail recipient in the address list. Figure 7.33 illustrates a sample routing slip.

M'SOFT 7

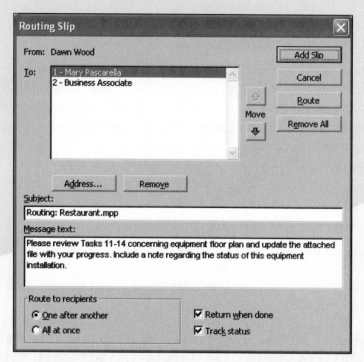

FIGURE 7.33

10 **Save *Restaurant*.**

You added a routing slip. Keep the *Restaurant* project file open and continue with the next lesson. If you prefer to complete the project later, close the file and exit.

TO EXTEND YOUR KNOWLEDGE . . .

SENDING A ROUTING SLIP

Once you have addressed and created the routing slip, you need to send it. To send a routing slip, choose File, Send To, Other Routing Recipient. From the Routing Slip dialog box, click Route and the project file is routed to the recipients as addressed.

VIEWING A ROUTING SLIP

From your e-mail program, open the routed e-mail message. The e-mail message contains the project file as an attachment. Double-click on the attachment to open the project file and launch Microsoft Project. Review and modify the project as per the message contained in the routing slip.

SENDING THE PROJECT FILE TO THE NEXT ROUTING RECIPIENT

If the creator of the routing slip has chosen the *One after another* option in the Routing Slip dialog box, the project file needs to be sent to the next recipient. These instructions can be seen in the content of the e-mail message written as: *The project below has a routing slip. When you are done reviewing this project, choose Next Routing Recipient from the Send To menu in the Microsoft Office Project File menu to continue the routing.* To send the project file to the next routing recipient, choose File, Send To, Next Routing Recipient.

LESSON 8: Sending a Schedule Note Message

A *schedule note message* is either a picture of selected tasks or an attached project file that is automatically addressed to members of the project team. When you need to send information about critical tasks to assigned resources or ask resources to report on the status of their task assignments, you can schedule a note and send it to them as an e-mail message. This feature is useful to communicate with the project team as well as stakeholders to send or receive project information. When sending a schedule note, you can display the view, including any sheet views as well as custom fields that you require.

In this lesson, you select a range of tasks and send only those tasks as a picture to an e-mail recipient.

To Send Schedule Note Messages

1 Open *Restaurant*, if necessary, and close any open side panes.

2 Click *Task Usage* on the View Bar.

3 Highlight Tasks 41 (*Plans and approvals*) through 47 (*Construction can begin*).

4 Choose File, Send To, Mail Recipient (as Schedule Note).
The Send Schedule Note dialog box appears (see Figure 7.34).

FIGURE 7.34

If you have problems . . .

Depending on the e-mail program you are using and the settings or virus protection programs in use, you may receive warning dialog boxes stating something similar to *A program is trying to access e-mail addresses you have stored in Outlook. Do you want to allow this? If this is unexpected, it may be a virus and you should choose 'No'.* Proceed by clicking Yes or as directed.

5 Under *Address message to*, uncheck the *Project manager* check box.
Now, only *Resources* should be selected (see Figure 7.35).

FIGURE 7.35

6 Check *Picture of selected tasks*, if necessary, and then click OK.
Your e-mail application is launched and a new e-mail message form is created with a completed *To* text box showing the e-mail addresses of each resource from the project plan. In addition, the selected tasks are attached as a BMP (bitmapped picture) file (see Figure 7.36).

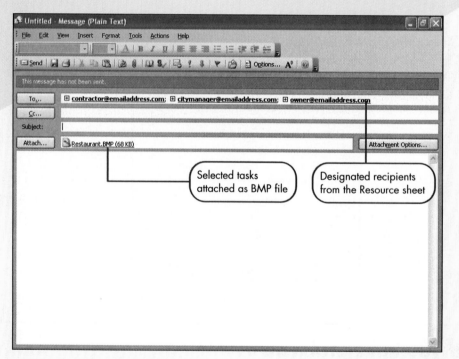

FIGURE 7.36

7 Click in the *Subject* text box, and type `ACTION: Please review the attached.`

8 In the message area, type `Attached please find several tasks. Please review to ensure this is a comprehensive list and advise me of any additions or changes you feel are necessary. Student Name (where Student Name is your name).` You completed the specifications to send the selected tasks as a note. At this point, clicking OK would complete the process. Instead, you close without sending.

9 Click Close and do not save your changes to the e-mail form.

10 Save *Restaurant* and then close it.

TO EXTEND YOUR KNOWLEDGE . . .

ADDING E-MAIL ADDRESSES TO THE RESOURCE SHEET

You can include e-mail addresses as part of the information that you maintain with the resources data that you have entered. To add e-mail addresses, choose View, Resource Sheet and then choose Insert, Column and select *E-mail Address* in the *Field name* text box; click OK. The E-mail Address column is added to the resource sheet where you can then type the e-mail address for each resource.

SUMMARY

In this project, you learned many ways you can customize Microsoft Project and share information. First, you modified the timescale to display hours rather than days. Then, you also created a custom field, a custom view, and a custom report. You learned how to share a custom view, report, and calendar by copying to the *Global.mpt* file by using the Organizer so that is available to other project files. Finally, you took a look at several e-mail functions by sending a project file as an attachment, routing a file for feedback, and sending a scheduled note message to members of the project team.

You can extend your learning by reviewing concepts and terms and by practicing variations of skills presented in the lessons. Use the following table as a guide to the numbered questions and exercises in the end-of-project learning opportunities.

M'SOFT 7

LESSON	MULTIPLE CHOICE	DISCUSSION	SKILL DRILL	CHALLENGE	DISCOVERY ZONE
Customizing the Timescale	5		1	2	2
Creating a Custom Field	1	2		1	
Creating a Custom View	7	1	2	3	1
Creating a Custom Report	3	1	3		
Using the Organizer to Share Custom Views, Reports, and Calendars	6, 8, 9	1		4	
E-Mailing a Project File	4			5	
Routing a Project File	10	3	4		
Sending Schedule Note Messages	2		5		2

KEY TERMS

attachment	MAPI	schedule calculations
bottom tier	maps	schedule note message
combination view	middle tier	screen control
controls	modules	sheet view
count	Organizer	single view
crosstab report	recipient	table control
custom field	routing	top tier
filter control	routing slip	
group control		

CHECKING CONCEPTS AND TERMS

MULTIPLE CHOICE

Circle the letter of the correct answer for each of the following.

1. Which of the following does *not* happen when you assign a value list to a custom field? [L2]

    a. Data entry is restricted.

    b. Accuracy of data entry is ensured.

    c. A wizard automatically generates a list of acceptable values.

    d. Data entry is consistent.

2. Which method of communicating a project plan would you use if you only want to include a small portion of a project plan? [L8]

    a. E-mail the project file

    b. Routing slip

    c. Scheduled note message

    d. Instant messaging

3. Which report type presents data in column and row format with totals? [L4]

    a. Task report

    b. Resource report

    c. Calendar report

    d. Crosstab report

4. What happens to a project file when you e-mail it? [L6]

    a. It is inserted as part of the message text.

    b. It is sent as an attachment to the e-mail message.

    c. A routing slip is attached to the project file.

    d. The project file becomes shared and changes from multiple users are incorporated.

5. What is the default setting for the timescale? [L1]

    a. Top tier = Week, Middle tier = Day, Bottom tier = Hour

    b. Middle tier = Week, Bottom tier = Day

    c. Middle tier = Day, Bottom tier = Hour

    d. Top tier = Year, Middle tier = Month, Bottom tier = Day

6. Why would you want to copy a custom report to the global file? [L5]

    a. It automatically appears in all existing projects.

    b. It is available in all new project files.

    c. It can be accessed in any Microsoft Project program because it becomes part of the software code.

    d. Copying it to the global file makes it accessible via the Web.

7. What is a combination view? [L3]

    a. A view that displays two projects at once.

    b. A view that displays tasks and costs at once.

    c. A view that displays one view in the left and one view on the right.

    d. A view that displays one view in the top of the window and one view in the bottom of the window.

8. Which of the following elements cannot be copied by using the Organizer? [L5]

    a. Views

    b. Reports

    c. Tasks

    d. Calendars

9. To which file does the Organizer allow you to copy project elements? [L5]

 a. Project.mpt

 b. Global.mpt

 c. Template.mpt

 d. Project1.mpp

10. Which method would you use if you wanted to receive feedback about your project file from a group of people? [L7]

 a. E-mail

 b. Routing

 c. Scheduled note

 d. Instant messaging

DISCUSSION

1. What are the benefits of being able to create a unique customized view or report? How does the Organizer enhance the benefits of creating these unique elements, and why would you make them available to the global template file? [L3, L4, L5]

2. Provide at least two examples of some unique custom fields that you could create in your own project plans and the purposes that they would serve. Include the field name and the type of field it would be: text, date, cost, and so on. [L2]

3. Describe a scenario where using the routing feature could help you incorporate feedback from other individuals involved with your project plan. Discuss why it might be better to route a file to each individual one at a time, rather than to multiple individuals all at once. [L7]

SKILL DRILL

Skill Drill exercises reinforce project skills. Each skill reinforced is the same, or nearly the same, as a skill presented in the project. Detailed instructions are provided in a step-by-step format. The exercises relate to a single file, and you should work them in order.

1. Modifying the Resource Usage View

As the fund-raiser coordinator of a local civic organization, you organize an auction each year as a fund-raiser for charity. From past experience, you know that a project plan is necessary to keep things running more smoothly. To make it easier to visualize the status of the project plan, you decide to modify the Resource Usage view to help you see the cost of all tasks completed by each resource.

To modify the Resource Usage view, follow these steps:

1. Open the *EPr1_0702* file, save it as Fundraiser_Auction, and then close any open side panes.

2. Choose <u>V</u>iew, <u>V</u>iew Bar, and then click Resource Usage.

3. Choose F<u>o</u>rmat, T<u>i</u>mescale.

4. Under *Middle tier formatting*, click the <u>U</u>nits drop-down arrow and select *Days*.

5. Click the <u>L</u>abel down arrow and choose the first option (*Mon Jan 28, '02*).

6. Click the Bottom Tier tab, click the <u>U</u>nits down arrow, and then select *Hours*.

7. Click the *Label* down arrow, choose the third option (*1/28 11 AM*), and then click OK.

8. Choose F̲ormat, Detail S̲tyles.

9. In the *A̲vailable fields* list, select *Cost* and then click the S̲how button.

10. Click the *C̲ell background* drop-down arrow, choose *Lime*, and then click OK.

11. Scroll horizontally to the right to view *Jan 2, 8 AM*.

12. Save *Fundraiser_Auction* and leave it open for the next exercise.

2. Creating a Custom View

As you continue to work with the fund-raiser project plan, you determine you need a custom view. You need to view the work of each resource for each task.

To create a custom view, follow these steps:

1. Open *Fundraiser_Auction*, if necessary, and then click *More Views* on the View Bar.

2. In the More Views dialog box, click Resource Allocation and then click N̲ew.

3. Click S̲ingle View, if necessary, and then click OK.

4. Specify the options for this view as shown in the following table and then click OK.

N̲ame:	**Work by Resource**
S̲creen:	Resource Usage
T̲able:	Work
G̲roup:	No Group
F̲ilter:	Resources - Work
Hi̲ghlight filter:	Checked

5. Click *Apply* in the More Views dialog box.

6. Scroll to see the work for the Auction Coordinator for January 1, 2006.

7. Scroll down to view the Copy Shop resource.

   Notice the Copy Shop is black text. It is not a work resource.

8. Save *Fundraiser_Auction* and leave it open for the next exercise.

3. Creating a Custom Report

On at least a weekly basis, you must provide a report to organization leadership concerning the assignments given to each volunteer. You decide to create a custom report that lists the volunteers and their assignments. You also want to show what work has been completed on each task.

To create a *Resource Assignments* report, follow these steps:

1. Open *Fundraiser_Auction*, if necessary, and then choose V̲iew, R̲eports.

2. Click C̲ustom, and then click S̲elect.

3. In the *R̲eports* list, select *Resource (Material)*.

4. Click the N̲ew button.

5. Select *Resource*, and then click OK.

6. Specify the options for this report on the Definitions tab as follows:

Name:	**Resource Assignments**
Period:	Months
Table:	Entry - Work Resources
Filter:	All Resources

7. Click the Details tab.

8. Check the *Schedule* check box, and then click OK.

9. Click the Preview button.

10. Click within the report and view the data.

11. Click Close to exit without printing. (If you prefer to print, you can click the Print button to immediately start the print process at default settings.)

12. Click Close, and then click Close in the Reports dialog box.

13. Save *Fundraiser_Auction* and leave it open for the next exercise.

4. Routing a Project Plan

Now that the *Fundraiser_Auction* project plan is designed, you need to send it to the organization leaders and the volunteers. You expect to receive some feedback concerning the tasks and the schedule. The easiest way to do so is to route the file to all stakeholders.

To route the *Fundraiser_Auction* project plan, follow these steps:

1. Open *Fundraiser_Auction*, if necessary, and then choose File, Send To, Routing Recipient.

2. Click Address.

3. Select the first e-mail recipient from the list of names, click the *To* button, and then click OK.

4. In the *Message* text box, type **Please review the attached project plan and notify me of any changes you see that are necessary. Thanks for your input.**

5. Under *Route to recipients*, click *All at once*.

6. Check the *Return when done* check box.

7. Click Add Slip.

8. Save *Fundraiser_Auction* and leave it open for the next exercise.

5. Sending Schedule Note Messages

You need to regularly send reminders to volunteers and leaders concerning their specific tasks. A note message is most appropriate in this case to highlight tasks that need attention. Now you want to send a copy of the advertisement tasks to the project manager.

To send a scheduled note message, follow these steps:

1. Open *Fundraiser_Auction*, if necessary, and then click *Gantt Chart* on the View Bar.

2. Highlight Tasks 25 (*Coordinate advertisements*) through 32 (*Distribute yard signs*).

3. Choose File, Send To, Mail Recipient (as Schedule Note).

4. Under *Address message to*, uncheck all boxes except *Project manager*.

5. Check *Picture of selected tasks*, if necessary, and then click OK.

6. Click in the *Subject* text box, and type **Auction advertisement.**

7. In the message area, type **Attached are the tasks necessary to properly advertise our auction fundraiser. Please be certain that each task is handled promptly. Thank you.**

8. Click Close and do not save your changes to the e-mail form.

9. Save *Fundraiser_Auction* and then close it.

CHALLENGE

Challenge exercises expand on or are somewhat related to skills presented in the lessons. Each exercise provides a brief narrative introduction, followed by instructions in a numbered-step format that are not as detailed as those in the Skill Drill section. The exercises relate to a single file, and you should work them in order.

1. Creating a Customized Calculated Field

You are an insurance claims processing specialist and a member of the Provider Information Maintenance System (PIMS) team. Your job is to assist the project manager by maintaining the deliverables of a software implementation in Microsoft Project. The PIMS team is testing and implementing a new software program to be used by your company. This software maintains data on physician records, Medicare, and procedure codes. The data and their accuracy are vital to how claims are processed. The project file is tracking a test upload of provider information in an effort to gather data on how long it should take the mainframe system and the claims processing specialists to review and clean up a data download of provider updates.

Now, you need to add a calculated custom field to determine which task items are over the budgeted amount of $100. To create a custom field, follow these steps:

1. Open *EPr1_0703*, save it as **PIMS**, and then close any side panes, if necessary.

2. Use Help to research custom calculated fields and how to use them.

3. Create a new custom field called **Cost Warning** using the Text1 field.

4. Click Formula in the Customize Fields dialog box.

5. In the 'Formula for Cost Warning' dialog box, click the Function button, point to General, and click *IIf(expression, truepart, falsepart)*.

   The formula is added to the *Cost Warning* = text box.

6. Double-click the word *expression*, click the Field button, point to *Cost*, and then point to *Cost* in the second column and click it.

7. Click the greater than symbol (>), and type **100**.

8. Double-click the word *truepart* and type **"Overbudget"** (making sure you include the quotation marks).

9. Double-click the word *falsepart* and type **"On Target"** (making sure you include the quotation marks).

The formula appears as *IIf([Cost]>100, "Overbudget", "On Target")*

10. Click OK, click OK on the warning screen that appears, then click OK again to return to the Gantt chart.

11. Add the Text 1 (Cost Warning) field to the left of the Duration field in Gantt Chart view and then add the Cost field to the left of the Duration field as well.

Notice that for each item over $100 a message appears that the task is over budget, while the other tasks that are under $100 have a message stating the task is on target.

12. Save *PIMS* and leave it open for the next exercise.

2. Creating a Custom Crosstab Report

As you are working with the project plan, you decide you need to compare the tasks in the project to their costs. You need to know which tasks' costs are higher than a specified goal. You want to look at the tasks for this month only.

To create a custom crosstab report, follow these steps:

1. Open *PIMS* and close any side panes, if necessary.

2. Use Help to research the use of a crosstab query and how to create one.

3. Open the Reports dialog box and create a new report called **Costs Greater Than Specified Amount** based on the Crosstab report type.

4. Use Tasks and Cost for the row data and 1 month for the column data.

5. Use the Cost Greater Than filter, and include totals for the Row and Column data.

6. Preview the report, specify $150 when prompted, and then close it.

7. Save *PIMS* and leave it open for the next exercise.

3. Creating a Custom View That Includes Baseline and Progress Lines

In Lesson 3, you created a custom single view. Now you create a specific view that includes baseline data and progress lines to better track and compare the amount of time it is taking the new PIMS software to complete the tasks in this test run. A single view is not complete; thus you create a custom combination view.

To create a custom view, follow these steps:

1. Open *PIMS* and close any side panes, if necessary.

2. Create a new combination view and name it **Software Upgrade**.

3. The top portion of the view should display the Resource Usage view and the bottom portion of the view should display the Task Details Form.

4. Apply the view to the PIMS project plan.

5. Click on each specialist's name, view the Task Details Form portion of the view, and note how it changes.

6. Modify the view so that the top portion displays Task Usage and the Bottom portion of the view displays the Resource Sheet; then apply the view.

7. Switch to Gantt Chart view and remove the horizontal split bar.

8. Save *PIMS* and leave it open for the next exercise.

4. Copying Custom Views Using Organizer

You need to create a new custom view that includes progress lines and a modified timescale. You also want to copy this view to the global template so that it is available for all Microsoft Project files.

To create and copy a custom view, follow these steps:

1. Open *PIMS* and close any side panes, if necessary.

2. Move the split bar so that more of the Gantt chart is visible.

3. Create a new single view named **Software Progress** with the following options:

    Screen: Gantt Chart

    Table: Summary

    Group: No Group

    Filter: All Tasks

4. Apply the view and modify the timescale so that the middle and bottom tiers of the Gantt chart units are expressed in days.

5. Add progress lines that are displayed in relation to the baseline.

6. Using the Organizer, copy the Software Progress view to the *Global.mpt* file.

7. Open any existing lesson file that you have already created; apply the Software Progress view to it; and then close the file without saving your changes.

8. Open the Organizer and remove the Software Progress view from the *Global.mpt* file.

9. Save *PIMS* and leave it open for the next exercise.

5. E-Mailing Resource Information

You would like to receive some input on the resources that are currently assigned to the PIMS project and plan to e-mail this information to the project manager. Because you need the project manager to review the entire project plan, you send the project file as an attachment to your inquiry e-mail.

To set up sending resource information via e-mail, follow these steps:

1. Open *PIMS* and close any side panes, if necessary.

2. View the Resource Sheet and select all of the resources.

3. Under *Address message to*, uncheck the <u>R</u>esources check box.

4. E-mail the highlighted resources as a picture.

5. In the body of the e-mail message form, type **Review Resource Assignment** as the subject.

6. In the message text box, type **Please review the attached picture and let me know if you think we should add people to the project team as I suspect the workload is becoming too great for some.**

7. Close the e-mail message without sending it and do not save the e-mail message.

8. Save *PIMS* and close the project file.

DISCOVERY ZONE

Discovery Zone exercises require advanced knowledge of topics presented in *Essentials* lessons, application of skills from multiple lessons, or self-directed learning of new skills. The exercises are independent of each other, so you may complete them in any order.

1. Researching View Help Topics on Microsoft Online

In this project, you have learned about custom views and other custom elements. You used both single views and combination views. Another important view to learn about is the Network Diagram view. Select Microsoft Project Help from the Help menu and click the *Get the latest news about using Project* link. From the Web page, scroll down to locate the *Viewing Project Information* section and click the *Viewing Project Information* link. Research the topics on *Work with the Network Diagram view* and *Grouping Information in a View* as well as any other topics on views that look interesting to you.

2. Sending a Schedule Note of a PERT Analysis View

You have learned about different e-mail options that allow you to send the entire project file or certain pieces of it to mail recipients. In this exercise, you try working with a new view and sending a picture of it to the Project Manager. Type **PERT** in the *Type a question for help* box and look through the Help topics that appear. Open *EPr1_0702* and save it as **PERT**. Turn on the PERT Analysis toolbar and then click PERT Entry Sheet from the PERT toolbar and enter some optimistic, expected as well as pessimistic durations in the appropriate fields for some of the tasks. Select all the tasks and send them as a picture to the project manager, using the *Scheduled Note Message* option. When you get to the actual *Send* option in your e-mail program, save the message instead and close it without sending.

PROJECT 8

INTEGRATING PROJECT DATA

OBJECTIVES

IN THIS PROJECT, YOU LEARN HOW TO

- Import a task list from Excel

- Export task sheet information into an Excel worksheet

- Copy and paste a Gantt chart

- Link and embed Project data into Word and Excel

- Insert objects into task notes and add hyperlinks to tasks

- Use the Outlook address book to add resources

WHY WOULD I DO THIS?

Project data can be shared between Microsoft Project and other applications such as Microsoft Word, Excel, and PowerPoint. When you are creating new project files, some of the data you would like to use might be contained in another application file. Microsoft Project provides the tools that allow you to use information from other programs quite easily. The fact that you don't have to retype the data is a big time-saver and, more importantly, eliminates the chance of introducing typing errors. In addition to being able to use information from another application file, you can also share project data with other programs. This can be helpful when you would like to share information from your project file with other individuals, who might not have Microsoft Project on their system. Perhaps you would simply like to share a snapshot of a Gantt chart as a picture or present the task list in a Word document. Microsoft Project also provides menu options to easily share data contained in Microsoft Outlook. You can utilize the address book in Outlook to create your resource pool, including contact information such as e-mail addresses.

VISUAL SUMMARY

In this project, you are a member of an external consulting team that specializes in streamlining corporations to make them more cost-effective and efficient. Your team has been hired by a company that is in the process of reorganizing its corporate management staff in an effort to improve internal processes. The project file you are using is in the final stages of creation. Tasks have been entered, but you need to add more. Resources have not yet been entered or assigned to tasks and no work progress has been entered. Your efforts in this project file include importing and exporting task sheet data, linking and embedding data with other programs so that it can be used in new ways, and adding resources from Microsoft Outlook. You use the Export Wizard and use a map to transfer data between Microsoft Project and Microsoft Excel. Also, you copy and paste the Gantt chart into an Excel worksheet, link the task sheet to a Word document so that it automatically updates, embed a pie graph into the project file, and import contacts from the Outlook address book into the resource sheet (see Figure 8.1).

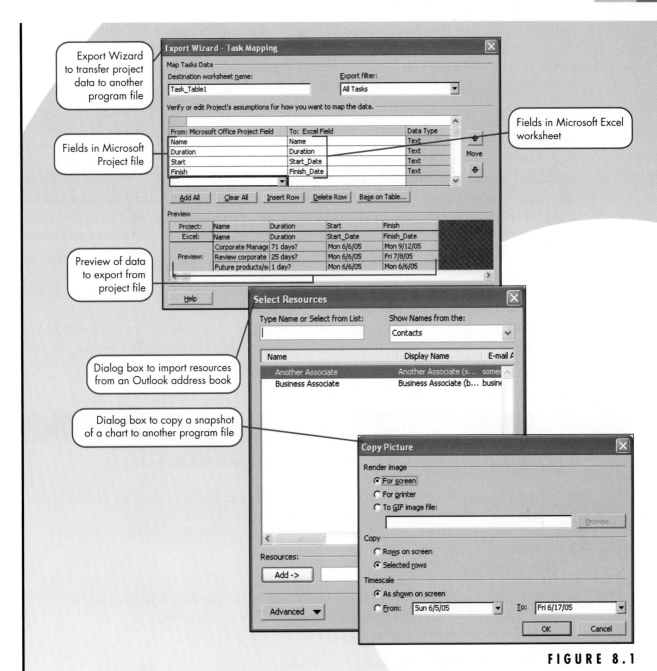

FIGURE 8.1

LESSON 1:   Importing a Task List from Excel

Generally, a project plan involves a group of resources working toward the same goal. That being the case, it is possible that some project data have been entered into another application file by one team player and could easily be imported into the project file. To *import* data into Microsoft Project means transferring the data from another application file into Microsoft Project. Importing data is a useful feature that can save you quite a bit of time because you can recycle information without having to type it again. Importing also eliminates the chance of making typos. To import data, you utilize a *map,* which is a set of instructions that defines the data you import, the order, and the destination fields in Microsoft Project into which the data will be imported. For example, you might have a list of tasks that you have stored in an Excel workbook and the column heading is Task. When you import the Excel data, you must map the Task column from Excel to the Name column in Microsoft Project.

Microsoft Project provides three choices for importing data. You can import the data into a new blank project file. Doing so makes creating the initial project file quicker and more accurate. Another option is to *append* the data to the active file—meaning that you add the data to the end of the active project file. For example, a list of tasks may exist in an Excel worksheet and need to be added to an existing project file. You could append this list to the task table. A third alternative is to *merge* the data to the active file, which also adds the data to the end of the active project file. However, merging requires a *primary key* (a field that uniquely identifies each task) and for that reason this option is not used very often.

In this lesson, you first view a worksheet in Microsoft Excel. Then, you use the Import Wizard to map the data from Excel into Microsoft Project and append the data to an existing file. Merging is not appropriate because the project file does not contain primary key fields. You conclude the lesson by making some editing changes to the imported data so that the new information flows smoothly with the existing data already in the task table.

To Import a Task List from Excel

1 Click Start from the taskbar and move the mouse to All Programs.

2 Move the mouse pointer to the Microsoft Office folder and then to Microsoft Excel 2003; then click the left mouse button.

3 Choose File, Open.
The Open dialog box opens.

4 Click the drop-down arrow at the right end of the *Look in* box, and select the drive and folder containing the student files for this text.
The list of student data files displays.

5 Click the *EPr1_0801* filename, and then click Open.
The *EPr1_0801* workbook opens (see Figure 8.2). The workbook contains only one sheet of data, with a list of tasks. When importing data, it is not necessary for the source and destination files to reside in the same folder.

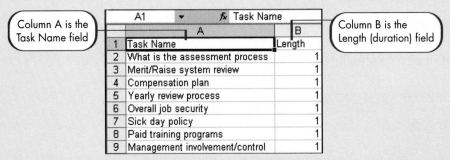

FIGURE 8.2

6 Choose File, Save As; then navigate to the location of your solution files, click in the *File name* text box, type Assessment, and then click Save.

7 View the data contained in the Excel worksheet.

There are two column headings in this worksheet: Task Name and Length. Typically, data in an Excel worksheet include column headings to provide a description for the data within that column. These headings become field names when imported into a project file.

8 Choose File, Close and then minimize the Excel program.

Microsoft Excel is minimized and resides on the taskbar. You keep it open to use it in several other lessons in this project.

9 Start Microsoft Project, open the *EPr1_0802* file, save it as Mgmt_Review, and then close any open side panes.

10 Choose File, Open.

The Open dialog box opens.

11 Click the *Files of type* drop-down arrow, select *Microsoft Excel Workbooks*, and then navigate to the folder where your solution files are located.

The list of files changes to display only Excel workbooks (see Figure 8.3).

FIGURE 8.3

M'SOFT 8

12 **Select the *Assessment* workbook and then click Open.**

The Import Wizard dialog box opens (see Figure 8.4). This dialog box is the first of several steps designed to walk you through importing data.

FIGURE 8.4

13 **Click Next.**

The Import Wizard – Map dialog box opens (see Figure 8.5).

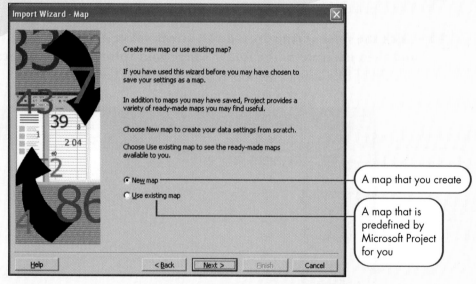

FIGURE 8.5

14 **Click the *New map* option, if necessary, and then click Next.**

The Import Wizard – Import Mode dialog box opens (see Figure 8.6).

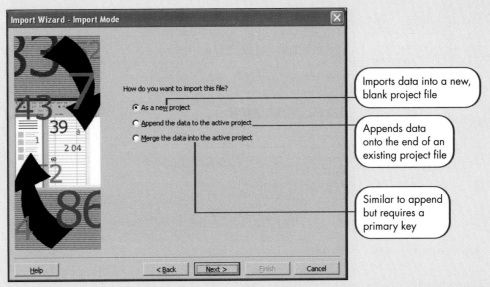

FIGURE 8.6

15 Click the *Append the data to the active project* option, and then click Next.
The Import Wizard – Map Options dialog box opens (see Figure 8.7).

FIGURE 8.7

16 Check the *Tasks* check box, verify that *Import includes headers* is also selected, and then click Next.
The Import Wizard – Task Mapping dialog box opens (see Figure 8.8).

Worksheet to use in the Excel workbook

Fields in the Excel workbook

Fields in the Project file

Mapping grid

FIGURE 8.8

17 **Click the *Source worksheet name* drop-down arrow and choose Sheet1, which is a worksheet in the *Assignment* workbook.**

The dialog box updates, showing the columns of data contained in the Excel worksheet along with the corresponding Microsoft Project field to which they will be mapped, in an area called the **mapping grid** (see Figure 8.9).

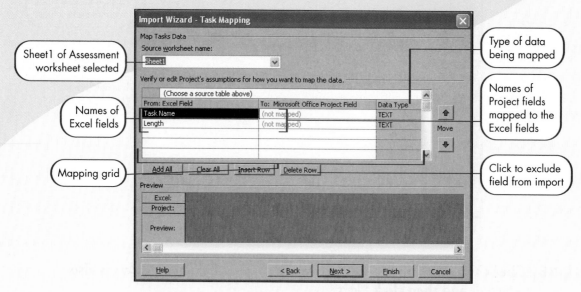

Sheet1 of Assessment worksheet selected

Names of Excel fields

Mapping grid

Type of data being mapped

Names of Project fields mapped to the Excel fields

Click to exclude field from import

FIGURE 8.9

18 **In the mapping grid, click the Task Name field under *To: Microsoft Office Project Field*.**

A drop-down arrow appears in the Microsoft Office Project field box.

19 **Click the drop-down arrow, scroll down the list, and choose *Name*.**

Now the *Task Name* Excel field is mapped to the *Name* Microsoft Office Project field.

20 Click in the Length field under *To: Microsoft Office Project Field*, click the drop-down arrow, scroll down the list, and then choose *Duration*.

The Import Wizard–Task Mapping dialog box now should look like Figure 8.10.

FIGURE 8.10

21 Click Next and then click Finish.

The eight tasks from the Excel worksheet are appended to the bottom of the task table in the project file.

If you have problems . . .

Sometimes blank rows precede the imported data. If so, highlight the blank rows and press Del.

---

22 Highlight Task 27 (*Merit/Raise system review*) through Task 33 (*Management involvement/control*) and click Indent on the Formatting toolbar.

The selected tasks become subtasks for Summary Task 26 (*What is the assessment process*).

23 Click Task 26 (*What is the assessment process*) and click Outdent on the Formatting toolbar.

Summary Task 26 and its subtasks are promoted to become subtasks of Task 1 (*Corporate Management Review*). The *Mgmt_Review* project file should look like Figure 8.11.

M'SOFT 8

	ⓘ	Task Name	Duration	Start	
20		Review functional jo	20 days?	Mon 7/11/05	
21		Review managemen	5 days?	Mon 8/8/05	F
22		Determine how inter	20 days	Mon 8/15/05	
23		⊟ **Functional division a**	**30 days?**	**Mon 6/6/05**	F
24		Identify job catagorie	10 days?	Mon 6/6/05	F
25		Review managemen	20 days?	Mon 6/20/05	F
26		⊟ **What is the assessn**	**1 day**	**Mon 6/6/05**	M
27		Merit/Raise system r	1 day	Mon 6/6/05	N
28		Compensation plan	1 day	Mon 6/6/05	N
29		Yearly review proce	1 day	Mon 6/6/05	N
30		Overall job security	1 day	Mon 6/6/05	N
31		Sick day policy	1 day	Mon 6/6/05	N
32		Paid training progran	1 day	Mon 6/6/05	N
33		Management involve	1 day	Mon 6/6/05	N

Imported tasks

FIGURE 8.11

24 **Save** *Mgmt_Review.*

Keep the *Mgmt_Review* project file open and continue with the next lesson. If you prefer to complete the project later, close the file and exit Microsoft Project.

TO EXTEND YOUR KNOWLEDGE . . .

USING THE EXCEL TASK LIST TEMPLATE

Excel provides a Task List template that is set up for the purpose of importing Excel data into Microsoft Project. Using this template takes the guesswork out of the mapping process because the column names in the template are the same as the column names used in the Task Sheet view in Microsoft Project. When it comes time to import the data, the columns of data automatically map because the column names are the same. To use the template, open Excel and choose File, New. From the New Workbook side pane, locate the *Templates* area and click the *On my computer* link. From the Templates dialog box, click the Spreadsheet Solutions tab and then double-click the Microsoft Project Plan Import Export Template to create a new blank file with columns that correspond to the default task sheet columns in Gantt Chart view. Within this template, there are individual worksheets for each portion of a project file, including Task_Table, Resource_Table, Assignment_Table, and Info_Table.

USING AN EXISTING MAP

Microsoft Project also provides preexisting maps that you can use when importing data. These predefined maps fit specific and unique situations. The import process is the same as in the lesson, except you would choose *Use existing map* in the Import Wizard. Some types of import maps include but are not limited to "Who Does What" Report, Default task information, Earned value information, and others.

LESSON 2: Exporting Task Sheet Information into an Excel Worksheet

To **export** data means that you transfer data from Microsoft Project to another software program. Exporting enables you to place project data into another application format, such as an Excel worksheet or Word document or even an Access database. This feature is useful for simply sharing the data in another file format or using the data for another purpose. For example, there might be information in the Microsoft Project task sheet that you want to use in an end-of-year report done in Microsoft Excel. Rather than retype the tasks, you can simply export them into the report. Maps are also used when exporting data from Microsoft Project and provide you with the opportunity to pick and choose the specific fields you want to export. Programs that support exported information from Microsoft Office Project 2003 include Microsoft Excel (as a workbook or PivotTable), another Microsoft Project file, Microsoft Access Database (MDB), and other Open Database Connectivity (ODBC) database programs. **ODBC** programs are compliant database formats that Microsoft supports. In addition, you can export data into **Hypertext Markup Language (HTML)** format, which is the standard World Wide Web convention for presenting text and graphics, or the **Comma Separated Values (CSV)** format, which is a file format in which fields are separated by commas or semicolons.

In this lesson, you use the Export Wizard to map the columns in the task table that you want to export to Microsoft Excel. Then, you start Excel and view the data that you exported.

To Export Task Sheet Information into Excel

1 Open *Mgmt_Review*, if necessary, and close any open side panes.

2 Deselect any selected group of tasks, if necessary, and then choose <u>F</u>ile, Save <u>A</u>s.
The Save As dialog box opens.

3 Navigate to the location of your solution files.

4 Click the *Save as type* drop-down arrow and choose *Microsoft Excel Workbook (*.xls)*.
Only Excel workbooks are listed now, and a suggested filename is given for the file you are saving (see Figure 8.12), which is the same as the project filename.

M'SOFT 8

FIGURE 8.12

5 **Click in the *File name* text box after the *w* in *Review* and type `_Export` so the filename is *Mgmt_Review_Export*; then click Save.**
The Excel file is saved as *Mgmt_Review_Export* and the Welcome screen for the Export Wizard dialog box opens.

6 **Click Next.**
The Export Wizard – Data dialog box opens.

7 **Verify that the *Selected Data* option button is selected; then click Next.**
The Export Wizard – Map dialog box opens (see Figure 8.13).

FIGURE 8.13

8 **Click the *New map* option button and then click Next.**
The Export Wizard – Map Options dialog box opens.

9 Check the *Tasks* check box, verify that *Export includes headers* is also selected, and then click **Next**.

The Export Wizard – Task Mapping dialog box opens and should appear as shown in Figure 8.14.

FIGURE 8.14

10 Click in the first cell under *From: Microsoft Office Project Field*.

11 Click the drop-down arrow in the cell, scroll down the list, select *Name* from the list, and then press ⏎Enter.

The Name field is inserted into the *From: Microsoft Office Project Field* column and is automatically added to the *To: Excel Field* column. The data type is automatically set.

12 Continue adding fields as shown in Figure 8.15.

FIGURE 8.15

13 Click <u>N</u>ext and then click <u>F</u>inish.

14 Minimize Microsoft Project, and maximize Excel from the taskbar.

15 Click the Open button; navigate to the location where your solution files are saved and select the *Mgmt_Review_Export* Excel file; then click <u>O</u>pen.

If you have problems . . .

Some columns may display crosshatches, which are overflow markers. You may also need to resize the column to see the entire name in all the columns. Move your mouse to the border between the column headers that need to be resized, and when the mouse appears as a left-right sizing arrow, double-click.

Your file should appear similar to Figure 8.16.

	A	B	C	D	E	F	G	H	I	J
1	Name	Duration	Start_Date	Finish_Date						
2	Corporate	71 days?	6/6/2005 8:00	9/12/2005 17:00						
3	Review co	25 days?	6/6/2005 8:00	7/8/2005 17:00						
4	Future pro	1 day?	6/6/2005 8:00	6/6/2005 17:00						
5	Identify sta	3 days	6/6/2005 8:00	6/8/2005 17:00						
6	Identify line	3 days	6/9/2005 8:00	6/13/2005 17:00						
7	Develop cc	5 days?	6/6/2005 8:00	6/10/2005 17:00						
8	Create out	10 days?	6/13/2005 8:00	6/24/2005 17:00						
9	Create out	10 days?	6/27/2005 8:00	7/8/2005 17:00						
10	Organizati	46 days?	7/11/2005 8:00	9/12/2005 17:00						
11	Identify ne	5 days?	7/11/2005 8:00	7/15/2005 17:00						
12	Develop or	10 days?	7/18/2005 8:00	7/29/2005 17:00						
13	Corporate	1 day?	8/1/2005 8:00	8/1/2005 17:00						
14	Human Re	30 days?	8/2/2005 8:00	9/12/2005 17:00						
15	Identify bu	45 days?	7/11/2005 8:00	9/9/2005 17:00						
16	Process m	15 days	7/11/2005 8:00	7/29/2005 17:00						
17	Review key	15 days?	7/11/2005 8:00	7/29/2005 17:00						
18	Assess int	30 days?	8/1/2005 8:00	9/9/2005 17:00						
19	Develop ac	5 days	7/11/2005 8:00	7/15/2005 17:00						
20	Create a fe	5 days?	7/11/2005 8:00	7/15/2005 17:00						

Task_Table1

Double-click column border to resize

Field name (column header)

Date fields import with both date and time

FIGURE 8.16

16 Choose <u>F</u>ile, <u>C</u>lose; save any changes; and minimize Excel.

If you have problems . . .

A warning box may appear concerning the Excel file version. If so, click Yes to save the file with the latest Excel file format and continue.

---

17 On the taskbar, restore your project file and then save the file.
Keep the *Mgmt_Review* project file open and continue with the next lesson. If you prefer to complete the project later, close the file and exit Microsoft Project.

TO EXTEND YOUR KNOWLEDGE . . .

EXPORTING A PROJECT FILE AS AN HTML DOCUMENT

You may find that you often need to share project data with individuals who do not have Microsoft Project installed on their computers. Stakeholders who have a strong interest in the status and overall success of the project plan often want to see the file and know what is going on, even though they don't own the application. In addition to exporting project data into a worksheet or Word document, you can also export it as an HTML document. Saving a Microsoft Project file as an HTML file has the advantage of providing all the information contained in the project file in World Wide Web format and enables individuals to see the information, although they are not able to modify or change it. To export a Microsoft Project file as an HTML document, choose File, Save As. From the Save As dialog box, click the *Save as type* down arrow, choose *Web Page (*.html, *.htm)*, and click Save. Step 1 of the Export Wizard dialog box appears, where you click Next. From Step 2 of the Wizard, choose either *New map* or *Use existing map,* depending on your preference, and click Next. From Step 3 of the Wizard, choose the type of data you want to export, which is either Tasks, Resources, or Assignments. Select any other HTML options, if you prefer, and click Next. From Step 4 of the Wizard, you map the Microsoft Project field to the HTML table field in the mapping grid, and then click Next. Click Next again, and then click Finish.

LESSON 3: Copying and Pasting a Gantt Chart

Sharing a Gantt chart with another program can be difficult because the charts tend to be oversized and often do not fit well in some file formats. It may require trial and error to get the result that you want. By default, when you choose to copy a Gantt chart, the procedure captures only what you see on the screen rather than the entire chart. You can modify this default by copying a range of tasks and specifying the begin and end dates for the timescale of the Gantt chart to capture exactly what you need. You are provided three options on how you would like to **render** the image, or capture the picture of the Gantt chart. You can choose *For screen*, which means the Clipboard captures the picture and it becomes something that you can use Edit, Paste to insert into the other program. *For printer* means it will go directly to your printer, and *To GIF image file* means that the image will be saved as a **Graphics Interchange Format (GIF)** file, a bitmapped graphics file format used by the World Wide Web.

In this lesson, you select a range of rows and specify a timescale for the Gantt chart. Then you copy it, using the *For screen* option. After you have copied the image, you paste it into a Microsoft Excel worksheet.

To Copy and Paste a Gantt Chart

1 Open *Mmgt_Review*, if necessary, and close any open side panes.

2 On the Gantt chart, point to the Task 1 (*Corporate Management Review*) Gantt bar and view the Summary ScreenTip.

Note the start date of *Mon 6/6/05* and the finish date of *Mon 9/12/05* (see Figure 8.17).

FIGURE 8.17

3 In the task table, select Task 1 (*Corporate Management Review*) through Task 33 (*Management involvement/control*) to select all the tasks.

4 Choose Edit, Copy Picture.
The Copy Picture dialog box opens (see Figure 8.18).

FIGURE 8.18

5 Under *Copy*, choose *Selected rows*, if necessary.

6 Under *Timescale*, choose the *From* option button.

7 Click the calendar drop-down arrow for the *From* date, and choose *Tue 6/28/05*.

8 Choose *Mon 9/12/05* as the *To* date.
Now the start and finish dates are selected for the Gantt chart to be copied to Excel (see Figure 8.19).

FIGURE 8.19

9 **Click OK.**

10 **From the taskbar, maximize Microsoft Excel, and then click New.**
A blank workbook opens in Excel.

11 **Choose Edit, Paste.**
The entire Gantt chart along with a portion of the task sheet is pasted as an image into Excel (see Figure 8.20).

FIGURE 8.20

12 **Choose File, Save As, and navigate to the location where your solution files are saved.**

13 **Click in the *File name* text box, and type Gantt_Chart.**

14 **Click Save.**

15 **Close the Excel workbook and exit Microsoft Excel, and then restore Microsoft Project from the taskbar, if necessary.**
Keep the *Mgmt_Review* project file open and continue with the next lesson. If you prefer to complete the project later, close the file and exit Microsoft Project.

LESSON 4: Linking and Embedding Project Data into Word and Excel

At times it is helpful to share data between files or even between programs called the source and destination files. The **source file** is where the data originate, and the **destination file** is where the data are pasted. Most commonly, people copy and paste data to share information. This method works fine unless the data have the potential to change.

Two other methods are available for sharing data: linking and embedding. To **paste link** means that data are created in a source file and then copied and linked in a destination file; a connection is automatically maintained between the two files. The linked object in the destination file is automatically updated when the source file is modified or changed. For example, if you copy a list of tasks in Microsoft Project (the source file) and paste link them into a Word document (the destination file), any time you change the task list in the project file, the Word document automatically updates. On the other hand, to **embed** means that an object is created in a separate program and then is inserted into the destination file. For example, you can create a bar graph using Microsoft Graph and insert the graph into a Microsoft Project file as an object. An **object** simply refers to the menu option used to insert other file types and describes any type of compatible file formats such as an Excel worksheet, a Microsoft Graph, a picture, and so forth. When you need to make changes to the embedded object, you access the source application used to create the object by double-clicking the object in the destination file. In doing so, you can access commands from the source application from within the destination file and make changes. Any changes you make to the embedded object are automatically reflected in the destination file.

Together, these sharing methods are called **Object Linking and Embedding (OLE),** which is a program-integration technology that you can use to share information between programs. All Microsoft Office programs support OLE, so you can share information through linked and embedded objects. Including objects such as pictures, charts, and other graphical images can give views or reports a finished look. They can clarify or enhance information as well as draw attention to a particular item you want to highlight. An obvious question is when to use linking and when to use embedding. Because a linked object changes each time its source changes, you would use linking for volatile information. For example, you might maintain monthly sales data in an Excel worksheet. You could then communicate that data to certain personnel through a memo or letter, including an excerpt of the worksheet. Obviously, the sales data change each month and those changes must be reflected in the monthly communication. On the other hand, you would use embedding if the data are not likely to change. For example, you might include a chart from Excel in an annual report created in Word. Data contained in an annual report are constant and not likely to change, so embedding is a good choice. Embedding is also the best choice when you want to include an object from another application, such as a graph, a sound file, or a video.

In this lesson, you link the task sheet data with a Microsoft Word document and view how the data automatically update in Word when you change information in the project file. You also embed a pie chart that was created in Microsoft Excel in the Milestone Date Rollup view in Microsoft Project. Then, you double-click the graph to launch the Microsoft Graph program and make a change to the color of the area surrounding the pie graph.

To Link Project Data with Word

1 Open *Mgmt_Review*, if necessary, and close any open side panes.
The *Mgmt_Review* file is the source file in this linking scenario.

2 Move the mouse to the Task Name column header and when it appears as a small, black down-pointing arrow, click and drag right to select the Duration, Start, and Finish columns.
The four columns are selected (see Figure 8.21).

	ⓘ	Task Name	Duration	Start	Finish	Predecessors
21		Review managemen	5 days?	Mon 8/8/05	Fri 8/12/05	20
22		Determine how inter	20 days	Mon 8/15/05	Fri 9/9/05	21
23		⊟ **Functional division a**	**30 days?**	**Mon 6/6/05**	**Fri 7/15/05**	
24		Identify job catagorie	10 days?	Mon 6/6/05	Fri 6/17/05	
25		Review managemen	20 days?	Mon 6/20/05	Fri 7/15/05	24
26		⊟ **What is the assessn**	**1 day**	**Mon 6/6/05**	**Mon 6/6/05**	
27		Merit/Raise system r	1 day	Mon 6/6/05	Mon 6/6/05	
28		Compensation plan	1 day	Mon 6/6/05	Mon 6/6/05	
29		Yearly review proce	1 day	Mon 6/6/05	Mon 6/6/05	
30		Overall job security	1 day	Mon 6/6/05	Mon 6/6/05	
31		Sick day policy	1 day	Mon 6/6/05	Mon 6/6/05	
32		Paid training progran	1 day	Mon 6/6/05	Mon 6/6/05	
33		Management involve	1 day	Mon 6/6/05	Mon 6/6/05	

Selected fields

FIGURE 8.21

3 Choose <u>E</u>dit, <u>C</u>opy Cell.

4 Click Start on the taskbar; point to All Programs, Microsoft Office; and then click Microsoft Word.
Microsoft Word opens with a blank document, which serves as the destination file for this exercise.

5 Close any open task panes, and then choose <u>E</u>dit, Paste <u>S</u>pecial.
The Paste Special dialog box opens (see Figure 8.22).

Paste formatting options

Click to paste link the data to the source

Paste Special

Source: Microsoft Project Document
          C:\Mgmt_Review.mpp!LINK_2

As:

- ● Paste:
  - Microsoft Project Document Object
  - Formatted Text (RTF)
  - Unformatted Text
  - Picture (Windows Metafile)
  - Unformatted Unicode Text
- ○ Paste link:

OK

Cancel

☐ Display as icon

Result

Inserts the contents of the Clipboard as text with font and table formatting.

FIGURE 8.22

M'SOFT 8

6   Click the *Paste link* option button, and verify that *Formatted Text (RTF)* is selected in the *As* list box.

7   Click OK.

The contents of the project file are paste linked and pasted into Microsoft Word, using the ***rich text format (RTF)*** format, a file type used to transfer formatted text documents between applications. Your document should look like Figure 8.23.

Imported data

FIGURE 8.23

8   Choose File, Save As; then navigate to the location of your solution files, name the Word file `Linked_Mgmt_Review`, and then click Save.

9   Minimize Word; then restore the *Mgmt_Review* project file from the taskbar, if necessary.

10   Click Task 2 (*Review corporate vision*).

The Task 2 text now appears in the Edit bar above the column headings.

11   Double-click the word *vision* in the Edit bar, type `plan`, and then click Enter

The change is made (see Figure 8.24).

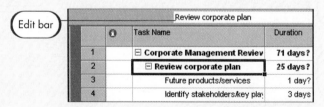

Edit bar

FIGURE 8.24

12   Save the *Mgmt_Review* project file and minimize it.

13 **From the taskbar, restore Microsoft Word and look at the**
_Linked_Mgmt_Review_ document.
Task 2 was automatically updated in the document (see Figure 8.25). Changes in the
source file are reflected in the destination file when a paste link exists between them.

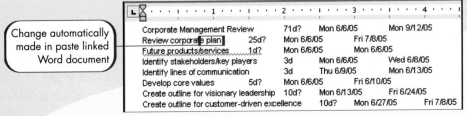

Change automatically
made in paste linked
Word document

Corporate Management Review	71d?	Mon 6/6/05 Mon 9/12/05
Review corporate plan	25d?	Mon 6/6/05 Fri 7/8/05
Future products/services	1d?	Mon 6/6/05 Mon 6/6/05
Identify stakeholders/key players	3d	Mon 6/6/05 Wed 6/8/05
Identify lines of communication	3d	Thu 6/9/05 Mon 6/13/05
Develop core values	5d?	Mon 6/6/05 Fri 6/10/05
Create outline for visionary leadership	10d?	Mon 6/13/05 Fri 6/24/05
Create outline for customer-driven excellence	10d?	Mon 6/27/05 Fri 7/8/05

FIGURE 8.25

14 **Choose _File_, E_x_it, and save the _Linked_Mgmt_Review_ Word document.**
Microsoft Word closes along with the _Linked_Mgmt_Review_ Word document.

15 **From the taskbar, restore the _Mgmt_Review_ project file.**

You have learned how to paste link information from Microsoft Project to Microsoft Word. In
the next set of steps, you embed a Microsoft Excel graph into the project file.

To Embed Excel Data in Microsoft Project

1 **Choose _V_iew, _M_ore Views, Milestone Date Rollup, and then click Apply.**

2 **Click the horizontal scroll button in the Gantt Chart once.**
The screen quickly moves to the status date of June 5, '05.

3 **Choose _I_nsert, _O_bject.**
The Insert Object dialog box opens (see Figure 8.26).

FIGURE 8.26

4 Click the *Create from File* option button.

5 Click the Browse button and navigate to the location where your student files are saved.

6 Select the *EPr1_0803* file, and click Insert.

7 Click OK in the Insert Object dialog box.

The worksheet with the pie graph is inserted into the Gantt chart area of the Milestone Date Rollup view (see Figure 8.27). The *Mgmt_Review* file is the destination file, and the *EPr1_0803* Excel file is the source file in this embedding scenario.

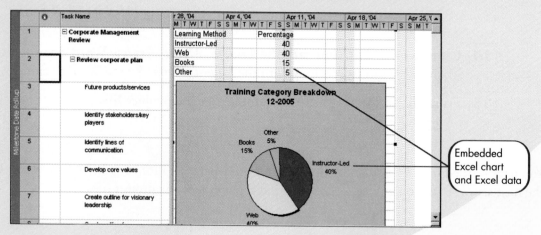

FIGURE 8.27

8 Click Save.

9 Double-click the embedded pie graph.

A message displays warning that you are about to activate an OLE object (see Figure 8.28).

FIGURE 8.28

10 Click Yes.

Notice that the Microsoft Graph program has been opened, as indicated by the Chart menu on the menu bar (see Figure 8.29). Also note that the Excel formula bar displays below the Microsoft Project toolbars.

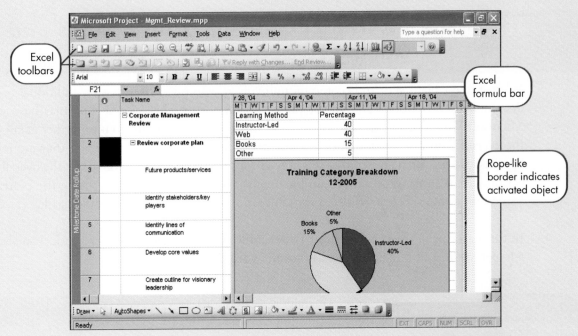

FIGURE 8.29

11 **Double-click on the gray area around the pie chart.**
The Format Chart Area dialog box opens (see Figure 8.30).

FIGURE 8.30

12 **Click on the light blue color in the last row, third from right, and then click OK.**
The area surrounding the pie chart is now light blue instead of gray.

13 **Click anywhere in the task sheet, and then click Save.**
The Microsoft Graph program closes.

Keep the *Mgmt_Review* project file open and continue with the next lesson. If you prefer to complete the project later, close the file and exit Microsoft Project.

LESSON 5: Inserting Objects into Task Notes and Adding Hyperlinks to Tasks

When project plans start to become more involved, you often find that an additional body of documentation is created around the project to support it. For example, you may have several Microsoft Word documents that support a number of task items and go into further detail about those tasks. You can include these documents as notes for the task to which they are related. Spreadsheets are often created that might have more detailed information about the overall project budget. All this information can be attached to your project file by using the Notes and Hyperlink features. A *hyperlink* is a clickable word or picture that opens another file.

In this lesson, you insert a Microsoft PowerPoint slide as a note object for a task. You also add a hyperlink to a task that opens a Microsoft Word document.

To Insert Objects into Task Notes

1 Open *Mmgt_Review*, if necessary, and close any open side panes; then choose **View**, **Gantt chart**.

2 Double-click **Summary Task 9** (*Organizational and personal learning*) and click the Notes tab.
The Notes tab of the Summary Task Information dialog box contains several commands for formatting text and inserting objects into a note (see Figure 8.31).

FIGURE 8.31

 3 Click the Insert Object button.
The Insert Object dialog box opens.

4 Click the *Create from File* option button.

5 Click Browse and navigate to the folder where your student files are located.

6   Select the *EPr1_0804* PowerPoint file and click Insert.

7   Click OK.
The contents of the PowerPoint file are inserted as a task note (see Figure 8.32).

FIGURE 8.32

8   Click OK.
A note icon appears in the Indicator column.

9   Select Summary Task 26 (*What is the assessment process*), and then choose **I**nsert, Hyper**l**ink.
The Insert Hyperlink dialog box appears (see Figure 8.33).

FIGURE 8.33

10   Using the Look in drop-down list, navigate to where your student files are located, select the *EPr1_0805* document, and then click OK.
A hyperlink icon appears in the Indicator column (see Figure 8.34).

M'SOFT 8

22		Determine how inter	20 days	Mon 8/15/05	
23		⊟ **Functional division a**	**30 days?**	**Mon 6/6/05**	F
24		Identify job categorie	10 days?	Mon 6/6/05	F
25		Review managemen	20 days?	Mon 6/20/05	F
26	🖨	⊟ **What is the assessn**	**1 day**	**Mon 6/6/05**	**M**
27		Merit/Raise system r	1 day	Mon 6/6/05	N
28		Compensation plan	1 day	Mon 6/6/05	N
29		Yearly review proce	1 day	Mon 6/6/05	N
30		Overall job security	1 day	Mon 6/6/05	N
31		Sick day policy	1 day	Mon 6/6/05	N

Hyperlink icon

FIGURE 8.34

11 **Click the hyperlink icon.**
The Microsoft Word document *EPr1_0805* opens (see Figure 8.35).

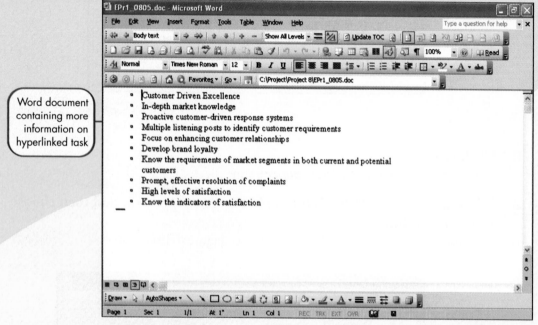

Word document containing more information on hyperlinked task

FIGURE 8.35

If you have problems . . .

If you utilize security measures on the computer, a warning dialog box may appear. If the warning dialog box appears now, simply click Yes to continue.

12 **Review the document and then choose File, Exit.**
Microsoft Word closes.

13 **Save *Mgmt_Review*.**
Keep the *Mgmt_Review* project file open and continue with the next lesson. If you prefer to complete the project later, close the file and exit Microsoft Project.

LESSON 6: Using the Outlook Address Book to Add Resources

Most of us utilize an e-mail program to process a good percentage of our day-to-day work. We send and receive e-mails. We maintain names, addresses, e-mail addresses, and phone numbers in our Outlook contacts file. Some of us use the Appointment feature to keep track of meetings and other events. If you have Microsoft Outlook, Microsoft Outlook Express, or Microsoft Outlook Exchange installed on your company server, you can add resources to your project plan from the e-mail address book. Doing so saves you time because you do not need to retype information in the resource sheet. However, the only address book that Microsoft Project can utilize is the Outlook address book.

In this lesson, you add the Email Address column to the Resource Sheet view. Then, you add resources from Microsoft Outlook to the resource sheet.

To Add Resources from Microsoft Outlook

1 Open *Mmgt_Review*, if necessary, and close any open side panes; then choose View, Resource Sheet.
The Resource Sheet view displays.

2 Right-click the Type column header and choose Insert Column.
The Column Definition dialog box opens.

3 Select *Email Address* from the *Field name* drop-down list, and then click OK.
The Email Address column is inserted to the left of the Type column (see Figure 8.36).

FIGURE 8.36

4 Choose Insert, New Resource From, Address Book.
The Select Resources dialog box appears (see Figure 8.37).

M'SOFT 8

Contacts in the Outlook address book

Click to add selected address to e-mail

FIGURE 8.37

5 From the *Name* list, click the first resource you want to add and then click the Add button.

6 Click the second resource you want to add in the *Name* list box, and then click Add.
Repeat as needed until all the resources you need have been added.

7 Click OK.
The resources you added along with their e-mail addresses are be inserted into the Resource sheet, similar to Figure 8.38.

Imported resources

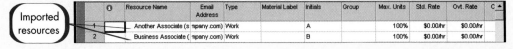

FIGURE 8.38

8 Save *Mmgt_Review* and close it.

SUMMARY

In this project, you learned how Microsoft Project shares information with other software programs. A task list was imported from Excel and appended to an already existing file. From the default Gantt Chart view, the task sheet was exported from Microsoft Project into an Excel worksheet. You linked task sheet data with a Microsoft Word document and saw how the data automatically update when changes are made in the original file. A pie chart created in an

Excel worksheet was incorporated into the Milestone Data Rollup view in Project. The Insert Object button in the Notes tab of the Task Information dialog box was investigated. You learned how to add objects into a note and how to add a hyperlink to a task. Finally, you learned how to import resources from Microsoft Outlook into the resource sheet.

You can extend your learning by reviewing concepts and terms and by practicing variations of skills presented in the lessons. Use the following table as a guide to the numbered questions and exercises in the end-of-project learning opportunities.

LESSON	MULTIPLE CHOICE	DISCUSSION	SKILL DRILL	CHALLENGE	DISCOVERY ZONE
Importing a Task List from Excel	1, 4, 9	3	1	1	1
Exporting Task Sheet Information into an Excel Worksheet	8, 10	3	2	2	
Copying and Pasting a Gantt Chart	7	1		3	
Linking and Embedding Project Data into Word and Excel	2, 5	1, 2		4	
Inserting Objects into Task Notes and Adding Hyperlinks to Tasks	6	1	3		
Using the Outlook Address Book to Add Resources	3		4		2

KEY TERMS

append

Comma Separated Values (CSV)

destination file

embed

export

Graphics Interchange Format (GIF)

hyperlink

Hypertext Markup Language (HTML)

import

map

mapping grid

merge

object

Object Linking and Embedding (OLE)

Open Database Connectivity (ODBC)

paste link

primary key

render

rich text format (RTF)

source file

MI'SOFT 8

CHECKING CONCEPTS AND TERMS

MULTIPLE CHOICE

Circle the letter of the correct answer for each of the following.

1. Which of the following is not specified when creating a map to append Excel data to a project file? [L1]

   a. To and From fields

   b. Worksheet name

   c. Filters

   d. Primary key

2. Which method would you use if you need two programs to create a file but only want one file to maintain? [L4]

   a. Copy and paste

   b. Embed

   c. Link

   d. Merge

3. What project data can be imported from an address book? [L6]

   a. Tasks

   b. Resources

   c. Work

   d. Schedules

4. What specification is necessary to import data into Project? [L1]

   a. Module

   b. Macro

   c. Merge code

   d. Map

5. Which method of sharing data does not allow changes made in the source file to be reflected in the destination file? [L4]

   a. Copy and paste

   b. Embed

   c. Link

   d. Merge

6. What do you use to access an outside data source within Microsoft Project? [L5]

   a. Hyperlink

   b. Map

   c. Network diagram

   d. Macro

7. Which of the following is not an allowable rendering method when copying a chart in Microsoft Project? [L3]

   a. Screen

   b. HTML

   c. Printer

   d. GIF

8. Which program supports exported project data? [L2]

   a. Word

   b. Access

   c. Excel

   d. All of the above

9. To import additional resources to a project file without using a primary key, which method would you use? [L1]

   a. New file

   b. Append

   c. Merge

   d. Map

10. What format is used as the World Wide Web standard? [L2]

    a. HTML

    b. XML

    c. ODBC

    d. CSV

DISCUSSION

1. In the previous project you learned how to e-mail project files; in this project you learned about different copy, paste, link, and embed options. How do these features complement each other? How are they different? [L3–L5]

2. Explain the differences between linked data and embedded data, and describe a scenario where each option could apply. [L4]

3. Describe what a map is and how it is utilized when importing and exporting data to and from Microsoft Project. What are the two mapping options? [L1, L2]

SKILL DRILL

Skill Drill exercises reinforce project skills. Each skill reinforced is the same, or nearly the same, as a skill presented in the project. Detailed instructions are provided in a step-by-step format.

You should complete all of the Skill Drill exercises in sequence.

1. Importing a Task List from Excel

You have been assigned by your supervisor to conduct a critical business analysis of the Purchasing department of your corporation. Your supervisor hopes that this analysis will flush out any duplication in processes, identify outdated technologies, and isolate steps to improve the processing of internal purchasing orders. Your job in this project is to help the lead project manager create the initial project plan to submit to your supervisor for approval. Because some tasks already reside in an Excel workbook, you decide to import them rather than type them from scratch.

To import a task list from Excel, follow these steps:

1. Click Start from the taskbar and click on Microsoft Excel 2003 from the Microsoft Office Folder.

2. Choose File, Open.

3. Click the down arrow at the right end of the *Look in* box, and select the drive and folder containing the student files for this text.

4. Click the *EPr1_0806* filename, and then click Open.

5. Choose File, Save As and name the file **Options_Analysis**.

6. View the data contained in the Excel spreadsheet.

7. Choose File, Close; and then minimize the Excel program.

8. Start Microsoft Project, open the *EPr1_0807* file, save it as **Business_Definition**, and then close any open side panes.

9. Choose File, Open.

10. Click the *Files of type* drop-down arrow;,select *Microsoft Excel Workbooks*, and then navigate to the folder where your student files are located.

11. Select the *Options_Analysis* Excel file, and then click <u>O</u>pen.

12. From the Import Wizard dialog box, click <u>N</u>ext.

13. Click the *New map* option, if necessary, and then click <u>N</u>ext.

14. Click the *Append the data to the active project* option, and then click <u>N</u>ext.

15. Check the *Tasks* check box, verify that *Import includes headers* is also selected, and then click <u>N</u>ext.

16. Click the *Source worksheet name* drop-down arrow and choose *Sheet1*.

17. In the mapping grid, click the Task Name field under *To: Microsoft Office Project Field*. Click the drop-down arrow and choose *Name*.

18. Click <u>N</u>ext and then click <u>F</u>inish.

19. Use the vertical scroll button to scroll to row 25 to view the imported data.

20. Select Task 25 (*Options Analysis*) through Task 32 (*Issues*) and click Outdent on the Formatting toolbar.

21. Select Task 26 (*Financial costs*) through Task 32 (*Issues*) and click Indent on the Formatting toolbar.

22. Save the *Business_Definition* project file and leave it open for the next exercise.

2. Exporting the Task Sheet as an Excel File

The project manager informs you that now that you have a good start on creating the project file, your supervisor wants to take a look at the file and then schedule a meeting with you to discuss changes that you might need to make. However, your supervisor does not have Microsoft Project on her system. To facilitate her request, you export the file as an Excel spreadsheet so she can review the task list at her convenience.

To export the task sheet to Excel, follow these steps:

1. Open *Business_Definition*, if necessary, and close any open side panes.

2. Choose <u>F</u>ile, Save <u>A</u>s.

3. Click the *Save as type* drop-down arrow and choose *Microsoft Excel Workbook (*.xls)*.

4. In the *File name* text box, click after the *n* in *Definition* and type **_Export**, and then click <u>S</u>ave.

5. From the Export Wizard dialog box, click <u>N</u>ext.

6. Click the *Selected Data* option and click <u>N</u>ext.

7. Click the *New map* option button and then click <u>N</u>ext.

8. Check the *Tasks* check box, verify that *Export includes headers* is also selected, and then click <u>N</u>ext.

9. Under *Verify or edit Project's assumptions for how you want to map the data*, click in the first cell under *From: Microsoft Office Project Field*, select *Name* in the list, and then press ⏎Enter.

10. Then, select *Duration* and press ⏎Enter.

11. Click <u>N</u>ext and then click <u>F</u>inish.

12. Minimize Microsoft Project, and maximize Excel.

13. Click Open on the Excel Standard toolbar; *Business_Definition_Export*; and then click <u>O</u>pen.

14. Verify that the data are accurate; then choose <u>F</u>ile, E<u>x</u>it to close the Excel file and exit the Excel program.

15. Click the *Business_Definition* Project file from the taskbar, if necessary, and save it, leaving it open for the next exercise.

3. Inserting a PowerPoint Slide into a Note

After your supervisor reviews the project file, she wants you to attach a PowerPoint file to the task where business data problems are listed. This process ensures that the standard corporate form is utilized.

To attach a PowerPoint slide to a note, follow these steps:

1. Open *Business_Definition*, if necessary, and then close any open side panes.

2. Double-click Task 12 (*List problems with business data*) and click the Notes tab.

3. Click the Insert Object button.

4. From the Insert Object dialog box, click the *Create from File* option button.

5. Click Browse and navigate to the folder where your student files are located. Select the *EPr1_0808* PowerPoint file and click <u>I</u>nsert.

6. Click OK.

7. Save *Business_Definition* and leave it open for the next exercise.

4. Adding Resources from Microsoft Outlook

Your supervisor has given you and the project manager the go-ahead to begin adding resources to the project plan and assigning work to the team who will be conducting the critical business analysis. However, she wants to ensure that you include everyone's e-mail address. The project manager provided the list of resources and informs you that most of them can be found in the corporate address book and that you can import them from Outlook.

To import e-mail addresses from Microsoft Outlook, follow these steps:

1. Open *Business_Definition*, if necessary, and close any open side panes; then choose <u>V</u>iew, Resource <u>S</u>heet.

2. Right-click the Type column header and choose Insert <u>C</u>olumn.

3. Select *Email Address* from the *Field <u>n</u>ame* drop-down list, and then click OK.

4. Choose <u>I</u>nsert, New Resource Fro<u>m</u>, Address <u>B</u>ook.

5. From the *Name* list, click the first resource you want to add and then click the Add button.

6. Click the second resource you want to add in the *Name* list box and then click Add.

7. Click OK, then click OK again.

8. Save *Business_Definition* and close it.

CHALLENGE

Challenge exercises expand on or are somewhat related to skills presented in the lessons. Each exercise provides a brief narrative introduction, followed by instructions in a numbered-step format that are not as detailed as those in the Skill Drill section. The exercises relate to a single file, and you should work the exercises in order.

1. Importing Resource Lists

As the technical editor for a large firm, you are creating a handbook to accompany a customized in-house computer program. This handbook requires a group effort with many departments involved. You have an Excel workbook that lists each employee assigned to the handbook project. Each department has a worksheet within the workbook, including employee names, hourly cost, and availability. You must import this workbook of data into your project file to supplement the resource sheet.

To import a resource list, follow these steps:

1. Start Excel; open *EPr1_0809* and save it as **Resources.xls**.

2. View the Programmers and Software Testers worksheets, and then exit Excel.

3. Open *EPr1_0810*, save it as **Handbook**, and then switch to Resource Sheet view.

4. Open the *Resources* workbook within Microsoft Project, and begin the importing process, using a new map.

5. Choose to append the data to the open project file; select to import *Resouces* and include headers in the import.

6. In the Import Wizard – Task Mapping dialog box, choose to import the Programmers worksheet; then map the Excel Employee field to the Project Name field, the Excel Hourly Rate field to the Project Standard Rate field, and the Excel Available Time field to the Project Max Units field.

7. Import the resources on the Software Testers worksheet, using the same procedures.

8. Save *Handbook* and leave it open for the next exercise.

2. Exporting Project Data as HTML

Your company has several branches in various cities within a three-state region. Your company uses a WAN (Wide Area Network) to disseminate information to all branches. You need to share the task and resource information with the entire company, and the best way is to export the data into an HTML file to post on the company intranet. So you use an existing map to export a task and resource PivotTable.

To export project data as HTML, follow these steps:

1. Open *Handbook* and close any side panes, if necessary.

2. Use Microsoft Project Help to learn how to save project information as a Web page.

3. Save the project file as an HTML file.

   The Export Wizard opens.

4. Choose to use an existing map.

5. Choose the Task and Resource PivotTable map.

6. Complete the wizard, using defaults.

7. Open a browser, and then open the *Handbook.html* file in your solution files.

8. Look through the Web page and then close the browser.

9. Save *Handbook* and leave it open for the next exercise.

3. Copying a Portion of a Network Diagram to an Excel Workbook

You need to send an Excel workbook to the department head to inform her of the tasks involving the technical writers. You have a worksheet listing those tasks, but you think a diagram would be beneficial as well. So you copy a picture of the network diagram in the project file and paste it in the worksheet.

To copy part of a network diagram to a workbook, follow these steps:

1. Open *Handbook* and close any side panes, if necessary.

2. Switch to Network Diagram view, and then change the zoom to 85% (Hint: Use View, Zoom).

3. Use the Copy Picture option to copy the screen.

4. Open Microsoft Excel, open *EPr1_0811*, and then select cell A7.

5. Paste the picture; then drag the bottom-right corner handle to make the image larger, filling the range A7 to J31.

6. Save the workbook as **Writers** and close it.

7. Save *Handbook* and leave it open for the next exercise.

4. Embedding a Calendar from a Project File into a Word Document

Each week, you plan to distribute a memo to all stakeholders to inform them of the next few weeks' activities concerning the handbook creation. You have decided to embed a copy of the calendar from your project file into the memo.

To embed a calendar, follow these steps:

1. Open *Handbook* and close any side panes, if necessary.

2. Display the View Bar and switch to Calendar view.

3. Save the project file and minimize Microsoft Project.

4. Start Word and open *EPr1_0812*.

5. Use the Insert Object menu option to embed the *Handbook* project file after the first paragraph.

6. Resize the embedded calendar to 3.48″ (height) by 6.13″ (width). Use Help to learn how to resize an object in a Word document if it is unfamiliar to you.

7. Save the Word document as **Schedule**.

8. Double-click the calendar and note the changes to the application window.

9. Click outside of the calendar, save the document again and close Word.

10. Close *Handbook*.

DISCOVERY ZONE

Discovery Zone exercises require advanced knowledge of topics presented in *Essentials* lessons, application of skills from multiple lessons, or self-directed learning of new skills. The exercises are independent of each other, so you may complete them in any order.

1. Using the Excel Task List Template

Microsoft Office provides continuity between programs as well as collaborative features. Data can be shared between Microsoft Project and Excel easily. In fact, Microsoft Excel contains a template designed to make importing Excel data into Microsoft Project simple.

Start Microsoft Excel and click the On my computer link under Templates in the New Workbook task pane. Click the Spreadsheet Solutions tab and select Microsoft Project Plan Import Export Template. Look through the workbook, particularly the Info Tab. Then, create some records on each worksheet. Save the workbook as **Template_Data**, and then close it.

In Microsoft Project, import the *Template_Data* workbook. Use the wizard to include all the worksheets. Save the new project file as **Template_Data**. Close the project file.

2. Using Resource Pools

In Project 4, you learned about resources and how to assign them to specific tasks. There are times when resources are used within multiple projects. A resource pool is a set of resources that are available for assignment to project tasks and can be used exclusively by one project or can be shared by several projects. When resources are used repeatedly, a resource pool saves a great deal of time.

Use Help to research the topic "Use another project's resources in your project." Then, create a new project file and name it **Resource_Pool**. In the resource sheet, create a list of resources to be shared with other projects. Open any existing project file and save it as **Shared_Resources**. Share the resources from the *Resource_Pool* project file with the *Shared_Resources* project file. Save and close both files once you have verified that the resources were shared correctly.

INTEGRATING PROJECTS

Essentials 2003: Microsoft Project

The Integrating Projects exercises provide additional hands-on practice working with Microsoft Project. Each exercise requires the application of skills from multiple projects; a cross-reference accompanying each exercise title tells you which projects introduced the skills applied in the exercise. The exercises are independent of each other and can be worked in any order.

You follow a checklist as you create and enhance each complete product. Many of the exercises include opportunities to make decisions about the best approach and features to use in a particular situation.

1 CREATING A SOFTWARE DEPLOYMENT PROJECT PLAN

Based on Projects 1, 2, 3, and 8

Roddenberry's and Associates has recently decided to create an internal information management systems team to handle training, computer end-user support, e-mail administration, and virus protection and recovery. You work in the Human Resources division of this company and are responsible for processing new hires. You must create a project plan to manage the job creation portion of this newly developed information systems department. The purpose of this project plan is to determine the job types needed in this new department, to develop an overall department structure or hierarchy, and to track operating expenses associated with creating this new team. Figure PrIP.1 illustrates the final project plan.

	❶	Task Name	Duration	Start	Finish	Predecessors
1		⊟ **Business Analysis**	**6 days?**	**Mon 4/3/06**	**Mon 4/10/06**	
2		Determine use and function of dept. for firm	1 day?	Mon 4/3/06	Mon 4/3/06	
3		Review business goals/vision/mission statement	1 day?	Mon 4/3/06	Mon 4/3/06	
4		Determine department structure/hierarchy	1 day?	Mon 4/3/06	Mon 4/3/06	
5		Determine job types	1 day?	Mon 4/3/06	Mon 4/3/06	
6		Verify job types with human resources	1 day?	Mon 4/3/06	Mon 4/3/06	
7		⊟ **Phase II**	**6 days?**	**Mon 4/3/06**	**Mon 4/10/06**	
8		Create Information Systems analysis plan	2 days	Mon 4/3/06	Tue 4/4/06	
9		Implement plan	5 days	Tue 4/4/06	Mon 4/10/06	3
10		Identify support infrastructure	2 days	Tue 4/4/06	Wed 4/5/06	4
11		Summarize business needs	2 days	Tue 4/4/06	Wed 4/5/06	5
12		Identify market needs	1 day	Tue 4/4/06	Tue 4/4/06	6
13		Summarize operating expenses	1 day?	Mon 4/3/06	Mon 4/3/06	

	❶	Resource Name	Email Address	Type	Material Label	Initials	Group	Max. Units	Std. Rate	Ovt. Rate
1		Manager	ddress.com	Work		Mgr	Sr. Mgmt	100%	$75.00/hr	$0.00/hr
2		Computer Training	ddress.com	Work		CT	Train	300%	$150.00/hr	$0.00/hr
3		Director	ddress.com	Work		Dir	Sr. Mgmt	100%	$150.00/hr	$0.00/hr
4		Human Resources	ddress.com	Work		HR	HR	100%	$50.00/hr	$0.00/hr
5		Marketing	ddress.com	Work		Mrk	Mrk	200%	$100.00/hr	$0.00/hr
6		Accounting	ddress.com	Work		AP	AP	300%	$300.00/hr	$0.00/hr
7		FedEx		Material		FedEx			$0.00	

FIGURE PrIP.1

IP Exercise Checklist

❑ Open a new project file and save it as **IS_Deploy**.

❑ Set the start date as *4/3/2006*.

❑ Define the Project Working Times using the Standard calendar with the default work week of Monday–Friday, with the default 8-hour work day, 40-hour work week.

❑ Enter the following tasks:

Business Analysis

Determine use and function of dept. for firm

Review business goals/vision/mission statement

Determine department structure/hierarchy

Determine job types

Verify job types with human resources

❑ Indent Task 2 (*Determine use and function of dept. for firm*) through Task 6 (*Verify job types with human resources*) below Task 1 (*Business Analysis*) to make Task 1 a summary task.

❑ Import the next set of tasks from the *EPr1_IP01* Excel workbook. Use a new map and append the data to the existing project plan. Map only the task information on Sheet1. In the mapping grid, review the map assignments to verify that all fields are mapped to the correct and corresponding column in the task sheet.

❑ Indent Task 8 (*Create Information Systems analysis plan*) through Task 13 (*Summarize operating expenses*) below Task 7 (*Phase II*) to make Task 7 a summary task.

❑ Modify the scheduling constraint on the newly imported tasks, using the default constraint of *As Soon As Possible*.

❑ Add the Email Address column after the Resource Name column in the resource sheet and then enter the following resources:

Resource Name	Email Address	Type	Initials	Group	Max. Units	Std. Rate	Cost/Use
Manager	mgr@emailaddress.com	Work	Mgr	Sr. Mgmt	100%	$75.00/h	(blank)
Computer Training	training@emailaddress.com	Work	CT	Train	300%	$150.00/h	(blank)
Director	direct@emailaddress.com	Work	Dir	Sr. Mgmt	100%	$150.00/h	(blank)
Human Resources	hr@emailaddress.com	Work	HR	HR	100%	$50.00/h	(blank)
Marketing	market@emailaddress.com	Work	Mrk	Mrk	200%	$100.00/h	(blank)
Accounting	ap@emailaddress.com	Work	AP	AP	300%	$300.00/h	(blank)
FedEx	(blank)	Material	FedEx	(blank)	(blank)	$0.00	$5.00

❑ Preview (or print if you prefer) the Working Days report.

❑ Save and close the *IS_Deploy* project file.

2 MODIFYING TASKS AND ASSIGNING RESOURCES

Based on Projects 3, 4, and 5

You work in the Human Resources division of Roddenberry's and Associates and are managing a project file for a newly developed information systems department. Considerable work has been done on the file and you are now ready to finalize the project plan and implement a second phase so that you can begin using it to track the progress of the information systems department deployment. To complete the file, you must specify the different task predecessors to create links between tasks. You also use the outline features to better view the different phases of the project plan. You then need to assign resources to their task assignments.

IP Exercise Checklist

❑ Open *EPr1_IP02* and save it as **Final_IS_Deploy**.

❑ Use the following table to link tasks:

Task ID	Task Name	Predecessors
10	Identify dept. goals - long/short	9SS
11	Promote/Hire dept. employees	10FF
12	Complete new hire application form	11
13	Complete 941	12SS
14	Interview process with leadership	9
16	Make offers	15
17	Set start dates	16
18	Infrastructure Review	17
19	Identify standard computer workstation	9
21	Determine connectivity LAN/WAN needs	20
22	Determine server needs	21
23	Develop detailed infrastructure plan	22
26	Implement plan	3
27	Identify support infrastructure	4
28	Summarize business needs	5
29	Identify market needs	6
30	Summarize operating expenses	7

❑ Use Outdent and Indent to outline the project plan and organize the tasks as follows:

 ❑ Task 8 (*Staff Information Systems department*) through Task 23 (*Develop detailed infrastructure plan*) as subtasks for Task 1 (*Phase 1*)

 ❑ Task 9 (*Identify leadership*) through Task 13 (*Complete 941*) as subtasks for Task 8 (*Staff Information Systems department*)

 ❑ Task 15 (*Select candidates*) through Task 17 (*Set start dates*) as subtasks for Task 14 (*Interview process with leadership*)

 ❑ Task 20 (*Decide upon software package*) through Task 23 (*Develop detailed infrastructure plan*) as subtasks for Task 19 (*Identify standard computer workstation*)

❑ View the resource sheet and familiarize yourself with the resources. Then switch to Gantt Chart view and assign resources to each task as appropriate. Remember: Multiple resources may be assigned to one task.

❑ Save a copy of the baseline.

❑ View the Tracking Gantt to preview (or print if you prefer) the baseline.

❑ Save the project file, and then close *Final_IS_Deploy*.

3 USING A TEMPLATE TO CREATE A NEW PROJECT FILE

Based on Projects 2, 4, 5, and 8

You are a department administrative professional for a large manufacturing firm. Your company recently received a federal training grant. In order to be eligible for the federal money, however, all corporate employees must receive several hours of OSHA (Occupational Safety and Health Administration) training. Your supervisor has asked you to be the communications liaison between her and several employees managing this large-scale training project. Your job is to work at the direction of your supervisor as well as a group of training professionals, to create and maintain a project plan that the group will use.

To get started with creating the project plan, use an already existing template from Microsoft templates online and modify the start date. You customize this template. A hyperlink to a Word document listing the different departments to receive OSHA training is added and resources are entered in the resource sheet. You also assign these resources to the tasks listed in the project file and save a baseline.

IP Exercise Checklist

❑ Start Word, open *EPr1_IP03*, and save it as **Target_Department**.

❑ View the *Target_Department* document and then exit Word.

❑ Create a new Project file using the Training rollout initiative and plan located at Templates on Office online in the Meetings and Projects category and the Project Management sub-category, and save it as **Training**.

❑ Familiarize yourself with the tasks in this template.

❑ Set the start date and the status date to *Sun 3/5/06*.

❑ Create a hyperlink from Task 6 (*Create list of target departments*) to the *Target_Department* Word document you saved.

❑ Create a list of resources in Resource Sheet view. Be sure to add at least eight work resources and two material resources. Assign the resources to the following groups:

Group

Planning

Training

Vendor Management

Marketing

Registration and Staff Support

ROI Team

❑ For each task, assign a resource or multiple resources as you see fit.

❑ Save a baseline for the project.

❑ Preview (or print if you prefer) a Who Does What report.

❑ Save and close the *Training* project file.

4 MONITORING THE PROGRESS OF A TRAINING ROLLOUT INITIATIVE

Based on Projects 1, 3, 4, 5, 6, and 7

You are a department administrative professional for a large manufacturing firm that is implementing a large-scale OSHA (Occupational Safety and Health Administration) training program to receive a federal grant. Working at the direction of a group of training professionals and your supervisor, you update the project plan as instructed. With the project plan well under way, you start tracking how well the training program is progressing. Using a variety of values including percentage complete and remaining duration, update the task progress as communicated to you from the team. You also need to communicate the overall project status to your supervisor.

IP Exercise Checklist

❑ Open the *EPr1_IP04* project file and save it as **Training_Initiative**.

❑ View the Tracking table and display the Tracking toolbar.

❑ Mark the following tasks as complete:

Task 3 (*Define project objectives and describe mission statement*)

Task 4 (*Ensure total participation by training team support staff*)

Task 6 (*Create list of target departments*)

Task 13 (*Define vendor deliverables - can they meet our needs?*)

Task 29 (*Reserve training rooms*)

Task 31 (*Order training manuals and necessary material*)

Task 52 (*Call 1*)

Task 53 (*Call 2*)

Task 54 (*Call 3*)

❑ Mark the following tasks as 75% complete:

Task 7 (*Perform departmental training needs analysis*)

Task 14 (*Obtain vendor commitment to training rollout schedule*)

Task 43 (*In-house instructors*)

Task 44 (*Outsourced instructors*)

❑ Mark the following tasks as 50% complete:

Task 16 (*Obtain approval for purchase orders to cover vendor invoices*)

Task 18 (*Create a list of training recipients by department*)

Task 26 (*Determine course dates, start and end times, and locations*)

❏ Mark the following tasks as 25% complete:

Task 8 (*Compile results and present findings to training coordinator*)

Task 9 (*Prioritize training delivery according to critical need*)

Task 33 (*Order promotional material*)

❏ Modify the Actual Finish date for Task 3 (*Define project objectives and describe mission statement*) to *Tue 3/7/06.*

❏ Modify the Remaining Duration for Task 7 (*Perform departmental training needs analysis*) and Task 8 (*Compile results and present findings to training coordinator*) to display *3 days.*

❏ View the Entry Table and remove the lag time between Task 21 (*Initiate end-user placement matrix*) and Task 22 (*Finalize project budget*).

❏ Split Task 7 (*Perform departmental training needs analysis*) at *Tue 3/14/06.*

❏ View the Project Statistics and then preview (or print if you prefer) the Project Summary report.

❏ Save and close the *Training_Initiative* project file.

5 COMPLETING AND E-MAILING A MAINTENANCE SCHEDULE PROJECT FILE

Based on Projects 3, 4, 5, 7, and 8

You have recently been hired as a property manager by a large property management company. The community you are responsible for is very exclusive and is in a large metropolitan area. The property was recently purchased by the company that hired you and several maintenance issues have been identified. Your first job is to work with your maintenance staff to identify those items that require immediate maintenance. You also utilize this list as a quarterly maintenance tool to check everything on a more regular basis. In addition, because so many items are expected to be repaired, this schedule needs to be approved by the vice president of leasing.

Complete the task table by adding durations and specifying predecessors. Import resources from an Excel spreadsheet, modify task information, and create a custom view to apply when sending the project plan as an attachment for review. Figure PrIP.2 illustrates your plans for the completed project plan. Save your work periodically as you make your changes.

FIGURE PrIP.2

IP Exercise Checklist

❑ Open the *EPr1_IP05* project file and save it as **Repair_Schedule**.

❑ Review the current list of tasks to familiarize yourself with the project plan.

❑ Using the table below, complete the task durations and predecessors.

ID	Task Name	Duration	Predecessors
3	Check faucets for leaks, corrosion	20d?	
4	Check drains for clogs	20d?	3SS
5	Check toilets for stability and leaks	20d?	4SS
6	Drain water heaters, check for leaks	60d?	5SS
7	Complete maintenance checklist for each unit	2d?	
8	Submit copy to property manager and resident	1d?	7
9	Develop repair schedule	5d?	8
10	Notify residents	5d?	9
11	Complete repairs	60d?	10
13	Clean and replace HVAC filters	25d?	
14	Clean all kitchen exhaust fans	25d?	13SS
15	Empty and clean fridge drain pans	15d?	14SS
16	Check dishwashers for leaks	20d?	15SS
17	Check outlets for wear	30d?	
18	Test all smoke detectors	30d?	17SS
19	Complete maintenance checklist for each unit	5d?	
20	Submit copy to property manager and resident	1d?	19
21	Develop repair schedule	5d?	20
22	Notify residents	5d?	21
23	Complete repairs	25d?	22
25	Inspect foundation of each building	10d?	
26	Inspect all ducts and vents for clogs	10d?	25SS
27	Check sprinkler system	1d?	
28	Inspect for proper drainage	1d?	27
29	Submit repair list to property manager	1d?	
30	Hire repair crews	5d?	29
31	Develop schedule of repairs	1d?	30
32	Complete repairs	15d?	31

❑ Insert a recurring meeting task with the name *Telephone conference with corporate* above Task 2 (*Plumbing*) that meets every other week on Tuesday. Make the end date for the recurring task *Mon 8/22/05*.

❑ Check the spelling and correct any spelling mistakes that exist in the file.

❑ Switch to Resource Sheet view and import the *EPr1_IP06* Excel file, using a new map and appending the data to the existing project plan. Map only the resources on Sheet1. In the mapping grid, review the map assignments to verify that all fields are mapped to the correct and corresponding column in the resource sheet.

❑ Complete the resource sheet by adding the following material resources:

Resource	Type	Cost/Use
Heating/AC filter	Material	2.50
Smoke alarm	Material	15.75
Toilet kit	Material	5.25

❑ Create a custom view with the following attributes:

Attribute	Selection
View Type:	Combination View
Name:	Task Detail for Supervisor
Top:	Resource Usage
Bottom:	Task Details Form

❑ Apply the Task Detail for Supervisor view.

❑ E-mail the project file as an attachment to one individual. Rather than sending the e-mail, save the file. From the Save as type: drop-down, choose Outlook Message Format (*.msg) and save the file where your solution files are located. Close the e-mail form without sending it.

❑ Save the *Repair_Schedule* project file and close it.

6   USING A ROUTED PROJECT FILE

Based on Projects 4, 7, and 8

You are a property manager at a large, upscale urban rental community. You have created a project plan to track and regularly check items in the rental units and the overall property that require regular maintenance. The project file you created was routed to several people in the leasing division of the property management company for which you work. The last recipient has sent the routed file back to you, and you need to review the changes that have been made to it.

In the following steps, you open the project file, save it with a new name, and review the changes. In addition, the task items you created should be paste linked into a Microsoft Word document and saved as an HTML document. The company you work for wants this information shared with other community managers so they can develop their own maintenance plans.

IP Exercise Checklist

❑ Open the *EPr1_IP07* project file and save it as **Repair_Schedule_Routed**.

❑ Switch to Gantt Chart view and close the lower pane in the view by double-clicking the split line.

❑ Review the project file and the resources.

❑ Switch to Resource Usage view and review the task assignments for the Maintenance Staff resource. Notice that this resource is overallocated and needs to be leveled.

❑ Modify the Maintenance Staff resource so that it now has Max. Units of 500%—which reflects that the staff will have five full-time employees during the project time frame.

❏ Remove the Maintenance Staff from the following tasks, and apply the Leasing Assistant instead, accepting the default SmartTag options as prompted.

Task ID	Task Name
24	Develop repair schedule
25	Notify residents
36	Develop repair schedule
37	Notify residents

❏ Switch to Gantt Chart view and save the project baseline.

❏ Select the Task Name, Duration, Start, and Finish columns in the task sheet and copy these columns.

❏ Save *Repair_Schedule_Routed* and minimize it.

❏ In a new blank Word document, link the columns that you copied in the *Repair_Schedule_Routed* project file as Formatted Text (RTF). Save the file in the same directory where your other solution files are located, and name it **Paste_Link_Repair_Schedule**. Exit Microsoft Word.

❏ In the *Repair_Schedule_Routed* project file, double-click Task 25 (*Notify residents*) and insert a Note object created from a file. Use the *EPr1_IP08* Excel file as the linked file.

❏ Insert the same *EPr1_IP08* Excel file as a Note object for Task 37 (*Notify residents*).

❏ Save the file as a Web page (*.html; *.htm) file and name it **Web_Ver_Repair_Schedule**. Use a new map and export only the tasks, making sure the *Export header row/Import includes headers* option is selected. From the mapping grid, export the following columns of data:

From: Microsoft Project Field	To: HTML Table Field
Name	Name
Start	Start
Finish	Finish
Resource Names	Resource Names

❏ Preview (or print if you prefer) a Who Does What report.

❏ Save the *Repair_Schedule_Routed* project file and close it.

M'SOFT IP

FILE GUIDE

Guide to Files in Essentials: Microsoft Project 2003

P#-L# or P#-ex type	Original Student File	Student File Saved As	Related Solution Notes
Project 1			
P1-L1 thru L7	EPr1_0101.mpp	Apartment_Brochure.mpp	
P1-SD1 thru SD4	EPr1_0102.mpp	Software_Deployment.mpp	
P1-SD5			No files; explore Help topics
P1-CH1 thru CH3	New project (template)	New_Business.mpp	
P1-CH4	EPr1_0103.mpp	Software.mpp	
P1-DZ1			Creative Solution exercise (explore Help topics); solution not provided
P1-DZ2			Creative Solution exercise (Web research on project management); solution not provided
Project 2			
P2-L1	New project	New_Hires.mpp	
P2-L2 thru L5	EPr1_0201.mpp	New_Hire_Orientation.mpp	
P2-L6	New project (template)	OFFMOVE.mpp	
P2-SD1 thru SD2	New project	Board_New_Member.mpp	
P2-SD3	EPr1_0202.mpp	Forms_Procedures.mpp	
P2-SD4	EPr1_0203.mpp	PO_Routing.mpp	
P2-CH1 and CH2	EPr1_0204.mpp	Manual_Schedule.mpp	
P2-CH3	EPr1_0205.mpp	Magazine_Article.mpp	
P2-CH4	New project (template)	Building_Plan.mpp	
P2-DZ1	New project	Production.mpp	Creative Solution exercise (project calendars); solution not provided

P = Project   L = Lesson   SD = Skill Drill   CH = Challenge   DZ = Discovery Zone   IP = Integrating Projects

Creative Solution exercises permit individual choices that produce unique solutions

P#-L# or P#-ex type	Original Student File	Student File Saved As	Related Solution Notes
P2-DZ2			Creative Solution exercise (create a template from project of choice); solution not provided

Project 3

P#-L# or P#-ex type	Original Student File	Student File Saved As	Related Solution Notes
P3-L1	New project	Conference_Preplanning.mpp	
P3-L2 thru L7	EPr1_0301.mpp	Conference_Plan.mpp	
P3-SD1	New project	Cruise_Planning.mpp	
P3-SD2 thru SD5	EPr1_0302.mpp	Club_Cruise.mpp	
P3-CH1	New project	Signs_Graphics.mpp	
P3-CH2 and CH3	EPr1_0303.mpp	Apartment_Artwork.mpp	
P3-CH4	EPr1_0304.mpp	Training_Portal.mpp	
P3-DZ1	New project	Accounting_Software.mpp	Creative Solution exercise (project templates); solution not provided
P3-DZ2	New project	Constraint.mpp	Creative Solution exercise (task constraints); solution not provided

Project 4

P#-L# or P#-ex type	Original Student File	Student File Saved As	Related Solution Notes
P4-L1 thru L6	EPr1_0401.mpp	Business_Model.mpp	
P4-SD1 thru SD5	EPr1_0402.mpp	Virus_Recovery.mpp	
P4-CH1 thru CH5	EPr1_0403.mpp	Temps_Hiring_Plan.mpp	CH4 is a Creative Solution exercise (level resources); solution file is a representative solution and will vary depending upon CH4
P4-DZ1			Creative Solution exercise (template); solution not provided
P4-DZ2			Creative Solution exercise (costs); solution not provided

Project 5

P#-L# or P#-ex type	Original Student File	Student File Saved As	Related Solution Notes
P5-L1 thru L6	EPr1_0501.mpp	Fundraiser.mpp	
P5-L7	EPr1_0502.mpp	Programming.mpp	
P5-SD1 thru SD6	EPr1_0503.mpp	Software_Manual.mpp	

P = Project   L = Lesson   SD = Skill Drill   CH = Challenge   DZ = Discovery Zone   IP = Integrating Projects

Creative Solution exercises permit individual choices that produce unique solutions

P#-L# or P#-ex type	Original Student File	Student File Saved As	Related Solution Notes
P5-CH1 thru CH4	EPr1_0504.mpp	Direct_Market.mpp	Creative Solution exercise (project tracking); solution not provided
P5-DZ1			Creative Solution exercise (using Help); solution not provided
P5-DZ2			Creative Solution exercise (create views using a template); solution not provided

Project 6

P#-L# or P#-ex type	Original Student File	Student File Saved As	Related Solution Notes
P6-L1 thru L6	EPr1_0601.mpp	Ad_Campaign.mpp	
P6-SD1 thru SD4	EPr1_0602.mpp	Request_For_Proposal.mpp	
P6-CH1 thru CH4	EPr1_0603.mpp	Orientation.mpp	
P6-DZ1			Creative Solution exercise (multiple progress lines); solution not provided
P6-DZ2			Creative Solution exercise (reports); solution not provided

Project 7

P#-L# or P#-ex type	Original Student File	Student File Saved As	Related Solution Notes
P7-L1 thru L8	EPr1_0701.mpp	Restaurant.mpp	
P7-SD1 thru SD5	EPr1_0702.mpp	Fundraiser_Auction.mpp	
P7-CH1 thru CH5	EPr1_0703.mpp	PIMS.mpp	
P7-DZ1			Creative Solution exercise (Help, views); solution not provided
P7-DZ2	EPr1_0702.mpp	PERT.mpp	Creative Solution exercise (Help, PERT analysis); solution not provided

Project 8

P#-L# or P#-ex type	Original Student File	Student File Saved As	Related Solution Notes
P8-L1 thru L6	EPr1_0802.mpp	Mgmt_Review.mpp	
P8-L1	EPr1_0801.xls	Assessment.xls	Import Excel data into Mgmt_Review
P8-L2		Mgmt_Review_Export.xls	Export Mgmt_Review data to Excel
P8-L3		Gantt_Chart.xls	Copy Gantt chart from Mgmt_Review to a new Excel workbook

P = Project   L = Lesson   SD = Skill Drill   CH = Challenge   DZ = Discovery Zone   IP = Integrating Projects

Creative Solution exercises permit individual choices that produce unique solutions

M'SOFT FG

P#-L# or P#-ex type	Original Student File	Student File Saved As	Related Solution Notes
P8-L4 (part 1)		Linked_Mgmt_Review.doc	Link Mgmt_Review data to a new Word document
P8-L4 (part 2)	EPr1_0803.xls		Embed an Excel chart and data in Mgmt_Review
P8-L5	EPr1_0804.ppt EPr1_0805.doc		Insert a slide (EPr1_0804.ppt) into Mgmt_Review; then add a hyperlink that opens the Word file EPr1_0805
P8-L6			Import resources from Microsoft Outlook to Mgmt_Review
P8-SD1 thru SD4	EPr1_0807.mpp	Business_Definition.mpp	
P8-SD1	EPr1_0806.xls	Options_Analysis.xls	Import Excel data into Business_Definition
P8-SD2		Business_Definition_Export.xls	Export Business_Definition data to Excel
P8-SD3	EPr1_0808.ppt		Insert slide (EP1_0808.ppt) into Business_Definition
P8-CH1 thru CH4	EPr1_0810.mpp	Handbook.mpp	
P8-CH1	EPr1_0809.xls	Resources.xls	Import Excel data (Resources.xls) into Handbook
P8-CH2		Handbook.html	Export Handbook data as HTML (Handbook.html)
P8-CH3	EPr1_0811.xls	Writers.xls	Copy part of a network diagram in Handbook to Excel (Writers.xls)
P8-CH4	EPr1_0812.doc	Schedule.doc	Embed a calendar from Handbook into a Word document (Schedule.doc)
P8-DZ1	New Excel workbook from template; New project file	Template_Data.xls Template_Data.mpp	Creative Solution exercise; add data of choice to Excel template and save as Template_Data.xls; then import those data into a new project file Template_Data.mpp; solution not provided
P8-DZ2	New project Choice of any existing project file	Resource_Pool.mpp Shared_Resources.mpp	Creative Solution exercise; get Help on sharing resources; then share resources from Resource_Pool with Shared_Resources; solution not provided

Integrating Projects

P#-L# or P#-ex type	Original Student File	Student File Saved As	Related Solution Notes
IP1	New project EPr1_IP01.xls	IS_Deploy.mpp	Create new project IS_Deploy; includes importing Excel data (EPr1_IP01.xls)
IP2	EPr1_IP02.mpp	Final_IS_Deploy.mpp	Creative Solution exercise; assign resources and save/view a baseline

P = Project   L = Lesson   SD = Skill Drill   CH = Challenge   DZ = Discovery Zone   IP = Integrating Projects

Creative Solution exercises permit individual choices that produce unique solutions

P#-L# or P#-ex type	Original Student File	Student File Saved As	Related Solution Notes
IP3	EPr1_IP03.doc New from template	Target_Department.doc Training.mpp	Creative Solution exercise; use online template to create Training.mpp; set up project file; create hyperlink to a Word document; add and assign resources to tasks; save a baseline; and view a report
IP4	EPr1_IP04.mpp	Training_Initiative.mpp	Track progress and enter actuals; create lag time for one task; split a task; and view Project Statistics
IP5	EPr1_IP05.mpp EPr1_IP06.xls	Repair_Schedule.mpp	Enter durations and predecessors for select tasks; insert a recurring task; check spelling; import an Excel worksheet (EPr1_IP06.xls); add material resources; create a custom view; and e-mail the project file as an attachment
IP6	EPr1_IP07.mpp EPr1_IP08.xls New Word document	Repair_Schedule_Routed.mpp Paste_Link_Repair_Schedule.doc Web_Ver_Repair_Schedule.html	Level resources; create a baseline; link the project file to the Paste_Link_Repair_Schedule.doc file; insert the EPr1_IP08.xls file as a note in the Task Information for two tasks; export the project data as Web_Ver_Repair_Schedule.htm Web page; and view a report

M'SOFT FG

P = Project   L = Lesson   SD = Skill Drill   CH = Challenge   DZ = Discovery Zone   IP = Integrating Projects

Creative Solution exercises permit individual choices that produce unique solutions

MICROSOFT PROJECT 2003 TASK GUIDE

A book in the *Essentials* series can serve as a handy reference beside your computer even after you complete all the projects and exercises. When you need a refresher for the sequence of steps or a shortcut to achieve a result, look up the task category in the alphabetized listing that follows. Then turn to the page number listed in the second column to locate the step-by-step exercise or other detailed description. Entries without page numbers describe tasks that are closely related to those presented in the projects.

Project Task	Page	Mouse	Menu Bar	Shortcut Menu	Shortcut Keys
Baseline, save	458	Click `Track ▾` on Project Guide toolbar, click *Save a baseline plan to compare with later versions* link, and click `Save Baseline`	**Tools | Tracking | Save Baseline**		
Baseline, view data	459		**View | Tracking Gantt**		
Calendar, apply to a task	397	Click 📁 on Standard toolbar and the Advanced tab and click the C**a**lendar drop-down	**Project | Task Information | Advanced tab | Calendar drop-down**		
Calendar, creating a new custom	356		**Tools | Change Working Time | New | complete dialog box**		
Calendar, modify Project Working Times	361	Click *Define general working times* on the Tasks side pane	**Tools | Change Working Time | Complete dialog box**		
Calendar, modify work week	361		**Tools | Options | Calendar tab | enter number in *Hours per week* box**		
Calendar, set start date	356	Click *Set a date to schedule from* on the Tasks side pane	**Project | Project Information**		
Column, hide a column in the Task Table	330		**Select column | Edit | Hide Column**	**Right-click column heading | Hide column**	
Column, view Indicator column icon ScreenTip	328	Point and pause on the icon in the Indicator column			

Project Task	Page	Mouse	Menu Bar	Shortcut Menu	Shortcut Keys
Constraint, set	400	Click on Standard toolbar and the Advanced tab and click the *Constraint type* drop-down	P<u>r</u>oject | Task Information | Advanced tab | Constraint Type		
Copy a Gantt chart (from Gantt Chart view)	573		<u>E</u>dit | Copy Picture | complete dialog box | switch to destination file | <u>E</u>dit | <u>P</u>aste		
Costs, enter fixed costs	424	In Cost table, click in Fixed Cost field and type data	<u>V</u>iew | Ta<u>b</u>le: Entry | <u>C</u>ost; click in Fixed Cost field and type data		
Critical path, view the critical path	504		<u>V</u>iew | Tracking Ga<u>n</u>tt		
Current Date, Modify	360		P<u>r</u>oject | <u>P</u>roject Information		
Custom field, create using a value list	529		<u>T</u>ools | <u>C</u>ustomize | Fiel<u>d</u>s; name field; Value List; enter list		
Custom report, create	535		<u>V</u>iews | <u>R</u>eports | C<u>u</u>stom | <u>S</u>elect | <u>N</u>ew | Complete dialog box		
Custom view, create	533		<u>V</u>iew | <u>M</u>ore Views | <u>N</u>ew | Complete dialog box		
Duration, change default	382		<u>T</u>ools | <u>O</u>ptions | Schedule tab; enter number in *Duration is entered in* box		
E-mail a project file	543		<u>F</u>ile | Sen<u>d</u> To | M<u>a</u>il Recipient (as Attachment)		
Embed Excel data in Project	579		<u>I</u>nsert | <u>O</u>bject | Create from file; select file | OK		
Exit Microsoft Project	341	in upper-right corner	<u>F</u>ile | <u>E</u>xit		Alt + F4
Export, data as HTML	573		<u>F</u>ile | Save <u>A</u>s | change *Save as type to Web Page* | <u>S</u>ave | complete wizard		

Project Task	Page	Mouse	Menu Bar	Shortcut Menu	Shortcut Keys
Export, data into an Excel Worksheet	569		File | Save As | change *Save as type* to *Microsoft Excel Workbooks* | Save | complete wizard		
Finish Date, set	356		Project | Project Information		
Format, view details (from Resource view)	523		Format | Detail Styles		
Getting Started task pane, Close	353	☒ in upper-right corner of the pane			
Gridlines, adding to Gantt chart	334	Right-click the Gantt chart and choose Gridlines	Format | Gridlines		
Help, accessing web-based	339	Click ⊘	Help | Microsoft Office Online		F1 or Alt+H
Help, display Microsoft Help task pane	339	Click ⊘ on the Standard toolbar	Help | Microsoft Project Help		F1 or Alt+H
Help, *Type a question for help* box	337	Click *Type a question for help* box, type term or question, press ↵Enter			
Help, version of Project	340		Help | About Microsoft Project		Alt+H and A
Hyperlink, insert	583		Insert | Hyperlink | complete dialog box		
Import, from Excel	562		File | Open | change *File of type* to *Microsoft Excel Workbooks* | complete wizard		
Insert, recurring task	386		Insert | Recurring Task | Complete dialog box		
Join line, view the ScreenTip	331	Point and pause on the join line			
Link, create	391	Click ▥ and click the Predecessors tab and choose constraint from the Type drop-down	Project | Task Information | Predecessors tab | Complete dialog box	Click in the Predecessors field in the task table for the successor task and type the Task ID for the link task followed by FF, SS, FS, or SF	

Project Task	Page	Mouse	Menu Bar	Shortcut Menu	Shortcut Keys
Link, project data with Word (with selected data)	577	Click [icon]	Edit | Copy Cell | switch to Word document | Edit | Paste Special | Paste link button		Select data, Ctrl+C, switch to Word document, Edit, Paste Special, Paste link button
Link, remove	496	Click [icon] on the Standard toolbar or double-click join line on Gantt chart and choose Type down-arrow	Project | Task Information | Predecessors tab; select link and press Del.	Right-click Gantt bar; Unlink tasks	Click in the Predecessors field in the task table for the successor task and press Del
Link, tasks	391	Select tasks to link and click [icon] on the Standard toolbar or Click in the Predecessors field in the task table for the successor task and type the Task ID for the link task	Project | Task Information | Complete dialog box		
Milestone task, create	386	Click in the Duration cell for the task and type 0			
Milestone, view the ScreenTip	332	Point and pause on the black diamond			
Modify the timescale	523		Format | Timescale | Complete dialog box		
Move, to beginning of the task table	326				Ctrl+Home
Organizer, copy a custom item	539		Tools | Organizer | appropriate tab | select item | Copy		
Organizer, remove item from global file	541		Tools | Organizer | appropriate tab | select item | Delete		
Organizer, rename an item	542		Tools | Organizer | appropriate tab | select item | Rename		
Outlining, create subtask	394	Select tasks and click [icon] on the Formatting toolbar			
Outlining, create summary task	394	Select tasks and click [icon] on the Formatting toolbar			

Project Task	Page	Mouse	Menu Bar	Shortcut Menu	Shortcut Keys
Outlining, show outline by levels	395	Click `Show ▾` on Formatting toolbar and choose the outline level to display	Click expand (+) or collapse (-) buttons		
Print, current view	335	Click 🖨 on the Standard Toolbar	File | Print		Alt+F and P
Print Preview, current view	335	Click 🔍 on the Standard Toolbar	File | Print Preview		Alt+F and V
Progress line, add to Gantt chart	494	📊 on the Tracking toolbar	Tools | Tracking | Progress Lines | Dates and Intervals tab | Complete dialog box		
Progress lines, remove	494		Tools | Tracking | Progress Lines | Dates and Intervals tab; deselect *Always display current progress line*		
Progress, tracking by adding Status column to task table	494		Insert | Column | Choose Status from Field name drop-down	Right-click column heading, Insert Column, Choose Status from Field name drop-down	
Project file, close	341	Click ✖ (to right of *Type a question for help* box)	File | Close		Ctrl+F4 or Ctrl + W
Project file, create from a template	366		File | New | click *On my computer;* or File | New | click *Templates on Office Online*		
Project file, open	321	Click 📂 on the Standard toolbar	File | Open		Alt+F and O or Ctrl+O
Project Guide side pane, Show/Hide	326	Click 📋 on the Project Guide toolbar			
Project Guide Toolbar, show	354	Right-click on a toolbar and choose *Project Guide*	View | Toolbars | Project Guide		
Project, Save As, (copy)	324		File | Save As		Ctrl+A or Alt+F and A or Alt+F2

Project Task	Page	Mouse	Menu Bar	Shortcut Menu	Shortcut Keys
Report, preview	All		View | select Category and click Select and then choose report		
Report, print	All		View | select Category and click Select and then choose report | Print		
Resources, add using Outlook Address Book (from Resource Sheet view)	585		Insert | New Resource From | Address Book		
Resources, assign to a task (from Gantt Chart view)	425	Type resource name in the Resources Name field of desired task in the task table or Click 🖳 on the Standard toolbar and choose the Resources tab or Click 🔳 on the Standard toolbar and type name in the first blank row	Tools | Assign Resources; click the resource name and click Assign		Alt + F10
Resources, change assignment units (from Gantt Chart view)	427, 432, 454	Double-click task, select Resources tab, and use spinner to change Units amount. Respond to smart tags appropriately, or Click 🖳, select Resources tab, and use spinner to change Units amount	Project | Task Information	Right-click task and choose Task Information	
Resources, edit resource (from Resource Sheet view)	421	Double-click resource and make modifications, or click 🖳	Project | Resource Information	Right-click task and choose Resource Information	

Project Task	Page	Mouse	Menu Bar	Shortcut Menu	Shortcut Keys
Resources, insert resource (from Resource Sheet View)	419	In Resource Sheet view, click in blank row, type resource name, press Tab↹ to move to each successive field	Insert | New Resource | Complete dialog box		Insert
Resources, sort resources (from Resource Sheet view)	419		Project | Sort | click sorting preference		
Resources, unassign resource from task (from Gantt Chart view)	432	Select task, click 🧩 on the Standard toolbar, click resource name, and click Remove			Click in the Resource Names field for the task and press Del
Resources, view initials (from Gantt Chart view)	429		Select task(s) | Format | Bar | Bar Text tab; select Resource Initials in the Right position		
Route a project file	544		File | Send To | Routing Recipient | Address | Complete dialog box		
Routing slip, view (from e-mail program)	546	Double-click attachment to e-mail from e-mail program			
ScreenTip, view the summary task	328	Point and pause on the black Gantt bar			
ScreenTip, view the task relationships	332	Point and pause on the blue Gantt bar			
Send project to next routing recipient (assumes *One after another* option used)	546		File | Send To | Next Routing Recipient		
Send scheduled note message	547		File | Send To | Mail Recipient (as Scheduled Note)		
Spell check	455	🔤✓	Tools | Spelling		F7
Split a task	499	Click ⬚ on the Standard toolbar		Right-click task and choose Split task	
Split bar, move	331	Click the bar and drag left or right			

Project Task	Page	Mouse	Menu Bar	Shortcut Menu	Shortcut Keys
Split, modify duration	503	Drag the right edge of the second Gantt bar to adjust the duration of the unfinished portion of task			
Split, modify resume date	503	Drag the second Gantt bar to adjust the resume date			
Split, remove	503	Drag one Gantt bar to touch the other			
Status Date, modify	360	Click *Set a date to schedule from* on the Tasks side pane	<u>P</u>roject | <u>P</u>roject Information		
Task Bar, view ScreenTip	328	Point and pause on the progress bar			
Task Information dialog box, view	329	Double-click on the task or Select task and click ⬚ on the Standard toolbar	<u>P</u>roject | Task Information		⬆Shift+F2
Task notes, insert objects into	582	Double-click task, click Notes tab, click ⬚			
Task, create lag time	471	Click in the Predecessors field and type a positive number (or '+' and a number) after the Predecessor listed; or Click ⬚, Predecessors tab, type positive number (or '+' and a number) after the Predecessor listed in Lag column			

Project Task	Page	Mouse	Menu Bar	Shortcut Menu	Shortcut Keys
Task, create lead time	471	Click in the Predecessors field and type a negative number (or '-' and a number) after the Predecessor listed; or Click ▢, Predecessors tab, type negative number (or '-' and a number) after the Predecessor listed in Lag column			
Task, cut (with item selected)	385	Click ✂ on the Standard toolbar	**Edit** | **Cut Task**	**Right-click task to cut** | **Cut Task**	Ctrl+X
Task, paste (with item cut or copied)	386	Click ▢ on the Standard toolbar	**Edit** | **Paste**	**Right-click task row where you want the task** | **Paste**	Ctrl+V
Task, specify duration	381	Click in the Duration column and type a number and the letter *D* for Day, *M* for Minute, *H* for Hour, or *W* for Week			
Task, view constraint dates	474		**View** | **Table: Entry** | **More Tables** | select **Constraint Dates** | **Apply**		
Tasks side pane, view	327,354	Click [Tasks ▾] on the Project Guide toolbar			
Tasks, collapsing	331	Click ▭ on Formatting toolbar, or click [-] beside summary task in the task table			
Tasks, enter actuals	467		**View** | **More Views** | select **Task Sheet** | **Apply** | **View** | **Table** | **Tracking**		
Tasks, enter new	384	Click *List the tasks in the project* on the Tasks side pane and begin typing in the Task Name column in row 1 or Click in the Task Name column from Gantt chart view in row 1 and begin typing	**Insert** | **New task**	**Right-click any row selector and choose New Task**	Insert

Project Task	Page	Mouse	Menu Bar	Shortcut Menu	Shortcut Keys
Tasks, enter percent complete	463	Double-click task or click , click General tab, use spinner to change Percent complete field	View | Toolbars | Tracking | use any percentage complete button		
Tasks, expanding	328	Click on Formatting toolbar, or click [+] beside task in the task table			
Tasks, set constraint date	474	Click , click Advanced tab, click Constraint date drop-down arrow and choose constraint date	Project | Task Information | Advanced tab		
Tasks, set constraint type	474	Click , click Advanced tab, click Constraint type drop-down arrow and choose constraint type	Project | Task Information | Advanced tab		
Tasks, set deadline	476	Click , click Advanced tab, click Deadline drop-down arrow and select date	Project | Task Information | Advanced tab		
Tasks, view percent complete in task table (from Gantt chart view)	464	Point and pause on progress bar in Gantt chart to view ScreenTip	Insert | Column | % Complete	Right-click column heading, Insert Column, % Complete	
Tasks, view Task Usage	454	Click on the View Bar	View | Task Usage		
Toolbars, show Formatting and Standard toolbars on two rows	321		Tools | Customize | Toolbars | Options tab; check Show Standard and Formatting toolbars on two rows	Right-click any toolbar | Customize | Options tab | Check Show Standard and Formatting toolbars on two rows	
View project statistics	508	Click			
View variance data (from Gantt Chart view)	459		View | Table: Entry | Variance		

Project Task	Page	Mouse	Menu Bar	Shortcut Menu	Shortcut Keys
View, change	All	Click desired view on View Bar	View | select desired view or More Views		
View, project progress	467		View | Tracking Gantt		
View Bar, turn it on	334		View | View Bar		
WBS code, define	397	Double-click task and click the Advanced tab or Click on Standard toolbar, click the Advanced tab, and enter code	Project | WBS | Define code		
WBS code, view	397	Double-click task and click the Advanced tab or Click on Standard toolbar and click the Advanced tab	Project | Task Information | Advanced tab		
Work, reschedule	501	Click on the Tracking toolbar			

GLOSSARY

All key terms appearing in this book (in bold italic) are listed alphabetically in this Glossary for easy reference. If you want to learn more about a feature or concept, use the Index to find the term's other significant occurrences.

Accrue At field   A field in the resource information that defines when a cost for a resource is incurred and when actual costs are charged to the project (start, end, or prorated).

actual duration   The field that shows the span of actual working time for a task so far, based on the scheduled duration and current remaining work or percent complete.

actual finish   The date when a task actually ends.

actual start   The date when a task actually begins.

actual work   The amount of work that has been performed on a task or assignment; also called *actuals*.

actuals   The amount of work that has been performed on a task or assignment; also called *actual work*.

append   A method of importing data into Microsoft Project that adds the data to the end of the active project file without the use of a primary key.

As Late As Possible (ALAP)   A constraint that allows you to start a task as near as possible to the scheduled project finish date.

As Soon As Possible (ASAP)   A constraint that allows you to start a task as soon as possible in relation to the scheduled start date.

assignment units   The percentage of a work resource's time, or units, that is allocated to a task.

attachment   A file that is included with an e-mail but is not part of the e-mail message.

base calendar   A calendar that can be used as a project and task calendar that specifies default working and nonworking time for a set of resources.

baseline   The original project plan (up to 11 per project) used to track the project's progress. It represents a "snapshot" of the schedule at the time that you save the baseline and includes information about tasks, resources, and assignments.

bottom tier   The bottom level of the timescale.

budget   The amount of money slated for the completion of a project plan.

Budget report   A report that lists all project tasks and costs.

Code field   A field in the Resource Sheet view that can be used to contain any type of custom data about a resource.

combination view   A view containing two views; the bottom pane view shows detailed information about the tasks or resources in the top pane view.

Comma Separated Values (CSV)   A file format in which each field is separated by a comma or semicolon.

consolidated resources   Multiple interchangeable resources with the same knowledge and skills concerning a project, such as a group of engineers; also called *group resources*.

constraint   A restriction set on the start or finish date of a task. For instance, you can specify that a task must start on or finish no later than a particular date. Constraints can be flexible (not tied to a specific date) or inflexible (tied to a specific date).

constraint icon   An icon that appears in the Indicator column if a task has a scheduling constraint.

constraint triangle   The three critical components of a project: budget, time, and scope.

controls   The various elements that comprise a view.

Cost/Use field   Resource field that assigns a flat rate or fee for the use of a resource that can be in place of, or in addition to, other cost variables. For work resources, a per-use cost accrues each time the resource is used. For material resources, a per-use cost is accrued only once.

count   The unit of time that appears between labels in the timescale.

critical path   The series of tasks that must be completed on time for a project to finish on schedule. Each task on the critical path is a *critical task*.

critical task   A task that, along with its predecessors, drives the overall finish date of the project.

crosstab report   A report in which the data are presented in column and row format with totals that can be applied to the column, the row, or both, like a spreadsheet.

current date   The system date that can be used as an optional start date for new tasks rather than the project start date and is the Microsoft Project 2003 default setting.

custom field   A field used to store unique data that can be any number, cost, text string, date, or even formula. Custom fields are used to track information that Microsoft Project, by default, does not monitor.

deadline A target date indicating when you want a task to be completed.

default A setting that a program uses automatically unless you specify a different setting.

default working time The hours a resource normally works on a project.

deliverables Tangible and measurable results, outcomes, or items that must be produced to complete a task or series of tasks.

destination file The file where linked or embedded data are pasted.

duration The total span of active working time that is required to complete a task—generally the amount of working time from the start to finish of a task, as defined by the project and resource calendars. The default duration is days, but you can change it to minutes, hours, weeks, or months.

earned value The cost of work up to the status date.

effort-driven scheduling The adjustments that Microsoft Project makes to lengthen or shorten the duration of a task based on the amount of resource units assigned to it, but without changing the total amount of work for the task.

embed To create an object in a separate program and then insert it into a destination file; once embedded, the inserted object becomes part of the destination file.

entry bar A toolbar that displays the contents of the current field.

entry table The default task table used to enter and edit tasks.

export To copy data from Microsoft Project to another software program.

field A column of data that represents a category of information.

filter control A control that limits or highlights those tasks for a view that fit the criteria.

Finish field The date that a task is scheduled to be complete.

Finish No Earlier Than (FNET) A constraint that requires a task to finish on or after a specific date.

Finish No Later Than (FNLT) A constraint that requires a task to finish on or before a specific date.

Finish-to-Finish (FF) A link in which a predecessor task finishes and the successor task also finishes.

Finish-to-Start (FS) A link in which the successor cannot begin until the previous task or predecessor is complete.

fixed cost A set cost for a task that remains constant regardless of the task duration or the work performed by a resource.

flexible constraint A constraint that is not tied to a task on a specific date but rather takes into account other task dependencies and constraints.

Formatting toolbar A toolbar that provides shortcuts to frequently used commands for changing the appearance of field contents.

Gantt bar A horizontal bar within a Gantt chart showing task information, due date, and task dependencies.

Gantt chart A project management tool that can be used to represent the timing of tasks required to finish a project and to measure the progress toward completing the tasks.

Gantt Chart view The default view for a project; includes the task table and the Gantt chart.

global template (global file) A collection of default settings controlling everything from startup view options to how Microsoft Project calculates formulas; the default global template for Microsoft Project is *global.mpt.*

Graphics Interchange Format (GIF) A bitmapped graphics file format used by the World Wide Web.

group control A control used to combine or rearrange tasks or resources in a project according to specific criteria, such as task duration, priority, resource overallocation, or finish date.

Group field A resource field that provides a keyword to be used in sorting, grouping, and filtering resources.

group resources Multiple interchangeable human resources with the same knowledge and skills concerning a project, such as a group of engineers; also called *consolidated resources.*

hyperlink A clickable word or object that opens another file, e-mail message, or Web site.

hyperlink icon An icon in the Indicator column that associates the resource or task to a Web page or document.

Hypertext Markup Language (HTML) The standard World Wide Web convention for presenting text and graphics.

ID field A field in the task information or resource information that contains an automatically supplied number used to identify a task or resource.

import To copy data from another program into Microsoft Project.

Indicator column A field in the task information or resource information that provides information about the state of a task or resource.

individual resource An individual person or asset used as a resource.

inflexible constraint A constraint that ties a task to a specific date.

Initials field A field that provides a brief name for a resource in the Gantt Chart or Network Diagram views.

lag time A delay between tasks that have a dependency.

lead time An overlap between tasks that have a dependency.

leveling An automatic Microsoft Project feature used to balance the workload for a resource by adding delays and splits in the project plan.

map A set of instructions that defines the data you import or export, the order, and the destination fields in Microsoft Project into which the data will be imported or exported.

MAPI Acronym for *Messaging Application Programming Interface,* the standard programming interface supported by Microsoft for accessing electronic messaging.

mapping grid   The columns of data that are to be imported or exported, along with the corresponding Microsoft Project field to which they will be mapped in the Export Wizard or Import Wizard dialog boxes.

Material Label field   A field in Resource Sheet view that defines the unit of measure (quarts, boxes, gallons, and so on) for material resources.

material resource   Any resource that is used up through the work involved in a task, such as gasoline.

Max. Units field   A field in Resource Sheet view that defines the maximum percentage, or units, that a resource is available to be scheduled for any tasks. The maximum units value indicates the highest capacity at which the resource is available for work; the default value is 100%.

menu bar   A toolbar that contains common menu items that, when activated, display a list of related commands.

merge   A method of importing data to the end of the active project file; requires a primary key.

middle tier   The middle level of the timescale.

milestone   A task that marks the completion of one or more tasks yet has no duration of its own. A milestone is a reference point marking a major event in a project and is used to monitor the project's progress.

module   Programming code that performs an action.

Must Finish On (MFO)   A task with an associated date that controls when the task finishes.

Must Start On (MSO)   A task with an associated date that controls when the task starts.

noncontiguous link   A join between tasks that are not adjacent.

nondefault working time   Work day hours that are not available for the project plan.

nonworking time   Any time that work is not being completed, such as holidays or vacation time.

note icon   An icon in the Indicator column that provides text about the resource that the user added.

object   In OLE, shared information that is compatible in format and can be used among different files and programs such as a Microsoft Graph chart or an Excel spreadsheet. The program used to create the object and the object type determines the programs that can be used to edit the object, as well as how it can be edited.

Object Linking and Embedding (OLE)   A program-integration technology that you can use to share information between programs.

ODBC   Acronym for *Open Database Connectivity,* a compliant database format that Microsoft supports.

Organizer   A tool that allows you to copy Microsoft Project elements such as views, reports, and project base calendars between the open file and the global file.

overallocation icon   An icon in the Indicator column that reveals that a resource has too much work assigned to it for the time frame involved or has been assigned to two tasks at the same time.

overflow markers   Crosshatch characters (###) that indicate the entry in a field is too wide to fit in the column.

Overtime Rate (Ovt. Rate) field   A field in Resource Sheet view that assigns charges per unit of overtime work for a work resource.

paste link   An object or data created in a source file and inserted into a destination file; objects in the destination file are automatically updated to reflect changes in the source object.

percent complete   Term to denote how much of a task has been completed; expressed as a percentage.

phases   The major steps for a group of related tasks that are present throughout the project life cycle.

predecessor task   A task that must start or finish before another task can start or finish.

Predecessors field   A field that shows any tasks that must be considered before

calculating the start or finish date of the current task.

primary key   A field that uniquely identifies each task.

priority   A numeric setting between 0 and 1000, used when leveling resources across multiple project files.

progress bar   A visual representation in a Gantt bar that depicts the progress of work on a task.

progress date   The date used to set a progress line. It can be the current date (computer clock) or the status date, which is user-specified in the Progress Information dialog box.

progress line   A vertical line added to the Gantt chart on a particular date of interest, including peaks to the left for tasks behind schedule and peaks to the right for tasks ahead of schedule.

project   A self-contained group of tasks performed to achieve a specific objective.

project calendar   The working days and hours, the number of hours in a given week, and any nonworking time such as holidays or vacation time used in a project.

project finish date   The date when a project is scheduled to be completed.

Project Guide   A side pane that is accessed from the Project Guide toolbar that provides step-by-step instruction to guide you through the process of creating and managing a project.

project manager   The individual who oversees all aspects of a project, including the assignment of tasks, resources, and budgeting.

project start date   The date when a project begins. By default, projects are scheduled from the project start date.

project statistics   Project data displayed in the Project Statistics dialog box—including the current project start date, project baseline data, the project finish date, the duration, work, and cost of the overall project.

Project Summary report   A report that outlines actual and baseline data for the overall project plan.

M'SOFT

recipient   The person to whom you are addressing an e-mail message.

recurring task   A task that repeats with some pattern, such as weekly, monthly, or biweekly.

remaining duration   The amount of time left to work on a task before the task is completed.

remaining work   The amount of hours still required to complete a task.

render   To capture a picture of data.

resource   Anything needed to complete a task, such as an employee, a vendor, a conference room, a building, or equipment. Each task has at least one resource.

Resource calendar   A calendar assigned to each resource to reflect unique scheduling considerations such as the type of work day and vacation schedules.

resource cost   The costs incurred due to the expense of using a resource.

Resource Names field   A field that shows the resources assigned to work on the task.

resource pool   A set of resources available for assignment to project tasks. A resource pool can be used exclusively by one project or can be shared by several projects.

Resource Usage report   A report designed to provide assignment hours for each resource by week.

response pending icon   An icon in the Indicator column that shows a resource has not responded to an e-mail notification about task assignment.

resume date   The new start date for the rescheduled portion of a task.

Rich Text Format (RTF)   A file type used to transfer formatted text documents between applications.

routing   A way to send the project file to one or more individuals for comments and modifications and have the file returned to the originator after the routing recipients have reviewed the project.

routing slip   A project file that contains e-mail address information along with instructions and message text for the e-mail recipients.

schedule calculations   Values that Microsoft Project calculates, such as work hours. Schedule calculations are automatic by default but can be made manually, if necessary.

scheduled note message   Either a picture of selected tasks or an attached project file that is automatically addressed to members of the project team and sent as an e-mail message.

scheduling formula   The formula that Microsoft Project uses to schedule a task (*Duration = Work / Units*).

scope   The performance expectations (quality) of a project plan.

screen control   The underlying structure for an entire onscreen view.

scrollbar   A horizontal or vertical bar that enables you to move the project window vertically and horizontally so that you can see other parts of the work area.

scrollbox   A square object within a horizontal or vertical scrollbar that you can drag to move quickly within the window.

sheet view   The spreadsheet-like presentation of data, such as a task table.

side pane   A pane displayed on the left side of the Microsoft Project window. The side pane contains Project Guide information.

single view   A view such as the Gantt Chart view or Network Diagram view.

source file   The file where linked or embedded data originate.

split task   To divide a task by inserting a time delay, thereby creating two or more segments.

stakeholders   Individuals who have an interest in the success of the project plan.

Standard Rate (Std. Rate) field   A field in Resource Sheet view that assigns a charge per unit of normal working time for a work resource.

Standard toolbar   A toolbar that provides shortcuts to common tasks including Save, Print, Cut/Paste (Move), and Copy/Paste.

Start field   A field that specifies when the task is scheduled to begin.

Start No Earlier Than (SNET)   A constraint that schedules the task to start on or after a specified date.

Start No Later Than (SNLT)   A constraint that schedules the task to start on or before a specified date.

Start-to-Finish (SF)   A dependency in which, as soon as a predecessor task starts, the successor task can finish.

Start-to-Start (SS)   A dependency in which both the predecessor and successor task start at the same time.

status bar   The bar at the bottom of the Microsoft Project window that provides information about the current actions or settings.

status date   A date you specify when reporting progress information for a task or when calculating earned value totals.

subtask   A task that is part of a summary task.

successor task   A task that cannot start or finish until another task starts or finishes.

summary task   A task that is made up of subtasks and summarizes those subtasks.

table control   The list of fields you want in a view, determined by the screen that you choose.

task dependency   A dependency in which the start or finish of one task depends on the start or completion of another task; also called *task link*.

Task ID   An automatic number assigned to each task, shown on the left side of each row.

task link   A dependency in which the start or finish of one task depends on the start or completion of another task; also called *task dependency*.

Task Name field   A field that describes the task; it can contain up to 255 characters.

task pane   A window within an Office application that provides commonly used commands. Its location and small size allow you to use these commands while still working in the open file.

task table   A list of tasks displayed on the left side of the project window in Gantt Chart view.

tasks   Specific activities within a project that have a start date, duration, and completion time.

template   A model providing generic tasks and resources, which you can then modify to suit your individual project plan specifications.

time constraint   The deadline of the overall project as well as how much time each individual task requires.

timeline   The horizontal bar graph displayed on the right side of the Gantt chart.

timephased   Type of graph or chart that shows how tasks, resources, or assignments are distributed over time.

timescale   The time period legend appearing across the top of the Gantt chart.

title bar   A bar at the top of the Microsoft Project window that displays the name of the software and the name of the active project—either a default name, such as *Project1*, or a user-determined filename.

To-do List report   A report of the assigned tasks for a particular resource, including the week the task begins and the start date of the task.

toolbar   A set of buttons onscreen. Each button provides a shortcut to a frequently used command.

top tier   The top level of the timescale.

total cost   The sum of all resource costs and fixed costs.

Tracking Gantt view   A Gantt chart that displays a baseline Gantt bar beneath the current Gantt bar and highlights the critical tasks by displaying them in red.

Tracking toolbar   A toolbar used to update the percent complete for a task.

***Type a question for help* box**   A box at the right end of the menu bar in which you enter a keyword or phrase to specify a new Help topic or redisplay a previous Help topic.

Type field   A resource information field that identifies a resource as a work resource or a material resource.

unlink   To remove a task dependency.

wizard   A feature of Microsoft Office programs that guides you step-by-step through an activity.

work   The time assigned to a resource to complete a task; also represents the total labor required to complete a task.

Work Breakdown Structure (WBS) codes   The default outline numbers automatically assigned to each task that identify the task's hierarchical position within your project plan.

work resource   Any resource, such as a human resource, that contributes to the project through work and effort but is not used up by the task performed.

work unit   The amount of time it should take a resource to complete a task.

Working Days report   A report for printing a project's calendar, which displays the working days and times and any exceptions (the nonworking days).

working time   Any time that work is being completed. Working time may be the typical 8:00 A.M. to 5:00 P.M. time frame, but it can also include holidays and other nonworking times, such as evenings and weekends.

M'SOFT

INDEX

M'SOFT

M'SOFT

M'SOFT

M'SOFT